Dignāga's Investigation of the Percept

Dignāga's Investigation of the Percept

A Philosophical Legacy in India and Tibet

DOUGLAS DUCKWORTH
MALCOLM DAVID ECKEL
JAY L. GARFIELD
JOHN POWERS
YESHES THABKHAS
SONAM THAKCHÖE

OXFORD
UNIVERSITY PRESS

OXFORD
UNIVERSITY PRESS

Oxford University Press is a department of the University of Oxford. It furthers the University's objective of excellence in research, scholarship, and education by publishing worldwide. Oxford is a registered trade mark of Oxford University Press in the UK and certain other countries.

Published in the United States of America by Oxford University Press
198 Madison Avenue, New York, NY 10016, United States of America.

CIP data is on file at the Library of Congress
ISBN 978–0–19–062370–8 (pbk)
ISBN 978–0–19–062369–2 (hbk)

This book is dedicated to the memory of Leslie Kawamura, a valued member of this team who did not live to see the completion of the project.

Contents

Acknowledgments ix

List of Contributors xiii

Introduction xv

PART I: *Studies and Translations*

1. The Subject Matter of *Investigation of the Percept*: A Tale of Five Commentaries—MALCOLM DAVID ECKEL, JAY L. GARFIELD, and JOHN POWERS 3

2. *Investigation of the Percept*—DIGNĀGA 38

3. *Autocommentary to Investigation of the Percept*—DIGNĀGA 40

4. "To Please Beginners": Vinītadeva's *Subcommentary on Investigation of the Percept* in Its Indian Context—MALCOLM DAVID ECKEL 48

5. *Subcommentary on Investigation of the Percept*—VINĪTADEVA 78

6. Introduction to *Ornament for Dignāga's Thought in Investigation of the Percept*—DOUGLAS DUCKWORTH 105

7. *Ornament for Dignāga's Thought in Investigation of the Percept*—GUNG THANG DKON MCHOG BSTAN PA'I SGRON ME 112

8. Ngawang Dendar's Commentary: Philosophy Through Doxography—JOHN POWERS 118

9. *Beautiful String of Pearls:* A Commentary on *Investigation of the Percept*—NGAG DBANG BSTAN DAR 131

10. Introduction to *Summary of the Essence: A Commentary on Investigation of the Percept*—JAY L. GARFIELD, JOHN POWERS, and SONAM THAKCHÖE 169

11. *Summary of the Essence: A Commentary on Investigation of the Percept*—YESHES THABKHAS 175

PART II: *Tibetan Texts*

12. *Investigation of the Percept* and Its *Autocommentary*: The Tibetan Text of 216
dMigs pa brtag pa—DIGNĀGA 218
dMigs pa brtag pa'i 'grel pa—DIGNĀGA 220

13. *Subcommentary on Investigation of the Percept:* The Tibetan Text 225
dMigs pa brtag pa'i 'grel bshad (*Ālambanaparīkṣā-ṭīkā*)—VINĪTADEVA 227

14. *Ornament for Dignāga's Thought in Investigation of the Percept*: Tibetan Text 259
dMigs pa brtag pa'i 'grel ba phyogs glang dgongs rgyan zhes bya ba bzhugs so—GUNG THANG DKON MCHOG BSTAN PA'I SGRON ME 260

15. *Beautiful String of Pearls: A Commentary on Investigation of the Percept*: Tibetan Text 264
dMigs pa brtag pa'i 'grel pa mu tig 'phreng mdzes zhes bya ba bzhugs so—NGAG DBANG BSTAN DAR 265

16. *Summary of the Essence of the Commentaries on Investigation of the Percept*: Tibetan Text
dMigs brtag 'grel pa snying po bsdus pa—YESHES THABKHAS 289

English-Tibetan-Sanskrit Glossary 319

Bibliography 323

Index 347

Acknowledgments

RESEARCH FOR THIS project was supported by a four-year Discovery grant from the Australian Research Council; our research would not have been possible without it. We are grateful for additional support from Yale-NUS College and the Singapore Ministry of Education. Thanks also to the Centre for South and Southeast Asian Studies of the College of Asia and the Pacific at the Australian National University for supplementary research funds. Douglas Duckworth's research on this project was aided by a Columbia University Library Grant and a Summer Research Award from Temple University.

Sonam Thakchöe wishes to thank the University of Tasmania for its ongoing support for the Asian philosophy program, which allowed him to devote time and resources on this research. He also acknowledges the Central University of Tibetan Studies for permission to access its resources; in particular, he is grateful to Mr. Sonam Tsewang, Librarian, and Mr. Pasang Dorjee, Research Assistant for Geshe Yeshes Thabkhas, for their assistance in finding some of the relevant manuscripts for this project.

A number of people provided assistance in a variety of ways, and we sincerely thank all of them. We are particularly grateful to Paul Hackett, who has developed a powerful search engine that allows scholars to find quotations or approximations throughout the Tibetan Buddhist canon. This has expanded to include a vast range of noncanonical Tibetan literature, as well as Buddhist works in other languages. Paul enabled us to track down all of the direct quotations in our texts and to determine that other material phrased as quotes was either from sources that are no longer extant, except as paraphrases, or perhaps hazy memories of the authors. Paul also provided searchable electronic texts of all the Tibetan works mentioned in commentaries, with which we identified relevant pages for quotations and better understood their philosophical context.

Geshe Yeshes Thabkhas of the Central University of Tibetan Studies gave two days of lectures on Dignāga's *Investigation of the Percept* (*Ālambana-parīkṣā*). This seminar was arranged by Joshua and Diana Cutler of the Tibetan Buddhist Learning Center in Washington, New Jersey. Our thanks to them for organizing the seminar and for hosting the members of our group who attended.

A number of colleagues joined us in group meetings and made valuable contributions. The late Professor Leslie Kawamura of the University of Calgary came to the Australian National University in 2010 and participated in an intensive workshop on the *Ālambana-parīkṣā*, providing many cogent insights on the Chinese translations of the text. Professor Toru Funayama of Kyoto University and Dr. Michael Radich of the Victoria University of Wellington also contributed to workshops and aided in the translation and editing of difficult texts. Professor Guy Newland of Central Michigan University joined in a meeting during the final stages of the translation of Gungtang Könckok Denbe Drönme's *Ornament for Dignāga's Thought in Investigation of the Percept*. We gratefully acknowledge their contributions to this project.

This project was originally conceived as a group endeavor involving scholars from the disciplines of religious studies and philosophy with expertise in Indian, Tibetan, and East Asian Buddhism. We anticipated that our research would result in a single volume that would comprise the intellectual history of the *Ālambana-parīkṣā* from its composition in sixth-century India through a millennium and a half of commentary and debate in India, Tibet, and East Asia. A group of eleven core members met together for six intensive workshops over four years and maintained an ongoing interchange of ideas and translations. As the project developed, it became clear that the output should be divided into two streams producing separate books, one addressing Indian and Tibetan literature and one focusing on the Chinese literature.

Nonetheless, our joint workshops provided invaluable cross-fertilization of research and yielded insights that have significantly improved our work, including discussion and translation of Chinese materials relating to the *Ālambana-parīkṣā* and its philosophical legacy in East Asia. We particularly thank Professor John Makeham of LaTrobe University, one of the two Chief Investigators on this project (along with John Powers and Partner Investigator Jay Garfield), who worked on the initial grant proposal and who has been involved in every facet of the research since then. John is an outstanding scholar of Chinese philosophy and one of the most intellectually generous people we know. His input into this project from its inception has made our work possible and has added immeasurable benefit to our collective research. We also wish to thank our other colleagues in the East Asia team: Professor Eyal Aviv of George Washington University, Dr. John Jorgensen of the Australian National University, Professor Ching Keng and Professor Chen-kuo Lin of National Chenching University, and Dr. Dan Lusthaus of Harvard University. Their work on East Asian materials raised a number of important issues in our discussions.

A panel on our research into the *Ālambana-parīkṣā* was held at the 2012 Annual Meeting of the American Academy of Religion. Feedback from colleagues who attended helped with evaluation of results to that point and in defining future directions.

Academics at the Tibetan Buddhist Resource Center (TBRC) generously provided pdf versions of the Tibetan texts used in this study, and the data on their website also contained helpful background information. The Digital Dictionary of Buddhism, developed and maintained by Professor Charles Muller of Tokyo University, has been a superb resource for Chinese materials and for understanding the range of connotations of technical terms. The GRETL (Göttingen Register of Electronic Texts in Indian Languages) site maintained at the University of Göttingen makes available a large number of critically edited Sanskrit Buddhist texts. SAT Daizōkyō and the Chinese Buddhist Electronic Texts Archive (CBETA) have provided edited and critically punctuated Chinese texts used in this study. The development and free deployment of such invaluable resources have revolutionized academic research in Buddhist Studies, and we wish to extend our sincere thanks for their generosity in making them available.

Finally, the academic institutions that employ team members have played important roles in making our work possible. The Australian National University (and in particular Professor Ken George, Director of the School of Culture, History and Language of the College of Asia and the Pacific) has been highly supportive and has granted sabbatical leave and research funding on several occasions.

The project has employed a number of research assistants who have made important contributions. Ms. Kalsang typed two of our Tibetan texts, and Mr. Tenzin Choephak also helped with the editing and interpretation of some Tibetan terms.

We have benefited from feedback from many other colleagues in Buddhist Studies and related fields at conferences and exchange of emails, from two anonymous reviewers for the press, as well as the generous scholars who develop and maintain electronic resources that have facilitated our research. We are sincerely grateful to all of them.

Contributors

Douglas Duckworth is Associate Professor in the Department of Religion at Temple University. He is the author of *Mipam on Buddha-Nature: The Ground of the Nyingma Tradition* (2008) and *Jamgön Mipam: His Life and Teachings* (2011). He also introduced and translated *Distinguishing the Views and Philosophies: Illuminating Emptiness in a Twentieth-Century Tibetan Buddhist Classic* by Bötrül (2011).

Malcolm David Eckel is a Professor of Religion and Director of the Institute for Philosophy and Religion at Boston University. His scholarly interests range across the religious traditions of Asia, particularly the philosophy and practice of Mahāyāna Buddhism in India, Tibet, China, and Japan. He received his B.A. from Harvard, his M.A. from Oxford, and his Ph.D. in the Study of Religion from Harvard. His publications include *Bhāviveka and His Buddhist Opponents* (2008); *Understanding Buddhism* (2002); and *To See the Buddha: A Philosopher's Quest for the Meaning of Emptiness* (1992). He has edited two volumes of essays: *India and the West: The Problem of Understanding* and *Deliver Us from Evil.* At Boston University he has served as Director of the Core Curriculum (2007–2013) and Distinguished Teaching Professor of the Humanities (2002–2005). In 1998, he won the university's highest teaching award, the Metcalf Award for Teaching Excellence. Before joining Boston University, he served as Associate Professor and Administrative Director of the Center for the Study of World Religions at Harvard Divinity School.

Jay L. Garfield is Doris Silbert Professor in the Humanities and Professor of Philosophy at Smith College, Visiting Professor of Buddhist Philosophy at the Harvard Divinity School, Professor of Philosophy at Melbourne University, and Adjunct Professor of Philosophy at the Central University of Tibetan Studies. His most recent books include *Engaging Buddhism: Why It Matters to Philosophy* (2015), *Moonpaths: Ethics and Emptiness* (with the Cowherds, 2015), *The Moon Points Back: Buddhism, Logic and Analytic Philosophy* (edited with

Koji Tanaka, Yasuo Deguchi, and Graham Priest, 2015), and *Madhyamaka and Yogācāra: Allies or Rivals?* (edited, with Jan Westerhoff, 2015).

John Powers is a Research Professor in the Alfred Deakin Institute for Citizenship and Globalisation at Deakin University, and a Fellow of the Australian Academy of Humanities. He is the author of fourteen books and more than sixty book chapters and academic articles. He is the recipient of a national teaching award from the Australian Learning and Teaching Centre and an Excellence in Supervision Award from Australian National University. He is the co-chair of the Yogācāra Studies Group of the American Academy of Religion. His publications include *A Bull of A Man: Images of Masculinity, Sex, and the Body in Indian Buddhism* (2009) and *Historical Dictionary of Tibet* (with David Templeman; 2012).

Yeshes Thabkhas is Professor emeritus of Indian Buddhist Philosophy at the Central University of Tibetan Studies. He completed his Geshe Lharampa degree at Drepung Loseling Monastic University in 1948 and joined the faculty of the Central Institute of Higher Tibetan Studies (now the Central University of Tibetan Studies) in 1972, where he taught until his retirement in 1990. He is the author of several books, including *A Straightforward Analysis of Interpretable and Definitive Meanings in the Treatise "Essence of Eloquence"* (Vāṇa dbus bod kyi ches mtho'i gtsug lag slob gnyer khang, 1997). Geshe Yeshes Thabkhas has lectured in the United States, India, and Nepal and has collaborated with and taught many of the leading scholars of Buddhist Studies in the West.

Sonam Thakchöe is Senior Lecturer in Philosophy in the School of Humanities at the University of Tasmania and Director of the University of Tasmania Buddhist Studies in India Program. He holds an Ācārya degree from the Central University of Tibetan Studies and a Ph.D. in Philosophy from the University of Tasmania. He is the author of *The Two Truths Debate: Tsongkhapa and Gorampa on the Middle Way* (2007), a coauthor (with the Cowherds) of *Moonpath: Ethics and Emptiness* (2015) and *Moonshadows: Conventional Truth in Buddhist Philosophy* (2011). He has also published several academic articles.

Introduction

Investigation of the Percept *and Its Reception in India and Tibet*

This book charts the unusual and sometimes puzzling intellectual history of Dignāga's (*c.* 480–540) *Investigation of the Percept* (*Ālambana-parīkṣā*) and autocommentary (*vṛtti*) in India and Tibet. *Investigation of the Percept* is a short epistemological text inquiring into the nature of the object (*ālambana*) of perception. Dignāga defines the percept as that which is the cause of perceptual cognition and appears to perceptual consciousness. He then asks whether the percept is an external object or an internal cognitive object. He argues that neither macroscopic external objects nor the fundamental particles that constitute them can serve this function. External objects lack causal power, in virtue of not being substantially real; fundamental particles do not appear to perception. Only an internal cognition, he argues, can serve both functions. The text comes with a brief autocommentary and was the subject of commentaries by two Indian scholars, Dharmapāla and Vinītadeva, as well as by three Tibetan scholars, Ngawang Dendar, Gungtang Könchok Denbe Drönme, and Yeshes Thabkhas. We present the text along with its Indian and Tibetan commentaries in this volume, demonstrating the way that these eight terse verses serve as the platform for an extended philosophical project and revealing the richness of commentary as a genre of philosophical expression.

Investigation of the Percept was written in the early sixth century and generated significant interest and commentary among both Buddhist and non-Buddhist philosophers. Influential analyses of the text were composed by Dharmapāla (Hufa 護法, *c.* sixth century) and Vinītadeva (*c.* 645–715) in India, but it was not until the eighteenth century that a Tibetan commentary was written by the third Gungtang Rinpoche, Könchok Denbe Drönme (Gung thang dKon mchog bstan pa'i sgron me, 1762–1823). This was soon followed by another commentary by the Mongolian scholar Ngawang Dendar (Ngag dbang bstan dar, 1759–1840). There are also numerous detailed examinations of the text in China, most of which engage with Dharmapāla's interpretations. The ideas Dignāga advances were highly significant for subsequent Buddhist epistemology, and *Investigation of the Percept* was translated into Tibetan and Chinese. Unfortunately, there are no extant Sanskrit versions of the root verses or the autocommentary, but fragments have been preserved in texts by Buddhist and non-Buddhist authors.[1]

The philosophical positions defended in *Investigation of the Percept* were criticized by a number of Indian scholars, including Bhāviveka (*c.* 490–570) and Śāntarakṣita (*c.* 725–728). Chapter five of Bhāviveka's *Blaze of Reasoning: Autocommentary on Verses on the Heart of the Middle Way* (*Madhyamaka-hṛdaya-kārikā-tarkajvālā*) contains an analysis of Dignāga's presentation of perception and the percept. The "Investigation of External Objects" (*Bahir-artha-parīkṣā*) section of Śāntarakṣita's *Compendium of Metaphysics* (*Tattva-saṃgraha*) discusses the ramifications of Dignāga's rejection of the externality of the percept and cites his explanation of perception as an entirely internal process in *Investigation of the Percept.*

There are no surviving Sanskrit versions of the two Indian commentaries by Dharmapāla and Vinītadeva, both written within a century of its composition. Dharmapāla's work was translated into Chinese but not Tibetan and forms the basis of the East Asian commentarial tradition. It appears to have had little impact in India or Tibet on analyses of *Investigation of the Percept.* Neither Bhāviveka nor Śāntarakṣita mentions Dharmapāla in their discussions of Dignāga's thought. Vinītadeva's commentary mentions Dharmapāla twice, once in reference to an argument he presents but does not endorse, and a second time in a presentation of an argument he claims not to understand. He addresses a number of Dharmapāla's commentarial points but diverges from him throughout his exegesis. Dharmapāla's views are known in the Tibetan commentarial tradition only through Vinītadeva's brief discussions.

In Tibet, the Buddhist Epistemological (*Pramāṇa*) tradition—of which Dignāga is regarded as the patriarch—was enormously influential, particularly in the Gelukpa (dGe lugs pa) and Sakyapa (Sa skya pa) orders, but *Investigation of the Percept* received little attention until the eighteenth century. For Tibetan epistemologists, Dignāga's most important text was his *Compendium of Epistemology* (*Pramāṇa-samuccaya*). This work was read almost

1. Some of these have been published in articles and books, which are listed in the Bibliography. Some previously unidentified fragments have been gathered by Harada Wasō 原田和宗 (unpublished manuscript), who generously gave permission to cite them.

exclusively through the lens of Dharmakīrti's (*c.* seventh century) *Commentary on the Compendium of Epistemology* (*Pramāṇa-vārttika*), which became the standard for understanding Dignāga's thought in the Gelukpa tradition.

Tibetan scholars generally discussed Dignāga's work in the context of Dharmakīrti studies. Prior to the publication of Gungtang's *Ornament for Dignāga's Thought in Investigation of the Percept* in 1788, the text had largely been neglected in India and Tibet for more than 1000 years. Gungtang's work was followed by Ngawang Dendar's *Beautiful String of Pearls: A Commentary on Investigation of the Percept*, which was probably written near the end of his life. The text received no subsequent attention in Tibet until the present time.

In light of Dharmakīrti's eclipse of Dignāga in the Tibetan philosophical world and the relatively minor role *Investigation of the Percept* plays in Indian Buddhist epistemological literature, it is not surprising that this text has received less attention in Tibet than in East Asia. Surprisingly, two scholars in remote regions of Tibet suddenly developed an interest in it in the eighteenth century after a period of long neglect. It is also noteworthy that each commentary focuses almost exclusively on Dignāga's text itself, and neither can be regarded as a subcommentary on Vinītadeva's work, a relatively rare posture for a Tibetan commentary on an Indian Buddhist treatise. Neither author gives any indication of why he chose to analyze this text after it had languished so long in obscurity, nor does either indicate who requested the commentary, further deepening the mystery surrounding this episode in the literary history of *Investigation of the Percept*. Moreover, Ngawang Dendar does not mention Gungtang's work, nor does he directly address any of his commentarial points. Hence, there is no indication in the text that his decision to write a commentary was influenced by the work of his senior contemporary.

After this brief resurgence of interest in *Investigation of the Percept*, no Tibetan scholar of whom we are aware commented on the complete text until the late Geshe Lobsang Gyatso (dGe bshes bLo bzang rgya mtsho, 1928–1997) delivered a series of talks over several days in 1995 in Dharamsala, India. They were not recorded, and so his interpretations were not preserved. The most recent Tibetan commentary, by Geshe Yeshes Thabkhas (dGe bshes Ye shes thabs mkhas, 1929–), was given in lectures in 2014 and later edited as a formal written commentary and translated. This commentary appears in this volume. Members of the research team attended the lectures and asked a number of questions related to East Asian interpretations of *Investigation of the Percept*, particularly issues pertaining to Dharmapāla's exegesis. These issues were addressed in detail, and so this text represents a dialogue between the Tibetan scholastic tradition's understanding of Dignāga's thought and how it has been interpreted in China.

Investigation of the Percept *in China*

While in Tibet Dignāga has largely been interpreted through a Dharmakīrtian lens, China received Dignāga's works without Dharmakīrti's extrapolations, a situation that can be likened to a philosophical tradition that follows Plato (Dignāga) but without access to Aristotle (Dharmakīrti).[2] In East Asia, one of the primary Indic sources for discussions of Yogācāra philosophy was Dharmapāla, whose ideas were widely disseminated by Xuanzang 玄奘 (602–664), particularly in his *Treatise on Mere Cognition* (*Cheng weishi lun* 成唯識論), and also in his translations of Dharmapāla's major works. In Tibet Dharmapāla had little influence. The only translated treatise in the Tibetan canon attributed to him is a short text, *Clarification of Entry into the One Hundred Dharmas* (*Śatadharma-prakāśa-mukha-śāstra;* Tib. *Chos brgya gsal pa'i sgo'i bstan bcos*), which contains a listing of 100 dharmas.

Paramārtha (Zhendi 眞諦, 499–569) produced the first Chinese translation of *Investigation of the Percept* sometime between 558 and 569,[3] and Xuanzang published an interpretive translation in 657, which apparently added words in order to make it more comprehensible and possibly to correct what he regarded as errors in the earlier version.[4] In 710 Yijing 義淨 (635–713) published a notoriously difficult edition titled *Explanation of Investigation of the Percept* (*Guan suoyuan lunshi* 觀所緣論釋).[5] Yijing's text contains most of Dharmapāla's commentary but does not discuss the last two verses of the text. No reason is given for this omission. Despite its being characterized by Chinese Buddhist literati as impenetrable in parts,[6] this translation became highly influential and was the basis of subsequent commentaries, including Mingyu's 明昱 (1527–1616) *Explanation of Investigation of the Percept* (*Guan*

2. Eli Franco made this comparison in a comment at a panel at the International Association of Buddhist Studies conference in Vienna in August 2014.

3. This was originally titled *Sichen lun* 思塵論 (*Treatise on the Object of Cognition*), but in Chinese Buddhist canons today it is referred to as *Wuxiang sichen lun* 無相思塵論 (*Treatise on the Object of Cognition Devoid of Attributes*): T 1619.31.882–883.

4. This is referred to in Chinese canons as *Guan suoyuanyuan lun* 觀所緣緣論 (*Treatise Investigating the Percept Condition*): T 1624.31.888–889.

5. T31 no. 1625.

6. In the preface, Wang Ye 王野 describes its language as "odd" (*qi* 奇) and "difficult" (*xian* 嶮), and he states that readers could not understand it. Mingyu (*Explanation of Investigation of the Percept*: 818c) states that when he first read the text, it was like "staring at a wall" and he was unable even to punctuate it.

suoyuan yuan lunshi 觀所緣緣論釋).[7] Xuanzang's version was more widely cited, however, no doubt because of its greater readability.

Investigation of the Percept was quoted and debated in a number of Chinese works, including Chapters 70 and 71 of Yongming Yanshou's 永明延寿 (904–975) encyclopedic *Records of the Mirror of Orthodoxy* (*Zongjing lu* 宗鏡錄),[8] which discusses its ideas regarding the percept, the percept condition (*ālambana-pratyaya*), and how cognition operates.

After this initial period of interest during the Tang dynasty (618–907), there appears to have been a hiatus until the Ming dynasty (1368–1644), when there was a general resurgence in engagement with Yogācāra and study of Buddhist epistemology. This revival of interest was partly prompted by critiques of Buddhism by Christian missionaries, who used logic and Western science in their attempts to convert Chinese. Buddhists seeking an indigenous resource to combat attacks on their culture found logic and epistemology in the Indian Epistemological tradition, and as they deployed Buddhist reasoning procedures in developing arguments for Buddhism's ability to stand on its own and defend itself against criticism by foreigners, Dignāga again became prominent because of his association with logic and reasoning.[9]

A new treatise entitled *Anthology of Commentaries on Investigation of the Percept* (*Guan suoyuanyuan lun jijie* 觀所緣緣論集解) was published by Zhenjie 真界 (d.u.) in 1599, but this work attracted little interest.[10] Mingyu published *Explanation of Investigation of the Percept* in 1609. He later wrote another work, *Reconciled Explanation of Investigation of the Percept* (*Guan suoyuanyuan lun huishi* 觀所緣緣論會釋), which apparently was prompted by concerns relating to differing terminology in the translations of Yijing and Xuanzang.[11] The renewed interest in *Investigation of the Percept* continued with Zhixu's 智旭 (1599–1655) *Straightforward Explication of Investigation of the Percept* (*Guan suoyuanyuan lun zhijie* 觀所緣緣論直解), published in 1647.[12]

---

7. XZJ 83.363a–399b.

8. T 48.2016.415a–957b.

9. This is discussed in Makeham (2014), which traces the history of early Chinese Yogācāra studies, their revival during the Ming period, and the efflorescence of interest in Yogācāra during the Qing and Republican periods.

10. It was not included in the Taishō or in subsequent supplementary canons in China. The only known extant copy is a woodblock print held in the library of Nagoya University.

11. The commentaries of Zhenjie and Mingyu have been translated by John Jorgensen and are part of the East Asian materials for this project.

12. XZJ 83; CBETA X51. No. 831.

This brief resurgence of attention to Dignāga's work was followed by another hiatus, but in the twentieth century Chinese scholars once again turned their attention to *Investigation of the Percept*, and new commentaries were written. It also figured in discussions of Buddhist philosophy generally, particularly in relation to Yogācāra and Buddhist logic. The first new commentary was Zhang Kecheng's 張克誠 (1865–1922) *Superficial Interpretation of Investigation of the Percept* (*Guan suoyuanyuan lun qianshuo* 觀所緣緣論淺說). It is not dated, but it may have been written as early as 1912.[13] In 1914 Ouyang Jingwu 歐陽竟無 (1871–1943) published *Interpretive Exposition of Investigation of the Percept* (*Guan suoyuan yuan lun shijie* 觀所緣緣論釋解), which focused on Dharmapāla's reading of the text.

The most significant study of this period in China was Lü Cheng's 呂澂 (1896–1989) *Translation and Comparative Exposition of Investigation of the Percept* (*Guan suoyuan shi lun huishi* 觀所緣釋論會譯), published in 1928. Lü's approach was innovative among Chinese intellectuals: he had studied both Sanskrit and Tibetan in the China Institute for Inner Learning (*Zhina Neixue Yuan* 支那內學院) in the early 1920s, and he used his linguistic skills to compare Chinese and Tibetan versions of the text. His stated goal was to discern "Genuine Buddhism" (*Zhenshi Foxue* 真實佛學) and to free it from the false accretions that he believed had found their way into Chinese traditions. In his estimation, Yogācāra is a core source of Genuine Buddhism—a Buddhist school that contains sophisticated discussions of logic and epistemology developed by some of the greatest minds of Buddhism's formative period. Lü and other Chinese reformers regarded it as an indigenous intellectual resource that could withstand the onslaught of Western ideas. He never fully articulated what doctrines and practices should characterize Genuine Buddhism, but his analysis of *Investigation of the Percept* was intended as an example of proper methodology for understanding a normative Indian work.[14]

Inception and Design of the Project

This book is the result of a four-year collaborative research project. It is built upon a previous collaborative effort that examined the resurgence of interest in Yogācāra in China in the nineteenth and twentieth centuries and the role

13. It has been translated by John Makeham and is part of the East Asian materials for this project.

14. See Lusthaus (2013 and 2014) for a discussion of Lü Cheng's approach to Genuine Buddhism and his analysis of *Investigation of the Percept*.

Yogācāra played in the development of Buddhist modernism. That research produced an edited volume, *Transforming Consciousness: Yogācāra Thought in Modern China* (New York: Oxford University Press, 2014), edited by John Makeham, which charts the reception of Yogācāra in modern China and analyzes the thought of the major figures in its revival.

The present research endeavor is designed to examine a parallel development in Tibet: Yogācāra has generally been relegated to secondary status behind Madhyamaka in the Land of Snows but, as in China, Yogācāra studies enjoyed a renaissance in the nineteenth and twentieth centuries in Tibet, and a number of new commentaries on Yogācāra texts were composed during that period. Reformers such as Khenpo Shenga (mKhan chen gZhan phan Chos kyi snang ba, 1871–1927) devised new curricula for intensive study centers that included works like Vasubandhu's (*c.* fourth century) *Differentiation of the Middle and Extremes* (*Madhyānta-vibhāga*) and *Differentiation of Phenomena and Ultimate Reality* (*Dharma-dharmatā-vibhāga*).[15] Mipam (Mi pham rnam rgyal rgya mtsho, 1846–1912) and other "Non-Sectarian" (Ris med) scholars took a fresh look at Indian texts and composed works that often interpreted them in significantly new ways. As E. Gene Smith notes,

> The nonsectarian tradition emphasized a different aspect of religious education: scriptural exposition (*bshad pa*). . . . In their exposition seminaries (*bshad grwa*), monastic educators continued to teach a small number of classical Indian Buddhist *śāstras* in their Tibetan translations as the curriculum. Their students were expected to master these works through oral exposition and the study of editions provided with interlinear explanatory annotations (*mchan*). The basic aim was comprehension, not only of the words and arguments, but also of the doctrinal implications. This reorientation toward the Indian originals, it was felt, would eliminate many controversies that arose through variant expositions of the same texts by different Tibetan exegetes.[16]

A resurgence of interest in Yogācāra among scholars following the Non-Sectarian approach to Buddhist literature led to the composition of dozens of new commentaries on Indian Yogācāra texts that had largely been ignored for centuries. While mainly concerned with preserving and transmitting tantric lineages in danger of disappearing, Non-Sectarian lamas also pursued an

15. These commentaries are collected in Khenpo Shenga (1978).

16. Smith (2001: 246).

agenda of returning to ancient Indic sources and reading them on their own terms, not relying on traditional commentaries that were characterized as misleading or inaccurate. This was similar to Lü Cheng's approach, and it revolutionized Tibetan intellectual life, particularly in the Kagyu (bKa' brgyud), Nyingma (rNying ma), and Sakya orders. Gelukpa scholars also began to rediscover long-neglected Indian works such as *Investigation of the Percept* but, like Gungtang and Ngawang Dendar, their analyses were situated within the traditional Geluk commentarial tradition and relied on it in their discussions.

In light of this parallel renewal of interest in the same body of literature and in many of the same texts by Tibetan and Chinese scholars, we wondered whether there was mutual influence or if Chinese and Tibetan scholars were aware of each other's work. Tibetans would generally deny that there is any significant Chinese influence on their religion or scholarship. A common theme in autochthonous discussions of Tibetan Buddhism is that it preserves the pure tradition of India's Nālandā University, which in turn maintained the best of Indian Buddhism in a direct lineage from Śākyamuni Buddha.[17] The reality is more complex, and from at least the seventh century there has been cultural exchange between China and Tibet.

In the early period of transmission of the Dharma to Tibet, Chinese lineages exerted significant influence. Traditional sources report that conflicts between Indian and Chinese Buddhist missionaries came to a head in a "great debate" held at Samye (bSam yas) Monastery in the eighth century under the aegis of King Tri Songdetsen (Khri Srong lde btsan, r. 754–c. 799). The opponents were a Chinese group led by the Chan master Heshang Moheyan (和尚摩诃衍, fl. eighth century), a proponent of "sudden awakening" (*dunwu* 頓悟; Tib. *cig car 'jug pa*), and Indian monks led by Kamalaśīla (fl. 740–795), who championed a gradualist paradigm (*rim gyis 'jug pa*) that was normative in institutions like Nālandā. Modern scholarship has demonstrated a number of problems with the traditional account, and Luis Gómez has provided convincing evidence that it was probably a later fiction that summarized a series of confrontations as a single winner-take-all contest between rival factions that the Chinese side lost.[18]

Although the historicity of the "debate" may be questionable, most Tibetan Buddhists believe the story, and an enduring legacy is that Chinese Buddhism was condemned as heretical and Indian Buddhism became normative. When the Dharma was revived in Tibet in the eleventh century, there was

---

17. See, for example, Tenzin Gyatso (1995: 40), 228 and Thurman (2008: 39).

18. Gómez (1983a,b).

no question that India would be the sole source. Nonetheless, cultural and religious contacts between Tibet and China continued throughout the following centuries, particularly in the borderlands in eastern Tibet that lie near Chinese cultural regions.[19] Kumbum (sKu 'bum), a large monastery located on the downslope from the Tibetan Plateau leading toward Chinese lands, was one such point of contact. The eastern regions of Tibet were also the centers of the Non-Sectarian efflorescence in modern times and the locale where many of its leading figures lived and worked. Another meeting point for Tibetan and Chinese Buddhists was Wutai Shan, a sacred mountain in Shanxi Province where religious exchange was common.[20] The mountain today has several monasteries where Tibetans, Chinese, and Mongolians jointly practice a form of Tibetan Buddhism.

In light of these factors, it seemed possible, even probable, that the parallel resurgence of interest in Yogācāra among Chinese and Tibetan Buddhists in the modern period could have been a result of mutual influence, that one group might have inspired the other, or that some scholars worked in tandem. We were, however, unable to identify any evidence for such influence, despite the tantalizing fact that both of the eighteenth-century Tibetan exegetes of *Investigation of the Percept* lived in areas adjacent to China, and despite the fact that Ngawang Dendar spent time in Beijing. But this remains circumstantial at best because neither commentary provides evidence that its author was aware of distinctively East Asian interpretations of the text, and no Chinese authors are mentioned.

As we note above, the China Institute for Inner Learning taught Tibetan and Sanskrit and was an influential center for the dissemination of Tibetan culture. Some Chinese scholars who studied there, such as Lü Cheng, became fluent in Tibetan and worked on Yogācāra texts, but Chinese seldom traveled to Tibet for long-term or intensive study. Many Tibetan lamas went to China during the Manchu Qing dynasty (1644–1911) and the Republican

---

19. Kapstein (2009: 1–14). Sino-Tibetan interactions in the borderlands are also the subject of Makley (2007) and Nietupski (2011). Kolås and Thowsen (2005) examine the present-day dynamics of this cultural interaction.

20. See Tuttle (2006). A number of prominent Tibetans visited the mountain, including Pakpa Lodrö Gyeltsen ('Phags pa blo gros rgyal mtshan, 1235–1280), the sixth Dalai Lama, Tsangyang Gyatso (Tshangs dbyangs rgya mtsho, 1683–1706), and the fifth Karmapa, Teshin Shekpa (De bzhin gshegs pa, 1384–1415). *The Blue Annals* (Roerich 1995: 220, 335–336, 669, 679) reports a number of visits by Tibetan monks. Zhenhai Temple (鎮海寺), situated on Wutai Shan, was also the seat of the Jangya (lCang skya) incarnations, particularly Jangya Rolbe Dorje (lCang skya Rol pa'i rdo rje, 1717–1786), who served as intermediaries between governments in Tibet, China, and Mongolia.

period (1912–1949),[21] but Chinese interest in "Lamaism" (Lamajiao 喇嘛教, the standard way of referring to Tibetan Buddhism in China) was mainly concerned with the purported magical powers of Tibetan lamas, and not their scholarship.[22] This trend continues today as thousands of Chinese make the journey to monasteries in eastern Tibet and receive teachings and empowerments from lamas, but most are attracted by the mysteries of Tibetan tantric Buddhism and the supramundane abilities associated with its luminaries, rather than study of ancient philosophical texts.[23]

During the nineteenth and twentieth centuries, some foreigners went to Tibet, and some from Buddhist countries studied at monastic universities. These include the Japanese monk Kawaguchi Ekai 河口慧海 (1866–1945), who stayed in Tibet from 1900 to 1902 and who brought back a number of copies of Buddhist texts, and the Buryat Mongol Agvan Dorjieff (Ngag dbang blo bzang rdo rje, 1854–1938), who reached central Tibet in 1873. He studied at Drepung Monastic University in Lhasa and distinguished himself as a scholar. Dorjieff became a tutor to the thirteenth Dalai Lama, Tupden Gyatso (Thub bstan rgya mtsho, 1876–1933), and served as an emissary between the Tibetan government and the Russian government of Tsar Nicholas II (1894–1917).

There are few accounts of Chinese making the difficult and hazardous journey to Tibet prior to the invasion by China in the 1950s. Many Chinese view Tibet as a dangerous and unhealthy place, and Buddhists in China commonly regard Tibetan traditions as deviant and heterodox. The mutual negative stereotypes, coupled with the distance between interior China and the Tibetan Plateau and the difficulties of traveling between the two regions, were factors that inhibited cultural collaboration between Buddhists.

One Chinese monk who did study in Tibet was Fazun 法尊 (1902–1980), who in 1925 traveled to eastern Tibet and spent three years there before continuing to Lhasa. He attended lectures at Drepung but never formally enrolled in its academic program. He initially intended to study for the *geshe* (*dge bshes*)

---

21. Chia Ning (1992) reports that Qing imperial registers indicate that more than 100 high-ranking Tibetan reincarnate lamas (*sprul sku*) resided in Beijing during the late imperial period, and during the reign of the Qianlong 乾隆 emperor (1711–1799) more than 1200 lamas were registered with the Court for Managing the Frontiers. Nietupski (2009) discusses Tibetan lamas from Labrang Monastery (bLa brang bKra shis 'khyil) who taught in China and became known as "Chinese lamas" (rGya nag pa bla ma).

22. The best study of this phenomenon to date is Tuttle (2005). Tuttle argues that the presence of Tibetan lamas in China was a crucial element in Chinese coming to view Tibetan Buddhism as part of Chinese culture and was a factor in a growing perception of Tibet as part of Chinese territory.

23. See, for example, Yü (2012: 75–125) and Kapstein (2009: 7).

degree, but in 1933 he was recalled to China, and in 1935 became director of the Sino-Tibetan Institute of World Buddhist Studies (Shijie Foxue yuan Han Zang cang jiaoli yuan 世界佛學苑漢藏教理院; Tib. rGya bod lung rigs bslab grwa khang), located at Jinyun Monastery (縉雲寺) on Jinyun Mountain near Chongqing.

The institute opened in 1932 as one of the seminaries established by Taixu 太虛 (1890–1947) to provide academic training for young monks and lay Buddhists. It continued operations until 1950, and more than 200 students graduated. Fazun made Gelukpa texts a core aspect of the curriculum, including Tsongkhapa's (Tsong kha pa bLo bzang grags pa, 1357–1419) *Great Exposition of the Stages of the Path* (*Lam rim chen mo*; Ch. *Puti dao cidi guang lun* 菩提道次第廣論) and *Great Exposition of Mantra* (*sNgags rim chen mo*; Ch. *Mizongdao cidi guanglun* 密宗道次第廣論). Fazun translated these works into Chinese, and he assigned several Yogācāra works as required reading for students, along with Madhyamaka treatises, some sūtras, and a range of other works that are widely studied in Gelukpa monastic universities.[24] He also wrote the first Chinese textbook for the study of Tibetan language and a Tibetan-Chinese dictionary. On his trip to Tibet he was accompanied by other monks, including Dayong 大勇 (1893–1929) and Huishen 慧深 (d.u.).[25] They were joined in Kangding 康定 (Tib. Dar rtse mdo) by Nenghai 能海 (1886–1967). Dayong died during his visit, but Nenghai was one of the few Chinese who made it to Lhasa, where he studied for several years.

Following the declaration of Tibet's independence by the thirteenth Dalai Lama in 1913, an official ban was imposed, and Chinese nationals were expelled from the country. This made it virtually impossible to travel to central Tibet, although contact between Chinese and Tibetans continued at shared holy sites like Wutai Shan and monasteries in eastern parts of the Tibetan Plateau that were under Chinese control or were governed independently by local chieftains. A few Chinese still managed to travel to Tibet, including Bisong (碧松; also known as Luosang Zhenzhu 洛桑珍珠, 1916–), who entered Tibet in 1937

---

24. His life and activities are described by Sullivan (2007 and 2008). Sullivan notes that Fazun's writings introduced many Chinese to Tibet and its culture. Fazun wrote a history of Tibet based on Tibetan sources (Fazun 1940), which was the first such work in China, and he also promoted the Gelukpa order following his return to China.

25. The group referred to itself as "Team to Study the Dharma Abroad in Tibet" (Liu Zang xuefa tuan 留藏學法團). They started off with great enthusiasm, but most never reached Tibet, and some died during the journey. Only a few made it to Tibetan cultural areas. Another program sponsored by the Mongolian and Tibetan Affairs Commission (Mengzang Weiyuanhui 蒙藏委員會) sent about twenty monks to study in Tibet.

and became the first Chinese scholar to earn the rank of *geshe hlarampa* (*dge bshes lha rams pa*, the highest degree in the Gelukpa scholastic system).

This intellectual traffic was almost entirely one way: many academic Buddhists such as Lü Cheng and Fazun looked to Tibet as a source for recovering the true Dharma and finding textual resources unknown in China that would help them in purging their tradition of false accretions. Tibetans, however, had no such conceptions regarding Chinese Buddhism, and when they traveled to China they did so as teachers, and not as students of the Dharma. Even today the sense among Tibetans that they have preserved the unbroken Nālandā lineage remains strong, but Yao Zhihua reflects a widespread sentiment when he states that as a student he realized that many young scholars like himself had a suspicion: "Chinese Buddhism is wrong, or, at least, there is something wrong with Chinese Buddhism."[26] Chinese often looked to Tibetan Buddhism for more authentic sources, and there was "a common hostility toward Sinicized Buddhism."[27] Similarly, Fazun declared: "In Tibet there is a perfect Buddhism, which one could study, translate, and promulgate."[28]

Research Focus

In light of these factors, in retrospect it is probably not surprising that we failed to find evidence of influence by Chinese on Tibetan Yogācāra scholarship or examples of collaborative study between Chinese and Tibetans on this literature. After searching in vain for examples of influence across the border in the revival of interest in Yogācāra in the modern period, the research team turned its attention to examination of texts that received commentaries by Chinese and Tibetans, particularly those with a long history of debate and analysis in India, Tibet, and China. The corpus of Yogācāra is vast, and it contains some of the most abstruse philosophical and scholastic material in Buddhist canonical literature. The volume of new material on Yogācāra in Tibet and China during the nineteenth to twenty-first centuries made a comprehensive study impossible, and so the group decided to follow the lead of Lü Cheng and focus on *Investigation of the Percept* because it is an important Indian work that has been the subject of renewed commentarial interest in Tibet and China in several periods, including the nineteenth and twentieth centuries.

---

26. Yao (2009b: 281).

27. Yao (2009b: 281).

28. Bianchi (2009: 209).

The initial goal was to engage in close study of the text and its commentaries from the sixth century to the present in order to discern the sources of the commentators and to uncover any evidence of awareness of and engagement with one another's tradition by Tibetans or Chinese. This study also failed to yield any positive evidence, but the exercise has nonetheless been valuable: *Investigation of the Percept* has a long history in India, Tibet, and China, one punctuated by times of renewed interest and commentary followed by periods of neglect. While there is some broad overlap between these phases in China and Tibet, these events appear to have occurred independently, and neither side gives any sign of awareness of the other's activities. Moreover, close study of Chinese and Tibetan commentaries reveals that each side had its own approaches to the text and asked different questions in interpreting it, reflecting in part the absence of Dharmakīrti in China and divergences in the respective emphases of Dharmapāla and Vinītadeva, each of whom was foundational for one, but not the other, tradition.

This divergence begins with translations. Some early Tibetan exegetes were fluent in Sanskrit, and study of Indic texts used both Sanskrit and Tibetan sources. Historically, few Tibetan Buddhists have learned Chinese, and Chinese translations are generally regarded in Tibet as less authoritative than those in their own canon. Chinese commentators based their work on Chinese translations, and until Lü Cheng analyzed *Investigation of the Percept* in the 1920s, none appear to have worked with Tibetan texts in studying it. Another factor, as we noted, was the Indian commentaries with which each group engaged: Dharmapāla became the standard Indic resource for interpretation in East Asia, and Dharmapāla's omission of any analysis of the last two verses meant that Chinese exegetes commonly focused on Dignāga's discussion of atomism and paid less attention to his presentation of cognition in verses 7 and 8. An example is Mingyu's *Explanation of Investigation of the Percept*, most of which (818a–833c) is concerned with atomism and other topics of the first six verses. Vinītadeva, in contrast, thematizes Dignāga's ideas in the context of idealism and uses this as his guiding interpretive frame.

As the research team worked in parallel on Indian, Tibetan, and Chinese sources relating to *Investigation of the Percept*, it became increasingly clear that the traditions of India and Tibet on the one hand, and of East Asia on the other, were highly divergent. Key terms were used differently in Chinese texts in comparison to how they were glossed in Sanskrit sources and the implied glosses in Tibetan equivalents. And the project grew: as new sources were discovered and translated, the group's output became too large for a single volume. The size of the combined material and of the research team, as well as the disjunction between these two bodies of literature, led us to divide our work into two publications, the present one focused on Indian and Tibetan literature, and another on Chinese translations of and commentaries on *Investigation of the Percept.*

Some Comments on Methodology

We have been discussing *Investigation of the Percept* as though it were a single text, but this is rarely the case with classical Buddhist works. There is no reason to doubt that a monk named Dignāga wrote some Sanskrit verses and an autocommentary in the sixth century or that these became known as *Ālambana-parīkṣā* and *Ālambana-parīkṣā-vṛtti,* but these were lost centuries ago. Sanskrit fragments exist in the works of other Indian authors, but there is no way to ascertain the degree to which they quoted accurately, misrepresented him, or paraphrased. Like so many other treatises of this genre and period, *Ālambana-parīkṣā-vṛtti* was copied and redacted, and in this process errors and emendations inevitably made their way into the manuscripts. There may have been more than one Tibetan translation, and as the canon was edited textual variants developed, all of which we have noted in our critical edition. In China three translations from Sanskrit manuscripts were included in the canon, and each of these translations interprets and renders the text in different ways, including three equivalents for many technical terms and variants in phrasing that indicate that Paramārtha, Xuanzang, and Yijing disagreed in their understanding of the Sanskrit manuscripts with which they were working and that they may have been working with different Sanskrit editions.

The expansion of the corpus grounded in *Investigation of the Percept* continued with the composition of commentaries. The first of these, by Dharmapāla and Vinītadeva, were based on Sanskrit manuscripts, but later exegetes in Tibet and China probably only read their own languages and so appropriated Dignāga's work in terms of their respective traditions' translations and interpretations.

Scholars often speak loosely of "Sanskrit originals" as if a newly discovered Sanskrit manuscript is necessarily earlier (and thus more authoritative) than translations into other languages and supersedes them, but many of the extant Sanskrit versions of Buddhist texts are handwritten copies made in Nepal from the fifteenth to seventeenth century, and so they represent the most recent—and often most corrupt—edition of a given text. Such manuscripts are the end of a process of copying and revision that probably began shortly after the composition of a given work and that with the advent of digitized texts has probably reached its terminus. The errors, mistaken emendations, or misreadings of scribes in these textual lineages became part of the transmission of each text.[29] If such a Sanskrit version of *Investigation of the Percept* were to be discovered, it would be one more part of the corpus, and it would need to be edited in light of Tibetan and Chinese translations as well as commentaries. Even then, the result would be an example of how a particular scholar or group of scholars thinks the text should read, and not *the Ālambana-parīkṣā*.

Barring the invention of time travel, there is no way to recover Dignāga's original text—and even if it were possible, would it be *the Ālambana-parīkṣā*? It would have a certain claim to precedence, but later versions that were the results of copying and emendation were the basis of the commentaries through which Buddhists in India, China, and Tibet read his work, and so the copies in the libraries of the great Indian monastic universities might have been historically more influential than what Dignāga originally wrote. There is no way to ascertain today, or even cogently speculate about, what relation there may have been between subsequent copies and Dignāga's drafts and final version. Nor would such speculation settle anything. The same is true of the manuscripts that were transmitted to China and Tibet. So, the text we have today is really a family of literature, not an individual ür-text.

Contemporary scholars have two main choices when they translate an ancient Indian text like *Investigation of the Percept*: they can concentrate on one particular presently attested version, either in Tibetan or Chinese, or they can make a composite edition using available textual materials and their own intuitions and informed judgments in deciding what to follow for particular terms or passages. In the case of one particular edition, the result is a translation of a real text that is part of a lineage that may or may not constitute an unbroken line back to Dignāga. In the case of the composite edition, the result is simply one more version that in turn becomes part of the corpus.

Our team chose the former course and used the Derge (sDe dge) editions as the basis for translating *Investigation of the Percept* and Vinītadeva's commentary. The Derge has become a de facto standard in Tibetan because of its easy accessibility and generally careful editing, but it is corrupted in parts. Other Tibetan versions sometimes provide clearer readings, and so we have used them for necessary emendations. Where Sanskrit fragments were available, they aided in deciding between competing possible readings of some

---

29. An Indian tradition holds that the most prolific consumers of Sanskrit manuscripts are worms and ants. See Lutgendorf (1991: 57), where he refers to "his majesty the white ant." The voracious appetites of worms and ants for manuscripts create numerous problems, including holes and missing portions. It also means that manuscripts must be copied in each generation; those that are not are often lost forever. Many of the copyists were not literate in Sanskrit and mechanically retained errors. The ongoing corruption of manuscripts led to multiplication of textual problems that must be sorted out by contemporary editors.

passages. The two editions of the commentaries of Gungtang and Ngawang Dendar are each almost identical, and so few decisions regarding variants were needed. Our goal has been to produce translations that make the best philosophical sense of the extant texts and not to attempt reconstruction of texts that no longer exist. Moreover, we have tried to translate each text on its own terms in order to reflect the differences between distinct readings of Dignāga's treatise.

In addition to translations of *Investigation of the Percept* and the commentaries from India and Tibet, we provide editions of our texts and introductory essays for each translation that contain short biographies of the authors and discussions of their most significant philosophical contributions to this corpus of literature. Because this is an intellectual history of a particular work, the focus of the essays is the thought of Dignāga and his commentators and what each contributed to the development of Buddhist epistemology. Inasmuch as Dharmapāla's commentary influenced the East Asian exegetical tradition and had little impact in Tibet, we discuss its most useful insights for understanding Dignāga's thought and have left the task of translating and analyzing it to the East Asia cohort of the research team.

Our translation policy has been to produce readable English versions of Tibetan texts, including Tibetan translations of Indian Sanskrit treatises. We have tried as much as possible to use natural philosophical English to translate texts, supplying Sanskrit or Tibetan equivalents only where necessary to clarify or to indicate an unusual or possibly contentious translation choice. We have limited the use of philological square brackets to cases where we are explicitly interpolating material to clarify an otherwise obscure passage. In particular, where Tibetan or Sanskrit grammar allows subjects or verbs to be dropped when clear from context or antecedents, but where English requires explicit use for grammaticality or clarity, we have inserted the necessary lexical items without the use of brackets, reflecting our principle that the English translation should be as close as possible in meaning to the source text, while also remaining grammatical and clear in English. Since this volume includes editions of the source texts, specialists will be able to compare our translations with the Tibetan texts we translate. To facilitate readability for nonspecialists and because answers to questions regarding the source texts can be found in the second section, we have endeavored to keep the texts as readable as possible and to avoid breaking the flow with unnecessary parenthetical insertions.

PART I

Studies and Translations

I

The Subject Matter of Investigation of the Percept

A TALE OF FIVE COMMENTARIES

Malcolm David Eckel, Jay L. Garfield, and John Powers

Dignāga: Life and Times

Unlike their Tibetan successors, Indian Buddhists had little interest in the details of the lives of great figures. Not surprisingly, then, information about Dignāga's (*c.* 480–540)[1] life is sketchy and often contradictory in Indian sources. Several Tibetan texts (written centuries after his death) provide more details, but their reliability is questionable. Such accounts probably contain little in the way of accurate biographical information regarding their subjects, but they do indicate how Buddhist traditions have viewed them and how they became important as exemplars of particular qualities or activities. Chinese

1. Tibetan translators rendered his name as "Direction Elephant" (*Phyogs kyi glang po*). The Tibetan term *glang po* has a range of connotations, including "elephant" or "mountain." Nāga (Tib. *glang*) can refer either to elephants or to mythological beings who are shape shifters; they have the bodies of snakes and are associated with water. *Diś* (Tib. *phyogs*) can refer to space, region, or direction. This connotation is also reflected in the Chinese translation of his name as Yulong 域龍: 域, which refers to direction or space and 龍 is a common translation for *nāga*. Fangxiang 方象is similar to the Tibetan: 方 means "direction" and 象 is used to translate *nāga*. It appears that the Tibetan and Chinese translators used terms involving various connotations of the components of his name. Another possibility is suggested by Monier-Williams's (1979: 479 col. 3) discussion of *dik-karin* ("direction-elephant"), which he describes as "one of the mythical elephants which stand in the four or eight quarters of the sky and support the earth." Chenna 陳那 is an attempt at a phonetic rendering of Dignāga and is how Xuanzang and Yijing treat his name.

travelogues by Xuanzang[2] and Yijing,[3] who journeyed to India about a century after his death and reported traditions concerning his activities, contain relatively less mythological material but are still hagiographical in tone.

According to Tibetan sources, Dignāga's origins lie in South India, and he was a native of Kāñcī.[4] Chinese tradition, however, states that he resided near Veṅgīpura (Pingquiluo 瓶耆羅), the capital of Andhra (Andaluoguo 案達羅國). Tāranātha (1575–1634; 1990: 176–179) says he was born in a brahman family in the city of Siṅgavakti. He became a student of Nāgadatta, a master of the Vātsīputrīya subsect of the Pudgalavāda school, who believed in a conventional self (*pudgala*) that is supervenient on the aggregates (*skandha*). During his meditation practice, Dignāga sought in vain for such a self, at one point stripping off all his clothes and searching among the constituent elements of his body and mind. Judging Dignāga to be an apostate, Nāgadatta demanded that he leave his order.

Both Tāranātha and Pudön (Bu ston Rin chen grub, 1290–1364; 1986: 149–152) agree that Dignāga subsequently found Vasubandhu and became his student. Pudön states that Dignāga was more learned than his teacher in logic and excelled in debate. He earned the epithet "Bull of Reasoning" (Tarka-puṅgava). The notion that he was Vasubandhu's student has been questioned by some scholars in light of a passage in the *Compendium of Epistemology* in which Dignāga indicates qualms about *Rules for Debate* (*Vādavidhi*), a work generally credited to Vasubandhu. According to Jinendrabuddhi,[5] however, Dignāga only questions the provenance of a particular passage and suggests that it might be an interpolation.[6] As suggested at the beginning of this chapter, the dates of Indian figures are seldom well attested and are often the subject of speculation by scholars using limited or contradictory evidence. Vasubandhu's probable dates, however, are in the fourth century, and it is unlikely that the two lived at the same time or in the same place.

Tāranātha says that Dignāga engaged in intensive solitary meditation in a cave named Bhoṭaśela in Oḍiviśa and attained advanced meditative states.

---

2. Xuanzang, *Great Tang Dynasty Record of Western Regions* (*Da Tang xiyu ji* 大唐西域記), T 2087.51.867–947. Xuanzang (*c.* 602–664) traveled to India from 629 to 645.

3. Yijing, *A Record of Buddhist Practices Sent Home from the Southern Seas* (*Nanhai jigui neifa zhuan* 南海寄歸內法傳). T 2125, vol. 54. He left for India in 671 and returned in 695.

4. Dharmapāla is also associated with this city and region.

5. Regarding problems with identifying this figure and his works, see Hayes (1993).

6. Jinendrabuddhi (2005, vol. 1: 86) states that Dignāga highlights "the impossibility of the defective *Rules of Debate* passage's being written by him."

Dignāga later studied at Nālandā University, where he debated with non-Buddhists led by Sudurjaya. Dignāga defeated Sudurjaya and his fellow heretics and became a renowned teacher. Tāranātha relates that Dignāga composed more than 100 works. He later returned to solitary meditation in Oḍiviśa.

Pudön and Tāranātha report a debate with a non-Buddhist philosopher named Kṛṣṇamunirāja. The latter sneaked into Dignāga's cave on two occasions and erased a verse Dignāga had written in chalk expressing his desire to develop a logic system for the benefit of sentient beings. Kṛṣṇamunirāja was defeated three times, and Dignāga said that he should convert to Buddhism. Kṛṣṇamunirāja responded by shooting flames from his mouth that burned Dignāga's possessions and almost incinerated Dignāga as well. Dignāga despaired that he had been unable to help this one being and thought to renounce Mahāyāna Buddhism and embrace the Lesser Vehicle, but Mañjuśrī appeared and convinced him to remain true to his convictions. Following this incident, Mañjuśrī became Dignāga's personal tutor.

The Tibetan accounts agree that Dignāga later traveled to Southern India, where he continued to defeat non-Buddhist opponents in debate. He also rebuilt Buddhist sites that had fallen into disrepair. He converted the minister of the king of Oḍiviśa, who subsequently built sixteen major monasteries. Dignāga spent the rest of his life in solitary retreat. He was content with very little and did not even have an attendant. He passed away in a forest in Oḍiviśa.

Xuanzang characterizes Dignāga as an advanced meditator and describes conversations between him and Mañjuśrī. The bodhisattva of wisdom advised him to expound the *Treatise on the Levels of Yogic Practice* (*Yogācāra-bhūmi-śāstra*) for the benefit of beings.[7] Dignāga first composed treatises on logic and reasoning but later taught his students about the *Treatise on the Levels of Yogic Practice.*

Dignāga is widely credited with revolutionizing the field of logic or reasoning (*hetu-vidyā*). Yijing states that eight of Dignāga's logic treatises had become part of the standard curriculum for Indian monks by the time of his visit. Xuanzang reports that he visited a *stūpa* on a hill near Veṅgīpura where Dignāga wrote his logic treatises.[8] He indicates that Dignāga was prophesied to expound the principles of reasoning that had been set out by the Buddha but that were subsequently neglected.

Among other innovations, Dignāga championed the idea that there are only two reliable instruments of knowledge (*pramāṇa*): (1) perception (*pratyakṣa*);

---

7. Xuanzang, *Great Tang Dynasty Record of Western Regions*, T 2087.51.930b.

8. Xuanzang, *Great Tang Dynasty Record of Western Regions*, T 2087.51.930b.

and (2) inference (*anumāna*). In *Introduction to Logic* (*Nyāya-mukha*, which survives only in Chinese: *Yinming zhengli men lun* 因明正理門論), he defines perception as "devoid of conceptual constructions" (*kalpanāpodha*), that is, of false ideas derived from dreams, memory, desires, or hallucinations. He composed a number of influential works, the most important of which was *Compendium of Epistemology*. This text is best known through the interpretations of Dharmakīrti's (*c.* seventh century) *Commentary on the Compendium of Epistemology*, which became one of the most influential epistemological treatises in India and Tibet. Dignāga also composed the *Wheel of Reasons* (*Hetu-cakra*), which discusses procedures for reasoning, and a commentary on Vasubandhu's *Treasury of Abhidharma* (*Abhidharma-kośa*) titled *Commentary on the Treasury of Abhidharma Called "Lamp of the Essence"* (*Abhidharmakośa-vṛtti-marmapradīpa-nāma*).[9]

The Subject Matter of the Text: Fundamental Particles and Perception

Investigation of the Percept is a terse text that encodes a number of subtle philosophical points and outlines refutations of the positions of various opponents. Depending on how it is read, in the first five verses and their autocommentary Dignāga presents and rebuts two (or three) positions: (1) that the percept[10] of cognition consists in fundamental particles (*rdul phra rab*; Skt. *paramāṇu*);[11]

9. The title of this text can be construed in various ways. It is a voluminous work that discusses a wide range of philosophical topics within the purview of the scholastic Abhidharma tradition. Vasubandhu explains (commentary on verse 2cd; Wogihara 1932–1936 II: 8–9) that *abhidharma* (literally "higher/superior dharma") means "stainless wisdom" (*amala-prajñā*), and the treatise leads to its attainment. This in turn is conducive to attainment of the supreme dharma (*paramārtha-dharma*), that is, nirvana. He explains *kośa* as a sheath, like the scabbard of a sword. His treatise is the "sheath of Abhidharma" in the sense that it is drawn from Abhidharma, as a sword is taken out of its sheath.

10. Tib. *dmigs pa*; Skt. *ālambana*. Xuanzang, *Treatise Investigating the Percept Condition* (*Guan suoyuanyuan lun* 觀所緣緣論, T 1624.31.888–889) renders this term as *suoyuan* 所緣, perceptual objects. Paramārtha (*Treatise on the Object of Cognition Devoid of Attributes*; *Wuxiang sichen lun* 無相思塵論, T 1619.31.882–883) uses *chen* 塵, literally "dust." It often is used to refer to objects in general and translates Sanskrit *artha*, *viṣaya*, or *gocara*. In some contexts, it can refer to a tiny object or to a stain or pollution. Paramārtha's usage in this context is idiosyncratic.

11. The Chinese translators render this term in several ways: Paramārtha has: *linxu* 鄰虛, virtually empty space. Xuanzang renders it as *jiwei* 極微, absolutely subtle/tiny. In Indian Abhidharma literature, this term refers to the smallest possible particles, which may be material or constitutive properties of things, such as color. In this sense, its meaning corresponds

(2) that it consists in collections (*'dus pa*; Skt. *samūha*)[12] of such particles; or (3) that the percept is a representation or collection of representations (*rnam pa*; Skt. *ākāra*) derived from fundamental particles.

Dharmapāla distinguishes the third of these as a distinct position requiring a distinct refutation. Vinītadeva follows his lead in his commentary on verse 3: "Having refuted these two positions, [Dignāga] presents a third position."(42–43)[13] The two eighteenth-century Tibetan commentators, Gungtang Könchok Denbe Drönme and Ngawang Dendar, treat what Dharmaplāla takes as the third position as a version of the second position, or as a hybrid of positions one and two that shares their respective defects.

Verse 1 discusses the first position; verse 2 analyzes the second; and verse 3 presents what some commentators take to be the third. On this view, the critique of the third position begins in verse 3 and extends into verses 4 and 5. The final three verses of *Investigation of the Percept* present Dignāga's own account of the nature of the percept, and they do so in a way that is consistent both with Dignāga's own idealism and with the realism of certain of his Buddhist interlocutors. In each case, the terse formulation of the verse is expanded into explicit argument in the autocommentary.

---

to the Latin term *atomus* or the Greek *átomos*—something that cannot be divided. In modern usage, however, "atom" refers to the smallest quantity of an element that can be involved in a chemical reaction. Atoms have components such as neutrons, protons, and electrons, whereas *paramāṇu* are by definition partless.

The Tibetan translation uses three different terms to represent Dignāga's words for fundamental particles: *rdul phra rab* or *phra rab rdul* (for the Sanskrit *paramāṇu*, as in verse 1); *rdul phran* (for the Sanskrit *aṇu*, as in verse 1); and *rdul phra mo* (as in the commentary on verse 1). The Sanskrit equivalent of the third of these terms is not known directly from Sanskrit sources, but it appears that *rdul phran* in verse 1 is simply the short, verse form of *rdul phra mo* in the prose of the commentary. In other words, it is likely that *rdul phran* and *rdul phra mo* both represent the Sanskrit *aṇu*. To accommodate distinctions that appeared in later Tibetan commentaries, we have chosen to translate these three terms differently, as "fundamental particles" (for *rdul phra rab* and *phra rab rdul*), "particles" (for *rdul phran*), and "minute (or subtle) particles" (for *rdul phra mo*). Dignāga, however, does not seem to have distinguished different types of particles for the purposes of his argument in this text. He uses the terms interchangeably, as he does, for example, in the text and commentary on verse 3.

12. The Tibetan term *'dus pa* can render a number of Sanskrit terms, including *samūha* or *saṅghāta*. Dan Lusthaus (personal communication) points out that Yijing transliterates this as *mu a* 謨阿, which suggests that *samūha* was the original term. He appears to have omitted the character *san* 三, which is commonly used for this transliteration. An example is Yijing's translation of another text attributed to Dignāga, *Treatise on Apprehending the Designations of Causes* (*Quyin jiashe lun* 取因假設論, T.31.887b19). The reading of *samūha* is also supported by Bhāviveka's summary of the third argument in *Verses on the Heart of the Middle Way* (*Madhyamaka-hṛdaya-kārikā*) 5.31: Eckel (2008: 406).

13. This is discussed by Eckel in his analysis of Vinītadeva's commentary (88).

In the autocommentary, Dignāga states that the purpose of the text is to respond to those who maintain that the percept "is fundamental particles (because that is what causes cognition), or that it is collections (because that is what appears to cognition: 220)." This statement suggests that he wants to refute two positions: first, that perceptual cognitions are caused by fundamental particles; and second, that cognition involves an appearance of a collection of fundamental particles.

Dignāga plays his philosophical cards close to his robe. He wants to present an analysis of cognition that is acceptable to realists but that also undergirds his own idealist position. That is, although he himself is an idealist, this text is not meant as a defense of idealism per se. Rather, it is intended as a defense of a particular view of the structure of perception, one that is acceptable independent of one's broader ontological commitments; it is primarily epistemological, not ontological, in force.

The text has a clear structure, refuting a set of positions that Dignāga takes to constitute a family of philosophical views, despite the variation among them; it is a family from which he wishes to distance himself. Nonetheless, it is not immediately obvious what these positions have in common, nor why they are to be considered together. At the end of the autocommentary, Dignāga makes this commonality clear:

> A cognition arises with the appearance of an object, depending on the capacity called "eye" and on an internal object, without being disclosed as the percept. These two cause one another and have done so from beginningless time. Sometimes the representation of the object of cognition arises from the maturation of the capacity, and sometimes the capacity arises from the representation. Saying these two are different or not different from cognition is a matter of preference. (224)

Let us unpack this a bit, with the help of other remarks in the autocommentary. Dignāga takes his opponents to be those who think that fundamental particles are the causes of external objects, or that cognition involves an appearance of fundamental particles. First, note that the term *internal object* contrasts with a term used elsewhere, *external object* (*phyi rol gyi don*; Skt. *bāhyārtha*).[14] In the context of this discussion, an external object must be read as meaning the *appearance* or the *apprehension* of objects as external. Dignāga is examining the *percept* here; in the second verse in particular and its autocommentary, he makes it clear that the phenomenon whose cause he is interrogating is the

14. Paramārtha: *waijing* 外境, external objects. Xuanzang: *waise* 外色, external form.

object perceived as external. He states that two criteria must be met for something to be considered a percept in the relevant sense: (1) it must be the *cause* of cognition; and (2) it must be that which *appears* in the cognition.[15] Each of the positions he considers satisfies one of these two criteria but fails the other: fundamental particles may be causal, but they do not appear in cognition. Collections may appear, but they cannot be causal. Thus, each position fails one of the two criteria; together they constitute a kind of logical space of epistemic near misses in this domain.

Dignāga's final remark suggests that even a materialist opponent must accept his contention that cognition has merely the appearance of an object and is an internal phenomenon. So, he takes himself to have demonstrated that although idealism can provide a satisfactory account of how perception functions, that account is also the best way for even a materialist to explain perception. Dignāga, despite being clear about his own ontological position, also indicates that he is concerned only with epistemology in this treatise.[16]

Terminology

A word about words is in order here. *Ālambana* is a technical term with a complex semantic range and is used in this literature in the context of two other related terms, each with its own complex semantic range: *viṣaya* (Tib. *yul*) and *artha* (Tib. *don*). Each can be used to refer to perceptual content in *some sense of object*, but each has its own etymology and associations. *Ālambana* derives from the Sanskrit root *lamb*, meaning "to hang down, sink, cling to, suspend, depend or rely on, seize, maintain,"[17] with the prefix *ā*, "near, toward." The term *ālambana* has a range of connotations, including "depend on, rest on,

15. Although this twofold criterion predates Dignāga, the origin is unclear. The dialectical context shows that he regarded it as noncontroversial and acceptable to all relevant parties to these debates. Mingyu takes this position in his commentary, *Explanation of the Treatise Investigation of the Percept* (*Guan suoyuan yuan lunshi ji* 觀所緣緣論釋記, XZJ 83.827a04). He quotes Dharmapāla as stating that these criteria are found in the scriptures (*ajimo* 阿笈摩; Skt. *āgama*), and his own commentary asserts that both Mahāyāna philosophers and Hīnayānists hold this position . He does not specify whether or not it would also be accepted by non-Buddhists.

16. Dignāga is clearly an idealist, and indeed he has just argued that both the appearance of the object and the capacity of the sense faculty are cognitive. Nonetheless, he has not argued here directly for any particular ontological commitment regarding distal causes of the appearance. He claims that the idealist has the most economical explanation of appearance but that he has not refuted materialism on metaphysical grounds. So, he has shifted the burden of proof from the idealist to the materialist.

17. Monier-Williams (1979): 897 col. 1. Whitney (1945): 146.

support, sustain, foundation, base, reason, or cause."[18] In philosophical literature, an *ālambana* serves as a support of cognition. It refers to the attributes of things apprehended by the senses and the mental consciousness. In his autocommentary on the *Treasury of Abhidharma* (*Abhidharma-kośa-bhāṣya*), Vasubandhu defines *ālambana* as follows: "the percept refers to the domain of cognition" (*citta-dhātu*).[19] Dignāga comments that percepts are "the objects (*viṣaya*; Tib. *yul*) of the six cognitions, the visual up to the mental."[20]

Dignāga's choice of terminology in *Investigation of the Percept* is significant. Referring to the object of perception as "*ālambana*" is neutral with regard to its ontological status. It only indicates that it is the object of perception (and satisfies the two epistemic criteria noted earlier), but not that there is an independently existent or external object from which it arises. An image perceived in a dream—which like the percepts of waking consciousness can prompt emotional responses and resultant activities—is also a percept. In Buddhist philosophical literature, it is often neutral with regard to whether or not it is external: in the *Ornament for Mahāyāna Discourses* (*Mahāyāna-sūtrālaṃkāra*), for example, Asaṅga (*c.* fourth century) indicates that it has three senses: internal, external, or both.[21]

The same is true of the term *viṣaya*, which Dignāga uses to gloss *ālambana*. Derived from the Sanskrit root *viṣ*, meaning "to act, to do, perform," it can refer to a region or domain.[22] In Buddhist epistemology, it often denotes the range of the senses and their objects. It can also mean something with which one is engaged, an object of concern or attention. In epistemology, this can be anything that is noticed or cognized, and like *ālambana* it does not imply a judgment regarding its ontological status. In the *Treasury of Abhidharma*, Vasubandhu differentiates the two terms:

---

18. Monier-Williams (1979): 153 col. 2. Edgerton (1985): 105.

19. Vasubandhu, *Abhidharma-kośa-bhāṣya*, verse 33b commentary (Wogihara 1932–1936 I: 65). Our translation of *citta-dhātu* as "domain of cognition" (rather than "mental realms" or other possible readings) is influenced by the Tibetan translation, *rnam par shes pa'i phung po*, literally "aggregation of consciousness," which indicates that the Tibetan translators understood Vasubandhu to be including all the phenomena that are apprehended by cognition, perceived as data from the sense faculties and the mind.

20. Dignāga, *Commentary on the Treasury of Abhidharma Called "Lamp of the Essence"* (*Abhidharmakośa-vṛtti-marmapradīpa-nāma*. Tib. *Chos mngon pa'i mdzod kyi 'grel pa gnad kyi sgron me zhes bya ba*), sDe dge edition: 99b.

21. Asaṅga, *Ornament for Mahāyāna Discourses* (*Mahāyāna-sūtrālaṃkāra*), GRETL e-text, commentary on Chapter 11, verses 5–7.

22. Whitney (1945): 161. Monier-Williams (1979): 997 col. 1–2. Edgerton (1985): 502. Monier-Williams states that it can also be derived from *vi* + $\sqrt{}$*si*, meaning "to extend."

> What is the difference between *viṣaya* and *ālambana*? That which is the activity in any given sense faculty is the *viṣaya*, and that which is apprehended by the mind and mental factors is the *ālambana* (*yaccittacaittairgṛhyate tadālambanam*).[23]

Dignāga's commentary explains that the *ālambana* is associated with cognitive processes. It is the immediate cognitive object of the mind, and at the beginning of *Investigation of the Percept* he is noncommittal regarding the question of whether or not it originates within the perceptual process itself or in an external object.

In this context, in *Investigation of the Percept* Dignāga sometimes uses the related term *artha* (Tib. *don*) in critiquing positions he rejects, such as the view that the percept is an external object. *Artha* has a more robust sense of reality than *ālambana* or *viṣaya*. Derived from the root *arth*, meaning "to strive to obtain, desire, request," *artha* can refer to objects of desire such as wealth or other material things, and it has a sense of something concrete and tangible.[24] It appears widely in Sanskrit literature, where among other things it is one of the four aims of life along with sensual pleasure (*kāma*), religious duty (*dharma*), and release (*mokṣa*) from cyclic existence.

Artha can refer to one's goal or objects of desire, a cause, motive, or reason, wealth, property, or sense objects. In the last-named sense, it tends to connote something that is tangible and real, something that can be obtained and used in the real world. But it also conveys the idea of *intentionality* in Brentano's sense: that goal or object of desire is identified in relation to a cognitive agent or state. We can think of the problematic with which this literature is concerned as the relationship between the *percept* and the *intentional object*, or between the *de re* cause of perception and its content. In light of these considerations, it is significant that Dignāga focuses on the *ālambana*, which serves as the foundation of cognition but which, like a dream image, may not be founded on an external object. Nonetheless, the distinction between these terms is not systematic, and at times Dignāga uses the other two terms, *viṣaya* and *artha*, interchangeably with *ālambana*. Vinītadeva also glosses them as synonyms, and so in our translation both are rendered as "object."

---

23. Vasubandhu, *Abhidharma-kośa-bhāṣya*, verse 40a (Wogihara 1932–1936 I: 59). He adds that the mind and mental factors have both *viṣaya* and *ālambana*, but the sense faculties only have *viṣaya*. In his subcommentary, Yaśomitra (fl. *c.* 850 CE) glosses "activity" (*kāritra*) as "human activity" (*puruṣakāra*), meaning that it refers to the workings of the sense faculties, the eye, ear, and so on. The colors, sounds, and the like with which they are concerned are their fields of operation.

24. Monier-Williams (1979): 91 col. 1–2.

It is philosophically significant that Dignāga inquires about the link between *ālambana* and *viṣaya*. In this literature, *viṣaya* is that which is perceived, that which is contacted in perception. An *ālambana* is something that serves as a support, or a foundation, on which cognition depends. So, although Dignāga argues in the end that the *ālambana* is internal to cognition, he leaves open at the outset the possibility that an external object is the *ālambana*, and he does not entirely preclude that possibility in the conclusion. Indeed, it is important to his analysis that this conclusion is consistent with both realist and idealist systems; as we have noted, the ontological status of the external world and the objects believed by realists to populate it are not officially Dignāga's concern in this text, and its conclusions are intended to apply to perception, however the ontological status of its object is understood.

Yeshes Thabkhas argues that Dignāga uses the terms *don/artha* and *yul/viṣaya* differently and that he is concerned directly with the relation between the *ālambana* and the *artha* on one hand and the *viṣaya* on the other. Dignāga construes *don/artha* as an object toward which a cognition directs its attention—its intentional object—and he reads *yul/viṣaya* as a more generic term for object in general, that he uses to denote the referent, or *de re* object of perception. Because it is not clear that Dignāga and Vinītadeva draw a clear distinction between the meanings of these two terms (although if one accepts Yeshes Thabkhas's reading, they do), we have used the neutral term *object* to translate both of these terms in those texts. But we translate *don* as *intentional object* and *yul* as *object* (or sometimes, to be more explicit, *referential* object) in Yeshes Thabkhas's commentary to reflect his reading.

What Gives Rise to Cognition?

Dignāga's explanatory categories and questions arise from the Abhidharma tradition, and the positions he considers and rejects derive from that tradition. In particular, his concern with the percept reflects a concern with the percept condition in perception (the *ālambana-pratyaya*), which figures in the Abhidharma taxonomy of four conditions. We therefore begin there in explaining the context for his central question, "what gives rise to cognition?" We will then turn to the realist and representationalist positions that he considers and rejects.

According to Abhidharma philosophers, four conditions give rise to things: (1) the causal condition (Skt. *hetu-pratyaya*; Tib. *rgyu rkyen*); (2) the homogeneous immediately preceding condition (Skt. *samanantara-pratyaya*; Tib. *mtshung pa de ma thag pa'i rkyen*); (3) the percept condition (Skt.

ālambana-pratyaya; Tib. *dmigs rkyen*); and (4) the dominant condition (Skt. *adhipati-pratyaya*; Tib. *bdag rkyen*).[25] In the case of visual perception, for example, the causal condition is the collection of dharmas that stimulate the eye. The homogeneous immediately preceding condition comprises the mind and mental processes. The percept condition is the visible object. The dominant condition of the visual consciousness comprises the complete set of phenomena responsible for the cognition.[26] Dignāga is concerned with the percept condition and in particular with what the percept is in perception.

Dignāga begins by criticizing two principal theories regarding the percept: the realism of the Vaibhāṣika school and the representationalism of the Sautrāntika school. The Vaibhāṣika and Sautrāntika positions disagree regarding the nature of the percept. On the one hand, the Vaibhāṣikas are realists and argue that perceptual experience puts us in direct contact with external objects: "It is the organ of sight that sees visible matter when it is conjoined [with visual consciousness]."[27] The Sautrāntikas, on the other hand, "attribute sight, not to the organ of sight, but to visual consciousness ... if an organ sees, then the organ of a person occupied with hearing or touch consciousness would see."[28] The Sautrāntikas maintain that the percept is not an external object but a representation—a mental image that is constructed by the contact between sense organs and external objects. In veridical perception, the percept resembles the external object; in nonveridical perception it does not. The Sautrāntikas hence agree with the Vaibhāṣikas in affirming the existence of external objects in spite of the fact that they maintain that perception does not afford us direct access to them.

The Sautrāntikas defend this representationalism on the grounds of the Buddhist doctrine of momentariness: because everything is momentary, they argue, there is a time gap between the moment of contact between the sensory faculty and an external object and the moment of perceptual awareness. By the time perceptual cognition arises, the external object with which the sense faculty came in contact no longer exists. Therefore, this external object is not the percept because it does not now exist. The percept, Buddhist epistemologists

---

25. See Vasubandhu, *Commentary on the Treasury of Abhidharma*, II.61c (Pruden 1988–1990, vol. I): 296; Dharmatrāta, *Saṃyuktābhidharma-hṛdaya-śāstra* II.83 (Dessein 1999, vol. 1): 131; and Chim Jambeyang (mChims 'jam dpal dbyangs) (2009): 179–181.

26. *Commentary on the Treasury of Abhidharma*, II.62–II.64: Pruden (1988–1990, vol. 2): 360.

27. *Commentary on the Treasury of Abhidharma*, I.42a: Pruden (1988–1990, vol. I): 115; Tib. sDe dge, *mNgon pa*, vol. *ku*: 3b.

28. *Commentary on the Treasury of Abhidharma*, I.6cd: Pruden (1988–1990, vol. I): 120–121.

agree, must (a) appear in cognition and (b) be causally responsible for the content of the cognition in question. But the external object, the Sautrāntikas argue, cannot satisfy both criteria. Nonetheless, in perceptual cognition we are aware of something, and therefore there must be an intentional object of perceptual cognition. That internal object, they maintain, is the percept condition of perceptual cognition, and so that is the percept.

The Vaibhāṣikas's direct realism and the Sautrāntikas's representationalism both affirm the reality of physical objects, which they also agree are reducible to fundamental particles. They part company regarding the causal relation between those objects and perception, and so with regard to the nature of the percept. We will see that Dignāga parts company with both schools of thought, arguing that neither an external object nor the particles that compose it—nor a representation of an external object—can be a percept. We now turn to his strategy.

Dignāga's Opponents

The first position Dignāga seeks to refute—at least if we take his autocommentary at face value—is the assertion that fundamental particles, or what we might call the most basic bits of matter, cause us to perceive the objects we naively believe constitute the external world in the sense of being their *ālambana*—the thing that serves as the basis or foundation of that perception, both its simultaneous cause and the thing in virtue of which the cognitive state is perceptual.

The second position Dignāga opposes is that the percept is "a collection (because that is what appears to cognition: 220)." This is the notion that the intentional object of perception is in fact a collection of fundamental particles. On this view, when I see something such as a pot, the direct intentional object of perception is not a macroscopic object, but rather a swarm of atomic entities, which I mistakenly take to be a single object.

These two positions are in fact aspects of a single view that Dignāga is addressing, and that is a thesis about the nature of intentionality and of the percept in particular. The view that a percept must satisfy two conditions—it must be the *cause* of our perceptual experience, *and* it must be what *appears* to us in perception—is reasonable. After all, if I have a visual experience caused by a tree, but in which a pot appears (perhaps due to drug abuse or mirrors), it is plausible that neither the tree nor the pot is a genuine *percept*. The tree is a cause but is not perceived; the pot is hallucinated but is not perceived. We get a percept when the same thing is causal and figures as intentional content.

Now, Dignāga is not *attacking* what seems to have been a commonly held Indian view of the percept. On the contrary, he *takes it for granted*. Instead, he is considering and refuting a specific hypothesis about what the percept is in the case of ordinary perception, namely, that it is collections of particles that perform these two functions. This hypothesis derives from an understanding of the doctrine of the two truths as adumbrated in the Abhidharma. On this view, macroscopic wholes are composites of countless constantly changing fundamental particles. Inasmuch as they are impermanent and dependent for their identity on the conventional aggregation of their components, on the one hand, they are only conventionally real; they are not *substantially* real. On the other hand, given this understanding, the fundamental particles or dharmas that constitute them *are* substantially real. According to this formulation of the doctrine of the two truths, the conventional truth is that there are trees, pots, cups, and people; the ultimate truth is that there are momentary, dimensionless fundamental particles. Moreover, only what is substantially real can have causal power. Therefore, macroscopic wholes, despite the fact that they appear, cannot cause anything. Because a percept must *cause* perceptual experience, it might be concluded that fundamental particles, whether alone, together, or in combination, constitute the percept.

Dignāga thinks that is impossible, and he offers several arguments why. Verse 2 of *Investigation of the Percept* argues that collections are not substantially real (*rdzas su yod pa*; Skt. *dravya-sat*) and so can't be causes. Only individual dharmas, on Dignāga's view, are substantially real. Causality is found at that level. But of course individual particles don't appear in perception. As a result, one kind of thing (a particle) might *cause* perception, but another (a collection) *appears* in perception. No percept (that must perform *both* functions) is then to be found.[29]

In addition, according to verses 4–5 (directed at the third position but relevant here as well), fundamental particles all look the same. They are all very small and spherical. But percepts look different from one another. Although the particles that compose trees and pots might be identical in appearance, trees and pots look very different. Thus, since the objects that appear manifest

29. Dharmapāla comments that the first position will not work because cognition does not perceive an individual fundamental particle. The second fails because "there are no examples [of a group acting as] a cause" (Dharmapāla, *Explanation of Investigation of the Percept* (*Guan suoyuan lun shi* 觀所緣論釋), T 1625, CBETA vol. 00.0889b28). He adds a further qualification: a percept must "convey its appearance" (*ziti xiang xian* 自體相現) to cognition. Cognition does not directly perceive its objects; rather, the object of perception is really a representation or a collection of features, which cognition perceives and interprets as holistic things.

as different to perception, but fundamental particles appear to be identical, the fundamental particles cannot be what appear to sensory cognition.

The conundrum here concerns the nature of both fundamental particles and perception as they are understood in the Buddhist scholastic Abhidharma context in which Dignāga is working. Fundamental particles in this sense are not quite like atoms as they are understood in the Western tradition, and not even as they were conceived by early atomic theorists such as Democritus (*c.* 460–370 BCE). We could easily get sidetracked into the complex debates within the Abhidharma tradition regarding the nature and variety of those particles. Although echoes of those arguments can be heard in some of these five commentaries, they are beside the present point, and we stick to the broad framework on which there is consensus in the tradition.

First, fundamental particles are entirely partless and indivisible, the smallest building blocks of the world. Second, they are momentary, without even temporal parts. But third, they are not particles of *matter* per se, at least as that concept is deployed in Western materialism and atomism. There can be fundamental color particles, sound particles, solidity particles, and so on. So, they are more like property particles that, when aggregated or collected, constitute physical objects. The nature of their aggregation or collection, and the locus of causation in aggregates or collections, become issues in Dignāga's investigation and in those of his commentators. But the important thing to note here is that these fundamental particles are the genuine particulars in this framework, and they are extremely minute, far too small to be perceived.

Perception (*pratyakṣa*; Tib. *mngon sum*) is one of the two instruments of knowledge accepted by Dignāga and his successors; it is that instrument that takes as its object a *particular* (*svalakṣaṇa*; Tib. *rang mtshan*) as opposed to a universal (*sāmānya-lakṣaṇa*; Tib. *spyi mtshan*), the object of inference (*anumāna*; Tib. *rjes dpag*). Particulars, in this framework—and only particulars—are causally efficacious, and the epistemological credentials of perception rest on its being a direct causal process. The object of perception directly causes perceptual experience.[30] Exactly how this occurs is the subject matter of these

30. This condition gives rise to an interesting proposal made by Dharmapāla, as reported by Mingyu, in defense of a particular understanding of Dignāga's idealism. Dharmapāla, in his discussion of the prefatory remarks in the autocommentary, suggests that the percept is the direct perceptual object of the mental sense faculty (*manas-vijñāna*). This could both be the cause of (mental) perception and exist as it appears, satisfying the two conditions for qualifying as a percept and closing the case for idealism. Interestingly, Vinītadeva, commenting on this suggestion, writes: "the master Dharmapāla wrote at length to discuss the percept of mental cognition. This statement might be a correct understanding, but his idea is too profound for me to comprehend (230)." One can appreciate Vinītadeva's commentarial quandary. He does not wish to attribute a heterodox view to Dharmapāla, but he has no

five commentaries. Fundamental particles, however, as real particulars, seem like the right kinds of things to do the causal work, but the wrong kinds of things to be perceived. Aggregations of them seem more like the perceptible furniture of our world, but they are not equipped to cause anything. Hence the problem: how do we get causation and intentional content together?

The Third Position

At this point, Dignāga suggests a possible third position: "Some maintain that collected features are the cause (221)." He explains that macro-objects have many aspects, such as shape, color, and solidity, but only a few of these are perceived by a particular sense at a particular time. Dharmapāla expands on this position:

> In a locus where there are fundamental particles, each has an image of the collective, and it is precisely this collective particle whose image appears in accordance with its having many or few fundamental particles. They are all real existents. In the locus where there are fundamental particles, there is the image of an aggregated whole that produces an image of itself in cognition because it is a real thing. That is what should be the percept since it satisfies both criteria.[31]

The opponent, on this reading, argues that the percept comprises fundamental particles, but it is not a mere *collection*: it is the combined features (*'dus pa'i rnam pa*; Skt. *saṃcitākāra*) of the fundamental particles that comprise macro-objects, which coalesce into an image that is conveyed to perception. As we might put it in more contemporary terminology, it is a higher-level object that supervenes on, but is not reducible to, those fundamental particles. This is indeed a more sophisticated position—whatever its eventual philosophical difficulties—and it makes sense that Dignāga works up to it and devotes so much attention to its refutation.[32]

---

other way to represent the position. For if the object of mental perception appears correctly, it appears as a synthetic whole—as a macroscopic object assembled from the input of the external senses—then it appears as conceptualized and is hence *unreal*, and not an object of *perception*. Dharmapāla may have been anticipating Kant on the synthetic unity of manifolds of perception, but this position, while brilliant, would not be an orthodox Buddhist one.

31. Dharmapāla, *Explanation of Investigation of the Percept*: 00.0890c13.

32. Ching Keng (during group meetings) points out that there is another way to read the third position, namely, as suggesting that in fact it is not the particles that are the percepts,

An analogy suggested by Mingyu's *Explanation of Investigation of the Percept* (829a) is a group of people attempting to move a heavy log. If each tries individually in sequence, the log will not move. The group of individuals acting sequentially lacks causal efficacy. But if the whole group works together and pulls at one time, they can move the log. Thus they all cooperate, each contributing a certain amount of causal efficacy. In his shorter commentary on *Investigation of the Percept*, Mingyu speaks of a group of fundamental particles, each helping the others to produce a collective impression on cognition:

> As the collective is constituted of particles, the particles help each other, and each has one part that appears as an image of the collective in the five sense objects. This image is substantially existent. Each is able to generate the arising of a semblance of its own image in cognition: this indicates that the particles constitute the collective and are able to serve as a percept condition for the five sensory cognitions.[33]

A group of things like the trees that constitute a forest is, in this sense, conventionally existent. The trees have no collective causal efficacy. But a collective of particles acting in concert, each possessing characteristics such as

---

but rather the representation transmitted to consciousness by the particles, where each particle transmits a tiny representation of the whole (particles of a cup each transmitting a cup particle, etc.). He finds this reading in Kuiji's *Account of the Twenty Verses on Mere Cognition* (*Weishi ershi lun shuji* 唯識二十論述記, 2 *juan* (CBETA, T43, no. 1834, p.0992, c27-993a4): "For these reasons, [the masters of the *Nyāyānusāra*, such as Saṅghabhadra] claim: dharmas such as matter, etc., have many features, among which only a portion is the object of direct perception. For this reason, several particles help each other by [adding up to] the image; and [in each group of particles] there is an image of a collection. This image [in each particle] is real. Each image in each particle can produce a cognition that resembles itself; hence it can serve as a percept condition for the five sense consciousnesses. This is like the case where many particles accumulate to be [seen as] a mountain, etc.: the image of a mountain in each particle accumulates to form the image in the measure of a mountain. When the five sensory consciousnesses, eye-consciousness etc., have a mountain, etc. as their percept, what happens is that several particles help each other to contribute to the image of a mountain, which is obtained by all five sensory consciousnesses and hence becomes their percept condition. If not, then one would commit the fallacy of having no percept condition."

As Keng points out, this view has Abhidharma antecedents, and one could make sense of Dignāga's refutation on this reading. Nonetheless, the reading we present here is that adopted by Vinītadeva and the Tibetan commentators studied in this project, as well as other Chinese commentators (see, for example, Mingyu's commentary quoted above). See also Hattori (1988) for a compelling alternative reading.

33. Mingyu, *Reconciled Explanation of Investigation of the Percept* (*Guan suoyuanyuan lun huishi* 觀所緣緣論會釋): 081c. This is a commentary on Xuanzang's translation of *Investigation of the Percept*. Mingyu wrote two commentaries, both of which are cited in the Bibliography.

color, solidity, and other features, is able to convey an impression of a macro-object to cognition.

According to Vinītadeva, the proponents of this view assert that these features belong to fundamental particles, not to the collections per se.[34] If they were *sui generis* features of collections, this position would suffer from the defects of the second position, but because they pertain to fundamental particles they can serve as causes of perceptual cognition, and thus satisfy the conditions that they be causal and that they appear in cognition. They also accord with the representationalist paradigm mentioned earlier in that they do indeed (at least according to the opponent) convey their aspects to cognition.[35]

Dignāga (in verses 4 and 5) responds that fundamental particles are infinitesimally small and spherical in shape, and so they are indistinguishable from one another. At the level of fundamental particles, there are no distinguishable features. Moreover, the distinctions between such macro-objects as pots and cups can only apply to things that are conventionally real, but fundamental particles are ultimately real because they cannot be broken down into anything more basic. That is, he argues that there is no explanation of how such distinct phenomena could share a single supervenience base.

The opponent responds that features become manifest through aggregation: when a sufficient number of fundamental particles are conjoined, differences appear. But Dignāga responds that differences in number should not matter because fundamental particles are just tiny spheres, and so the opponent cannot account for differences in shape, color, or other qualities in macro-objects. Vinītadeva comments:

> One might think that collected features are macro-objects, but because they are substantially real, they must be partless. This is not the case. If something has parts, then it is not substantially real. And if it has no parts, then how could it have any differences in configuration? Whatever has parts can be configured in various ways, but things that are partless cannot (93).

Mingyu explains that proponents of this position have confused levels of analysis: because fundamental particles are indistinguishable, they

34. Vinītadeva, *Subcommentary on Investigation of the Percept* (*Ālambana-parīkṣā-ṭīkā*; Tib. *dMigs pa brtag pa'i 'grel bshad*), sDe dge edition: 361–362, 81.

35. This denial of causal power to the supervenient phenomenon indeed does collapse this position into a variant of the second, justifying the Tibetan assimilation of the two.

are incapable of producing cognitions, either individually or in concert. Distinctions of shape, color, solidity, and so forth appear only when they combine to form elements, which are the constituents of things that are perceptible.[36]

Although Tibetan exegetes did not recognize this "third position" as a separate thesis,[37] it was widely influential in East Asia, where it is regarded as the most plausible of the three. It was therefore the subject of extensive commentary and discussion. Dharmapāla's commentary, in which this position is described and analyzed in depth, became the most influential exposition in East Asia of *Investigation of the Percept* by an Indian author. Dignāga, Vinītadeva, and Dharmapāla all agree that positions one and two are clearly deficient, but some East Asian commentators have viewed the third position as a stance that merits serious attention.

Dignāga's Own Position

With the presentation and refutation of the third option, Dignāga concludes his analysis of his opponents' positions and then proceeds to present his own. He begins by pointing out that all we ever perceive are internal phenomena; we have no direct access to anything external, but merely posit externality on the basis of how things are perceived and subsequently interpreted by the mind.

> But an internal cognitive object,
> Which appears to be external, is the object
> Because it is cognition itself,
> And because it is its condition. [6]

Dignāga expands on this idea in the autocommentary. He explains that "even though there is no external object, one that appears to be external

36. Mingyu, *Explanation of Investigation of the Percept*: 829b21.

37. During lectures on the *Ālambana-parīkṣā* and its Tibetan commentaries in July 2014, Geshe Yeshes Thabkhas was asked if he regarded this as a distinctive position. He replied that it could be construed that way, but he had no sense of a Tibetan tradition that upheld this view. There are, however, Indic sources that construe this as a distinctive position, including Bhāviveka's *Verses on the Heart of the Middle Way* (Eckel 2008: 247–253) and the eighth-century philosophers Śubhagupta and Kumārila. All three options are discussed in the "Investigation of the External Object" (*Bahir-artha-parīkṣā*) section of the *Compendium of Metaphysics* (*Tattva-saṃgraha-pañjikā*, 1965–2084). Kamalaśīla ends his commentary on this section of *Investigation of the Percept* by quoting and affirming its conventional validity in verses 7 and 8.

but is only internal is the percept condition.... Internal cognition appears as the object and arises from it, so it has the two characteristics (44)."[38] Thus, in the autocommentary to this verse, he says, "a percept condition only exists internally (44)." In other words, the perceptual process itself is entirely internal, and therefore the immediate object of perception is also an internal phenomenon. The sense faculties that convey the images of things to the mind are internal factors, and so the implied conclusion is that externality is posited on the basis of this activity but is not directly revealed.

In verses 6 and 7, Dignāga also argues that both the perceived object and the sense faculties are important conditions of perception. No matter how many pot-particles are present externally, he says, without a functioning eye and visual system one won't see a pot. So, the visual faculty and its components must be taken to be part of the causal story in perception. But this, Dignāga sees, raises an important difficulty: if the percept is both the cause and the object of perception, then the visual faculty—or at least some part of the visual process—must be the percept because it is causally efficacious. As he notes in the commentary to verse 5cd:

> Cognitions of things that are substantially real, such as color, do not disappear even when things that are connected with them are removed.[39] Thus it makes sense that objects of sensory awareness are not external (43).

---

38. This refers to the two characteristics of a percept as defined in the commentary on verse 2a.

39. D (Derge) differs from P (Peking), N (sNar thang), and S (gSer bris); it reads: "*rdzas su yod pa rnams la ni 'brel pa can bsal du zin kyang kha dog la sogs pa bzhin du rang gi blo 'dor bar byed do.*" P, N, and S have the same reading except for a negation at the end: *'dor ba **med***. D's reading is an argument that presents the opponent with an unwanted consequence: if macro-objects such as pots and cups were substantially real, as he contends, then perception of them should remain even if their particles (for example, particles of color or solidity) are removed, but this is clearly not the case. The alternative phrasing in P, N, and S would read: "Even if one were to remove things that are associated with substantially real things, one's awareness of things like their color would not disappear." These differences may reflect a textual variant that is found in Paramārtha's and Xuanzang's translations, as noted by Lü Cheng (1928). Paramārtha's text follows the "would *not* disappear" version, whereas Xuanzang's text has "would disappear." Lü Cheng states that the Peking version agrees with Paramārtha, whereas what he calls the "Amdo version" (i.e., sDe dge) agrees with Xuanzang.

Vinītadeva (94) restates this argument in the following inference: "a whole is not substantially real, because it is an aggregate of many things at one time, in the same way as horses are not substantially real."

Dignāga then concludes in verse 6 that the percept is "cognition itself (44)." The point is as follows: putatively external causes of cognition, like pots, or collections of pot-particles, fail to be percepts in virtue of failing simultaneously to satisfy the two criteria for that status. But more than that, they are too distal to count. To the extent that they are causes at all, it is only through the mediation of the sensory organs and their associated perceptual and cognitive faculties. Those are the proximal causes. Even without the distal causes, stimulation of these proximal entities could give rise to perceptual experience. So the sense faculties—or processes or representations internal to them—are what play the properly causal role here.

One might respond that these factors doom the reality of the percept. But Dignāga argues (verses 7–8) that this is not so. For the object, or appearance in sensory consciousness, is just that—an appearance, and it contains no information regarding externality or material constitution. (Compare Berkeley and Hume in the West on this point.) The appearance, then, can be both the cause and the intentional content of perception, thus satisfying the two conditions. Hence, the percept is simply the appearance in the sense faculty.[40]

Dignāga's text is very brief, comprising eight terse verses and an autocommentary covering only about two and one-half Tibetan folio pages. The argument is more ostended than presented, and a lot of room is left for interpretation. Hence it is that this text inspires a rich commentarial tradition. Although the treatise at first appears to be concerned primarily with Indian atomic theory and reductionism with regard to macroscopic objects, we see quickly that this theory is at best a subsidiary concern and is leading to an exploration of the nature of perceptual cognition. Atomic theory is introduced only to set the stage for Dignāga's main project: an analysis of the nature of percepts and perception.

Instead, *Investigation of the Percept* raises three principal philosophical issues. First, there is the question of idealism and the status of the external world. Dignāga remarks that his analysis of the intentional object of perception makes sense whether the distal object of perception is internal or external. This suggests that the analysis in the text is consistent and would have to

---

40. The Chinese versions stress that it is the appearance of an image (*ākāra*) that resembles the *ālambana*. As Hattori (1968: 3, n. 16) notes, in this text, "Dignāga proves that the object of cognition (*ālambana*) is nothing other than the appearance of an object in cognition itself." Hattori adds that the analysis of perception in *Investigation of the Percept* forms the basis for his more expanded discussion of direct perception (*pratyakṣa*) in the *Compendium of Epistemology*. Arnold (2005: 22–23) argues that Dignāga's position in *Investigation of the Percept* is that "cognition can be explained satisfactorily if we posit mental phenomena as the 'objects' intended thereby—and, indeed, that we cannot coherently posit any nonmental, external objects as what is directly intended by cognition."

be accepted whether one is an idealist or a materialist. Perhaps this analysis simply "brackets" the question of the ontological status of the external world in a phenomenological investigation of perception;[41] perhaps it demonstrates that we are never in contact with an external world in perception; perhaps it is an attack on the very reality of the external world. The text underdetermines these issues. Dignāga's presentation is consistent with the idealism evident in the rest of his corpus and with that attributed to him by all the commentators on this text.

Second, the text raises questions about intentionality. Just what is the intentional object of perceptual experience? Is it a representation, or what is represented? Is it something internal or external to consciousness? This is a deep and important question.

Finally, there is a question about the role of representation in perceptual knowledge. Is our knowledge of the external world (if there is one) mediated by representations, or is it direct? If so, are representations mere vehicles, or instruments, by means of which we gain knowledge of external objects, or are they the only real objects of consciousness? Once again, the text underdetermines the answer to these questions.

Despite this neutrality at one level, Dignāga is playing a subtle game that lends aid and comfort to the idealist. After all, once he has established that both the percept and percept condition are internal to cognition and that the causal sense faculties are also internal factors, there is really no need for an external world. According to the Indian philosophical principle of "conciseness" (*laghutva*, literally "lightness," the Indian equivalent of Ockham's Razor), a philosophical position that requires the fewest assumptions should be preferred. So if an internal analysis of perception is able to account for all relevant aspects, by implication there is no need to make the added assumption of an external world, particularly because any knowledge about it can only come from internal sense data or mental cognition. Thus, Dignāga subtly coaxes the materialist opponent toward the inevitable conclusion that the external world is unknown and unknowable and that

41. If this is indeed Dignāga's intention, it would resonate with a central contention of Dan Lusthaus's (2002) presentation of Yogācāra. He argues that Yogācāra is not idealist, as it is commonly characterized. Rather, he argues, Yogācāra thinkers bracketed the question of the existence of external objects in a manner similar to Husserl's epoché. This is a possible interpretation of what Dignāga says in this section, but neither he nor any other Yogācāra philosopher explicitly adopts this position. Lambert Schmithausen (2005) has criticized Lusthaus's reading, defending an idealist interpretation of Yogācāra texts. See also Richard Hayes's (1987: 132, 177–178) interpretation of Dignāga's position in *Investigation of the Percept* as phenomenalism and as a fundamental skepticism about the relation between purported external objects and perception.

idealism makes sense of how perception actually operates without the need for additional metaphysical assumptions.

Vinītadeva, in his subcommentary composed in the eighth century at Nālandā University, focuses on the question of idealism. Gungtang Könchok Denbe Drönme, writing in the early eighteenth century in a scholastic Tibetan context, addresses the nature of intentionality. Ngawang Dendar, writing a few decades later, takes up the question of representationalism. Yeshes Thabkhas, writing in the twenty-first century. goes further to develop the ethical implications of the text. Together, these commentaries constitute a deep engagement with Dignāga's work, each one taking up where its predecessor leaves off. Considering them together reveals the richness of this scholastic tradition.

Vinītadeva: An Argument for Idealism

Vinītadeva was Sthiramati's (*c.* sixth century) student, and Sthiramati, along with Dharmapāla, was largely responsible for the consolidation of Yogācāra as a recognizable philosophical school committed not only to the doctrines of the three natures (*svabhāva*) and three naturelessnesses (*niḥsvabhāvatā*) articulated in the *Discourse Explaining the Thought* (*Saṃdhinirmocana-sūtra*), but also to a thoroughgoing idealism, articulated most forcefully in his commentary on Vasubandhu's *Thirty Verses* (*Triṃśikā-kārikā*). Vinītadeva inherits the idealism of Sthiramati and Dharmapāla and defends an idealist reading of *Investigation of the Percept*.

Vinītadeva makes this interpretative goal explicit in his commentary on the first verse: "This treatise is composed in order to refute external objects and to affirm that they are internal (79)." Two comments are necessary immediately. The first is straightforward: Vinītadeva interprets Dignāga's attack on fundamental particles as constitutive of objects of experience as an attack on the cogency of any account of external objects, similar to the attack on the possibility of material objects mounted by Vasubandhu in the *Twenty Verses* (*Viṃśatikā* or *Viṃśaka*). We will explore this reading in more detail later in this chapter.

Vinītadeva sees this attack as a defense of the idea that the percept is *internal*, but he also contends that *there is no percept in the sense of the interlocutor*. That is, for one who believes that perception connects us to the external world, because a percept is the external object that is the cause and the content of our perception, there simply can be no percept. Vinītadeva writes: "to maintain that something is a percept means to accept that something is apprehended (81)." A few lines earlier, he characterizes the position of the opponent as follows: "Not all debaters maintain that external objects are the percept.... They maintain that the mind also has a percept that is an external object. For this reason, its percept is to be refuted at the same time (95)." So, where it appears that Dignāga presents himself as *identifying* the percept, Vinītadeva thinks of Dignāga as *refuting* the idea that the percept is external to consciousness.

Let us first examine the argument for idealism. Vinītadeva begins by arguing that there is something incoherent about the idea of fundamental particles themselves, an argument deriving from Vasubandhu. Either the particles are partite or they are impartite. If they are partite, they are not substantially existent, and so they can't be real causes; but if they are impartite, they have no dimensions or shape, and so they can't combine to constitute anything with dimension.

Vinītadeva, following Dignāga closely, then argues that there is a tension between thinking of fundamental particles as causes and as contents of consciousness. On the one hand, if they are minute causes, they are not what is represented; but if they are what is represented, then, being aggregates, they are not causally responsible for those representations. All of this argument is worked out in the commentary on verse 1. The commentary on verse 2 also follows Dignāga closely, arguing that neither individual fundamental particles nor collections can be percepts: the individual particles are not represented, and the collections are not causal.

It is in the commentary to verse 5 that Vinītadeva's idealism comes to the fore. Again, recalling Vasubandhu's argument against the reality of material objects in *Twenty Verses*, Vinītadeva argues first that because fundamental particles are nondifferentiated, they could never aggregate to form distinct things. There could be no explanation of how different things are colored differently, or why some things are pots and others cups. So things cannot be composed of fundamental particles. Vinītadeva concludes from this argument that the objects of cognition are not external objects because any external object must be composed of fundamental particles. (We can assume that here he relies on Vasubandhu's argument in *Twenty Verses* against infinite divisibility.)

Vinītadeva expands on this point in the commentary on verse 6, noting that externality involves existence in space, but he compares space to the reflection of the moon in a mirror. The moon appears to be in the mirror even though it is not. Similarly, the objects we experience appear to be in space, but they are not. Because they are not, they are not external. Once again, we are driven to an idealistic conclusion. Nonetheless, Vinītadeva argues, this does not mean that there is no percept condition for the arising of conscious experience. He says, "This is because while there may be no external object, there is still an internal appearance that merely seems to be external, and that is the percept condition (95)." He compares this to the appearance of floaters to a person suffering from opthalmia.

Vinītadeva concludes that the percept can only be an internal object. Only an internal object can be both the cause of cognition and its content. In his discussion of the problem raised by the apparent simultaneity of cause and effect in the case where an internal object is both the cause and the content of a representational state, Vinītadeva emphasizes that we often have instances of simultaneous causation, as when bundles of reeds support one another in a stack. Similarly, in perception a single state can have both an apprehended and an apprehending aspect. Although one is the cause of the other, they are simultaneous. The important point here is not the interesting account of simultaneous causation, but rather the analysis of perception as a single cognitive state in which both content and subject are internal to the mind.[42]

A bit later, in the commentary on verse 7, Vinītadeva considers the objection that the eye itself is a condition of visual perception and appears to be an external physical object. As a good idealist, he bites the bullet, asserting that "in our view, the eye is only internal, just as the object is internal, so how could this problem arise? (99)" And to put all such objections to rest, he points out that any causal argument on the reality of external objects is bound to fail:

> Thus it is possible to infer fire in general from smoke, but not a particular sort of fire such as one of grass or leaves. Similarly, it is possible to infer a cause in general from the cognitive nature of the effect, but not its specific cause, such as one that is derived from material elements (99–100).

In the commentary to the concluding verse, Vinītadeva gives a strong reading of Dignāga's claim that "it is not contradictory for this capacity also to be

42. This point follows from earlier discussions in Buddhist philosophy, particularly in Yogācāra sources. Asaṅga's *Compendium of the Mahāyāna* (*Mahāyāna-saṃgraha*; Ch. *She dasheng lun* 攝大乘論) had already referred to two such "parts" or aspects: *nimitta* [*bhāga*]; Ch. *xiang fen* 相分) and *darśana* [*bhāga*]; Ch. *jian fen* 見分; that is, the object/image part and the perceiving/seeing part: *Theg pa chen po'i bsdus pa*, sDe dge edition: D 4048, *sems tsam*, vol. *ri*: 15a. Taishō, 31, no. 1594, p.141, b11, Xuanzang's translation of the *Mahāyāna-saṃgraha*.

Dignāga added a third part, the self-verifying aspect or the part that confirms the perceiving part (*svasaṃvṛtti*; Ch. *zizheng* [*fen*]自證[分]). This is related by Kuiji 窺基 (632–682) in his *Account of the Treatise on Mere Cognition* (*Cheng weishilun shuji* 成唯識論述記), Taishō, 43, no. 1830: 319, a22. Dharmapāla later added a fourth part: confirmation of the self-verifying part. In the Chinese commentarial tradition on *Investigation of the Percept*, the two parts—perceiving/subject part and image/object part—became a central focus of analysis.

in cognition (100)." The capacity is, of course, the sense faculty, the capacity to perceive. Vinītadeva strengthens this idea with the observation that cognition "is the basis that is pervaded by karma," (100) providing a positive reason for thinking that cognition is the basis for the capacity for perception. He thereby turns a neutrality with respect to idealism into an argument for a positive assertion. A few lines later, he interprets Dignāga's remark that it makes no real difference whether or not the capacity is cognitive to mean that in either case "all it does is produce something like the mere perceptual cognition (100)."

None of this is to say that the idealism Vinītadeva emphasizes is not present in Dignāga's text. Of course it is. Indeed, we might say, the very fact that Dignāga argues that his account can work in either an idealist or a nonidealist framework is a *prima facie* argument for an idealist stance. After all, no realist thinks that realism has a problem explaining perception: external objects cause perception. But realists often see the explanation of perception as a problem for the idealist: if there is no external world, what causes all of these perceptual states? Dignāga argues that the idealist can respond to this challenge; hence, he offers aid and comfort to that position, even if he does not argue directly for it. It therefore makes sense to read this text as idealistic, albeit with reservations. But where Dignāga hedges and allows the possibility that a materialist might maintain a realist ontology and still accept his analysis, Vinītadeva explicitly endorses an idealist interpretation and takes the defense of idealism as the central task of the text. As we turn to Gungtang's commentary, we will see a different approach.

Gungtang: An Exploration of Intentionality

Gungtang is writing in a Geluk doxographical context and in a frame of reference that takes the tradition of thinking about intentionality initiated by Dharmakīrti for granted. Although Gungtang reads *Investigation of the Percept* as a Yogācāra text, nonetheless, unlike Vinītadeva, he does not read it as especially idealistic. Instead, he takes Dignāga to be working out a theory of intentionality. He begins by identifying the topic of the text as "apprehender and apprehended," (116) that is, as the relationship between subject and object. And unlike Dignāga in his autocommentary, or Vinītadeva in his subcommentary,[43]

43. Gungtang—unlike Vinītadeva, who is working from Dharmapāla's commentary on Dignāga's autocommentary—is not writing a *subcommentary* on Dignāga's commentary, but rather is commenting *directly* on the root text, bypassing both Dignāga's autocommentary and Vinītadeva's subcommentary, although he is clearly aware of both. He generally addresses broad themes in *Investigation of the Percept*, whereas Vinītadeva and Ngawang Dendar devote significant attention to commentary on individual passages and terms.

Gungtang considers the definition of the percept by the opponent to be "that which appears as it exists." So, Gungtang believes that Dignāga—instead of demonstrating either that external objects can't satisfy both the causal and the intentional condition, or that there are no external objects in the first place—is demonstrating that nothing in fact exists as it appears; that appearance is subjectively constructed.

In his commentary on verse 1, Gungtang sets up a dilemma for the opponent, parallel to but not identical to what Dignāga sets up in the autocommentary: the percept would be apprehended through either a sequential causal process or a simultaneous representation. If, on the one hand, the process were causal, the causality would have to reside in the fundamental particles in which the perceived object consists. But then because what consciousness apprehends would not be a set of fundamental particles, the mode of existence and the mode of apprehension of the object would differ, and it could not be a percept as understood by the opponent. If, on the other hand, the mode of apprehension were through a simultaneous representation, the same problem would arise: what is represented is singular; what exists is manifold, and the condition proposed for being a percept is violated.

Note that here the argument is explicitly concerned with the relation between the intentional object of cognition and the object apprehended by that intentional state. Gungtang takes as the target the perfectly natural position that the intentional object is an instrument by means of which the percept is grasped, either because it represents it through some kind of similarity relation or because it is caused by it in the right way. Gungtang argues that neither of those options makes sense if one takes accurate perception to deliver the object in appearance just as it exists in reality.

This theme of the relation between the immediate intentional object of cognition and the object grasped in successful perception continues as Gungtang considers the verses that address the relation of fundamental particles to the objects they constitute. In his discussion of verses 2–5, Gungtang makes some very important points. He addresses the relation between unity and multiplicity as it arises in representation; he analyzes the causal story of the occurrence or representation; and he discusses the relation of causality to the representational relation. We consider each of these relations in turn.

First, Gungtang notes:

> These are aggregated cognitively; they are not aggregations of external particles. Nonetheless, the term "*of which*" is used to refer to appearing in this way due to the power of predispositions.... In that case, contrary to the previous position, even if appearance makes sense, sensory

cognitions *"do not"* arise *"from them"* i.e., aggregations. Failing this second criterion, it is not a percept. It is not causal (113).

Gungtang raises two issues here, one of which—the order of causality—we will set aside for a moment. Because Gungtang is reading *Investigation of the Percept* as a Yogācāra text within the Geluk doxographical system, he is thinking of the order of causality between the mental and the physical world as going from the mental to the physical. We need not worry about that order here. The important point for our purposes is, rather, that physical aggregations do not correspond to cognitive aggregations. Even when the physical is composite, the representation that delivers that composite to us can be singular. And the representation delivers the composite to us as a unity. So, once again, whatever is represented does not exist as it appears.

Gungtang then deploys the simile of two moons—not the moon and that in the mirror mentioned by Vinītadeva, but the two moons seen by a person with an eye ailment or by someone who may have had too much to drink:

> The appearance of two moons is not produced by two moons in someone to whom they appear. Therefore, their appearance is only due to defective sense faculties. In the same way, when composite collections (*bsags pa'i 'dus pa*) appear as external objects, they do not have the power to produce anything because they are not substantially existent (113–114).

The point of the example is clear: The causes of conscious appearances do not exist independently in the way that they appear. One moon gives rise to two. The cause is a single moon; the appearance is double. The congruence needed for genuine perception is absent. In perception, on the first option, aggregations appear to be singular. Internal appearances—representations—are not directly caused by what they represent; they are caused by our cognitive processes, perhaps stimulated by, or in cooperation with, external objects. As a Buddhist, Gungtang also assumes that individual karma and the innate predispositions with which each type of being is endowed play a role in how the cognitive apparatus of a particular perceiver operates. But this means that intentionality cannot be parsed in terms of causation, any more than it can be parsed in terms of resemblance. If it could be, then not only would double moons be the cause of drunkards' perceptual states, but our own cognitive processes would be the objects of our representations, not merely their supporting causes.

Gungtang concludes this discussion with a set of general observations about objects and representations. He points out again that when we represent wholes, *they* are the intentional objects of our cognition, not the parts they comprise. This is his gloss on verse 3cd ("features of minute particles are not the objects of cognition" 114). He concludes that although external objects may or may not be compounds, representations of them are not compounds of representations; intentional objects have a unity and integrity that defy that kind of decomposition. Once again, this argument entails that if to be a percept is to exist in the manner of appearance, then external objects cannot be percepts.

Gungtang next turns to what he considers Dignāga's own position regarding the percept: "It is defined as follows: it is nothing other than a self-presenting internal apprehension—an entity that is a cognitive object (115)." Let us pause on this definition for a moment before turning to one of Gungtang's more interesting remarks on the percept. The percept is self-presenting (*rang mdangs*). That is, it is not grasped as the object of a distinct cognitive act, but itself is internal to a cognitive act. We might compare this view to Sellars's (1977) analysis of early modern Western accounts of intentionality, according to which a representation of a blue triangle is not an act directed upon blueness and triangularity, or even upon specific instances thereof. Rather, it is an act that *is* blue and triangular, not in the normal predicative sense of *is*, but rather in that it is intrinsically *of a blue triangle*, that its intentional content is part of its nature, not extrinsic to it. The idea that perceptual states are intrinsically representational, though perhaps present in Dignāga's and Vinītadeva's texts in embryo, is an important advance on Gungtang's part, reflecting a synthesis of Geluk philosophy of mind with Dignāga's epistemology.

Moreover, the percept is internal. That is, like Vinītadeva, Gungtang takes the immediate intentional object to be itself internal, and not an external object toward which the mind is directed. (Note that this position is rather broadly set out here and would be consistent either with Vinītadeva's idealism or with a more modest Husserlian position.) And finally, the percept is the object of knowledge. When I see a pot, the object of knowledge is not an external entity or an aggregation of pot atoms, but rather an internal representation of a pot. And of course, while this does not demand an idealist interpretation, it pushes one in that direction.

In what may be the most important and original (though, not surprisingly, deeply inflected by Tsongkhapa's philosophy of mind) passage of Gungtang's commentary, returning to lunar examples, he writes:

> The representation does not appear as it exists. For example, when an image of the moon appears in a mirror, spatiality also appears. The moon appears to be different from its action of reflecting. Although it is apprehended with an appearance of externality, the object (*don*) is that

which exists internally. Thus, while it (*don*) has a wide semantic range, in this context it is the percept condition (115).

Let us parse this passage with some care. First note the conclusion. The *representation* does not appear as it really exists. Gungtang is not merely saying that the object represented does not exist as it appears, but that the representation also does not exist as it appears. So, even though the cognition may be self-presenting in one sense, it does not present itself transparently, in its mode of existence. The structure of intentionality, as Tsongkhapa argued,[44] is opaque to consciousness.

Consider the elegant analogy: When we see the moon in a mirror, the moon appears to be different from the mirror in which it is reflected. But it is not. The reflection is not related to the mirror as the moon in the sky is related to the mirror; the latter is distinct from the mirror, but the former is not. Nonetheless, when we see the reflection, it is presented to us as though it is distinct; we don't experience ourselves as *seeing the mirror* but rather as *seeing the moon using the mirror*. Similarly, when we experience an intentional state, like the perception of a pot, we experience its object—the *appearance of the pot* (*not even the pot itself*)—as distinct from the state. But it is not. It is internal to it, not distinct from it. Nonetheless, because of this mode of appearance, we refer to it as the "object" of the state, just as we refer to the appearance of the moon in the mirror as "the moon." It is for this reason that this *aspect* of the intentional state is singled out as the percept condition, even though many factors are involved in the perception. There is nothing uniquely causal about it. A bit later, Gungtang emphasizes this point by referring to it as the "nominal percept condition" (116) (*dmigs rkyen btags pa ba*).

Gungtang concludes his commentary by giving it a clearly idealistic spin, responding to an objection that if the object is internal, perception is nonveridical. He argues that on a Yogācāra position, *everything* is internal to cognition, and so the causes and objects of perception are all purely ideal. He asserts that in writing his commentary he has adopted the viewpoint of Yogācāra and has framed his interpretation in accordance with the doctrinal commitments attributed to it by the Geluk tradition. Here he follows not only Vinītadeva but also Geluk doxographic orthodoxy. But the principal point of his commentary is summed up in his closing remark: "According to others, the percept is the apprehended object; this is what we take to be the self of phenomena. This is

---

44. Tsongkhapa, *Instructions on the View of the Profound Path of the Middle Way Consequence School* (*dBu ma thal 'gyur pa'i lugs kyi zab lam dbu ma'i lta khrid*): Collected Works, vol. *sha*: 578: 3.

what *Investigation of the Percept* by our Philosopher, the great master Dignāga, has refuted (117)."

Nothing exists as it appears, not even that which is internal. Intentionality is not determined by causal factors, nor by resemblance; but rather it is an intrinsic property of intentional acts.

Ngawang Dendar: The Role of Representations

Ngawang Dendar is also a Gelukpa exegete, and, like Gungtang's, his exegesis reflects Geluk doxographic thought. But whereas Gungtang's commentary is a short work by a young scholar,[45] Dendar's is the careful composition of a mature, and justly renowned, monastic professor. His concern for doxography is evident, and his use of the doxographic hierarchy to unpack the text is a scholastic *tour de force*. Dendar begins his commentary with a survey of atomic theory as the Geluk scholastic system takes it to be understood by each Buddhist philosophical school. The discussion is erudite and detailed, but it is only preliminary to his concern with the ways in which the mind engages external objects, where his primary concern with the role of representations comes to the fore.

Dendar begins by noting that the Vaibhāṣikas are nonrepresentationalist direct realists with regard to perception. They deny the reality, and hence the causal efficacy, of aggregations, reducing them to their atomic constituents, and they assert that fundamental particles appear directly to perception.[46]

Both the Sautrāntika position and those of all of the more sophisticated philosophical schools, Dendar points out, are representationalist. The Sautrāntikas, he argues, see representations as resembling that which they represent. He uses the analogy of a crystal placed on a blue cloth: just as all of the facets of the crystal become blue, the visual cognition that apprehends blue becomes blue in the same sense as the blue object. Moreover,

---

45. He states in the colophon that his short commentary is just a collection of lecture notes written down as he heard them, with little augmentation on his part. This is no doubt a modest assertion from a very precocious *geshe lharampa*, but it does reflect the fact that he wrote it when he was twenty-three years old.

46. Ngawang Dendar (Ngag dbang bstan dar), *Beautiful String of Pearls: A Commentary on Investigation of the Percept* (*dMigs pa brtag pa'i 'grel pa mu tig 'phreng mdzes*): TBRC W7301, sKu 'bum edition: 227. *Ngag dbang bstan dar gSung 'bum, ja*: 21ff. Our edition compares this with a typeset edition of the sKu 'bum edition, *"mKhas pa'i dbang po A lag sha bsTan dar lha rams pa'i gsung 'bum"* (*stod cha*) (Gansu: bLa brang tshug lag deb phreng, Kan su'u mi rigs dpe skrun khang, 2004).

the Sautrāntikas, in virtue of commitments both to the veridicality of perception and to an atomic reductionist account of aggregations, believe the direct objects of perception are representations (*rnam* pa; Skt. *ākāra*) that are transmitted by things to cognition and then become the objects of cognition.

Dendar attributes to the Sautrāntikas a twofold criterion for being the percept condition: "(1) to convey its own representation to sensory cognition; and (2) to be that sensory cognition's cause (138)." This twofold condition should remind us of those suggested in Dignāga's autocommentary and by Vinītadeva, but with a twist: the emphasis on the conveyance of a representation. Dendar, in the context of responding to a worry about the nonsimultaneity of perceived and perceiver, explains the process as follows:

> Although there is no blue at the time of the apprehension of blue, there is no problem in terms of their not being an apprehender and an apprehended. This is because when the visual faculty that is the dominant condition of that visual cognition and blue—the percept condition—come together, then immediately in the next moment a visual cognition arises having a representation of blue. At that moment, although there is no blue, the representation of blue certainly remains in the perspective of cognition (144).

The Cittamātra (Yogācāra) position, he argues, is different only in that on this view the representation is caused not by contact with a physical blue object, but rather by a predisposition in consciousness. (Once again, the reading is decidedly idealist.)

When Dendar comments on the refutation of the opponent in the opening verses of the text, he puts the dilemma in representational terms: "Fundamental particles may be causes of sensory cognitions such as the visual, but a sensory cognition does not have the appearance of these—that is, a representation that is like those fundamental particles (149)." A few sentences later, Dendar emphasizes the importance of representations in this context: "The statement that sensory cognition cannot have fundamental particles as its object means that a cognition is that which ascertains the identity of an object because it has the representation of that object (149)."

Here is how Dendar sums up the destructive dilemma set up in the first two verses:

> If something is the percept condition of a sensory cognition, then it is said that a representation like itself appears in that sensory cognition and also that it is the condition of the arising of that sensory cognition.

> A collection of many particles does not produce a sensory cognition in this way, because it is not substantially real. For example, when a person sees a double moon because of defective sense faculties . . . it is just a single moon appearing to be double. But even though it is a single moon appearing as double to a sensory cognition, the single moon is not the *cause* of the sensory cognition; and, for that reason, it also is not the object that is called the percept condition of that cognition. As in this example, a collection of fundamental particles is shown not to be the cause because it is not substantially real. Therefore, a collection of particles is not the cognition's percept in this context (151–152).

The target here is the idea that a macroscopic object—a collection of fundamental particles—is the percept. If it were, it would have to produce a representation "like itself." Just producing any old representation won't do. This use of the double moon example is particularly elegant. The double moon doesn't resemble anything in reality, and in particular not a single moon; so it is not a representation of a real object. That much is obvious. But Dendar takes things one step further and understands the analogy differently from Gungtang: the double moon is not *caused by* the single moon either (and of course not by a double moon). It is caused by having had too much to drink or by an ocular defect. The causes and conditions of the perception are a combination of the moon in the sky and one or more physical impediments. So the moon fails *both* tests for its status as the drunk's percept.

Just so, Dendar thinks, for collections of particles. First, collections are not real; only the particles are, and so the collections are not the causes of our representations. Rather, our predisposition to see aggregations as entities is the relevant cause. But second, our representation doesn't look like a collection; it looks like a unitary object. So, just like the double moon, collections of particles fail *both* tests for percepthood.

When Dendar comes to the final arguments of the text, he reads Dignāga as taking the *appearance in sensory cognition*—that is, the representation—as the percept. In his commentary to verse 6 he says:

> Even without an external object, it is possible for there to be a percept condition. Even without an external object, the cognitive object itself—which has the nature of internal cognition and exists internally while appearing to be external—is precisely the object—that is, the percept condition.
>
> A visual consciousness that apprehends blue acquires the nature of blue. Therefore, the appearance of blue in visual cognition is not

> only the appearing object that appears in visual cognition, but also its condition.
>
> Why? Internal consciousness appears as the object, and it also arises from it. Therefore cognition is its percept and is also its condition. Since it has both of these characteristics, the percept condition simply exists internally (160–161).

The idealistic reading is obvious here. But that is not the most important issue in this passage. The point instead is that the representation (the appearance to cognition) is that which satisfies the two conditions for being the percept. It conveys its own representation, and it is the cause of perception. The appearance of blue, according to Dendar, leads the cognition of blue to represent things as blue in virtue of that visual consciousness being blue itself (in some sense); and it also causes that cognition. Dendar is insistent on the difference between the representation and the cognition:

> Even though the appearance of blue in visual cognition and the visual cognition itself are simultaneous, they do not deviate in the sense that when one is present, the other arises; and when the opposite is the case, the other does not arise. Therefore, even though the condition and the conditioned are simultaneous, it is not wrong for them to be causal and effective entities (161).

Dendar does not say what it is for the cognition to "acquire the nature of blue (160)." But once again, as in the case of Gungtang, we can say that it acquires the nature of blue insofar as it becomes a state that has blueness as its intentional content. Although the Sautrāntikas may have a similarity theory of representation, Dendar certainly does not attribute that view to the Yogācāras, since in their case there is no external matter to which the cognitive state can be similar. And we don't want to say that a mental state is *literally* blue, but only that it has blue as its content.

But note that Dendar differs from Gungtang on another matter here. In foregrounding the idea of representation as the topic of the text, and in taking the nature of cognition to be essentially representational, Dendar must draw a clear distinction between representation and its content. So, although Gungtang emphasizes the identity of the moon and the mirror and regards talk of the moon as object as merely *nominal*, for Dendar the representation is the percept itself and is a causal factor in cognition. This is not only a difference in emphasis in reading Dignāga's text: it is a very different interpretation of that text and a different account of the nature of cognition.

Reading *Investigation of the Percept* as representationalist in the context of Yogācāra doxography forces one to address the question: "is this a true-representationalist (*satyākāra*) position or a false-representationalist (*alīkākāra*) position?" On the former, the representations themselves are nondeceptive in their mode of appearance. They appear as representations, and their mode of appearance and mode of existence are the same; qua representations, they are nondeceptive. On the latter, they are deceptive, either in appearing not to be representations, despite being so (for instance, appearing to be external objects), or having contents or characteristics that are at odds with the way they are experienced (for instance, being composed of many representations of fundamental particles despite appearing to be singular representations of macroscopic wholes). Dendar raises this issue but drops it without resolution. It seems, however, that to be consistent with his own initial position he should adopt the true-representationalist perspective because he holds that representations are concordant with that which they represent. This, however, is very much a subsidiary issue.

Yeshes Thabkhas: Epistemology and Ethics

Yeshes Thabkhas is a contemporary Gelukpa scholar who specializes in the study of Indian Buddhist literature. Like Gungtang and Ngawang Dendar, his reading reflects Geluk doxography and situates this text firmly in the Yogācāra tradition. His commentary reflects on those of Vinītadeva, Gungtang, and Ngawang Dendar, frequently endorsing or commenting on their readings, and clarifying difficult points in the text through juxtaposing them.

Yeshes Thabkhas's reading is distinctive in that he draws explicitly *ethical* conclusions from the text. He argues that epistemology and ethics are closely intertwined in the Buddhist tradition. A consequence of the internality of the percept, he argues, is that we are responsible not only for what we think, say, and do, but also for how we see the world. Emotions—whether salutary or dysfunctional—arise in the very act and moment of perception, and they condition the way in which we see our circumstances, our fellows, and ourselves. The transformation of consciousness that is the goal of Buddhist practice is, on his view, a transformation of perceptual consciousness.

Reading this scholarly commentary on *Investigation of the Percept* and on the commentarial tradition reminds us that Buddhist Studies is not purely historical. The Buddhist commentarial tradition is alive and well, and this commentary is one more moment in it, not simply a reflection on the past.

Final Thoughts on the Scholastic Process in India and Tibet

We have been examining a sequence of texts in a scholastic commentarial tradition. The term *scholastic* often is uttered in a pejorative tone. But that is unwarranted.[47] The genre of commentary can be a fertile ground for developing philosophical insight that may exist *in potentio* in a text but that requires hermeneutical reflection and dialogue to bring to full fruition. Dendar notes that whereas Dignāga's text is brief, its content is vast. The vastness of that content does not emerge even in Dignāga's autocommentary. Nor does it emerge in complete form in any one of the three subsequent commentaries preserved in Tibetan works or in the numerous discussions of the text in China. Instead, each of these works develops a portion of the insight that animates Dignāga's project. Only by combining them can we see just how much is packed into the eight *ślokas* that comprise the root text of *Investigation of the Percept.*

We hope that this exercise helps the reader to see the complex relationships among these treatises. We also hope that it demonstrates the value of a historically articulated commentarial tradition and indeed also the value of reading not a single commentary on a text, but an entire sequence of exegeses. The meaning of Dignāga's text was not present when it was composed. It arose instead as it was read, and we can expect that it will continue to develop as we ourselves read and comment on it. That is what it is to be an "eminent text," and it is that eminence that leads us to continue to engage with it.

47. See José Cabezón (1998) for a discussion of the importance of scholastic commentary as a genre.

2

Investigation of the Percept[1] (Ālambana-parīkṣā)[2]

Dignāga

TRANSLATED BY DOUGLAS Duckworth, Malcolm David Eckel, Jay Garfield, John Powers, and Sonam Thakchöe

Homage to all buddhas and bodhisattvas!
Even if sensory cognition were caused by fundamental particles,
It would not have particles as its object
Because they do not appear to cognition,
Any more than the sense faculties do.[3] (1)
It does not come from that of which it has the appearance

1. While this text was composed in metered verse and is represented in Tibetan in four-line verse, the line and verse breaks are not syntactically important, and sentences flow between lines and verses. We have chosen to represent it in verse instead of more natural prose because that is the way the text is presented in the Tibetan canon and because the commentaries often take lines or groups of lines as units for discussion.

2. Chinese: *Guansuoyuan yuan lun* 觀所緣緣論 or *Wuxiang sichen lun* 無相思塵論. The translation is based on the sDe dge edition, #4205, *Tshad ma* vol. *ce*, ff. 86a1–86a5. The text used here is Tibetan Buddhist Resource Center (TBRC) W23703-1490: 171.1–5. For alternative English translations, see Hayes (1987), Sastri (1938), and Tola and Dragonetti (1982). Wayman (1979) translates parts of the text.

3. There is an alternate reading of this line: "cognition arises as its appearance." This is consistent with Dharmakīrti's understanding of perception and with Vinītadeva's understanding of this verse. This reading is underdetermined by the Tibetan translations of Dignāga's text. The translation we adopt is also supported by the Tibetan and reflects the structure of Dignāga's argument more closely.

Because, like a double moon, collections are not substantially real.
Thus, neither kind of external object
Makes sense as an object of cognition. (2)
Some maintain that collected features are the cause.
Features of minute particles
Are not the object of cognition,
Any more than things like solidity are. (3)
According to them, cognitions of things like pots
And cups would be identical.
If they are distinguished by different features,
These do not belong to substantially real particles, (4)
Because there is no difference in their dimensions.[4]
Therefore, these belong to something that is not substantially real
Because the cognition that has the appearance of them
Disappears when particles disperse. (5)
But an internal cognitive object,
Which appears as though external, is the object
Because it is cognition itself,
And because it is its condition. (6)
Even though they are simultaneous,
It is its condition because it is invariably concomitant.
It is sequential because of a transfer of capacity.
A sense faculty is a co-operating sense capacity. (7)
It is not contradictory for this capacity also to be in cognition.
Thus, the object and
The capacity cause one another and
Have done so from beginningless time. (8)

---

4. Dignaga's verses run on from verse 4 to verse 5; in order to make sense of this in English, we have transposed some material from 5a to 4d.

3

Autocommentary to Investigation of the Percept (Ālambana-parīkṣā-vṛtti)[1]

Dignāga

TRANSLATED BY DOUGLAS Duckworth, Malcolm David Eckel, Jay Garfield, John Powers, and Sonam Thakchöe

In Sanskrit: *Ālambana-parīkṣā-vṛtti*; in Tibetan: *dMigs pa brtag pa'i 'grel pa.*

[171.5] Homage to all buddhas and bodhisattvas!

Some maintain[2] that the percept[3] of a sensory (e.g., a visual) cognition[4] is an external object.[5] They must suppose that it is fundamental particles[6] (because that is what causes cognition), or that it is a collection[7] (because that is what

1. Paramārtha (P): *Wuxiang sichen lun* 無相思塵論. Xuanzang 玄奘 (600–664) (X): *Guan suoyuanyuan lun* 觀所緣緣論. This text is translated from the Derge edition, TBRC *bsTan 'gyur*, W23703-1490: 171.5–174.

2. Tib. *rtog grang*. Lü Cheng 呂澂 (L): *ji* 計, calculate. P: *zhi* 執, accept. X: *yuling* 欲令, allow.

3. Tib. *dmigs pa*; Skt. *ālambana*. L, X: *suoyuan* 所緣, perceptual objects. P: *yuan* 緣, indirect cause.

4. L, X, P: *yanshi* 眼識, visual consciousness. Vinītadeva (Derge: 349) interprets "a sensory (e.g., a visual) cognition" (*mig la sogs pa'i rnam par shes pa*) as including mental perception.

5. Tib. *phyi rol gyi don*; Skt. *bāhyārtha*. L, P: 外境, external objects. X: *waise* 外色, external form.

6. Tib. *rdul phra rab*; Skt. *paramāṇu*. L: *wei* 微, subtle thing. P: *linxu* 鄰虛, fundamental particle. X: *jiwei* 極微, subtle atom.

7. Tib. *'dus pa*; Skt. *samūha*. L, P: *ju* 聚, cluster. X: *hehe* 和合, combination.

appears[8] to cognition). In the first case: **Even if sensory cognition were caused by fundamental particles, it would not have particles as its object because they do not appear to cognition, any more than the sense faculties do.**[9] (1abcd)

An "object" is defined as something whose identity[10] is ascertained by a cognition[11] because a cognition arises with its representation. [172] Minute particles may be the cause of this cognition, but it does not have their appearance; this is also true of the sense faculties. Thus, first of all, minute particles are not the percept.[12]

A sensory cognition may have the appearance of a collection,[13] **but it does not come from that of which it has the appearance.**[14] (2a) It makes sense that

---

8. Tib. *snang ba;* Skt. *ābhāsa.* L: *xian* 現, appear. P: *si* 似, appear. X: *xiang* 相, image (Skt. *ākāra*).

9. Tib. *dbang po;* Skt. *indriya.* L, P, X: *gen* 根, faculties. This verse is quoted by Prajñākaragupta (*c.* seventh century) in the *Subcommentary on the Commentary on the Compendium of Epistemology* (*Pramāṇavārttika-bhāṣya* (1953: 336) "*yady apīndriyavijñapteḥ kāraṇaṃ paramāṇavaḥ / atadābhatayā nāsyā akṣavad viṣayo 'ṇavaḥ.*" Kamalaśīla preserves another version of this verse in *Extensive Commentary on the Compendium of Metaphysics* (*Tattvasaṃgraha-pañjikā,* ed. Śāstri, 1968, vol. 2: 711): "*yady apīndriyavijñapter grāhyāṃśaḥ karaṇaṃ bhavet / atadābhatayā tasyā nākṣavad viṣayaḥ sa tu.*" Compare also Bhāviveka's *Verses on the Heart of the Middle Way* (*Madhyamaka-hṛdaya-vṛtti-tarkajvālā*), 5.32: "Of these [two options], a cognition of material form does not have the form of a single particle as its object (*gocara;* Tib. *spyod yul*) because it does not have the appearance of that particle, just as it does not have the form of the eye as its object": "*tatrāṇurūpam ekam tu rūpabuddher na gocaraḥ / atadābhatayā yadvad akṣarūpaṃ na gocaraḥ.*" Our translation follows Prajñākaragupta's Sanskrit in interpreting the Tibetan.

10. Tib. *rang gi ngo bo;* Skt. *svabhāva.*

11. This is quoted by Siṃhasūri (*c.* seventh century: 1966) in the *Commentary on the Wheel of Logic According to the Nyāya Text-Tradition* (*Nyāyāgamānusāriṇī Nyāyacakravṛtti*): "*viṣayo hi nāma yasya jñānena svabhāvo 'vadhāryate.*" This, along with other quotations from *Investigation of the Percept,* was identified by Harada Wasō 原田和宗, unpublished manuscript.

12. L, X: *suoyuan* 所緣, perceptual objects. P: *chen* 塵, "dust," object. Vinītadeva (355–356) formulates this argument as two different inferences (*prayoga*): (1) "fundamental particles are not the percept, because they do not produce a cognition that has their appearance, just like the sense faculties"; or (2) "fundamental particles are not the percept because one does not grasp their identity, just as with the sense faculties."

13. As discussed in the Introduction, the Tibetan term *'dus pa* can translate the Sanskrit *samūha,* as in Bhāviveka's summary of this argument in *Madhyamaka-hṛdaya-kārikā* 5.31 (Eckel 2008: 406). It also can translate *saṃhata* (as in Vasubandhu's *Thirty Verses* (*Triṃśikā,* v. 11) or *saṃghāta* (as in his *Treasury of Abhidharma Commentary Abhidharmakośa-bhāṣya* on 2.22). Eckel discusses this in his introduction to Vinītadeva's commentary (59).

14. This is quoted in Dignāga's *Compendium of Epistemology* (Steinkellner 2005: 6) 1.15 (2.3 in Hattori's [1968] numbering) and Prajñākaragupta's *Subcommentary on the Commentary on the Compendium of Epistemology* (1953: 339): "*yadābhāsaṃ na tat tasmāc [citrālambaṃ hi pañcakam].*"

an object[15] is a percept if it produces an appearance of itself.[16] This is because it is said to be a condition for the arising of cognition. A collection, however, is not like this **because it is not substantially real, like a double moon.**[17] (2b)

When a person sees a double moon because of defective sense faculties,[18] there may be an appearance of that double moon, but it is not the object of that cognition. In the same way, a collection is not a percept because it is not substantially real and, for that reason, is not a cause.[19] **Thus, neither kind of external object makes sense as an object of cognition.** (2cd) Because in each case one of the criteria is not satisfied,[20] no object, whether it is an "external minute particle" or an "aggregation," can be a percept.

With regard to the matter at hand,[21] **some**[22] **maintain that collected features are the cause.**[23] (3ab) They maintain that while all objects have many features,[24] they are perceived with only a few features.[25] Fundamental particles have the causes that produce cognitions that have the appearance of collections.

---

15. Tib. *don*; Skt. *artha*.

16. Tib. *rang snang ba'i rnam par rig pa*; Skt. *svābhāsa-vijñapti*. L: *xianji zhi shi* 現已之識, self-manifesting cognition. P: *liaobie qi tixiang* 了別其體相, perception of essence and characteristics. X: *shi dai bi xiang* 識帶彼相, cognition connected with characteristics.

17. Tibetan: *rdzas su med*; Skt. *dravyāsat*; L: *feishi shi* 非實事, unreal thing. P: *wuyou ti* 無有體, nonexistent entity. X: *ti shi wu* 體實無, nonexistent entity.

18. Tib. *dbang po ma tshang ba*; Skt. *vikalpendriya*. L: *genque sun* 根缺損, impaired faculties. P: *genluan* 根亂, confused faculties. X: *yan cuoluan* 眼錯亂, erroneous eye.

19. Vinītadeva (87) formulates this argument as two inferences: (1) "a collection is not a cause, because it is not substantially real, like a double moon"; or (2) "a collection is not a percept because it is not a cause, like a double moon." He attributes this formulation to Dharmapāla.

20. Tib. *yan lag gcig ma tshang ba*. L: *que yifen* 闕一分, lacking one part. P: *yifen bu* 一分不, without one part. X: *que yizhi* 闕一支, lacking one branch.

21. Vinītadeva explains that "the matter at hand" refers to opponents who believe that there are external objects (88–89).

22. According to Vinītadeva (88), "some" (*kha cig*) refers to Vāgbhaṭa (Pha khol) and others.

23. Tibetan: *sgrub pa*; Skt. *sādhana or sādhaka*; L: *neng chengli* 能成立, literally "what is able to be proven." P: *li* 立, established. According to Vinītadeva (88), the word *sgrub pa* (Skt. *sādhaka* or *sādhana*) means "cause" (*rgyu*).

24. Read *du ma can yin pa'i* rather than *du ma can yin pas*. This reading is supported by Vinītadeva's use of *'on kyang* later in his commentary. He explains (89): "material things are composed of the four great elements and, moreover, because they have such aspects as blue, fragrance, sweetness, and roughness, they have many aspects." The source is *Abhidharmakośa* 2.22ab: "A fundamental particle is composed of eight things (*aṣṭadravyaka*)."

25. Vinītadeva (89) attributes this position to Buddhadeva. His position is discussed in note 42 in the translation of Vinītadeva's text.

Features of minute particles are not the object of cognition any more than things like solidity are.[26] (3cd) Things like solidity may exist,[27] but they are not the object of visual cognition. The same is true of minute particles.

According to them,[28] **cognitions of things like pots and cups would be identical.** (4ab) There may be many minute particles in things like pots and cups, but they are not different at all.

If they are distinguished by different features: (4c) That is to say, if someone thinks that distinctive features, such as the neck of a pot, distinguish different cognitions, then these distinctive features belong only to things like pots. But **these do not belong to substantially real**[29] **particles because there is no difference in their dimensions.** (4d-5a) Fundamental particles may be substantially distinct,[30] but there are no differences in their spherical shapes. **Therefore, these differences belong to something that is not substantially real.** (5b)

These distinctive features belong only to things that are conventionally real[31] [173] but not to minute particles. Things like pots are just conventionally real **because the cognition that has the appearance of them disappears when particles disperse.** (5cd) Cognitions of things that are substantially real, such as color, do not disappear even when things that are connected with them are removed.[32] Thus, it makes sense that objects of sensory awareness are not external.

---

26. L: *jianxing* 堅性, hard nature. X, P: *jian* 堅, hard.

27. L: *you* 有, exist. P, X: *shiyou* 實有, truly exist.

28. That is, according to those who think that fundamental particles have "collected features" that become perceptible when they are gathered together with other fundamental particles.

29. Tib. *rdzas su yod pa*; Skt. *dravya-sat*. L: *fei shiyou* 非實有, not really existent. P: *shi shiyou* 是實有, is truly existent. X: *shi* 實, real.

30. Tib. *rdzas gzhan*; Skt. *anya-dravya*. L: *ceng wuyou shu* 曾無有殊, not substantially different. P: *wuyouyi* 無有異, without any differences. X: *wu chabie* 無差別, lacking distinctions.

31. Tib. *kun rdzob du yod pa*; Skt. *saṃvṛti-sat*. P: *jiaming you* 假名有, nominal existence. X: *jia* 假, designation. Lü Cheng translates *kun rdzob du yod pa* (Skt. *samvṛti-satya*) with a term that means illusion: *huanyou* 幻有, which commonly translates Sanskrit *māyā*, so his translation would read: "differences only exist as illusory existence."

32. D differs from P, N, and S; it reads: "*rdzas su yod pa rnams la ni 'brel pa can bsal du zin kyang kha dog la sogs pa bzhin du rang gi blo 'dor bar byed do.*" P, N, and S have the same reading except for a negation at the end: *'dor ba* ***med***. D's reading is an argument that presents the opponent with an unwanted consequence: if macro-objects such as pots and cups were substantially real, as he contends, then perception of them should remain even if their particles (e.g., particles of color or solidity) are removed, but this is clearly not the case. The alternative phrasing in P, N, and S would read: "Even if one were to remove things that are

But an internal cognitive object,[33] **which appears as though external, is the object.**[34] (6ab) Even though there is no external object, one that appears to be external but is only internal is the percept condition.[35] **Because it is cognition itself and because it is its condition:**[36] (6cd) Internal cognition appears as the object and arises from it, so it has the two characteristics.[37] Thus, a percept condition only exists internally.

Objection: First, if cognition appears in this way, how do you understand that its condition arises in the same place and at the same time?

Reply: **Even though they are simultaneous, it is a condition because it is invariably concomitant.**[38] (7a) That is, even though they occur simultaneously, it can be a condition that arises from other conditions because they are invariably

---

associated with substantially real things, one's awareness of things like their color would not disappear." These differences may reflect textual variants that are also found in Paramārtha's and Xuanzang's translations, as noted by Lü Cheng (1928a). Paramārtha's text follows the "would **not** disappear" version, while Xuanzang's has "would disappear." Lü Cheng states that the Peking version agrees with Paramārtha, while what he calls the "Amdo version" (i.e., Derge) agrees with Xuanzang.

33. Tib. *nang gi shes bya;* Skt. *antarjñeya-rūpa.* L: *neisuozhi zhi tixing* 內所知之體性, essential nature of an internal perceptual object. P: *neichen xiang* 內塵相, internal object characteristic. X: *neise* 內色, internal form.

34. This is quoted in the *Commentary on the Compendium of Metaphysics* (vol. 2: 710): "*yad antarjñeyarūpaṃ tu bahirvad avabhāsate / so 'rthaḥ.*" It would be possible to translate *antarjñeya-rūpa* as "the identity of an internal cognitive object," echoing the terminology in the autocommentary on verse 1, where Dignāga defines an object (*don;* Skt. *artha*) as "something whose identity is ascertained by a cognition." But here the word *rūpa* simply designates the internal cognitive object itself.

35. Tib. *dmigs pa'i rkyen;* Skt. *ālambana-pratyaya.* L: *suoyuan yuan* 所緣緣, causal condition perceptual object. P, X: *yuanyuan* 緣緣, conditioning factor perceptual object.

36. L, P, X: *yuan* 緣, condition. This verse is quoted in the *Commentary on the Compendium of Metaphysics* (vol. 2: 710): "*vijñānarūpatvāt tatpratyayatayāpi ca.*"

37. This refers to the two characteristics of a percept as defined in the commentary on verse 2a.

38. To say that two things are invariably concomitant means that they invariably occur together in a causal relationship (and not merely coincidentally, like the two horns of a cow). The Chinese translators seem to have construed this as having a stronger sense than did the Tibetans. Lü Cheng, Paramārtha, and Xuanzang all use *jueding* 決定, which has connotations of certainty or ineluctability, but the probable Sanskrit original, *avyabhicārin* (attested by the quote by Pārthasārathimiśra cited below), means "not deviating, not failing, not going astray, fidelity." The upshot is that they cause each other in an autopoietic relationship that is constant and regular. This is reflected in Paramārtha's translation, which combines *jueding* with *suisheng* 隨生, "arise in response to, arise together." Similarly, Xuanzang combines *jueding* with *xiangsui* 相隨, "follow, accompany, conform to."

This verse is quoted by Pārthasārathimiśra (c. eleventh century: 1978) in *Jewel Mine of Logic* (*Nyāya-ratnākara*): "*pratyayo 'vyabhicāritvāt saha.*"

concomitant. Logicians[39] say that being present or absent is also the defining character[40] of the sequential arising of cause and effect.

Alternatively, **it is sequential because of a transfer of capacity.** (7b) In sequence also, it is not contradictory for the appearance of an object to cause a capacity located in cognition to produce an effect that is similar to itself.[41]

Someone may ask: "If the percept condition is just an internal object, then how does visual cognition arise by depending on this and also on the eye?" **A sense faculty is a cooperating sense capacity.**[42] (7cd) It can be inferred from its result that a sense faculty is a capacity, but it is not derived from material elements. **It is not contradictory for this capacity also to be in cognition.** (8a) This capacity can exist in cognition, and it can exist in something that is inaccessible.[43] It makes no difference in the production of the result.

Thus, the object and the capacity cause one another and have done so from beginningless time. (8bcd) A cognition arises with the appearance of

---

39. The reading follows Vinītadeva and sNar thang, which indicate that this refers to people, and not to reasoning. Vinītadeva's text (223) reads: "*gtan tshigs pa dag*," but all the Tibetan texts of *Investigation of the Percept* read: "*gtan tshigs*."

40. Tib. *mtshan nyid*; Skt. *lakṣaṇa*. Paramārtha's translation clarifies the dynamic between cause and effect: "If the cause precedes and the effect follows, then the effect is consequent on the cause; the cause is not consequent on the effect. If a cause has an effect, then the effect necessarily exists. If a cause has no effect, then that potential effect necessarily does not exist. Effects consequent on causes may or may not appear. This is the defining character of 'cause and effect'." Xuanzang translates this passage as: "Logicians say that existence and nonexistence [or presence and absence] are mutually consequent. Even though they arise simultaneously, still they also achieve existence, because this is the defining character of 'cause and effect'." See also Vinītadeva's discussion on pages 45–46.

41. The Tibetan reads differently from the Sanskrit of Kamalaśīla's (1968: 710) quotation of this passage in *Extended Commentary on the Compendium of Metaphysics*: "It is not contradictory for the appearance of an object sequentially to cause a potential to be present in cognition, in order to cause an effect to arise that is similar to itself" (*athavā śaktyarpaṇāt kramāt// krameṇāpi so 'rthāvabhāsaḥ svāvabhāsānurūpakāryotpattaye śaktiṃ vijñānādhārāṃ karotīty avirodhaḥ*, quoted by Pārthasārathimiśra in the *Jewel Mine of Logic* (1978: 222). Kamalaśīla's version is probably less accurate.

There are two variants in the Tibetan of this passage: *don du snang ba* (N) for *don du snang bas* (D), and *skyed par byed par* (D) for *skyed par byed pa'i* (N and Ngawang Dendar). The Sanskrit supports N's reading of *snang ba* (*arthāvabhāsaḥ*), and D's reading of *skyed byed par* (*utpattaye*).

42. Normally, the pronoun *yat* (Tib. *gang*) would mark the subject of the sentence (see Tubb and Boose 2007: 1.84.1), but it seems more probable to take this verse as a definition of a sense faculty (*indriya*; Tib. *dbang po*).

43. Tib. *bstan du med pa*. Skt. *anidarśana*. The term "*bstan du med pa*" is commonly used in the *Treasury of Abhidharma* to refer to a sense faculty like the eye that is "inaccessible" in cognition. It is often translated as "invisible," but it can also refer to sounds and other phenomena that are not perceived by a particular sensory faculty.

an object, depending on the capacity called "eye" and on an internal object, without being disclosed as the percept.[44] These two cause one another and have done so from beginningless time. Sometimes the representation of the object of cognition[45] arises from the maturation of the capacity, and sometimes the capacity arises from the representation. Saying that these two are different or not different from cognition is a matter of preference.[46] Thus, it makes sense[47] for an internal percept to be the object because it has the two characteristics.

Here ends the *Commentary on Investigation of the Percept* by the Master Dignāga.

---

44. We have slightly altered the wording to better reflect the import of the passage. The Peking version of the autocommentary reads: "*ma phye ba*" (*phye* can be the pf. of *'byed*, "to open or separate," or it can be the equivalent of *'bye ba*, "to open or divide"). This reading is confirmed by the version of the *ṭīkā* in S. D reads "*ma bstan pa*," while the D version of Vinītadeva reads: "*ma phye ba*." To make matters more confusing, the N version of Vinītadeva reads: "*ma gye ba*," probably a scribal error.

Negi (2000, vol. 10: 4214, col. 2) lists two significant equivalents of *ma phye ba: abheda* and *avibhāga*. The Tibetan term *ma phye ba* occurs twice in the *Commentary on the Treasury of Abhidharma*: once as *anirdhāraṇa* (in the commentary on 7.33; Wogihara 1932–1936. II: 640) and once as *abhedena* (in *the Treasury of Abhidharma* 6.40ab; Wogihara 1932–1936. II: 489). In the first case, it means that a particular point is *not specified* in a particular verse; in the second case, it means that there is *no difference* between two categories. A more likely meaning in this context, however, is *phye ba* as *apāvṛtta* or *udghāṭita* in the sense of "opened, uncovered, or disclosed" (hence D's correction to *ma bstan pa*). The idea is that a cognition appears as an object without being "disclosed" as the percept.

45. Translated in accordance with N: *shes pa'i yul.*

46. Paramārtha appears to have understood this differently from how the Tibetan translators read it. The Tibetan indicates that one is free to take either stance, but Paramārtha translates: "Some claim that cognition is different from those two; some claim that it isn't different from the two; and some are unable to say." Xuanzang provides a gloss that is closer to the Tibetan reading: "Regarding whether the two forms—the capacity and the object—and cognition are the same or different or whether they are neither the same nor different: one may say as one wishes."

Note that Dignāga's phrase "one is free to say" (*ci dgar brjod par bya'o*) appears as "cannot say" in both Bhāviveka (*brjod par mi 'dod de*) and Vinītadeva (*brjod par bya ba ma yin no*). It is possible that *ci dgar* represents a misreading (or mistaken transmission) of the Sanskrit term that is reflected by *mi 'dod de* in Bhāviveka. Both could involve versions of the Sanskrit word *iṣṭa*. The expression *ci dgar* could translate *yatheṣṭam*, while *mi 'dod de* could translate *aniṣṭam*. Negi (2000, vol. 3: 1101, col. 2) lists *yatheṣṭam* as a possible equivalent of *ci dgar*. Either one would be possible, but the support from Vinītadeva favors the reading in Bhāviveka.

47. Translated in accordance with N: *mdzad pa rdzogs.*

Texts

Dignāga. *Autocommentary to Investigation of the Percept* (*Ālambana-parīkṣā-vṛtti*; Tib. *dMigs pa brtag pa'i 'grel pa*). (1) sDe dge (D) edition, TBRC *bsTan 'gyur*, W23703-1490: 171.5–174; (2) Co ne (C): Tibetan Buddhist Resource Center (TBRC) W1GS66030, vol. 174: 175–177; (3) dPe bsdur ma (B): TBRC W1PD95844, vol. 97: 432–436; (4) gSer bris (S): #3705; TBRC W23702, vol. 183: 474–476; (5) Peking (Pe cing) (P): #5703, *tshad ma* vol. *ce*: 86a.5-87b.2 (vol. 130, p. 73); (6) sNar thang (N): #3702, *tshad ma* vol. *ce*: 180b1–182a2; (7) Paramārtha (Zhendi 眞諦), *Wuxiang sichen lun* 無相思塵論: T 1619.31.882–883; (8) Xuanzang 玄奘 *Guan suoyuanyuan lun* 觀所緣緣論: T 1624.31.888–889.

———. *Investigation of the Percept* (*Ālambana-parīkṣā*; Tib. *dMigs pa brtag pa*). (1) sDe dge edition (D), #4205, *Tshad ma* vol. *ce*: 86a1–86a5. TBRC W23703-1490: 171.1–5; (2) Co ne (C): TBRC W1GS66030, vol. 174: 174–175; (3) dPe bsdur ma (B): TBRC W1PD95844, vol. 97: 430–431; (4) gSer bris (S): #3705; TBRC W23702, vol. 183: 474–476; (5) Peking (Pe cing) (P): #5703, *tshad ma* vol. *ce*: 177a7–177b5 (vol. 130: 73–74); (6) sNar thang (N): #3702, *tshad ma* vol. *ce*: 119.3–6.

4

"To Please Beginners"

VINĪTADEVA'S *SUBCOMMENTARY ON INVESTIGATION OF THE PERCEPT* IN ITS INDIAN CONTEXT

Malcolm David Eckel

VINĪTADEVA'S SUBCOMMENTARY ON Dignāga's *Investigation of the Percept* (*Ālambana-parīkṣā-ṭīkā*) is one of only two known commentaries on this text in the Sanskrit tradition, and it is the only one to survive in Tibetan translation. But it would be misleading to think that this text, along with the Chinese translation of the commentary by Dharmapāla, exhausts the interpretive resources available to us for understanding Dignāga's text in its original Indian setting. This short text, consisting of only eight verses with a brief autocommentary, had a much more substantial intellectual presence in the Indian tradition than its size would suggest. It was widely quoted and discussed as a source for understanding "mind-only," the signature doctrine of the Yogācāra tradition, from the time of its original appearance in the sixth century until the eighth century and beyond, and not just in the Buddhist sources that took a proprietary interest in its positions but in other systematic accounts of Indian thought.[1]

This chapter has two goals. The first is to identify some of the distinctive features of Vinītadeva's subcommentary so that it can help us understand some of the unexpected and creative ways in which Dignāga's text was used in later Tibetan and Chinese traditions. The second is to situate Vinītadeva's subcommentary in the context of other Indian responses to Dignāga's ideas—to

1. Many of the Sanskrit quotations of Dignāga's text are embedded in Jain sources. These are noted in the footnotes to the translation.

read it, in other words, as part of an evolving commentarial tradition in the wider sense of the word, in which Dignāga's ideas are quoted, interpreted, and applied to an evolving Buddhist discussion of perceptual objects and perceptual cognition. It would be too much to say that there is a single "Indian" reading of Dignāga's text, but Vinītadeva gets us closer to the understanding of the text in its original language and original setting than the Tibetan and Chinese commentaries that occupy other parts of this complex study. In part, this involves a careful study of its language and its use of typical Sanskrit rhetorical resources. But its "meaning" also has to do with the way its arguments were appropriated and applied to other challenges in other settings. So this introduction is meant not only to examine the relationship between Vinītadeva and Dignāga, but also to situate both texts in the larger intellectual world in which Dignāga's text played such a distinctive part.

We know very little about Vinītadeva himself, other than what we can glean from the works that have been preserved in Tibetan translation and in a few Sanskrit fragments.[2] Vinītadeva is best known as a commentator on the short logical works of Dharmakīrti: he was part of a cadre of similar commentators who are dated roughly to the eighth century.[3] But Vinītadeva had other interests as well. He wrote a subcommentary on Vasubandhu's *Twenty Verses* and another on Sthiramati's commentary on Vasubandhu's *Thirty Verses*.[4] To these can be added his subcommentary on Dignāga's *Investigation of the Percept*. Funayama (2001: 321) observes quite aptly that "Vinītadeva's activity is best appreciated as a scholar who was quite well versed in a variety of fields of Buddhist academism." In other words, he was a generalist. To this we can add that he shows the virtues of a teacher. In the concluding verses of his subcommentary on *Investigation of the Percept*, he asks scholars to be patient and not find fault, since his goal is simply to "please beginners." His subcommentaries on Vasubandhu and Dignāga give the impression of school texts, meant to introduce beginning students to the classic texts of the tradition rather than to break new critical ground. In this sense, they give a solid, accurate, and readable account of the basic issues in the texts as they were understood in the decades after the appearance of Dharmakīrti. It is well known that

2. For a list of Vinītadeva's surviving works, see Jaini (1985: 470).

3. For a detailed analysis of the date of Vinītadeva and his relationship to other commentators in the epistemological tradition, including Śākyabuddhi, Arcaṭa, Śāntarakṣita, Jinendrabuddhi, Kamalaśīla, and Śāntabhadra, see Funayama (1995; 2001).

4. Both of these fall into the category of subcommentaries (*ṭīkā*) since they comment not only on the root verses but on another commentary. In the case of the *Twenty Verses*, it is Vasubandhu's autocommentary; in the case of the *Thirty Verses*, it is Sthiramati's commentary.

Dharmottara (eighth century) harshly criticized Vinītadeva's subcommentary on the *Drop of Logic* (*Nyāyabindu*), but Funayama (2001: 320) notes that this does not diminish his importance as a gauge of "the actual philosophical circumstances before the appearance of Dharmottara." The same can be said of his subcommentary on Dignāga. It tells us a great deal about the way the text and its argument were viewed in the time of Dharmakīrti and thereafter.

Introduction: The Subject Matter, Purpose, and Connection of the Text

Vinītadeva begins his analysis in the conventional, formulaic style common in other eighth-century commentaries, especially in the Buddhist epistemological tradition: he defines the subject matter (*abhidheya*), purpose (*prayojana*), and connection (*saṃbandha*) of the text.[5] Vinītadeva gives a succinct justification: "The connection, the subject matter, and the purpose of the text should definitely be stated. Otherwise, students (*śrotṛ*) who have previous knowledge will not accept a text without connection, subject matter, and purpose (78–79)." This formula is repeated almost word-for word in his other commentaries. In the subcommentary on the *Thirty Verses*, he says: "The connection, subject matter, and purpose of the text should definitely be stated at the very beginning. Otherwise, students who have previous knowledge will not accept a treatise without connection, subject matter, and purpose. For this reason, these three should be stated to encourage students (*śrotṛ-jana*)."[6] Vinītadeva's subcommentary on the *Twenty Verses* begins with a similar formula: "This opening statement, 'In the Mahāyāna, it is established that the three worlds are mind-only,' directly states the purpose, subject matter, and connection of the text. The connection is understood by implication. These definitely should be stated. Otherwise, a text that lacks these three would not be accepted by students who have previous knowledge."[7] This language is sufficiently common in other texts to make many of the Sanskrit equivalents

5. The origin of this formula is unclear, but Kumārila (*c.* seventh century) uses similar language in the *Verse Commentary* (*Ślokavārttika*): "If the goal of any text or activity is not stated, why would it be accepted?" (*sarvasyaiva hi śāstrasya karmaṇo vāpi kasya cit / yāvat prayojanaṃ noktaṃ tāvat tat kena gṛhyatām*; quoted in Funayama 1995: 184).

6. *rab tu byed pa'i 'brel pa dang brjod par bya ba dang dgos pa rnams gdon mi za bar thog mar brjod dgos so // gzhan du na 'brel pa med pa dang / brjod par bya ba med pa dang dgos pa med pa'i rab tu byed pa ni nyan pa po rtog pa sngon du gtong ba rnams nyan par khas mi len to // de'i phyir nyan pa po'i skye bo spro ba bskyed pa'i don du 'di gsum brjod par bya'o //*

7. *theg pa chen po la khams gsum pa rnam par rig pa tsam du rnam par gzhag ces bya ba tshig dang po 'dis ni rab tu byed pa 'di'i dgos pa dang / brjod par bya ba'i rang gi ngo bo dang / dgos pa'i yang dgos pa dngos su ston to // 'brel pa ni don gyis brtag par bya'o // rab tu byed pa'i 'brel pa dang /*

clear. For example, Vinītadeva uses a common formula to relate the text and its purpose as "means and end" (*upāya-upeya*): "The refutation and affirmation of these two are the purpose. Since this text achieves this purpose, this text is the means to this purpose. Therefore, the text and its purpose are connected as means and end." This language of "means and end" occurs again in Dharmottara's *Subcommentary on the Drop of Logic* (*Nyāyabindu-ṭīkā*): "The connection between the treatise and its purpose is a relationship of means and end (*upāyopeyabhāvaḥ prakaraṇaprayojanayoḥ saṃbandha iti*)."[8] In the conventional world of eighth-century commentaries, Vinītadeva's formulas are certainly not unique.

If these formulas are so common, what do they tell us about Vinītadeva's interests and goals? First, it is obvious from the simplicity of his language that he was not interested in the complex epistemological issues that occupied other eighth-century commentators. As Funayama has ably explained, the simple statement that the subject matter, purpose, and relevance are given "to encourage students" (*nyan pa po'i skye bo spro ba bskyed pa'i don du*) provoked a lively controversy among other commentators about what could and could not be known from the opening line of a text.[9] In most cases, Vinītadeva lets this question pass by almost without notice. In only one case does he recognize a problem. Funayama has argued that Arcaṭa (*c.* 700–750) differentiates himself by arguing that it is not enough to "encourage" students; the author also had to respond to the suspicion that the text is useless.[10] Vinītadeva is not as expansive as Arcaṭa (or as Arcaṭa's critic, Kamalaśīla) on this topic, but he is aware of the problem when he puts the suspicion in the mouth of an opponent: "What is the point of this refutation and affirmation? They are completely unnecessary (*'gog pa dang / rab tu sgrub pa 'di dag gis ci zhig bya ste / de dag ni gang du yang mi mkho'o*: 79)." Funayama has argued that Vinītadeva represents a stage in the eighth-century commentarial tradition when scholars were less sophisticated and less critically aware. Certainly he does not show the same complexity of analysis that we find in Arcaṭa or Kamalaśīla, but I wonder whether this simplicity is just a reflection of his ambitions for this text. If he is writing for

---

brjod par bya ba dang / dgos pa rnams nges par brjod par bya'o // gzhan du na 'brel pa med pa dang / brjod par bya ba med pa dang / dgos pa med pa dang / dgos pa'i yang dgos pa med pa'i rab tu byed pa ni rtog pa sngon du gtong ba'i nyan pa po dag khas mi len te //

8. Dharmottara, *Commentary on the Drop of Logic* (*Nyāyabindu-ṭīkā*): 12.

9. Funayama (2001: 311). This phrase appears in Vinītadeva's subcommentary on the *Thirty Verses* quoted earlier. It also appears in his own *Commentary on the Drop of Logic* (*Nyāyabindu-ṭīkā*).

10. Funayama (1995: 188–189) and (2001: 311).

beginners and asks scholars for their patience, perhaps he thinks these are questions better left for another time or for another author.

What then did Vinītadeva see as the purpose of the text? In the formulaic language of his opening paragraphs, he makes one intellectual move that is worth noting before reading more deeply. Dignāga's opening sentence says: "Some maintain that the percept of a sensory (e.g., a visual) cognition is an external object. They must suppose that it is fundamental particles (because that is what causes cognition), or that is a collection (because that is what appears to cognition) (79)." Vinītadeva notes that this sentence tells us about the subject matter: this is a text about different views of a percept. He goes on to say that the purpose and connection are known by implication (Tib. *shugs kyis*; Skt. *sāmarthyāt*). The purpose is to refute external objects and affirm internal ones; and this purpose is connected to the text as the end is to the means.

By drawing this implication out of Dignāga's opening sentence, Vinītadeva is alerting the reader to a symmetry that is not obvious in Dignāga's own words. Vinītadeva interprets the argument as having two parts: it refutes an external view of the percept, and it affirms an internal one. What it means to "refute" and "affirm," and what constitutes "external" as opposed to "internal," remain to be seen, but we know from the start that we are dealing with a structured sequence of ideas that mirrors the structure of other texts in this tradition. Although he does not say it explicitly, what is at stake is the fundamental balance between affirmation and denial that characterizes the middle path.

Verses 1 and 2: The Initial Dilemma

Dignāga begins the substantive argument of his text with a simple dilemma: if the percept of a sensory cognition is an external object, it has to consist of either fundamental particles or a "collection" of these fundamental particles. He then rejects these two options with two specific arguments: "Even if sensory cognition were caused by fundamental particles, it would not have particles as its object because it does not have the appearance of these [particles], any more than the sense faculties do (82)," and "[A sensory cognition] does not come from that [collection], because [a collection] is not substantially real, like a double moon." Vinītadeva unpacks these arguments in the way one would expect from a commentary of this type. He defines terms, often providing synonyms for the key technical vocabulary; he analyzes compounds; he responds to objections; then he restates the argument in ways that make its structure become clear. These strategies are typical of Sanskrit commentaries. I will only comment on a few of the features that situate the text in its historical setting.

First, it is useful to note that Dignāga picks up and advances an argument against external objects that has precedent in a text by Vasubandhu, the *Twenty Verses*, a work that also received Vinītadeva's commentarial attention. A comparison helps identify ways in which Dignāga has advanced the argument. The *Twenty Verses* begins with an assertion and an example: "Consciousness arises with the appearance of an object, just as people with an eye disease see unreal hairs and flies; there is no object at all."[11] Hanneder has pointed out that this statement may have originally been part of the text's prose introduction then turned into a verse by Vasubandhu himself or a later redactor.[12] Be that as it may, the initial formulation of mind-only serves as the focus of a series of objections, expressed in verse: "If cognition has no object, there cannot be any specificity of place and time, no lack of specificity of personality (*santāna*), and no effective action."

Vasubandhu's commentary explains more clearly what the opponent has in mind. "Specificity of place and time" means the perception of a particular object only appears in certain places and certain times, not in all places and all times. Without an external object to specify its appearance, this would seem to be impossible. "Lack of specificity of personality" means that it is possible for more than one person to see the same object at the same time. And "effective action" means that the object can bring about a real effect. Matilal (1986: 230) points out that all three of these objections presuppose a causal theory of perception: If there is no real object to cause our perception, why does it appear at one time or place and not another? Without a common external cause, there would be no way to explain a common perception. And without an external cause, there would be no way to explain how the things we perceive have real effects.

Vasubandhu's responses to these three objections are quite straightforward: he offers a series of counter-examples that provide the necessary explanation. Specificity of time and place is established as it is in a dream: In a dream someone sees a certain thing, like a city, a garden, a woman, or a man, in a certain place and time and not at all places and times. A dream can also answer the objection about effective action: A dream of an imaginary sexual object can

---

11. This translation is based on the Tibetan: *rnam par shes pa 'di nyid don su snang ba 'byung ste / dper na rab rib can rnams kyis skra zla la sogs pa pa med par mthong ba bzhin te / don gang yang med do //* (Derge no. 4057: Śi 4a–10a). Lévi (1932: 175) provides a Sanskrit version based on a Nepali manuscript: "*vijñaptimātram evedam asadarthāvabhāsanāt / yadvat taimirikasyās atkeśoṇḍrakādidarśanam / na deśakālaniyamaḥ saṃtānāniyamo na ca / na ca kṛtyakriyā yuktā vijñaptir yadi nārthataḥ.*"

12. As noted by Taber (2010: 281).

cause a real physical effect in the person who is having the dream. And in the case of shared illusions, Vasubandhu cites the experience of beings in hell. Because of the similarity of their previous karma, they all perceive the same punishments, even though the punishments have no reality outside their own minds. These three responses manage the three objections by giving counterexamples, but they do not actually give an argument *against* external objects.

For this argument, we have to turn to verse 11, where Vasubandhu says: "An object (*viṣaya*) is not a single thing, it is not many fundamental particles, and it is not a combination, because no fundamental particle is established." The commentary explains that "not one" means that it is not a "whole" (*avayavin*) in the sense imagined by the Vaiśeṣikas. It is not "many" because fundamental particles are not apprehended separately. And it is not a combination because a single fundamental particle is not established as a real thing (*dravya*). Why is it not a real thing? Vasubandhu develops an argument based on the indivisibility of fundamental particles. If a particle is defined as the smallest possible unit of matter, it cannot be subdivided into anything else. But to "combine" with other particles in such a way that it creates extension in space, it has to have different sides. Or, as Vasubandhu puts it, "If a fundamental particle is connected at the same time to six other particles on six sides, it must have six parts because the location of one would not be the location of the other. If the location of a single particle is the location of all six, then all of them would have the same location, and every cluster of particles would be the size of a single particle. And because they would not be distinguished from one another, no cluster would be visible."[13] This argument about the extension of clusters of fundamental particles had enduring influence on the analysis of external objects into the eighth century and beyond.[14]

But this is not the direction that Dignāga chooses to follow in *Investigation of the Percept*. His argument against the claim that external objects can be percepts is based on an assumption that the percept of a cognition has to satisfy two separate conditions: It has to be the cause of the cognition, and it has to appear in the cognition. These two conditions can be stated separately, or they can be condensed in a single sentence: a percept has to produce a cognition that appears as itself.[15] The original source of these two conditions is not

13. *ṣaḍbhyo digbhyaḥ ṣaḍbhiḥ paramāṇubhir yugapad yoge sati paramāṇoḥ ṣaḍaṃśatā prāpnoti | ekasya yo deśas tatrānyasyāsaṃbhavāt | atha ya evaikasya paramāṇor deśaḥ sa eva ṣaṇṇāṃ | tena sarveṣāṃ samānadeśatvāt sarvaḥ piṇḍaḥ paramāṇumātraḥ syāt parasparāvyatirekād iti na kaścit piṇḍo dṛśyaḥ syāt ||* (from Vasubandhu's commentary on verse 12).

14. As in Śāntarakṣita's *Compendium of Metaphysics* verses 1991ff.

15. As in the autocommentary on verse 2a: *don gang zhig rang snang ba'i rnam par rig pa bskyed de ni dmigs pa yin par rigs te.*

known, although we do know that the conditions preceded Dignāga. In the *Commentary on the Treasury of Abhidharma*, Vasubandhu applies the same two conditions to the production of a cognition:

> In that case, what does cognition do? It does not do anything. An effect is said to correspond to (*anuvidhīyate*) [its cause], because it comes into being by resembling (*sādṛśyena*) it, even though it does not do anything. In the same way one says that "cognition cognizes" because it comes into being by resembling [its cause], even though it does not do anything. And what is its resemblance? The fact that it has a representation of that [object] (*tadākāratā*). This is why it is said to cognize an object (*viṣaya*), not a sense organ (*indriya*), even though it also arises from a sense organ.[16]

This passage from Vasubandhu is reflected almost word-for-word in a quotation Vinītadeva uses to elaborate Dignāga's claim that "a percept produces a cognition that appears as itself": "If a cognition corresponds (Tib. *rjes su byed*; Skt. *anuvidhīyate*) to the identity of an object (*artha*), and if this [object] produces [that cognition], it is reasonable for that [object] to be a percept condition, but not otherwise."[17] Where does this definition come from? Vinītadeva answers by quoting another unidentified text: "An object is a percept if it causes mind and mental phenomena to arise, and, when they arise, causes the idea that this object is experienced (85)." The terminology is not an exact replica of Dignāga's own account of the two conditions, but for Vinītadeva it is close enough to show that the distinction is not Dignāga's own creation. It is likely that it was part of the general Abhidharma discussion of perceptual cognition.

Once Dignāga has armed himself with this distinction, it is relatively easy for him to formulate his arguments. Not surprisingly, they take the form of the standard three-part inference for which Dignāga is famous. Following Vinītadeva, the argument of the first verse can be formulated as follows:

(1) A sensory cognition does not have fundamental particles as its object,
(2) because it does not have the appearance of those [particles],
(3) as in the case of the sense faculties.

---

16. This passage is discussed by Kellner (2014: 279). My translation follows Kellner's, with some modifications to adapt it to the terminology used in our translation. The Sanskrit text is found in the *Commentary on the Treasury of Abhidharma*: 473–474.

17. In the commentary on verse 2a.

Here the subject of the inference is sensory cognition (*indriya-vijñapti*); "does not have particles as its object" (*nāsyā viṣayo 'ṇavaḥ*) is the inferred property; "because it does not have their appearance" (*atadābhatayā*) is the reason; and "as in the case of the sense faculties" (*akṣavad*) is the example. This formulation makes it clear that the inference, in a sense, is "about" sensory cognition. In keeping with what is often called the "epistemological turn" in Dignāga's writings, this inference focuses on the status of cognition rather than the status of external objects.[18] This way of formulating the inference also makes good sense of the compressed syntax of the verse.

The abstract property in the reason *atadābhatayā* ("not-appearing-as-those-ness") is best understood as belonging to the genitive, "of sensory cognition," in the first half of the verse. If so, the word "those" in the reason ("not-appearing-as-those-ness") has to refer to fundamental particles. Putting the reason together with the subject yields the final inference, "Sensory cognition does not . . ., because its does not have the appearance of those." If the syntax seems obscure, the best way to understand it is by analogy with the standard inference about fire on a mountain: "There is fire on the mountain because there is smoke on the mountain, as in a kitchen." Here the subject (*dharmin*) of the inference is "mountain" (*parvatasya*); the inferred property is "possessing fire" (*agnivattvam*); and the inferential property is "possessing smoke" (*dhūmavattvāt*). Literally, the inference means that the mountain has the property of possessing fire because it has the property of possessing smoke. When the abstractions are stripped away, it means simply that the mountain has fire because it has smoke. Dignāga's argument is capable of the same simplification: "A sensory cognition does not have fundamental particles as its object, because it does not have the appearance of those particles." Judging from his explanation of this verse, Vinītadeva preferred the simplicity of this option.

Oddly enough, this is not the only available interpretation. Vinītadeva also quotes two inferences from Dharmapāla. Dharmapāla wrote within a generation or so of Dignāga and gives a glimpse of the way Dignāga was read in the middle of the sixth century. Dharmapāla translates the first verse into two different inferences:

(1) Fundamental particles are not a percept,
(2) because they do not produce a cognition that has their own appearance,

---

18. See, for example, McCrea and Patil (2010: 5).

(3) like the sense faculties.
(1) Fundamental particles are not a percept,
(2) because their identities are not ascertained,
(3) like the sense faculties.

The key to both of these inferences is the identification of fundamental particles as the subject and the interpretation of *atadābhatayā* ("not-appearing-as-those-ness")—the inferential property—as their property rather than a property of sensory cognition. Understood this way, the inferential property means that fundamental particles do not appear as themselves. Obviously, Dharmapāla read the verse differently than Vinītadeva, as Vinītadeva himself indicates when he says: "These two inferences were formulated by the master Dharmapāla. I have copied them, but I did not formulate them (85)."

It would be natural to imagine that Dharmapāla's reading is the exception and that Vinītadeva represents a more literal and accurate reading of the text, but Dharmapāla's interpretation is supported by an unexpected source. As a representative of the rival Madhyamaka tradition, Bhāviveka (*c.* 500–560) would not normally be considered a commentator on Dignāga. But he read Dignāga carefully, quoted him, and occasionally translated Dignāga's arguments into verses for debate. Bhāviveka rewrites Dignāga's first verse in the following way:

> Here, the form of a single particle is not the object (*gocara*)
> of a cognition of form,
> because it does not have the appearance of that [object],
> just as the form of the eye is not the object.[19]

The commentary adds the following explanation:

> The form of a single particle is the subject. "Not the object of a cognition of form" is its property. The combination of the subject and the property is the thesis. "Because it does not have the appearance of that [object]" is the reason. This reason is explained as follows: "the appearance of that" means "the appearance of the object (*viṣaya*)." To

19. *tatrāṇurūpam ekaṃ tu rūpabuddher na gocaraḥ / atadābhatayā yadvad akṣarūpaṃ na gocaraḥ // Verses on the Heart of the Middle Way* (*Madhyamaka-hṛdaya-kārikā*) 5.32, Eckel (2008: 247).

> say that [a particle] does not have that appearance means that it does not appear in a cognition of that [object]. In other words, it is not the object. (Adapted from Eckel 2008: 247)

Bhāviveka confirms Dharmapāla's identification of a "particle" as the subject of the inference (although he puts it in the singular rather than the plural), and he attributes the inferential property ("not having the appearance of that") to a particle rather than to cognition. But he gives a different interpretation of the word "that." Here it is interpreted as referring not to particles, but to the object that the particles are not.

What should we make of these differences? Which of these readings is preferable? Vinītadeva's has the virtue of preserving the central position that "cognition" (*vijñapti*) occupies in Dignāga's original verse. By making this move, he confirms the importance of cognition in the argument of the text as a whole. On the other hand, this treatise is not just about cognition; it is also about the *percept* of cognition. It makes sense to expect the first verse to focus on something that the percept is not. It also would make sense in debate to identify and analyze possible views about the "object" (however that is designated in Sanskrit) of cognition. There are arguments to be made on both sides. But whichever side one prefers, this disagreement shows that the appropriation of texts in sixth-century India was not a static or stable process. Arguments were adapted and reformulated in different settings, as interpreters explored the implications of their cryptic expressions. These differences are a taste of the complexities that lie ahead in this study of translations and commentaries from China and Tibet.

Dignāga's second verse presents fewer challenges to his commentators, although it maintains his focus on cognition: "[A sensory cognition] does not come from that [collection] of which it has the appearance because, like a double moon, [a collection] is not substantially real." Here "sensory cognition" is carried down from the preceding verse. Vinītadeva starts by identifying an argument in the first part of the verse: "A cognition may have the appearance of a collection, but it does not have a collection as its percept. This is because the cognition does not arise from it (85)." But this argument needs to be supported by the inference that unfolds in the second part, an inference that has a "collection" as its subject. Combining the autocommentary with the verse, we read: "A collection is not like this (i.e., it does not produce a cognition that appears as itself), because, like a double moon, it is not substantially real (86)." It is at this point in the text that Vinītadeva introduces the quotation that supports Dignāga's two criteria for a valid percept: it has to produce a cognition that appears as itself. A so-called collection of particles may satisfy the second of these criteria—it may appear in a cognition—but it cannot satisfy the first, for the simple reason that Buddhists do not accept that "collections" made up of multiple entities constitute a real thing (*dravya*).

Dharmapāla offers two formulations of this argument, neither of which is surprising: "A collection is not a cause, because it is not substantially real, like a double moon" and "A collection is not a percept, because it is not a cause, like a double moon." Bhāviveka differs somewhat, but his argument is still quite similar: "The form of many particles is not an object of cognition, because it is not a real thing, like a double moon." He makes the similarity explicit in the commentary by explaining that the form of many particles is a collection (Tib. *'dus pa*; Skt. *samūha*), and collections, like an army or a forest, are not considered real things (Eckel 2008: 247).

It would be possible to linger over this point and explore the antecedents of the two positions Dignāga rejects in these opening verses. If so, it would take us into the many twists and turns in the tradition of "Indian atomism" that have been ably charted by Gangopadhyaya (1980). But it would take us away from the main thrust of Dignāga's argument. At this point in the text, Dignāga is not making a historical argument as much as he is establishing a clear intellectual dilemma. Valid percepts have to satisfy two conditions—they have to cause cognitions, and they have to appear in cognitions—and particles cannot satisfy these two conditions, either singly or together. These two stipulations prepare him to deal with a more complex and difficult position developed in verses 3 to 5, in which an opponent argues that it is possible to think of particles in such a way that they satisfy both of Dignāga's conditions. This position takes us much more deeply into the Indian account of external objects than is possible based on verses 1 and 2 alone.

Verses 3 to 5: Dignāga's Third Position

Up to this point, the argument has been forceful and clear, as long as we accept Dignāga's two criteria. But the situation becomes more complex in verse 3. Vinītadeva explains: "Now that [Dignāga] has refuted these two positions, he presents a third position, saying: 'Also among these.' That is, among the positions of those who say that there are external objects, some, such as Vāgbhaṭa, think that the collected features of fundamental particles are the cause of sensory cognition (88)." While Vinītadeva associates this third position with Vāgbhaṭa, it stands in for a view that had much wider circulation, including not just representatives of the Buddhist Abhidharma but also Brahmanical philosophers like Uddyotakara (sixth century) and Kumārila. What is meant by the third position? In his autocommentary Dignāga explains the third verse by saying: "Fundamental particles have the causes that produce cognitions with the appearance of collections." In other words, the opponent is trying to satisfy both of Dignāga's criteria at once. The opponent is claiming that fundamental particles have "features"[20] that cause cognitions to perceive the appearance of collections. How can they do this? The answer requires a much closer look at the term that I have translated as "collected features."

In the Tibetan translation, the term *'dus pa'i rnam pa* does not give us much to go on. The translators do not distinguish the term "collected" (*'dus pa*) here from the "collection" discussed in the second verse, but we have reason to believe that the terminology shifts in verse 3 from one kind of "collection" to another. The Chinese translators provide evidence that the word for "collection" in verse 2 is the Sanskrit *samūha*. They do not clearly establish the Sanskrit equivalent of the second term, but they do consistently distinguish the second from the first. What might this second term be? Here we are helped again by an unlikely source. In response to Dignāga's critique of the second position (that the percept is a collection), Bhāviveka distinguishes between two kinds of collections, a *samūha* (Tib. *'dus pa, Verses on the Heart of the Middle Way* 5.38) and a *saṃcita* (Tib. *bsags pa, Verses on the Heart of the Middle Way* 5.35). He agrees that a *samūha* cannot function as a percept, but he argues that a *saṃcita* can. How? A *samūha* is like an army or a forest; it is not a real thing even conventionally. But a *saṃcita* consists of homogeneous (*tulya-jātīya*) particles that are located in the same place (Eckel 2008: 247–252). This *saṃcita* is real conventionally and can function as an object of perception.[21]

We find further confirmation for Dignāga's use of the term "collected features" (*saṃcitākāra*) in Sthiramati's commentary on the first of the *Thirty Verses*:

> (1) [Some say that] the five kinds of sense cognition have a *saṃcita* (D *bstsags*, P,N *bsags*) as their *ālambana*, because they have its representation

---

20. In this context, it would also be possible to translate *ākāra* as "aspect" rather than "feature," following the second option in the definition of "aspect" cited by Kellner (2014: 287) from the *Oxford English Dictionary*: "one of the ways in which things may be looked at, or in which they present themselves to the mind." The key point is that the *ākāra* belongs to the thing that presents itself, not to the mind that perceives it.

21. Dan Lusthaus (personal communication) provides the following comment based on Puguang's 普光 (d. 664) commentary on the *Abhidharmakośa, Record of the Treasury of Abhidharma* (*Jushelun ji* 俱舍論記; T41, No. 1821.109a14–15): "Since Puguang, in his commentary on the *Kośa*, clearly identifies Xuanzang's equivalent for the third position atom-group as *saṃcita* by transliterating it into Chinese *san-mu-shi-ta* 三木訖底 (or something that then sounded like *saṃcita*), I think the case is pretty well settled that *samūha* is the first type of group and *saṃcita* is the second."

> (*tadākāratvāt*). But a *saṃcita* is nothing more than a group (Skt. *saṃhati; Tib. 'dus pa*) of parts (Skt. *avayava*; Tib. *cha shas*), because there is no cognition of the representation of a collection (*saṃcitākāra*) apart from its parts (*tadavayavān apohya*). Therefore, cognition arises with the representation of a collection (*saṃcitākāra*) without any external object. (2) And collected (*saṃcita*) fundamental particles are not its *ālambana*, because these particles do not have that representation (*atadākāratvāt*). This is because particles in a collected state (*saṃcitāvasthāyām*) have no additional factor (*ātmātiśaya*) other than what they have when they are in an uncollected state. Therefore, collected particles are not the percept, like uncollected [particles]. (3) Someone else thinks: a fundamental particle by itself is imperceptible (*atīndriya*) if it does not depend on (or cooperate with) others (*anyanirapekṣya*), but many [fundamental particles] that depend on each other (*parasparāpekṣya*) are perceptible (*indriyagrāhya*). But these [fundamental particles] also have no additional factor, whether they depend on each other or not,[22] so they either are perceptible individually or they are not perceptible at all. If fundamental particles are the object (*viṣaya*) of cognition when they depend on (or cooperate with) one another (parsparam apekṣamāṇānām) there can be no distinction between the cognitions of a pot and a wall, because fundamental particles do not have that representation (*atadākāratvāt*). And a cognition that has one kind of image (*anyābhāsa*) cannot have an object with another representation (*anyākāra*), because that would lead to an unacceptable conclusion (*atiprasaṅgāt*).[23]

Sthiramati helps us take a useful step forward. He distinguishes a *saṃcita* from a *samūha*, as Bhāviveka did, and he places *saṃcita* in compound with the term *ākāra*, as Dignāga apparently did. What's missing in this passage is

---

22. Lit. in the dependent or independent states.

23. The Sanskrit is found in Buescher (2007): 44: *sañcitālambanāś ca pañcavijñākāyās tadākāratvāt / na ca sañcitam avayavasaṃhatimātrād anyad vidyate / tadavayavān apohya sañcitākāravijñānābhāvāt / tasmād vinaiva bāhyenārthena vijñānaṃ sañcitākāram utpadyate / na ca paramāṇava eva sañcitās tasyālambanaṃ paramāṇūnām atadākāratvāt / na hy asañcitāvasthātaḥ sañcitāvasthāyāṃ paramāṇūnāṃ kaścid ātmātiśayaḥ / tasmād asañcitavat sañcitā api paramāṇavo naivālambanam / anyas tu manyate ekaika paramāṇur anyanirapekṣo 'tīndriyo bahavas tu parasparāpekṣā indriyagrāhyāḥ / teṣām api sāpekṣanirapekṣāvasthayor ātmātiśayābhāvād ekāntenendriyagrāhyatvam atīndriyatvaṃ vā / yadi ca paramāṇava eva parasparāpekṣā vijñānasya viṣayībhavanti / evaṃ sati yo 'yam ghaṭakuḍyādyākārabhedo vijñāne sa na syāt paramāṇūnām atadākāratvāt / na cānyanirbhāsasya vijñānasyānyākāro viṣayo yujyate 'tiprasaṅgāt /*. According to Dhammajoti (2012: 220–221), Kuiji identifies Sthiramati's third position with Saṅghabhadra.

the idea that the *saṃcita* can function as a third position, different from the idea that the percept consists either of fundamental particles or collections. Sthiramati still leaves us with two questions: First, what kind of work can a *saṃcita* do that a *samūha* cannot, and is it possible for the term *ākāra* in the compound *saṃcitākāra* to belong not just to collections, but also to fundamental particles?

We can begin to answer these questions by considering Cox's account of the dispute between the Vaibhāṣika Saṅghabhadra (fourth-fifth centuries) and the Sautrāntika author Srīlāta (330–410) on the nature of perception.[24] It seems that Śrīlāta took the position that perceptual cognition depends on objects that do not exist as real entities. Saṅghabhadra replied to Śrīlāta by distinguishing between what Cox calls "composites" (*sāmagrī, samghāta, samnipāta, samhata?*) of fundamental particles and "aggregations" (*saṃcita?*). According to Saṅghabhadra, an "aggregation" makes possible a perception of fundamental particles in a way that a "composite" cannot.[25] How can this be? Saṅghabhadra does not explain, but we can find a possible answer by considering the broader Abhidharma discussion of the causal effectiveness of groups, as in Yaśomitra's commentary on the concept of aggregates (*skandha*)

---

24. Cox (1988: 74): "Saṅghabhadra (NAS 4 p.350.c.5—p.352.a.25) argues at length against the Dārṣṭāntika-Sautrāntika master, Śrīlāta, who claims that the five externally directed types of perceptual consciousness depend upon object-fields that do not exist as real entities. Śrīlāta claims that single atoms are not the object-support of perceptual consciousness because they do not constitute the content of perception. The five externally directed types of perceptual consciousness rely only upon composites (*ho-ho*) of atoms, and these composites, as such, do not exist as real entities. Therefore, the five externally directed types of perceptual consciousness do not apprehend actually existing object-fields. Saṅghabhadra responds by distinguishing the term 'composite' (*ho-ho, sāmagrī, samghāta, samnipāta, samhata?*), used by Śrīlāta, from aggregation (*ho-chi, saṃcita?*). Saṅghabhadra claims that atoms form an aggregation, not a composite, and this aggregation then allows direct perception to occur. (See also *Nyāyānusāra* 32 p. 522.a.5–10.) The actually existing object-field that causes perception is still, however, the individual atom. (See *Nyāyānusāra* 4 p. 352.a. 18–19.) This composite (*ho-ho*), as proposed by Śrīlāta, exists only provisionally, and hence it is apprehended only by mental perceptual consciousness. Saṅghabhadra's attempt to salvage the Sarvāstivādin theory that atoms in aggregation are the object-field of the five externally directed types of perceptual consciousness by distinguishing *ho-ho* from *ho-chi* constitutes an innovation not found in the Vibhāṣā commentaries." These issues have also been discussed in more detail by Dhammajoti (2012).

25. Dhammajoti (2012: 230) summarizes Saṅghabhadra's position in the following way: "Saṅghabhadra holds that each individual atom in itself is actually efficacious. But it is only when they are *saṃcita* (physically assembled together) that their combined efficacy becomes strong enough to generate a cognition. However, this *saṃcita* state is not a conceptualized whole, but a physical collocation or aggregation of the atoms. Moreover, since from the Sarvāstivāda-Vaibhāṣika perspective, this takes place in the very first moment, thanks to simultaneous causality, the cognitive object is a real existent."

in the first chapter of *Treasury of Abhidharma*. Here the question is whether aggregates are merely nominal (*prajñapti-sat*) entities or whether they have real causal effect.

> Do the five sense cognitions have *saṃcitas* as their location and percept (*āśraya-ālambana*)? On this point [Vasubandhu] says: "No. Because all are the cause individually (*ekaśaḥ samagrāṇāṃ kāraṇabhāvāt*)." Why? Because all the things that arise together (*samuditānām*) are the cause individually (*ekaśaḥ*), or singly (*pratyekam*). This is because many fundamental particles of the sense organs are the cause individually, when they depend on (or cooperate with) one another (*parasparam apekṣamāṇānām*), but not when they are not combined (*na asaṃhatānām*). For example, when many people are trying to pull a log, they are not effective if each one pulls individually, but if they arise (or get) together (*samudita*) and depend on (or cooperate with) one another, they are effective.... The same is true of the fundamental particles that constitute the sense organs and their objects. They are not effective in producing a sensory cognition individually (*pratyekam*), but they are effective when they arise together (*samudita*).[26]

Yaśomitra's example begins to make the point clear. When a group of people get together to move a log, everyone has to pull. But it is not the "group" that does the pulling; each individual person has to make his or her individual effort. The same is true of an object of perception: it takes each individual particle pulling together to give the impression of a group.

A glance at the terminological variety of these passages, from Saṅghabhadra to Sthiramati and Yaśomitra, shows us two important things about the shape of this dispute. First, while there seems to be a discernible bias in favor of the term *saṃcita* to designate an effective combination of parts, it is not the only possibility. At one point Yaśomitra drops his guard and uses the term *saṃhata*. The same is true of Bhāviveka. He generally uses the term *saṃcita* for the positive form of a collection but occasionally drops in a term like *saṃghāta* (as in the commentary on *Verses on the Heart of the Middle Way* 5.35). This can be explained in part by his use of conflicting traditional sources, but that does not explain the inconsistency in the sources themselves. My impression is that two contradictory tendencies were at work in this literature. There was a desire to draw clear distinctions between different kinds of collections, combinations, or aggregations (call them what you will) to show how some kinds

26. Yaśomitra, vol. 1: 61.

of aggregations have real effects. But the terminology was fluid. We read in Yaśomitra, for example, that particles are effective when they "arise together" (*samudita*). This corresponds to Bhāviveka's idea that a *saṃcita* consists of homogeneous (*sajātīya*) particles located in the same place. Yaśomitra's usage is mirrored in some sources that use the term *samudāya* in place of *saṃcita*.[27] In English we might call this a "co-arising"; or, in the spirit of Bhāviveka, it might be called a "collocation." In spite of the attempts at consistency, it is hard to avoid the impression that we are dealing with a loose collocation of terms—perhaps a *samūha* rather than a *saṃcita*—out of which certain thinkers tried to draw a sense of clarity, with only partial success.

It would be wrong to get the impression, however, that the issues involved in Dignāga's third position were superficial or inconsequential. It only takes a glance at the sequence of opponents in Śāntarakṣita's "Investigation of External Objects" in *The Compendium of Metaphysics* (*Tattvasaṃgraha*, verses 1965–2084) to see that the issue of a causal aggregation was heavily contested in the eighth century. Śāntarakṣita introduces this argument with a generic objection to the doctrine of mind-only (verse 1965): "If the four elements do not exist apart from cognition, why do they appear distinctly and clearly?" Then Śāntarakṣita responds with the same dilemma Dignāga used in *Investigation of the Percept* (verse 1967): "When an external object appears, what is it that appears? Is it a fundamental particle, or is it a whole (*avayavin*)?" Once he has stated Dignāga's dilemma, he gives the standard refutation of the first option (verse 1968): "In the first case the representations of fundamental particles are not cognized separately, because they do not appear in a cognition of them as partless, many, and corporeal."

After making this point, Śāntarakṣita shifts immediately to Dignāga's third position and formulates an objection in the words of the eighth-century author Śubhagupta (verse 1970): "[Fundamental particles] arise together and appear as themselves, and they do not cease to be partless in these conditions." When Śāntarakṣita questions their perceptibility, Śubhagupta makes the move for which he is known in Tibetan doxography[28] (verse 1972): "Just as there is an

---

27. Dharmakīrti treats *saṃcita, samudāya,* and *sāmānya* as synonyms in *Commentary on the Compendium of Epistemology* (*Pramāṇa-vārttika*) 2.194ab.

28. Dreyfus (1997: 363) explains: "Śubhagupta (c. 650–750 C.E.) is a critic of Dharmakīrti. He is usually classified as a Vaibhāṣika, but his theory is different from the usual epistemology of this school. Śubhagupta distinguishes two stages in the cognition of external objects. The first stage is non-conceptual, in which we contact aggregated atoms without imposing any form. In the second, conceptual stage, a mental cognition imposes a coarse (*sthūla, rags pa*) form on the aggregation of atoms. This form is the product of a synthesis and, therefore, illusory. Depending on this synthesis (in which perception and mental cognition are involved), we apprehend things as extended in space and time. Śubhagupta's theory

illusion of permanence when there is a sequence of similar moments, there also is an illusion of a gross object when one apprehends contiguous homogeneous [particles]." Kamalaśīla explains: "Bhadanta Śubhagupta proposes an escape. He says: 'Just as there is a perceptual illusion of permanence in the case of sound and so forth when there is a sequence of similar moments . . ., there also is a mental illusion 'gross' when homogeneous (*sajātīya*) particles are apprehended together in the same place (*avicchinna-deśa*)." While Śubhagupta's argument has its novel features, what is most striking is how much his position echoes the language we encountered in earlier texts. We have "homogeneous particles that arise in the same place," as in Bhāviveka, and we have the idea that the individual members of a group "appear as themselves," like the individuals that come together to pull on a log.

What can we say then about the "features" (Skt. *ākāra*; Tib. *rnam pa*) that play such a crucial role in Dignāga's term "collected features" (*saṃcitākāra*)? How do they figure in the argument? Śāntarakṣita raises the issue first as an objection attributed to the Jain Sumati (eighth century; verses 1981–1982):

> Since all things have both general characteristics (*sāmānya*) and particulars (*viśeṣa*), particles are thought to have two forms (*rūpa*), the common and the uncommon. In this case, since the common form is the object of visual cognition, it is possible for a cognition of [many] particles to have a single feature (*ākāra*).

Śāntarakṣita dismisses this objection by saying simply: "How can it be reasonable for one thing to have two forms (*rūpa*)?" But then he takes the question a step further by citing an objection from the Buddhists' arch-opponent, Kumārila (seventh century; verses 1986cd–1987): "It is not impossible for one thing to have contradictory [features (*ākāra*)] because they are perceived. There is no divine pronouncement that a single thing can have only one *ākāra*, because it should be accepted as it is apprehended."

This formulation of the argument still leaves a crucial question: If fundamental particles come together to have "collected features" (*saṃcitākāra*) that make them perceptible as a group, where do these collected features come from? Do these "features" (if that is the right word) exist in the particles independently of their aggregation, or are they produced in some way by the act of aggregation itself? Sthiramati rejected the idea that there could

---

differs from the usual Vaibhāṣika view, which denies that cognition has any aspect at all. Śubhagupta does not deny that determinate cognition has an aspect but asserts that this aspect is false or illusory (*alikākāra, rdzun pa'i rnam pa*)."

be any additional factor (*ātmātiśaya*) that would make particles perceptible in a group: "Particles in a collected state (*saṃcitāvasthāyām*) have no additional factor (*ātmātiśaya*) other than what they have when they are in an uncollected state." But what if this "factor" arises in the particles themselves? If so, how could it come to be? Dharmakīrti mentions one possible model in the *Commentary on the Compendium of Epistemology* (3.195–196): "Because of a connection with other things, different particles arise; these are said to be a collection (*saṃcita*), and cause the arising of cognition. And this distinctive property (*viśeṣa*) of particles does not occur without other particles; so this cognition does not determine a single thing, and thus is said to have an aggregation (*sāmānya*) as its object."[29] Here a connection (*saṃbandha*) with other particles causes particles to arise with a distinctive property, and this distinctive property makes them perceptible as an aggregation (*sāmānya* understood as *saṃghāta* or *saṃcita*).[30] It is as if a "connection" with other people makes it possible for grouped individuals to have a property called "capability" or "effectiveness" (*sāmarthya*) that allows them to pull a log.

Interestingly enough, Dignāga seems to have a different model in mind when he sketches the opponent's position in *Investigation of the Percept* 3ab and commentary: "(Verse) Some maintain that collected features are the cause. (Commentary) They maintain that, while all objects have many features, they are perceived with only a few features. Fundamental particles have the causes that produce cognitions with the appearance of collections (88–89)."[31] Apparently, Dignāga's opponent is claiming that fundamental particles have many features, whether or not they are collected, and some of these, called

---

29. *arthāntarābhisambandhāj jayante ye 'ṇavo 'pare / uktās te sañcitās te hi nimittaṃ jñānajanmanaḥ // aṇūnāṃ sa viśeṣaś ca nāntareṇāparān aṇūn / tad ekāniyamāj jñānam uktam sāmānyagocaraṃ //* The commentator Manorathanandin glosses the term *sāmānya* in verse 3.196 as *saṃghāta*, "aggregation." In his commentary on verse 3.194, he equates it with a *saṃcita*.

30. Dunne (2004: 103) has a clear explanation of the model Dharmakīrti has in mind: "Dharmakīrti's point is that when the term 'aggregated' is applied to infinitesimal particles, it does not refer to their formation of some single entity; instead, it is a way of expressing a distinctive property that *each* infinitesimal has obtained by virtue of its production being conditioned by the proximate presence of the other, surrounding infinitesimal particles. This distinctive property is the ability, when causally assisted by other infinitesimal particles, to participate in the causal complex (*hetu-sāmagrī*) that produces a perceptual cognition. And since other infinitesimal particles are required for a particle to arise with such a property, a single perception is actually being caused by multiple infinitesimal particles that are simultaneously apprehended. Hence, a single perception is not related to a single infinitesimal particle, but rather to many infinitesimal particles."

31. Another way to interpret the Tibetan translation of this line would be to say that "the causes that produce . . . are [located] in fundamental particles." Judging from the translation available to us, this seems to be Dharmapāla's interpretation.

"collected features," become perceptible when they are collected together with other particles. Here the analogy would be to a "capability" or "effectiveness" that is inherent in each individual person but only becomes manifest when they work together to pull a log. Of the two possibilities, the second sounds more plausible, at least superficially, but the idea that fundamental particles have many features (is the number finite or infinite?) that only become manifest in certain situations may cause more problems than it solves, especially when the particles themselves are conceived only as momentary events. In any case, the model associated with Dignāga's opponent seems not to have died in the sixth century. This appears to have been the model Kumārila had in mind when he said that "there is no divine pronouncement that a single thing can have only one *ākāra*."

Unfortunately, it is impossible to say much more in this short space about the details of the argument between Śāntarakṣita and Kumārila, fascinating though it may be. As the larger argument unfolds, Śubhagupta continues to appear at strategic moments, and there is even a cameo appearance from the Naiyāyika Uddyotakara. Read in its entirety, Śāntarakṣita's chapter on the "Investigation of External Objects" functions as a sophisticated introduction to the theory of perception in eighth-century epistemology, but at the heart of the chapter is an engagement with the arguments of Dignāga's *Investigation of the Percept*. At the end, Śāntarakṣita returns to Dignāga's final definition of the object (*artha*) of perception as "an internal cognitive object that appears to be external" (*yad antarjñeyarūpaṃ tu bahirvad avabhāsate*). This is the conclusion of his argument, as it was for Dignāga, but Śāntarakṣita appropriates it in the distinctive way that is characteristic of eighth-century Madhyamaka: for him it is conventional but not ultimate. It may be possible for objects to appear through an internal evolution of the mind, but he says that "we do not maintain this to be real" (*tāttvikī neṣyate asmābhis*). "The wise remove the stains from the proof of mind-only; we have gone in this direction in the analysis of ultimate truth" (verse 2084). We will return to these points when we consider the conclusion of Dignāga's text.

With this background in mind, we can see how Vinītadeva unravels some of the difficulties of Dignāga's third position. Verse 3ab simply states the opponent's view: "Some maintain that collected features are the cause." This is followed by the statement in the autocommentary that attributes these collected features to fundamental particles: "Fundamental particles have the causes that produce cognitions with the appearance of collections (90)." Here the claim is that fundamental particles have what it takes not only to cause cognitions but also to convey the appearance of a collection. In other words, they satisfy the two criteria of a valid percept.

But what should we make of the statement in verse 3cd that seems to contradict what has just been said: "Features of minute particles are not the object of cognition any more than things like solidity are?" Is this the start of Dignāga's own refutation, or is it part of the opponent's position? If these words belong to the opponent, how are they consistent with the claim that starts the verse? Vinītadeva helps us in two ways. First, he makes it clear that Dignāga's refutation does not start until verse 4, so verse 3cd must belong to the opponent. Second, he unpacks the reference to *visual* cognition in Dignāga's brief explanation of the verse. According to the opponent, it is understood that features such as solidity, wetness, and heat exist, but they are not the objects of *visual* cognition. They have to be perceived by other senses. So it is possible to imagine that there are other features (in this case, "collected features") that are not visible. This is not one of the clearest lines in the text, but it makes sense in terms of the model of "collected features."

Dignāga's refutation of the third position follows the pattern that he has already established in verses 1 and 2: If there is a perceptible feature (called in this case a "collected feature"), it has to belong either to fundamental particles or to a collection. If it belongs to fundamental particles, it cannot be used to distinguish different types of gross objects, like a pot or a cup, because the particles of clay that make up these objects are indistinguishable. On the other hand, if it belongs to the distinctive features of a pot or a cup—like the neck in the case of a pot—then the perceptible feature belongs to the collection, not to the fundamental particles. And if the distinction between a pot and a cup belongs to a collection, then it can only be conventionally real and not ultimately real. It is understandable that Śubhagupta would argue that "there is an illusion of a gross (or macro-) object when one apprehends contiguous homogeneous [particles]." This is a way of saying that the perception of extension in time or space in the perception of a macro-object is a form of conventional reality. It is also easy to see why someone would say that there really is no third position in Dignāga's text. No matter how the third position is constructed, Dignāga would say that it is reducible to one of the positions in his initial dilemma.

Vinītadeva generally does not spend much time dealing with the objections of brahmanical opponents. Those normally lie beyond the intramural purpose of his text. But Dignāga's claim in verse 5b that "distinctive features" belong only to things that are conventional (*saṃvṛti-sat*) and not to real things (*dravya-sat*) elicits an obvious objection from the side of a Vaiśeṣika who holds that a "whole" (*avayavin*) constitutes a real substance (*dravya*): "How do you know that things like pots are conventionally real? (93)"

Vinītadeva takes verse 5cd to be a response to this objection: "Because the cognition that has the appearance of these [pots and cups] disappears when particles are removed." A Vaiśeṣika responds by saying: "When individual particles are removed, the contact that makes [a pot] a substance is broken. In that case, if the pot is broken, the cognition of the pot does not arise." Dignāga then asks where the real substance or the "whole" (*avayavin*) that constitutes a pot goes when the pot is broken. Does it continue to exist in the fundamental particles? And if it does continue to exist, does it exist completely or only partially? If it still exists completely, there must be as many new wholes as there are parts, and so on. Vinītadeva summarizes this argument with his last formal inference in the text: "A whole is not substantially real (*dravya-sat*), because it depends on many things at one time, in the same way that horses are not [substantially real] (94)." With the refutation in this inference, he is ready to turn to the second goal that he announced at the beginning of the text—to affirm that objects are internal.

Verses 6–8: Internal Cognitive Objects

Vinītadeva marks the transition in a way that initially seems quite straightforward:

> By refuting the opponents' system in this way, [Dignāga] has completely refuted the percept. It will be further refuted by what he himself accepts. To show how the percept is defined (Tib. *rnam par gzhag pa*; Skt. *vyavasthita*) in his own system, he says: "But an internal cognitive object" and so forth (95).

Now that he has finished his refutation, he is moving on to the affirmative dimension of his argument by showing what he himself accepts. But what should we make of the claim that he has "completely" (*rnam pa thams cad du*) refuted the percept? It is tempting to add a qualification to the statement and say that Dignāga has completely refuted the percept "as the opponents understand it." But that is not what the sentence says. Is there any way to make this statement consistent with what follows?

For now, it is best to say that this inconsistency alerts us to a problem that may not be fully resolved within the limits of this text. In Dignāga's own writings, it may need to wait until he discusses the "two forms" (*dvirūpa*) of cognition in the first chapter of the *Compendium of Epistemology*, and even then it may only be resolvable by reference to the two truths. We see this, for example, in Kamalaśīla's commentary on the conclusion of Śāntarakṣita's analysis of external objects. This is the text that gives us the Sanskrit of two of Dignāga's final verses.

> "We do not maintain that this is real" means that the master [Dignāga] has explained at length that there cannot be any percept apart from fundamental particles. If the percept condition is completely negated, it is a contradiction of common sense (*pratīti-bādhā*) and also a contradiction of something that we accept, because it says in a sūtra that there are four conditions, which are defined as the percept, the dominant, the immediately preceding, and the causal. To show that there is no contradiction, his explanation is consistent with the kind of percept condition that is accepted conventionally in the sūtra and among common people, but not ultimately. Ultimately, no cognitions have any percept.[32]

This sounds as if the Madhyamaka concept of two truths has been smuggled into the interpretation of Dignāga's text, but we know that the concept of conventional reality already plays a role in his argument. Perhaps it does here as well. For the moment, that remains to be seen.

Another point to notice in Dignāga's opening statement is the ambiguous use of the term *rūpa* in the phrase here translated as "internal cognitive object" (*antar-jñeya-rūpa*). It is more common to translate *rūpa* as "form." Here we take it as an echo of the term *svabhāva* in the definition of an object in the autocommentary on verse 1: "An object is defined as something whose identity is ascertained by a cognition" (*viṣayo hi nāma yasya jñanena svabhāvo 'vadhāryate*: 41). This interpretation is confirmed by the Tibetan translation, where *rūpa* is expressed by the Tibetan *ngo bo* to match the term *rang gi ngo* in the earlier translation of *svabhāva*. To say that something is the "identity of an internal cognitive object" is simply to say that it is the internal cognitive object itself.

But Vinītadeva and Dharmapāla show that there is another possible interpretation. Vinītadeva says: "This verse means: It is only the representation (Tib. *rnam pa*; Skt. *ākāra*) of a cognitive object, which appears as if it were separate, that is, the object (Tib. *yul*; Skt. *viṣaya*) of cognition." Dharmapāla has a similar explanation (in Michael Radich's translation): "What is termed 'the

32. *yataḥ paramāṇvāder vyatiriktasyālambanatvaṃ na yujyata iti vistareṇa pratipādyācāryeṇa—mā bhūt sarvathā 'lambanapratiṣedhe pratitibādhā, tathā—ālambanād-hipatisamanant arahetupratyayatvalakṣaṇāś catasraḥ pratyayitā iti sūtre vacanād abhyu- petabādhāpi" iti avirodhapratipādanāya yathāvida ālambanapratyayo 'bhipretaḥ sūtre loke ca tathā pratipāditaṃ saṃvṛttyā, na paramārthataḥ / paramārthatas tu nirālambanāḥ sarva eva pratyayā //* (commentary on verse 2083).

proper nature of . . . an object' is the aspect [of consciousness] that is apprehended (*grāhyāṃśa); that means consciousness which has transformed into the image (*ākāra) of the object (*viṣaya)" This ambiguity in the meaning of *rūpa* bedevils the interpretation of several key passages at the end of the text, so it is important to keep these two possibilities in mind. It can refer to the identity or nature of an internal cognitive object, or it can refer to the representation of the object in cognition. These are distinguishable interpretations, but in the end "representations" and "internal cognitive objects" are simply aspects of cognition itself.

Why should we think that an "internal cognitive object" (*antar-jñeya-rūpa*) is an object (*artha*)? The second half of verse 6 gives two reasons: "because it is cognition itself" (Skt. *vijñāna-rūpatvāt;* Tib. *rnam shes ngo bo'i phyir*) and "because it is its condition" (Skt. *tat-pratyayatayāpi ca;* Tib. *de'i rkyen nyid kyang yin phyir ro*). Dignāga's commentary on this verse makes clear what is at stake: "Internal cognition appears as the object, and arises from it, so it has the two characteristics [of a valid percept] (44)." Dignāga has given us an account of a valid percept that "only exists internally."

It is worth pausing for a moment and asking what kind of argument Dignāga has just given for his position. In the refutation of external objects in the first part of the text, his arguments were framed as or were easily translated into standard three-part inferences, with assertions, reasons, and examples. In effect, all he has done here is assert that his "internal object" meets the two crucial conditions. He has not given us an argument that there *is* such a thing as an "internal object"; he has simply set up two alternatives (external and internal), eliminated one, and affirmed the other. As Kellner (2010) has noted in another context, this argument functions as a form of abduction: it is "inference to the best explanation." In his investigation of Kumārila's argument against Buddhist views of cognition, Taber (2010) has noted how difficult it is to identify positive arguments for the claim that it is the nature of cognition to have no external objects. Perhaps this is one of the reasons. Dignāga's argument is structured to show that external objects are impossible in their own right. All that remains is to give a consistent account of cognition itself.

The first step is to provide an explanation of causation. If the object of cognition (or the percept) is cognition itself and also the condition of cognition, how does the second give rise to the first? Dignāga offers two models: one in which the object of cognition is simultaneous with the cognition, and another in which the two occur sequentially. The first of these options seems forced, but it is a standard option in Indian theories of perception and needs to be accounted for by Dignāga's model of the percept. The second involves what Dignāga calls a sequential "transfer of capacity" (*śakty-arpaṇa*): "In sequence also, it is not contradictory for the appearance of an object (*arthāvabhāsa*) to cause a capacity located in cognition to produce an effect that is similar to itself."[33] The term "capacity" (*śakti*) might seem odd in this context—it would be more common to call it a "trace" (*vāsanā*) or a "seed" (*bīja*)—but this term helps Dignāga respond to a new objection: If the cognition of an object is generated only by an internal object, why does it seem to depend on senses like the eye? Dignāga's answer is that the so-called senses are just sense capacities that are located in cognition itself. This leaves him with a model of mutual causation (verse 8bcd): "The object and the capacity cause one another and have done so from beginningless time." For the Sanskrit of this final verse, we are indebted once again to Bhāviveka.[34]

We can learn a great deal about Dignāga's argument by looking at the way Bhāviveka reads it. In logical procedure, he was a devoted follower; in the substance of his argument, he was a persistent critic; and in both cases he was a careful reader. He frames Dignāga's argument by attributing the following claim to his opponent: "The three worlds are mind-only, and there are no external objects."[35] The first part of the sentence grounds the Yogācāra position in scripture, and the second part gives him the proposition that serves as the focus of his argument. His first move is to say that the denial of external objects contradicts a point that has already been accepted and also contradicts common sense. The "point that has already been accepted" is the traditional statement that "visual cognition depends on the eye and material forms." When he has raised this objection, the opponent has to give an inference in support of his claim. The inference starts like this: "A cognition of form has no object, because it arises with that kind of image (or appearance) (*tathābhāsodayāt*), like cognition in a dream." The terminology in the reason is already familiar to us from Dignāga's argument against external objects in *Investigation of the Percept*, although Dignāga uses it somewhat differently.

---

33. *athavā śaktyarpaṇāt kramāt // krameṇāpi so 'rthāvabhāsaḥ svāvabhāsānurūpakāryotpattaye śaktiṃ vijñānādhārāṃ karotīty avirodhaḥ*, quoted by Pārthasārathimiśra in the *Jewel Mine of Logic* (*Nyāya-ratnākara*, p. 222). Kamalaśīla preserves a different (and less accurate) version: *athavā śaktyarpaṇāt kramenāpi so 'rthāvabhāsaḥ svāvabhāsānurūpakāryotpattaye śaktiṃ vijñānācārāṃ karotīty avirodhaḥ* (*Commentary on the Compendium of Metaphysics* [*Tattvasaṃgraha-pañjikā*]] vol. 2: 710).

34. Bhāviveka quotes this verse in *Verses on the Heart of the Middle Way* 5.39abc and commentary: "In *Investigation of the Percept*, I [Dignāga] have firmly established the following position: 'Even without an external object, the capacity and the object cause one another (*asaty api ca bāhye 'rthe dvayam anyonyahetukam / śaktir viṣayarūpaṃ ca*).' (Comm.) and have done so from beginningless time."

35. *'di lta ste khams gsum pa 'di ni sems tsam ste / phyi rol gyi do med do zhes dam bcas pa grang yin pa* (Eckel 2008: 232, 399).

Bhāviveka responds to this claim by arguing that dreams arise from external objects that were previously seen and were recollected by memory. The argument then shifts to the assertion that cognition arises with two images (or appearances)—the image of itself (*svābhāsa*) and the image of an object (*viṣayābhāsa*). This shift to the "double image" (*dvyābhatā*) of cognition then leads to Bhāviveka's discussion of Dignāga's final claim in the commentary on *Investigation of the Percept* (verse 8bcd). Bhāviveka tracks Dignāga's terminology quite closely but with enough differences to make a useful comparison. In effect, it is commentary by paraphrase. Dignāga reads like this:

> A cognition (*vijñāna*) arises with the image of an object, depending on the capacity called "eye" and on an internal object (Tib. *nang gi gzugs* / Skt. *antaḥ-rūpa*), without being disclosed as the percept. These two cause one another and have done so from beginningless time. Sometimes the object-representation (*viṣayākāra*) of cognition arises from the maturation of the capacity, and sometimes the capacity [arises] from that representation. Saying that these two are different or not different from cognition is a matter of preference (45–46).

Bhāviveka's version reads:

> To produce a result that is consistent with itself, the image of the object (*viṣayābhāsa*) sequentially (*krameṇa*) transfers a capacity (*śakti*) to the continuum of consciousness. Sometimes it remains merely the capacity for the representation of that [object]. At other times, from the maturation of the capacity, a cognition arises with the representation of the image of the object. One cannot say (lit. one does not maintain that it is sayable, *brjod par mi 'dod de*) whether cognition is identical to or different from these two—namely the capacity and the appearance of the object. Consciousness has a double image, as potential and as object.[36]

---

36. The translation follows Eckel (2008: 236), with changes to accommodate the terminology of our translation of *Investigation of the Percept*. The Tibetan reads: *'dir smras pa / yul du snang ba des rang dang rjes su mthun pa'i 'bras bu bskyed par bya ba'i phyir rim gyis rnam par shes pa'i rgyun nus pa dang ldan par byed cing lan 'ga' ni de'i rnam pa'i nus par gnas so // lan 'ga' ni nus pa yongs su smin pa las rnam par shes pa yul du snang ba'i rnam par skye'o // rnam par shes pa ni nus pa dang yul du snang ba de gnyis las gcig pa nyid dang tha dad pa nyid du brjod par mi 'dod de / rnam par shes pa nyid nus pa dang yul gyi ngo bo nyid gnyis su snang ba yin no zhe na /* (Eckel 2008: 401–402).

These passages clearly have the same model in mind: the capacity causes the image of the object and the object-image returns the favor. It is also clear that this reciprocal causation takes place *within cognition itself.* Bhāviveka leaves no doubt about this point when he specifies the subjects in Dignāga's penultimate sentence. When Dignāga says, "Saying that these two are different or not different from cognition is a matter of preference," it should already be clear from the context that the words "these two" refer to the "capacity" and the "object-representation" (or "object-image") mentioned in the preceding sentence, but Bhāviveka makes this identification explicit. He specifies further that the capacity and the object-image constitute the "double image" of consciousness.[37]

But Bhāviveka's value goes beyond his careful parsing of this final passage. He also helps us situate the cryptic phrases of *Investigation of the Percept* in the context of Dignāga's other work. Bhāviveka has already given us a hint of this larger context by discussing this passage in his analysis of the double image of consciousness. He specifies the context further just a few verses later by adding an argument about the instrument and result of cognition (*pramāṇa* and *pramāṇa-phala*):

> If the opponent thinks that [the mind] has a double image because it has an instrument of knowledge and a result [we] do not agree, because they are established another way.
>
> [We] think that the instrument of knowledge is the cognition that knows the object of knowledge when [this cognition] is arising and bearing the image of the object. (*Verses on the Heart of the Middle Way* 5.24–25; Eckel 2008: 239)

Bhāviveka's argument is based on verses 1.8cd–10 of Dignāga's *Compendium of Epistemology*. For our purposes, the key idea is found in verse 1.8cd:

> (1.8cd) Because it is understood to include an action, [a cognition is figuratively called an "instrument," when in fact] the result is the instrument of knowledge.

37. Bhāviveka may also clarify another puzzling aspect of Dignāga's passage. Dignāga's phrase "one is free to say" (*ci dgar brjod par bya'o*) appears as "cannot say" in both Bhāviveka (*brjod par mi 'dod de*) and Vinītadeva (*brjod par bya ba ma yin no*). It is possible that the word *ci dgar* represents a misreading (or mistaken transmission) of the Sanskrit term that is reflected by *mi 'dod de* in Bhāviveka. Both could involve versions of the Sanskrit word *iṣṭa*. The term *ci dgar* could translate *yatheṣṭam*, while *mi 'dod de* could translate *aniṣṭam*. Either one would be possible, but the support from Vinītadeva favors the reading in Bhāviveka.

> Here the result is not different from the instrument of knowledge, as it is for externalists. But the cognition that constitutes the result (*phala-jñāna*) is understood to be accompanied by an action, because it arises with the representation of an object (*viṣayākāra*). Based on this understanding, it is called an instrument of knowledge figuratively (*upacaryate*), even though it has no action, just as an effect is said to take the form of a cause when it arises in a way that resembles the cause, even though it does not do this. The same is true here.

As Kellner (2010) has pointed out in her careful interpretation of this passage, these verses involve more than a few perplexities, but Dignāga structures his position in a way that helps us understand what he had in mind in the final passage of his autocommentary on *Investigation of the Percept*. His commentary on verse 1.8cd shows that his analysis of the result and the instrument of knowledge operates on two levels. On one level there appear to be two things: an instrument and a result. But this distinction is only established figuratively, based on the "understanding" that the cognition is accompanied by an action. In other words, it is as if cognition has two forms (an instrument and a result), but actually there is only cognition itself.

If this passage gives the impression that Dignāga is invoking a concept of two truths in the style of a Mādhyamika, this would not be a mistake, although it took his commentators to draw out the implications of his words. In his commentary on this passage, Jinendrabuddhi (eighth century) explains:

> To be designated figuratively is to be designated conventionally (*vyavahriyate*). This means that the nature (*svarūpa*) of conventional instruments and objects of knowledge is stated in order to remove the illusions of those who misunderstand. But in a transcendent sense (*lokottaram eva*) the ultimate (*pāramārthika*) instrument of knowledge is imperishable and free from the faults of delusion and discrimination, and its object (*gocara*) is the real object of knowledge.[38]

38. *upacaryata iti vyavahriyate / etenaitat sūcayati—vyāvahārikasya pramāṇasya prameyasya cedaṃ svarūpam uktam atrāpi vipratipannānāṃ sammohanirāsāya / lokottaram eva tu vibhramavivekanirmalam anapāyi pāramārthikaṃ pramāṇaṃ tasyaiva ca gocaro bhūtaṃ prameyam iti /* (Jinendrabuddhi 2005, vol. 1: 74–75).

And again:

> Ultimately (*tattvataḥ*) [consciousness] has no division; it is only characterized as divided into the representation of subject and object (*grāhakākāra* and so forth) by those who are overwhelmed by ignorance. Therefore, this definition (*vyavasthā*) of the instruments and objects of knowledge is made according to appearances (*yathādarśanam*), not according to reality (*yathātattvam*). How can something that is undivided appear as if it were? Pieces of clay and so forth appear to have the form of something like an elephant, even though they do not have the form of an elephant, for those whose eyes are overwhelmed by mantras and so forth, and something that is large appears small from a distance in the desert. In a similar way, a cognition appears like this (i.e., as divided) to those who have been blinded by ignorance, even though it is not like this.[39]

The language here is a direct reflection of the distinction between the two truths, and not just in a generic sense. The term translated as "according to appearances" (*yathādarśanam*) is a distinctive feature of Jñānagarbha's definition of the two truths, a definition that he shared with other Mādhyamikas of the eighth century (Eckel 1987: 89).

How do these passages help us interpret Dignāga's final position in *Investigation of the Percept*? After he has described the reciprocal causation of the object-representation and the capacity, he says: "Saying that these two are different or not different from cognition is a matter of preference." Bhāviveka and Vinītadeva interpret this sentence as a negation, "One cannot say whether these two are identical to or different from consciousness (102)," but the point is the same: it is not possible to specify whether these two are the same or different. With the *Compendium of Epistemology* in mind, Dignāga's meaning should be clear. From a conventional point of view, consciousness can be distinguished into different aspects. In *Investigation of the Percept*, these aspects are called "capacity" and "object-representation"; elsewhere they may be called something else. But ultimately these different aspects are identical to

---

39. *naiva tattvatas tasya vibhāgo 'sti, kevalam avidyopaplutais tadgrāhakākārādivibhāgavad iva lakṣyate / ato yathādarśanam iyaṃ pramāṇaprameyavyavasthā kriyate, na yathātattvam iti / kathaṃ punar avibhaktaṃ sat tathā pratibhāsate / yathā mantrādyupaplutākṣāṇāṃ mṛcchakalādayo hastyādirūparahitā api hastyādirūpāḥ pratibhāsante, yahtā ca dūre maruṣu mahānalpo 'py ābhāsati, tathedam apy avidyāndhānāṃ jñānaṃ atathābhūtam api tathābhati /* (Jinendrabuddhi 2005, vol. 1: 73–74).

consciousness itself, and consciousness is one. Vinītadeva makes this point in the final paragraph of his subcommentary:

> If one analyzes how they exist, then these capacities are conventionally real because they are distinguished in context. For this reason, it is impossible to specify whether they are different from cognition or identical to it. So the two alleged problems do not apply. But when one relies on mundane convention, it is possible to say, as a matter of preference, that cognition is different from them and sometimes is not different. This is because, for ordinary people, conventional things are sometimes said to be different, like sandalwood and its scent, and sometimes not to be different, like a pot and its material form (102–103).

The scent may be distinguishable from sandalwood conventionally, but actually the two are identical. In other words, there is no sandalwood without a sandalwood scent, and no sandalwood scent without sandalwood. The same is true of a pot and its material form.

It is widely known that Dignāga developed a more complex and ambiguous approach to the reality of external objects in his *Compendium of Epistemology*, where he argued that the concept of self-cognition could apply to cognitions of external objects as well as to cognitions that are entirely internal.[40] The relationship between these two options was widely discussed in the Indian commentarial tradition, and the disputes live on in contemporary scholarship, as in Dreyfus (1997), Dunne (2004), McCrea and Patil (2010), and Kellner (2011). But it is clear from a careful reading of *Investigation of the Percept* that this more complex approach to external objects belonged to another phase in Dignāga's work, when he focused more explicitly on the issues that surround the instruments of knowledge. It would be a major error of interpretation to read this more complex theory of knowledge back into *Investigation of the Percept*, where the goal is simply to refute external objects and articulate a model of internal causation that accounts for the traditional view of a percept. As Vinītadeva said, scholars should be patient; this task alone is enough to please the beginners who start their analysis of external objects with this compact and elegant text.

40. The key verses in Dignāga's "Compendium" are 1.8cd–10. For a close reading of this passage in relation to Jinendrabuddhi's commentary, see Kellner (2011).

5

Subcommentary on Investigation of the Percept (Ālambana-parīkṣā-ṭīkā)

Vinītadeva

TRANSLATED BY DOUGLAS Duckworth, Malcolm David Eckel, Jay Garfield, John Powers, and Sonam Thakchöe

[349] The title in Sanskrit is: *Ālambana-parīkṣā-ṭīkā*. In Tibetan it is: *dMigs pa brtag pa'i 'grel bshad.*

Homage to all buddhas and bodhisattvas!

> Having bowed my head
> To the Omniscient One
> With compassionate intention,
> I undertake this subcommentary on "*Investigation of the Percept.*"

Commentary on Verse 1

The first words, "Some maintain that the percept of a sensory (e.g., visual) cognition[1] is an external object,"[2] state both the subject matter of the text and the cause of error. The purpose and relevance can be inferred by implication. Moreover, the implication is clear from the context. The relevance of this

1. This includes visual, auditory, tactile, olfactory, gustatory, and mental cognitions.

2. Preface to Dignāga's autocommentary.

treatise, the subject matter, and the purpose should definitely be stated. If this is not done, students who have prior knowledge will not accept a treatise that lacks relevance, subject matter, and purpose. Therefore, here the text states:

> Some maintain that the percept of a sensory (e.g., visual) cognition is an external object. They must suppose that it is fundamental particles (because that is what causes cognition), or that it is collections (because that is what appears to cognition).[3]

This states that the subject matter is something to be rejected. The phrases "because that is what causes cognition" and "because that is what appears to cognition" state the cause of error. The purpose and relevance are stated by implication. Regarding this, the implication [350] can be understood as follows: This treatise is composed in order to refute the existence of external percepts and to affirm that they are internal.

Therefore, because this treatise is composed in order to refute the existence of external objects and to affirm the existence of internal ones, by implication the purpose is precisely to refute and affirm. This text is clearly the means. This is because those with prior knowledge will not engage with a text that has no purpose, nor will they engage with one that is not a means. Here, external percepts, which will be refuted by reason, and internal ones, which will be affirmed, are the subject matter. The refutation and affirmation of these two[4] are the purpose. Moreover, because this treatise achieves this purpose, this treatise is the means to this purpose. Therefore, the treatise and the purpose are connected as means[5] and goal.[6] Thus, it is settled that this treatise is composed in order to refute external objects and affirm internal ones.

After this has been settled, someone might raise the following question:[7] "What is the point of this refutation and affirmation? They are completely unnecessary."

---

3. This is a shortened version of Dignāga's autocommentary preface.

4. Text correction: read *de gnyis* in accordance with D, S, N, and P.

5. Tib. *thabs*; Skt. *upāya*.

6. Tib. *thabs las byung ba*; Skt. *upeya*. Compare Durveka Miśra's (*c.* tenth century) *Light on Dharmottara* (*Dharmottara-pradīpa*, a commentary on Dharmottara's *Nyāya-bindu-ṭīkā*) (1955: 12): "*darśita evopāyopeyebhāvaḥ prakaraṇaprayojanayoḥ sambandha iti.*"

7. D, T: *brgyal*; read *brgal*.

Response: Refuting what is to be rejected and affirming what is to be accepted constitute the actions of rejecting and accepting these two. That is to say, the refutation is provided in order to reject external objects. In other words, one realizes from the refutation that external objects are to be rejected; thinks that they should be rejected; and then rejects them. Similarly, one realizes from the affirmation that internal objects are to be accepted; thinks that they should be accepted; and then affirms them. Therefore, this explains that refutation and affirmation are the purpose of the text because they reject the external objects that are to be rejected and accept the internal ones that are to be accepted.

Objection: Just as the first words state that the subject matter is something to be rejected, they also should state [351] what is to be to be accepted.

Response: Those who assert external objects are greatly harmed by their imagination of external objects. For this reason, the very first words are said to refute them at the outset. A later verse, "**an internal cognitive object, which appears to be external, is the object**,"[8] asserts that they are internal. This is a preliminary overview.

Now I will discuss the meaning of the parts. The statement, "**Some maintain that the percept of a sensory cognition**,"[9] says "**some**" because not all debaters maintain that external objects are the percept. The term "sensory" means the eye and so forth. The term "and so forth" includes everything from the auditory and so forth up to the mind. That is, they maintain that the mind also has a percept that is an external object. For this reason, its percept is to be refuted at the same time. What is the point of this position? In his presentation, Dignāga does not negate its object separately. This is why the master Dharmapāla wrote at length in his own commentary to distinguish the percept of mental cognition. This might be a correct understanding, but his idea is too profound for me to comprehend.

"**Cognitions**" are cognitions such as the visual.[10] Because there are many types of senses, it is clear that there are also many types of cognition. It also is clear that there are many terms for cognition, just as one can say, for example, that both copper and a leaf are "red."

In the phrase, "**percept of a sensory cognition is an external object**," "external object" means one that is external, that is to say, "not included in

8. Verse 6.

9. Preface to the autocommentary.

10. This is redundant in the original text. The explanatory phrase only differs from the one it is glossing in that it contains the plural particle *dag*.

cognition." An object (Tib. *don*; Skt. *artha*) is something that is cognized; that is, it is defined as "something that is known" (Tib. *shes par bya*; Skt. *jñeya*) and "apprehended" (Tib. *gzung bar bya*; Skt. *grāhya*). Here, the word "object" (Tib. *don*; Skt. *artha*) is used as a synonym of "object" (Tib. *yul*; Skt. *viṣaya*); it does not refer to something that is substantially real. [352] This is because a collection (Tib. *'dus pa*; Skt. *samūha*) also is said to be an object, but it is not substantially real. To maintain that something is a percept means to accept that it is apprehended.[11]

The phrase "**must suppose that it is fundamental particles**" means that these debaters accept that the intentional object of cognition is either extremely minute particles or collections. These are fundamental particles because they are particles and they are very subtle. In other words, they are extremely subtle because nothing else is more subtle.

Collections of fundamental particles arise and cease, but others maintain that these fundamental particles individually are the percept when they are collected. Visible form and taste may be collected into one, but they are apprehended individually by the senses because the senses have their own specific capabilities. In this way, cognition, too, is definitely able to discriminate substances. For this reason, they accept that individual particles are the percept, but not wholes.

If they are extremely subtle, how can they be a percept, even when they are collected?

In response, Dignāga says: "**because that is what causes cognition.**"

The opponents maintain that they are the percept, even though they are subtle, because they are substantially real and thus function as the causes of cognition. They think that a percept is a cause. This is because conditions reveal percepts internally and because conditions also are causes. When the opponents imagine that fundamental particles are the percept, this idea that they are causes is the cause of error. That is to say, those who maintain external objects maintain that they are percepts because they are the causes of cognition. In the phrase "because that is what causes it," the word "it" refers to cognition.

To introduce the second position, Dignāga says: "**they must suppose . . . that it is a collection of these (because that is what appears to cognition).**" They might think that the percept of cognition is a collection of fundamental

11. The purpose of this sentence is to define the percept (*ālambana*) as something apprehended (*ālabhya*), probably using the Sanskrit term *grāhya* as a synonym to make the meaning clear. A similar definition occurs in Dharmapāla, *Explanation of Investigation of the Percept* (*Guan suoyuan lun shi* 觀所緣論釋, T 1625: 0.4).

particles. [353] A collection of these is a combination of these. Here the word "these" refers to fundamental particles, so "a collection of these" is "a collection of fundamental particles."

If one asks, "Why do they maintain that a collection is the percept," Dignāga responds: "**because that is what appears to cognition.**" They maintain that a collection is a percept because cognitions always arise with the appearance of collections. Here as well, when they imagine that a collection is a percept, the cause of error is the idea that a cognition appears as a collection. They think that because a cognition appears as a collection, a collection that is different from individual particles is the percept. That is, they maintain that the appearance with which cognition arises is its object.

"With the appearance of that" means that a cognition has the appearance of that. Here the word "that" refers to a collection. The grammatical analysis is: It has the appearance of this and it is a cognition. The final compound is: "arising of cognition with the appearance of that." These are the opponents' positions. They think that fundamental particles or collections are the percept because they are consistent with the definition of "percept."

Commentary on Verse 1

In order to refute the first position, Dignāga says:

> **Even if a sensory cognition were caused by fundamental particles,**
> **It would not have particles as its object**
> **Because they do not appear to cognition,**
> **Any more than the sense faculties do.**[12] (1)

Fundamental particles are not actually substantially real. If one thinks that they have parts, then it would follow that they only exist conventionally; but if one thinks that they do not have parts, it would follow that they could not have such things as shadows and shade.[13] Therefore, how can they be causes?

---

12. This verse is quoted by Prajñākaragupta in his *Subcommentary on the Commentary on the Compendium of Epistemology* (*Pramāṇavārttika-bhāṣya*) (1958: 336): "*yady apīndriyavijñapteḥ kāraṇaṃ paramāṇavaḥ / atadābhatayā nāsyā akṣavad viṣayo 'ṇavaḥ.*" Kamalaśīla preserves another version of this verse in his *Extended Commentary on the Compendium of Metaphysics* (*Tattvasaṃgraha-pañjikā*, ed. Dvārikādāsa Śāstri 1958, vol. 2: 711): "*yady apīndriyavijñapter grāhyāṃśaḥ karaṇaṃ bhavet / atadābhatayā tasyā nākṣavad viṣayaḥ sa tu.*"

13. See Vasubandhu's *Twenty Verses* (*Viṃśatikā*): 14.

On the other hand, if one accepts that fundamental particles are causes, then they could not[14] be percepts. Even if fundamental particles were the causes of cognition, they could not be the percept because they do not produce a cognition that has the representation[15] of fundamental particles, [354] like the sense faculties. Even though sense faculties are causes of cognitions, the opponent does not maintain that they are their objects. This is because cognition does not arise with the representation of a sense faculty.

In the term "sensory cognition," the word "sensory" includes the sixth sense faculty, the mind. The reason for this has already been explained.[16] The meaning of "**fundamental particles**" is already understood. The phrase, "**even if** . . ." states the opponent's position. In the phrase, "it does not have the appearance of these," to have the appearance of these is to appear as these. The word "these" refers to fundamental particles. Not to have the appearance of these is not to appear as these. Here the instrumental case should be viewed as a reason. This means: "because it does not have the representation of fundamental particles." The word "it" refers to "sensory cognition." The phrase, "**It would not have particles as its object, any more than the sense faculties do,**" means "just as the sense faculties are not the object, so fundamental particles also are not." Here the term "sense faculties" refers to the dominant condition.[17]

Is it really a problem if a cognition does not have a representation of fundamental particles? If fundamental particles are the source that produces cognition, why can't they be the object?

---

14. Translated in accordance with N: read *dgag* instead of *dag*.

15. In this text, the Tibetan term *rnam pa* (Skt. *ākāra*) has different usages. When referring to the system of Dignāga and Vinītadeva, it refers to the representation of an object that is presented to cognition. In other places, particularly when discussing other philosophical traditions, it can mean an aspect or feature of an object. Our translations of Indic and Tibetan texts reflect these varying usages.

16. As Mingyu's long commentary on Dharmapāla makes clear, Dharmapāla assigns a special role to the mental sense faculty. While the external sense faculties, on his account, may be causally sensitive to external particulars, the mental sense faculty takes the sensations generated by the external senses as its objects and unites them in a single appearance. This appearance is what we take to be the percept but is a conceptual construction, and it is distinct from what is caused by any external particles. Dharmapāla explains the impossibility of this complex appearance being the percept in terms of the distinctness of the operation of multiple channels of external causation on the senses from the unitary conceptually mediated representation delivered by the mental sense faculty. This is the position that Vinītadeva claims above not to understand. See Mingyu, *Explanation of the Treatise Investigation of the Percept* (*Guan suoyuan yuan lunshi ji* 觀所緣緣論釋記). XZJ 83: 82a03. Mingyu's commentary incorporates all of Dharmapāla's text and comments on it.

17. Tib. *bdag [rkyen]*; Skt. *adhipati-[pratyaya]*.

In response, Dignāga says: **"an object is defined as something whose identity is ascertained by a cognition."**[18] That is, an object is something whose identity is ascertained when a cognition arises with a representation of that.[19] The particle "*ni*" means "because." In the phrase, **"identity is ascertained,"** the term "identity" refers to specific and general characteristics.[20] To ascertain it is to know it—in other words, to determine and apprehend it.

The phrase **"because that is what appears to cognition"** means that a cognition cannot ascertain an object unless it arises with the representation of that object. Therefore, a cognition ascertains an object such as blue when it arises with the representation of such things as blue. [355] What is the point? One can use the conventional expression "this cognition ascertains an object," but there is no action that is characterized as ascertaining. It is like saying that a son takes the form of the father when he arises with features that are similar to the father's. Similarly, one can say that one "apprehends an object" when a cognition arises that has features similar to those of the object.

On this point, someone might think: "The same applies to fundamental particles: if cognition arises with their representation, then it ascertains their identity."

In response, Dignāga says: **"minute particles may be the cause of this cognition."**[21] Fundamental particles may be the cause of a cognition, but if a cognition does not correspond to their individual representations, how can it ascertain their identities? If a cognition does not ascertain them, how can fundamental particles be the object?

The phrase **"minute particles may be the cause"** means "they may be the causes of cognition." Here, as an example, Dignāga says: **"any more than the sense faculties do."** The sense faculties are causes of cognition, but a cognition that arises with a representation of an object does not ascertain their identities, and so they are not considered to be objects. Fundamental particles should be viewed in the same way. The percept cannot just be a cause because it would follow that the sense faculties would be a percept.

So, having disproved that fundamental particles are the percept, in conclusion Dignāga says: **"thus, first of all, minute particles are not the percept."**[22]

---

18. Verse 1 commentary. Skt. "*viṣayo hi nāma yasya jñānena svabhāvo 'vadhāryate.*"

19. The construction here is quite elliptical. The commentary below makes it clear that it is cognition that arises with the representation of the object.

20. D: *rang gi mtshan nyid* (Skt. *svalakṣaṇa*) and *spyi'i mtshan nyid* (Skt. *sāmānya-lakṣaṇa*).

21. Commentary on verse 1.

22. Verse 1 commentary.

This means that fundamental particles are not the percept because it is not reasonable according to the definition of a percept.

Here the formal argument is: Fundamental particles are not the percept because they do not produce a cognition that has their own appearance, like the sense faculties do. The inverse property is that which is apprehended. If they were a percept but did not produce a cognition that has their appearance, this would result in an undesirable consequence. This is an argument that contains a refutation. [356]

Alternatively, fundamental particles are not the percept because their identity is not apprehended, just as in the case of the sense faculties. The inverse property is that which is apprehended. The apprehended aspect is proven to be the percept. If a thing whose identity is not apprehended were the percept, there would be an undesirable consequence. This is an argument that contains a refutation. These two formal arguments were formulated by the master Dharmapāla. I have copied them, but I did not formulate them. Thus, first of all, that fundamental particles are the percept is refuted.

Commentary on Verse 2

In order to refute that collections are the percept, Dignāga says: "**a sensory cognition may have the appearance of a collection**. . . ." A cognition may have the appearance of a collection, but a collection is not the percept. This is because that cognition does not arise from it.

Even if we grant that it does not arise from that, why not understand a collection to be a percept? Because Dignāga says: "**it makes sense for an object to be a percept if it produces an appearance of itself.**"[23] That is, it is reasonable for any object that appears as itself—or that produces a cognition of the appearance of itself—to be a percept. It is said: "If a cognition corresponds to the form of an object, and if this object produces that cognition, then it is reasonable for it to be a percept condition, but not otherwise."

What is the source of the statement, "Only that which produces a cognition is the percept?" Dignāga says: "**So it is said to be a condition for the arising of cognition.**"[24] Similarly, a treatise explains: "A percept is the cause of the arising of a cognition." A treatise also states: "An object is a percept if it causes the arising of a mind and mental phenomena, and, when they arise, causes the idea that this object is experienced." It also states: "An object is a percept if it

23. Verse 2a commentary.

24. Verse 2a commentary.

causes mind and mental phenomena to arise, and, when a mind and mental phenomena arise, causes the idea 'that object is experienced.'"[25] [357]

Therefore, the statement "a percept is the cause[26] for the arising of cognition..."[27] asserts that a percept condition is what gives rise to a cognition. Because it is well known in this position that a cognition has the representation of this percept, it is not stated. Therefore, it is said that an object is a percept if it has both of these characteristics.

In this context, if someone thinks that "a collection produces a cognition," Dignāga responds: "**collections, however, are not like this.**"[28] That is, a collection does not produce a cognition. If it does not produce a cognition, then how could it be a percept? Why doesn't it produce a cognition? Dignāga says: "**because collection are not substantially real.**" (2b) Since a collection is not substantially real, it follows that it cannot produce a cognition. Things that are not substantially real cannot produce effects. As he will later prove, a collection is not substantially real.

As an example for the statement, "something that is not substantially real does not produce a cognition," Dignāga says: "**like a double moon.**" (2b) That is, a double moon cannot be the thing that causes a cognition that has the appearance of a double moon because it is not substantially real. Similarly, a collection is not a thing that causes a cognition in which it appears.

Someone might object: "If a double moon does not produce this cognition, then it would lack a cause."

In response, Dignāga says: "**because of defective sense faculties.**"[29] It is not the case that it has no cause. It is due to[30] defective sense faculties that someone sees a double moon. That is, when someone's visual faculties are impaired due to ocular defects,[31] there arises a cognition with the appearance of a double moon. But it is not produced by a double moon. Because this cognition is not produced by it, the cognition of a double moon may have the appearance of a double moon, but that is not its object. This means that

---

25. We have not been able to identify the sources of these passages.

26. Vinītadeva's text reads: *rgyu mtshan*; the *Ālambana-parīkṣā* reads: *rkyen*.

27. This refers to the second of the passages quoted above.

28. Verse 2a commentary.

29. Commentary on verse 2b.

30. D inserts the negative particle *mi* before *'gyur*. This is omitted in S, P, and N. Our translation follows the latter reading.

31. Tib. *rab rib*; Skt. *timira*.

a double moon is not the object, because it does not produce this cognition. Here the term "defective" (*ma tshang ba*) [358] means "impaired" (*nyams pa*).

Having established the example in this way, in order to apply it to his point, Dignāga says: "**in the same way, a collection is not a percept because it is not substantially real and, for that reason, is not a cause.**"[32] A double moon is not a cause of cognition because it is not substantially real; and because it is not a cause, it is not an object. Similarly, a collection is not a cause of cognition because it also is not substantially real; and because it is not a cause, it is not its object.

Here the formal argument is: a collection is not a cause because it is not substantially real, like a double moon. The inverse property pertains to cognition.[33] The lack of functionality in insubstantial things is an argument that contains a refutation. Alternatively, a collection is not a percept because it is not a cause, like a double moon. The inverse property is the apprehended aspect. The apprehended aspect is proven to be a cause and a percept. If something could be a percept even if it is not a cause, then even such things as double moons could be percepts. Therefore, this would entail an absurd consequence: this is an argument that contains a refutation. These two arguments also were formulated by the master Dharmapāla.

Having refuted both positions, in conclusion Dignāga says: "**thus, neither kind of external object makes sense as an object of cognition.**" (2cd) According to the approach that has just been explained, it is not reasonable for either kind of external object to be an object of cognition. "External" means not included in cognition. "**Neither**" refers to the position of fundamental particles and the position of collections. "**Of cognition**" means "of knowledge."

Why is this impossible? In response, Dignāga says: "**because in each case one of the criteria is not satisfied.**"[34] This is because in the case of fundamental particles, causality is present, but their representation is absent. In the case of collections, their representation is present, but causality is absent.

32. Commentary on verse 2b.

33. As with the previous formal argument, Vinītadeva is directing his readers' attention to the second element, "because it is not substantially real." In Indian debate literature, to be substantially real (*dravya-sat*) is to be causal, and a double moon is not a cause. He makes this problem explicit below when he says: "because it is not a cause." In order for the opponent to meet the challenge of Dignāga's double moon example, the double moon would have to be the cause of the cognition of a double moon, but it is not. This paragraph is somewhat obscure in the text, perhaps because Vinītadeva is not presenting and developing his own arguments, but rather he is summarizing how Dharmapāla comments on this point. As with the previous discussion of Dharmapāla's commentarial stance on a section of *Investigation of the Percept*, Vinītadeva's final sentence may imply that he does not necessarily endorse it.

34. Verse 2cd commentary.

Therefore, because in each case one of the criteria is not satisfied, the objects referred to as "fundamental particles" and "collections" are not percepts. It is said that "a percept has two aspects: it conveys its own representation [359] and it is the cause. And because these aspects are absent in fundamental particles and in collections, neither of them is an object." When it says that "an object has these two properties,"[35] it is referring to these two aspects as two properties.

Commentary on Verse 3

Now that he has refuted these two positions, he presents a third position, saying: "**also among these, some maintain that collected features are the cause.**" (3ab) That is, among the positions of those who say that there are external objects, some, such as Vāgbhaṭa,[36] maintain that collected features of fundamental particles are the causes of sensory cognitions. They say that fundamental particles also have collected features, and everything that fundamental particles have is substantially real. Because these collected features are substantially real, they can serve as causes of cognitions. Because these are macro-objects,[37] they convey their identity to cognition. In this way, fundamental particles are referred to as "another kind of object." The particle ***ni*** should be understood to mean "also." Here collected features are represented as macro-objects. **Cause** (Tib. *sgrub pa*; Skt. *sādhana*) means "cause" (*rgyu*; Skt. *hetu*).

Isn't it well known that the features of fundamental particles are extremely subtle? If so, how could they have collected features that are macro-objects? If this were possible, then how could one thing have two features?

---

35. Tib. *chos*; Skt. *dharma*.

36. Tib. Pha khol. This name could also be Vābhaṭa, as in Vasubandhu's *Differentiation of the Middle and Extremes* (*Madhyānta-vibhāga*), 3511. The Tibetan Pha khol, "father-servant," presupposes Vābhaṭa, but the only figure we have been able to find who is referred to by this name is Vāgbhaṭa (*c*. seventh century), the author of the influential medical texts *Eight-Limbed Essential Collection* (*Aṣṭāṅga-hṛdaya-saṁhitā*) and *Eight-Limbed Compendium* (*Aṣṭāṅga-saṃgraha*). It is not clear how Vinītadeva construes his position, and he provides no textual citations. The *Eight-Limbed Compendium* discusses how elements combine to make larger wholes—for instance, on p. 195 of the SARIT version edited by R. P. Das and R. E. Emmerick, revised by Dominik Wujastyk: http://sarit.indology.info/exist/apps/sarit/works/sarit_aṣṭāṅgasaṅgraha. The places in which Vāgbhaṭa discusses particles or collections relate to medical topics, including embryology and preparation of medicines, and not perception, and so it is not clear how these might relate to the topic at hand in this text. Perhaps Vinītadeva is extrapolating from Vāgbhaṭa's medical works or is drawing on an oral tradition regarding Vāgbhaṭa's position on minute particles and collections.

37. Tib. *rags pa*; Skt. *sthūla* or *audārika*.

Dignāga says: "**while all objects have many features, they are perceived with only a few features.**"[38] There is no problem[39] because all material things have many features. That is, material things are composed of[40] the four great elements and have many features because they have features such as blueness, fragrance, sweetness, and roughness. And just as fundamental particles have many features, they also have collected features.

Someone might ask: "If all objects have many features, [360] then why are they not cognized as having all of these features?" Dignāga responds: "**they are perceived with only a few features.**"[41] They maintain that objects may have many features, but only a few are directly perceived, not all. This is because the sense faculties have specific capacities and thus do not apprehend all objects. This follows the position of the venerable Buddhadeva.[42] In this context, the ten sense media[43] are just the material elements.

Thus, having established that they have many features, to apply this to the point at hand, Dignāga says: "**fundamental particles**. . . ."[44] To say that

38. Verse 3ab commentary.

39. Tib. *nyes pa*; Skt. *doṣa*.

40. Lit. have the nature of: *ngo bo nyid*.

41. Verse 3ab commentary.

42. Bhadanta Buddhadeva (Tib. bTsun pa Sangs rgyas lha) is mentioned in the *Commentary on the Treasury of Abhidharma* along with a group of other Bhadantas: Dharmatrāta (Chos skyob), Dharmasubhūti (Chos ldan rab 'byor), Ghoṣaka (dByangs sgrog), Vasumitra (dByigs bshes), and Kumāralāta (gZhon nu len). These are the four masters of the *Great Exposition* (*Mahāvibhāṣa*). Vasumitra is the author of the *Five Categories* (*Pañca-vastuka*). Ghoṣaka is the author of the *Nectar of Abhidharma* (*Abhidharmāmṛta*). Vasumitra maintained that the present moment possesses efficacy, which is not the case with past or future moments. Ghoṣaka held that the characteristic of efficacy of the elements is different in the present, and Dharmatrāta is associated with the position that each moment is different but that the capacity aspects of a present moment are present in its own nature. Buddhadeva held that the nature of past, present, and future moments is contingent and relative because each has its identity in relation to the others.

43. Tib. *skye mched*; Skt. *āyatana*. This refers to the five senses and their objects. A commentary on the *Treasury of Abhidharma* attributed to Sthiramati (Anhui 安慧) found in the Dunhuang caves contains an extended discussion that expands on Vasubandhu's refutations of Buddhadeva (*Treasury of Abhidharma* I.35c in the *Commentary*). It presents Buddhadeva as saying that material phenomena are derived from the four great material elements (*dazhong* 大種; Skt. *mahābhūta*) and are not separate from them. Qualities such as solidity cannot be perceived by the eye, according to Buddhadeva, because they lie outside its purview. Each perceptual realm (*chu* 處; Skt. *āyatana*) is delimited, and the capacity of a particular sense faculty only allows it to perceive certain features from the range of qualities of a given object. See *Commentary on the Real Meaning of the Treasury of Abhidharma* (*Apitdamo Shelun shi* 阿毗達磨俱舍論實義疏; Skt. *Abhidharmakośa-tattvārtha-ṭīkā*; three *juan*; (CBETA, ZW01, no. 7, p. 169, a6–7).

44. Verse 3ab commentary.

"fundamental particles have the causes that produce cognitions that have the appearance of collections" means that they produce cognitions of the collected features of fundamental particles.

Someone might ask: If you assert that fundamental particles have collected features, shouldn't you just say that fundamental particles have collected features? Why do you say that fundamental particles are the causes that produce a cognition with the appearance of a collection?

Dignāga says this in order to show that the percept has two parts. By saying "fundamental particles have the causes that produce cognitions that have the appearance of collections,"[45] he shows that they are the causes. By saying "appearance of collections," he asserts that they convey their features and also that they have collected features. Because an object conveys to cognition a feature that it has, but not one that it does not have, he definitely says that fundamental particles have collected features.

Someone might ask: "If fundamental particles have the features of macro-objects, then why refer to them as "fundamental particles?" Why are they not apprehended as having only[46] subtle features?

In response, Dignāga says: "**features of minute particles are not the object of cognition.**" (3c) To explain this, he says: "**any more than things like solidity are.**" There are objects such as solidity, wetness, and heat, but [361] because specific capacities of sense faculties ascertain them, they cannot be the objects of visual cognitions. Similarly, minute particles also are not their objects. It is for this reason that they are called "fundamental particles." The word represented by "*ni*" should be interpreted in an emphatic sense.[47]

Commentary on Verse 4

After presenting the third position, Dignāga provides the following refutation: "**According to them, cognitions of things like pots and cups would be identical.**" (4ab) This is a response to those who maintain that fundamental particles have collected features. What collected features do they accept fundamental particles as having? First, it is well known among ordinary people that fundamental particles are collected as things like pots, cups, and bowls, or

45. Verse 3ab commentary.

46. Text emendation: read *nyid* for *nye*.

47. In verse 6, the particle *ni* is used to translate the Sanskrit *tu*. It also can be used to represent the Sanskrit *hi*. Here Vinītadeva is saying that the Sanskrit particle (whichever it is) is being used in an emphatic sense to identify solidity and so forth as the subject of the sentence.

things like pillars or scents. Among these, what features do they maintain that fundamental particles have? If they say that they have a pot feature, then all collections of things like cups would be cognized as pots. If they say that they have cup features, then all collections would be cognized as cups, and there would not be different cognitions: "In some cases there is a pot, and in other cases there is a cup."

It is said: "If a cognition arises that corresponds to the identity of an object and if an object has a single identity, how can there be different cognitions of it?"

On this point, someone might think: "In a pot, there are many[48] fundamental particles, but in a cup there are fewer. Similarly, it should be understood that there are many or few fundamental particles in other things as well. Therefore, distinctions between cognitions are created by the quantity of fundamental particles."

In response, Dignāga says: "**There may be many minute particles in things like pots and cups, but they are not different at all.**"[49] In this case, it is impossible for different cognitions to be created by the number of fundamental particles. This is because while there may be many fundamental particles in a pot and fewer fundamental particles in a cup, their collected features still comprise [362] fundamental particles, and there cannot be any distinctions between them.

Therefore, there is still a problem. "Where there are many fundamental particles, there is a big pot, and where there are fewer, there is a smaller pot." This is all there is to it.[50] It will not work here to assert: "When collected features are the same, the cognition of a pot comes from many, and cognition of a cup comes from few."

To give another opponent a chance to speak, Dignāga says: "**If they are distinguished by different features.**" (4c) To explain this, he says: "**If someone thinks that distinctive features, such as the neck of a pot, distinguish different cognitions.**"[51]

---

48. This follows the readings of S and B: *mang*. T reads: *med*, which makes no sense. This reading is confirmed by the presence of *mang* in the following line.

49. Verse 4ab commentary.

50. Tib. "*'di tsam zhig tu 'gyur bar zad kyi*." Negi (2000, vol. 6: 2559) gives *'di tsam zhig* as an equivalent of *etāvat*. Thus *'di tsam zhig tu* could be *etavatā*. The definition of *etāvat* (by Macdonnell) is "so great, so much, of such a kind." The term *etāvan-mātra* means "of such a measure, so great, so much; so little" (http://dsalsrv02.uchicago.edu/cgi-bin/romadict.pl?query=etAvAt&display=simple&table=macdonell).

51. Verse 4c commentary.

Someone might think: "The neck of a pot points upward and it is narrow. In the middle, its chamber is broad. Things like this are its distinctive features. The distinctive features of a cup are such things as its broad opening and its narrow bottom." Therefore, due to these distinctive features, there are different cognitions of such things as pots and cups." In the phrase "distinctive features" (*rnam pa'i khyad pa*), the word "feature" means "shape" (*dbyibs*; Skt. *saṃsthāna*): that is, its configuration (*bkod pa*; Skt. *saṃ*) and state (*gnas pa*; Skt. *stāna*).[52]

To show that these different features are not objects, Dignāga says: "**distinctive features belong only to things like pots.**"[53] We do not deny that the distinctive features that you attribute to such things as pots and cups are distinct, but substantially real fundamental particles do not have distinctive features. Why? Dignāga says: "**because there is no difference in their dimensions.**" (5b) This is because there is no difference in the dimensions of fundamental particles as "spheres."[54]

Commentary on Verse 5

Someone might ask: "Aren't the fundamental particles of a pot one thing and those of a cup another thing? Why can't there be differences in their dimensions?"

In response, Dignāga says: "**Fundamental particles may be substantially distinct, but there are no differences in their spherical shapes.**"[55] The fundamental particles of such things as pots and cups may be substantially different, but spheres have no differences. [363] Therefore, fundamental particles have no distinctive features. So according to you, regardless of how many fundamental particles there are and what they are, all are substantially real. Similarly, regardless of how small the dimensions of fundamental particles are, all are spheres. And fundamental particle spheres are identical. Therefore, how could they be differentiated?

52. These two words represent the two parts of the word *saṃ-* (together) and *sthāna* (state).

53. Verse 4c commentary.

54. Ngawang Dendar clarifies this point: "They are not different in size, because they are as small as anything can be; and they are not different in shape because, according to you Sautrāntikas, they are nothing but spheres. Therefore, the fundamental particles of such things as pots and cups may be substantially different, but there is no difference in their equally spherical shape (156)."

55. Verse 5a commentary.

One might think that collected features are macro-objects, but because they are substantially real, they must be partless. This is not the case. If something has parts, then it is not substantially real. And if it has no parts, how could it have any differences in configuration? Whatever has parts can be configured in various ways, but things that are partless cannot.

Thus, having refuted that fundamental particles have distinctive features, in conclusion Dignāga says: "**Therefore, these differences belong to something that is not substantially real.**" (5b) Why? The features that have been explained in this way are partless and cannot have different configurations. Therefore, you should understand that they are not substantially real.

To explain the meaning of the verse, the author of the treatise says: "**distinctive features. . . .**"[56] These distinctive features belong only to things that are conventionally real, because they have parts. They do not belong to fundamental particles, because the latter are partless.

According to the Vaiśeṣikas, things like pots are substantially real, and so they might say: "How do you know that things like pots are conventionally real?" In response, Dignāga says: "**Things like pots are just conventionally real.**"[57] This should be understood in accordance with the statement: "Things like pots are conventionally real." So when individual fundamental particles are removed,[58] cognition that has the features of a pot does not arise.[59] In the phrase "**because the cognition that has the appearance of them disappears when particles disperse,**" (5cd) for cognition to have the appearance of a thing [364] means that it appears as that thing. The word "**them**" refers to pots. The word "**appearance**" refers to a semblance. A cognition that has the appearance of them has the appearance of them and is a cognition. "**Disappear**" means that the cognition in which it appears as that would disappear. This is what is meant by "**cognition that has the appearance of them disappears.**"

---

56. Verse 5b commentary.

57. Verse 5b commentary.

58. T reads: *brtsal*. N and P indicate that this should be read as "remove": *bsal*.

59. Vasubandhu, *Treasury of Abhidharma* 6.4: "If there is no cognition of something like a pot when it is broken, or of something like water when other things have been removed by the mind, it is conventionally real; otherwise it is ultimately real." The *Commentary* explains: "If there is no cognition of something like a pot when it is broken into parts, it is conventionally real. This is because there is no cognition of a pot when it is broken into parts. And if there is no cognition of something like water when other dharmas have been removed by the mind, this also is known as conventionally real. This is because there is no cognition of water when dharmas such as material form are removed by the mind."

Someone might say: "A cognition of the features of something like a pot is not produced when individual fundamental particles are removed. How could this sort of pot be conventionally real?"

Dignāga responds: "**if one were to remove things that are associated with substantially real things, then awareness of things like their color would not**[60] **disappear.**"[61] If things are substantially real, then cognition of them will not disappear even if things associated with them are removed—like color, for example. If things like pots were substantially real, then even if one were to remove things associated with them, cognition of them would not disappear.

Someone might say: "When individual fundamental particles are removed, the connections that make them substantially real are broken. Therefore, either a cognition of a pot does not arise because the pot is destroyed, or it does not arise because it is utterly nonexistent."

Response: Are you asserting: "If the substance of a whole such as a pot—which is different from fundamental particles—is broken, then at that time it still exists in those fundamental particles?" Would you say that it exists in them to the extent of their number or that it exists singularly? On the one hand, if it did not include the parts it comprises, then the whole would exist in them but would not exist partially. And if you say, "it does not exist singularly," then you would have to accept that "it exists in them to the extent of their number." In that case, there would be as many wholes of such things as pots as there are fundamental particles. There would no longer be one whole.[62]

The formal argument is: A whole is not substantially real because it is an aggregate of many things at one time, just as such things as horses are not substantially real. [365] The negative property is the specific characteristic. If a whole were an entity, then, in light of the points that have been explained, it would make no sense for it to be composed of many things at once. This argument is a refutation.

In this way, having argued that "it makes no sense for an external object to be the percept" according to all three positions, Dignāga concludes by saying: "**thus it makes sense that objects of sensory awareness are not external.**"[63] Why? Because he has argued that: "Since it is not reasonable for fundamental

---

60. This follows the reading of N, P, and S: *'dor ba med.*

61. Verse 5cd commentary.

62. There is a useful account of the Vaiśeṣika theory of parts and wholes in Potter (1977: 74–79).

63. Verse 5cd commentary.

particles to be the percept, it is proven that sensory cognitions do not have external objects as their objects."

Commentary on Verse 6

By refuting the opponent's system in this way, Dignāga has completely refuted his view of the percept. It will be further refuted by a presentation of how Dignāga's own system defines the percept. Thus he states:

> **An internal cognitive object,**
> **Which appears to be external, is the object**[64]
> **Because it is cognition itself,**
> **And because it is its condition.** (6abcd)

This verse means: "It is only a representation of the cognitive object,[65] which appears in cognition as if it were separate, that is the object of cognition." "**Internal**" means "within." This should be understood as cognition itself. The term "internal" has the meaning of the locative of "self"; that is, it means "internal to cognition." The phrase "**internal cognitive object**" means "the representation of the object, which is the apprehended aspect." The word *ni* (but) should be understood as having an emphatic and an adversative meaning.

The phrase "**appears to be external**" means "it manifests as if it were external; in other words, as if it were separate from cognition." A condition of its appearance in that way is the appearance of space. Space appears to cognition as if it were separate from cognition, and so it reveals the apprehended object. For example, when a reflection of the moon appears on the surface of a mirror, it appears as if it were separate, as if it were in a well, by virtue of a reflection of space.

Someone might ask: "if there is no external object, then does cognition have no percept condition at all?"

Dignāga says: "**Even though there is no external object.**"[66] [366] Here there is no problem of there being no percept condition. This is because while there may be no external object, there is still an internal appearance that merely seems to be external, and that is the percept condition. For example, someone

64. The *Commentary on the Compendium of Metaphysics* (vol. 2, p. 710) quotes the Sanskrit for this passage: "*yadantarjñeyarūpam tu bahirvad avabhāsate / vijñānarūpatvāt tatpratyayatāpi ca.*"

65. Tib. *shes bya*; Skt. *jñeya*.

66. Verse 6ab commentary.

with ocular defects may have a cognition that has a representation of things like hairs and flies, as if there were features of things like hairs. Thus it is said: "If this apprehended object can have the characteristics of a percept, then it is said to be the percept condition."

Again, someone might ask how this can have the characteristics of a percept. In response, Dignāga says: "**because it is cognition itself.**" (6c) Why? Due to the maturation of predispositions toward the fabrication of things like blue and yellow, cognition arises with the representations of things like blue and yellow. Because it has the representations of things like blue, it is explained as having these representations. And because representations such as blue are the conditions of this cognition, they are established as its cause. **Its condition** is the condition of this. The word "**it**" refers to cognition. Cognition itself is the condition of cognition. In the phrase "**because it is its condition,**" the use of the instrumental case should be understood to indicate a reason.

As a way of explaining the meaning of the verse, the treatise's author concludes by saying: "**internal cognition appears as the object and arises from it.**"[67] Why? Due to the representation of an object that exists internally, cognition has that representation, and it arises when that representation of an object is present. Therefore, because cognition has these two characteristics, it is reasonable for the percept to be internal.

Thus, it is said: "Cognition appears with a representation in which an internal object is depicted. Thus, it has a representation of this internal object." For example, it is as if its representation were an image drawn on a wall. Why? Because it is said that: "It arises when the apprehended aspect is present. Therefore, that cognition arises from it. Thus, because both aspects of a percept are present, it is reasonable for it to be a percept." [367]

Commentary on Verse 7

To give an opponent a chance to speak, Dignāga says: "appears as the object" and so forth,[68] even if it is granted that a cognition appears as a cognitive object internally. That is, it arises as if it were a representation depicted by the representation of a cognitive object. If you say this, then "how do you understand that" a representation of a cognitive object that arises "in the same place and at the same time" is a condition of that cognition? If so, then you would have to accept that a cognition causes itself, and this would have absurd consequences. If the apprehending aspect also produces the apprehended aspect,

67. Verse 6cd commentary.

68. Introduction to the commentary on verse 7.

then wouldn't it absurdly follow that the right and left horns of a cow produce each other? This is the objection.

In reply, the author says: "**Even though they are simultaneous, it is a condition**, which also arises from other conditions **because it is invariably concomitant.**" (7a) To explain this, he says: "**they are invariably concomitant.**"[69] There is no problem here. Why? Even though the apprehended aspect arises at the same time and is invariably concomitant, it is the percept condition of a cognition that also arises from other conditions, namely, the immediately preceding and dominant conditions. This is because a cognition does not arise without an apprehended aspect. It is just like this: cognition is supported in the way that a bundle of reeds support each other.[70] It is not the case that they work as a unit, nor should one single out any one condition.

Someone might ask: Why does cognition not arise without being assisted by an apprehended aspect?

This is because it cannot depend on something that cannot assist it, and it cannot arise without assistance. Even if what does not assist is absent, cognition will not fail to arise. Even if the apprehended aspect is the cause in this way, so be it.[71]

What is the contradiction? The right and left horns of a cow are not invariably concomitant, and so they are not cause and effect. In some cases, something acting on itself is accepted, as in the case of a lamp. [368] It illuminates itself by itself.

Someone might say: A particular thing rarely acts on itself. What about the phrase: "Anything that is cause and effect must have the characteristic of invariable concomitance?"[72]

Dignāga says: "**Logicians say that being present or absent is the defining character of the sequential arising of cause and effect.**"[73] That is, "logicians say

---

69. Verse 7a commentary.

70. See Ngawang Dendar: 161. This image is of reeds that are pointed inward to a peak, and all support each other. This reference appears in the *Compendium of Mahāyāna* and is quoted in Dendar's commentary on this passage. See Lamotte (1973, ch. 1, sect. 17).

71. The sNar thang, gSer bris, and Peking have a different reading: "In this way, cognition would be both the apprehended aspect and the cause; so be it."

72. There are two possible readings based on the different Tibetan versions. sDe dge reads: *ka las she*, but sNar thang reads: *ka la zhe*; Peking reads: *las zhe*. If translated according to sDe dge, it would read "where is this coming from?" In this case, the opponent would be disagreeing with the example of the lamp.

73. Verse 7a commentary. This reads differently from any of the *Investigation of the Percept* texts we have consulted. These say: *gtan tshigs*, which can mean reason, but Vinītadeva's verse reads: *gtan tshigs pa dag*, which indicates that it refers to people.

that" something being present or absent when something else is present or absent is the "defining character of the sequential arising of cause and effect." When one thing is present whenever another is present and absent whenever another is absent, then one is the cause and the other is the effect. In this case, the cognition is present when the apprehended aspect is present, and it is absent when the other is absent. Therefore, even though these two arise simultaneously, it is established that they are cause and effect.

Those who use the language of argument are called "**logicians.**" This is synonymous with "dialectician." "**Possessing this**" means possessing presence and absence. "**Cause and cause-possessor**" (*rgyu dang rgyu dang ldan pa*) means "cause and effect" (*rgyu dang 'bras bu*).

At this point, having explained that object and subject are simultaneous things, now, in order to explain that object and subject are sequential things, Dignāga says: "**It is sequential because of a transfer of capacity.**" (7b) When the apprehended aspect transfers a capacity, it is the object that produces the apprehending aspect sequentially. This is because when the apprehended aspect ceases, it transfers a capacity to the fundamental consciousness.[74]

If this capacity establishes cooperative factors in the next moment, then in the very next moment it produces a cognition corresponding to itself. If it does not establish cooperative factors in the second moment, then it will establish one in another moment, either the third or the fourth. When the capacity has come to fruition, then it will produce a cognition corresponding to itself. According to this position, the following problems are not possible: "Because it is contradictory for it to act on itself; because it is contradictory for it to arise in the same place; and because it is contradictory for it to arise simultaneously." [369] This is because in a previous cognition, the apprehended aspect—which is a representation of something such as blue—gives rise to subsequent cognitions that have representations such as blue. This is why these problems are not even remotely possible.

Someone might think: "If the capacity produces the cognition, then it is the capacity that is the object, not the previous apprehended aspect."

Dignāga says: "**in sequence also**" and so forth.[75] There is no problem because the apprehended aspect sequentially produces an effect that corresponds to itself and creates a capacity that is located in the fundamental consciousness. If that apprehended aspect did not establish that capacity, then that capacity could not produce this kind of cognition. Therefore, because the

74. Tib. *kun gzhi rnam par shes pa*; Skt. *ālaya-vijñāna*.

75. Verse 7b commentary.

cognition that arises from that capacity arises from that very apprehended aspect, there is no contradiction at all. According to this position, it is entirely reasonable for it to have both characteristics. This is because the apprehended aspect produces a subsequent cognition that corresponds to itself, and so it has both characteristics.

At this point, in order to allow the opponent to speak, Dignāga says: "Someone may ask: "**If the percept condition is just an internal object, then how does visual cognition arise by depending on this and also on the eye?**"[76] If you maintain that a percept condition is only an internal object, then how could a visual cognition arise depending on an internal object and also on the eye? This is because a form that has appeared to a previous moment of the eye produces a cognition of itself with the eye that is simultaneous with it. When this occurs, if the internal object did not appear to a previous moment of the eye, then how can you say that "an internal object, along with a simultaneous moment of the eye, produces a visual cognition? If it never occurs in front of an eye, then how could it appear?" This is the objection.

The author responds: "**A sense faculty is a cooperating sense capacity.**" (7cd) If sense faculties were material, there would be a problem. But we maintain [370] that a sense faculty is a capacity that cooperates with the object. Therefore, in our view, the eye is only internal, just as the object is internal. So how could this problem arise? The phrase "**cooperating capacity**" should be understood to mean "a capacity that cooperates with an object." If one thought that the capacity of a sense faculty is not like this, then there would be no connection between the sense faculty and the object. And then to call it the capacity of a sense faculty would be infelicitous.[77]

"But how do you know that a sense faculty is a capacity?" In response, Dignāga says: "**a sense faculty is a cooperating sense capacity.**" (7cd) Why? Because it can be inferred from its result that a sense faculty is a capacity that has the nature of cognition and is not derived from material elements. This is because it is possible to infer a cause in general from an effect, but not a specific cause, because logical entailment is not possible with a particular indicator.

Thus, it is possible to infer fire in general from smoke but not a particular sort of fire such as one of grass or leaves. Similarly, it is possible to infer a

76. Verse 7b commentary.

77. Vinītadeva is playing on connotations of terms that cannot be reflected in English. The Tibetan reads: *dbang po'i dbang po*, which literally means "capacity of a sense faculty." This appears to gloss capacity (*nus pa*) in the previous line. This is what enables the senses to function in cooperation with their intentional objects.

cause in general from the cognitive nature of the effect, but not that it has a specific cause, such as one that is derived from material elements. That is, it is impossible to infer specific causes, such as the following: according to the Vaibhāṣikas, sense faculties are derived from elements; according to Bhadanta Buddhadeva, they are material elements; according to the Yogācāras, they are cognition; according to the Mādhyamikas, they are conventional things; according to the Sāṃkhyas, they are the ego.[78] Therefore, by inferring a capacity that is a cause in general, one infers nothing but a capacity.

Commentary on Verse 8

On this point, someone might think, "A capacity is based on something that has a capacity, and it is not possible for a capacity to have no basis.[79] The thing that has a capacity is the sense faculty, and this is derived from material elements. This proves that a sense faculty is derived from material elements." [371]

In response, Dignāga says: "**It is not contradictory for this capacity also to be in cognition.**" (8a) If it definitely requires a basis, then cognition is simply this basis. That is to say, it is accepted by both sides because it is the nature of cognition to be the cognition of a specific object and also to have the nature of self-cognition. For this reason, cognition is the basis that is pervaded by karma. Why would it not make sense for a capacity to be based in cognition? Cognition and capacity are not mutually exclusive.

On this point, someone might think: "A capacity that is located in something derived from material elements produces one kind of effect, and one that is located in cognition produces a different effect."[80] This is how we know that: "a sense faculty is definitely derived from material elements."

Anticipating this concern, Dignāga says: "**this capacity can exist in cognition**" and so forth.[81] Here the basis makes no functional difference. Whether the capacity is located in cognition or is located somewhere else, in either case,

---

78. Tib. *nga'o snyam pa*; Skt. *ahaṃkāra*. Literally, "I-making." This is one of the four parts of the "inner organ" (*antaḥkaraṇa*) in some schools of classical Indian philosophy. The others are intelligence (*buddhi*), mind (*citta*), and mentation (*manas*). I-making is the factor that causes one to develop the concept of self.

79. This passage is translated in accordance with sNar thang, which provides a clearer reading.

80. In other words, something that results from transformations of elements will be fundamentally different from something that is entirely mental.

81. Verse 8a commentary.

all it does is produce something like the mere perceptual cognition. So there is no distinction in the production of an effect.

The phrase "**it can exist in something that is inaccessible**"[82] means that the nature of the sense faculty accepted by the opponent cannot be known by the sense faculties and so cannot be investigated. If something cannot be investigated, it cannot be perceived. For this reason, the sense faculties as accepted by the opponent are inaccessible.

But what is the cause of the capacity that constitutes the sense faculties? To conclude, Dignāga says: "**These two cause one another and have done so from beginningless time.**"[83] Just as a cognition arises from the capacity that constitutes the sense faculty, the capacity arises in turn from a preceding cognition that sets in motion a sense faculty. And the preceding cognition also arises from a preceding sense faculty capacity. Thus, [372] both the sense faculty capacity and the cognition of what has the representation of the object cause one another, and since there was no time when this causal sequence began, these two should be viewed as beginningless.

To explain the meaning of this verse, the author says: "**A cognition arises with the appearance of an object, depending on the capacity called 'eye' and on an internal object.**"[84] Depending on a sense faculty called "eye" and an internal object that arose either simultaneously or previously, cognition arises with a representation of an indeterminate object. According to those who say that objects are external, a cognition arises only from a determinate object, but in this case it is not like that. For this reason, Dignāga explains: "**without being disclosed as the percept.**"

Others say: You have said that "cognition appears with an inexpressible object." This does not appear to be relevant to the point at hand. Here inexpressibility is not necessary at all. This is because all particulars are inexpressible. If cognitions arise with their appearances, what does this actually prove?

Someone might reply: "But a cognition that arises with the representation of the object is inexpressible."

If you say this, is it inexpressible because it does not exist at all, or because it is a particular? In the first case, if you say that it is inexpressible because it does not exist, this is unreasonable because something that does not exist can be expressed, like the horns of a rabbit. If you are saying that it is inexpressible because it is a particular, this has already been answered.

---

82. Verse 8a commentary.

83. Verse 8ab commentary.

84. Verse 8bcd commentary.

In the passage "**depending on the capacity called** 'eye'," [85] "and so forth" refers to "the eyes and so forth."

Someone might say: "From where does this capacity arise?" Dignāga responds: "these two cause one another." [86] Regarding the statement, "The capacity also arises from a previous cognition that sets in motion a sense faculty, and that cognition in turn arises from a previous capacity, and that capacity also is a cognition that sets in motion [373] a sense faculty": because it arises from a previous cognition, the causal sequence is beginningless. Thus, this indicates that the capacity of a sense faculty and cognition are cause and effect. The statement "these two cause each other and have done so from beginningless time" means that the capacity of the object and cognition cause one another and have done so from beginningless time.

To explain their mutual causation, Dignāga says: "Sometimes the representation of the object of cognition[87] arises from the maturation of the capacity." [88] Sometimes the cognition with the representation of an object arises from the maturation of a capacity that is called "predispositions toward fabrication," and sometimes a capacity arises from a cognition that has a representation of an object. Here there is no interruption of this causal sequence, and so it should be understood to be beginningless.

Someone might say: "Are the capacities of the sense faculties and objects different from cognition or not? If they are different, then these are just words, and the object that one takes to be excluded is the same. This is because you have accepted that the sense faculty and the percept are not included in cognition. But if they are not different, then you cannot make the claim that 'the capacity is the sense faculty and also is the object'."

Dignāga responds: "**Saying these two are different or not different from cognition is a matter of preference.**" [89] If one analyzes how they exist, then these capacities are conventionally real because they are distinguished in context. For this reason, it is impossible to specify whether or not they are different from cognition. So the two alleged problems do not follow. But when one relies on mundane convention, then it is possible to specify, as a matter of preference, that cognition is different from them, and sometimes it is not

85. Verse 8bcd commentary.

86. Verse 8bcd commentary.

87. Translated in accordance with sNar thang: *shes pa'i yul.*

88. Verse 8bcd commentary.

89. Verse 8bcd commentary.

different from them. This is because, for ordinary people, conventional things are sometimes said to be different, [374] like sandalwood and its scent. And sometimes they are said to not be different, like a pot and such things as its material form.

Having shown in this way that for both positions the percept is internal, Dignāga concludes by saying: "**it is a matter of preference.**"[90] From this explanation, since a percept that is not different from cognition, in the way that has just been described, has both characteristics. Therefore, it makes sense that it is the object.

Through the merit obtained
By elucidating the *Commentary*
On Investigation of the Percept,
May all beings attain buddhahood.
Because this subcommentary by Vinītadeva
Was composed in order to delight beginners,
The ten realms have been left out.
Therefore, scholars should be patient.
I acknowledge that this text may contain errors,
But not for lack of analysis.
As far as I can understand it,
This text is error free.

The master Vinītadeva surveys everything that can be known and as a debater gnaws on the heads of heretics like a lion among elephants. This completes his *Subcommentary on Investigation of the Percept.* Having requested a translation by the Indian scholar Śākyasiṃha and the chief editor and translator, the monk Beltsek, this has been concluded.

Texts

Vinītadeva. *Subcommentary on Investigation of the Percept* (*Ālambana-parīkṣā-ṭīkā*; Tib. *dMigs pa brtag pa'i 'grel bshad*). (1) T: sDe dge bsTan 'gyur, Tshad ma vol. *zhe* (190), ff. 175a3–187b.5: Tibetan Buddhist Resource Center (TBRC), vol. 3452, Work #22704, pp. 349–374. (2) D: Asian Classics Input Project bsTan 'gyur, sDe dge #4241, vol. *zhe* (190), ff. 175a–187b. (3) N: sNar thang bsTan 'gyur, Tshad ma vol. *ze*: TBRC vol. 3452, Work # 22704, ff. 186b.1–200b.6.

90. Verse 8bcd commentary.

(4) S: gSer bris bsTan 'gyur, Tshad ma vol. 201, pp. 485–522 (ff. 243a–261b). (5) P: Peking (Pe cing) bsTan 'gyur, Tshad ma vol. *ze* (138, pp. 45–51), ff. 183a.7–197b.7. (6) C: Co ne bsTan 'gyur, Tshad ma vol. *zhe* (ff. 167b.4–180a): TBRC vol. 190, pp. 338–363. (7) B: dPe bsdur ma bsTan 'gyur, Tshad ma (Pe cing: Krung go' bod rig pa'i dpe skrun khang, 1994–2000; TBRC W1PD95844), pp. 467–500.

6

Introduction to Ornament for Dignāga's Thought in Investigation of the Percept (dMigs pa brtag pa'i 'grel pa phyogs glang dgongs rgyan)

Douglas Duckworth

Introduction: The Author

The third Gungtang, Könchok Denbe Drönme, was the most prolific of the Gungtang incarnation line. He was born in southern Dzöge (mDzod dge'i smad) in Ngawa (rNga ba)[1] and was recognized as the Gungtang reincarnation at the age of five by his teacher, the second Jamyang Sheba, Könchok Jikme Wangbo ('Jam dbyangs bzhad pa dKon mchog 'jigs med dbang po, 1728–1791).[2] When he was seven, he became a novice monk and entered Labrang Tashikyil (bLa brang bkra shis 'khyil), a large monastery in his homeland of Amdo founded by the first Jamyang Sheba, Ngawang Dzöndrü ('Jam dbyangs

1. Welmang Könchok Gyaltsen (dPal mang dKon mchog rgyal mtshan, 1764–1853) (1974: 238.2). For a critical edition of Gungtang's religious biography (*rnam thar*), see Steinkellner (1981) and Dargyay (1981).

2. dPal mang dKon mchog rgyal mtshan, *gSung 'bum* vol. *na*: 246–247.

bzhad pa Ngag dbang brtson 'grus 1648–1721/1722). After studying at Labrang, when he was seventeen he traveled to Lhasa and continued his studies at the Gomang (sGo mang) college of Drepung monastery. When he was twenty, he took full ordination from the eighth Dalai Lama, Jampel Gyatso ('Jam dpal rgya mtsho, 1758–1804), and quickly advanced to receive his *geshe lharampa* degree (the highest degree in the Geluk monastic system) when he was just twenty-two years old.[3]

After returning to his homeland and teaching at Labrang Tashikyil, Gungtang was appointed to serve as the abbot of a Gomang monastery in Ngawa (rNga ba'i sgo mang), a monastery founded by the second Jamyang Sheba, Könchok Jikme Wangpo. A year later, when he was thirty-one, Gungtang took over as the twenty-first throne holder of Labrang and served for seven years. He simultaneously served as throne holder of Gönlung monastery (dGon lung byams pa gling) from 1796 to 1797; this was the seat of the third Tuken, Losang Chokyi Nyima (Thu'u bkwan bLo bzang chos kyi nyi ma, 1737–1802) and the third Jangya, Rolpe Dorje (lCang skya Rol pa'i rdo rje, 1717–1786). Gungtang's connections with the third Tuken and Jangya, who had strong ties with the Qianlong Emperor 乾隆 (1711–1799), gave him access to Beijing and the Qing Court. The ties between Gönlung and Labrang monasteries extended the influence of the Geluk tradition in Amdo,[4] which had risen to dominate central Tibet a century earlier led by the fifth Dalai Lama, Ngawang Losang Gyatso (Ngag dbang blo bzang rgya mtsho, 1617–1682), with Mongolian support.

Gungtang not only held administrative positions of considerable power but was also a formidable scholar. His collected works were contained in twelve volumes in the Labrang monastery edition, 189 titled works in 8052 carved blocks,[5] which have recently been reprinted in an eleven-volume set (one volume has been lost) of bound books in Beijing.[6] He wrote on a wide range of topics of the monastic curricula, such as Abhidharma, Madhyamaka, and logic. The genres of his writing were not limited to

---

3. dPal mang dKon mchog rgyal mtshan, *gSung 'bum* vol. *na*: 274.5.

4. See Nietupski (2011: 132–133).

5. Nietupski (2011: 27).

6. *Gungtang's Collected Works* (*Gung thang bstan pa'i sgron me'i gsung 'bum*).

scholastic textbooks, however. He composed texts on a wide range of subjects, including Mahāmudrā,[7] a fascinating text on Amdo dialect,[8] and even a treatise on how to make rain.[9]

In addition to his commentary on *Investigation of the Percept*, the first known indigenous Tibetan commentary on the text, Gungtang also wrote a commentary on the "Mind-Only" chapter of Tsongkhapa's *Essence of Eloquence* (*Legs bshad snying po*).[10] For a Geluk scholar, his attention to Yogācāra is noteworthy. It is also worth mentioning that in this commentary he (subtly) critiqued Gyeltsap's (rGyal tshab Dar ma rin chen, 1364–1432) interpretation of a key passage in *Differentiation of the Precious Lineage* (*Ratnagotra-vibhāga*), traditionally attributed to Asaṅga (*c.* fourth century). Gyeltsap had attempted hermeneutical acrobatics to describe the text's reference to what is not empty (by claiming that the meaning of not empty is to be not empty of a *lack* of inherent existence rather than not empty of the potential for awakening).[11] Gungtang's critique of an authoritative commentary on this point shows not only his aptitude as a critical reader (he was not simply putting the square peg of his tradition's Prāsaṅgika-Madhyamaka interpretation into the round hole of the buddha-nature [*tathāgathagarbha*] doctrine); it also shows his creatively independent intellect, one capable of challenging even the revered authorities of his own tradition.

Gungtang wrote a lengthy commentary on Tsongkhapa's *DifficultPoints of Mind and the Fundamental Consciousness* (*Yid dang kun gzhi'i dka' ba'i*

---

7. Gungtang, *Phyag chen khrid kyi zin bris zhal lung bdud rtsi'i thigs phreng*, *Gungtang's Collected Works* (*bla brang* ed.), vol. 4: 89–146. Gungtang describes how the teaching of Geluk Mahāmudrā (*dge ldan phyag chen*) traces to an esoteric lineage from Tsongkhapa, who in a letter to his teacher, Rendawa (Red mda' ba gZhon nu blo gros, 1349–1412), had claimed that he had unique instructions called "Mahāmudrā" from the "Great Madhyamaka" (dBu ma chen po), but that he did not teach it because it was not a suitable time for its propagation (ibid., 91–92). See also Dalai Lama and Berzin (1997: 230).

8. Gungtang, *Phal skad tshul du gnang ba'i zab chos*, *Gungtang's Collected Works*, vol. 10: 504–510. This has been translated in T. J. Norbu (1995).

9. Gungtang, *'Phags mchog thugs rje chen po la brten pa'i char 'bebs bya tshul*, *Gungtang's Collected Works* (*bLa brang* ed.), vol. 9: 205–220.

10. Gungtang, *Legs bshad snying po las sems tsam gyi skor gyi mchan 'grel rtsom 'phro nang rig gzhung brgya'i snang ba*, *Gungtang's Collected Works* (*bLa brang* ed.), vol. 3: 1–165.

11. Gungtang, *Legs bshad snying po las sems tsam gyi skor gyi mchan 'grel rtsom 'phro nang rig gzhung brgya'i snang ba*, *Gungtang's Collected Works* (Zhol ed.) vol. 2: 824–825. See also Lobsang Rabgye (1990: 88–89).

gnas),[12] a text that Tsongkhapa composed at Sakya after studying with the Sakya master Rendawa, and before his famed "conversion" to Prāsaṅgika.[13] In addition to Yogācāra, Gungtang seems to have had a certain affinity for the Sakya tradition, and Sakya Paṇḍita (Sa skya Paṇḍita Kun dga' rgyal mtshan, 1182–1251) in particular. He cites Sakya Paṇḍita in a biography he composed of his teacher,[14] and in his *Treatises on Water and Trees*,[15] a popular compilation of poetry that imparts advice on worldly affairs and religion through similes of water and trees, acknowledging his debt to Sakya Paṇḍita, who pioneered this Tibetan genre of popular advice in both form and content in his *Elegant Sayings of the Sakya*.[16] Gungtang can be said to share a connection with Sakya Paṇḍita politically (in terms of his ties to Mongol support), philosophically (in terms of his interest in Yogācāra), and poetically (in terms of his literary style).

Gungtang's inspiration from the Sakya, a tradition in which Yogācāra plays a more constitutive role in its core philosophy than it does for the Gelukpas, is particularly telling in that he seems to show a sincere interest in the philosophy of "Mind-Only." Nevertheless, like a good incarnate lama with diplomatic duties to prominent Geluk monasteries, he presents his tradition's Prāsaṅgika-Madhyamaka as the supreme view.

Gungtang's Commentary on Investigation of the Percept

In *Investigation of the Percept*, Dignāga demonstrates that the concept of matter is incoherent, and Gungtang's commentary expands on his arguments. The analysis revolves around an argument against a view that the precept exists as it appears. Gungtang begins his commentary by presenting a realist view of perception and then interrogating it.

---

12. Gungtang, *Yid dang kun zhi'i dka' gnad rnam par bshad pa mkhas pa'i 'jug ngogs, Gungtang's Collected Works* (bLa brang ed.), vol. 2, 243–362. Tsongkhapa's text has been translated and studied in Sparham (1993). Gungtang's commentary has been studied and translated in Wilson (1984).

13. Wilson (1984: 47–48).

14. Gungtang (1990: 170).

15. The text is actually a compilation of two treatises: the tree treatise and the water treatise. Gungtang, *Legs par bshad pa shing gi bstan bcos lugs gnyis yal 'dab brgya ldan, Gungtang's Collected Works* (bLa brang ed.), vol. 11: 7–19; and *Legs par bshad pa chu'i bstan bcos lugs gnyis rlabs 'phreng brgya ldan, Gungtang's Collected Works* (bLa brang ed.), vol. 11: 21–39. English translation: Gungtang (1991).

16. See Davenport (2000: 10–11).

Gungtang first attacks a position that claims that fundamental particles constitute the content of perception. Commenting on verse 1, Gungtang argues that it is incoherent to maintain that the content of perception is fundamental particles because these particles are not perceived: What is perceived is never particles; we always perceive macro-objects, not micro-ones. Gungtang shows that the use of fundamental particles to explain perception is question-begging; their existence is only presumed from the divisible constitution of macro-objects. He thus argues that indivisible particles, which are not perceived, cannot serve as the basis of perception.

Gungtang then attacks a position that maintains that *compounds*, rather than particles, are what we really perceive. He does so with a gloss on Dignāga's statement that compounds are not substantially existent. He argues that compounds of particles cannot be the content of perception because the unities attributed to them are simply imputations—conceptual constructs—without substance. The integrity of compounds as singularities, like a forest or a garland, does not inhere in the entities themselves but is imputed by the mind. His arguments here, characteristic of the *reductio* style often associated with Madhyamaka, challenge the realist presumption that objects of perception exist externally as they appear.

Gungtang thus presents the first part of Dignāga's text as a sustained argument criticizing the possibility of a coherent account of perception in terms of external objects, as particles or in their combinations. He argues that Dignāga's position is that there are no real material causes for the perception of extended objects. Rather, these compounds are simply constructions or mental representations. He further argues that Dignāga maintains that the occurrence of these representations is not explained by the existence of something external because the perception of macro-objects from micro-objects—infinitesimally small, external particles—is incoherent. Thus, Gungtang shows that according to Dignāga's analysis, macro-objects are only conventionally existent and that for Dignāga the cause of the mental representation of extended external objects is the mind, not the external world.

Gungtang's presentation of Dignāga's arguments shows that *Investigation of the Percept* sheds light on the nature of supervenience and problems of emergence in terms of (1) the relation between extended things and that which is not extended, and (2) the relationship between mind and matter. With respect to the first problem, Dignāga echoes Vasubandhu's argument in the *Twenty Verses* that extended objects cannot be constituted by indivisible particles that lack extension.[17] The second problem—the relationship not between macro-objects

17. Vasubandhu, *Twenty Verses*, verses 11–14.

and micro-objects, but between cognition and matter—is known today as the "hard problem" of consciousness. It is the question: how can experience arise from matter, which does not share its nature? This problem is set up by the presumptions of a mental–physical dualism, but it is answered with monism. According to Gungtang, Dignāga's answer is not, however, a physicalist monism but rather panpsychism.

In his interpretation of Dignāga's account of the percept, Gungtang defines it as "nothing other than a self-presenting internal apprehension" (*nang gi 'dzin pa'i rang mdangs de nyid*). Even while percepts appear within a duality of an inner mind and outer object, these representations don't exist in the way that they appear. The percept is cognitively constituted and is a mental representation that is conditioned by a previous cognition. In Gungtang's interpretation of Dignāga, this cognition is the fundamental consciousness.

Gungtang certainly describes Dignāga as an epistemic idealist, given that he refers to the percept as an "internal entity." Yet we can discern a tension in this Yogācāra description—a tension between the respective meanings ascribed to subjectivity, internality, and cognition. That is, this explanation does not simply reduce the fundamental consciousness to the *subject*, as in a simplistic model of "mind-only" in which objective percepts are simply the products of a *subjective* mind. Rather, there is a more complex and arguably more nuanced causal story.

The fundamental consciousness, being nominally a "consciousness," may be identified with the subjective pole of perception. Yet the fundamental consciousness is the source of not only the subjective representations of mind, but also of objective representations of bodies, environments, and materials as well. Thus, the meaning of reflexivity with regard to this consciousness concerns the structure of self-illumination through which this consciousness presents itself *both* as subject *and* as object. Gungtang's presentation of the fundamental consciousness supports a form of panpsychism rather than simple subjective idealism because the fundamental consciousness constitutes the content of both *subjects* and objects. Thus, this emergent process comes from something that is not itself a *subjective* consciousness, but from what is said to be an "internal" consciousness nonetheless.

Gungtang presents the process of perception as the transformation of the fundamental consciousness, which perpetuates itself in a reflexive process. He responds to the objection that this kind of reflexive action is contradictory (like a finger pointing to itself) by claiming that the fundamental consciousness is structured as a representation of an external appearance apprehended by an apprehending subject. Even though the subject and object are simultaneous, they are not causally unrelated (like the two horns on the head of a bull) because the process is temporally structured. That is to say, even though an intentional object and the cognition that apprehends it are simultaneous, the co-emergent process of their arising is sequentially structured and causal. This is because a present intentional object arises from the predisposition of a previous cognition, and the object, in turn, shapes cognition by laying the seeds for its further perpetuation.

For Gungtang, Dignāga's account of perception entails a temporal, self-generating, and self-regulating process of conscious experience, which is driven by habituation to predispositions. This is the dynamic process of the fundamental consciousness. He says that the capacities for representing an external world reside in cognition, and cognition arises from the representations of these objects. In this way, the fundamental consciousness is autopoietic: It is a self-organizing, self-perpetuating system. It exemplifies the cognitive coupling of agent and environment, which mutually cooperate to create the world. In this system, moreover, the dualist's and physicalist's problem of emergence—how mind arises from matter—is skirted because, just as the fundamental consciousness (the transcendental structure of cyclic existence) is not spatially located *in here* or *out there*, it is also not bound by the temporality that it shapes. It therefore lacks a point of origin, so its process is "beginningless." Thus, the percept, like the fundamental consciousness, is said to have been there since beginningless time.

Gungtang's panpsychism hence captures the fact that the fundamental consciousness manifests both as subject and as object. Therefore, the reality of the *subject* along with its subject–object presentation can be denied while affirming the conscious process. In this framework, the mere flow of consciousness is affirmed in a causal story that denies the reality of any enduring entities, whether self or external objects. In that case, *internality*—as opposed to subjectivity, particularly in the absence of external objects—requires elaboration, as it is not clear what the distinction between external and internal could amount to. Gungtang, as a Gelukpa lineage holder, will argue that the commitment to the independent reality of such an "internal" mind falls into the error of subjective idealism with which the Geluk tradition charges Cittamātra (Mind-Only), one that, according to this tradition, is corrected by Candrakīrti's (*c.* seventh century) Prāsaṅgika-Madhyamaka.

7

Ornament for Dignāga's Thought in Investigation of the Percept (dMigs pa brtag pa'i 'grel pa phyogs glang dgongs rgyan)

Gung thang dKon mchog bstan pa'i sgron me

TRANSLATED BY DOUGLAS Duckworth, Jay Garfield, John Powers, and Sonam Thakchöe

Preface

[1] In this order: having paid reverence to the Buddha who is completely liberated from the snare of subject and object and relying on scholars, I will explain this treatise in accordance with Dignāga's thought. The topic to be explained here is *Investigation of the Percept.*

With regard to the title and translator's homage: the Sanskrit title is *Ālambanaparīkṣā.* In Tibetan it is *dMigs pa brtag pa.*

"Homage to all buddhas and bodhisattvas!" This part was easy.

Commentary on Verses 1 and 2

Now for the actual meaning. By way of examples that refute opponents' definitions of the percept—that it (1) arises from fundamental particles or (2) resembles collections of them—Dignāga makes various points with the two main refutations of entailment and other arguments. Here is the refutation of the opponent's thesis: if the percept is definitely apprehended, then how are minute particles apprehended? Is it by producing a representation, or is it like when a son takes on his father's form?[1] It might look like one would have to accept the latter position, but in this context this does not help. Because this has been refuted by the statement, "**even if sensory cognition were caused by fundamental particles, it would not have particles** serve **as its object**," (1ab) I will not bother to refute you here.

But there remains a much bigger problem to be resolved that is easy to see. According to you who do not accept the first horn of the dilemma—"**Because they do not appear to cognition**" (1c)—that very percept, the definitely ascertained "**object**" of the sensory cognition, "**would not have particles.**" (1bc) In virtue of the fact of its being a mere cause and its not being directly apparent, [2] because it cannot be the cause that produces a representation—which is the first criterion—you have failed to satisfy both criteria. Thus, it cannot be the percept, "**any more than the sense faculties can.**" (1d) The foundations [of your position] have been swept away!

Now Dignāga explains how collections will not work either. The argument from incoherence shows that when each individual thing is removed nothing appears. Hence, the indefinite pronoun "**that**" (*gang*) refers to whatever is left over and appears, that is, collections.[2]

These are aggregated cognitively; they are not aggregations of external particles. Nonetheless, the term "**of which**" (*ltar*) is used to refer to appearing in this way due to the power of predispositions. This is what the phrase "**of which it has the appearance**" (2a) means. In that case, contrary to the previous position, even if appearance makes sense, sensory cognitions "**do not**" arise "**from that**" that is, aggregations. Failing this second criterion, it is not a percept. It is not causal "**because, like a double moon, collections are not substantially real.**" (2b)

Here is how this example is now applied to the subject of the opponent's assertion. The appearance of two moons is not produced by two moons in someone to whom they appear. Therefore, their appearance is only due to

1. This example comes from Vinītadeva (sDe dge edition: 355). The idea is that sometimes one sees a son who closely resembles his father (*bus pha'i gzugs 'dzin pa*). One can thus say that he "takes on his father's form," or in English that he is the "spitting image" of his father. In this phrase, the Tibetan word *'dzin* also means "to apprehend," implying that the son acquires the characteristics of his father, just as the representation takes on the characteristics of what it represents.

2. *Gang* in Tibetan is an indefinite pronoun, but we use the definite pronoun "that" for ease of translation.

defective sense faculties. In the same way, when composite collections[3] appear as external objects, they do not have the power to produce anything because they are not substantially existent. Moreover, they arise internally due to distortions caused by mental predispositions to the view of self.[4] Thus, this example also has the power to eliminate inconsistencies. Then he summarizes: "**Thus, neither kind of** small or large **external object makes sense as** the percept condition or the perceptual object **of cognition.**" (2cd)

The Extensive Supplementary Explanation, [3] comprising such things as the opponent's rebuttal and refutation of that

According to some, such as Vāgbhaṭa,[5] even though minute particles do not appear with their own features, collectively existent substances must exist a little bit in each particle, like oil in sesame seeds; and so, "**some maintain that collected features are the cause.**" (3a). They exist: they produce or generate cognitions with their own representations.

This would make sense if there were appearances of the features of macro-objects. These characteristics would also be shared by fundamental particles. The opponent seeks to avoid the following problem: "Why is it that the features of fundamental particles are not accessible?" Since they are perceptible in some things,[6] how could they be completely inaccessible?

Therefore, although "**features of minute particles are not the object of cognition,**" (3cd) we do not commit the error of treating these features as the same. Earth's color is apparent, but "**things like solidity**" (3d)—although they are similar in being qualities of earth—are not seen because each sense faculty

---

3. Tib. *bsags pa'i 'dus pa.*

4. Predispositions to the view of self (*bdag lta'i bag chags*; Skt. *ātmadṛṣṭi-vāsanā*) are tendencies to perceive things as inherently possessing the characteristics imputed to them by thought.

5. Pha khol. See the discussion of this figure at the beginning of Vinītadeva's commentary on verse 3 (88 n. 36).

6. Geshe Yeshes Thabkhas (oral commentary) states that it refers to macro-objects composed of fundamental particles. Some aspects of things may be directly perceivable by one sense-cognition, but others will be inaccessible to that sense-cognition. A pot, for example, is a solid thing, but its solidity is not directly perceptible by sight. The earth element has such features as color, shape, and solidity, but only color and shape are directly perceived by the eye, while solidity is perceived by touch. He adds that it could also refer to the sense faculties: each has its own provenance, and so while the eye is perceiving color it does not perceive sounds or tastes, and so on.

has its particular capacity for ascertainment. And so it makes sense that their features also have a dual aspect.

So the opponent says, but this makes no sense. "**According to them, cognitions of things like pots and cups** (and pillars) **would be identical**"; (4ab) that is, when the features appear to the mind. Why? The mind constructs something that corresponds to a nonindependent object, but because the minute particles are indistinguishable, being identical in nature, diversity among cognitions makes no sense. Quantity would make no difference: because there would be no differences in nature, you could have awareness of pots of different sizes but no awareness of a cup.

Suppose someone were to maintain: "**they are distinguished by different features**" (4c)—distinctions in virtue of such differences as that between the base and the mouth of a pot. Such distinctions of shape [4] are features of divisible minute particles, but they cannot be posited for unchanging, self-existent substances such as those particles. This is because, being indistinguishable in dimension, they are alike in being as small as it is possible to be.[7] Since there would be no distinct parts of any material form, it would make no sense to distinguish between configurations. Therefore, in this context, distinctions between features are **not substantially real** (5b); they would only exist conventionally because it is possible to divide them into parts. For minute particles, this is impossible. "**The cognition that has the appearance of these** pots and cups **disappears when** each part of **particles disperse**" (5cd)—that is, the appearances of material things would cease.

Presentation of the Yogācāra Position

So, having refuted others and in order avoid undermining what is commonly acknowledged, we will now give our own account of the percept. "What is the percept?" It is defined as follows: it is nothing other than a self-presenting internal apprehension—an entity that is a cognitive object.

Suppose someone asks: "Because reflexive action is inconsistent, how could it appear?" The representation does not appear as it exists. For example, when an image of the moon appears in a mirror, spatiality also appears. The moon appears to be different from its action of reflecting. Although it is apprehended with an appearance of externality, the object (*don*) is that which exists internally. Thus, while it has a wide semantic range, in this context it is the percept condition.

---

7. This is based on Geluk doxography, according to which in the Sautrāntika system only the most minute particles are substantially real.

Why? As a result of familiarization with predispositions to linguistic expression,[8] [5] cognition is produced with its object—that is, with a representation of its object—within the framework of apprehender and apprehended. Furthermore, if there were no object, it would not arise. This is why it is said to be "its condition."

He now anticipates the following qualm: taking these two arguments in order, there is the error of inconsistency of reflexive action and the extremely absurd consequence of treating simultaneous conditions as causal, like the two horns of a cow.[9] Even though these two occur at the same time and have the same nature, it is possible for a thing to act on itself in some sense, like fire, but not without any distinctions being drawn. With respect to the first qualm, there is no problem because this can be understood on the basis of the explanation in terms of apprehender and apprehended. With regard to the second, because there is an invariable sequence of presence and absence, **"it is its condition because it is invariably concomitant."** (7a)

So having posited the *nominal* percept condition (*dmigs rkyen btags pa*)—that is, the apparent percept condition—we now present our main point. Through a previous moment of cognition, a capacity to generate an object is set in place in the mind that is called the fundamental consciousness. Because a subsequent object is put in place by a previous cognition that is the emplaced capacity to give rise to a representation of an object—**"it is sequential because of a transfer of capacity"** (7b)—the capacity is the percept condition of the cognition.[10] This is the *actual* percept condition.

---

8. Predispositions to linguistic expression (*mngon par brjod pa'i bag chags*; Skt. *abhilāpya-vāsanā*) are latent tendencies toward use of language deposited in the fundamental consciousness. They are discussed in *Establishment of Cognition-Only* (*Vijñaptimātratā-siddhi*): la Vallée Poussin (1929: 478–480). They are also examined in Gungtang's discussion of fundamental consciousness: Wilson (1984: 177–178; 387–394). According to the *Establishment of Cognition-Only*, this category comprises seeds that predispose a person to make differentiations regarding individual compounded phenomena. According to Jangchup Dzüntrül (Byang chub rdzu 'phrul (1985, vol. *cho* [205]: 221.3), this refers to "the fundamental consciousness that is infused with the predispositions of imputations" (*kun btags pa'i bag chags kyis bsgos pa kun gzhi rnam par shes pa*). These are latent tendencies toward future actions that are caused by one's own karmic actions. In Buddhist psychology, it is generally held that performance of a particular action or type of action predisposes an individual to continued performance of similar actions in the future. For more on the predispositions, see Rahula (1971: 74, 172), and Lamotte (1973: ch. I.2).

9. This refers to Vinītadeva's commentary (sDe dge p. 367), which points out that not all things that occur simultaneously are linked by causal relations. For example, cows generally have two horns that appear and grow simultaneously, but neither is the cause of the other.

10. English cannot reflect the way these pronouns are used here, and so we have opted for a natural reading.

Suppose someone argues as follows: "Since cognition arises from an external object and an eye just like a face in a mirror, and since on your view the percept would be merely internal, there would be nothing in front of you. In that case, how could cognition be produced?"

For you who assert the material nature of the simultaneously arising object and sensory faculties, the object must also be external matter. We, however, do not take the percept and the simultaneously arising sense faculties in this way. When one infers the nature of the cause from the effect, [6] while it is the specific capacity of the visual faculty in the mind, it is an entity that has ceased. Even though it has ceased, it can still be known to exist through such arguments as that establishing causal sequence. What goes for this goes for the sense faculties as well. The word "**and**" indicates that it does not just refer to capacity; it refers to both sense faculty and capacity. Although Vinītadeva explains capacity as "nothing but a cause," when applied to what follows this will raise some questions.

A challenge is anticipated: "Even though you assert that a sense faculty is something nonmaterial, since an unsupported capacity would not exist without a basis, its basis must be material." The account of the sensory capacities that are established as the support of cognition is **not contradictory** (8a) for us Proponents of Cognition Only. That is, because the capacity resides in cognition and because cognition arises from the capacity, unlike you we have no need to waste our time searching for anything external.

To summarize: **thus, the** (8b) cognitive representational **object and** the twofold **capacity**—the nature of the sensory faculties—**cause one another**; there is an autopoietic dynamic of arising and ceasing. Through this dynamic, this process has unfolded **from beginningless time**. (8bcd) Despite the fact that the opponents' arguments as presented earlier are rigorous, they are unable to undermine our position. According to others, the percept is the apprehended object; this is what we take to be the self of phenomena. This is what *Investigation of the Percept* [7] by our Philosopher, the great master Dignāga, has refuted. We have now completed the explanation of this extremely sublime root text of this philosophical system. This interpretation was written down with some trepidation as it came to his mind by the monk Könchok Denbe Drönme at the age of twenty-six in order to analyze this scripture a little so that doubts might be removed.

8

Ngawang Dendar's Commentary

PHILOSOPHY THROUGH DOXOGRAPHY

John Powers

Ngawang Dendar's Life and Times[1]

Ngawang Dendar (1759–1840),[2] also referred to as "Dendar Lharampa" (bsTan dar lha rams pa; Ch. 丹达拉然巴 Danda laranba), was born in Duomai (多麦), in the Alashan region (Tib. A lag sha; Ch. 阿拉善; Mon. Alašan ayimaɣ) of Inner Mongolia in Nianggawa (娘噶哇).[3] At a young age, he studied the various fields of knowledge. He traveled far from home, enduring hunger and cold and other difficulties to reach Lhasa, where he trained in the Gelukpa tradition. His institutional affiliation was Drepung Gomang.

Ngawang Dendar pursued the standard scholastic curriculum, which included study of sūtras, Madhyamaka philosophy, Perfection of Wisdom,

1. This biographical sketch is based on: (1) Töndor and Tenzin Chödrak (1993). The colophon indicates that it was composed by bShad sgra gung dBang phyug rgyal po. This collection contains biographies of about 700 Tibetan lamas up to the time of the 13th thirteenth Dalai Lama, arranged chronologically. (2) Nordrang Orgyen (2006); (3) Tashi Ngödrup (2008); and (4) Khotse Tsültrim (2006). The translation of these texts was a collaborative effort with Sonam Thakchöe.

2. These dates may be incorrect. Nordrang Orgyen (2006: 757) gives his birth date as 1751, the earth-rabbit year of the thirteenth sexagenary cycle. Khotse Tsültrim (2006: 659) gives the year as 1759. The colophon of Ngawang Dendar's last work, *Advice on Seven Topics on Mind Training: Short Path of Mahāyāna* (*bLo sbyong don bdun ma'i gtam theg mchog nye lam*; Ch. *Xiuxin qi yi chengyong yusheng chengjie jing* 修心七义常用语：胜乘捷径), indicates that it was composed in 1839 when he was eighty-two years old.

3. The Tibetan version of his biography refers to his birthplace as mDo smad yul gru chen mo'i bye brag.

the *Commentary on the Treasury of Abhidharma*, monastic discipline, and epistemology.

At the age of thirty, during the Great Aspiration Festival (sMon lam chen mo) in Lhasa, he underwent his final examinations. His biography reports that he fearlessly debated thousands of monks. His voice "bellowed like a lion's roar." As a result of his performance in oral debate, he was awarded the highest qualification in the Geluk system, *geshe lharampa*. His fame as a scholar grew, and he became known by the honorific epithet Dendar Lharampa.[4]

Ngawang Dendar received oral instructions from the leading scholars in Lhasa, including Longdol Lama Ngawang Losang (kLong rdol bla ma Ngag dbang blo bzang, 1719–1794) and Gachen Yeshe Gyeltsen (dKa' chen Ye shes rgyal mtshan, 1713–1793), the preceptor (*yongs 'dzin*) of the seventh Dalai Lama, Kelsang Gyatso (bsKal bzang rgya mtsho, 1708–1757). Ngawang Dendar's *Collected Works* reports that Gachen Yeshe Gyeltsen provided Dendar with many empowerments (*dbang*), oral scriptural transmissions (*lung*), and secret transmissions (*man ngag*).[5] Ngawang Dendar's main teacher for secular subjects was Longdol Lama, who instructed him in poetics and grammar and spelling.[6]

Ngawang Dendar gained renown as a debater and teacher. When he was thirty-one (in 1791), he was appointed abbot of Drepung Gomang College.[7] Following his tenure there, he returned to Mongolia and settled at Mipam Chöling (Mi pham chos gling) at Alasha Monastery (A lag sha'i g.Yon dgon). He concentrated on exposition, debate, and writing and reorganized the curriculum of the monastery based on these subjects. His erudition was described as unrivalled. He was particularly interested in poetics and examined the purported interruption of the instruction lineage of the Tibetan *Mirror of Poetry Treatise*.[8]

During his stay in Mongolia he had a life-altering experience. His elderly mother asked him to explain the verses of her daily prayer:

> I respectfully bow down to the lotus feet of Tārā,
> Who is worshipped with the crown jewels

4. *bsTan dar lha rams pa'i gsung 'bum*: 1; Khotse Tsültrim (2006: 659).

5. *bsTan dar lha rams pa'i gsung 'bum*: 1.

6. Nordrang Orgyen (2006: 757).

7. Khotse Tsültrim (2006: 659).

8. *Bod kyi snyan ngag gi bstan bcos me long*, the Tibetan translation of Dandin's *Kāvyādarśa*.

> Of 100 companion deities: Indra, Brahmā, the guru of gods, Ganeśa,
> Viṣṇu, Sūrya,[9] and so forth.[10]

Ngawang Dendar could not provide any more than a cursory response that it was "a prayer to Mother Tārā." His mother was unimpressed. She pointed out that he had attained the highest educational level in one of the greatest seats of learning in Tibet. Like a modern parent whose child has recently graduated from college, but who has difficulty explaining her subject, she questioned the quality of his education.

> Have you not completed the monastic education and received the *geshe lharampa* degree? Even our household officiant[11] can provide a full explanation of the meaning of this passage. Even I understand it![12]

His mother then offered a word-by-word exegesis of the prayer, which embarrassed the renowned scholar. His biography reports that he came to recognize the limitations of a purely academic approach to the Dharma.[13] Nevertheless, he later composed a treatise that explained its meaning in detail (*Ornamental Gem for the Crown Jewel of the Wise: Explanation of the "Crown Jewel of the Wise, Praise of Tārā"*),[14] which indicates that he did not turn away from scholarship altogether.

According to Mongolian oral tradition, he became an advanced meditator and developed miraculous abilities. Geshe Ngawang Wangyal, a Mongolian lama, recounted a story that once some of his fellow monks at Gomang suspected Dendar of having an affair with a woman. They secretly spied on his room and saw him smoking a pipe. He blew a cloud of smoke and then rested the pipe on it, and it remained suspended in the air. This convinced his observers that his conduct was blameless.

---

9. Padmo'i gnyen, "Friend of the Lotus," an epithet of Sūrya the sun god.

10. "*Legs bris dpal gyi bdag po gser gyi mngal // Lha yi bla ma glang gdong dpal gyi mgrin // Padmo'i gnyen sogs lha brgya'i gtsug rgyan gyis // Zhabs pad gus mchod sgrol ma'i zhabs la 'dud //*" (Khotse Tsültrim 2006: 660).

11. Tib. *'u tshang gi a mchod*. An *a mchod* is someone (lay or monastic) who performs ceremonies for the dead.

12. Khotse Tsültrim (2006: 660).

13. Khotse Tsültrim (2006: 660).

14. *sGrol bstod mkhas pa'i gtsug rgyan gyi rnam bshad mkhas pa'i gtsug nor gyi phra rgyan.*

At age fifty-one, Ngawang Dendar traveled to Labrang Tashikhyil. There he heard lectures on all three chapters of the *Mirror of Poetry* by Dorampa Lhashe (rDo rams pa Lha zhe, b. eighteenth century) at Belbung Monastery (dPal spungs) in Derge. He mastered the text and excelled in a written examination on the subject.[15]

Ngawang Dendar subsequently resided at Dome Kumbum Jambaling (mDo smad sKu 'bum 'Jams dpal gling) for a number of years.[16] After this, he traveled to Beijing, where he taught at the Yonghe Temple (Yung dgon; Ch. Yonghe gong 雍和宫). He lectured on various aspects of Buddhist doctrine and composed a treatise on the origins of the tea ceremony. He relied on a number of Chinese reference works for this purpose. He passed away in 1831 at the age of seventy-three.[17]

Ngawang Dendar's Literary Corpus

Ngawang Dendar's biography characterizes him as a hard worker and a stern teacher. It quotes his *Banquet of Worldly Ethics*[18] chastising his students:

> Half of your lives are spent sleeping. You try to devote the other half to eating and drinking. The rest of my disciples waste their time babbling about nothing. How wonderful! They are spoiled; how can they not be ashamed?

His written work, according to his biographers, included comparative analyses of treatises by past scholars in various fields, including poetry, literature, and philosophical scriptures. Ngawang Dendar also composed philosophical critiques, poetry, and treatises on grammar and literature. Most of his written works are extant. His biographers state that his compositions are generally concise and use fewer words than most such texts, but they are nonetheless replete with condensed meaning.

The lectures Ngawang Dendar gave to his students, his philosophical debates, and his composition of scholarly works are regarded as his main legacy. The list of his written works—thirty-seven entries in all—include treatises

15. *bsTan dar lha rams pa'i gsung 'bum*: 1; Khotse Tsültrim (2006: 660).

16. Khotse Tsültrim (2006: 660).

17. Nordrang Orgyen (2006: 757).

18. *bsLab bya'i mi chos dga' ston*; Ch. *Xuechu pian rendao xiyan*; 学处篇: 人道喜宴.

on philosophy, grammar, and spelling, explanations of ancient Tibetan terms, orthographies, and poetics. They were carved on wood blocks at Kumbum Monastery.[19]

Beautiful String of Pearls: A Commentary on Investigation of the Percept

As noted in the Introduction, Ngawang Dendar's commentary on *Investigation of the Percept* is a masterpiece of traditional scholarship. He provides detailed analyses of the text and a lucid interpretation that frames its philosophy as a form of representationalism consistent with Geluk doxographical understandings of the Sautrāntika school.

He introduces his commentary with a series of literary flourishes. The dedication verses use elements of the names of his teacher, Ngawang Losang (Ngag dbang blo bzang, 1719–1794), and Tsongkhapa in clever plays on words. He then explains the title: his work "strings together pearls of scripture" with a "thread of reason," and the result will "adorn the necks" of students who study it.

The commentary is divided into two parts, and these are further subdivided with subheadings in the standard Tibetan scholastic *sa bcad* (sections or subject headings) format. The first section situates *Investigation of the Percept* within the Gelukpa scholastic framework, particularly that of the Gomang tradition, which follows the tenet presentation of the second Jamyang Sheba—Könchok Jikme Wangbo—in his magnum opus, *Precious Garland of Tenet Systems.*[20] The second part examines the text line by line and gives a detailed analysis that emphasizes Dendar's understanding of its philosophy as a sophisticated representationalism.

The Gelukpa Doxographical System and Investigation of the Percept

According to Gelukpa doxography, Buddhist thought can be divided into four "tenet systems" (*grub mtha'*; Skt. *siddhānta;* literally "established conclusions"), two of which—Vaibhāṣika (Great Exposition School) and Sautrāntika (Sūtra School)—are classified as "Hīnayāna," while the other two—Cittamātra (Mind

19. *bsTan dar lha rams pa'i gsung 'bum:* i.

20. *Grub pa'i mtha'i rnam par bzhag pa rin po che'i phreng ba.*

Only; alternatively Yogācāra, "Yogic Practice") and Madhyamaka (Middle Way)—belong to Mahāyāna. These are further subdivided according to doctrines imputed to particular figures or lineages by Gelukpa exegetes.

The two Hīnayāna systems valorize the path of individual liberation and do not accept the bodhisattva ideal of pursuing buddhahood in order to liberate all sentient beings as a realistic goal for all practitioners. The Vaibhāṣikas base their philosophy on the *Great Exposition Treatise*[21] and propound a realist philosophy. They assert the real existence of fundamental particles and regard them as the building blocks of macroscopic phenomena. Such particles are not further divisible, and an individual fundamental particle lacks mass. When, however, they are grouped together, they become material, and further aggregation constitutes the objects of the world. There are various formulations of atomism, but a standard one holds that when seven fundamental particles group together in an equidistant arrangement, this is the smallest bit of matter.[22] Fundamental particles may be bits of matter, but they may also be qualities such as color and attributes such as solidity. Dendar lists eight substances (*rdzas*; Skt. *dravya*) of fundamental particles: earth, water, fire, air, form, smell, taste, and tactility. These are permanent entities and survive the cataclysm at the end of an eon. After an intermediate period, these indestructible entities again begin to recombine and form the phenomena of the universe.[23]

The Sautrāntikas are representationalists: they accept the existence of fundamental particles but assert that cognition has no direct access to them or to any external objects. Rather, the objects of perception, which are aggregations of these particles, transmit a representation (*rnam pa gtod pa*) that is apprehended by the senses or interpreted by the mind. This is the position

---

21. Skt. *Mahāvibhāṣa-śāstra*. This is an influential Abhidharma text, probably composed around 150 CE. The Chinese canon has three texts of this title: (1) *Abhidharma-mahāvibhāṣā-śāstra* (*Apidamo da piposha lun* 阿毘達磨大毘婆沙論, 200 fascicles: T1545); (2) *Abhidharma-vibhāṣā-śāstra* (*Apitan piposha lun* 阿毘曇毘婆沙論 (T 1546), translated by a team that included Buddhavarman 浮陀跋摩 and Daotai 道泰 in 437–443); and (3) *Vibhāṣā-śāstra* (*Piposha lun* 鞞婆沙論 (T 1547), translated by Saṅghabhadra 僧伽跋澄 in 383). The first of these (extant only in Chinese) is the text considered by the Gelukpas to be the foundation of the Vaibhāṣika system. It is believed to have been composed by 500 arhats and later compiled by Katyāyāniputra (Jiaduoyannizi 迦多衍尼子), and it was translated into Chinese by Xuanzang between 656 and 659. All three texts claim to be commentaries on the *Treatise on the Arising of Wisdom* (Skt. *Jñāna-prasthāna-śāstra*; Ch. *Apidamo fazhi lun* 阿毘達磨發智論: T 1544; or *Treatise on the Eight Aggregates*: Skt. *Aṣṭaskandha-śāstra*; Ch. *Ba jiandu lun* (八犍度論: T 1543).

22. Different Buddhist exegetes posit differing numbers of particles. This follows Dendar's discussion (*Beautiful String of Pearls*: 134). He cites Vasubandhu's *Treasury of Abhidharma*.

23. Ngawang Dendar, *Beautiful String of Pearls*: 134.

Dendar attributes to Dignāga, and the bulk of his analysis fleshes out this initial understanding.

> Other than by way of subjective cognition becoming like its object, there is absolutely no way for cognition to apprehend an object. For example, when a crystal is placed on a blue cloth, all facets of the crystal turn blue. In the same way, when a visual cognition apprehending blue sees blue, the color blue is transferred to the visual perspective, and so the subjective visual cognition becomes just like the blue object. The visual cognition apprehending blue is referred to as "a visual cognition that arises as a representation of blue." This is the criterion for the direct apprehension of blue (142).

The two Mahāyāna tenet systems uphold the bodhisattva ideal and apply the critique of emptiness to the doctrines of their Hīnayāna and non-Buddhist rivals. The Cittamātra system denies the real existence of either fundamental particles or macro-objects and asserts that all phenomena are products of mind. A core aspect of this system is the doctrine of "fundamental consciousness" as the most basic level of mind. It is composed of the "seeds" (*sa bon*; Skt. *bīja*) of past volitional actions, which leave predispositions toward future actions of concordant type. The fundamental consciousness at any given time is the sum total of these seeds, and the objects of cognition are derived from the maturation of "stable predispositions" (*bag chags brtan*) that appear as external but are in reality solely aspects of mind.

The Madhyamaka school, characterized by the Gelukpas as the highest Mahāyāna system, subjects the tenets of all lesser schools to critique in terms of emptiness. All phenomena are empty of intrinsic nature (*rang bzhin*; Skt. *svabhāva*), and all philosophical systems ultimately fail because of basic unacknowledged contradictions in their tenets. Madhyamaka is further subdivided into (1) the Svātantrika (Autonomy) school, which according to the Gelukpas is so-named because its proponents employ autonomous syllogisms in their refutations of opponents; and (2) the highest philosophical tradition, the Prāsaṅgika (Consequence) school, which holds no tenets of its own and uses *reductio ad absurdum* (*thal 'gyur*; Skt. *prasaṅga*) arguments to demonstrate the flaws in opponents' systems.

In Geluk presentations of tenets, each of these schools is described as having a standard list of philosophical positions accepted by its members, all of whom are aware of their affiliations and self-consciously attempt to remain consistent within the school's conceptual boundaries. Moreover, these systems each have a founder, who the Buddha prophesied would become the "opener of the chariot way" of his tradition. The analogy is that the Buddha taught four distinct systems, but following his death disciples misrepresented his ideas and the tenets became confused, like a chariot track that is overgrown with vegetation. At preordained times, great scholars appeared in the world, each with a specific mission to clear away wrong views and to correctly present each of these tenet systems as intended by the Buddha. For the Sautrāntika school, this figure was Dignāga.

Although Gelukpa doxography neatly characterizes each of these schools and presents a coherent vision of their philosophical commitments, it is replete with conceptual problems. For example, the "opener of the chariot way" of Cittamātra, Asaṅga, spent his life working within the doctrinal constraints of Mind Only, but he was really a third-level bodhisattva. According to Geluk orthodoxy this state can only be attained by someone who has directly realized the Madhyamaka view of emptiness. So, on this account, Asaṅga wrote voluminously, laying out a system to which he did not himself adhere. Dignāga, the "opener of the chariot way" of one of the two main "Hīnayāna" systems, belonged to a Mahāyāna lineage, the Yogācāra, but according to Geluk doxography followed the tenets of Sautrāntika in his writings.

Further issues arise when we consider what we can say with confidence about Sautrāntika and its purported members. Contemporary nontraditional scholars generally agree that little is known with any certainty about Sautrāntika. Their opponents lumped philosophers together as members of this tradition mainly on the basis of what they rejected. They are primarily distinguished by their opposition to key tenets of orthodox Sarvāstivāda. The earliest attested use of the term "Sautrāntika" is probably in Vasubandhu's commentary on the *Treasury of Abhidharma*, where he identifies some of the positions he argues against as Sarvāstivāda and his own perspective as Sautrāntika. But these are mainly refutations rather than presentations of a coherent system of tenets. According to Charles Hallisey, Sautrāntikas

> are best understood as thinkers who held a variety of doctrinal positions. They were grouped together by opponents more for their common rejection of orthodox Sarvāstivādin thought and texts than for any consistent doctrinal position or shared textual basis of their own . . . the term creates an image of commonality among thinkers and doctrinal positions on the basis of what they are not and what they reject rather on the basis of any consistently shared characteristics among these thinkers and doctrinal positions. In both cases, the name also creates the image of a community where there probably was none.[24]

24. Hallisey (2007: 676).

The Gelukpas, however, attribute a coherent set of philosophical commitments to them and identify a group of people as members, including Dignāga and Dharmakīrti. According to Jamyang Sheba, Sautrāntikas are "the Sūtra School" because they rely on the Buddha's words rather than on philosophical treatises (*bstan bcos*; Skt. *śāstra*).[25] They are divided into two groups: (1) those who follow scripture (*lung gi rjes su 'brang pa'i mdo sde pa*); and (2) those who follow reasoning (*rig pa'i rjes su 'brang pa'i mdo sde pa*). This raises another problem: some members of a school characterized as "followers of scripture" are categorized as followers of reasoning *instead of scripture*. This issue is not discussed by any Geluk exegete of whom I am aware.

Dignāga and Dharmakīrti are the main examples of followers of reasoning. Dignāga's core text is *Compendium of Epistemology* and Dharmakīrti's are the *Seven Treatises on Epistemology*.[26] In their presentation of the two truths, they characterize ultimate truths (*don dam bden pa*; Skt. *paramārtha-satya*) as objects that appear to an ultimate awareness—that is, one that is "not mistaken with regard to its appearing object."[27] Conventional truths (*kun rdzob bden pa*; Skt. *saṃvṛti-satya*) are merely valid conventionally: they are able to perform functions (*don byed nus pa*; Skt. *artha-kriyā-śakti*), and so they are true on the conventional level.

The Sautrāntikas disagree with the Vaibhāṣikas in not positing substantially real entities, and they differ from Cittamātra in not discussing the fundamental consciousness. They also accept the doctrine of momentariness: each phenomenon comes into being, abides, and disintegrates in a single moment, giving rise to a successive moment concordant with itself. These three factors occur simultaneously. According to Ngawang Belden's (Ngag dbang dpal ldan, b. 1797) *Annotations for the Great Exposition of Tenets* (*Grub mtha' chen mo'i mchan 'grel*), "things made from the collection and aggregation of causes and conditions are momentary because they last only for the moment of production."[28]

---

25. Hopkins (2003: 245).

26. Tshad ma sde bdun. These are: *Commentary on the Compendium of Epistemology* (*Pramāṇa-vārttika*; Tib. *Tshad ma rnam 'grel*); *Ascertainment of the Instruments of Reasoning* (*Pramāṇa-viniścaya*; Tib. *Tshad ma rnam nges*); *Drop of Reasoning* (*Nyāya-bindu*; Tib. *Rigs thigs*); *Drop of Logic* (*Hetu-bindu*; Tib. *gTan tshigs thigs pa*); *Investigation of Relations* (*Sambandha-parīkṣā*; Tib. *'Brel ba brtag pa*); *Reasoning for Debate* (*Vāda-nyāya*; Tib. *rTsod pa'i rigs pa*); and *Proof of Other Continuums* (*Saṃtānāntara-siddhi*; Tib. *rGyud gzhan grub pa*).

27. Hopkins (2003: 247).

28. Hopkins (2003: 265).

Sautrāntikas on Perception

Dendar characterizes the Sautrāntika position as quasi-realist: they assert that the percept of sensory cognitions is an external object, but what is actually apprehended is a representation of it. The thing itself, though real, is necessarily inaccessible because the mind only receives impressions caused by sense data. Neither individual fundamental particles nor collections of them can be apprehended directly. We do not perceive fundamental particles; we perceive macroscopic objects, not their tiny constituent parts that are the cause of perception. And collections are merely conventionally real and so cannot be causal. Dendar summarizes Dignāga's position as follows: "a cognition is that which ascertains the form of an object, because it has the representation of that object (149)." According to Geshe Gendün Lodrö's (dGe bshes dGe 'dun blo gros) explanation of the Sautrāntika position:

> When an eye consciousness looks at a table in front of itself, that table is seen by perceiving an aspect similar to the table. This is not called "indirect," but it is perception by way of an image.... If one did not see the object by way of an aspect, then either one would not see it at all, or the consciousness would have to actually contact the object ... and then there would be no explanation for why we do not see through walls and so forth.[29]

Dendar compares the way perception and recognition operate to the experience of seeing a son who is the "spitting image" of his father when he was young (152). One is seeing the son, but in a sense the father appears. The son is not the cause of the father-perception, nor is the father the cause. The father is not actually apprehended; rather, one has a perception, caused by a mental event prompted by past visual association with the father. What one sees is not exactly the son but is also not the father either. Our cognitions of other things in the world are like this: there is a bare perception of a quality like blue, which is then overlaid with conceptual thoughts and interpretations. These latter events, not their representational contents, are the constituents of the worlds of individual sentient beings.

Dendar characterizes Dignaga's own position as idealist. In Gelukpa doxographical terms, this position appears to elide the distinction between the Sautrāntika and Cittamātra systems. The Sautrāntika system asserts the real

---

29. Hopkins (2003: 276).

existence of external objects, while the Cittamātra does not. It may be that Dendar sees the position of the first five verses as according with Sautrāntika and that he believes that in presenting his own view Dignāga adopts a Cittamātra perspective. He does not explicitly state this belief, however.

Dendar first points out that many examples of perceptions arise in the absence of external objects, for example, dream images. They are perceived as real and prompt emotional—and sometimes physical—reactions, even though they are purely internal. He then states that for all cognitions, the appearance and the cognition are simultaneous. The question arises: how then can there be causality? The answer occupies most of the rest of the commentary and explores some of Dignaga's most interesting philosophical moves.

Dendar points out that there is sequence in that first blue appears and then there is apprehension of blue. The first moment is the arising, and although the blue thing that was perceived, being momentary, is no longer present when it is perceived, the fact that there is sequence is sufficient to maintain causality. Moreover, this sequence is invariable: when the thing appears, a cognition of it is produced. They are not merely incidentally co-extensive, like the two horns of a cow. A cow's horns appear together, but neither is the cause of the other. Dendar notes that Vasubandhu discusses this idea in relation to the notion of "simultaneous cause" (*lhan cig 'byung ba'i rgyu;* Skt. *sahabhū-hetu*). He adds that the Abhidharma thinkers recognize that cause and effect can be simultaneous and that this does not necessarily entail that they are substantially different. He lauds this explanation as an elegant one that accords with the Cittamātra position that perception and its cause are both internal (154–155).

Now Dendar explains how causality works within this idealist framework. The appearance of something like blue within a previous cognition "transfers a capacity" to be perceived as it is to a subsequent sensory cognition with a representation of blue. Because they occur sequentially, causality is said to occur even though when the cognition arises the previous moment of blue is no longer present.

> Consider the capacity that is established in cognition when the immediately preceding condition of the sense cognition that appears as blue ceases. This acts sequentially as the percept condition of the subsequent sensory cognition, because it is the condition that transfers the representation of blue to its own effect—namely the subsequent sensory cognition that appears blue. It is generally accepted that "the percept condition transfers the capacity." I think, however, that we should say that "the percept condition transfers the representation (163)."

Dendar now considers an objection: if one asserts that cognition and its object both exist internally, then how can one account for the fact that sensory perceptions require things like eyes? A blind person has no visual perceptions, and so, in the absence of physical sense organs, perception should be impossible. Dendar answers by pointing out that in Buddhist epistemology it is not the gross matter of the eye, for example, that makes perception possible. Rather, it is the "eye sense faculty" (*mig gi dbang po*; Skt. *cakṣur-indriya*), a form of subtle matter that empowers the eye to do its work. When a person dies, the eye no longer functions, even though its gross matter is unchanged from one moment to the next. So Buddhists posited a type of subtle capacity that is necessary for operation of the senses but cannot be perceived by them. Dignāga describes the sense faculty as "a co-operating sense capacity" (*lhan cig byed dbang nus pa*). (7cd)

Unlike their realist Buddhist opponents, the Sautrāntikas do not characterize the sense capacities as material form. So sense capacities, like the rest of our cognitive apparatus, are internal phenomena. Dendar points out that the Sautrāntikas posit the sense faculties as subtle material form, while the Cittamātras claim that they are located in cognition. In either case, he asserts, the effect would be the same.

> Both the visual cognition that has the representation of an object and the capacity that is the visual sensory faculty are mutually causal. If one attempts to track down its origin, one will realize that it has proceeded since beginningless time (165).

If one maintains a consistently idealist position, there is no contradiction in a cognition arising on the basis of an internal form with the aid of a sense capacity. The conclusion is that this is in fact the way perception operates, and the percept—the focus of this treatise—is not an external object, but rather something that merely appears as such. The capacity and the cognition set in motion a causal series that leads to production of subsequent moments of concordant type, which in turn continue the sequence into the future. This process has been going on since beginningless time in a manner that Gungtang Könchok Denbe Drönme characterizes as an "autopoietic dynamic" (*res mos kyi tshul du skye 'gag dus mnyam pa'i 'brel ba*; see p. 117). Everything required for this process to occur and continue is accounted for in this idealist system.

> Sometimes cognition arises as the representation of the object from the maturation of the capacity—which consists of predispositions in the

same continuum—and sometimes the capacity arises from a cognition that has the representation of the object (165).

There is no need to search for anything external. The capacity is neither substantially identical to nor different from the cognition that has it. In terms of how cognition functions, one can choose either option. Dendar concludes that Dignāga has shown that the percept condition and the perceiver can be both simultaneous and sequential without the need to posit external objects. This presentation satisfies the requirements of the realist position as well, but in the end Dendar clearly reads Dignāga as presenting an idealist analysis.

9

Beautiful String of Pearls

A COMMENTARY ON *INVESTIGATION OF THE PERCEPT* (*dMigs pa brtag pa'i 'grel pa mu tig 'phreng mdzes*)

Ngag dbang bstan dar

TRANSLATED BY DOUGLAS Duckworth, Malcolm David Eckel, Jay Garfield, John Powers, and Sonam Thakchöe

[216] I am mindful of the supreme teacher (Ngag dbang blo bzang), whose eloquent speech (*ngag*)

> Generously bestows the supreme understanding (*blo gros mchog*) of the
> Master's (*Thub dbang*, i.e., Buddha's) teachings
> And who brings good (*bzang*) fortune to everyone.[1]
> May his infinite, sublime glory sustain us!
> [218] Homage to the master Ratnasambhava,[2]
> Born from the bountiful cloud that is the two accumulations,[3]
> Imbued with an array of profound qualities of wisdom and love,

---

1. Ngawang Dendar is obliquely referring to his teacher, Ngawang Losang (Ngag dbang blo bzang, 1719–1794). In the Tibetan text, the components of his name are highlighted by small circles underneath each part of the name.

2. In Mahāyāna meditation theory, Ratnasambhava (Rin chen 'byung gnas) is associated with destruction of pride, and this is presumably why he is invoked in the dedicatory verses.

3. The two accumulations (*tshogs gnyis*; Skt. *saṃbhāra-dvaya*) are: (1) the accumulation of merit (*bsod nams gyi tshogs*; Skt. *puṇya saṃbhāra*); and (2) the accumulation of wisdom (*ye shes gyi tshogs*; Skt. *jñāna-saṃbhāra*).

Who showers a soft, nourishing rain of thousands of auspicious texts.
I praise both Dignāga and Dharmakīrti, the sun and the moon,
Who dispel the darkness of misconceptions with rays of reason
And who limn the vast expanse of the three domains of knowledge,
Traversing the celestial course of wisdom and analysis.
I bow to the second conqueror, Losang Drakpa (bLo bzang grags pa),
Who has transcended this existence.
Through his excellent (*bzang*) understanding (*blo gros*) of the profound doctrines of the sūtras and tantras,

Which exceeds (*'gongs pa*) the scope of ordinary scholars,
He is renowned (*grags snyan*) as the great elucidator.[4]
I joyfully explain *Investigation of the Percept*
Primarily in order to facilitate my own understanding,
But also in order to provide an easy introduction to the literature of the noble land of India for a few bright students;
I here condense other commentaries.
Therefore, I string these pearls of scripture
On this thread of reason,
And offer it as an ornament to grace the necks of those deserving students
Who love epistemology.

Section One: Preliminary Remarks

This commentary on the epistemological treatise *Investigation of the Percept* comprises two sections: (1) preliminary remarks; and (2) the meaning of the text.

Preliminary Remarks

The Indian title is *Ālambana-ṭīkā*, and the Tibetan name is *dMigs pa brtag pa*. It begins: "Homage to all buddhas and bodhisattvas!"

4. As in the above verse, Ngawang Dendar uses elements of the name of Tsongkhapa Losang Drakpa (Tsong kha pa bLo bzang grags pa). The syllables are in the proper order in Tibetan, an order that cannot be replicated in English.

The Meaning of the Text

[219] This section has two parts: (1) a general explanation of the four principles of the text beginning with the purpose; and (2) the actual explanation of the text.

General Explanation of the Four Principles of the Text Beginning with the Purpose.

If a treatise has a purpose, then intelligent people will engage with it; but if not, then they will not do so. This is why the purpose is stated.[5] Moreover, given that it has a purpose, it makes no sense for a treatise to lack a subject matter. Therefore, one should explain the subject matter before the purpose. The purpose has to be established on the basis of the treatise; therefore, there is a connection between the purpose and the treatise.

The Actual Explanation of the Text

This section has two parts: (1) an overview; and (2) the meaning of the parts.

OVERVIEW

The overview has three parts: (1) how external objects exist; (2) how they appear to the mind; and (3) how the percept condition functions.

How External Objects Exist—From the perspective of those who maintain that there are external objects, "external objects" are things that exist without depending on an internal cognition. And so their mode of existence is different from that of the environment and its inhabitants that do depend on internal cognition; they maintain that these are not substantially cognitive. Furthermore, they maintain that in the end one arrives at the fundamental particles that constitute external macro-objects;[6] so these "fundamental particles" are the fundamental units of all material form[7] and are not conceptually divisible into parts. Although the mind attributes many parts to them such as "an eastern part and a western part," these are not aspects of their nature. Because these are not bisected or split into parts, the Śrāvakas assert that they

---

5. This echoes the introduction to Vinītadeva's commentary: 78–79.

6. Tib. *phyi don rags pa.*

7. Tib. *gzugs*; Skt. *rūpa.*

are partless. *Ornament for Seven Epistemological Texts That Dispels Darkness in the Mind* states:

> This is their nature. The meaning of "partless" is that they do not have multiple substantially distinct eastern or western parts that are different from themselves. However, in general, [220] being "partless" does not mean lacking eastern and western sides. While every fundamental particle is substantially different from the fundamental particles to the east and west of it, those other ones are not part of it. Therefore, even though it has an eastern side, this does not entail that it has spatial dimension. In the same way, it does not follow from the fact that every shortest moment has a predecessor and a successor that it has temporal dimension as part of its nature. This is what it means to be partless. In general, having a predecessor and a successor does not entail having temporal dimension. Otherwise, a shortest moment would be incapable of effective action and could not be a cause.[8]

Thus, regarding the way in which fundamental particles arise, the *Treasury of Abhidharma* similarly states: "Apart from sound, fundamental particles have eight substances." In the Desire Realm,[9] as soon as a material form arises, the eight substances—the particles of the four elements and those of material form, odor, taste, and texture—necessarily arise simultaneously with it.[10] In this way, a particle of the eightfold substance is designated as an aggregated particle (*bsags rdul*), and its parts are designated as substantial particles (*rdzas rdul*); they are both equally fundamental particles.

According to Pūrṇavardhana: "There are two kinds of fundamental particles: substantial fundamental particles and aggregated fundamental

8. Kedrup (mKhas grub dGe legs dpal bzang, 1385–1438), *Ornament for Seven Epistemological Texts That Dispels Darkness in the Mind* (*Tshad ma sde bdun gyi rgyan yid kyi mun sel*, a study of seven treatises attributed to Dharmakīrti): 48b.

9. This is one of the three realms of existence according to traditional Buddhist cosmology. It is called the "Desire Realm" ('Dod khams; Skt. Kāma-dhātu) because the dominant affliction of its inhabitants is desire. The other two realms are the Form Realm (gZugs khams; Skt. Rūpa-dhātu) and the Formless Realm (gZugs med khams; Skt. Ārūpya-dhātu).

10. Vasubandhu, *Treasury of Abhidharma*, 2.22ab (Wogihara 1932–1936 II: 700): "*kāme 'ṣṭadravyako śabdaḥ paramāṇur anindriyaḥ*." "In the Desire Realm, a soundless fundamental particle that is not accessible to the other sense consists of eight substances." The *Commentary on the Abhidharma* explains: "Here 'particle' means the most subtle combination (*saṃghāta*) of material form." The eight substances are the gross elements, plus material form, smell, taste, and tangibility (see Eckel 2008: 249).

particles."[11] According to some others, this does not make sense because an aggregated fundamental particle would have to be larger than a substantial particle. This follows because an aggregated particle is constituted by combining eight substantial particles. But this does *not* follow. For example, were that the case, when one pours water on a pile of sand, the volume of sand and the volume of water would be doubled; they are combined in the same space, but that pile of sand does not grow any larger.

Suppose someone replies: "It would absurdly follow that earth particles[12] [221] are nonobstructive because they do not exclude water particles from their own location." This is not a problem. You would have to accept that the meaning of some particles excluding others in a location is excluding particles of the same type, not particles of a different type. This is because you would have to accept that odor particles and particles of material form exist in the same place. Although this is refuted in the *Ornament for the Commentary on the Treasury of Abhidharma*,[13] I explain it in order to develop the minds of beginners. A smallest particle and a fundamental particle are not the same. As the *Treasury of Abhidharma* states: "A moment of a smallest particle is like a fundamental particle. . . ."[14] A particle is composed of seven smallest particles, and so it is a little larger than a fundamental particle.

However, some others say: "It doesn't make sense for Śrāvakas to maintain that there are fundamental particles because the *Commentary on the Four Hundred*[15] states: "It makes no sense for our schools to accept substantial

---

11. Pūrṇavardhana (Gang spel, *c.* 700–800), *Supplement on the Features of the Commentary on the Treasury of Abhidharma* (*Chos mngon pa mdzod kyi 'grel bshad mtshan nyid kyi rjes su 'brang ba*; Skt. *Abhidharmakośa-ṭīkā-lakṣaṇa-sariṇī*): 131a: "*rdul phra rab ni rnam pa gnyis te / rdzas kyi rdul phra rab dang / bsags pa'i rdul phra rab po.*"

12. Tib. *sa rdul.*

13. Chim Jambeyang (mChims 'Jam pa'i dbyangs, thirteenth century), *Ornament for the Treasury of Abhidharma* (*mDzod 'grel mngon pa'i rgyan*; Skt. *Abhidharmakośālaṃkāra*, a commentary on the *Verses of the Treasury of Abhidharma*).

14. Vasubandhu, *Treasury of the Abhidharma* 3.85bcd: "*paramāṇvakṣarakṣaṇāḥ / rūpanāmādhvaparyantāḥ paramāṇur aṇus tathā.*" "A fundamental particle, a syllable (*akṣara*), and a moment (*kṣaṇa*) are the smallest units (lit. limit) of matter, language, and time. A *paramāṇu* is like an *aṇu*." In the commentary, Vasubandhu ascribes this position to the Ābhidharmikas (Vaibhāṣikas). He explains that seven *paramāṇus* equal one *aṇu*. La Vallée Poussin (1971: 177) has a note identifying parallel passages in Buddhist and Jain literature.

15. Candrakīrti, *Commentary on the Four Hundred* (*Catuḥśataka-ṭīkā*; Tib. *dBu ma bzhi brgya pa'i ṭīka*): 154ab: "*de'i phyir ji ltar bye brag pa rnams kyi ltar bde bar gshegs pa rnams la rdzas kyi rdul phra rab ces bya ba yod pa ma yin no / de'i phyir de bzhin gshegs pa rnams nam yang rdul phra rab rtag pa nyid ston par mi mdzad de / rang nyid kyis de ltar ma gzigs pa'i phyir ro.*"

fundamental particles as the Vaiśeṣikas do."[16] But this does not follow. The Vaiśeṣikas accept that there is a distinct, individual, substantial particle for each of the eight substances, such as an isolated fire particle that does not depend at all on the other three elements, or an eightfold particle that does not depend at all on a composite[17] of the eight substances. Moreover, they assert that these particles are permanent. They assert that following the end of an eon, after all macro-objects have disintegrated, there remain only isolated substantial particles, from which all macro-objects subsequently develop.

Although the Śrāvaka schools do not maintain that there are substantial particles that do not depend on aggregations of the eight substances, [222] they do maintain that there is a separate substantial particle that exists in combination with the eight substances and is a disconnected fundamental particle.[18] Not only does the scholar Bhāviveka accept fundamental particles; he also clearly states that fundamental particles are partless.[19] In the *Great Exposition of the Stages of the Path*, in the context of the explanation of this scholar's position, it states: "Since it appears that he accepts that there are minute particles,[20] he must accept that these partless minute particles are the percept condition."[21]

---

16. Gyeltsap, *Good Explanation of the Four Hundred Commentary* (*bZhi brgya pa'i rnam bshad legs bshad snying po*, a commentary on Āryadeva's *Four Hundred*): 104b): "*gal te me'i rdzas kyi rdul phra rab la 'byung ba gsum med pas bud shing med par yang me yod do zhe na / gal te me'i rdul phra rab la bud shing med na des na shing med pa'i me yod do ste yod pas rgyu med pa'i me yod par thal bar 'gyur bas bye brag pa ltar rdzas kyi rdul phran khas blangs par mi bya'o.*"

17. Tib. *tshogs pa.*

18. Tib. *zla med kyi rdul phra rab.*

19. In Bhāviveka's reckoning, each particle is "composed of the eight substances (*rdzas*; Skt. *dravya*)—earth, water, fire, air, form, smell, taste, and tactility—none of which have characteristics (*mtshan nyid 'ba' zhig*) or functions (*las 'ba' zhig pa*) that show their individuality to be intrinsically real and [specific] functional." See Bhāviveka's *Blaze of Reasoning: A Commentary on the Verses on the Heart of Middle Way* (*Madhyamaka-hṛdaya-vṛtti-tarkajvālā*), dBu ma vol. *dza*, 62a: "*gang gi phyir de dag gi rdul phra rab kyang 'dus pa'i ngo bo nyid de / sa dang chu dang me dang rlung dang gzugs dang dri dang ro dang reg pa zhes bya ba rdzas brgyad 'dus pa yin pas de'i phyir gang gis so so la ngo bo nyid dang las rnam par gzhag par bya ba'i mtshan nyid 'ba' zhig pa ni gang la ci yang med la / las 'ba' zhig pa yang gang la ci yang med do.*" For more on this argument, see Bhāviveka's *Verses on the Heart of the Middle Way* (*Madhyamaka-hṛdaya-kārikā*), III.248–250), dBu ma *dza*, 13a *and Blaze of Reasoning*, III.248–250; dBu ma *dza*: 119a.

20. Tib. *rdul phra ba.*

21. Tsongkhapa, *Great Exposition of the Stages of the Path* (*Lam rim chen mo*: 401b): "*rdul phra rab bsags pa'i re re nas dbang shes kyi rgyu dang de yang rdzas yod du bzhed pa dang rdul phra ba'i yang mthar thug par yang bzhed par snang bas rdul cha med dmigs rkyen du bzhed do.*"

At this point, one might wonder: "Does this acceptance of true existence follow from the scholar Bhāviveka's acceptance of partless entities? This is entailed by the statement in the *Great Commentary on the Wheel of Time, the Light of Reality*: "Any proponent of a philosophical system, however advanced, that posits partless entities must maintain their true existence."[22]

But this does *not* follow. This scholar accepts that there are partite fundamental particles on the grounds that they have four characteristics—such as arising—that are part of their very nature. Since a fundamental particle has no parts into which it could be divided, a minute particle is said to be partless. For this reason, this scholar would not accept that the partlessness of fundamental particles entails the partlessness of minute particles. On the contrary, while you might say that, he accepts the converse entailment.

This is how fundamental particles form macro-objects: because fundamental particles and aggregated particles do not differ in size, when seven aggregated particles—not seven distinct substantial particles—coalesce, a macro-object starts to form. Moreover, [223] the increase in size is proportional to the number of fundamental particles of the four elements that aggregate; but there is no increase in size in an aggregation of fundamental particles of smell and taste. For instance, no matter how many sound particles aggregate, they are still not apparent to visual cognition. Regarding the reason why sound particles do not appear in this way, someone might ask: "Even when many minute sound particles aggregate, nothing unifies them into a single entity. Thus, it is impossible for them to form a pile."

Some others say that when sound particles coalesce, since the four elements are weak and the sound particle is the principal one, it is not visible. If one were to say this, then one would have to accept that things like the sound of a conch are visible forms that are macro-objects.

Sautrāntika-Cittamātras assert that because neither macro-objects nor continuua substantially exist, neither are entities. Sautrāntikas assert that to be a macro-object or a continuum entails being substantially real and an entity. Thus, they seem to assert that to be a material macro-object is to be

---

22. Kedrup, *Clarification of the True Nature of the Great Commentary on the Wheel of Time* (*Dus 'khor 'grel chen de nyid snang ba*; full title: *dPal dus kyi 'khor lo'i 'grel chen dri ma med pa'i 'od kyi rgya cher bshad pa de kho na nyid snang bar byed pa*, a commentary on the "Lokadhātu-paṭala" chapter of the *Vimalaprabhā* commentary on the *Kālacakra-tantra*). The passage appears in a discussion of the views of Buddhist tenet systems according to Geluk doxography: "[282b] *grub mtha' smra ba gong 'og su'i lugs la yang cha med kyi dngos por 'dod phyin chad de bden dngos su 'dod pa yin la / 'dir ni skye 'jig thams cad bden med du bzhed par sngar yang bsgrubs shing / lta ba'i mdor bsdus* [283a] *la sogs par yang bsgrub par 'gyur ba'i phyir dngos po cha med lugs 'dir khas len pa'i gnas mad do.*" Our thanks to Paul Hackett, who located this passage and provided help throughout the project.

permanent. This is the argument: suppose there are material forms. It would absurdly follow that they are permanent macro-objects because they would have the property of being macroscopic. This can be proven through an exercise of the Epistemologists' reasoning.

If they could not prove this, then how could they demonstrate that a specific instance of a pot is permanent? In this context, some critical thinkers argue as follows: Consider a pot. It would be permanent as the negation of what it is not. So it would have the property of being the negation of what it is not. Some people say these are not relevantly similar because then the negation of what is other than a pot is objective exclusion by a pot. [224] Therefore, one would have to assert that this is an entity.

Some people think this makes no sense. If something is a pot and is permanent, then one would have to assert that it is the negation of not being a pot that is permanent. Otherwise, if it were a cognitive object that is a possible existent, then its existence as permanent could not be established. In brief, as it says in the *Autocommentary on the Investigation of the Percept*, the meaning of the assertion that macro-objects that are aggregations of many particles do not substantially exist is: "a collection is not a percept because it is not substantially real and, for that reason, is not a cause (42)." Thus, it is not the cause of sensory cognition because it is not substantially real.

Moreover, not being the cause of sensory cognition means not being its percept condition. Thus, because macro-objects made of particles are not causes, it makes no sense to say that they are different from permanent phenomena. Similarly, it is clear that collections of particles are not substantially real. *The Great Exposition of the Stages of the Path* states:

> According to Cittamātras, individual fundamental particles are not the objects of sensory cognitions because they do not appear, and compounds of many of them are not the objects of sensory cognitions because they are not substantial.[23]

So, one might ask: "Are aggregations and aggregations of particles also not entities?" The learned do say that these are not entities. The *Ornament for Epistemological Treatises* says: "Therefore, sensory cognition does not perceive universals, composites, and aggregations,\ because these three are not entities."[24] If you want to know more, see such statements as: "Aggregates and

23. Tsongkhapa, *Great Exposition of the Stages of the Path* (*Lam rim chen mo*); *Gsung 'bum* vol. 13 (*pa*): 401a.

24. Gendun Drup (dGe 'dun grub, 1391–1474), *Ornament of Reasoning: Great Exposition of Epistemological Treatises* (*Tshad ma'i bstan bcos chen mo rigs pa'i rgyan; Gsung 'bum*, vol. 5 (*ca*): 27b.

composites . . ." in the "Perception Chapter"[25] [225] and in the *Ornament* and other texts by Gyeltsap and Kedrup that explain the meanings of such statements. To set out the critical points of this literature: In general, an isolated minute particle[26] cannot produce sensory cognition. However, when many fundamental particles are configured together, as in such aggregations as pots, the word "aggregations" designates their component fundamental particles; in the same way, perceiving each of them is simply called perceiving the aggregation. But the composite or aggregation on its own is not the percept.

Although it is explained in this way, I have a further thought: Since Cittamātras do not maintain that there are any subtle or coarse particles, they say that aggregations are nonentities. When Sautrāntikas assert that aggregations are nonentities, don't they assert that the collection of the five aggregates is the person? Suppose that the answer is "no." Wouldn't this contradict the statement in *Clarifying the Thought: Explanation of the Introduction to the Middle Way*:

> According to the understanding of many in our school, they maintain that the eightfold aggregation of particles that are configured together in such material objects as pots are pots. That is why they say that they give rise to a pot as an object.[27]

The assertion that the aggregation of the five aggregates is a person also raises the following question: Since an aggregation is nominally real, how could it be the basis for the designation of the person? I suspect that this would be inconsistent with their commitment to the necessity of the basis of that which is nominally real being substantially real.

On the other hand, the scholar [226] Bhāviveka asserts that aggregations of many particles appear to sensory cognition, but collections of many particles do not appear.[28] Thus, he distinguishes between aggregations and collections.

---

25. Dharmakīrti (1968: 151), *Commentary on the Compendium of Epistemology* (*Pramāṇavārttika*; Tib. *Tshad ma rnam 'grel*, "Pratyakṣa-pariccheda" (Tib. mNgon sum le'u): "*sañcitaḥ samudāyaḥ sāmānyaṃ tatra cākṣadhīḥ*." Tib (Derge: 2.194ab): "*bsags pa dang ni tshogs pa yin / zhes sogs.*"

26. Tib. *zla med kyi rdul phran.*

27. Tsongkhapa, *Clarifying the Thought: Explanation of the Introduction to the Middle Way* (*dBu ma 'jug pa'i rnam bshad dgongs pa rab gsal*, a commentary on Candrakīrti's *Introduction to the Middle Way [Madhyamakāvatāra]*): "*rang gi sde pa mang pos bum pa'i gzugs la sogs pa'i rdul brgyad de ltar 'dab 'byor du gnas pa'i tshogs pa rnams bum pa yin pas / de la bum pa'i blor 'gyur ro zhes smra ba de yang shing rta'i dpe 'dis bsal bas na de ni rigs pa ma yin pa nyid do.*" *gSung 'bum*, vol. 3 (*ga*): 218b.

28. See Eckel (2008: 252 and 408). Bhāviveka introduces this phrase as a definition of a combination (*bsags pa*; Skt. *saṃcita*), but the Tibetan translation uses the term *tshogs pa*.

Moreover, the fundamental particles in an aggregation such as a pot are particles of the same kind. Thus, they are called an "aggregation." He maintains that individual fundamental particles appear in sensory cognition when this aggregation appears in sensory cognition, just as it is necessary to perceive fingers when perceiving a fist. The fundamental particles of the various kinds of trees that exist in an aggregation such as a forest are not of the same type. Therefore, they are called an aggregation. They do not appear in sensory cognition.

Furthermore, someone might wonder whether it is necessary to say that many particles constitute an entity. The "Perception Chapter" states: "Many fundamental particles produce an additional factor and together are causes of cognition."[29] Someone might wonder whether many particles can be a single entity because the *Ornament for Seven Epistemological Texts* states: "Perceiving many particles capable of producing sensory cognition is called 'perceiving an aggregation'; but this is merely an expression."[30] In that case, should you say that (a) the shortest moment is on the order of one one-hundredth of a short span; or (b) should you accept that, as it is as stated in *Ornament for Seven Epistemological Texts*: "The shortest moment is one one-hundredth of a short span; but does one one-hundredth of these shortest moments constitute the shortest duration of time?"[31]

If you accept the latter, then you could say that one three hundred sixty-fifth of this interval should be accepted as the shortest moment of time. In that case, someone with a fastidious intellect should investigate whether or not it is

---

29. Dharmakīrti, *Commentary on the Compendium of Epistemology* (2.223): "*ko vā virodho bahavaḥ saṃjātātiṣayāḥ pṛthak / bhaveyuḥ kāraṇaṃ buddher yadi nātmendriyādivat.*" Manorathanandin explains: "It is said: 'Since particles (*paramāṇavaḥ*) are not accessible to the senses (*atīndriyāḥ*) individually, they also are not objects of cognition when they are combined.' He responds: 'If many particles produce an additional factor (*atiśaya*) by approaching (*upasarpaṇa*) one another, a combination (*saṃhata*) is produced that is capable of generating a cognition, and they can be . . . a cause of cognition. Then, what is the contradiction, as in the case of the senses and so forth? The senses and so forth are not causes of cognition individually, but they are when they come together (*milita*). Particles are just like this. For, as far as we are concerned, particles do not have a permanent identity (*nityasvabhāva*), as they do for our opponents."

30. Kedrup, *Ornament for Seven Epistemological Texts That Dispels Darkness in the Mind* (*Tshad ma sde bdun gyi rgyan yid kyi mun sel*): "*mdo las / rnam par shes pa'i tshogs lnga ni bsags pa la dmigs pa can yin no zhes gsungs pa'i phyir zhe na / de ltar gsungs pas bsags pa la dmigs mi dgos par thal / dbang shes skyed nus kyi rdul du ma la dmigs pa la bsags pa la dmigs pa zhes brjod pa tsam yin pa'i phyir.*" Gsung 'bum, vol.5 (*ca*): 27b.

31. Kedrup, *Tshad ma sde bdun gyi rgyan yid kyi mun sel*, p. 31a: "*dus mtha'i skad cig ma brgya 'thud pa rgyun yin kyang dus mtha'i skad cig ma brgya po dus thung ba'i mthar thug pa yin no.*"

necessary to accept that this shortest moment of time is of the same duration as an instant of completion of an action. [227]

How External Objects Appear to the Mind—The Vaibhāṣikas assert that macro-objects are not substantially real and so do not appear to sensory cognition; and that while fundamental particles appear, they do not appear through representations. This is because visual cognitive apprehension of blue apprehends blue immediately without a representation. One might ask: "How can this be?" They assert that perception is nonrepresentational for two central reasons: (1) like the apprehended myrobalan fruit and the apprehending hand, the apprehender and the apprehended must be simultaneous; and (2) they do not maintain that the subject takes on the object as a representation through the power of the representation of the object to transfer itself to subjective cognition. On the other hand, they certainly maintain that there are merely cognitive representations. As the *Treasury of Abhidharma* states: "A cognition that has a percept apprehends with a representational cognition."[32] If you really want to understand this, the *Treasury of Abhidharma* itself says: "Mind and mental factors have a support, a percept, and a representational cognition and are associated in five ways..."[33] and "the path of release and the uninterrupted path respectively involve representations such as peace and extension."[34] The details are eloquently set out.

Regarding the way in which Sautrāntikas and more advanced schools maintain that cognition is representational, *Introduction to the Middle Way* states: "whatever the mind represents is its object."[35] When a representation

32. Vasubandhu (1975: 7.13), *Treasury of Abhidharma*: "*dravyataḥ ṣodaśākārāḥ prajñākāraḥ tayā saha / ākārayanti sālambāḥ sarvam ākāryate tu sat.*" "Things have sixteen *ākāras*. An *ākāra* is *prajñā*. With this [wisdom, which also is *ākāra*] those [dharmas] that have percepts convey (*ākārayanti*) [presumably the percept]." Ngawang Dendar quotes this passage as follows: "*rnam pa shes rab dang bcas pa'i / dmigs dang bcas pas 'dzin par byed.*" The *Commentary on the Treasury of Knowledge* points out a problem in this verse: "In this case, *prajñā* cannot have an *ākāra*, because it cannot be connected to another *prajñā*."

33. Vasubandhu, *Verses of the Treasury of Abhidharma* (mNgon pa, vol. *ku*: 5a): "*rten dang dmigs dang rnam bcas dang / mtshungs par ldan pa'ang rnam pa lnga.*" Pradhan (ed.), *The Abhidharmakośa of Vasubandhu*, II.34cd: "*sāśrayā lambanākārāḥ saṁprayuktāśca pañcadhā.*" "[Mind and mental phenomena] have a location, a percept, and a representation (*ākāra*), and they are associated in five ways." Dendar quotes this passage as follows: "*de nyid las / rten dang dmigs dang rnam bcas dang / mtshungs par ldan pa rnam pa lnga / zhes dang.*"

34. Vasubandhu, *Verses of The Treasury of Abhidharma* (Pradhan ed., VI.49c): *śāntādyudārādyākārāḥ.*" "[The ordinary *vimukti* and *ānantarya* paths have, respectively] the *ākāras* of peace and so forth, and extent and so forth." Tib. (mNgon pa, vol. *ku*, p. 20b): "*zhi sogs rags sogs rnam pa can.*"

35. Candrakīrti, *Introduction to the Middle Way* (*Madhyamakāvatāra; dBu ma la 'jug* pa), XI.13, dBu ma vol. *'a*, p. 216ab: "*gang tshe skye med de nyid yin zhing blo yang skye ba dang bral ba // de tshe de rnams sten las de yis de nyid rtogs pa lta bu ste // ji ltar sems ni gang gi rnam pa can*

of a blue object arises for a visual cognition apprehending blue, because it thereby apprehends blue, it is said that there is apprehension and an apprehender of blue. Other than by way of subjective cognition becoming like its object, [228] there is absolutely no way for cognition to apprehend an object.

For example, when a crystal is placed on a blue cloth, all facets of the crystal turn blue. In the same way, when a visual cognition apprehending blue sees blue, the color blue is transferred to the visual perspective, and so the subjective visual cognition becomes just like the blue object. The visual cognition apprehending blue is referred to as "a visual cognition that arises as a representation of blue." This is the criterion for the direct apprehension of blue.

According to the Sautrāntikas, since macro-objects are not substantially real, not only do they not appear to sensory cognition, they do not even appear as macro-objects. If they did appear in this way, then they would have to appear as partite. If they appeared in this way, then they would have to appear as partite to a nonerroneous sensory cognition, and then one would have to say that the whole and the parts are two different things. On the other hand, they maintain that since the visual cognition apprehending blue engages with the presence of blue, all of the fundamental particles existing in a blue aggregation appear. This is because the blue particles and the blue are indistinguishably coextensive—that is, substantially identical.

Even though fundamental particles are perceived by sensory cognition, they are not objects whose appearances can be ascertained. Thus, it is said: "Since it is a sensory object, it is not a fundamental particle."[36] The Cittamātras also maintain that macro-objects are not real, because blue macro-objects appear to cognition due to the fact that sensory cognition apprehending blue is an erroneous cognition.

How the Percept Condition Functions— This section has three parts: (1) the position of the Vaibhāṣikas; (2) the position of the Sautrāntikas; and (3) the positions of the Cittamātras.

The Position of the Vaibhāṣikas— Since the Vaibhāṣikas are not representationalists, they do not maintain that representations of either micro- or macro-objects are conveyed to sensory cognition. [229] Since they accept the

---

[216b] *du 'gyur ba de yis yul //de yongs shes pa de bzhin tha snyad* [*nye bar*] *brten nas rig pa yin.*" Although Ngawang Dendar cites only a portion of the text, we have produced the whole passage to bring out the full sense of Candrakīrti's passage.

36. Dharmakīrti, *Commentary on the Compendium of Epistemology* 1.87 (Shastri ed., p. 37): "*aviśeṣo viśiṣṭānām ainindriyatvam ato 'naṇuḥ / etenāvaraṇādīnām abhāvaś ca nirākṛteḥ.*" Tib: "*ma grub khyad par can rnams ni // dbang yul de phyir rdul phran min // 'dis ni sgrib byed la sogs pa // med pa dag kyang bsal ba yin.*"

simultaneity of causes and effects, they maintain that even though blue is the percept condition of the visual cognition apprehending blue, they are simultaneous. This is because they maintain that when something is a percept condition, the cognition that apprehends it is about to cease, and it carries out its activity in the present. Suppose someone asks: "How do you know this?" The *Treasury of Abhidharma* states:

> Two causes carry out their activity
> When the effect is ceasing;
> Three when it is arising.
> Other conditions are the opposite of this.[37]

This is how I know! Here is what this means: Since both the simultaneous cause and the conjoined cause are simultaneous with their effects, the effect is about to cease, and they carry out their activity in the present. It states: "Two causes carry out their activity when the effect is ceasing." The relation between the three causes—the homologous (*skal mnyam*) cause, the omnipresent (*kun 'gro*) cause, and the ripening (*rnam smin*) cause—and their effects is sequential. So, they occur when their effects are about to arise. To explain that they carry out their activity in the future, it states: "Three when it is arising." The immediately preceding condition and the percept condition—which are other than these two classes of cause—are the opposite of what has been explained. The immediately preceding condition carries out its activity on its future effect; the percept condition carries out its activity on its present effect. To explain this, it states: "Other conditions are the opposite of this."

The Position of the Sautrāntikas To be a sensory cognition's percept condition [230] is to have two characteristics: (1) to convey its own representation to sensory cognition; and (2) to be that sensory cognition's cause. They also hold that what cause means is this: the percept—which is called the sensory object's percept condition—or the thing that is apprehended—which is called the apprehended object. Thus, the "Perception Chapter" states: "Apart from the cause, nothing at all is apprehended."[38] Moreover, since the meaning of

---

37. Vasubandhu, *Treasury of Abhidharma*, Pradhan ed., 2.63: "*nirudhyamāne kāritraṃ dvau hetū kurutaḥ trayaḥ / jāyamāne tato 'nyau tu pratyayau tadviparyayāt.*" Ngawang Dendar: "*de gang las shes zhe na / mdzod las / rgyu gnyis po dag 'gag pa la / bya ba byed do gsum po ni / skye la'o de la gzhan pa yi / rkyen dag de las bzlog pa yin / zhes byung ba las shes pa'i phyir.*"

38. Dharmakīrti, *Commentary on the Compendium of Epistemology* (Tshad ma, vol. *ce*, p. 127a): "*rgyu yi dngos po ma gtogs pa // gzung ba zhes bya gzhan ci'ang med.*" *Pramāṇavārttikakārikā*: "*hetubhāvād ṛte nānyā grāhyatā nāma kācana*" Pandey (ed., 1989): II.224ab.

"cause" is held to be that which is prior to its effect, they do not assert the simultaneity of cause and effect. So, the "Perception Chapter" also states: "All causes are prior to their effects."[39]

Suppose someone asks: "How is blue apprehended by a cognition apprehending blue, given that the blue would have ceased at the time of the arising of the visual cognition that apprehends it?" Listen, fortunate ones, and I will explain this. Although there is no blue at the time of the apprehension of blue, there is no problem in terms of their not being an apprehender and an apprehended. This is because when the visual faculty that is the dominant condition of that visual cognition and blue—the percept condition—come together, then immediately in the next moment a visual cognition arises having a representation of blue. At that moment, although there is no blue, the representation of blue certainly remains in the perspective of cognition. *That* is what is meant by "cognition's apprehension of blue."

On the other hand, someone might ask: "According to the Vaibhāṣika tradition, even today there is the memory of previous eons. So there must be memory. If memory apprehends its object immediately, then the previous eon would have to exist today." There is no problem because this is a tradition that accepts the present existence of the past. [231] Or one might think that it would make sense to say that the name of the previous eon is the percept condition.

Now suppose someone asks: "Doesn't perceptual cognition have a present object?" Why would you ask this? Does it comprehend a past object at the time when it exists? The explanation of perceptual cognitions as having present objects is as follows: Having a present object does not mean that whatever is the object of perception must exist at the time of perception. If that were the case, then there would be no perception of what perception cognizes—that is, its cause. It makes no sense to say that in general the only objects are in the present. If that were the case, then even a thought that is the memory of yesterday's sunshine would have a present object.

This can be explained as follows. It is written: "The present is not far from the immediate past."[40] Just so, there is a potential for a representation of whatever occurred prior to the perception—up to and including what immediately

---

39. Dharmakīrti, *Commentary on the Compendium of Epistemology* (Tshad ma, vol. *ce*, p. 127b: "*phyis kyang nye bar mi sbyor phyir // rgyu rnams thams cad sngar yod yin.*" Pandey (ed.), II.246cd: "*prāgbhāvaḥ sarvahetūṇāṃ nāto 'rthaḥ svadhiyā saha.*"

40. Ngawang Dendar: "*'das ma thag pa la da lta yod ma thag pa.*" He does not indicate his source, but this follows from his discussion of the *Treasury of Abhidharma*, and it is similar to *Commentary on the Treasury of Abhidharma* 5.62 (Pradhan ed., p. 321, line 10): "How can the immediate past be far from the present?" (*yad anantarātītam utpadyamānaṃ vā tat kathaṃ dūram*). Note that *ma thag pa* translates both *anantara* and (*na*) *dūram*.

preceded it—to arise right after an ordinary person's perception. But there is no potential for it to arise thereafter. Therefore, since it has the potential to cognize the object that was just present, perception is simply said have a present object. In this context, in the Sautrāntika tradition it is necessary to ask: "What is the percept condition of a reflexive awareness experiencing the first moment of a visual apprehension of blue?" This does not contradict the statement in the "Perception Chapter": "A previous cognition knowing an object has neither an example nor evidence."[41] That is, although the past is merely nonexistent in the present, [232] the direct cause of a present perception is said to be in the past.

The Position of the Cittamātras— Although they do not maintain the existence of any particles whatsoever—whether macroscopic or microscopic—the appearance of macro-objects to sensory cognition is an erroneous appearance due to the force of predispositions. But the object itself does not through its own power deliver a representation. Therefore, they do not assert that macroscopic or microscopic material objects are percept conditions.

So, suppose someone asks: "What is the percept condition of a visual cognition apprehending blue?" In this context, everything—such as blue—that appears as an object of sensory cognition is present through the power of predispositions. Therefore, that predisposition for the arising of the appearance of blue in the prior cognition is the percept condition for the visual cognition of blue. This is also Gyeltsap's interpretation. His *Memorandum to the Perception Chapter* of instructions from Je [Rinpoche, i.e., Tsongkhapa] states:

> The previous implanting[42] cognition imbeds a cognition of a blue appearance in the immediately preceding condition of the sensory cognition of a blue appearance. That has the power to leave an imprint that gives rise to the representation of a blue object. This power is the percept condition of sensory cognition.[43]

---

41. Dharmakīrti, *Verses of the Commentary on Compendium of Epistemology* (Tshad ma, vol. *ce*, p. 125a): "*don rig 'das pa dpe dag dang // bral zhing rtags ni yod min te.*" Pandey ed., II.180ab: "*atītam apadṛṣṭāntam aliṅgañ cārthadarśanam.*"

42. Text correction: the text reads: *sgod byed*; corrected to: *sgos byed.*

43. Tsongkhapa, *Memorandum to the Perception Chapter* (*mNgon sum le'u'i brjed byang*), *gSung 'bum* (*sku 'bum par ma*). TBRC W22272: 56 ff. [*sKu 'bum byams pa gling*] [199-?]: "*de'ang bsgo byed shes pa snga mas bzhag pa'i sngor snang dbang shes kyi de ma thag rkyen gyi steng na/ sngor snang shes pa de gzung bya sngon po'i rnam ldan du bskyed pa'i lag rjes 'jog pa'i nus pa yod la/ nus pa de nyid dbang shes de'i dmigs rkyen yin* (*te / phyi rol don khas len pa rnams kyis shes pa yul gyi rnam ldan du skyed byed du 'jog pa bzhin no*" (*rGyal tshab chos rjes'i drung du gsan pa'i*

Moreover, in the *Commentary on the Compendium of Metaphysics*, the scholar Kamalaśīla states:

> Moreover, as an alternative, [Kamalaśīla quotes Dignāga]: "This is not contradictory because although there is sequence its appearance as an object—the potential that produces an effect that is similar to the appearance[44] of the object itself—acts as the support of consciousness." [233] Because this transmits the capacity that is a cause—that is, a sign—that produces an effect similar to itself in a cognition that is not different from that object, appearances are shown to be causal.[45]

This appears to be Gyeltsap's source. This is also Kedrup's interpretation when the *Ornament for Seven Epistemological Texts* states:

> The capacity—which has a nature of predisposition in the previous cognition for a similar one—is the dominant condition for the production of the subsequent sensory cognition having the representation of an object that is its own effect. Thus, this way of positing it as its percept condition is an extremely profound framework from the doxographical tradition.[46]

In brief, in this system, when the sensory cognition to which blue appears is dormant, it essentially transforms into a potential. Moreover, when that potential subsequently ripens, a part of it is the blue that appears to a visual

---

mngon sum le'u'i brjed byang; Tsongkhapa's Collected Works [sKu 'bum byams pa gling par khang], vol. 15: 755.

44. Ngawang Dendar follows P, N, and S: "*snang ba'i*"; D has *snang bar*, which would also be suggested by the Sanskrit of Kamalaśīla's quotation.

45. Kamalaśīla, *Commentary on the Compendium of Metaphysics*: "*gzhan yang yang na / nus pa 'jog phyir rim gyis kyang / don tu snang ba de ni rang dang mthun pa'i 'bras bu skyed par byed pa'i nus pa rnam par shes pa'i rten can byed pa mi 'gal lo.*" The Sanskrit text reads: "*athavā śaktyarpaṇāt krameṇāpi so 'rthāvabhāsaḥ svānurūpakāryotpattaye śaktiṃ vijñānācārāṃ karotīty avirodhaḥ*" (Śāstri ed., 1968: vol. 2:710). This means that the object-appearance transfers a potential to cognition, and this potential causes the arising of an effect that is consistent with the original object-appearance. Kamalaśīla is quoting *Investigation of the Percept* 7b and commentary.

There are two textual variants here: *don du snang ba* (N) for *don du snang bas* (D), and *skyed par byed par* (D) for *skyed par byed pa'i* (N and Ngawang Dendar). Kamalaśīla's Sanskrit supports *snang ba* (*arthāvabhāsaḥ*) and *skyed byed par* (*utpattaye*). Our translation of Ngawang Dendar follows the reading *skyed par byed pa'i*. The translation of the Sanskrit should follow the reading *skyed par byed par*. If one follows Dendar's reading, this would read: "It is not contradictory for the object-appearance sequentially to cause a potential to be present in cognition, and this potential causes an effect to arise that is similar to the object-appearance itself."

46. Kedrup, *Ornament for the Seven Epistemological Treatises*: 88ab.

cognition apprehending blue, and another part is the visual cognition that has the representation of blue. For this reason, blue and a visual cognition apprehending blue are "substantially identical" because they arise from the same substance, that is, the appropriating cognition. Since they are substantially identical, they cannot be causally related. For this reason, blue is also not said to be the percept condition of a cognition apprehending blue.

Well then, suppose someone asks: "Isn't it the case that for this tradition, to be a percept condition of sensory cognition is to be necessarily observed simultaneously with the sensory cognition? Why do they say that this potential within the previous cognition is the percept condition?"

That very predisposition in a previous cognition that causes the appearance of blue later appears as blue. [234] At that moment, the predisposition itself masquerades as blue, and one presumes that one is seeing blue. But really one just sees a predisposition. For example, when a single moon appears as two, there is no second moon apart from the one moon. Therefore, it is actually a single moon that is observed. Here's why: For those who presume that there is a fundamental consciousness, the essential point is the assertion that predispositions are the object of observation of the fundamental consciousness.

Moreover, in their tradition, since blue and the visual cognition apprehending blue are substantially identical, these two are simultaneous. Therefore, since there is no blue prior to the arising of a visual cognition apprehending blue, wouldn't you have to say that the dominant condition of the visual cognition—that is, the visual faculty—is what sees blue?

Moreover, in general, they also assert that the visual faculty is the potential and a predisposition. Thus, it is difficult to say whether or not they accept a visual object. If there is blue at the same time as the dominant condition—the visual faculty—then it and the visual cognition that apprehends it would arise sequentially. Therefore, how could one force blue into the very nature of the perception that apprehends it? Moreover, someone with a sharp intellect should inquire into whether or not the visual faculty—which is the dominant condition for seeing blue—and the visual cognition it supports are simultaneous.

The Meaning of the Text[47]

Although there are only eight verses in Master Dignāga's root text, their meaning is vast. In short, the main point is to refute the position[48] that the object

---

47. This is referred to as "the meaning of the parts" (*yan lag gi don*) earlier in the text.

48. We read *grub* here as *grub pa'i mtha'*.

that appears in a sensory cognition is an external object [235] and to prove that it has the nature of being internal to cognition.[49]

The explanation of the meaning of the verses and the associated autocommentary has two parts: (1) how to refute the claim that the percept condition is an external object; and (2) how to prove that it is purely mental.

How to Refute the Claim That the Percept Is an External Object

The first section has three parts: (1) a general refutation; (2) a specific refutation; and (3) a summary of these points.

General Refutation

The first section has three parts: (1) a refutation of the claim that fundamental particles are the apprehended object; (2) a refutation of the claim that macro-objects are the apprehended object; and (3) the conclusions drawn from these.

REFUTATION OF PARTICLES AS THE APPREHENDED OBJECT

According to the Sautrāntikas—who maintain that the percept of a cognition such as a visual cognition is an external object—(1) either fundamental particles are the percept conditions of sensory cognitions because they satisfy the definition of "being the cause of sensory cognition"; or (2) a collection of these fundamental particles is the percept condition because a sensory cognition perceives a collection of particles[50] and arises with the appearance of this collection—that is, with a representation that resembles it—and thus satisfies the meaning of "being the object of the appearance."

Here, to begin, the claim that the first position makes no sense is explained in connection with the commentary that introduces the first verse. Dignāga says:

> **Even if sensory cognition were caused by fundamental particles,**
> **It would not have particles as its object**
> **Because they do not appear to cognition,**
> **Any more than the sense faculties do.** (1abcd)

49. This echoes verse 6 of the root text.

50. Dendar uses *rdul*; the root text reads: *rdul phra rab*.

Here is what this means: Master Dignāga initially assumes for the sake of argument the position that fundamental particles are the causes of sensory cognitions. Fundamental particles may be causes of sensory cognitions such as the visual, but a sensory cognition does not have the appearance of these—that is, a representation that is like those fundamental particles. [236] For this reason, the appearing object in sensory cognition is not a minute particle, just as the opponent maintains that, although the visual faculty is a cause of visual cognition, it is not its percept.

I comment as follows: the statement that a sensory cognition cannot have fundamental particles[51] as its object means that a cognition is that which[52] ascertains the form of an object because it has the representation of that object. The minute particles that are present in a blue aggregation may be a cause of a sensory cognition that apprehends blue, but they cannot be the appearing object in that sensory cognition, any more than the sense faculties can. This is why, to begin, fundamental particles are not the percept in the context of the "percept condition."

Here "even if sensory cognition were caused by fundamental particles"[53] and "even if they were the cause" are only assumed for the sake of argument, since no fundamental particles[54] are accepted in the position of the Cittamātra. In the *Illumination of the Path to Liberation: Explanation of the Commentary on the Compendium of Epistemology, an Unerring Illumination of the Path to Liberation*, it says:

> In *Investigation of the Percept*, it says: "Even if sensory cognition were caused by fundamental particles." This has the same meaning as the statement in the *Compendium of Epistemology*. This is not meant to be an assertion that fundamental particles are established by authoritative cognition. But if they were, even if we were to grant that they are causes, they could not be percept conditions. Having assumed this for the sake of argument, Dignāga proceeds to refute the claim that these are percept conditions.[55]

51. The verse reads: *rdul phran* (Skt. *aṇu*), but Dendar uses *rdul phra rab*; Skt. *paramāṇu*.

52. Dendar's interpretation is based on the Tibetan *gang gis*, which is a mistaken translation of the word "*yasya*" in Sanskrit. The Sanskrit makes it clear that this sentence is a definition of an object and does not refer to the cognition that perceives it.

53. Dendar has changed the word order in the first two verses.

54. Read *rab* for *rags*.

55. Gyeltsap, *Illumination of the Path to Liberation: Explanation of the Commentary on the Compendium of Epistemology, an Unerring Illumination of the Path to Liberation* (*Tshad ma*

In *Ocean of Reasoning: Extensive Exposition of the Commentary on the Compendium of Epistemology*, it says:

> If they themselves accept this, then they have to accept, in their own position, that when there is a cognition the particles of the visual sense faculty are causes of perceptual cognition. [237] But it would be truly amazing for a Cittamātra to accept particles.[56]

But do Cittamātras really accept material form? Those who do not think carefully say this glibly.[57] However, according to Tsongkhapa's *Commentary on the Middle Way*,[58] there are Cittamātras who accept material forms; he cites such texts as Asaṅga's *Compendium of the Mahāyāna* and *Compendium of Ascertainments*,[59] and Vasubandhu's *Commentary on the Distinction of the First Factor of Dependent Arising*.[60] However, in the end, in the Cittamātra system the external world is rejected, and so it must be that such things as material form also do not exist because it is obvious that what holds for the external world must also hold for material form.

---

rnam 'grel gyi tshig le'ur byas pa'i rnam bshad thar lam phyin ci ma log par gsal bar byed pa), Zhol Par khang edition, vol. *cha*, fol. 288b.3.

56. Kedrup, *Ocean of Reasoning: Extensive Exposition of the Commentary on Epistemology, Chapter on Direct Perception* (*Tshad ma rnam 'grel gyi rgya cher bshad pa rigs pa'i rgya mtsho las mngon sum le'u rnam bshad bzhugs so*. (1) Zhol edition, Tohoku #5505, fol. 113b.1. (2) Beijing: Mi rigs dpe skrun khang, 1990: 734. In this section, Kedrup discusses Dignāga's hypothetical stance, accepting for the sake of argument that fundamental particles are the cause of sensory cognitions. If this were Dignāga's actual position, according to Kedrup, then he would have to accept that fundamental particles are the real causes of sensory cognition. This would entail that Cittamātras accept fundamental particles and also their externality. This would be odd given that, according to Geluk doxography, Cittamātras posit that mind alone is real.

57. This is a rhetorical question. He is saying that, according to Geluk doxography, it would be impossible for Cittamātras—who according to this system maintain that mind alone is real and that external objects do not exist—to posit material form. But he states that Tsongkhapa does indeed claim that some Cittamātras posit it. As we will see just below, however, Dendar also believes that Tsongkhapa thinks that these Cittamātras are mistaken in doing so in light of the doctrinal commitments he imputes to them and that the force of the logic of their system ultimately requires a rejection of external forms.

58. This refers to Tsongkhapa's commentary on Candrakīrti's *Introduction to the Middle Way*, *Clarifying the Thought: Explanation of the Introduction to the Middle Way* (*dBu ma la 'jug pa'i rgya cher bshad pa dgongs pa rab gsal*).

59. Skt. *Viniścaya-saṃgrahaṇī*; Tib. *gTan la dbab pa'i bsdus pa*.

60. This refers to Vasubandhu's *Commentary on the Distinction of the First Factor of Dependent Arising* (*Pratītyasamutpādādivibhaṅga-bhāṣya*; Tib. *rTen cing 'brel bar 'byung ba dang po dang rnam par dbye bshad pa*): (1) P 5496, vol. 104: 277–306; (2) To. 3995: *bsTan 'gyur (dpe bsdur ma)*; W1PD95844: 717–876. It discusses the *Pratītyasamutpāda-sūtra*.

These are difficult points, and I am concerned about being too verbose. Tsongkhapa regarded this as a difficult point, and so I do not think that I can say whatever I want.

REFUTATION OF THE CLAIM THAT MACRO-OBJECTS ARE THE APPREHENDED OBJECT

To begin, for the sake of argument he assumes that collections appear in sensory cognition, but they are not its cause. So Dignāga says:

> **A sensory cognition does not come from that of**
> **which it has the appearance**
> **Because, like a double moon, collections are**
> **not substantially real.**[61] (2ab)

An object may appear to be a collection of many blue particles to a particular visual cognition that apprehends blue, but the visual cognition that apprehends blue does not arise from a collection of blue particles because a collection of many blue particles is not substantially real. For example, it is like a single moon that appears as a double moon. It would make sense for something like a blue object to be [238] the percept that is called the percept condition if it appears as itself—that is, if it produces a cognition of itself or like itself. So a treatise states:

> An object is a percept if it causes mental states and mental processes to arise and, when they arise, prompts the conventional designation that this object is experienced.[62]

If something is the percept condition of a sensory cognition, then it is said that a representation like itself appears in that sensory cognition and also that it is the condition of the arising of that sensory cognition. A collection of many particles does not produce a sensory cognition in this way because it is not substantially real. For example, when a person sees a double moon because of defective sense faculties—that is, because his senses have been damaged by an eye disease—it is just a single moon appearing to be double.

---

61. This is quoted in Dignāga's *Compendium of Epistemology*: "*yadābhāsā na sā tasmāt*" (1,15a) and in Prajñākaragupta's *Subcommentary on the Compendium of Epistemology*: 339.

62. Vinītadeva quotes this definition in his commentary on verse 2 (85). Neither Dendar nor Vinītadeva indicates the source. A search of the Tibetan canon and another using standard Chinese equivalents of key terms in C-BETA did not produce any probable corresponding text.

But even though it is a single moon appearing as double to a sensory cognition, the single moon is not the *cause* of the sensory cognition; and, for that reason, it also is not the object that is called the percept condition of that cognition. As in this example, a collection of fundamental particles is shown not to be the cause because it is not substantially real. Therefore, a collection of particles is not the cognition's percept in this context.

Here the statement that neither fundamental particles nor collections are the object of a sensory cognition is intended to refer to the appearing object or the determinate object.[63] And the statement that the visual cognition that apprehends blue apprehends blue means that the visual cognition that apprehends blue and blue are merely similar. Apart from this, no other activity of apprehension can be characterized as similar to the act of a hand apprehending a pot.

For example, even though it is said that the form of the father is apprehended in a son who is similar to the father, [239] in this case there is neither a son who apprehends nor a father-form that is apprehended.[64]

Although a single moon is not really a double moon, it must be said that a single moon is substantially real because a single moon is an entity. This is because it is the percept condition of a sensory cognition of a single moon appearing to be double.[65] This point is confirmed in both the *Ornament for Epistemological Treatises* and the *Ornament for Seven Epistemological Texts That Dispels Darkness in the Mind*. Thus, although it conveys the representation of a single moon to the sensory cognition that appears as a double moon, it does not convey it correctly.

SUMMARY

Dignāga says:

> **Thus, neither kind of external object**
> **Makes sense as an object of cognition.** (2cd)

---

63. The function of the word *lam* (or *la ma*) that precedes *sgro 'dogs* is unclear.

64. It is impossible to convey the Tibetan connotation of this metaphor. Dendar plays with various uses of the term *'dzin pa*, which means "grasp," "apprehend," and so on, and has the English senses of both ascertaining something with the senses and physically grasping something. This extension of the metaphor refers to a Tibetan idiom in which a son who is the "spitting image" of his father is declared to "hold his father's form." But the English "apprehend" cannot be used in this way.

65. This seems to contradict the claim he made on the preceding page. In the first case he provides a Yogācāra analysis, and in this he is switching to a Geluk position. He does this throughout the text: in some cases, he presents the Yogācāra perspective, and in others he appears to be reminding his listeners that it ultimately fails from the Geluk perspective.

In this way, neither (1) the position that external fundamental particles are the percept condition nor (2) the position that a collection is the percept condition makes sense of external objects as the appearing objects of cognition. Why not? If an external object were the percept condition, then it would have to have both of the following characteristics: (1) it would have to transmit its own representation to the cognition; and (2) it would have to cause the cognition. The position that fundamental particles are the percept condition fails to account for the transmission of their representation, and the position that a collection is the percept condition fails to account for their being the cause. Therefore, these objects—external minute particles and aggregations—are not percepts in the sense of percept conditions.

Specific Refutation

In the specific refutation, there are two parts: (1) a refutation of distinct representations of fundamental particles; and (2) a summary of the refutation of distinct representations. [240]

REFUTATION OF DISTINCT REPRESENTATIONS OF FUNDAMENTAL PARTICLES

The first section has two parts: (1) a statement of the position; and (2) a refutation of this position as making no sense.

Statement of the Position—Dignāga says:

> **Some maintain that collected features are the cause.** (3a)

"Among these" who take the position that there are external objects[66] means "also among these." Some maintain the following: fundamental particles are the causes because they are substantially real; and since they have a nature of being collections of eight substantial particles, they are represented as collections in sensory cognition—that is, they manifest representations of macro-objects. For this reason, they maintain that these fundamental particles are causal since, as percept conditions, they account for the transmission of their own representation. That is, they are causes of sensory cognition.[67]

---

66. This is a reference to the opponents who were mentioned in the first line of the autocommentary.

67. Here Dendar, following Dignāga's autocommentary, is glossing "causal" (*sgrub*) with "cause" (*rgyu*).

Suppose someone asks: If fundamental particles have no parts, then how can they manifest the features of a macro-object? The answer is: All external objects have multiple features because they have a nature of being four elements, plus visible form, smell, taste, and touch.

Now suppose someone replies: "In that case, the visual cognition that apprehends the visible form of a pot should perceive the tangible fundamental particles of the pot." We reply: They maintain that certain fundamental particles of a pot are perceived as having certain features, but for that reason they do not maintain that every feature—such things as the visible form that is seen by the eye and the tangibility that is sensed by the body, which are specific to the capacities of each of the five senses—give rise to all features. This is why they say that fundamental particles are the causes that produce cognitions that have the appearance of a collection.[68]

Suppose someone asks: If fundamental particles are manifest in a sensory cognition that has the representation of a macro-object, why don't fundamental particles themselves appear? Dignāga says:

Features of minute particles
Are not the object of cognition,
Any more than things like solidity are. (3bcd)

This means that it is not the case that all the fundamental particles in the aggregation of a pot are the apprehended object of visual cognition, just as such things as solidity—soft and hard particles—do not appear in the aggregation as a pot. [241] He presents the following example: "things like solidity may exist": they are in the locus of an object but are not objects of a visual cognition due to the distinctive capacities of the five faculties.[69] "The same is true of minute particles."

In the commentary on the root verse that begins: "**Some maintain that collected features are the cause,**" (3a) although it is not explicitly stated that fundamental particles have parts, in light of the way it is expressed, the opponent's position is that fundamental particles appear as collective representations in sensory cognition. Thus, if a collection-representation appears in an unmistaken cognition, then it must appear as a macro-object; and if it appears as a macro-object, then it must definitely appear with parts. This is why it says in Jamyang Sheba's *Precious Garland of Tenet Systems*:

68. The opponent here seems to be Naiyāyikas and Vaiśeṣikas.

69. In other words, a pot may have various capacities such as hardness, but the eye faculty will not be able to perceive them because they lie outside its area of operation.

> In the commentary on the root verses of *Investigation of the Percept*, in the context of the debate between the Sautrāntikas and the Cittamātras, the Sautrāntikas maintain that when there is an aggregation of fundamental particles that have parts, each conveys[70] a representation that is like itself.[71]

I think that this is an elegant explanation. In the *Elucidation of Investigation of the Percept*, it says that this objector is Vāgbhaṭa.[72]

Refutation of This Position as Making No Sense—In the refutation of this position as making no sense, there are three parts: (1) refutation of the opponent's position; (2) anticipation of the opponent's response; and (3) refutation of this response.

Refutation of the Opponent's Position

First, Dignāga says:

> **According to them, cognitions of things like pots**
> **And cups would be identical.** (4ab)

Here is what this means: How can anyone say that fundamental particles appear to sensory cognition with the representation of a macro-object? You say that a macro-object is something like a pot or a cup. So when there is a representation of fundamental particles, [242] is it like a pot or like a cup? Either way, according to your position, when you perceive a pot, you would think that it is a cup; and when you perceive a cup, you would think that it is a pot. These two cognitions would be identical to each other.

You might respond that a pot is bigger than a cup and that this is due to the number of fundamental particles in a pot or a cup. But while there may be this difference, there is no difference at all in the way fundamental particles are represented in macro-objects.

---

70. The text reads: *gtod pa*, pf. *gtad* or *btad*.

71. Jamyang Shebe Dorje ('Jam dbyangs bzhad pa'i rdo rje, 1641–1721), *Sun of the Field of Samantabhadra: Explication of Tenet Systems* (*Grub mtha'i rnam bshad kun bzang zhing gi nyi ma*). *Grub pa'i mtha' rnam par bzhag pa 'khrul spong gdong lnga'i sgra dbyangs kun mkhyen lam bzang gsal pa'i rin chen sgron me*: 211). In this section, Jamyang Shebe Dorje cites the *Autocommentary to Investigation of the Percept* in order to argue that there are some Sautrāntikas who assert that fundamental particles are partite (*cha bcas*).

72. Pha khol. See the discussion of this figure at the beginning of Vinītadeva's commentary on verse 3 (88 n. 36).

Anticipation of the Opponents' Response

Dignāga says:

> **If they are distinguished by different features.** (4c)

An opponent might think: "A pot is represented as having such things as a long neck and a round chamber, and a cup is not. So, since a cup is distinguished by being different with respect to these particular features, one can distinguish the cognition of a pot from the cognition of a cup." This is the opponent's position.

Refutation of the Opponent's Response

"These differences," such as a long neck, "belong only to things like pots, but. . . . " In connection with this statement, Dignāga says:

> **These do not belong to substantially real particles**
> **Because there is no difference in their dimensions.** (4d–5a)

Differences in representation do not belong to substantially real minute particles. Why? Because fundamental particles are not different in size and shape. They are not different in size because they are as small as anything can be; and they are not different in shape because, according to you Sautrāntikas, they are nothing but spheres. Therefore, the fundamental particles of such things as pots and cups [243] may be substantially different, but there is no difference in their equally spherical shape.

SUMMARY OF THE REFUTATION OF DIFFERENT FEATURES

In the summary of the refutation of different features, there are two parts: (1) why it makes sense for macro-objects to differ in shape; and (2) why macro-objects are nominally real.

Why It Makes Sense for Macro-objects to Differ in Shape

Dignāga says:

> **Therefore, these differences belong to something that**
> **is not substantially real.** (5b)

Since dissimilar representations cannot belong to fundamental particles, these differences are not substantially real. That is, they only exist in conventionally real things but do not belong to minute particles.

Dignāga says that macro-material-forms such as pots "are conventionally real." Here the explanation that pots are conventionally real refers to the Sautrāntikas who follow the *Treasury of Abhidharma*; it is not a position that follows the *Commentary on Epistemology* because in the "Perception Chapter" it says: "Whatever is efficacious is ultimately real."[73] This is because it is explained that everything that is efficacious is ultimately real.

The statement that the shape of fundamental particles is spherical belongs to the Sautrāntikas who follow the *Commentary on Epistemology*, but it is not reasonable according to the approach of the Abhidharma. When the *Treasury* says, "It would be apprehended by two sense faculties, and it is not in a fundamental particle,"[74] it is explaining that fundamental particles do not have any shape. Why? A Śrāvaka school maintains that shape is imputed to color. If shape belonged to fundamental particles, then it could not be separate from their color, and their color would have to be considered their nature. In that case, [244] I think that they might wonder whether fundamental particles have parts. If someone does not have a clear understanding of this way of imputing shape to color, then, as in Jinendrabuddhi's position, the sensory cognition of a yellow conch would be mistaken with respect to the color of the conch but authoritative with respect to its shape. This is why Jinendrabuddhi says there is no distinction between the shape that is seen by a visual cognition that appears white and the shape that is seen by a visual cognition that appears yellow, because both of them are the shape of the conch.

According to Master Dharmottara, this does not make sense because when a visual cognition that apprehends a yellow conch appears in the shape of a conch, it does not appear in the shape of a white conch. It appears in the shape of a yellow conch; and because the yellow conch does not exist,[75] this visual cognition is thus mistaken about the shape of the conch because the appearance of a shape such as long is many color particles arranged in a line appearing as long rather than an appearance of something such as an objective long

73. Dharmakīrti, *Compendium of Epistemology* 2.3a: "*arthakriyāsamarthaṃ yat tad atra paramārthasat.*"

74. Vasubandhu, *Treasury of Abhidharma*, 4.3cd: "*dvigrāhyaṃ syāt na cāṇau tat.*" This section of the *Treasury of Abhidharma* (Wogihara 1932–1936 II: 346–347) discusses the Sautrāntika position, according to which shape is not real (*nāsti saṃsthānaṃ dravyataḥ*). Vasubandhu states that according to them when color is repeated in a linear pattern, perception discerns the object as something that is "long" (*ekadiṅmukhe hi bhuyasi varṇa utpanne dīrghaṃ prajñapyate*; Wogihara II: 348). But shape is not separate from the thing to which it is imputed. If it were, Vasubandhu argues, it would have to be grasped by two sense faculties. He further argues that material form is nonobstructive; if it had the property of obstruction, this would have to reside in the smallest particles, but they have no such qualities. Moreover, minute particles have no shape (because they are all spherical).

75. This summarizes the argument in Dharmottara's *Investigation of the Instruments of Knowledge* (*Pramāṇa-parīkṣā*; Tib. *Tshad ma brtag pa*), sDe dge edition, Tshad ma vol. *zhe*, ff. 213a.4–236b.1: 210b–211a. The discussion relates to someone with a medical condition that causes visual perception to see the world as yellow. White things such as a conch appear with a yellow cast. But Dendar, following Dharmottara, states that when one perceives this object,

shape. For this reason, there is no way to grasp the shape alone without grasping the white of the conch. This is how his refutation works.

Well then, how does a person get to a conch? Doesn't a different authoritative cognition ascertain the texture of the conch? I think that it must be the case that when one analyzes, one analyzes a yellow conch, and when one gets to it, one gets to a white conch. In Gyeltsap Je's *Memorandum to the Perception Chapter*, it says: "The sound of a conch comes from something that has a particular color and shape, and [245] getting to the conch depends on another authoritative cognition."[76] In brief, to be precise, it is clear that things like the round chamber and long neck of a pot are the pot, but the shape of the round chamber and long neck are not the pot.[77]

In the *Great Exposition of Calming Meditation*, it says: "We maintain that the thing that has a round chamber and a long neck and so forth is a pot; but the shape of the round chamber and so forth is not the pot."[78] Suppose someone says: "According to the Cittamātra system, although things are not made of particles, particles do exist. This is because the fundamental particles that constitute a macro-object exist, and because their shape is spherical. As it says in the *Autocommentary on Investigation of the Percept*: 'Fundamental particles may be substantially distinct, but there are no differences in their spherical shapes (43).'"

---

one sees both its color and shape; there is no way to apprehend length independently of the color. One is really basing the judgment about its length on a configuration of color particles arranged in a line; because one misperceives their color, one also misperceives their shape. The two are indelibly cognitively linked.

76. Tsongkhapa, *Memorandum to the Perception Chapter* (*mNgon sum le'u'i brjed byang*). *gSung 'bum* (*sku 'bum par ma*); rGyal tshab Dar ma rin chen, *Mngon sum le'u'i brjed byang*. *rGyal tshab rje gSung 'bum*. Zhol par ma, vol. 5: 581–678. TBRC W676 (New Delhi: Mongolian Lama Guru Deva, 1982): 647. http://tbrc.org/link?RID=O2CZ7509|O2CZ75092CZ7561$W676. Dendar seems to be saying that one can engage with something even if one is mistaken in one sensory modality, as long as one accurately apprehends it through another authoritative cognition. In the cited section from the *Memorandum*, Gyeltsap criticizes Devendrabuddhi's claim that a visual cognition apprehending a yellow conch is not authoritative with respect to the color of the conch, but is authoritative with respect to its shape. Gyeltsap's point appears to be that if a visual cognition is nondeceptive with regard to the conch's color, it could not be deceptive with regard to its shape. A visual cognition apprehending a yellow conch does not get us to the conch, and so we require another authoritative cognition such as touch.

77. This is a subtle differentiation. The shape of a pot is an abstraction and is unable to perform the functions of a pot. The round chamber can hold water, and the neck can be used to pour it, but a pot's shape cannot do either of these things.

78. Tsongkhapa, *Great Exposition of Calming Meditation* (*Lhag mthong chen mo*, a section of the *Great Exposition of the Stages of the Path*), Asian Classics Input Project (ACIP) edition, p. 466a (http://www.asianclassics.org/release6/flat/S5392L_T.TXT).

Generally, in Cittamātra texts, there are many references to macro-material-forms and particles. In Vasubandhu's *Exposition Establishing How Action Works*, it says: "'Aggregation refers to a body, because it is an aggregation of fundamental particles that are elements or derived from elements."[79] There are similar statements in many sections [of the *Levels of Yogic Practice*][80] such as the *Compendium of Ascertainments*. There is much here to investigate.

Now suppose someone asks: "If macro-objects exist, then a macro-object-pot must also exist. In that case, what is the basis for mistaking a pot for an external object?" It is all right to refer to "this macro-object-pot," even though Tsongkhapa does not say this. In the commentary on *Introduction to the Middle Way*, [246] he says:

> The mistaken perception of a snake because of a rope does not arise from a basis where there is no rope. And a mistaken perception of something like a pot does not arise in empty space where there is no clay. In the same way, in the absence of external objects, what would be the basis of the mistake that would yield the resultant mistaken conception of the externality of such things as blue?[81]

For this reason, it is definitely necessary to accept that the cause of the mistake of externality is impure dependent nature appearing as a duality of substantially distinct subject and object. So, one thinks that there is a ground for positing the so-called dependent nature after having sought it.[82] We can hold our heads high and proclaim that in the context of False-Representation Cittamātra,[83] there are neither material form macro-objects nor fundamental

---

79. Vasubandhu, *Exposition Establishing How Action Works* (*Karma-siddhi-prakaraṇa*; Tib. *Las grub pa'i rab byed*) Derge, Sems tsam vol. *shi*: 144a.

80. Sa sde'i lung; this refers to five sections of Asaṅga's *Levels of Yogic Practice*: (1) *Compendium of Domains* (*Vastu-saṃgraha*; Tib. *gZhi bsdu ba*); (2) *Hierarchy of Domains* (*Bhūmi-vastu*; Tib. *Sa'i dngos gzhi*); (3) *Compendium of Ascertainments*; (4) *Compendium of Enumerations* (*Paryāya-saṃgraha*; Tib. *rNam grang bsdu ba*); and (5) *Compendium of Explanations* (*Vivaraṇa-saṃgraha*; Tib. *rNam par bshad pa'i sgo bsdu ba*). See *The Great Tibetan Dictionary* (*Bod rgya tshig mdzod chen mo*: 2899).

81. Tsongkhapa, *Clarifying the Thought: Explanation of the Introduction to the Middle Way* (*dBu ma 'jug pa'i rnam bshad dgongs pa rab gsal*) (vol. 19): 206. In this section, Tsongkhapa is presenting the Yogācāra position prior to outlining his refutation of it.

82. Text correction: *btsal*, from *'tshol ba*.

83. This refers to a Tibetan doxographical division of "Sems tsam rnam brdzun pa" (Skt. Alīkākāra Cittamātras), who take representations to be deceptive. For a description of the positions of the False-Representation and True-Representation Cittamātras, see Dreyfus (1997: 434).

particle macro-objects. I leave it to future scholars to set out the system of True-Representation Cittamātras. We can draw these distinctions in this context.

Why Macro-objects Are Nominally Real

Dignāga says:

> **Because the cognition that has the appearance of them**
> **Disappears when particles disperse.** (5cd)

Here is what this means: In the case of nominally real material-macro-objects like pots, when each of their individual fundamental particles is removed, the cognition that appears to have the representation of something like a pot vanishes. If a pot were a substantially real macro-object, then there would be a problem: cognitions of color and so forth would likewise be removed even when the fundamental particles that are connected with them are removed. Thus, neither minute particles nor macro-objects can be percept conditions and, for this reason, it makes sense that the appearing objects [247] of sensory cognitions are not external objects.

PROOF THAT THE PERCEPT CONDITION IS BY NATURE INTERNAL TO THE MIND

In the proof that the percept condition is internal to the mind, there are two parts: (1) presenting the position that the percept condition is simultaneous; and (2) presenting the Master's own approach.

Presenting the Position That the Percept Condition Is Simultaneous

The first section has two parts: (1) the opponent's position; and (2) the refutation of the argument against this position.

Dignāga says:

> **An internal cognitive object,**
> **Which appears as though external, is the object**
> **Because it is cognition itself,**
> **And because it is its condition.** (6abcd)

Here is what this means: Even without an external object, it is possible for there to be a percept condition. Even without an external object, the cognitive object itself—which has the nature of internal cognition and exists internally while appearing to be external—is precisely the object—that is, the percept condition.

A visual consciousness that apprehends blue acquires the nature of blue. Therefore, the appearance of blue in visual cognition is not only the appearing object that appears in visual cognition but also its condition.

Why? Internal consciousness appears as the object, and it also arises from it. Therefore, cognition is its percept and also its condition. Since it has both of these characteristics, the percept condition simply exists internally.

REFUTATION OF THE ARGUMENT AGAINST THIS POSITION

To begin, even if the opponent grants or concedes that the percept is only internal and that appearing objects appear in this way, isn't the visual cognition that apprehends blue in the same place as its counterpart, that is, the appearance of blue? And aren't they simultaneous? How does Dignāga explain that they are the condition and that which is conditioned?[84] Dignāga says:

> **Even though they are simultaneous, it is a condition because it is invariably concomitant.** (7a)

Even though the appearance of blue in visual cognition and the visual cognition itself are simultaneous, they do not deviate in the sense that when one is present, the other arises; and when the opposite is the case, the other does not arise. Therefore, even though the condition and the conditioned are simultaneous, it is not wrong for them to be causal and effective entities. The cognition would have as its condition the arising of the percept condition, which is different from both the immediately preceding condition and the dominant condition. This is because an argument (*gtan tshigs*)—that is, a reason (*rgyu mtshan*)—is characterized in the following way:[85] When a certain thing is present, another thing is present; and when a certain thing is absent, the other is absent. When one thing is present when the other is present and absent when the other is absent, in a mutual way, like a house and its beams,[86] this is defined as cause and effect. And this definition applies not only to simultaneous causes and effects, but also to sequential causes and effects.

---

84. This is a complex paraphrase of the objection in the autocommentary that introduces verse 7a.

85. The Sanskrit term *hetu* can be translated into Tibetan as either *rgyu* (cause) or *gtan tshigs* (reason). In Dendar's version, the autocommentary mistranslated *hetu* as *gtan tshigs*, but it should have been *rgyu*. Dendar has noticed this and glosses it as *rgyu mtshan*. The Tibetan term *rgyu mtshan* has the same ambiguity as the English word "reason": that is, it can be used either causally or to indicate a justification. Dendar relies on this ambiguity in glossing the unambiguously justificatory *gtan tshigs* in terms of the ambiguous *rgyu mtshan* as a way of moving toward the unambiguous *rgyu*.

86. "House and beams" (*gdung khyim*) is a misinterpretation of Sanskrit "bundle of reeds" (*naḍakalāpa*; Tib. *mdung khyim*) in the passage from the *Compendium of Mahāyāna* quoted below.

Some say that two lines and the first half of another present the True Representationalists and that two lines plus the second half of that other present the percept condition according to the False Representationalists.[87] According to Kedrup Je, there is a clear explanation of the position of the Cittamātras who accept the simultaneity of cause and effect. In *Clarifying the Thought: Great Commentary Definitively Elucidating Epistemological Treatises*, [Gyeltsap] refutes the claim that it makes no sense for Cittamātras to think like this.[88] But in the general approach of the Cittamātra, it makes no sense for cause and effect to be simultaneous, so I wonder whether any Cittamātras think like this. In the *Compendium of Mahāyāna*, it says:

> Suppose someone asks: how could the fundamental consciousness and afflictions cause one another if they are simultaneous? [249] It is like a butter lamp where the arising of the flame and the burning of the wick[89] are simultaneous, or like a house and its beams[90] that support one another simultaneously without falling down. They seem to be mutual causes of one another.[91]

Regarding the meaning of this, Master Vasubandhu says: "In this way, this presents the simultaneous cause."[92] Therefore, in *Clarifying the Thought: Great*

---

87. This could be interpreted in various ways, but we believe that he means that the former position (True Representationalists) is presented in verses 7a and 7cd and that that latter position (False Representationalists) is presented in 7b, c, and d. Another possibility is that both positions accept all of verse 6 but that True Representationalists accept only 7a, while False Representationalists accept 7b.

88. This refers to Gyeltsap's *Clarifying the Thought: Great Commentary Definitively Elucidating Epistemological Treatises* (*bsTan bcos tshad ma rnam nges kyi ṭīk chen dgongs pa rab gsal*); TBRC Work W669.

89. Read: *snying po tshig pa.*

90. Read: *mdung khyim* (Skt. *naḍakalāpa*). The Tibetan is a misreading of the Sanskrit, which would be translated as "bundle of reeds." This image is of reeds that are pointed inward to a peak, and all support each other. The Tibetan spelling would be *gdung khyim*, so apparently a scribe made this error and it was transmitted into the canon. Two quotations cited by Negi (2000, vol. 6: 2519–2520) in the definition of *mdung khyim* suggest that *naḍakalāpa* is a common comparison for things that function simultaneously. Chandra Das's definition of *mdung khyim* is: "A shade for travellers made on the wayside by throwing a piece of cloth over three pikes or poles; a frame to lean spears against": *A Tibetan-English Dictionary* (2000: 674).

91. Asaṅga, *Compendium of Mahāyāna*: Derge, Sems tsam vol. *ri*, ff. 6a–6b.

92. Tib. *lhan cig 'byung ba'i rgyu*. Vasubandhu, *Commentary on the Compendium of Mahāyāna*: Derge, Sems tsam vol. *ri*, 131a. This passage is found in Lamotte (1973, ch. 1, sect. 17). See also Keenan (2006: 20).

Commentary Definitively Elucidating Epistemological Treatises, it says: "This is merely the assertion of earlier scholars like Vasubandhu when he follows Abhidharma: cause and effect can be simultaneous; it does not follow that cause and effect are substantially different."[93] What an elegant explanation!

Master Dignāga's Own Position

In the presentation of Master Dignāga's own position, there are five parts: (1) the actual presentation of his own approach; (2) a refutation of an objection; (3) an explanation that cognition is the location of the capacity; (4) a summarizing conclusion; and (5) an explanation of miscellaneous issues.

ACTUAL PRESENTATION OF HIS OWN APPROACH

Explaining in accord with the previous masters, or, to unpack the meaning of what is said here:

> **It is sequential because of a transfer of capacity.** (7b)

The appearance of blue within a previous cognition apprehending blue has the capacity to produce a subsequent sensory cognition with a representation of blue. This capacity is the condition that conveys the blue appearance to the subsequent sensory cognition with the representation of blue. For this reason, it acts sequentially as the percept condition of the subsequent sense cognition.

Putting it concisely, the formal argument should be advanced as follows: Consider the capacity that is established in cognition when the immediately preceding condition of the sense cognition that appears as blue ceases. [250] This acts sequentially as the percept condition of the subsequent sensory cognition because it is the condition that transfers the representation of blue to its own effect—namely, the subsequent sensory cognition that appears blue. It is generally accepted that "the percept condition transfers the capacity." I think, however, that we should say that "the percept condition transfers the representation." This is the right way to think.

This way of stating the formal argument concisely accords with *Clarifying the Thought: Great Commentary Definitively Elucidating Epistemological Treatises*.

---

93. Gyeltsap, *Clarifying the Thought: Great Commentary Definitively Elucidating Epistemological Treatises* (2006, vol. 21: 131). In this section, Gyeltsap cites *Examination of the Percept* in his discussion of the three conditions: percept condition, dominant condition, and immediately preceding condition. According to Yogācāra, sensory cognitions arise from them. Gyeltsap is mainly discussing the nature of the percept condition, and he relies on Dignāga's presentation.

According to the autocommentary, there is another way for a percept condition to act, namely, sequentially. The appearance of an external object in a sensory cognition produces a capacity, located in mental cognition, that produces a subsequent effect consistent with its appearance.[94] So this is not contradictory. This is how it should be understood.

REFUTATION OF AN OBJECTION

Suppose someone asks: "But if you maintain that only internal visible form is the percept condition, then how can the arising of a visual cognition depend not only on an internal visible form—which is the percept condition—but also on the visual sense faculty—which is the dominant condition? Your so-called internal visible form cannot be different from a visual sense faculty, and that does not appear in a visual cognition. So how could this be a percept condition? Regarding this, the Master says:

> **A sense faculty is a cooperating sense capacity.** (7cd)

If we maintained that the visual sense faculty is material form, this would be a valid point. But there is no problem because we maintain that the nature of the capacity that governs the simultaneous activity of the two—blue and the visual cognition that apprehends blue—[251] is not only the condition for the later sensory cognition; there is also the visual sensory faculty itself. So there is no such problem.

The visual sensory faculty that sees blue is a capacity because occasionally it does not arise even in the presence of both the percept condition—that is, the visual sensory cognition that apprehends blue that is its effect—and the immediately preceding condition. On the basis of this evidence, it is possible to draw an inference about the existence of the general nature of a capacity, stating that "there is the capacity to see only blue without having the capacity to see such things as sounds and scents." However, one cannot draw any inference about the particular details of the elements or such things as material forms that are derived from them.

EXPLANATION THAT COGNITION IS THE LOCATION OF THE CAPACITY

Dignāga says:

> **It is not contradictory for this capacity also to be in cognition.** (8a)

94. This refers to Gyeltsap's *Clarifying the Thought* (2006, vol. 21: 131–133).

A sensory faculty is a capacity, so it is not contradictory for it and the cognition that has it to be simultaneous as the location and that which is located. Whether it is as the Cittamātras say—that the capacity is located in cognition—or as the Sautrāntikas say—that the eye is located in material form itself that is not previously evident and is derived from the gross elements—in either case there is no difference with regard to their production of effects.

SUMMARY OF THESE POINTS

Dignāga says:

> **Thus, the object and**
> **The capacity cause one another and**
> **Have done so from beginningless time.** (8bcd)

In this way, both the visual cognition that has the representation of an object and the capacity that is the visual sensory faculty are mutually causal. If one attempts to track down its origin, one will realize that it has proceeded since beginningless time.

It is possible for cognition to have arisen depending on the capacity called "eye" [252] and for cognition to have arisen depending on an internal visible form. We do not maintain that the cognition that appears as the object arose because of the power of the apprehended object. For this reason, it is said that the cognition that appears as the object is "not made evident" by the percept. That is, it arises without being disclosed by the percept.

The capacity and the cognition that has the capacity cause one another, and the sequence has proceeded in this way from time immemorial. This is so because sometimes cognition arises as the representation of the object from the maturation of the capacity—which consists of predispositions in the same continuum—and sometimes the capacity arises from a cognition that has the representation of the object.

Although this capacity cannot be said to be substantially identical to or different from the cognition that has this capacity, nominally one is free to say that these two are either different or identical.

In this way, even without external objects—whether one maintains that the percept condition and the perceiver are simultaneous or sequential—in either case, it makes sense that this internal percept is the object of observation because it satisfies both criteria.

EXPLANATION OF EXTRANEOUS POINTS

It is well known that the particle "*ni*" is used to separate, to emphasize, and to fill out. There are many ways of using it other than these. In *Investigation of the Percept*, it says: "**Even if sensory cognition were caused by fundamental particles, it would not have particles as its object because they do not appear to cognition.**"[95] Here the word "*ni*" means "because." It says in Vinītadeva's [253] *Subcommentary on Investigation of the Percept*: "The word "*hi*" (*ni*) means 'because.' "[96] For example, in the statement "a pot is impermanent," it is correct to say that it is impermanent because it is a pot.[97]

Again, the particle "*ni*" in the phrase "in this" (*'di la ni*) in the *Autocommentary to Investigation of the Percept* [in the introduction to verse 3ab] functions as the word "also" (*yang*; Skt. *api*). This is because it says in the *Subcommentary*: "The particle '*ni*' should be understood to mean '*yang*.' "[98] It is correct to say "also" (*yang*) here instead of "*ni*."

Again, the particle "*ni*" in in the phrase "things like solidity" in the *Subcommentary* [on verse 3cd] has the meaning of "themselves" (*nyid*). This is because it says in the *Subcommentary*: "The meaning of the particle '*ni*' should be interpreted as '*nyid*.' "[99] This is like saying "pots themselves are impermanent" for "pots are impermanent."

Again, the particle "*ni*" in the root [verse 6ab], "**an internal cognitive object**," has both an emphatic and a delimiting function because it says in the *Subcommentary*: "The word '*ni*' (Skt. *tu*) should be viewed as having an emphatic and adversative meaning." For example, first, when there is reason to say that Devadatta is a man, there also is reason to say that he is certainly a

95. Dendar's comments focus on the third *pāda* of verse 1: *der mi snang phyir de yul ni*. He is differentiating possible meanings of the particle *ni*, which is used to translate Sanskrit *hi*, *tu*, and *api*.

96. Here Vinītadeva (Derge p. 354) is referring to the "*ni*" at the beginning of the first sentence in the commentary on verse 1: "*yul zhes bya ba ni*" (Skt. *viṣayo hi nāma*). This sentence explains *why* particles cannot be the object. The particle "*hi*" often has a causal meaning, as explained in Speijer's *Sanskrit Syntax* (1886: section 429): "*Tu*, *hi*, and the enclitic *u* are, like *ca* and *vā*, subjoined to the first word of the sentence. *Hi* was at the outset an emphatic, a weak 'indeed,' but generally it is a causal particle, at least in prose."

97. This probably means something like: For example, the statement "a pot (*ni*) is impermanent" means that it is impermanent because it is a pot." Unfortunately, Dendar's point is based on a misunderstanding of Vinītadeva's commentary.

98. Again Dendar has misunderstood Vinītadeva's commentary (88). Dendar is talking about the particle "*ni*" in the phrase (*'di la ni*) that introduces verse 3ab. Vinītadeva's comment on "*ni*" occurs at the end of his subcommentary on the autocommentary that follows this verse and refers to the phrase "*don thams cad ni*" ("all objects"). Since "*ni*" and "*yang*" can have many uses and many Sanskrit equivalents, it is difficult to know exactly what is being said. It seems likely that Vinītadeva is saying that "*ni*" (perhaps the Sanskrit "*hi*") is being used in an emphatic sense.

99. Again Vinītadeva (90) seems to be saying that "*ni*" is used in an emphatic sense to mark the subject of the sentence.

man. And, second, it has the adversative or delimiting function. For example, it is like the particle "*ni*" in the phrase "by the power of desire, hatred, and ignorance."[100]

Epistemological treatises negate external objects
And establish that everything that appears is the nature of mind.
Am I not fortunate to wish freely to understand them
In these final times?
Even though the ghost-bird that rules four realms of rebirth[101]
Cannot bear this approach and casts an evil omen,
Who can block the power of an eloquent teaching
To illuminate with its light a wise person's mental space?
Since this is drawn from pure, reliable sources,
And because it stands up to analysis by my mind,
I believe that this text is free from grievous errors of false teachings[102]
That are utterly inconsistent with the classical treatises.
However, because the system of cognition[103] is profound,
And because I cannot fathom its depths,
There may be some cases where I mistook a hat for a shoe;[104]
And you should treat them as flaws of my own intellect.
When small children speak incorrectly,
Their parents love them even more.
I am also full of ignorance and uncertainty,
So it makes good sense to treat me with even greater love.
May this work be a Samantabhadra offering cloud
Presented to the father and son, Dignāga and Dharmakīrti.

---

100. He appears to be glossing this as meaning: "*only* by the power of desire, hatred, and ignorance."

101. This probably includes the realms of humans, animals, hungry ghosts (*preta*), and hell beings. The "ghost bird" can refer to owls, who move silently in the dark and are camouflaged by their coloring. In Tibetan literature, the "ghost bird that rules the realms of rebirth" is a malevolent creature that looks like an owl, and Dendar indicates that it has a baleful glance, like that of an owl.

102. This appears to be obliquely referring to the third quatrain of Vinītadeva's concluding verses (103).

103. Tib. *rnam rig*; Skt. *vijñapti*. This refers to the philosophical tradition of Vijñapti-mātratā or Yogācāra.

104. This metaphor refers to someone making a decision based on partial or incomplete evidence, often on the spur of the moment. One is looking for a shoe and picks up a hat instead because it bears some superficial resemblance.

May it please and delight these supreme beneficiaries
And pacify all the world's negativities.
Out of the conjugal union of scripture and reasoning
that are like dark clouds
Resound the eloquent teachings of the rolling drum
of summer thunder.
May those who are eager to learn dance like peacocks
And be beautified by the womb of benefit and happiness.[105]
In the expansive lotus garden of the fine Epistemological tradition,
Study and reflection are like the constant playful buzzing of bees.
May the wise enjoy the honey of the profound meaning
And may this splendor never diminish.
May I also in all my lives gain confidence in this
Epistemological tradition
That does not need to rely on others.
And may I attain unrivalled authority
In explaining the meaning of logical reasoning.

This subcommentary on the *Investigation of Percept* known as *Beautiful String of Pearls* was written by Alasha Lharampa Ngawang Dendar (A lag sha lha rams pa Ngag dbang bstan dar). By this may the Victor's previous teachings remain a long time.

This is printed at Kumbum Jambaling (sKu 'bum byams pa gling).
sarva maṅgalaṃ/

All the best!

105. The image here is the dark clouds of the Indian monsoon, which bring the rain that sustains life. When they form, rolling thunder echoes across the land, which sounds like the beating of a large drum. Peacocks and other animals eagerly greet the rain, and their joy is compared to that of scholars involved in studying epistemology.

10

Introduction to Summary of the Essence

A COMMENTARY ON INVESTIGATION OF THE PERCEPT

Jay L. Garfield, John Powers, and Sonam Thakchöe

Biography

Geshe Yeshes Thabkhas[1] was born on March 10, 1930, in a small country town in Lhokha Chede Shol (Lho kha lce bde zhol), located in Gongkar Dzong (Gong dkar rdzong) in the vicinity of Lhasa. His birth name was Tsering Puntsok (Tshe ring phun tshogs). During his youth, Tsering Puntsok spent much of his time spinning wool, herding animals, and doing other tasks commonly allocated to children in his country.

When he was seven, Tsering Puntsok moved to Lhasa and stayed with his father, who was then working as an employee of the aristocrat Göshamba (rGod gsham pa). There he spent six years in two elementary schools, where he was introduced to the Tibetan alphabet, calligraphy, grammar, and literature.

At the age of thirteen, Tsering Puntsok chose to become a monk and enrolled at Drepung Lhopa Khangtsen ('Bras spungs lho pa khang mtshan)

1. This brief sketch of Geshe Yeshe Thabkhas's life is based on a detailed biography compiled by one of his students, Jamyang Gyatso ('Jam dbyangs rgya mtsho: 2012: 1–105) which was electronically published as a pdf. We are grateful to Passang Dorjee, Geshe Yeshes Thabkhas's current Research Assistant at the Central University of Tibetan Studies, from whom we first came to know of its existence and from whom we acquired an electronic copy.

and was given the name Yeshes Thabkhas. He was accepted as a student of Lhopa Khenpo (Lho pa mkhan po), the abbot of Loseling (bLo gsal gling) College. Within two years, however, his teacher died.

The next several years proved challenging for Yeshes Thabkhas. Suffering from poverty and lack of proper guidance, he neglected his studies, lost interest in reading philosophical texts, and even declined to participate in debates. His life turned around when Jamyang Nyishar ('Jam dbyangs nyi shar) took a personal interest in him and rekindled his interest in learning.

At the age of eighteen, Yeshes Thabkhas received novice ordination from Takdra Rinpoche (sTag brag Rin po che, 1874–1952), one of the tutors of the fourteenth Dalai Lama. He was given the ordination name Ngawang Tudop (Ngag dbang mthu stobs). From this time onwards, Yeshes Thabkhas was able to fully concentrate on his studies. He excelled and became a renowned debater, distinguishing himself at the great debate festivals in Lhasa.

At the age of twenty-three, Yeshes Thabkhas received full ordination vows from Tsulkhang Gyepa Khenpo (Tshul khang rGyas pa mkhan po). He studied with some of the greatest teachers of the time, including Khensur Yeshe Tupden (mKhan zur Ye shes thub bstan) and Geshe Sönam Gönpo (dGe bshes bSod nams dgon po). Yeshes Thabkhas followed the Dalai Lama into exile in the wake of the failed 1959 uprising against Chinese rule. On the way to India, Yeshes Thabkhas met Yeshe Tupden and Geshe Belden Drakpa (dPal ldan grags pa), who joined their group. They traveled through Lhodrak (Lho brag), the birthplace of the great translator Marpa (1012–1097) and then reached Bhutan. They settled at a Tibetan refugee settlement named Bhagsar (sBa gsar) near the border between Bhutan and Siliguri in the Indian state of Bengal. Yeshes Thabkhas later moved to Ladakh with Yeshe Tupden, Belden Drakpa, and some other geshes. Many of his colleagues were not as fortunate. His friend and debating partner Ami was one of the many Tibetans who died in Chinese labor camps.

When the Central Institute of Buddhist Studies was founded in Leh, Ladakh, in 1959, Yeshes Thabkhas was appointed Director and began teaching students. He spent the next thirteen years in Ladakh.

In 1972, Yeshes Thabkhas was appointed as a lecturer in Indian Buddhist philosophy at the Central Institute of Higher Tibetan Studies (now the Central University of Tibetan Studies). He remained on the faculty until he officially retired as Professor in 1990 at the age of sixty. He has continued to teach and to pursue research in retirement and remains at the Central University of Tibetan Studies as Emeritus Professor.

Yeshes Thabkhas's scholarship encompasses not only Indian Buddhist philosophy, but also a broad spectrum of Tibetan traditions. His wide-ranging intellectual interests are particularly evident in his monograph on Tsongkhapa's seminal work on hermeneutics, *Essence of Eloquence Differentiating the Interpretable and the Definitive*, titled *Straightforward Analysis of Interpretable and Definitive Meanings in the Treatise "Essence of Eloquence" Composed by Tsongkhapa Losang Drakpa*.[2] Yeshes Thabkhas has also composed a commentary and critical edition of Kamalaśīla's *Commentary on the Rice Seedling Discourse*.[3] He was the Tibetan advisor for the three-volume English translation of Tsongkhapa's masterpiece, *Great Exposition of the Stages of the Path to Awakening*.[4]

Geshe Yeshes Thabkhas was twice asked by the Dalai Lama to become abbot of Loseling Monastery, but both times he declined, citing teaching and research commitments. He has had numerous appointments at tertiary institutions, including several semesters as a visiting professor at the University of Virginia, and he has taught at Buddhist centers in Europe, Japan, and North America. Even though he is now officially retired, he maintains a busy teaching schedule and is involved in a number of research projects.

The Commentary

One of Geshe Yeshes Thabkhas's latest academic activities is the present commentary on Dignāga's *Investigation of the Percept*. This work had its origins in the oral teachings for the *Investigation of the Percept* research project he gave at the Tibetan Buddhist Learning Center in Washington, New Jersey, in 2014. The transcript of lectures on the text and its commentaries at Tibet House in New Delhi earlier that year was integrated with the transcript of these teachings into a single document, which was then presented to him as a draft manuscript. He edited this draft, clarifying some points and adding more material to further develop his analyses, resulting in a unitary Tibetan scholastic commentary, with a title, dedication verses, and a colophon.

Yeshes Thabkhas is a scholar of formidable learning. He has distinguished himself as one of the leading figures of his tradition in Middle Way philosophy and Epistemology. His wide-ranging study of Indian treatises is unusual for Gelukpa scholars, who generally know this literature primarily through Tibetan commentaries or textbooks that summarize their main points. Few

---

2. *Shar tsong kha pa blo bzang grags pas mdzad pa'i drang ba dang nges pa'i don rnam par 'byed pa'i bstan bcos legs bshad snying po.*

3. Tib. *Ārya-śālistambaka-ṭīkā*; Tib. *'Phags pa sā lu ljang pa rgya cher 'grel pa.*

4. *Byang chub lam rim chen mo*: Lamrim Chenmo Publication Committee (2000).

have devoted the same amount of time and energy to exploring in detail the arguments presented in works that are regarded as seminal but seldom read in isolation, independently of Tibetan exegetical treatises. This is largely due to a common belief that Indic philosophical works are too difficult for most scholars to understand. The distinctive feature of Yeshes Thabkhas's scholarship is his intimate familiarity with a broad range of Indian Buddhist literature as well as his immersion in the Tibetan commentarial tradition. Both of these aspects of his scholarship are evident in this commentary.

Yeshes Thabkhas is also, like any Tibetan scholar, reticent to teach any text for which he does not have oral lineage. Fortunately, he received the oral transmission for *Investigation of the Percept*, itself a rare phenomenon given the scant attention to this text in Tibet. It is probably no coincidence that the two authors of Tibetan commentaries, Gungtang and Ngawang Dendar, studied at Drepung Monastic University, as did Yeshes Thabkhas. This reflects the fact that Dignāga's work was part of the curriculum at this seat of learning and suggests that some of its scholars may have studied his philosophy independently of the commentarial lens of Dharmakīrti or of Gelukpa scholastic exegeses.

Yeshes Thabkhas's reading of any Indian philosophical text, like those of Gungtang and Ngawang Dendar, is framed by Geluk doxography, and he construes it as a Cittamātra text that responds to Sautrāntika. He also explicitly responds to Gungtang and Ngawang Dendar, situating his own analysis in this lineage. And for the first time in the history of readings of this text, we see a Tibetan commentator responding to ideas deriving from the Chinese commentarial tradition.

Yeshes Thabkhas's commentary is distinctive in a number of respects. First, he begins by carefully distinguishing the senses of *percept* (*dmigs pa;* Skt. *ālambana*), *intentional object* (*don;* Skt. *artha*), and *object* (*yul;* Skt. *viṣaya*). As he notes, these terms are often taken to be synonyms, and indeed they are sometimes used interchangeably even in commentaries on *Investigation of the Percept*. Nonetheless, he argues, they should be carefully differentiated.

A percept is the object immediately apprehended in perception, even if it is not conceptualized. The intentional object may or may not be perceptual but, in the case of perception, the percept only becomes an intentional object to the degree to which it is ascertained, or thematized cognitively. The object (which plays no further role in this commentary) is any object that falls in the domain of perception or cognition, whether or not it is thematized. Here Yeshes Thabkhas follows the tradition of the *Treasury of Abhidharma* in its analysis of language and thought, a tradition that is also reflected in the works of Dignāga (who composed a commentary on it and who, as indicated in notes to previous texts in this book, adheres to the terminological conventions he uses there).

In drawing this distinction, Yeshes Thabkhas introduces another innovation to this commentarial lineage. As we have seen in this volume, the apparently simple analogy of the double moon is deployed in a distinctive manner by each commentator. Yeshes Thabkhas introduces yet one more way to understand this trope. He points out that the single moon that is the cause of perceptual experience in the analogy represents the *percept,* but the double moon is the *intentional object.* He emphasizes that *Investigation of the Percept* is not concerned with this content of thought, but rather specifically with the percept—the content of perception. So the analogy of the double moon is reinterpreted not as an argument for idealism or as an example of an illusion, but rather as a way of distinguishing the different kinds of relations that subjectivity bears to its object.

Yeshes Thabkhas represents the overall structure of the text as a grand formal argument mounted by Dignāga as a representative of Cittamātra against the Vaibhāṣika and Sautrāntika positions, according to which the percept is external to cognition. Following the Chinese tradition grounded in Dharmapāla's commentary on *Investigation of the Percept,* Yeshes Thabkhas distinguishes three possibilities for any proponent of the thesis that external objects are percepts: that they are (1) fundamental particles; (2) collections of fundamental particles; or (3) collective features of fundamental particles. He divides the refutation section of the text into three distinct arguments, each aimed at one of these possibilities. This is a different framework from those we see at work in Gungtang or Ngawang Dendar, in which the third position is presented as a variant of the second.

Another distinctive feature of Yeshe Thabkhas's analysis is his attention to the ethical implications of this text. While *Investigation of the Percept* is clearly epistemological in focus, Buddhist philosophy is predicated on the close connection between epistemology and ethics, a linkage that begins in the four noble truths and the earliest accounts of dependent arising and runs through the history of Buddhist thought. In this tradition, the entire point of epistemological reflection is to facilitate moral development and liberation. While this dimension of the treatise is not thematized by Dignāga or any of his earlier commentators—whether Indian, Tibetan, or Chinese—Yeshes Thabkhas takes ethical implications to be important topics of reflection.

There are two important ethical consequences to which Yeshes Thabkhas draws our attention. First, he points out that the fact that the percept is internal means that we are responsible for the way we see the world; and that our perspective on "reality" is a function not only of the world we see but also of the way in which we have constituted ourselves as perceivers through our past actions and habits. Second, he asserts near the end of his commentary that reflecting on the fact that the percept can be simultaneous with—as well as anterior to—perception can lead us to see why emotions such as anger can arise in the context of perception itself, and therefore why attention to the cultivation of perceptual responses is so morally urgent.

In the later part of his commentary, Yeshes Thabkhas devotes himself to answering an important question: Does Cittamātra accept any material form? He concludes by noting that while Dignāga does not specifically refute the existence of an external world as an object or intentional object, his treatise does argue that the *percept*—the immediate object of perceptual experience—is entirely internal; that even if one were to develop or defend a mediated account of the perception of the external world, nothing in the external world itself can ever be perceived immediately.

But how far should we take the Cittamātras's refutation of external reality? Does it entail the rejection of the existence of material form altogether? None of the previous Indian or Tibetan commentators on *Investigation of the Percept*—Vinītadeva, Gungtang, or Ngawang Dendar—take any decisive stance on this question. In fact, Vinītadeva and Gungtang are silent on this issue, but Ngawang Dendar's commentary explicitly touches on it and claims that it is a *difficult question*. He also draws our attention to the position Tsongkhapa takes on this issue, but Dendar does not provide much discussion about it (150–151). Yeshes Thabkhas, however, dedicates two significant sections of his commentary (verse 1cd and his concluding discussion) to analyzing it. He concurs with Dendar that the question of whether or not Cittamātra accepts material form is complex and that it has received little critical attention.

A final word on this commentary: it is easy in Buddhist Studies to think of ourselves as antiquarians, studying the texts of a lost civilization. This very recent treatise, which has its roots in the efflorescence of Buddhist epistemological philosophy in the sixth century and follows on from two commentaries written in the eighteenth century and another oral discussion by Geshe Lobsang Gyatso in the twentieth, reminds us that these works and the issues they raise are still of vital concern to Buddhists. This commentary also reminds us that the scholarly tradition in which Dignāga himself figured is very much alive.

11

Summary of the Essence

A COMMENTARY ON INVESTIGATION OF THE PERCEPT

Yeshes Thabkhas

TRANSLATED BY DOUGLAS Duckworth, Jay Garfield, John Powers, and Sonam Thakchöe

Preface

I respectfully salute the assembly of Indian and Tibetan scholars
Including Dignāga and Dharmakīrti, who masterfully explain
The critical points of the profound emptiness of duality.
I will now endeavor to compose a brief commentary on
Investigation of the Percept.

Having paid my respects, I will now briefly offer my commentary on Master Dignāga's *Autocommentary on Investigation of Percept* as I have been invited to do so by some people who are interested in the text.

The Sanskrit title of the text is *Ālambana-parīkṣā-vṛtti*, and the Tibetan title is *dMigs pa brtag pa'i 'grel ba*. The Tibetan term for *ālambana* is *dmigs pa*, "percept"; *parīkṣā* is *brtag pa*, "investigation"; and *vṛtti* is *'grel pa*, "commentary."

Analysis of the Title

Suppose someone now asks: What is the difference between "percept" (*dmigs pa*; Skt. *ālambana*), "object" (*yul*; Skt. *viṣaya*), and "intentional object" (*don*;

Skt. *artha*)?[1] In general, percept, object, and intentional object can have the same meaning. For instance, form, sound, scent, taste, and texture are generally described as five percepts, five intentional objects, and five objects. The three, however, can be differentiated with respect to that to which they refer in specific contexts. Just because something is the percept of a cognition, it is not necessary to maintain that it is the object or intentional object of that cognition.

Consider, for example, a cognition that directly knows emptiness. Because it observes a percept that comprises all phenomena, they must be posited as the percept of wisdom that knows the emptiness of apprehender and apprehended. In this context, the percept of this wisdom is *all phenomena*, but they do not constitute its object. For instance, after one has perceived a percept that is a material form, when one directly knows that the material form and the perceiver are not substantially different, the material form is the percept of that wisdom, but it is not its object. Consider, on the other hand, the example of a visual cognition apprehending blue. The blue is the object of the visual cognition apprehending blue; it also must be its intentional object and its percept.

In general, in this treatise, *Investigation of the Percept*, the matters to be investigated include: What is the percept? What is its nature? How is a percept conveyed to cognition through a representation? So we will examine whether the percept condition that appears due to conveying a representation to cognition emerges from an external object that conveys a representation or whether it emerges from the maturation of latent predispositions internal to cognition.

Sautrāntika realists assert that a representation arises when an external object conveys a representation. Dignāga investigates the question, "So what would the nature of such a percept be like?"

But suppose one asks, "If *percept, intentional object*, and *object* have the same meaning, instead of naming this treatise *Investigation of the Percept*, if we were to name it *Investigation of the Object* or *Investigation of the Intentional*

---

1. Note that each of these terms has many other meanings. Our translation choices reflect how they are employed in *Investigation of the Percept*, but they are used in differing ways in other works and genres of Indian and Tibetan literature. As noted in Chapter 1, "The Subject Matter of *Investigation of the Percept*: A Tale of Five Commentaries" (3–37), in our translation of Dignāga's text and the other commentaries we have used "object" to translate both *yul* (Skt. *viṣaya*) and *don* (Skt. *artha*). It is not clear that either Dignāga or Vinītadeva distinguishes them. Gungtang and Ngawang Dendar may use them in distinct senses more regularly, and Geshe Thabkhas draws a clear distinction between them. So for this commentary we translate *yul* as "object" and *don* as "intentional object" to reflect how he understands their usage in *Investigation of the Percept*.

Object, would the change in the phrasing of the title make any difference in the commentarial meaning or mode of expression, or not?"

In this context, the analysis does not concern the object of conceptual cognition. This treatise analyzes the actual way in which perceptual cognitions experience things when they apprehend objects that are percept conditions—forms, sounds, scents, tastes, and textures—after they are produced due to the conveyance of each individual aspect of an object to cognition. It is not a discussion that is concerned with the objects of conceptual cognitions. Thus, it is more appropriate for the text to be titled *Investigation of the Percept*. If it were titled *Investigation of the Object*, there would be a problem that its scope would be too broad because *object* would encompass all cognitions, including conceptual ones.

The phrase "Homage to all buddhas and bodhisattvas" is the statement of homage paid by the translators.

Introduction

The Buddha turned the Dharma wheel in three stages. The first, the turning of the Dharma wheel of the four noble truths, discusses phenomena as if external objects were real. Moreover, in the context of the first Dharma wheel, in consideration of his primary audience, the two Śrāvaka schools—who regard all worldly phenomena such as forms and sounds as if they are directly perceived externally—the Teacher, Buddha, presents external objects as truly existent. There is no apparent critical analysis of whether or not they really exist in the way they are perceived. That is, as it is said in the third chapter of the *Commentary on the Compendium of Epistemology*:

> With indifference to its meaning,
> Gazing like an elephant,
> Solely in accordance with mundane minds,
> He introduces an analysis of the external.[2]

When the Buddha taught the Dharma wheel of the four noble truths, he understood the nonexistence of external objects such as material forms and the way things really are, but on this occasion he taught in a way that was noncommittal, like the way an elephant gazes. For example, when a great elephant walks from one location to another, its field of experience encompasses many

2. Dharmakīrti, *Commentary on the Compendium of Epistemology* (*Pramāṇa-vārttika*), sDe dge edition: 126b. See also Tshul khrims rin chen (1982–1985: 174).

things that exist on either side of the road, but he moves in whatever direction he pleases as though he does not even see them. Likewise, although the Buddha perceives the nonexistence of external objects, he teaches as though he does not perceive it, in accordance with the mundane perception that perceives external objects as existent. Thus, he teaches the Dharma to trainees.

During the turning of the first Dharma wheel, the Buddha did not provide explanations like that of the nonexistence of external objects in the way that they appear. For this reason, certain disciples of the first wheel developed the belief that the intention of the first wheel is that phenomena exist as external objects and exist by way of their own character.

Moreover, in the context of the teaching of the first Dharma wheel, cognitions arise because each conveys its representation when the five objects—forms, sounds, scents, tastes, and textures—appear to sensory cognitions. That is, the Buddha taught that a visual cognition arises from a form that is a percept condition, a visual sense faculty that is a dominant condition, and a previous moment of mental cognition that is an immediately preceding condition. In brief, because he taught that an external object is its cause and a visual cognition is its effect, he indicated that external objects exist. So for the benefit of the trainees of the first wheel—the two Śrāvaka schools, Vaibhāṣikas and Sautrāntikas, who assert the existence of external objects—he taught that external objects exist in order to accommodate them.

Someone may ask: In that case, what is the defining character of the percept's "percept condition" in the systems of those who posit external objects?

A percept is an intentional object that is experienced as a percept condition and that is perceptually experienced as an apprehended object. A percept or apprehended object is a truly existent external object; it is the object of engagement that is directly perceived by sense faculties such as the visual.

But what do they claim is the reason why direct perceptions of sense faculties directly perceive external objects? According to the Sautrāntikas, here is how one proves that there are external objects: They assert: "A blue thing exists externally, and due to conveyance of its representation to a visual cognition internally, because it is its percept condition, a visual cognition apprehending blue perceives blue as a blue apprehended object."

In that case, the Cittamātra asks the Sautrāntika, "What is the proof for the existence of external objects?" and "How do external objects exist as apprehended objects?" The Sautrāntika replies by citing the *Commentary on the Compendium of Epistemology*: "It resembles it and it arises from it; and, as it were, it has the characteristic of being experienced."[3]

---

3. Dharmakīrti, *Commentary on the Compendium of Epistemology*: 130b.

As the text says, when each percept condition—form, sound, scent, taste, and texture—conveys its representation, because that sensory cognition arises with the representation of that object, it is said to be "produced by it." With regard to the phrase "It resembles it," because that cognition arises as a representation of its object, that cognition "resembles that object."[4]

As Gungtang's commentary on *Investigation of the Precept* says, according to the presentation of the system of the Sautrāntikas, the opponent's definition of the percept is "what arises from it and resembles it." In short, they assert: "It satisfies the two criteria: (1) the subject arises from the object; and (2) a representation of the object appears to the subject and resembles it; for this reason, an external object serves as the percept condition of an internal cognition." This is what it means for a percept to be perceptually experienced after serving as a percept condition, and it is also what it means for a percept to be perceptually experienced after serving as an apprehended object for direct perception. Dendar Lharampa also defines *percept condition* in the same way:

> It would make sense for something like a blue object to be the percept that is called the percept condition if it appears as itself—that is, if it produces a cognition of itself or like itself. So a treatise states: "An object is a percept if it causes mental states and mental processes to arise and, when they arise, prompts the conventional designation that this object is experienced." If something is the percept condition of a sensory cognition, then it is said that a representation like itself appears in that sensory cognition and also that it is the condition of the arising of that sensory cognition (151).

According to the Vaibhāṣika system, external objects exist. These external objects are also the percept conditions of cognitions. Nonetheless, on their view, these external objects are the objects of engagement directly experienced by sensory cognitions. Therefore, they do not assert that unless these cognitions directly engage an object the object serves as a percept condition due to internally conveying its representation to the subject. So a visual cognition apprehending blue does not arise with the representation of that object. Thus, that cognition and that object do not need to satisfy the criterion of resembling each other.

According to the Cittamātra system, external objects such as blue appear as though they exist. Nonetheless, they maintain that the arising of all of their

4. Dharmakīrti, *Commentary on the Compendium of Epistemology*: 130b.

intentional objects is merely due to the maturation of predispositions in the fundamental consciousness that are implanted by such things as a visual cognition that apprehends internal blue things.

There are two distinct aspects of the maturation of predispositions: (1) in one way, a portion of a predisposition arises with the nature of a cognition, as in a dream cognition; and (2) in another way, the maturation of a single portion arises with the nature of a representation of an object. For these two reasons, they argue, it is logically proven that the experience of both a visual cognition apprehending blue and a representation of blue are only derived from the maturation of predispositions internal to cognition.

They are not experienced *as posited by the subjects*; rather, these objects are experienced as representations conveyed to the subject. In reality, however, they are like dreams. Just as in dreams there are no external objects, but due to the power of the maturation of predispositions in the fundamental consciousness various objects appear with the nature of dream cognitions. When various representations appear in a dream cognition—such as objects that are attractive or unattractive, happiness and suffering, birth, aging, and death—all are within cognition, although they appear as though they exist externally.

The outline of the subject matter of this treatise has two parts:

(1) **refutation of the assertions of both realists and proponents of external objects, who posit that the percept is an external object; and**
(2) **presentation of the Cittamātras's own system, which demonstrates that the percept exists internally.**

Refutation of the Assertion of Realists Who Posit That the Percept Is an External Object

(1) **The refutation of realists who posit that the percept is an external object has three parts:**
   1.1. **Refutation of the assertion that fundamental particles are apprehended objects;**
   1.2. **Refutation of the assertion that macro-objects are apprehended objects; and**
   1.3. **Refutation of the assertion that features of collected particles are apprehended objects.**

Refutation of the Assertion That Fundamental Particles Are Apprehended Objects

The term "**Some**" refers to certain Buddhist philosophers because it singles out the Vaibhāṣikas and Sautrāntikas—the two Śrāvaka schools—who advocate the true existence of external objects, and because the two are the principal disciples of the first turning of the Dharma wheel, who expressly assert external objects. These philosophers **maintain that the percept of a sensory (e.g., visual**, auditory, olfactory, etc.**) cognition is an external object**.

But the Cittamātras repudiate the true existence of external objects. There are four principal arguments that are traditionally employed to refute this. They are:

(1) Master Asaṅga's argument from dreams and reflections in the *Compendium of Mahāyāna*;
(2) Master Vasubandhu's argument that refutes the partlessness of fundamental particles in the *Twenty Verses*;
(3) Master Dharmakīrti's argument that refutes the definition of perception as arising from and resembling its object in the *Commentary on the Compendium of Epistemology* (explained previously); and
(4) Master Dignāga's argument that refutes apprehended objects—both collections of particles and fundamental particles—in *Investigation of the Percept*.

This text, *Investigation of Percept*, presents refutations of both the Vaibhāṣikas's and Sautrāntikas's accounts of the percept condition. Nonetheless, its primary focus is a refutation of the Sautrāntika position that, as a result of the perceptual experience of a percept condition, something like a visual cognition apprehending form has the characteristic of being experienced. According to the *Commentary on the Compendium of Epistemology*, "It resembles it and it arises from it; and, as it were, it has the characteristic of being experienced."[5] As it is said in Gungtang's commentary, this refutation refutes the entailment through examples (112–113).

The Sautrāntikas's argument demonstrating that the percept condition exists as an external object is as follows:

The subject is: a visual cognition apprehending form.

The predicate is: it perceptually experiences form as its percept condition; and it perceptually experiences form as its intentional object.

---

5. Dharmakīrti, *Commentary on the Compendium of Epistemology*: 130b.

> The reason is: because a visual cognition apprehending form arises from that form; and because when a visual cognition apprehending form apprehends form, it apprehends it due to the appearance of a representation of form to that cognition and resembles it.
>
> The example is: just as a visual cognition apprehending blue arises from blue; and because it has a representation of blue it resembles it.

The Cittamātra refutes the Sautrāntika's argument demonstrating that the percept is an external object. According to Gungtang's commentary, this is undermined by stating that the error that the premise is not established is committed. Here is how the refutation works: A visual cognition apprehending form perceptually experiences form as its percept condition and as its apprehended object. This much we Cittamātras also accept. However, your (the Sautrāntika's) argument—the proof that a visual cognition apprehending form has a percept condition that is an external form—is not true and is not a valid argument. This is because it does not satisfy the three criteria of a valid argument. In order to satisfy the three criteria, three things—the premise, its positive entailment, and its contrapositive entailment—must be satisfied. But in your reasoning the premise is not established.

The subject of the premise—a visual cognition apprehending form—is the basis of dispute, and the predicate—the reason—does not arise from a form. Form appears in a representation within that visual cognition apprehending form, but there is no representation that appears as it. This is the refutation.[6]

In order to present a detailed refutation of the premise, Master Dignāga poses these questions: When you Vaibhāṣikas and Sautrāntikas assert that an external object is the percept: (1) do you assert that **fundamental particles** are the percept because they are the **cause** of sensory **cognition**? Or (2) do you assert that a collection of fundamental particles is the percept because a sensory **cognition arises with the appearance of these** collections?

---

6. Here Yeshes Thabkhas is anticipating the structure of the rebuttal of the realist's argument. The structure of the critique goes like this: For the realist to establish that external objects are percepts, it is not enough to show that there is a perception ostensibly of external objects; the idealist grants that. Instead, an independent argument is needed to show that the cause of that perception is an external object, and that requires showing in a non-question-begging way that whenever there is an apparent perception of an external object there is an external object that causes it and that appears in that perception. That, Dignāga will show, cannot be done.

Neither alternative is acceptable. As Master Dignāga has argued, even if we grant for the sake of argument that fundamental particles are the causes that give rise to sensory cognitions, it is not possible for them to be their percept conditions. In the same way, even if we grant for the sake of argument that representations of collections of fundamental particles appear to sensory cognitions, it is not possible for them to be their percept conditions.

> **Even if sensory cognition were caused by fundamental particles,**
> **It could not have particles as its object**
> **Because they do not appear to cognition,**
> **Any more than the sense faculties do.** (1abcd)

Let us grant for the sake of argument that fundamental particles—the minutest ones—are the causes that produce cognitions or consciousnesses of sense faculties such as the visual, auditory, or olfactory. In that case, fundamental particles would have to appear to sensory cognitions due to conveying their representations internally; but they never appear in that way.

Sensory cognitions would have to apprehend these objects in virtue of their resemblance to their representations, but they never apprehend them that way. Therefore, fundamental particles are not the perceptual objects of sensory cognitions. If they were, the representations of fundamental particles would be apprehended by way of conveyance to sensory cognitions. This is because: (1) it would be necessary to ascertain that they resemble that object; and (2) one cannot ascertain that they resemble the object from perception of fundamental particles. For example, although the visual faculty is merely a cause that gives rise to a visual cognition, it does not appear to that visual cognition by way of conveying its representations to it.

In this context, according to Dendar Lharampa's commentary on *Investigation of Percept*, the phrases, "**Even if sensory cognition were caused by fundamental particles**" and "even if they were the cause" show that fundamental particles are merely discussed hypothetically, but no fundamental particles whatsoever are asserted in the Cittamātra system (149). He clarifies this point by citing Gyeltsap Je's *Illumination of the Path to Liberation: Explanation of the Commentary on Compendium of Epistemology*[7] and Kedrup Je's *Ocean*

7. Gyeltsap, *Illumination of the Path to Liberation: Explanation of the Commentary on the Compendium of Epistemology, an Unerring Illumination of the Path to Liberation* (*Tshad ma rnam 'grel gyi tshig le'ur byas pa'i rnam bshad thar lam phyin ci ma log par gsal bar byed pa*): 288b.3.

of Reasoning: Extensive Exposition of the Commentary on the Compendium of Epistemology.[8]

But do Cittamātras really accept form? According to Dendar Lharampa, "those who do not think carefully say this glibly": "indeed, they do accept it. However, Tsongkhapa has conceded that these are difficult points, and so I do not think that we can settle it by saying whatever we want (150–151)."

Dendar Lharampa observes that Tsongkhapa concludes in *Clarifying the Thought: Explanation of the Introduction to the Middle Way* that there are Cittamātras who accept the existence of material form. He deduces this in citations from such texts as the *Compendium of Mahāyāna*, the *Compendium of Ascertainments*, and the *Commentary on the Distinction of the First Factor of Dependent Arising*. But in the Cittamātra system, when externality is rejected, things like form must also be nonexistent and, if things like form are posited, then externality must also be posited. This is how they saw it. However, in conclusion Tsongkhapa says that in the Cittamātra system, if the external world is rejected, it must be that such things as form also do not exist, and if form is posited, the external world must also be posited.

To summarize: Some scholars assert that "there is no form in the Cittamātra system." Some, however, argue, "If there is no form, it would absurdly follow that for the Cittamātra name and form—the fourth of the twelve links of dependent arising—would not exist. If form did not exist, it would absurdly follow that the five sense faculties and their five objects such as form would not exist. There would also be the absurd consequence that a buddha's form body would not exist. Because many errors result from these assertions, it is necessary to assert: "Even in the Cittamātra system there is existent form." A mere acceptance of form does not necessarily entail accepting that "external form exists." They propound tenets after making detailed distinctions.

Other scholars argue that as long as you assert "in the Cittamātra system, there are forms," although you may not have stated explicitly that "there are external forms," you have implicitly made a commitment to this position.

Generally speaking, Cittamātra literature is situated in the tradition that says "external form does not exist," rather than the tradition that says "there is no form." In fact, it is widely believed that "in Cittamātra, form exists, but there is no form that exists as an external object." Whatever the case may be, it does appear that there has not yet been any detailed research undertaken on

---

8. Kedrup, *Ocean of Reasoning: Extensive Exposition of the Commentary on the Compendium of Epistemology, Chapter on Direct Perception* (*Tshad ma rnam 'grel gyi rgya cher bshad pa rigs pa'i rgya mtsho las mngon sum le'u rnam bshad bzhugs so*): 113b.1.

this issue, the "difficult point"—whether or not form exists in the Cittamātra system. Therefore, we need to analyze this carefully.

In either case, in Master Dignāga's system, fundamental particles are not the objects of sensory cognitions because with regard to an "object": (1) a cognition that conveys its representation to cognition must arise with a representation of its object; and (2) because the object—whether it is blue, yellow, or something else—exists, it must be experienced by way of its **identity** being **ascertained.** This is because the cognition arises as a representation of the object that is its percept condition.

Even if we accept for the sake of argument the two Śrāvaka schools' assertion that **minute particles may be the cause of this** sensory **cognition**, this does not satisfy the definition of an object because fundamental particles would have to be apprehended or experienced by a sensory cognition through the conveyance of a representation, and they are unable to convey a representation. They cannot be the percept conditions of **the sense faculties** such as the visual: Even if they were the causes of the arising of visual cognitions, they are similarly unable to be percept conditions that convey representations to visual cognitions. **Thus, first of all, minute particles are not the percept** of sensory cognitions.

According to Gungtang, minute particles are not percepts—objects that are ascertained—because, while they may be mere causes, they do not appear. Thus, they also cannot be the causes that give rise to representations due to this. The point is that they fail to satisfy both criteria, and so they cannot be the percept.

Refuting the Claim That a Macro-object Is the Apprehended Object

According to Gungtang, the argument from incoherence—which shows that a collection does not appear when individual particles are removed—refutes collections as the percept (151–152). According to Dendar Lharampa, the meaning of Master Dignāga's statement, "**A sensory cognition may have the appearance of a collection,**" is: "For the sake of argument he assumes that collections appear in cognition, but they are not their cause (113)."[9] These statements show that not only do fundamental particles themselves not appear to cognition, but also, according to the Cittamātra system, collections of fundamental particles do not appear to cognition. For this reason, in this context he assumes for the sake of argument that this is the way in which collections appear to

9. This is not what Dendar Lharampa actually says. His commentary states that Dignāga assumes for the sake of argument that fundamental particles are the causes of sensory cognitions. He adds that fundamental particles "may be causes of sensory cognitions such as the visual, but a sensory cognition does not have the appearance of these." Geshe Thabkhas is apparently indicating that he does not really accept that these are causes.

cognition: "**A sensory cognition may have the appearance of a collection, but it does not come from that of which it has the appearance . . . because, like a double moon, collections are not substantially real.**" (2ab)

Collections that are dissimilar to fundamental particles have appearances of many dissimilar collective representations to such things as visual cognitions that seem to exist as external objects, but their appearance comes from the maturation of internal predispositions.

These sensory cognitions do not arise from the force of conveying representations from collections that are composite external objects. This is because a collection is not an efficient cause that gives rise to a sensory cognition, for the collection is not substantially real, like a visual cognition apprehending the single moon as a double moon. There is a visual cognition that apprehends the double moon, but the cause that produces it is not a double moon. A double moon is not substantially real because it does not have an ontological basis.

According to Gungtang's analysis, this refers to the subject of the opponent's assertion that "a collection appears to cognition." This is the way in which it is applied:

> The appearance of two moons is not produced by two moons in someone to whom they appear. Therefore, their appearance is only due to defective sense faculties. In the same way, when composite collections appear as external objects, they do not have the power to produce anything because they are not substantially existent. Moreover, they arise internally due to distortions caused by mental predispositions to the view of self. Thus this example also has the power to eliminate inconsistencies (113–114).

In this context, someone might ask: "What is the difference between a collection (*'dus pa*) and an aggregation (*bsags pa*)? When the Cittamātras refute that both are external objects, do they advance the same arguments, or do they use different arguments to refute them?

It does not appear that Cittamātras differentiate collected particles and aggregated particles. But in response to Master Dignāga's Cittamātra statements, "It does not come from that of which it has the appearance" and "because it is not substantially real, like a double moon," in *Blaze of Reasoning*, the Svātantrika master Bhāviveka—who does posit external objects—says:

> Because our thesis is that an aggregation of fundamental particles is the percept, your denial that collections are the percept does not undermine our position. What is the difference between an aggregation and

a collection? Things of concordant type that are situated in the same place are "composites." Collections of distinct things of concordant type situated in a single place, such as elephants, horses, or *haridru* and *haridra* trees, are collections. And such things, labeled "armies" or "forests," are "collections."[10]

As mentioned earlier, in order to elaborate on this a bit, in *Heart of the Middle Way* Master Bhāviveka states:

If the opponent
Argues that the forms of uncombined particles
Are not objects of engagement by the mind,
He proves something that we already accept.[11]

In his explanation of the meaning in *Blaze of Reasoning*, he says:

If the opponents are arguing that a single fundamental particle that is not a collection of forms is not the mind's object of engagement, they would be establishing a hypothesis that had already been established by the opponent. For this is something that we already accept.[12]

Because collections of fundamental particles are not substantially real, he does not accept them as the percept conditions of sensory cognitions. In the same text, he says:

If the opponents are arguing about the forms of combinations,
We do not accept the reason,
Because when fundamental particles are combined
with the forms of others
A cognition arises with the appearance of them.[13]

---

10. Bhāviveka, *Blaze of Reasoning: A Commentary on the Verses on the Heart of the Middle Way* (*Madhyamaka-hṛdaya-vṛtti-tarkajvālā*), commentary to verse 5.38 (adapted from Eckel 2008: 252). Geshe Thabkhas's citations of this and following passages differ slightly from Eckel's Tibetan edition, and the translation reflects these variations.

11. Bhāviveka, *Verses on the Heart of the Middle Way* (*Madhyamaka-hṛdaya-kārikā*), verse 5.34 (adapted from Eckel 2008: 249).

12. Bhāviveka, *Blaze of Reasoning*, commentary on verse 5.34 (adapted from Eckel 2008: 249).

13. Bhāviveka, *Verses on the Heart of the Middle Way*, verse 5.35 (adapted from Eckel 2008: 249).

Explaining the meaning of this passage, the *Blaze of Reasoning* says:

> If one takes an aggregation of fundamental particles of concordant type as the subject and asserts as a reason "it is not substantially real," that reason makes no sense. Why? We assert that when fundamental particles are combined or associated with other forms of concordant type, this is an object, or an entity. A cognition with the appearance of that arises as a representation of collected fundamental particles. Therefore, we assert that aggregations of fundamental particles of concordant type, such as a pot, consist of fundamental particles, but they are conventionally substantially real.[14]

As summarized above, in *Essence of Eloquence Differentiating the Interpretable and the Definitive*, Je Tsongkhapa states:

> When things like form and sound are collected, although each individual fundamental particle functions as the percept condition of a sensory cognition, they do not appear to it. Things like armies and forests, which are based on different kinds of things, are aggregations. Although they are not substantially real, fundamental particles of concordant type that are based on a single basis are aggregations and, like a pot, they are substantially real.[15]

In the *Treasury of Abhidharma*, in a context where the philosophical positions of the Vaibhāṣikas and so forth are expounded, it is claimed that even the tiniest particles incorporate a minimum of eight dharmas, and these particles are called "aggregated particles" (*bsags rdul*). And contained within each aggregated particle are eight substantial particles (*rdzas rdul*), among which the four material elements—solidity, wetness, heat, and motility—and the five evolutes—form, sound, scent, taste, and texture—can be differentiated.

It seems that from among these two kinds of minute particles, substantial particles are smaller, and aggregated particles are larger. But in the Vaibhāṣika system, it is asserted that there is no difference in size between substantial particles and aggregated particles. For example, when one pours a bowl of water into a bowl of sand, the volume in the bowl does not increase. Similarly,

---

14. Bhāviveka, *Blaze of Reasoning*, commentary on verse 5.35 (adapted from Eckel 2008: 250).

15. Tsongkhapa *Essence of Eloquence Differentiating the Interpretable and the Definitive* (*Drang nges legs bshad snying po*) (1988, Zhol edition: 52b); (1975, bKra shis lhun po edition: 586).

they assert that even though at least eight substantial particles exist within each aggregated particle, the measure of aggregated particles is no greater than that of substantial particles.

Whatever is the case, when Cittamātras refute external objects, it is necessary for them to refute the external existence of both collections and aggregations. The arguments that refute both are also the same; it does not appear that there are two different lines of reasoning. In the Cittamātra system, it is asserted that both collected particles and aggregated particles are merely imputed; because they are not substantially existent, they are not conditioned, and they are not entities.

In that cognitions of intentional objects such as forms, sounds, scents, or tastes that appear due to conveying their individual representations give rise to sensory cognitions such as the visual or auditory, **it makes sense that an object is a percept**; that is, this intentional object **is said to be a condition for** its arising due to conveying its representation to things like visual cognitions.

In the case of a visual cognition that apprehends the single moon as a double moon, since one has deluded faculties a factor of the conditions that would give rise to a cognition that apprehends the object as it really is is missing. Therefore, **there may be an appearance of that double moon** to a visual cognition, but the double moon is not the percept condition of the visual cognition that apprehends the single moon as a double moon. The double moon does not exist, and so it cannot be the basis. This example shows that because a collection **is not substantially real, it is not a cause.** Thus, it is not a percept.

According to Dendar Lharampa, "the statement that neither fundamental particles nor collections are the object of a sensory cognition is intended to refer to the appearing object or the determinate object (152)." This is because there are various sorts of objects, and this statement does not distinguish between things like the implicitly realized or ascertained object. The object in this context must be the one that can be ascertained with respect to the appearing object because the object must be able to convey a representation and it must be an object that is directly realized.

In this context, the meaning of the statement "a visual cognition that apprehends blue apprehends blue" is that a visual cognition that apprehends blue resembles blue; or it means that when a representation of blue is conveyed to a visual cognition apprehending blue it has a blue representation. For this reason, it is merely similar to blue but does not produce it. Apart from this, according to Dendar Lharampa,

> There is no other activity of apprehension that can be characterized as similar to the act of a hand apprehending a pot. For example, even

> though it is said that the form of the father is apprehended in a son who is similar to the father, in this case there is neither a son who apprehends nor a father-form that is apprehended (152).

Suppose someone asks: How should we explain the epistemic framework of object, intentional object, and percept with respect to a cognition apprehending a single moon as a double moon?

The percept of a cognition that apprehends a double moon is the single moon, but from the perspective of that cognition the single moon does not exist as the percept. The object and intentional object that are apprehended by that cognition refer to a double moon, not to a single moon.[16]

But, someone might continue, in the Sautrāntika system, because it distinguishes between the object and the percept, it is easy to differentiate between correct and incorrect with regard to cognitions. The object of cognition comprises such things as forms, sounds, scents, and tastes; and the percept refers to the representations of the objects that appear to those same cognitions. The cognition that apprehends a double moon is a mistaken cognition because although the percept of that cognition does not exist in the single moon, a double moon appears as though it exists in its object. Therefore, while a cognition that apprehends a single moon is correct, because a single moon appears in its percept, the single moon is also its object. In Dignāga's system, however, *percept* and *intentional object* do not refer to two different things. Because both are posited as stable predispositions internal to cognition, it would seem to be difficult to distinguish which might be erroneous with regard to cognition.

So, in this system, how should we posit the difference between an erroneous cognition that apprehends a double moon and a correct cognition that apprehends a single moon?

Irrespective of whether or not external objects exist, a single moon is able to perform its function just as it is viewed, whereas a double moon lacks the

---

16. Yeshes Thabkhas seems to be following Ngawang Dendar's lead on this point, but his interpretation is not uncontroversial. For Dignāga, both singularity and multiplicity with regard to a percept are conceptual constructs. According to the Abhidharma, no wholes are substantially real. A single moon is neither really one nor many: From a Sautrāntika perspective, it is merely a representation perceived as singular, double, or multiple. A single moon is neither one nor many because it is not substantially real, and so it cannot serve as a percept. According to the external realism of Sautrāntika, the percept is ineffable particulars, not macro-objects extended in space and time. For Cittamātras, the percept of a double (or single) moon is a purely mental phenomenon that arises from internal predispositions, and so in this system it is also not substantially real. Yeshes Thabkhas may be interpreting Dignāga in terms of Gelukpa-Mādhyamika semi-realism—that is, the notion that conventionally real objects are *conceptually constructed percepts* of cognition.

ability to perform its function in the way in which it is viewed. Thus, we can understand that a cognition that apprehends a single moon is correct and that a cognition that apprehends a double moon is erroneous. Similarly, when one poses the question, "In the Madhyamaka system too, since objects do not exist from their own side, what kinds of things are they," the Mādhyamika answers: "Even though they do not exist by way of their own nature, they are able to perform functions."

Even though the reason given above works well for Mādhyamikas because they posit external objects, it does not work for Dignāga's system, which does not posit external objects. In Dignāga's system, when a cognition that apprehends a double moon is present, that cognition's cause is a double moon, and a representation that appears to cognition is also a double moon.

Since the double moon thus fulfills both of the criteria of a percept, one might ask: "How might Dignāga explain to the Sautrāntika why the cognition that apprehends a double moon is mistaken and erroneous?"

In Dignāga's system, one must also distinguish erroneous cognitions in virtue of predispositions. He distinguishes between two different kinds of predispositions: Some are stable predispositions, and others are unstable predispositions. They are differentiated as follows: predispositions that produce cognitions that are concordant with their objects and are causally effective are "stable predispositions," and predispositions that are not concordant with their objects and causally ineffective are "unstable predispositions." Thus, they explain that correct cognitions arise in dependence upon stable predispositions, while erroneous cognitions arise in dependence upon unstable predispositions.

In the Cittamātra system, even though there are no external objects, it is necessary to present a definite framework for distinguishing what is causally effective and what is causally ineffective solely through the efficacy of predispositions. Thus, a single moon is presented as something that is able to perform a function, while a double moon is not able to perform a function.[17]

Likewise, it is necessary to present a definite distinction between deceptive and nondeceptive cognitions. Thus, a cognition that apprehends a single moon is presented as correct, while a cognition that apprehends a double moon is deceptive. Therefore, Dendar Lharampa says:

> Although a single moon is not really a double moon, it must be said that a single moon is real because a single moon is an entity. This is because

---

17. This probably needs to be nuanced. For Cittamātra, a single (or double) moon is not really causally efficient: The predispositions that give rise to such perceptions are, and this seems to be the point he is making here.

> it is the percept condition of a sensory cognition of a single moon appearing to be double. This point is confirmed in both the *Ornament for Epistemological Treatises* and the *Ornament for Seven Epistemological Texts That Dispels Darkness in the Mind.* Thus, although it conveys the representation of a single moon to the sensory cognition that appears as a double moon, it does not convey it correctly (152).

Similarly, in the Cittamātra system, it is necessary to be able to present a nondeceptive distinction between that which is real and that which is unreal. If one is not able to draw such a distinction, as a consequence one would encounter many problems, such as these: one would not be able to ascertain the mode of subsistence of entities; and there would be no reasonable argument that ascertains their mode of subsistence.

But in Dignāga's system, because percept and object are a single entity, from the perspective of a cognition that apprehends a double moon both the object and the percept condition are just that double moon. So the double moon is the cause that produces that cognition, and that cognition is also the cause that produces the representation of the double moon. Therefore, in this system a nonexistent phenomenon, a double moon, appears to be able to perform a function. So in what way is a cognition that apprehends a double moon deceptive? Why isn't it a veridical cognition? In this system, with regard to cognition, it is not possible to present a distinction between what is able or unable to perform a function in terms of whether the percept of a cognition and its object are similar or dissimilar. One might say: "Because there is no way to do this, it does not seem to be clear how one might posit a criterion for error with regard to cognition."

The single moon is able to perform a function just in the way one experiences a single moon. The experience of the single moon as a double moon, a hundred moons, and so forth cannot perform its function. This fact can be understood clearly from the way in which the six kinds of beings each see and experience things differently. In general, things such as forms and sounds are sentient beings' means of livelihood or resources. Depending on these resources, they encounter various sensations, either pleasant or unpleasant. From these pleasant and unpleasant sensations, various cognitions, such as desire and aversion, arise.

Things may be desirable or undesirable: For example, a single thing such as the Ganges River seems to exist in various ways, reflecting how it is experienced when viewed by the six kinds of beings. Humans experience water, gods perceive ambrosia, and aquatic animals such as hippopotamuses or fish use it as their abode. Beings like hungry ghosts, who lack the positive karma that would enable them to use water as a resource, experience it as pus or blood, or they do not experience anything at all.

Similarly, due to the power of their individual karmic predispositions, for some beings even moonlight can be a scorching blaze of heat, or sunshine can be an unbearably freezing cold experience. Moreover, when the bodies of humans like us have certain temperature-related afflictions, they will shiver in warm weather, even after putting on heavy clothing; and in cold weather, even without any clothing on our bodies we will burn as if from heat.

The gods in the Realm of Infinite Space only experience space and do not perceive any spatially obstructing phenomena. If one were a pig, for example, one would only experience happiness in filthy surroundings. It is clear that if one were to put a pig in a clean environment such as a palace, this would lead it to experience prison-like suffering. Similarly, when three persons look at another person, this could produce three different modes of appearance: an experience of joy from a friend's perspective, dislike from a enemy's perspective, and indifference from one who is indifferent.

This is the reason why there are these various ways of experiencing a single phenomenon. They are only produced by the power of the ripening of predispositions within the cognitions of individual sentient beings. They are not produced by the things themselves—external objects such as the sun or moon. If they were produced from externally appearing objects, everyone's feelings and visual experiences would have to be the same. This is because from the standpoint of an external object there cannot be the slightest difference in the way in which it conveys its representation to cognition.

From the side of external objects, it is impossible for there to be partial or discriminatory thoughts toward sentient beings. So it is impossible for the same object to convey a representation of a pleasant object to some sentient beings and to convey a representation of an unpleasant object to others. Thus, it is not possible for it to be a cause of happiness for some sentient beings and a cause of unhappiness for other sentient beings. So whether an object is pleasant or unpleasant, a source of happiness or suffering, suitable or unsuitable to be used as a resource, is solely due to the force of the karma of each individual sentient being. Thus, it is established that they are only produced from the impetus of ripening predispositions within the internal cognitions of individual sentient beings.

This is just like dreams: since in a dream cognition when one is deeply asleep, all objects appear to exist externally, one is not able to experience things as produced from the force of predispositions within one's own mind. While one is deeply asleep, one will enjoy enjoyable dream objects and will produce aversion toward aversive objects. While one is in the dream, even if another person says, "These objects are merely fabrications of your own mind," you will be unable to believe it. But as soon as you wake up from sleep and the dream no longer exists, all the enjoyable mental appearances and the fearful appearances will naturally cease.

Similarly, as long as ordinary beings have a desire to grasp apprehender and apprehended as substantially different, they will be unable to abandon the conception according to which external objects are taken to be truly existent. However, when they realize the emptiness of real difference between apprehender and apprehended, they naturally abandon the conception that grasps external objects as existent. Thus, the ultimate purpose of teaching Cittamātra is to dispel attachment to external objects.

We now return to the text: **Thus, neither kind of external object makes sense as an object of cognition.** (2cd) In that case, it makes no sense for either external minute particles or composites to be the objects that are experienced as the apprehended objects of sensory cognitions.

Someone might ask, "What is the reason why it is not reasonable for them to be objects that are experienced as apprehended objects?"

This is because one of the two criteria that must be satisfied is missing: It is a cause with regard to the circumstances of the apprehended object; and it must convey a representation that resembles it. For composites of particles, the missing part is that they must be the cause of the arising of sensory cognitions. For fundamental particles, the missing part is they do not appear as they are because they do give rise to representations. For these reasons, apprehended objects that are "external fundamental particles and composites" are not the percept. Dendar Lharampa sums this up as follows:

> In this way, neither (1) the position that external fundamental particles are the percept condition; nor (2) the position that a collection is the percept condition makes sense of external objects as the appearing objects of cognition. Why not? If an external object were the percept condition, then it would have to have both of the following characteristics: (1) it would have to transmit its own representation to the cognition; and (2) it would have to cause the cognition (153).

However, both fail to satisfy one of the two criteria:

> The position that fundamental particles are the percept condition fails to account for the transmission of their representation; and the position that a collection is the percept condition fails to account for their being the cause. Therefore, these objects—external minute particles and aggregations—are not percepts in the sense of percept conditions (153).

Accordingly, Gungtang's commentary states that the first and second verses cited above show concisely that it is not reasonable for either kind of micro- or macro-external objects to be the percept condition or the perceptual object of cognition. After the third verse, the text offers an extensive supplementary explanation comprising opponents' rebuttals and their refutations.

Refutation of the Claim That Collective Representations of Particles Are the Apprehended Object

In response to this, Dignāga says:

> **Some maintain that collected features are the cause.** (3ab)

Who is this opponent? According to the Chinese commentaries on *Investigation of the Percept*, there are three opponents: (1) the first opponent asserts that fundamental particles are the percept condition; (2) the second asserts that collections of fundamental particles are the percept condition; and (3) in the opinion of the third opponent, unlike that of the first two, collected representations of fundamental particles are posited as the percept condition. What is Geshe-la's thought on this matter?

The *Autocommentary* does not explicitly state who the present opponent is. However, Master Vinītadeva's commentary on *Investigation of Percept* identifies him as Vāgbhaṭa. Following his lead, Gungtang's and Dendar Lharampa's Tibetan commentaries also indicate that he is Vāgbhaṭa.

Although we do not find anything explicit in the Indian sources such as the *Autocommentary*, it does not seem incompatible with them to accept the positions maintained by the Chinese commentators. And the third opponent's position does appear to be similar to a position held by some who assert external objects. On this view, although partless minute particles are not able to appear individually, when they aggregate, not only does the aggregation appear to cognition, but because the minute particles contained in the aggregation are able to appear to cognition, they function as the percept condition. This would be like an aggregation of sesame seeds. When the aggregation of sesame seeds appears, each individual one also appears. Similarly, although each individual hair is not experienced, when aggregated into tufts, both the aggregation of hairs and the individual ones are experienced. Dendar Lharampa concurs and says:

> In the commentary on the root verse that begins: "**Some maintain that collected features are the cause,**" although it is not explicitly stated that fundamental particles have parts, in light of the way it is expressed, the opponent's position is that fundamental particles appear as collective representations in sensory cognition (154).

However, there is a problem here for the Cittamātras: If a collection of representations appears to a nonmistaken sensory cognition, then it must appear as a macro-object; and if it appears as a macro-object, then it must definitely appear as partite. Therefore, some opponents like Vāgbhaṭa hold that after individual minute particles each convey their own representations to a sensory cognition, they are unable to give rise to a cognition that resembles them. But they are productive as collections of sensory cognitions that have representations. Because they have the ability to give rise to them, collective representations are posited as perceptual objects of sensory cognitions. According to Dendar Lharampa, the opponent's position can be expressed as follows:

> "Among these" who take the position that there are external objects means "also among these." Some maintain the following: Fundamental particles are the causes, because they are substantially real; and since they have a nature of being collections of eight substantial particles, they are represented as collections in sensory cognition—that is, they manifest representations of macro-objects. For this reason, they maintain that these fundamental particles are causal since, as percept conditions, they account for the transmission of their own representation. That is, they are causes of sensory cognition (153).

A Cittamātra might ask: If fundamental particles have no parts, then how can they manifest the features of a macro-object?

The opponent would reply: This is because all external objects have multiple features because they have a nature of being the four elements, plus form, scent, taste, and touch.

Well then, the Cittamātra asks, if minute particles are able to give rise to a sensory cognition through conveying their collective representations, why couldn't each individual minute particle appear to cognition by conveying its representation?

Response: Individual minute particles cannot appear to cognition because all phenomena have two aspects: an aspect that appears and an aspect that does not appear. So from among the many aspects that all collective objects such as pots have—such as a shape aspect, a color aspect, or a texture aspect—only shape and color are directly experienced by a visual cognition, while it does not experience texture.

Because fundamental particles have many features such as a form aspect, a sound aspect, or a scent aspect, some of these are also objects of engagement by direct perception, while others are not directly experienced. The features of each individual particle may not be directly perceived, but **they maintain that . . . they are perceived with only a few features** that are able to convey their representations. Therefore, **fundamental particles have the causes that produce cognitions that have the appearance of collections.** This is the assertion of the third opponent.

Suppose someone asks: If fundamental particles are manifest in a sensory cognition that has the representation of a macro-object, why don't fundamental particles themselves appear? Dignāga says:

> **Features of minute particles**
> **Are not the object of cognition,**
> **Any more than things like solidity are.** (3bcd)

These two lines further clarify the third opponent's position. Although minute particles can convey the representation of a collection, they cannot convey the representations of the particles themselves because these minute particles are neither the precept condition nor the apprehended object of the cognition. It is like a pot, for example: The pot's shape and color are directly experienced by a visual cognition, but things like the pot's solidity and texture are not directly experienced by that same visual cognition.

For this reason, it is just like a pot: just as a pot has many features such as solidity, texture, and color, the pot's color and shape are objects of visual cognition; but such things as solidity and texture are not objects of visual cognition. In the same way, minute particles are able to convey objects of cognition in a collective aspect, but they are not able to convey them as objects of cognition that are representations of themselves individually.

> **According to them, cognitions of things like pots**
> **And cups would be identical.** (4ab)

Master Dignāga responds in this way: If aggregations of minute particles were apparent to cognition, there would be this problem: an aggregation of minute particles would have to exist without their having any distinctions whatsoever in terms of such things as form, shape, or size.

According to them, when one experiences a collective representation, one must necessarily experience it as a representation of a macro-object. But should they assert that this collective representation is experienced as the representation of a pot macro-object, or should they assert that it is experienced as a representation that is like the shape of a cup macro-object?

Neither alternative makes sense. Minute particles are identical, not differing individually in the slightest in terms of such things as shape and color. Thus, if one asserts that minute particles themselves convey a pot-like representation from their own side, it would follow that all minute particles would have to appear with pot-like representations. If, however, one asserts that minute particles themselves appear with a cup-like representation from their own side, then it would follow that all minute particles would have to appear with cup-like representations.

For this reason, there is a problem: as there would be no difference whatsoever between cognitions of minute particles that appear as pots, cognitions that appear as cups, and so forth, all cognitions of things like pots and cups would be identical.

There is absolutely no difference between minute particles in terms of their size. Therefore, a distinction in terms of the differing features of things like pots and cups such as a round chamber or a flat bottom would not apply to minute particles. Therefore, there may be many minute particles but, unlike pots and cups, there is no difference whatsoever in the way in which they appear to cognition.

If they are distinguished by different features; (4c) If someone thinks that distinctive features—such as a pot's neck, its round chamber, or its flat bottom—appear to cognition, and that from these representational distinctions there occur differences between cognitions, Master Dignāga replies by saying that these distinctions belong only to macro-objects such as pots: **These do not belong to substantially real particles because there is no difference in their dimensions.** (4–5a)

These variations in terms of representational differences do not belong to substantially real minute particles, as there is no difference between them in terms of things like their size. Although fundamental particles are different entities—individually distinct—there is no distinction in terms of things like color or shape insofar as they merely appear to cognition as spherical: **Therefore, these differences belong to something that is not substantially real.** (5b)

Thus, distinctive features such as those that vary in shape and color exist only in things that are **not substantially real**, but they do not exist in substantially real minute particles. This follows because **distinctive features belong only to things that are conventionally real** macro-objects, **but not to minute particles. Things like pots are just conventionally real**, and they have varying features such as color and shape.

In this context, the position of the scripture-based Sautrāntikas is being considered. The position of the scripture-based Sautrāntika is like that of the Vaibhāṣikas; they are very similar. Thus, they assert that conventional truths are things like pots: Cognitive apprehension of them ceases when they are destroyed or when individual parts are conceptually removed. And they assert that even when substantially existent things like impartite minute particles and impartite moments of cognition are destroyed or when their parts are individually removed by thought, cognitive apprehension of them does not cease; and therefore they assert that they are ultimate truths.

In accordance with the presentation of the *Commentary on the Compendium of Epistemology*, reason-based Sautrāntikas assert that the definition of ultimate truth is "ultimately able to perform a function;" and the definition of conventional truth is "not ultimately able to perform a function." Thus something that is able to appear to direct perception is an ultimate truth, and something that is not able to appear to direct perception is a conventional truth.

Because the cognition that has the appearance of them disappears when particles disperse: (5cd) Because things such as pots only exist conventionally, if one were to remove their minute particles, then one's cognition of the appearances of things like pots would diminish. Even if one were to conceptually remove parts like color that are associated with substantially real things, cognitions of them would not be extinguished, just like the immutable ultimate truth. **Thus, it makes sense that objects of sensory awareness are not external.**

The Cittamātras' Own Position

Now that he has refuted the position that the percept condition is external, what is the percept condition as it is posited in the Cittamātras's own system? If there were no explanation for how one experiences something as a percept condition or of how one experiences something as an apprehended object, wouldn't this contravene ordinary common sense?

The Cittamātras's system dismisses the idea that conflict with ordinary common sense is a problem, and so the Cittamātras's system advances an argument that the percept is internal: **An internal cognitive object, which appears as though external, is the object.** (6ab)

According to the Cittamātra system, the percept condition is explained as follows: It is the ripening of predispositions within cognition itself or the fundamental consciousness. As Gungtang's commentary has it: "In our own system, we unequivocally claim that the percept condition is nothing other than a self-presenting internal apprehension.[18] Only the appearance of cognition

18. Gungtang refers to the percept, not the percept condition. Yeshes Thabkhas indicates that this refers to both.

itself appears to cognition as its cognitive object. There is no substantially distinct external object."

Suppose someone asks: "Reflexive cognition is contradictory; so, because they are simultaneous and because they have an identical nature, how could a cognitive object—a self-luminous cognition—appear to that very cognition as its percept condition?"

The internal object is cognitive in both substance and in nature. Nonetheless, it appears to be unconnected to cognition, as though it were external. That external appearance is not an appearance of a representation that exists in that way. When an image of the moon appears in a mirror, an expanse of empty space also appears, and the moon appears to be different from and unconnected to its reflection. Analogously, an entity that exists internally and is only of the nature of cognition—which is apprehended in such a way that it appears to be external but really arises through production of a representation—is called the intentional object. The term *intentional object* can refer to many objects, but in this context it is the percept condition. Why is it the percept condition? Gungtang explains that this is because

> as a result of familiarization with predispositions to linguistic expression, cognition is produced with its object—that is, with a representation of its object—within the framework of apprehender and apprehended. Furthermore, if there were no object, it would not arise. This is why it is said to be "its condition." (116)

As a result of the maturation of predispositions for perceiving something as blue by a visual cognition within the fundamental consciousness, one portion arises as an entity with the appearance of a blue cognitive object, and another portion arises as a cognitive entity that has a representation of blue. Therefore, because there are two different ways in which something that seems to be blue appears to cognition, an internal cognitive entity that appears to exist externally is the percept condition of those sensory cognitions.

Thus, the percept condition comprises the intentional objects or objects that appear to cognition due to the power of the ripening of internal predispositions. These cognitive objects are not external objects. In the same way, just as dream cognitions are nothing more than representations that appear as though they exist externally, objects, such as blue and white, which are produced through the force of predispositions and are present to internal cognition, are the percept condition.

Because it is cognition itself, and because it is its condition: (6cd) Because that object, which appears to an internal cognition, is the percept condition, it is the intentional object of cognition. And the two—the intentional object and cognition—are not different in nature. This is because the intentional object is of the nature of cognition and because the object of internal cognition is also the percept condition of that cognition.

Internal cognition appears as the object, with a representation of the object. Thus, the first criterion, that "it resembles it," is fulfilled. And since that internal object functions as the percept condition, it gives rise to a cognition. Thus, it fulfills the second criterion: that "it arises from that." Because it satisfies these two criteria for the percept condition posited by you Sautrāntikas, the percept condition is merely an intentional object that exists internally.

But the opponent may have a doubt and ask: "If we were to grant for now that, as you Cittamātras assert, the percept condition is only an object that appears to cognition and depends on it, then the two—the cognition and the simultaneous appearance to cognition of the object it reveals—would arise at the same time or simultaneously. So how would that object serve as the percept condition of that cognition? It makes no sense for a concurrent cause and effect, like the two horns of a cow, to be each other's conditions. Thus, extremely absurd consequences would follow."

The opponent's critique may not undermine the view that posits simultaneous cause and effect, but it may undermine the view that asserts that cause and effect are sequential. **Even though they are simultaneous, it is its condition because it is invariably concomitant.** (7a)

Suppose someone asks, "According to the view that asserts that cause and effect are simultaneous, if cognition and its objects—its percept conditions—are simultaneous, how could the cause-effect relationship make sense?"

It does indeed make sense. Although the two are simultaneous, cognition serves as an invariably concomitant cause of an object. Similarly, the object serves as an invariably concomitant cause of cognition. Therefore, each mutually serves as the other's cause. This is so because it is reasonable to posit simultaneous cause and effect with regard to such things as simultaneous cause and concomitant cause. For example, when three reeds stand upright and mutually support each other, they are simultaneous, and yet they serve as each other's cause and effect in that they unfailingly support each other.

Even though they are simultaneous and concomitant, each unfailingly serves as the other's cause because we ascertain that they serve as each other's effect. Therefore, it is reasonable that each of them serves as a condition that gives rise to the other. **Logicians** (or dialecticians) assert: "If when one is present it serves as the other's support, and when one is absent, the other is also absent, because they have a relationship of being each other's cause and effect, both cause and effect arise sequentially."

As an example of simultaneous cause and effect, the Cittamātras describe the burning of a wick and a flame. The burning of the wick depends on the flame, and the arising of the flame depends on the burning of the wick. But the flame and the burning of the wick are simultaneous. They assert that this is the defining character of the burning of the wick giving rise to the flame.

It is sequential because of a transfer of capacity. (7b) Moreover, it is reasonable to posit sequential cause and effect in this context. According to Gungtang's commentary (116), cognition is the *actual percept condition* or the *percept condition that transfers capacity*; and the object that conveys a representation to that cognition, the *nominal percept condition*, is the *appearing percept condition*, or the *percept condition that is transferred.*[19] Therefore, the two are sequentially cause and effect.

The phrase "**is sequential**" means that it is also possible to posit object and subject as having sequential cause and effect. Because predispositions are the percept condition, when a predisposition ripens, a representation of a blue object arises from one portion, and the subject—for example, a representation of a cognition that apprehends blue—arises from another portion. Therefore, both the cognitive representation (*shes rnam*) and the object representation (*don rnam*) are produced from the ripening of predispositions.

The predisposition is the object; it both gives rise to a representation of the intentional object and is the cause of cognition. Thus, when the predisposition ripens: (1) it appears as a representation of an intentional object, for example, a representation of a blue object; (2) that same predisposition reflexively appears as a prior cognition, for example, a visual cognition that apprehends blue; and (3) the previous cognition, for example, a visual cognition apprehending blue, is able to give rise to an effect, for example, a subsequent cognition that apprehends blue that is latent in it and concordant with it. Therefore, there is no contradiction in a predisposition serving as the basis of cognition.

Take anger, for example. Anger, an unpleasant cognition, arises from the force of ripening predispositions in the fundamental consciousness. That anger is then established as a potential in the fundamental consciousness in the form of a latency. From that predisposition yet again, a cognition arises with a representation of anger, which is experienced as another unpleasant cognition.

Similarly, because the predisposition is the percept, a representation of a blue object appears as a result of the ripening of predispositions, and a

---

19. The Tibetan equivalents can be found in the Glossary.

subject—a cognition that apprehends blue—also arises. This is even true for a percept of the fundamental consciousness: When one experiences a blue object that establishes a predisposition, that predisposition is asserted to "masquerade as a representation of a blue object."

Someone may ask: "If, as you Cittamātras have explained, the percept condition is just a form produced by the power of ripening predispositions of an internal cognition, then how do you explain the dictum, 'In dependence upon an internal form and the visual faculty, visual cognition arises?' "

If such an internal cognitive form were the percept condition, there would be no need for the arising of a visual cognition to depend on the visual faculty. This is so because according to the Cittamātras's position, a form that is the percept condition does not have to appear to sensory cognition. And so a visual cognition arises solely in dependence on internal cognitive predispositions. This is the problem that the opponent wants addressed. The opponent's problem is addressed in Gungtang's commentary in this way:

> Suppose someone argues as follows: "Since cognition arises from an external object and an eye just like a face in a mirror, and since on your view the percept would be merely internal, there would be nothing in front of you. In that case, how could cognition be produced?" (117)

In the Sautrāntika system, which asserts the material nature of the simultaneously arising intentional object and sensory faculties, the intentional object must also be external matter.

> We, however, do not take the percept and the simultaneously arising sense faculties in this way. When one infers the nature of the cause from the effect, while it is the specific capacity of the visual faculty in the mind, it is an entity that has ceased. Even though it has ceased, it can still be known to exist through such arguments as that establishing causal sequence. What goes for this goes for the sense faculties as well. (117)

A sense faculty is a cooperating sense capacity. (7cd) Since the predisposition itself is the percept, it not only appears as a representation of blue; even the visual faculty is regarded as a **cooperating sense capacity**, unlike the Sautrāntikas's form, which is constituted by minute particles that are external and material. **It can be inferred from its result that a sense faculty is a capacity** that exists prior to cognition, **but it is not derived from the material elements** as the Sautrāntikas have proposed. The way in which capacity as sense faculty is posited in the Cittamātra system is clearly presented in Master Candrakīrti's *Introduction to the Middle Way*:

> Capacity, which is the support of one's consciousness, is
> Understood as a material sense faculty called "the eye."[20]

Capacity, which is the support of cognition, is understood as "the eye," which has a material sense faculty. The section on the Prāsaṅgika system's refutation states:

> If cognition arises from the ripening of its own seed,
> In the absence of a visual sense faculty, why does it not arise in the blind?[21]

If it is possible to experience a form in dependence upon the ripening of one's own seeds or capacities in the absence of a visual faculty, then why doesn't a cognition that experiences form arise in the blind? It would make sense for the blind to experience a form because they would have the capacity to give rise to a visual cognition. This is how the Prāsaṅgikas refute the Cittamātra position.

One might respond to the Cittamātra view that a sense faculty is a capacity that is different from something that is material in nature as follows: you posit capacity, but this capacity lacks a basis. Because it has no support, wouldn't it have to be excluded from the class of dependently arisen phenomena? If so, wouldn't this contradict your own statement?

Dignāga responds: **It is not contradictory for this capacity also to be in cognition.** (8a) It is **not contradictory** for a proponent of the system of cognition-only to also posit sense faculties in terms of capacity. As Gungtang explains, "because the capacity resides in cognition and because cognition arises from the capacity, unlike you we have no need to waste our time searching for anything external." (117)

Even though it makes sense that a capacity is a consciousness with a capacity, it also makes sense that things that exist as material form exist with the very nature of inaccessible cognition; and so it makes no difference with regard to how cognition is produced as an effect.

---

20. Candrakīrti, *Introduction to the Middle Way* (*Madhyamakāvatāra; dBu ma la 'jug* pa), sDe dge edition, dBu ma vol. *'a*: 207a.

21. Candrakīrti, *Introduction to the Middle Way*: 207a.

Thus, the object and the capacity cause one another and have done so from beginningless time. (8bcd) Thus, they are mutually causal in two ways: (1) as the nature of a cognition that has a representation such as blue or yellow; and (2) as a capacity that produces that cognition or a potential for a cognition. This is because each serves as the cause of the other. When cognition is latent, it is capacity, and when capacity ripens, it is cognition. Thus, the arising of a cognition depends on the existence of a former capacity, while the arising of a capacity also depends on the existence of a former cognition.

The way in which both a cognition and the capacity that gives rise to it are mutually causal has proceeded **from beginningless time**. Thoughts, whether virtuous or nonvirtuous, transfer predispositions to the mind. From those predispositions, thoughts once again arise; as a result of these, virtuous or nonvirtuous karma accumulates.

Due to the power of karma, a variety of saṃsāric experiences such as happiness and suffering arise. From the experience of happiness and suffering, afflicted minds such as attachment and aversion arise. The power of affliction implants virtuous or nonvirtuous predispositions in minds. Again, from those predispositions either virtuous or nonvirtuous mental states arise, and so one engages with the sufferings of cyclic existence.

Because this visual faculty is termed a capacity, a cognition arises with the appearance of an intentional object, **depending on the capacity called "eye"** and on a percept condition—a form that is present to an internal cognition. Without depending on them, and just by depending on the external object, a cognition does not arise.

These two—capacity and internal cognition—mutually produce one another. Thus, they reciprocally **cause one another and have done so from beginningless time**. Because subsequent cognitions must arise from predispositions of similar type, a cognition only arises from the ripening of a cognition—a latent capacity—within the fundamental consciousness. Therefore, when the cognition ceases, its latent capacity is implanted in the fundamental consciousness; and when it in turn matures, a cognition arises.

Sometimes the representation of the object of cognition arises from the maturation of the capacity, and sometimes when the representation of the cognitive object is present in a nonapparent manner the capacity is in its representation. These two—cognition and the object such as blue that appears to the cognition—could be described as conceptually different but not substantially different.

So an internal percept is the cause of cognition, and because it arises with a representation of its cognition it satisfies both criteria. Therefore, it appears as the percept condition or the object.

At this point, some Sautrāntikas might object to the Cittamātras as follows: You Cittamātras posit a capacity within cognition as the *actual percept condition* and the object as merely the *nominal percept condition*; so why don't you face the same problem that we Sautrāntikas face? According to you Cittamātras, minute particles may serve as the cause of the arising of a cognition, but they are not the percept condition because they do not appear to cognition. So we assert: "Thus, this does not satisfy the second criterion for a percept condition." It would follow, therefore, that capacity is also not the actual percept condition because even though it may cause a cognition to arise, capacity by itself does not appear to cognition. And so it does not satisfy the second characteristic of a percept condition.

The Cittamātras's statement, "even if we grant that minute particles serve as the cause," seems to assert a position similar to that of the Sautrāntikas, but only for the sake of argument. In the Cittamātra system, minute particles are not asserted as the cause of the arising of cognition; and so, according to them, the *actual* cause that serves to produce cognition is either a predisposition internal to cognition or a capacity.

Consider, for instance, a visual cognition having a representation of blue: The capacity or predisposition is the cognition's representation of blue that exists in a latent form in an inaccessible manner. When this capacity serves as the percept condition of a visual cognition that apprehends blue, after the capacity ripens or manifests, it takes on the nature of the object's representation and of subjective cognition.

Capacity or predisposition is like a bud from which a flower arises. When the capacity fully manifests, the capacity itself becomes the object and the subject. Thus, some treatises describe this as "capacity that disguises its nature as a representation of an object."

Someone might ask: is there a difference between predisposition and capacity?

In general, in the context of cognition, the members of the triad—*predisposition, capacity,* and *seed*—are synonymous. Predispositions, seeds, and capacities that are implanted by cognition are the same. Even so, we say, "a seed has the capacity to give rise to a sprout," but we do not say, "a seed has a predisposition to give rise to a sprout." *Seed* may refer to a capacity that exists in anything, but a *predisposition* is a capacity that is only associated with cognition. Thus, cognition arises from the maturation of predispositions, and when cognition ceases it exists as predispositions.

Like the Sautrāntikas, the Vaibhāṣikas also assert that blue and a visual cognition apprehending blue are the apprehended and the apprehender and that a cognition that apprehends blue experiences blue as an apprehended object by way of its nature. This much is not controversial even for the Cittamātras. Nevertheless, the Vaibhāṣikas do not assert that that apprehension of blue has a blue representation. The Cittamātras assert that the apprehension of blue must establish an object that has a blue aspect and that the apprehension of blue is established with a blue representation. This is because when I have the memory, "I have seen blue," the seeing subject and the apprehension of blue are the two modes in which a memory that has a representation of blue generates a cognition that has a representation of an object. The *Commentary on the Compendium of Epistemology* says:

> With regard to how they posit experience,
> There is no controversy whatsoever:
> Its object does not exist inherently.
> This too is proven through a correct memory.[22]

If the Vaibhāṣikas were correct, then apart from objects displaying different representations for each individual subject, if those objects and the subjective cognitions that realize them did not exist, then it would be impossible for thoughts of different objects or different memories to arise, such as "this form is like this," "this form is not like this." The *Commentary on the Compendium of Epistemology* says:

> There are distinctions regarding one's object of engagement,
> But there is no difference in terms of experience.
> So one cannot draw any distinctions such as,
> "This is like this" and "This is not like this."[23]

If a person who has such a cognition of blue in his continuum apprehends blue himself but this sort of blue apprehension does not appear; and if he lacks either a visual cognition in which he experiences this blue or knowledge of it, then he would lack awareness of how he saw or heard the object. It is said that beings would become like fools or the blind due to not having cognitions of the objects they experience themselves or that they hear or touch. In this

---

22. Dharmakīrti, *Commentary on the Compendium of Epistemology*: 134b.

23. Dharmakīrti, *Commentary on the Compendium of Epistemology*: 134a.

regard, Master Devendrabuddhi's *Subcommentary to the Commentary on the Compendium of Epistemology* states:

> For an opponent who does not even accept cognitive resemblance although he sees these two things, neither the object nor cognition can be established. In that case, if experience of the intentional object did not derive from something that resembles it, then from what would knowledge of the intentional object derive? There would be no cognition, and no self-awareness. There would also be no experience of anything other, and so this does not make sense. In that case, neither cognition nor the object of cognition would exist. If this were to happen, how could one say, "this is the intentional object right now," or "this is cognition"? How could one have cognition of the dyad of intentional object and cognition? If one were to abandon such linguistic conventions, all beings would be blind and fools.[24]

So, if some preceding cognitions were to lack clearly appearing individual representations of objects, later memories could not be differentiated; and there would be no memories that are distinguished in that way. For example, if one does not cognize the differences that exist between twin siblings, one will be unable to distinguish them from each other. Accordingly, the *Commentary on the Compendium of Epistemology* states:

> Differences are not distinguished
> Merely by having different experiences.
> When the differences are not clear,
> There is no difference in cognition, as in the case of twins.[25]

Moreover, if an object's representation did not appear to cognition, cognition would be unable to distinguish between far and near, or between objects that are occluded by other forms, which are either clear or unclear for sensory cognitions. Nor would there be any difference between the seen and the unseen. There would be no way to understand such differences. Thus, the *Commentary on the Compendium of Epistemology* states:

---

24. Devendrabuddhi, *Subcommentary to the Commentary on the Compendium of Epistemology* (*Pramāṇavārttika-pañjikā*): 3.242b6.

25. Dharmakīrti, *Commentary on the Compendium of Epistemology*: 134b.

> Distinctions such as those between near and far,
> Clear and unclear, would be impossible.[26]

As explained above, in the Cittamātra system there arose two divergent theoretical positions: (1) the assertion that "since there is no external material form, there is no form at all"; and (2) "in this system, even though there is no external material form, there is form." Je Tsongkhapa's position is: "In the Cittamātra system, there are no external forms, but there are forms."

In the *Autocommentary to the Introduction to Middle Way*, in the context of presenting the Cittamātras's position, it is argued in many places that there are no external forms. Likewise, it is said: "There are no apprehended objects apart from cognition, and there is no visual faculty apart from cognition." The negation "there is no form" is stated with the qualifying expressions "external" or "apart from consciousness." On this point, Je Tsongkhapa's *Clarifying the Thought: Explanation of the Introduction to the Middle Way* states:

> In the *Autocommentary to Introduction to the Middle Way*, in the context of presenting the Cittamātras' position, it is stated in many places that "there is no externality," and "there is not the slightest apprehended object apart from consciousness." There is no apprehended object such as form, but this is qualified by the statement, "apart from cognition"; and in the commentary on the verse, "the material sense faculty is understood to be the 'eye,'" it states that there is no visual faculty apart from cognition.[27]

Someone might wonder: Does this mean that you assert that things like forms and material sense faculties do not exist? In the Perfection of Wisdom sūtras and other works, there are two contexts, with and without the application of a qualification: (1) application of a qualification in "things do not exist *ultimately*"; and (2) without this application. Similarly, in the context of the autocommentary to *Introduction to the Middle Way*, there are cases both with and without the application of the qualification. However, when production is negated, a qualification is applied: "There is no production *ultimately*." The application should also be extended in this way in the context of treatises in

---

26. Dharmakīrti, *Commentary on the Compendium of Epistemology*: 134b.

27. Tsongkhapa, *Clarifying the Thought: Explanation of the Introduction to the Middle Way* (*dBu ma 'jug pa'i rnam bshad dgongs pa rab gsal*): 205.

which production is denied but in which such qualifications are not applied. In the same way, in this Cittamātra context, it is asserted that statements like "there is no form" should be qualified as: "there are no *external* forms." In *Clarifying the Thought*, Tsongkhapa states:

> The statement, "there is no visual faculty that is distinct from consciousness," qualifies the object of negation. Must we assert that the same qualification should be applied in a Cittamātra context? Or should we ask whether it is necessary to apply the qualification to the statement: "the five, forms and so forth, and the five material sense faculties do not exist?"
>
> Reply: In this commentary, there are both cases with and without the qualification. However, there are many cases where the qualification is applied to the object of negation in the refutation of production, and so even in contexts in which it does not appear it should be extended in the same way in all cases. We do the same here.[28]

In this Cittamātra system, even though there are no external forms, forms in general must exist. In the *Compendium of Mahāyāna*, Asaṅga describes the fundamental consciousness as the cause of all material sensory faculties, the domain in which all bodies, such as those of humans, are appropriated, and as what prevents the five material sense faculties from disintegrating while one is alive; and he describes the seeds or predispositions within the fundamental consciousness that establish environmental habitats as "seeds without feeling."[29]

Similarly, in the context of the *Commentary on the Distinction of the First Factor of Dependent Arising*, it is explained that due to the condition of the fundamental consciousness the fourth limb of dependent arising, name and form, is established.[30] This kind of form is explained as constituting forms that are elements and things derived from them. It is explained that this form does not exist in the Formless Realm, but it does exist in both the Desire Realm and the Form Realm. Thus, Tsongkhapa explains that there are countless instances in the Cittamātra system where form is asserted. Similarly, in *Clarifying the Thought*, Tsongkhapa states:

---

28. Tsongkhapa, *Clarifying the Thought: Explanation of the Introduction to the Middle Way*: 205.

29. Asaṅga, *Compendium of Mahāyāna* (*Mahāyāna-saṃgraha*): 3b2.

30. Vasubandhu, *Commentary on the Distinction of the First Factor of Dependent Arising* (*Pratītyasamutpādādivibhaṅga-bhāṣya*): 30b4.

> Presenting the opponent's position here, the *Compendium of Mahāyāna* describes it as follows: "Why is it called the appropriating consciousness?[31] This is because it serves as the cause of all material sense faculties and because it serves as the basis of the appropriation of all bodies. As long as one remains alive, it sustains the five material sense faculties, keeping them from disintegration."[32]
>
> It further states: "What is held in common consists of the seeds of worldly environments, and what is not held in common consists of the seeds of individual sources of perception. What is held in common is the seeds produced without feeling."[33] Seeds of worldly environments within the fundamental consciousness are described as "seeds of entities without feeling." Asaṅga's *Compendium of Mahāyāna* makes the same point.
>
> Again it says:
>
> The *Commentary on the Distinction of the First Factor of Dependent Arising* states: "Due to the condition of the fundamental consciousnesses, name and form are said to be established. Name includes the last four aggregates, and form includes elemental and derivative forms. Such forms do not exist in the Formless Realm, but they do exist in the other two realms."[34] In the Cittamātra system, there are innumerable teachings like this that show that it does assert form.[35]

Someone may object: Yes, there are assertions in this Cittamātra system like "such things as form exist," but such assertions are made with the intention that such things as form only exist as appearances to cognition; in fact, such things as form do not exist.

If that were the case, then for this system even worldly environments like the earth, which have no feeling, would also not exist. Their attributes—such as forms, sounds, scents, tastes, and tangible objects—would not exist. It would absurdly follow that beings who are experiencers, having appropriated

---

31. Tib. *len pa'i rnam par shes pa*; Skt. *ādāna-vijñāna*.

32. Asaṅga, *Compendium of Mahāyāna*: 3b.

33. Asaṅga, *Compendium of Mahāyāna*: 12a.

34. A search of the sDe dge edition of this text indicates that this is not a direct quote. It appears to summarize elements of the discussion of pages 21a–24b.

35. Tsongkhapa, *Clarifying the Thought: Explanation of the Introduction to the Middle Way*: 205. bKra shis lhun po edition: 308.

the form aggregate, would still lack visual and auditory sources of perception that would enable them to experience such things as forms and sounds. Thus, there would be no experiencers endowed with things like eyes, nor beings who experience happiness or suffering. Consequently, in this system such conventions would be untenable. And if such conventions were untenable, who would say, "This is good philosophy?" No one would assert such a thing. As *Clarifying the Thought* states:

> It is apparent that there are innumerable assertions that form exists in the Cittamātra system. If that were not the case, then it would appear that in Cittamātra all of the conventions they espouse such as form and sound—beginning with the form aggregate—would simply become untenable as conventional designations, and so they would have to designate fresh new conventions. There is not a single Indian Buddhist who would say, "this is good philosophy" after having seen such untenable conventions.[36]

Therefore, they do not assert that cognitive objects such as forms and sounds that are directly perceived—that appear far removed from cognitions that apprehend form—exist externally. Someone who propounds that things are internal to cognition says: "We are proponents of internal cognitive objects." This does not mean that they say: "There are no *forms* that are cognitive objects, but cognition does exist." *Clarifying the Thought* also states:

> The meaning of the label "proponents of internal objects of knowledge" is this: objects of knowledge are such things as forms and sounds, but they do not assert that they are external. Rather, they say: "We propound that they are things that are internal to cognition."[37]

Thus, according to this Cittamātra system, cognitions that have experiences of pleasure or pain from objects such as pleasant or unpleasant forms clearly experience feelings. On this basis, they assert that they exist. Similarly, because experiences of forms such as blue are also clearly experienced, they exist. Therefore, they are not nonexistent: They exist. However, we must make a clear qualification: Forms such as blue do not exist *externally*. On this

---

36. Tsongkhapa, *Clarifying the Thought: Explanation of the Introduction to the Middle Way*: 205–206.

37. Tsongkhapa, *Clarifying the Thought: Explanation of the Introduction to the Middle Way*: 206.

point, Master Devendrabuddhi's *Subcommentary to the Commentary on the Compendium of Epistemology* again states:

> According to other Yogācāras, all things such as blue are not nonexistent because things like happiness are clearly experienced. However, things like blue do not exist as external entities. For one who asserts that cognition apprehends them, it is unitary and it does not have two parts.[38]

This is well put.

> May the collection of virtues my endeavors have gathered here
> Thoroughly eliminate the darkness in the minds of beings
> Like the autumn moon and
> Become a cause that increases the brilliance of wisdom.

This completes *Summary of the Essence: A Commentary on Investigation of the Percept.*

---

38. Devendrabuddhi, *Subcommentary to the Commentary on the Compendium of Epistemology* (*Pramāṇavārttika-pañjikā*): 242b.

PART II

Tibetan Texts

12

Investigation of the Percept *and Its* Autocommentary

THE TIBETAN TEXT

Introduction

This edition is based on the Derge version of *Investigation of the Percept* (D): #4206, *tshad ma* vol. *ce*: 86a5–87b2; *Autocommentary*: #4205, *tshad ma* vol. *ce*: 86a1–86a5; TBRC W23703–1490: 171–174. It has been compared with five other Tibetan editions:

1. Co ne (C): TBRC W1GS66030, vol. 174: 174–175; *Autocommentary*: TBRC W1GS66030, vol. 174: 175–177.
2. dPe bsdur ma (B): TBRC W1PD95844, vol. 97: 430–431; *Autocommentary*: TBRC W1PD95844, vol. 97: 432–436.
3. gSer bris (S): #3705; TBRC W23702, vol. 183: 474–476.
5. Peking (Pe cing) (P): #5703, *tshad ma* vol. *ce*: 177a7–177b5 (vol. 130: 73); *Autocommentary*: #5704, *tshad ma* vol. *ce*: 86a5–87b2 (vol. 130: 73).
6. sNar thang (N): #3702, *tshad ma* vol. *ce*: 119.3–6; *Autocommentary*: #3703; *tshad ma* vol. *ce*: 180b1–182a2.

   We have also consulted two Chinese translations of *Investigation of the Percept*, particularly with regard to how they render technical terms:
7. Paramārtha (Zhendi 眞諦), *Wuxiang sichen lun* 無相思塵論: T 1619. 31.882–883.
8. Xuanzang玄奘 *Guan suoyuanyuan lun* 觀所緣緣論: T 1624. 31.888–889.

We have not attempted to create a definitive Ür-text of *Investigation of the Percept*; rather, this edition aims to present the best reading of the Derge edition, collated with the other sources in order to correct errors and to clarify textual issues. Every significant deviation between Derge and the other Tibetan editions has been noted, so readers can use the footnotes to determine whether other readings might be preferable. The formatting follows that of the translation in order to help readers to locate passages and terms.

dMigs pa brtag pa[1]

Phyogs kyi glang po
(*Dignāga*)

Edited by Malcolm David Eckel, Jay Garfield, Leslie Kawamura, Dan Lusthaus, John Makeham, and John Powers

[170.6]] RGYA gar skad du / ā laṃ ba na pa rī ksha[2] / bod skad du / dmigs pa brtag pa /

sangs rgyas dang byang chub sems dpa' thams cad la phyag 'tshal lo //

dbang po rnam par rig pa'i rgyu //
phra rab rdul dag yin mod kyi //
der mi snang phyir de'i yul ni //
rdul phran ma yin dbang po bzhin // (1)
gang ltar snang de de las min //
rdzas su med phyir zla gnyis bzhin //
de ltar phyi rol gnyis ka yang //
blo yi yul du mi rung ngo // (2)
kha cig 'dus pa'i rnam pa dag //
sgrub pa yin par 'dod par byed //
rdul phran rnam pa rnam rig gi //
don min sra nyid la sogs bzhin // (3)
de dag ltar na bum pa dang //
kham phor sogs blo mtshungs par 'gyur //
gal te rnam pa'i dbye bas dbye //

---

1. Peking (P), N (sNar thang): dmigs pa brtag pa bzhugs so || zhes 'khod.
2. P, N, gSer bris (S): *a lam ba ṇa pa riksha.*

de ni rdul phran rdzas yod la[3] // (4)
med de[4] tshad dbye med phyir ro //
de phyir de rdzas med la yod //
rdul phran yongs su bsal na[5] ni //
der snang shes pa nyams 'gyur zhing[6] // (5)
nang gi shes bya'i ngo bo ni //
phyi rol ltar snang gang yin der[7] //
don yin rnam[8] shes ngo bo'i phyir //
de'i rkyen nyid kyang yin[9] phyir ro // (6)
gcig cha'ang mi 'khrul phyir na rkyen //
nus pa 'jog phyir rim gyis[10] yin[11] //
lhan cig byed dbang nus pa yi[12] //
ngo bo gang yin dbang po'ang yin // (7)
de'ang[13] rnam rig la mi 'gal //
de ltar yul gyi ngo bo dang //
nus pa phan tshun rgyu can dang //
thogs med dus nas[14] 'jug pa yin // (8)
dmigs pa brtags pa[15] slob dpon phyogs kyi
glang pos mdzad pa rdzogs so[16] //

---

3. S: *pa.*

4. P, N, S: *de med.*

5. P, N, S: *gsal ba.*

6. P, N, S: *nyams par 'gyur.*

7. P, N, S: *de.*

8. S: *rnams.*

9. N: *rim gyis pa'i yin.*

10. P, N, S: *gyi.*

11. *N: rim gyis pa'i yin.*

12. P, N, S: *yin.*

13. S: *de yang.*

14. P, N, S: *thog ma med dus.*

15. N: dmigs pa brtag pa'i tshig le'ur byas pa.

16. S: dmigs pa brtag pa'i tshig le'ur byas pa / slob dpon phyogs kyi glang pos mdzad pa rdzogs so.

dMigs pa brtag pa'i 'grel pa[17]

Phyogs kyi glang po (*Dignāga*)

[171.5] RGYA GAR skad du / ā[18] laṃ ba na pa rī ksha[19] brṛ ttī ka /
bod skad du / dmigs pa brtag pa'i 'grel pa /
sangs rgyas dang byang chub sems dpa' thams cad la phyag 'tshal lo //
gang dag mig la sogs pa'i rnam par shes pa'i dmigs pa phyi rol gyi don yin par 'dod pa de dag ni de'i rgyu yin pa'i phyir rdul phra rab dag yin pa'am der snang ba'i shes pa skye ba'i phyir de 'dus pa yin par rtog grang na / de la re zhig //

dbang po rnam par rig pa'i rgyu //
phra rab rdul dag yin mod kyi //
der mi snang phyir de[20] yul ni //
rdul phran ma yin dbang po bzhin // (1abcd)

yul zhes bya ba ni shes pas gang gis[21] rang gi ngo bo nges par 'dzin pa yin te de'i rnam par skye ba'i phyir ro // rdul [172] phra mo dag gi ni de'i rgyu nyid yin du zin kyang de lta ma yin te dbang po bzhin no[22] // de ltar na re zhig rdul phra mo dag dmigs pa ma yin no // 'dus pa ni der snang ba nyid yin du zin kyang /

gang ltar snang de de las min // (2a)

---

17. P, N, C: *ltar bkod.*

18. P, N, S: *a.*

19. P, N: *ri ksha.*

20. P, N, S: *de'i.*

21. S omits *gang gis.*

22. S omits *no.*

don gang zhig rang snang ba'i rnam par rig pa bskyed pa de ni dmigs pa yin par rigs te[23] / 'di ltar de ni skye[24] ba'i rkyen nyid du bshad pas so // 'dus pa ni de lta yang ma yin te /

rdzas su med phyir zla gnyis bzhin // (2b)

dbang po ma tshang ba'i phyir zla ba[25] gnyis mthong ba ni der snang ba nyid yin du zin kyang de'i yul ma yin no // de bzhin du rdzas su yod pa ma yin pa nyid kyis[26] rgyu ma yin pa'i phyir 'dus pa[27] dmigs pa ma yin no //

de ltar phyi rol gnyis kar yang //
blo yi[28] yul du mi rung ngo // (2cd)

yan lag gcig ma tshang ba'i phyir phyi rol gyi rdul phra mo dang tshogs pa zhes bya ba'i don ni dmigs pa ma yin no // 'di la ni //

kha cig 'dus pa'i rnam pa dag //
sgrub pa yin par 'dod par byed // (3ab)

don thams cad ni rnam pa du ma can[29] yin pas de la rnam pa 'ga' zhig gis mngon sum nyid du 'dod do // rdul phra rab rnams la yang 'dus par snang ba'i shes pa skyed pa'i rgyu[30] yod do //

rdul phran rnam pa rnam rig gi //
don min sra nyid la sogs bzhin // (3cd)

ji ltar sra[31] nyid la sogs pa ni yod bzhin du yang mig gi blo'i yul ma yin pa ltar rdul phra mo nyid kyang de dang 'dra'o //

de dag ltar na bum pa dang //
kham phor sogs blo mtshungs par 'gyur // (4ab)

---

23. S: *ni dmigs pa yin par rigs te / yin par rigs te.*

24. D: *skya.*

25. S omits *ba.*

26. P, N, S: *kyi.*

27. P, N, S: *byas.*

28. P, N, S: *yis.*

29. S omits *ni rnam pa du ma can.*

30. P, N, S: *bskyed pa'i rgyu'i dngos po.*

31. P, N, S: *sra ba.*

bum pa dang kham phor la sogs pa'i rdul phra mo rnams la ni mang du zin kyang khyad par 'ga' yang med do //

gal te rnam pa'i dbye bas dbye // (4c)

gal te 'di snyam du mgrin pa la sogs pa'i rnam pa'i khyad par las gang gis ni[32] blo'i khyad par du 'gyur ba'i khyad par yod do snyam du sems na khyad par 'di ni bum pa la sogs pa la yod kyi /

de ni rdul phran rdzas yod la //
med de tshad dbye med phyir ro // (5ab)

rdul phra rab rnams ni rdzas gzhan yin du zin kyang zlum po la ni dbye ba med do //

de phyir de rdzas med la yod // (5b)

rnam pa'i dbye ba ni kun rdzob tu yod pa dag kho na la yod kyi [173] rdul phra mo rnams la ma yin no // bum pa la sogs pa ni kun rdzob tu yod pa nyid do[33] //

rdul phran yongs su bsal na ni //
der snang shes pa nyams 'gyur phyir // (5cd)

rdzas su yod pa rnams la ni 'brel pa can bsal du zin kyang kha dog la sogs pa bzhin du rang gi blo 'dor bar byed do[34] // de lta bas na dbang po'i blo rnams kyi yul ni phyi rol na ma yin par 'thad do //

nang gi shes bya'i ngo bo ni //
phyi rol ltar snang gang yin de[35] // (6ab)

don yin phyi rol gyi don med bzhin du phyi rol lta bur snang ba nang na yod pa kho na dmigs pa'i rkyen yin no //

don yin[36] rnam shes ngo bo'i phyir //
de'i[37] rkyen nyid kyang yin phyir ro // (6cd)

---

32. P, N, S: *na.*

33. P, N, S: *de.*

34. P, N, S: *ba med.*

35. P, N, S: *te.*

36. Omitted in D, C, S, B.

37. B: *de.*

nang gi rnam par shes pa ni don du snang ba dang / de las skyes pa yin pas // chos nyid gnyis dang ldan pa'i phyir nang na yod pa kho na dmigs pa'i rkyen yin no // re zhig de ltar snang ba nyid yin la ni rag la[38] // de'i phyogs gcig po lhan cig skyes pa go ji ltar rkyen yin zhe na //

gcig cha'ang[39] mi 'khrul phyir na rkyen // (7a)

lhan cig par gyur du zin kyang 'khrul pa med pa'i phyir gzhan las skye ba'i[40] rkyen du 'gyur te / 'di ltar gtan tshigs pa dag ni[41] yod pa dang med pa dag gi de dang ldan pa nyid na rgyu[42] dang rgyu dang ldan pa rim gyis skye ba dag gi yang mtshan nyid yin par smra'o // yang na //

nus pa 'jog phyir rim gyis yin // (7b)

rim gyis kyang yin te / don du snang ba[43] de ni rang snang ba dang mthun pa'i 'bras bu skyed par byed par[44] nus pa / rnam par shes pa'i rten can byed pas mi 'gal lo // gal te 'o na ni[45] nang gi gzugs kho na dmigs pa'i rkyen yin na / ji ltar de dang mig la brten na[46] mig gi rnam par shes pa skye zhe na /

lhan cig byed dbang nus pa yi[47] //
ngo bo gang yin dbang po'ang yin // (7cd)

dbang po ni rang gi 'bras bu las nus pa'i ngo bo nyid du rjes su dpag gi 'byung ba las gyur pa nyid du ni ma yin no //

de yang rnam rig la mi 'gal // (8a)

---

38. P, N, S: *reg na*. read reg for rag.

39. D, C, S, B: *na'ang*.

40. P, N, S: *skyes pa'i*.

41. Text correction: P, N, S omit: *yod pa dang med pa*. Vinītadeva makes it clear that this refers to reasoners and not reasons.

42. P, N, S: *ni rgyu dang rgyu 'bras*.

43. Text correction: D has *snang bas*, but P, N, S have *snang ba*. Kamalaśīla's Sanskrit citation in the *Tattvasaṃgraha-pañjikā* makes it clear that this is a nominative.

44. P, N, S: *pa'i*. Ngag dbang bstan dar follows the reading of P, N, and S.

45. P, N, S: omit *ni*.

46. P, N, S: *nas*.

47. P, N, S: *yis*.

nus pa'i rnam par shes pa la yod kyang rung / bstan du med pa'i rang gi ngo bo la yod kyang rung ste / 'bras bu skye da pa[48] la khyad par med do //

de ltar yul gyi ngo bo dang //
nus pa phan tshun rgyu can dang //
thog ma med du 'jug pa yin // (8bcd)

mig ces bya ba'i nus pa dang / nang gi gzugs la brten[49] nas rnam par shes pa don du snang ba dmigs kyis ma bstan pa[50] skye'o // 'di gnyis kyang phan tshun gyi rgyu can dang / thog ma med pa'i dus can[51] yin te[52] / res[53] 'ga' ni[54] nus pa yongs su [174] smin pa las rnam par shes pas[55] yul gyi rnam pa nyid[56] 'byung la res 'ga' ni de'i rnam pa la nus pa'o // rnam par shes pa las[57] de gnyis dang[58] gzhan nyid dang gzhan ma yin pa nyid du ci dgar brjod par bya'o // de ltar nang gi dmigs pa ni chos nyid gnyis dang ldan pa'i phyir yul du mthong ngo[59] //

dmigs pa brtags[60] pa'i 'grel pa slob dpon phyogs kyi glang pos mdzad pa'o[61] //

---

48. P, N, S: *bskyed.*

49. P, N, S: *rten.*

50. P, N, S: *phye ba.*

51. P, N: *ma.*

52. S: *thog ma med pa'i dus ma yin te.*

53. P, N, S: *re;* C, B: res; D: *re su.*

54. Variant: *na.*

55. P, N, S: *pa'i.*

56. P, N, S: *nyid du.*

57. P, N, S: *dang.*

58. S, B omit *dang.*

59. P, N: *yul nyid du 'thad do.*

60. P, N, S: *brtag.*

61. P, N, S: *mdzad pa rdzogs so.*

13

Subcommentary on Investigation of the Percept

THE TIBETAN TEXT

13.1 Introduction

This edition of *Subcommentary to Investigation of the Percept* is based on two Derge versions: (1) T: Derge *bsTan 'gyur*, Tshad ma vol. *zhe* (190): 175a3–187b.5: Tibetan Buddhist Resource Center (TBRC), Vol. 3452, Work #22704: 349–374; and (2) D: Asian Classics Input Project *bsTan 'gyur*, Derge #4241, vol. *zhe* (190), ff. 175a–187b. These have been compared with five other Tibetan editions:

1. N: sNar thang *bsTan 'gyur*, Tshad ma vol. *ze*: TBRC vol. 3452, Work # 22704: 186b.1–200b.6.
2. S: gSer bris *bsTan 'gyur*, Tshad ma vol. 201: 485–522 (ff. 243a–261b).
3. P: Peking (Pe cing) *bsTan 'gyur*, Tshad ma Vol. *ze* (138: 45–51), ff. 183a.7–197b.7.
4. C: Co ne *bsTan 'gyur*, Tshad ma vol. *zhe* (ff. 167b.4–180a): TBRC Vol. 190: 338–363.
5. B: dPe bsdur ma *bsTan 'gyur*, Tshad ma (Pe cing: Krung go'i bod rig pa'i dpe skrun khang, 1994–2000; TBRC W1PD95844): 467–500.

We have not attempted to create a definitive Ür-text; rather, this edition aims to present the best reading of the Derge edition, collated with the other sources in order to correct errors and to clarify textual issues. Every significant deviation between the Derge and the other Tibetan editions has been noted, so readers can use the footnotes to determine whether other readings might be preferable.

Formatting reflects that of the translation. This was adopted in order to make it easier for readers to find particular passages or terms.

dMigs pa brtag pa'i 'grel bshad (Ālambanaparīkṣā-ṭīkā)

'Dul ba'i lha (*Vinītadeva*)
Edited by Malcolm David Eckel, John Powers, and Sonam Thakchöe

[349] RGYA GAR skad du / ā laṃ bha[1] na pa rī kṣa[2] ṭī kā / bod skad du / dmigs pa brtag pa'i 'grel bshad / sangs rgyas dang byang chub sems dpa' thams cad la phyag 'tshal lo / /

thugs rjes zin pa'i dgongs pa can //
thams cad mkhyen la[3] spyi bo yis //
phyag 'tshal dmigs pa brtag pa yi[4] //
rnam par bshad pa rab tu bya //

gang dag mig la sogs pa'i[5] rnam par shes pa'i[6] zhes bya ba'i tshig dang po 'dis ni rab tu byed pa 'di'i brjod par bya ba dang / phyin ci log gi rgyu mtshan bstan to // dgos pa dang 'brel pa dag ni shugs kyis[7] dpag par bya ste / shugs kyang skabs su bab nas[8] bstan par bya'o // rab tu byed pa 'di'i 'brel pa dang / brjod

1. N, P: la ba.

2. N: kā; S: a laṁ ba na pa rī ksha ṭī kā; C: a laṁ bha na pa rī kshā ṭī kā.

3. N: mkhyen pa'i; S: mkhyen pa la.

4. C, N: yi: sa

5. N, S, P: pa.

6. Commentary preface.

7. N, P: kyi.

8. N, S, P: na.

par bya ba dang dgos pa rnams ni gdon mi za bar brjod dgos so // de lta ma yin na 'brel pa med pa dang brjod par bya ba med pa dang dgos pa med pa'i rab tu byed pa ni nyan pa po[9] rtog pa sngon du gtong ba dag khas mi len to // de lta bas na 'dir /

> gang dag mig la sogs pa'i rnam par shes pa'i dmigs pa phyi rol gyi don yin par 'dod pa de dag rdul phra rab rnams yin pa'am / de 'dus pa yin par rtog grang na[10] /

zhes bya ba 'dis ni spang bar bya ba'i rang bzhin gyi brjod par bya ba bstan to // **de'i rgyu yin pa'i phyir**[11] / zhes bya ba dang / **der snang ba'i shes pa skye ba'i phyir**[12] zhes bya ba 'dis ni phyin ci log gi rgyu mtshan bstan to // dgos pa dang 'brel pa[13] dag ni shugs kyis bstan to // de la shugs [350] ni 'di yin par khong du chud par bya ste / phyi rol gyi dmigs pa dag[14] dgag pa'i phyir dang / nang gi rab tu sgrub pa'i phyir rab tu byed pa 'di brtsam[15] mo // de lta bas na[16] phyi dang nang gi don dag[17] dgag pa dang / rab tu sgrub pa'i phyir rab tu byed pa 'di rtsom pas shugs kyis na[18] 'gog pa dang[19] rab tu sgrub pa dag ni dgos pa nyid yin la / rab tu byed pa ni thabs nyid yin par bstan par 'gyur te / 'di ltar rtog pa sngon du gtong ba rnams ni dgos pa med pa la yang 'jug par mi 'gyur la / thabs ma yin pa la yang ma yin no // 'dir rigs pas phyi rol gyi dmigs pa dgag pa dang / nang gi rab tu sgrub pa 'di ni brjod par bya ba yin no // de nyid[20] 'gog pa dang rab tu sgrub pa dag ni dgos pa yin no // dgos pa de yang rab tu byed pa 'dis byed pas[21] rab tu byed pa ni dgos pa 'di'i thabs yin no // de'i phyir rab tu byed pa dang / dgos pa dag[22] thabs dang thabs las byung ba'i mtshan nyid kyis

9. N, S: pa.

10. This is a shortened version of the commentary preface.

11. Commentary preface.

12. Commentary preface.

13. Text correction: T, D, N, P, S read 'brel ba, but all other instances in the text read 'brel pa.

14. N, S omit dag.

15. S: mtshams.

16. S, P: de bas na.

17. N, P omit dag.

18. N: kyi; omits na.

19. N, P omit dang.

20. Text correction: D, S, P: de gnyis; C: de ni.

21. N, S, P: byed pa.

22. C: dang.

'brel pa yin no // de lta bas na phyi dang nang gi don dag dgag pa dang / rab tu sgrub pa'i phyir rab tu byed pa 'di brtsam mo zhes bya bar gnas so // de ltar gnas pa la brgal[23] 'ga' zhig 'gog pa dang / rab tu sgrub pa 'di dag gis ci zhig bya ste / de dag ni gang du yang mi mkho 'o [24] zhes gleng bar byed na 'dir smras pa / dor ba dang / blang ba dag[25] 'gog pa dang rab tu sgrub par byed pa gang dag yod pa de dag ni / de gnyis 'dor ba dang len par byed pa yin no // 'di ltar phyi rol gyi don dor bar bya ba'i phyir 'gog par byed de / ci nas kyang 'gog pa las phyi rol gyi don dor bar bya ba nyid yin par shes nas dor bar bya'o snyam ste 'gog par byed do // de bzhin du rab tu sgrub pa las nang gi[26] don blang bar bya ba nyid yin par shes nas blang bar bya'o snyam ste / rab tu sgrub par byed do // de bas na phyi dang nang dor bar bya ba dang / blang bar bya ba dag[27] dor bar bya ba dang blang ba'i phyir 'gog pa dang / rab tu sgrub par byed pas dgos pa yang bshad pa yin no // de lta na 'o na ni ji ltar tshig dang po 'dis spang bar bya[28] ba'i rang bzhin gyi[29] brjod par bya ba bstan pa[30] de bzhin du / blang bar bya ba'i rang gi ngo bo yang bstan [351] dgos so zhe na / 'dir[31] smras pa / phyi rol gyi[32] don du smra ba rnams ni[33] phyi rol gyi don du yongs su rtogs pas shin tu gnod de / de'i phyir de kho na tshig dang pos bstan nas gtsor de dag[34] dgag par bya'o // phyis ni zhar la / nang gi ngo bo'i shes bya ni / phyi rol ltar snang gang yin te // don yin zhes bya ba 'dis nang gi len par byed de / re zhig 'di ni spyi'i don yin no //

yan lag gi don brjod par bya ste / **gang dag mig la sogs pa'i rnam par shes pa**[35] zhes bya ba ni rgol ba ril gyis dmigs pa phyi rol don yin par 'dod pa ni ma yin pas de'i phyir **gang dag** zhes[36] bya ba smos so // dbang po gang dag

23. Text correction: read brgal for brgyal.

24. N, S, P: mkho.

25. N: omits dag; S, C: blang bar dang.

26. N, S: gis.

27. S omits dag; N, P: dang.

28. S: blang bar byed.

29. S omits gyi.

30. N, S, P: par bya ba.

31. N, S, P: 'dis.

32. S: phyi rol gyis.

33. P: kyi.

34. N omits dag.

35. Commentary preface.

36. C: ces.

la **mig la sogs pa** yod pa de dag ni **mig la sogs pa**[37] ste / sogs pa smos pas ni rna ba la sogs pa yid[38] la thug pa'i bar gzung[39] ngo // 'di ltar yid[40] kyang phyi rol gyi don gyi[41] dmigs pa can du 'dod pa nyid de / de'i phyir de'i dmigs pa yang 'dir tshar gcig tu dgag par[42] bya'o // de gzhag[43] pas ci zhig bya ste / bstan bcos byed pa gang gis ni[44] de gzhag[45] par bya ba de'i yul logs shig tu 'gog par ni mi byed do // de'i phyir slob dpon chos skyong gis rang gi 'grel bshad las / yid kyi rnam par shes pa'i dmigs pa gzhag[46] pa'i phyir mang po zhig smos pa gang yin pa de ni de nyid shes[47] grang / bdag gis ni de'i bsam pa zab pa'i phyir mi rig[48] go/

mig la sogs pa dag gi rnam par shes pa ni / **mig la sogs pa'i rnam par shes pa'o**[49] // mig la sogs pa'i rnam pa mang po[50] nyid kho nas rnam par shes pa'i rnam pa yang mang ba nyid du bstan par 'gyur bas rnam par shes pa la mang po'i tshig bstan par bya ste dper na / zangs dang lo ma dag la dmar por[51] gyur pa zhes bya ba lta bu'o // **dmigs pa phyi rol gyi don**[52] zhes bya ba la / phyi rol gyi don ni phyi rol gyi ste / rnam par shes pa la ma gtogs pa zhes bya ba'i tha tshig go / rtogs par bya bas[53] na don te shes par bya zhing gzung bar bya'o zhes bya ba'i tha tshig go / don zhes bya ba'i sgra ni 'dir yul gyi rnam grangs yin par bstan par bya'i rdzas yod par byed pa ni ma yin te / [352] 'di ltar 'dus pa yang yul nyid du 'chad par 'gyur mod kyi / 'di rdzas su yod pa ni ma yin

37. Commentary preface.

38. S: yin.

39. P, N: bzung.

40. S: yin.

41. N, S, P omit don gyi.

42. N, S, P: pa.

43. N, S, P: bzhag; C: gzhag.

44. N, S, P: na.

45. N, S: bzhag.

46. N, S: bzhag.

47. N: shas.

48. S: rigs.

49. Commentary preface.

50. N, P: ba.

51. N: par.

52. Commentary preface.

53. N, S, P: ba.

no // **dmigs pa yin par 'dod pa**[54] zhes bya ba ni gzung ba yin par khas len pa zhes bya ba'i tha tshig go /

de dag rdul phra rab dag yin pa'am zhes bya ba ni[55] rgol ba[56] de dag rnam par shes pa'i yul rdul shin tu phra ba dag yin par khas len par 'gyur ba'am zhes bya'o[57] // de dag ni rdul yang yin la phra rab kyang yin pas / rdul phra rab dag ste / gang phan chad ches[58] phra ba[59] gzhan med pa'i phyir shin tu phra mo zhes bya ba'i tha tshig go /

rdul phra rab 'dus pa kho na skye zhing 'gag mod kyi / 'on kyang gzhan dag 'di dag 'dus pa re re yang dmigs pa nyid yin par 'dod de / ji ltar dbang po rnams kyi nus pa so sor nges pa'i phyir gzugs dang ro la sogs pa gcig tu 'dus pa dag kyang so sor nges pa'i dbang po'i gzung ba yin pa de bzhin du rnam par[60] shes pa yang rdzas yongs su gcod pa[61] la nus pa nges pa'i phyir / rdul re re zhing dmigs pa yin gyi spyi ni ma yin no zhes grag go / 'dus pa yin du zin kyang 'on kyang shin tu phra mo de dag ji ltar dmigs par 'gyur zhe na de'i phyir de'i rgyu yin pa'i phyir zhes bya ba smos te / de dag phra mod kyi / 'on kyang gang gi phyir rdzas su yod pas rnam par shes pa'i rgyu'i dngos por 'gyur ba de'i phyir dmigs par 'dod do // 'di'i bsam pa ni dmigs pa'i don ni rgyu'i don to snyam pa yin te / rkyen rnams ni nang du dmigs pa bstan pa'i phyir dang / rkyen yang rgyu yin pa'i phyir ro // rgyu nyid yin pa 'di yang gzhan gyi ltar rdul phra rab rnams dmigs pa nyid du[62] yongs su brtag[63] pa la phyin ci log gi rgyu mtshan yin te / 'di ltar de dag rnam par shes pa'i rgyu'i dngos por 'gyur ba na[64] phyi rol gyi don du smra ba rnams dmigs pa yin par 'dod do // de'i rgyu yin pa'i phyir zhes bya ba la / de zhes bya ba'i sgras[65] ni rnam par shes pa dang sbyar ro //

---

54. Commentary preface.

55. N, S, P omit ni.

56. S omits rgol ba.

57. N, S, P: pa'o.

58. S: ces.

59. N: phra rab.

60. S omits rnam par.

61. S: bcod.

62. N, S, P omit nyid du.

63. S: brtags.

64. D: ni.

65. N, S, P: sgra.

phyogs gnyis pa nye bar dgod pa'i phyir / **de 'dus pa yin par**[66] **rtog**[67] **grang na**[68] zhes bya ba smos te[69] / rnam par shes pa'i dmigs pa rdul phra rab 'dus pa yin par rtog grang na'o // de dag [353] 'dus[70] pa ni de 'dus pa'o // de zhes bya ba'i sgras ni 'dir rdul phra rab dag dang sbyar[71] te / des na rdul phra rab 'dus pa zhes[72] bshad pa yin no //

yang ci'i phyir de dag 'dus pa dmigs pa yin par 'dod[73] ce na / **der snang ba'i** rnam par[74] **shes pa**[75] **skye ba'i phyir**[76] zhes bya ba smos te / gang gi phyir mig la sogs pa'i rnam par shes pa ni rtag tu 'dus par snang bar skye ba[77] de'i phyir 'dus pa dmigs par 'dod do // 'dir yang 'dus pa dmigs pa nyid yin par yongs su brtag pa la phyin ci log gi rgyu mtshan ni 'dus par snang ba nyid yin no // gang gi phyir rnam par shes pa[78] 'dus par snang ba de'i phyir gzhan 'dus pa dmigs pa yin no snyam du sems te / 'di ltar rnam par shes pa gang ltar snang bar skye ba de ni de'i yul yin par 'dod do zhes bshad do // rnam par shes pa 'di la de lta bur snang ba yod pas 'di ni **der snang ba'o** // 'dir yang **der** zhes bya ba'i sgras[79] ni 'dus pa dang sbyar ro // de[80] ni der snang ba yang yin la rnam par[81] shes pa yang yin pas zhes tshig rnam par sbyar te / **der snang ba'i shes pa skye ba** zhes tshig bsdu'o //

De ltar na 'dir gzhan dag dmigs pa'i mtshan nyid du 'thad pa'i phyir rdul phra rab dang / 'dus pa dag dmigs pa nyid yin no snyam du sems so zhes bya ba ni phyogs snga ma yin no // de la re zhig phyogs snga ma bsal[82] ba'i phyir /

---

66. D: pa'i.

67. P: rtogs.

68. Commentary preface.

69. D: so.

70. N, S, P: lus.

71. P, N: sbyor.

72. N: shes.

73. S omits 'dod.

74. N, P: pa.

75. S: der snang ba shes pa.

76. Commentary preface.

77. P, N: bar.

78. Text correction following S: shes par.

79. N, S, P: sgra.

80. N: da.

81. N, S, P omit rnam par.

82. N: gsal.

dbang po'i rnam par rig pa'i rgyu //
phra rab rdul dag yin mod kyi // (1ab)

zhes bya ba la sogs pa smos so // rdul phra rab rnams ni yang dag pa'i don du na rdzas su yod pa ma yin te / cha shas dang bcas pa nyid du rtog na ni kun rdzob tu yod pa nyid du thal bar 'gyur[83] la / cha shas med pa nyid du rtog[84] na yang grib ma dang sgrib pa la sogs pa med pa nyid du[85] thal bar 'gyur te / de'i phyir 'di dag rgyu nyid lta ga la yin / 'on kyang rdul phra rab rnams rgyu nyid du khas blangs nas / dmigs pa nyid yin pa dgag[86] go / rdul phra rab rnams rnam par shes pa'i rgyu'i ngo bor 'gyur mod kyi / 'on kyang gang gi phyir de dag rdul phra rab kyi rnam pa can gyi rnam par shes pa mi skye ba[87] de'i phyir dmigs [354] pa ma yin te / dper na dbang po bzhin no // dbang po'i[88] rnam par shes pa'i rgyu'i dngos por 'gyur mod kyi de de'i yul yin par ni pha rol po mi 'dod do // 'di ltar rnam par shes pa dbang po'i rnam pa can du mi skye bas so // **dbang po'i rnam par rig pa'o**[89] zhes bya ba la / dbang po smos pas ni yid la thug pa'i bar dbang po drug car gzung ste / 'dir gtan tshigs ni bshad zin to // **phra rab rdul dag** (1b) ces bya ba 'di ni don[90] go bar zad[91] do // **yin**[92] **mod kyi** (1b) zhes bya ba 'dis[93] ni khas len pa'i rgol ba ston te[94] / **der mi snang phyir** (1c) zhes bya ba la / gang la de dag lta bur snang ba yod pa[95] de ni der snang ba ste / **der** zhes bya ba'i sgras[96] ni rdul phra rab dag dang sbyar ro // der mi snang ba ni[97] der mi snang ba ste / gsum pa ni 'dir gtan tshigs la blta[98] bar bya ste / de

83. D: gyur.

84. S: rtog pa.

85. N, S, P: med par (omit nyid du).

86. Text correction following N, S, P: dgag. D: dag.

87. N, S, P: mi skyed pa.

88. N, S, P: dbang po ni.

89. N, S, P: pa'i. Verse 1a.

90. S: don ni.

91. S: go bar byed.

92. S: yid.

93. S: 'di.

94. N, P: to.

95. N, S, P omit yod pa.

96. N, S, P: sgra.

97. S omits ni.

98. N, S, P: lta.

bas rdul phra rab kyi rnam pa can ma yin pa'i phyir zhes bshad pa yin no // de'i zhes bya ba ni dbang po'i rnam par rig pa'i 'o // **yul ni / rdul phran ma yin dbang po bzhin** (1cd) // zhes bya ba ni ji ltar dbang po rnams yul ma yin pa ltar rdul phra rab rnams kyang de dang 'dra'o zhes bya ba'i tha tshig go / **dbang po** zhes bya ba'i sgras ni 'dir dbang byed pa rnams brjod do //

gal te rnam par shes pa rdul phra rab kyi rnam pa can du ma gyur na de ni de nyid kyis nyes par 'gyur[99] grang / rdul phra rab rnams go skyed par[100] byed pa yin bzhin du / ci'i phyir yul du mi 'gyur zhe na /

de'i phyir[101] **yul** zhes bya ba la sogs pa smos te / 'di ltar yul ni gang gi rang gi ngo bo de'i rnam par skye bar nges par 'dzin pa de la bya'o // **ni** zhes bya ba'i sgra ni gang gi phyir zhes bya ba'i don to // **rang gi ngo bo nges par 'dzin pa** zhes bya ba la / rang gi ngo bo smos pas ni rang dang spyi'i mtshan nyid du[102] bsams[103] pa yin no // de[104] nges par 'dzin pa ni rtog[105] pa ste / yongs su gcod cing 'dzin pa zhes bya ba'i tha tshig go / **de'i rnam par skye ba'i phyir ro**[106] zhes bya ba ni yul gyi rnam par[107] skye ba ma gtogs par[108] gzhan du rnam par shes pas yul nges par gzung bar mi nus te / de'i phyir sngon po la sogs pa'i rnam par skye ba'i rnam par shes [355] pas sngon po la sogs pa'i don nges par 'dzin to[109] zhes bya'o[110] // 'di la gang zhig byed na / rnam par shes pa 'dis[111] yul nges par 'dzin to zhes tha snyad gdags par bya ba nges par 'dzin pa'i mtshan nyid kyi byed pa[112] ni 'ga' tsam[113] yang med do // ji ltar pa'i[114] rnam pa'i rjes su byed

99. D: gyur.

100. N, P: skyed pa; S: bskyed par.

101. P omits de'i phyir; S, N omit phyir: de'i yul.

102. N, S: nyid du pa.

103. N, S, P: bsam.

104. S: de'i.

105. N, P: rtogs.

106. Verse 1 commentary.

107. N, S, P: rnam pa.

108. S omits par.

109. N, S, P: 'dzin no. Verse 1 commentary.

110. N: zhes bya ba'i.

111. N, S, P: 'di.

112. N, S, P: bya ba.

113. N, S, P omit tsam; S: 'gal ba.

114. S, B: pha'i.

par[115] skye ba'i bus pha'i gzugs 'dzin to zhes bya ba de bzhin du / rnam par shes pa yul gyi rnam pa'i rjes su byed par[116] skye bas kyang yul 'dzin to zhes tha snyad gdags so //

de la 'di snyam du rdul phra rab rnams kyi yang de bzhin du de'i rnam par skye bas rang gi ngo bo nges par 'dzin to snyam du sems na /

de'i phyir rdul phra mo dag ni de'i rgyu nyid yin du zin kyang de lta ma yin[117] zhes bya ba la sogs pa smos te / rdul phra rab rnams ni de'i rgyu nyid yin du zin kyang / rnam par shes pa so sor nges pa'i rnam pa'i rjes su mi byed na de ni[118] ji ltar de dag gi rang gi ngo bo 'dzin par 'gyur / nges par mi 'dzin na yang ji ltar yul du 'gyur /

de'i rgyu nyid yin du zin kyang[119] zhes bya ba ni rnam par shes pa'i rgyu nyid yin du zin kyang ngo zhes bya ba'i tha tshig go / **'dir dper[120] dbang po bzhin no**[121] zhes bya ba smos te / ji ltar dbang po rgyu'i dngos por 'gyur yang / de'i rnam par skye ba'i rnam par shes pas rang gi ngo bo nges par mi 'dzin pas / yul nyid du mi 'dod pa ltar rdul phra rab rnams kyang[122] de dang 'dra bar blta bar bya'o // dbang po yang dmigs pa nyid du thal bar 'gyur du 'ong bas dmigs pa ni rgyu mtshan nyid tsam 'ba' zhig[123] ni ma yin no //

de ltar rdul phra rab rnams dmigs pa nyid[124] yin pa bkag[125] nas mjug bsdu ba'i phyir / **de ltar na re zhig**[126] ces bya ba la sogs pa smos te / dmigs pa'i mtshan nyid du mi rung ba'i phyir rdul phra rab rnams dmigs pa ma yin no zhes bya ba'i tha tshig go /

'dir sbyor ba ni rdul phra rab rnams dmigs pa ma yin te / rang snang ba'i rnam par shes pa skyed par byed pa ma yin pa'i phyir dbang po bzhin no //

---

115. N, S, P: pa'i.

116. N: byed pa'i; S, P: byed pa.

117. Verse 1 commentary.

118. S: de'i.

119. Verse 1 commentary.

120. N, S, P: dpe.

121. Verse 1 commentary.

122. N, S, P: dang.

123. S: 'ga' zhig.

124. S: dmigs pa yin nyid.

125. S: bkag pa.

126. Verse 1 commentary.

chos mi mthun pa[127] ni gzung ba'i cha'o // rang snang ba'i rnam par shes pa skyed par byed pa ma yin pa yang dmigs pa nyid yin na ha cang thal bar 'gyur ba ni gnod pa can gyi tshad ma'o // [356]

yang na rdul phra rab rnams ni dmigs pa ma yin te / rang gi ngo bo[128] nges par mi 'dzin pa'i phyir dbang po bzhin no // chos mi mthun pa ni gzung ba'i cha ste / gzung ba'i cha dmigs pa nyid yin par ni sgrub par 'gyur ro // rang gi ngo bo nges par mi 'dzin pa yang dmigs pa nyid yin na ha cang thal bar 'gyur ba ni gnod pa can gyi tshad ma'o // sbyor ba 'di gnyis ni slob dpon chos skyong gi[129] bshad pa bdag gis bris kyi rang gi[130] bshad pa ni[131] ma yin no // de ltar na re zhig rdul phra rab rnams dmigs pa nyid yin pa bkag pa[132] yin no //

'dus pa yang dgag pa'i phyir / **'dus pa**[133] **der snang ba nyid**[134] **yin du zin kyang**[135] zhes bya ba la sogs pa smos te / rnam par rig pa 'dus pa can du snang mod kyi / 'on kyang 'dus pa dmigs pa ni ma yin te / 'di ltar rnam par rig pa de de las mi skye bas so //

de las[136] mi skyer chug na yang dmigs par go ci'i phyir mi 'gyur te[137] / de'i phyir **don gang zhig rang snang ba'i**[138] zhes bya ba la sogs pa smos te / 'di ltar don gang zhig rang snang[139] ste bdag nyid du snang ba'i rnam par rig pa skyed pa de ni dmigs pa yin par rung ngo // 'di skad du rnam par shes pa don gang zhig gi ngo bo'i rjes su byed la / de yang skyed par byed pa yin na de'i tshe dmigs pa'i rkyen du rung gi gzhan du ni ma yin no zhes bshad pa yin no // skyed par byed pa kho na dmigs pa yin par 'gyur ro zhes bya ba 'di ga[140] las she na / **'di**

---

127. N, S, P: pa'i.

128. N, S, P: ngo bo gi.

129. N, S, P: gis.

130. N, P: gis.

131. N: na.

132. N, P: bkag pa nyid.

133. S, P: 'dus pa nyid.

134. S, P omit nyid.

135. Verse 1 commentary.

136. S: de ltar.

137. N, S, P: zhe na.

138. Verse 2 commentary.

139. S, N, P: snang ba.

140. N, P: gang.

ltar de ni[141] zhes bya ba la sogs pa[142] smos te / 'di ltar de ni bstan bcos las skye ba'i rgyu mtshan nyid du bshad do // bstan bcos las ni 'di skad du / don gang zhig sems dang sems las byung ba rnams skye ba'i rgyu mtshan yang yin la / de rnams skyes na don de nyams su myong ba'i tha snyad 'dogs par yang byed pa de ni dmigs pa yin no zhes 'byung ngo // 'di skad du / don gang zhig sems dang sems las byung ba rnams skyed par byed la / sems dang sems las byung ba de rnams skyes nas / don de la 'di ltar nyams su myong ngo zhes de lta[143] bu'i tha snyad 'dogs par byed pa'i don de ni [357] dmigs pa zhes bya'o zhes bshad pa yin no[144] // de'i phyir skye ba'i rgyu mtshan yang yin la zhes smos pas / dmigs pa'i rkyen skyed par byed pa nyid yin par grub[145] bo // de'i rnam pa can nyid ni phyogs 'di la rab tu grags pa'i phyir ma bshad do // de bas na[146] gnyis ka'i mtshan nyid dang ldan pa'i don gang yin pa de dmigs pa yin no zhes bya bar bshad pa yin no //

de la 'di snyam du 'dus pa yang skyed par byed pa yin no snyam du sems na / **de'i phyir 'dus pa ni de lta**[147] **yang ma yin te**[148] zhes bya ba smos te / 'dus pa ni skyed par byed pa ma yin no // de rnam[149] par rig pa mi skyed na ji ltar dmigs pa yin par 'gyur / ci ste skyed par byed pa ma yin zhe na / **rdzas su med pa'i**[150] **phyir** (2b) zhes bya ba[151] smos te / gang gi phyir 'dus pa rdzas su yod pa ma yin pa de'i phyir skyed par byed pa ma yin te / rdzas su med pa rnams la ni 'bras bu skyed pa'i nus pa med do // 'dus pa rdzas su med pa nyid ni 'og nas sgrub par byed do // gang rdzas su yod pa ma yin pa de ni skyed par byed pa ma yin no zhes bya ba 'di la dpe **zla gnyis bzhin** (2b) zhes bya ba smos te / 'di ltar rdzas su med pa'i phyir zla ba gnyis pa ni zla ba gnyis par snang ba'i shes pa'i rgyu'i dngos por mi 'gyur ro // de bzhin du 'dus pa yang rang snang ba'i shes pa'i rgyu'i dngos por mi 'gyur ro //

---

141. Verse 2 commentary.

142. N, S, P omit sogs pa.

143. S: de ltar.

144. N: na.

145. C: 'grub.

146. S, P omit na.

147. N, S, P: ltar.

148. Verse 2 commentary.

149. N: rnams.

150. N, S, P omit pa'i.

151. N, S, P omit bya ba.

gal te zla ba gnyis pas de mi skyed na / 'o na ni de'i[152] rgyu mtshan med pa can du 'gyur ro zhe na /

de'i phyir **dbang po ma tshang ba'i phyir**[153] zhes bya ba la sogs pa smos te / rgyu mtshan med pa can ni ma yin te / 'di ltar dbang po nyams pas zla ba gnyis su mthong bar mi 'gyur[154] ro // 'di ltar gang gi tshe mig gi dbang po rab rib gyis nyams par 'gyur ba[155] de'i tshe zla ba gnyis su snang ba'i shes pa skye bar 'gyur te / de zla ba gnyis pas skyed pa ni ma yin no // gang gi tshe de des ma skyed[156] pa de'i tshe / zla ba gnyis kyi shes pa zla ba gnyis par snang du zin kyang / de'i yul ni ma yin no // de bas na skyed par byed pa ma yin pa'i phyir yul du mi 'gyur ro zhes bshad pa yin no // 'dir **ma tshang ba** zhes bya ba'i [358] sgras ni nyams pa brjod do //

de ltar dpe la rab tu bsgrubs nas / dngos po la nye bar sbyor ba'i phyir / **de bzhin du rdzas su yod pa ma yin pa nyid kyi**[157] zhes bya ba la sogs pa smos te / ji ltar zla ba gnyis pa rdzas su med pa'i phyir shes pa'i rgyu ma yin la / rgyu ma yin pa'i phyir de'i yul ma yin pa de bzhin du 'dus pa yang rdzas su med pa'i phyir shes pa'i rgyu ma yin la / rgyu ma yin pa'i phyir de'i yul ma yin no //

'dir[158] sbyor ba ni / 'dus pa ni rgyu ma yin te / rdzas su med pa'i phyir zla ba gnyis pa bzhin no // chos mi mthun pa ni rnam par shes pa'o / rdzas su med pa rnams la nus pa med pa ni gnod pa can gyi tshad ma'o // yang na 'dus pa ni[159] dmigs pa ma yin te[160] / rgyu ma yin pa'i phyir zla ba gnyis pa bzhin no // chos mi mthun pa ni gzung ba'i[161] cha ste / gzung ba'i cha rgyu nyid yin pa dang[162] / dmigs pa nyid yin par ni sgrub par 'gyur ro // rgyu ma yin pa yang dmigs pa nyid yin na / zla ba gnyis pa[163] la sogs pa yang dmigs pa nyid yin par

---

152. N, P: de.

153. Verse 2b commentary.

154. S, P, N omit mi; present in D.

155. S, P: gyur pa.

156. N, P: bskyed.

157. Verse 2b commentary.

158. S, P: de'i.

159. S, N, P omit ni.

160. N: no.

161. D, P: mthun pa ni gzung pa'i; N: mthun pa'i.

162. S: chos mi mthun pa'i cha ste / gzung ba'i cha rgyu nyid pa dang.

163. S, P omit pa.

'gyur bas[164] ha cang thal bar 'gyur ba ni gnod pa can gyi tshad ma'o // tshad ma 'di gnyis kyang slob dpon chos skyong gis bshad pa yin no //

de ltar phyogs gnyis ka bkag nas mjug bsdu ba'i phyir / **de ltar phyi rol gnyi gar yang // blo yi yul du mi rung ngo** (2cd) // zhes bya ba la sogs pa smos te / de ltar bshad pa'i tshul gyis na gnyi ga ltar na yang phyi rol gyi don rnam par shes pa'i yul du mi rung ngo // phyi rol ni rnam par shes pa las ma gtogs pa'o // **gnyi gar** zhes bya ba la[165] ni rdul phra[166] rab kyi phyogs dang / 'dus pa'i phyogs ltar ro // **blo'i** zhes bya ba ni shes pa'i'o // ci'i phyir mi rung zhe na / de'i phyir **yan lag gcig ma tshang ba'i phyir**[167] zhes bya ba la sogs pa smos te / 'di ltar rdul phra rab kyi phyogs la ni rgyu nyid yod kyi de'i rnam pa nyid med do // 'dus pa'i phyogs la yang de'i rnam pa nyid yod kyi rgyu nyid med do // de lta bas na yan lag re re ma tshang ba'i phyir rdul phra rab ces bya ba dang / 'dus pa zhes bya ba'i don dmigs pa ma yin no // 'di skad du dmigs pa nyid kyi yan lag gi rnam pa gnyis te / rang gi rnam pa[168] 'jog [359] pa dang / rgyu nyid yin pa'o // 'di yang rdul phra rab dang / 'dus pa dag la med pas / de gnyis yul nyid ma yin no zhes bshad pa yin no // gang las yul ni chos nyid gnyis dang ldan pa'o zhes 'byung ba der yang yan[169] lag de gnyis kho na chos nyid gnyis kyi sgrar brjod par zad do //

de ltar phyogs[170] gnyis ka bkag nas phyogs gsum pa nye bar dgod pa'i phyir / **'di la ni kha**[171] **cig** ces[172] bya ba la sogs pa smos te / phyi rol gyi don du smra bas[173] phyogs 'di la yang pha khol la sogs pa kha cig rdul phra rab[174] 'dus pa'i rnam pa dag dbang po'i rnam par shes pa'i rgyur 'dod do // de dag 'di skad ces rdul phra rab rnams la ni 'dus pa'i rnam pa yang yod do // rdul phra rab rnams la gang cung zad ci yod pa de thams cad ni / rdzas su yod pa yin no // rdzas su yod pa'i phyir 'dus pa'i rnam pa de[175] rnam par shes pa'i rgyu nyid du 'gyur ro //

---

164. Read ba'i?

165. N, S, P omit la.

166. S omits phra.

167. Verse 2cd commentary.

168. N: rnam par.

169. S omits yan.

170. S, N, P omit phyogs.

171. N: nam kha. S, P: nam kha.

172. D: zhes. Verse 2cd commentary.

173. S, N, P: smra ba'i.

174. N adds rnam pa ni.

175. N, S, P omit de.

rags pa'i phyir na rnam par shes pa la rang gi ngo bo yang 'jog par 'gyur te / de bas na rdul phra[176] rab rnams tshul[177] gzhan gyi yul nyid yin no zhes zer ro // **ni** zhes bya ba'i sgra ni yang zhes bya ba'i sgra'i don du blta bar bya'o // 'dus pa'i rnam pa ni 'dir rags pa'i rnam pa'o // **bsgrub pa** zhes bya ba ni rgyu'o //

rdul phra rab rnams kyi[178] rnam pa ni rab tu phra bar grags pa ma yin nam / de bas na 'di dag la 'dus pa'i rnam pa 'di lta ga la yod srid pa yod du chug na yang gcig la rnam pa gnyis ji ltar rung zhe na /

don thams cad ni[179] **rnam pa du ma can**[180] zhes bya ba la sogs pa smos te / 'di ni 'dir nyes pa ma yin te / gang gi phyir dngos po gzugs can thams cad ni rnam pa[181] du ma can yin pas so // 'di ltar gzugs can[182] thams cad ni 'byung ba chen po bzhi'i ngo bo nyid yin la / de dag kyang sngon po dang dri zhim pa dang / mngar ba dang / rtsub pa la sogs pa'i rnam pa dang ldan pas rnam pa du ma can yin no // yang ji ltar rdul phra rab rnams la rnam pa du ma dang ldan pa 'di yod pa de bzhin du 'dus pa'i rnam pa 'di yang de dag la yod par 'gyur ro // gal te don thams cad rnam pa du ma can yin na / [360] ci'i phyir rnam pa thams cad du mi shes zhe na /

de'i phyir **de la rnam pa 'ga' zhig gis**[183] zhes bya ba la sogs pa smos te / 'di dag rnam pa du ma[184] can yin mod kyi 'on kyang rnam pa 'ga' zhig gis 'di dag **mngon sum nyid du 'dod** kyi / rnam pa thams cad du[185] ni ma yin te / 'di ltar de dag gi[186] nus pa so sor nges pa'i phyir dbang po rnams ni don thams cad 'dzin pa ma yin no // 'di ni btsun pa sangs rgyas lha'i gzhung lugs kyi rjes su 'brangs nas bshad pa yin te / de ltar na skye mched bcu ni 'byung ba[187] tsam du zad do //

---

176. S omits phra.

177. D, T: chul.

178. P omits rnams kyi.

179. P omits thams cad ni.

180. Verse 3ab commentary.

181. S omits pa.

182. S, N, P omit can.

183. Verse 3ab commentary.

184. D: 'du ma.

185. S: du ma.

186. N, S, P: gis.

187. N: bar.

de ltar rnam pa du ma can nyid du bsgrubs nas rnal[188] ma dang sbyar ba'i phyir rdul phra rab rnams la yang[189] zhes bya ba la sogs pa smos te / rdul phra rab rnams la yang **'dus par snang ba'i shes pa bskyed pa'i rgyu'i dngos po yod de**[190] / rdul phra rab rnams kyi 'dus pa'i rnam pa can gyi shes pa bskyed do zhes bya ba'i don to //

rdul phra rab rnams la 'dus pa'i rnam pa yod pa sgrub par byed pas rdul phra rab rnams la 'dus pa'i rnam pa yod do zhes brjod par bya ba ma yin nam / ci'i phyir 'di skad du rdul phra rab rnams la yang 'dus par snang ba'i shes pa skyed pa'i rgyu yod do zhes smras she na /

'dir smras pa / dmigs pa'i cha gnyis rab tu bstan pa'i phyir de skad ces smras te / de la **shes pa skyed pa'i rgyu'i**[191] **dngos po**[192] zhes bya ba[193] smras pas ni / rgyu nyid yin par rang gi sgras[194] bstan to // 'dus par snang ba zhes smras pas ni rnam pa 'jog pa dang 'dus pa'i rnam pa yod pa nyid kyang bsgrubs pa yin te / gang gi phyir don gyis ni[195] rnam par shes pa la rang gi bdag nyid la yod pa'i rnam pa 'jog gi med pa ni ma yin pa de'i phyir 'dus pa'i rnam pa yod par yang smras pa kho na yin no //

gal te rdul phra rab rnams la rags pa'i rnam pa yod na go / ji ltar de dag la rdul phra rab ces bya / ji ltar phra mo'i rnam pa de nyid[196] bzhin du yang mi 'dzin zhe na /

de'i phyir **rdul phran rnam pa** (3c) zhes bya ba la sogs pa smos so // de nyid rnam par dgrol ba'i phyir **ji ltar sra ba nyid la sogs pa**[197] zhes bya ba smos te[198] / ji ltar sra ba nyid dang / gsher ba dang / dro ba la [361] sogs pa'i yul rnams yod bzhin du yang / dbang po'i nus pa so sor nges pa'i phyir mig gi blo'i yul nyid[199] du mi 'gyur ba de bzhin du rdul phra mo yang de bzhin du yang mi 'gyur ro //

---

188. N, S, P: snal.

189. Verse 3ab commentary.

190. Verse 3ab commentary.

191. S, P: bskyed pa'i rgyu'i; N: bskyed pa'i rgyu ba.

192. Verse 3ab commentary.

193. N, S, P omit bya ba.

194. D: smras; N: S: sgris.

195. S, N, P omit ni.

196. Text correction: D, S, T: nye; read nyid.

197. Verse 3cd commentary.

198. S, N, P: zhes bya ba la sogs pa smos te.

199. N omits yul; S, P omit nyid.

rnam pa de nyid la brten nas kyang 'di dag la rdul phra rab ces tha snyad gdags so // ni zhes bya ba'i sgra ni nyid ces bya ba'i don du blta bar bya'o //

de ltar phyogs gsum pa nye bar bkod nas sun dbyung ba **de dag ltar na bum pa dang / kham phor la sogs blo** (4ab) zhes bya ba la sogs pa smos te / gang dag[200] rdul phra[201] rab rnams la 'dus pa'i rnam pa yod par khas len pa de dag la brgal zhing brtag par bya ste / rdul phra rab rnams la 'dus pa'i rnam pa gang zhig khas len / re zhig 'jig rten na ni bum pa dang / kham phor dang / phor bu[202] la sogs pa dang / ka ba dang dri la sogs pa la 'dus par grags so // 'di dag gi nang na rnam pa gang zhig rdul phra rab rnams[203] la yod par[204] 'dod / gal te bum pa'i rnam pa'o zhe na de'i tshe kham phor la sogs pa 'dus pa thams cad la bum pa'i blo 'byung bar 'gyur ro // 'on te kham phor gyi rnam pa'o zhe na / de'i tshe yang thams cad la kham phor gyi blo 'byung bar 'gyur gyi[205] kha cig la ni bum pa'i blo kha cig la ni kham phor gyi blo zhes bya ba blo tha dad pa dag yin[206] pa 'dir mi 'gyur ro //

'di skad du / blo ni yul la[207] rang gi ngo bo'i rjes su byed cing skye la / yul yang ngo bo[208] gcig pa yin na de ji ltar blo tha dad par 'gyur zhes bshad pa yin no //

de la 'di snyam du / bum pa la ni rdul phra rab mang[209] la / kham phor la ni ches nyung ste / de bzhin du ni gzhan dag la yang mang ba dang nyung ba nyid rig par bya'o // de'i phyir mang ba dang nyung ba nyid kyis byas pa'i blo'i khyad par 'di yod do snyam du sems na /

de'i phyir **bum pa dang kham phor la sogs pa'i rdul phra rab rnams la ni**[210] zhes bya ba la sogs pa smos te / 'di la ni / nyung ngu dang mang po nyid kyis byas pa'i blo'i khyad par mi rung ste / 'di ltar bum pa la rdul phra rab mang la / kham phor la ches nyung mod kyi / 'on kyang rdul phra rab tu gtogs pa

---

200. S: gang dag pa.

201. T omits phra.

202. S: phur bu.

203. N, S omit rnams.

204. N, P: la yod pa.

205. S: gyis.

206. N, S, P: gang yin.

207. S omits la.

208. S: ngo bo'i.

209. Text correction: T reads: med; S, B read: mang.

210. Verse 4ab commentary.

'dus[211] pa'i [362] rnam pa la rang la yod pa'i khyad par ni 'ga' yang med do // de'i phyir nyes pa de'i so na 'dug ste / gang du[212] rdul phra rab mang ba der ni bum pa che la[213] / gang du[214] ches nyung ba der ni bum pa chung ngo[215] zhes bya ba 'di tsam[216] zhig tu 'gyur bar zad kyi 'dus pa'i rnam par 'dra ba las mang po las ni[217] bum pa'i blo / nyung ngu la ni kham phor gyi blo 'byung ngo zhes bya ba 'dir ni mi 'gyur ro //

'dir gzhan gyi tshig gi go skabs bstan pa'i phyir / **gal te rnam pa'i dbye bas dbye** (4c) zhes bya ba smos so // de nyid rnam par dgrol ba'i phyir[218] / gal te **'di snyam du**[219] zhes bya ba la sogs pa smos te / gal te 'di snyam du bum pa'i mgrin pa ni gyen du blta la / de yang zhum pa yin / lto[220] ni rked[221] na 'dug la de yang yangs pa yin te / de lta bu la sogs pa ni[222] 'di'i rnam pa'i[223] dbye ba yin no // kham phor ni kha ni yangs la / zhabs ni zhum pa zhes bya ba la sogs pa rnam pa'i dbye ba yin te / de'i phyir rnam pa'i dbye ba'i sgo nas / bum pa dang kham phor la sogs pa'i blo rnams tha dad par 'gyur ro snyam du sems na'o // rnam pa'i khyad par las zhes bya ba la rnam pa zhes bya ba ni dbyibs te / bkod pa dang / gnas pa zhes bya ba'i tha tshig go /

rnam pa'i dbye ba yul ma yin pa nyid du bstan pa'i phyir / **khyad par 'di ni bum pa la sogs pa la yod kyi**[224] zhes bya ba la sogs pa smos te / khyod kyi bum pa dang gzhan[225] kham phor la sogs pa'i rnam pa'i khyad par bstan pa gang yin pa de dag gi khyad par 'di ni[226] yod de / de ni kho bo cag kyang mi bsnyon mod

---

211. S, N, P: lus.

212. S omits du.

213. S, N, P: bum pa ches.

214. N omits che la gang du.

215. N: ngu.

216. N, S, N, P omit tsam.

217. D, S: mang po las ni; N, S, P: mang po'i.

218. S omits phyir.

219. Verse 4c commentary.

220. S, T: lto; D: lho.

221. N, S, P: sked.

222. S: de lta bum pa la sogs pa ni.

223. S: rnam par.

224. Verse 4c commentary.

225. N, S, P omit gzhan.

226. N, S, P omit ni.

kyi[227] / 'on kyang rdul phra rab rdzas su yod pa gang dag yin pa[228] de dag la ni rnam pa'i dbye ba de med do // de ci'i phyir zhe na / **tshad dbye med phyir ro** (5b) zhes bya ba smos te / 'di ltar rdul phra rab rnams kyi tshad[229] zlum po zhes bya ba gang yin pa de la ni dbye ba med do //

bum pa'i rdul phra rab rnams kyang rdzas gzhan kho na yin la / kham por gyi yang rdzas gzhan ma yin nam / de ji ltar tshad dbye ba[230] med ce na / de'i **phyir rdul phra rab rnams ni**[231] zhes bya ba la sogs pa smos te / gang gi phyir bum pa dang / kham phor la sogs pa'i rdul phra rab rnams rdzas gzhan nyid yin du zin kyang zlum po la tha dad pa med [363] pa de'i phyir rdul phra rab rnams la rnam pa'i dbye ba med do // ji ltar khyed kyi ltar na rdul phra rab rnams las ji[232] dang / ji snyed pa yod pa de thams cad rdzas su yod pa de bzhin du / rdul phra rab rnams la tshad cung zad ci yod pa de thams cad kyang zlum po'i ngo bo nyid yin la / rdul phra rab rnams kyi zlum po yang ngo bo nyid gcig pa kho na yin no // de'i phyir ji ltar de dag gi dbye bas tha dad par 'gyur / 'dus pa'i rnam pa rags par 'dod mod kyi / 'on kyang rdzas su yod pa'i phyir de yang cha shas med pa nyid du 'gyur dgos so // de lta ma yin te / 'di cha shas dang bcas pa yin na rdzas su yod pa nyid du mi 'gyur ro // cha shas med pa'i phyir de la bkod pa tha dad pa lta ga la yod de / gang dag cha shas dang bcas pa de dag ni nus pa sna tshogs pas bkod par 'gyur gyi / cha shas med pa dag ni ma yin no //

de ltar rdul phra rab rnams kyi rnam pa'i dbye ba bkag nas mjug bsdu ba'i phyir / **de'i phyir de rdzas med la yod**[233] (5b) // ces[234] bya ba smos te / gang gi phyir de ltar bshad pa'i rnam pas[235] cha shas med pa rnams la bkod pa tha dad pa mi srid pa de'i phyir / de ni rdzas su med pa rnams kho na la blta bar bya'o //

bstan bcos byed pas mdo'i don bstan pa'i phyir / **rnam pa'i dbye ba ni**[236] zhes bya ba la sogs pa smos te / rnam pa'i dbye ba gang yin pa de ni / **kun rdzob tu**

227. N: kyis.

228. N. S, P omit pa.

229. D, S, N, P omit tshad.

230. S, N: dbyer; D: dbye ba; P: dbye.

231. Verse 5ab commentary.

232. N, S, P: ci.

233. N: yo byad.

234. N, P: zhes.

235. S: rnam pa'i.

236. Verse 5b commentary.

yod pa dag kho na la yod de[237] / cha shas dang bcas pa'i phyir ro / /rdul phra rab rnams la ni ma yin te / cha shas med pa'i phyir ro //

bye brag pa'i ltar na bum pa la sogs pa rdzas su yod pa nyid yin te / de'i phyir brgya[238] zhig la de bum pa la sogs pa kun rdzob tu yod pa'o zhes bya ba 'di ji ltar shes zhes smra bar gyur[239] na / de'i phyir **bum pa la sogs pa ni kun rdzob tu yod pa nyid**[240] ces bya ba la sogs pa smos te / bum pa la sogs pa ni kun rdzob tu yod pa nyid do zhes bya ba de ltar shes par bya ste / 'di ltar rdul phra rab re re nas yongs su brtsal[241] bar byas na yang bum pa'i rnam pa can gyi shes pa mi skye'o // **der snang shes pa nyams 'gyur phyir** (5d) // zhes bya ba ni shes pa 'di la de lta bur snang ba yod pas na[242] / 'di ni [364] der snang ba ste / de zhes bya ba'i sgras[243] ni bum pa dang sbyar ro // snang zhes bya ba'i sgras[244] ni 'dra bar brjod do // de ni der snang ba yang yin la / shes pa yang yin pas na / der snang[245] shes pa'o // de nyams pa ni der snang shes pa nyams pa ste / der snang[246] shes pa nyams pa[247] de'i phyir ro //

rdul phra rab re re nas yongs su bsal[248] na bum pa la sogs pa'i rnam pa can gyi shes pa mi skyed[249] zin kyang / ci de tsam gyi bum pa la sogs pa kun rdzob tu yod pa nyid du 'gyur ram zhe na / de'i phyir / **rdzas su yod pa rnams la ni**[250] // zhes bya ba la sogs pa smos te / 'di ltar gang dag rdzas su yod pa de dag ni / 'brel pa can bsal kyang rang gi blo yongs su mi 'dor te / dper na kha dog la sogs pa lta bu'o //

---

237. Verse 5b commentary.

238. N, S: brgya; D: rgyu.

239. S: smras par 'gyur.

240. Verse 5b commentary.

241. Text correction: D, T read: brtsal; pf. N, P: bsal; S: gsal.

242. N, P omit na.

243. Text correction: N, T, S: sgras; D: sgra.

244. S, N, P: sgra.

245. N: snang ba.

246. S, N: snang ba.

247. P: nyan pa; N: nyam po.

248. S: bsal bar.

249. S, N, P: shes pa ma skyer.

250. Verse 5cd commentary.

gal te bum pa la sogs pa yang rdzas su yod pa zhig yin par gyur[251] na ni de'i tshe de dag kyang rang dang 'brel pa can yongs su bsal kyang / rang gi blo mi 'dor bar 'gyur ro // rdul phra rab re re nas yongs su bsal bar byas nas[252] / rdzas rtsom par byed pa'i sbyor ba zhig pa'i phyir / bum pa zhig pas de'i phyir bum pa'i blo mi skye ba yin[253] nam / thams cad kyi thams cad du med pa'i phyir ni ma yin no zhe na /

'dir bshad pa gal te / rdul phra rab las ma gtogs pa bum pa[254] la sogs pa yan lag can gyi rdzas zhig[255] yod na / de'i tshe rdul phra rab dag la yod do zhes brjod par bya ba ci de dag la ji snyed[256] yod pa'i ngo bos yod dam / 'on te phyogs gcig gis yin / de la rtsom par byed pa'i cha shas ma gtogs pa gang dag gis ni de de la yod par 'gyur ba cha shas can gyi phyogs gcig gis yod pa ma yin no // gal te phyogs gcig gis yod pa ma yin no zhe na / de'i tshe ji snyed yod pa'i ngo bos yod do zhes bya bar gyur to // de'i phyir rdul phra rab dag ji snyed pa de snyed kyi bum pa la sogs pa'i[257] cha shas can du 'gyur te / des na cha shas can gyi gcig pa nyid nyams par 'gyur ro[258] //

'dir sbyor ba ni[259] cha shas can ni[260] rdzas su yod pa ma yin te / dus gcig tu dngos po du ma nye bar len pa'i phyir / rta ma yin pa nyid la sogs [365] pa bzhin no // chos mi mthun pa ni rang gi mtshan nyid do // dngos po'i ngo bo nyid yin na ni bshad pa'i rnam pas dus gcig tu dngos po du ma nye bar len pa nyid du mi 'thad pa ni gnod pa can gyi tshad ma'o //

de ltar na phyogs gsum char la yang / phyi rol gyi don dmigs pa nyid du mi 'thad do[261] zhes bsgrubs nas[262] mjug bsdu ba'i phyir / **de lta bas na dbang po'i**[263] zhes bya ba las sogs pa smos te / gang gi phyir de ltar rdul phra rab

251. S: 'gyur.

252. N, S, P: na.

253. N, S: ma yin.

254. N omits pa.

255. N, P: rdzas shig.

256. N, S, P: ji snyed pa'i.

257. N, S, P: pa.

258. N, S: 'gyur ba ni.

259. N, S omit 'dir sbyor ba ni.

260. N, S, P: gyi.

261. D omits do.

262. N, P: bsgrubs na; S: bsgrub pa nas.

263. Verse 5cd commentary.

rnams dmigs par mi rung ba de'i phyir dbang po'i blo rnams kyi[264] phyi rol gyi don gyi yul can ma yin no zhes bya bar grub bo //

de ltar gzhan gyi gzhung lugs bkag nas rnam pa thams cad du dmigs pa bkag nas[265] / khas blangs pa la grags pas[266] gnod par 'gyur du 'ongs pas[267] rang gi gzhung lugs la dmigs pa rnam par gzhag[268] pa bstan pa'i phyir / **shes bya nang gi ngo bo ni** (6a) zhes bya ba la sogs pa smos te / mdo'i don ni shes pa la / shes bya'i rnam pa beg bur chad pa lta bur snang ba gang yin pa de kho na shes pa'i yul yin no zhes bya ba yin no / **nang** zhes bya ba ni nang ste / de yang 'dir shes pa yin par blta bar bya'o // nang zhes bya ba'i sgra 'di ni rang bzhin gyis[269] bdun pa'i don yin te / des na shes pa la nang zhes bshad pa yin no // **shes bya'i ngo bo** (6a) zhes bya ba ni yul gyi[270] rnam pa gzung ba'i cha zhes bya ba'i tha tshig go / ni zhes bya ba'i sgras[271] ni nges par gzung ba dang / bar du chod pa'i don du blta bar bya'o // **phyi rol ltar snang** (6b) zhes bya ba ni phyi rol lta bur mngon pa[272] ste / rnam par chad pa lta bur zhes bya[273] ba'i tha tshig go / de de ltar snang ba'i rgyu mtshan yang nam mkha'i khams snang ba yin no // nam mkha' de ni rnam par shes pa la snang bas na / rnam par shes pa las beg[274] bur chad pa bzhin du / des gzung ba'i[275] char ston par byed de / dper na zla ba'i gzugs brnyan me long gi ngos su 'byung ba na / nam mkha'i khams kyi gzugs brnyan gyi dbang gis khron pa na 'dug pa ltar beg bur chad par snang ba bzhin no //

phyi rol gyi yul med na rnam par shes pa'i dmigs pa'i rkyen nyid 'ga' yang yod[276] pa ma yin nam zhe na / de'i phyir **phyi rol gyi don**[277] zhes bya ba la sogs [366]

264. N, S, P omit kyi.

265. S, P: bkag pa na; N: bkag na.

266. S: grags pa.

267. N, S, P: 'ong bas.

268. N, S: bzhag.

269. N, S, P: gyi.

270. S: gyis.

271. N, S, P: sgra.

272. S: mngon par.

273. N, T, C, P omit bya.

274. N: bag.

275. S: gzung bar.

276. N, S, P: med.

277. Verse 6ab commentary.

pa smos so // 'di la dmigs pa'i rkyen med pa'i[278] nyes pa med de / 'di ltar phyi rol gyi don med mod kyi / 'on kyang nang na phyi rol lta bur snang ba yod pa kho na bas / de ni dmigs pa'i rkyen du 'gyur te / dper na rab rib can gyis[279] skra shad dang / sha sbrang la sogs pa'i rnam pa can gyi blo la / skra shad la sogs pa'i rnam pa lta bu'o // 'di skad du gzung ba'i cha de ni dmigs pa'i mtshan nyid du rung ba'i phyir dmigs pa'i rkyen nyid du bshad do zhes bshad pa yin no //

yang 'di ji ltar dmigs pa'i mtshan nyid du rung zhe na / de'i phyir **rnam shes**[280] **ngo bo'i phyir** (6c) zhes bya ba la sogs pa smos te / gang gi phyir shes pa sngon po dang ser po la sogs pa[281] spros pa'i bag chags yongs su smin pa'i dbang gis sngon po dang ser po la sogs pa'i rnam pa dang ldan par skye ba de'i phyir / sngon po la sogs pa'i rnam pa can yin pas de'i rnam pa can nyid du grub la gang gi phyir sngon po[282] la sogs pa'i rnam pa de rnam par shes pa de'i rkyen yin pa de'i phyir rgyu nyid du yang grub bo // de'i rkyen ni de'i rkyen nyid de / de zhes bya ba'i sgra ni rnam par shes pa dang sbyor[283] ro // de'i ngo bo ni de'i rkyen nyid do // de'i rkyen nyid yin pa de'i phyir te / gsum pa 'di ni gtan tshigs la blta bar bya'o //

bstan bcos byed pas mdo'i don rnam par dgrol ba'i[284] thabs kyi mjug bsdu bar bya ba'i phyir **nang gi rnam par shes pa ni**[285] **don du snang ba dang**[286] zhes bya ba la sogs pa smos te / gang gi phyir rnam par shes pa ni nang na yod pa'i don gyi rnam pas de'i rnam pa can dang / don gyi rnam pa de yod na de skyes pa de'i phyir / chos nyid gnyis dang ldan pas na nang gi nyid dmigs pa yin par rigs so //

'di skad du / rnam par shes pa ni nang na yod pa'i don gyi rnam par bris pa'i rnam pa lta bur snang ngo // de lta bas na de'i[287] rnam pa can[288] yin te / dper na rgya[289] bris pa'i rnam pas de'i rnam pa can yin pa lta bu'o // gang gi phyir

278. S: med pa.

279. N, S, P: gyi.

280. S: rnam par shes pa'i.

281. S, N, P: la sogs pa'i.

282. S: sngon pa.

283. N, S: sbyar.

284. N, S, P omit ba'i.

285. N, S, P: rnam par shes pa'i.

286. Verse 6cd commentary.

287. Text correction: D: 'di'i.

288. N, S, P omit can.

289. Text correction: D: rgyu; T, S, N: rgya.

gzung ba'i cha yod na skyes pa de'i phyir / rnam par shes pa de ni de las skyes pa zhes kyang bya ste / de bas na[290] dmigs pa'i[291] cha gnyis ka yod pas 'di ni dmigs pa nyid du rigs so zhes bshad pa yin [367] no // 'dir gzhan gyi tshig gi go skabs bstan pa'i phyir / **re zhig de ltar snang ba nyid**[292] **yin la ni rag na**[293] zhes bya ba la sogs pa smos pa rnam par shes pa la nang na yod pa'i shes bya snang ba nyid ni yin la rag ste / 'di ltar de ni shes bya'i rnam pa des bris[294] pa'i rnam pa lta bur skye'o zhes bshad na de'i phyogs gcig tu gyur pa dang / lhan cig skyes pa shes bya'i rnam pa gang yin pa[295] de go ji ltar rnam par shes pa de'i rkyen du 'gyur / de lta[296] yin na ni bdag nyid la byed par khas blangs pa dang / ha cang thal bar 'gyur te / 'dzin pa'i cha yang gzung ba'i cha skyed par byed par[297] 'gyur la / ba lang gi rwa[298] g.yas g.yon kyang phan tshun skyed par byed pa nyid du thal bar 'gyur ba ma yin nam zhes bya ba ni[299] phyogs snga ma'o //

'di la bstan bcos byed[300] pas lan gdab par / **gcig cha'ang**[301] **mi 'khrul phyir na rkyen** (7a) // zhes bya ba smos so // de nyid rnam par dgrol ba'i phyir / **lhan cig par gyur du zin kyang**[302] zhes bya ba la sogs pa smos so[303] // 'di ni 'dir nyes par mi 'gyur te / gang gi phyir[304] gzung ba'i[305] cha ni lhan cig 'byung[306] bar 'gyur du zin kyang / rkyen gzhan rgyu dang mtshungs pa de ma thag pa dang / bdag po dag las skyes pa'i rnam par shes pa'i dmigs pa'i[307] rkyen nyid du 'gyur bas so //

---

290. S: de bas ni.

291. N, P: dmigs pa.

292. N, P omit nyid.

293. Verse 6cd commentary.

294. N, P: byis.

295. N, P omit pa.

296. N, S, C: ltar.

297. P omits byed par.

298. N: rā.

299. P: zhes bya ba'i.

300. S, N, P: ces.

301. Text correction: D: gcig na'ang.

302. Verse 7a commentary.

303. N, S, P: smos te.

304. S: gang gang phyir.

305. N, P: gzung ba'i phyir.

306. N, S, P: byung.

307. N, S, P omit dmigs pa'i.

'di[308] ltar gzung ba'i cha de med par rnam par shes pa de mi 'byung ste / de ni dbyug[309] pa la brten[310] pa'i tshul du dmigs par bya ba 'ga'[311] zhig du zad kyi / 'di rkyen ril gyi bya ba byed pa'am / rkyen re re la sgro gdags pa ni ma yin no //

gal te yang shes pa de gzung ba'i cha de las phan 'dogs pa mi re na ci ste / de med par yang mi 'byung ste / 'di ltar phan mi 'dogs pa la ltos[312] par mi 'gyur la / phan mi 'dogs pa ni / med du zin kyang 'ga' yang mi 'byung bar mi 'gyur ro //

gal te rnam pa 'dis gzung ba'i cha yang[313] rgyu nyid du 'gyur na ni 'gyur du zad de / 'gal ba ci zhig yod / ba lang gi rwa g.yas g.yon[314] dag[315] ni 'khrul pa'i phyir rgyu dang 'bras bu'i dngos po med do // bdag nyid la byed pa yang la lar 'dod pa nyid de / dper na mar [368] me lta bu'o // de ni bdag nyid kha nas[316] bdag nyid gsal bar byed do // cha'i bye brag gis ni bdag nyid la byed pa yang yod re skan / rgyu dang 'bras bu'i dngos po mi 'khrul pa'i rgyu mtshan can yin no zhes bya ba 'di ga las she[317] na /

'di ltar gtan tshigs pa dag ni yod pa dang med pa dag gi[318] zhes bya ba la sogs pa smos te / 'di ltar gtan tshigs pa dag ni yod pa dang med pa dag gi[319] yod pa dang med pa nyid gang yin pa de ni **rgyu dang rgyu dang ldan pa'i rim gyis skye ba dag gi yang mtshan nyid yin par smra ste**[320] / gang zhig yod na gang yod[321] la // de med na med pa de ni rgyu yin la[322] / cig shos ni rgyu dang ldan pa yin no // 'di la yang gzung ba'i cha yod na shes pa yod la med na med de /

---

308. N, S, P omit 'di.

309. S: dbyugs.

310. N: rtan.

311. N, S, P: 'ba'.

312. N, P: bltos.

313. N, S, P: dang.

314. S: g.yas g.yon ni.

315. N, S, P omit dag.

316. S, B: kho nas.

317. N: la zhe; S, P: las zhe.

318. Verse 7a commentary.

319. N, S, P: dag ni.

320. Verse 7a commentary.

321. N, S: gang yin.

322. N, S, P omit de med na med pa de ni rgyu yin la.

de lta bas na lhan cig 'byung ba de gnyis kyang rgyu dang rgyu dang ldan pa nyid du 'grub bo //

gtan tshigs pa dag ces bya ba ni gang dag gtan tshigs kyi tha snyad 'dogs pa de[323] dag ni gtan tshigs pa dag ste / rtog ge[324] pa zhes bya ba'i tha tshig go / de dang ldan pa nyid ces bya ba ni yod pa dang med pa dang ldan pa nyid do // rgyu dang rgyu dang ldan pa zhes bya ba ni rgyu dang 'bras bu dag ces bya ba'i don to //

de ltar re zhig yul dang yul can gyi dngos po dus mnyam pa[325] bstan nas / da ni rim gyis yul dang yul can gyi dngos po bstan pa'i phyir / **yang na / nus pa 'jog phyir rim gyis yin** (7b) // zhes bya ba smos te / yang na gzung ba'i cha de[326] nus pa 'jog pa na rim gyis skyed[327] par byed pa'i ngo bo'i yul du 'gyur te / 'di ltar gzung ba'i cha de 'gag pa na / kun gzhi rnam par shes pa la nus pa 'jog par byed do // nus pa de gal te skad cig ma gnyis pa la lhan cig byed pa rnams sgrub[328] na ni de'i tshe skad cig ma gnyis pa kho na la rang dang mthun pa'i rnam par shes pa skyed[329] do // gal te mi sgrub na ni de'i tshe skad cig ma[330] gsum pa'am / bzhi pa la[331] yang rung gang gi tshe 'di sgrub par 'gyur ba de'i tshe / yongs su smin nas rang dang mthun pa'i rnam par shes pa skyed par 'gyur ro // phyogs 'di la ni bdag nyid la byed pa 'gal ba'i phyir dang / phyogs gcig yin pa'i phyir dang / lhan cig skyes pa yin pa'i phyir zhes bya [369] ba la sogs pa'i nyes pa mi srid de[332] / 'di ltar shes pa snga ma la gzung ba'i cha[333] sngon po la sogs pa'i rnam pa yod pa gang yin pa de / sngon po la sogs pa'i rnam pa can gyi shes pa phyi ma skyed par byed do // de'i phyir nyes pa 'di rnams lta srid re skan /

gal te nus pas shes pa skyed na / de lta na 'o na ni nus pa kho na yul du 'gyur gyi / gzung ba'i cha snga ma ni ma yin no snyam du sems na /

---

323. N, P omit de.

324. S: rtogs ge.

325. Text correction: D: dngos po dus mtsham pa. N: dngos po dus mnyis; pf. S: dngos po dus mnyam par.

326. S, N, P omit de.

327. N, S, P: rim gyi bskyed.

328. N, P: bsgrub.

329. N, S, P: bskyed.

330. N, P omit ma.

331. N, S, P omit la.

332. S: mi srid do.

333. N, S, P: gzung ba'i phyir.

rim gyis kyang yin te[334] zhes bya ba la sogs pa smos te / 'di ni nyes pa med do[335] // 'di ltar rim gyis kyang gzung ba'i cha de ni rang[336] dang mthun pa'i 'bras bu skyed pa'i phyir kun gzhi rnam par shes pa'i rten can gyi[337] nus pa byed do // gal te gzung ba'i cha des nus pa de gzhag[338] par ma gyur na ni nus pa des shes pa de lta bu skyed par yang mi 'gyur ro // de'i phyir nus pa las skye ba'i shes pa de yang gzung ba'i cha de kho na las skyes pa yin pas 'gal ba 'ga' yang med do // phyogs 'di la ni chos nyid gnyis dang ldan pa shin tu yang 'thad de / 'di ltar gzung ba'i cha des[339] rang dang mthun pa'i shes pa phyi ma de skyed[340] pas de'i phyir chos nyid gnyis dang ldan pa yod do //

'dir gzhan gyi tshig gi go skabs bstan pa'i phyir **gal te 'o na nang gi gzugs kho na**[341] zhes bya ba la sogs pa smos te / gal te khyod nang gi gzugs kho na dmigs pa'i rkyen yin par 'dod na / de'i tshe ji ltar nang gi gzugs de dang mig la brten nas mig gi rnam par shes pa skye ste[342] / 'di ltar mig sngar snang bar gyur ba'i gzugs gang yin pa de[343] dang lhan cig pa'i mig gis[344] rang gi rnam par shes pa skyed na / nang gi gzugs ni mig sngar snang bar yang mi 'gyur na / de ji ltar nang gi gzugs de dang lhan cig pa'i mig gis mig gi rnam par shes pa skyed[345] ces brjod par bya / de ni nam yang mdun na mi 'dug na / de ji ltar snang bar 'gyur zhes bya ba ni phyogs snga ma'o //

bstan bcos byed pas 'di'i lan gdab par / **lhan cig byed dbang nus pa yi** // (7c) zhes bya ba la sogs pa smos te / gal te dbang po 'byung ba las gyur pa yin na ni de'i tshe nyes pa 'dir 'gyur na / kho bo [370] cag ni dbang po nyid du 'dod pa'i dngos po[346] yul lhan cig byed pa'i nus pa gang yin pa de[347] dbang po yin

334. Verse 7b commentary.

335. C: med de.

336. N: rab.

337. N: gyis.

338. N, S: bzhag.

339. N: de.

340. N, S, P: ste bskyed.

341. Verse 7b commentary.

342. S: skye de; N, S, P: skyed de.

343. S omits de.

344. N, S, P: gi.

345. N, S, P: bskyed.

346. N, S, P omit dngos po.

347. S: de ni.

par 'dod de / de'i phyir kho bo cag gi ltar na ji ltar gzugs nang gi yin pa de bzhin du mig kyang nang gi kho na[348] yin pas ji skad smras pa'i nyes par lta zhig ga la yod / lhan cig byed dbang zhes bya ba 'di ni yul dang lhan cig byed pa'i dbang por 'dod pa'i zhes bya bar de ltar blta bar bya'o // de lta ma yin gyi dbang po'i dbang po zhes byas nas ni 'brel pa med par 'gyur la / dbang po'i dbang po zhes brjod na mdzes par yang mi 'gyur ro //

yang dbang po nus pa'i ngo bo nyid yin no zhes bya ba 'di ji ltar shes she na /

de'i phyir / **dbang po ni**[349] zhes bya ba la sogs pa smos te / gang gi phyir dbang po ni rang gi 'bras bu rnam par shes pa'i mtshan nyid las nus pa'i ngo bo nyid du rjes su dpag gi / 'byung ba las gyur[350] pa nyid du ni ma yin pas so // 'di ltar 'bras bu las ni rgyu tsam rjes su dpag par nus kyi[351] / rgyu'i khyad par ni ma yin te / khyad par gyi rtags la khyab pa mi srid pa'i phyir ro // ji ltar du ba las me tsam rjes su dpag par nus kyi / me'i[352] khyad par rtswa dang lo ma la sogs pa ma yin pa de bzhin du / 'bras bu'i rnam par shes pa'i mtshan nyid las rgyu tsam rjes su dpag par nus kyi / rgyu'i khyad par 'byung ba las[353] gyur pa nyid la sogs pa[354] ni ma yin te / 'di ltar bye brag tu smra ba'i ltar na ni dbang po 'byung ba las gyur pa yin / btsun pa sangs rgyas lha'i ltar na[355] ni 'byung ba'i ngo bo nyid yid[356] / rnal 'byor spyod pa'i ltar na ni[357] rnam par shes pa'i ngo bo nyid yin / dbu ma pa'i ltar na ni[358] kun rdzob tu yod pa yin / grangs can pa'i ltar na ni nga'o[359] snyam pa yin pas de lta bu la sogs pa'i khyad par rjes su dpag par mi nus so // de lta bas na nus pa rgyu tsam du rjes su dpog par byed pas nus pa tsam rjes su dpog par 'gyur ro //

348. N, S, P: kho bo

349. Verse 7cd commentary.

350. S: 'byung bar gyur.

351. S: gyi.

352. S, N, P: me.

353. S: 'byung bar.

354. S: la sogs pa nyid.

355. N, S, P omit na.

356. Text correction: D, S, B: yin; T: yid.

357. N, S, P omit ni.

358. S, N, P omit ni.

359. N: ngo'i.

de la 'di snyam du nus pa ni nus pa dang ldan pa la ltos[360] te / nus pa can[361] gzhi med bar ni[362] mi rung ngo // nus pa dang ldan pa ni dbang po yin la / de yang 'byung ba las gyur pa yin pas dbang po 'byung ba[363] las gyur pa yin par grub [371] po snyam du sems na /

de'i phyir / **de yang rnam rig la mi 'gal**[364] // (8a) zhes bya ba smos te / gal te rten zhig gdon mi za bar dgos na / rnam par shes pa de nyid rten yin du zad de / 'di ltar rnam par shes pa la[365] ni yul so sor rnam par rig pa'i ngo bo yin pa'i phyir dang / rang rig[366] pa'i ngo bo yin pa'i phyir gnyi ga la grags so // de'i phyir de nyid las kyis yongs su bsgos[367] pa rten yin du zad de / nus pa ni[368] gang gis na de rnam par shes pa'i rten can du mi rung bar 'gyur ba rnam par shes pa dang lhan cig 'gal ba ni med do //

de la 'di snyam du 'byung ba las gyur pa la rnam par gnas pa'i nus pa yang 'bras bu gzhan skyed la / rnam par shes pa la gnas pa yang gzhan skyed do[369] // de lta bas na dbang po ni gdon mi za bar 'byung ba las gyur pa kho na yin par[370] shes par bya'o snyam du sems na de'i dogs pa bsu bar **nus pa ni rnam par shes pa la yod kyang rung**[371] zhes bya ba la sogs pa smos so // 'di la ni rten gyis byas pa'i khyad par med de / 'di ltar nus pa ni gal te rnam par shes pa la rnam par[372] gnas kyang rung / 'on te gzhan la rnam par gnas kyang rung / rnam pa thams cad du des ni gzugs mthong ba la sogs pa tsam zhig bya bar zad pas de'i phyir 'bras bu bskyed[373] par bya ba la khyad par med do //

---

360. Text correction: N, S: bltos; D: sogs.

361. S, N, P omit can.

362. S, N, P omit ni.

363. N, P omit ba.

364. S: mi 'gal zhing.

365. S: rnam par shes pa'i.

366. S: rang rigs.

367. S: bskos.

368. S, N: na.

369. N, S, P: skyed de.

370. N, S, P: gyur pa yin pa.

371. Verse 8a commentary.

372. N, S, P omit rnam par.

373. N, S, P: skyed.

bstan du med pa'i rang gi ngo bo la[374] zhes bya ba ni gzhan 'dod pa'i dbang po'i rang gi ngo bo ni dbang pos mi sod pa'i[375] phyir brtag par mi nus so // ma brtags pa yang bstan par mi nus te / de'i phyir gzhan 'dod pa'i dbang po ni[376] bstan du med pa'i rang gi ngo bo yin no //

'o na dbang po'i nus pa de'i rgyu gang yin[377] zhe na / mjug bsdu ba'i[378] thabs kyis de bstan[379] pa'i phyir / **de ltar yul gyi ngo bo dang** (8b) zhes bya ba la sogs pa smos te / ji ltar rnam par shes pa 'di dbang po'i nus pa las skye ba de bzhin du / dbang po'i nus pa 'di la yang / dbang po 'phen par byed pa'i rnam par shes pa yang snga ma las skye la / sngon gyi rnam par shes pa de yang dbang po'i nus pa yang snga ma las skye'o // de ltar [372] na 'di lta ste dbang po'i nus pa dang / yul gyi rnam pa can gyi rnam par shes pa 'di gnyis ni phan tshun gyi rgyu can du 'jug la / rgyu dang 'bras bu brgyud pa 'di'i dus kyi thog ma yang med pas 'di gnyis thog ma[380] med pa'i dus par[381] blta bar bya'o //

bstan bcos byed pas[382] mdo'i don bstan pa'i phyir / **mig ces bya ba'i**[383] zhes bya ba la sogs pa smos te / mig ces bya ba'i[384] dbang po'i nus par bstan pa gang yin pa dang / nang gi gzugs lhan cig skyes[385] pa'am / sngar byung ba la brten nas ma nges pa'i don gyi rnam pa can gyi rnam par shes pa skye'o // ji ltar phyi rol gyi don du smra ba ltar na nges pa'i don kho na las[386] rnam par shes pa skye ba ltar / 'di la ni de lta[387] ma yin pas de'i phyir 'di skad du / **rnam par shes pa don du snang ba dmigs kyis**[388] **ma phye**[389] **ba skye'o**[390] zhes bshad do //

---

374. Verse 8a commentary.

375. B, T: mi sod ba'i.

376. S, N, P: dbang po na.

377. S, N, P omit yin.

378. N, P: bsdu bas.

379. Text correction: D: bsnyan.

380. N, P: thog pa.

381. N, P: dus pa.

382. N, S, P: pa.

383. Verse 8bcd commentary.

384. N, S, P: ba.

385. N, S, P omit skyes.

386. N, S, P: kho nas.

387. S: ltar.

388. N, S, P: kyi.

389. Text correction: D: ma bstan; P, S: ma phye; N: gye.

390. Verse 8bcd commentary.

gzhan dag ni brjod du med pa'i don du snang ba zhes zer te / de ni don shin tu 'brel bar mi snang ste / brjod du med pa nyid ni 'dir cung zad kyang mi dgos so // 'di ltar rang gi mtshan nyid thams cad ni brjod du med pa ste / gal te der[391] snang ba'i shes pa skye ba yin na des na dngos su[392] ci zhig 'grub par 'gyur /

'on te don gyi rnam pa can gyi shes pa skye ba gang yin pa de brjod par mi nus so[393] zhe na / de la yang ci med pa'i phyir brjod par mi nus sam / 'on te rang gi mtshan nyid kyi[394] phyir re zhig gal te med pa'i phyir ro zhe na / de ni rigs pa ma yin te / 'di ltar med pa'i[395] ri bong gi rwa la sogs pa yang rjod[396] par byed do // 'on te rang gi mtshan nyid kyi phyir ro zhe na / 'di la ni lan btab zin to //

mig ces bya ba'i nus pa la brten nas[397] zhes bya ba 'dir sogs pa zhes bya ba'i sgra[398] ni[399] mngon par rtogs par bya ste / des ni mig la sogs pa zhes bya ba la[400] zhes bshad pa yin no // 'o na[401] nus pa de gang[402] las skye zhe na /

'di gnyis kyang phan tshun gyi rgyu can dang[403] zhes bya ba smos te[404] / nus pa de yang dbang po 'phen par byed pa'i rnam par shes pa snga ma las skye zhing / rnam par shes de yang nus pa yang snga ma las skye la / nus pa de yang dbang po 'phen par byed [373] pa'i rnam par shes pa zhes snga ma las skye bas / rgyu dang 'bras bu'i ngo bo brgyud pa 'di ni thog ma med pa'i dus can nyid yin no // de ltar na[405] re zhig dbang po'i nus pa dang / rnam par shes pa rgyu dang 'bras bu'i dngos por bstan pa yin no // 'di gnyis kyang phan tshun gyi rgyu can dang /

---

391. S: de'i.

392. S: dngos po.

393. N omits so.

394. S: kyis.

395. N, S: med pa.

396. N, S, P: brjod.

397. Verse 8bcd commentary.

398. N: da.

399. S, N, P: zhes bya ba 'di ni.

400. S, N, P omit la.

401. S: 'on te.

402. S: de dag.

403. Verse 8bcd commentary.

404. N omits te.

405. N, S, P omit na.

thog ma med pa'i dus[406] pa yin te / zhes bya ba'i tshig 'di kho nas / yul gyi nus pa dang rnam par shes pa phan tshun rgyu can[407] nyid dang / thog ma med pa'i dus can nyid du ston to //

phan tshun gyi rgyu can nyid bstan pa'i phyir / **res 'ga' ni nus pa yongs su smin pa las**[408] zhes bya ba la sogs pa smos te / res 'ga' ni spros pa'i bag chags zhes bya ba'i nus pa yongs su smin pa las rnam par shes pa'i[409] yul gyi rnam pa nyid du 'byung la / res 'ga' ni yul gyi rnam pa can gyi[410] sems las nus pa skye'o // 'di la yang rgyu dang 'bras bu'i brgyud pa[411] 'di'i rgyun chad pa med pas thog ma med pa'i dus can nyid du shes par bya'o //

yang ci dbang po dang yul gyi nus pa 'di dag rnam par shes pa las tha dad pa zhig yin nam / 'on te ma yin / gal te tha dad pa[412] na de'i tshe ming tsam zhig la ldog par rtogs par zad kyi don ni mthun te / rnam par shes pa la ma gtogs pa'i dbang po dang / dmigs pa dag khas blangs pa'i phyir ro // 'on te tha mi dad na ni de'i tshe nus pa 'di ni dbang po'o // 'di ni[413] yul lo zhes bya ba'i rnam par gzhag[414] pa 'dir mi 'gyur ro[415] zhe na /

de'i phyir **rnam par shes pa dang / de gnyis**[416] zhes bya ba la sogs pa smos te / gal te dngos kyi tshul dpyad na ni / de'i tshe nus pa rnams gnas skabs kyi khyad par gyi bdag nyid yin pas kun rdzob tu yod pa'i phyir / rnam par shes pa las gzhan nyid dam / gzhan ma yin pa[417] nyid du brjod par bya ba ma yin no // de'i phyir ji skad smras pa'i nyes pa gnyi gar thal ba[418] med do // 'on te 'jig rten gyi tha snyad la brten na ni[419] / de'i tshe ci dgar res 'ga' ni rnam par shes pa de dag las gzhan pa nyid du brjod par bya la / res 'ga' ni gzhan ma yin pa nyid du'o // 'di ltar kun rdzob tu yod pa rnams ni 'jig rten na res 'ga' ni tha

406. N: nus.

407. Text correction: D: rgyu mtshan; pf. S, N, P: rgyu can.

408. Verse 8bcd commentary.

409. N, S, P: shes pa.

410. S, N, P: gyis.

411. S, N, P: brgyud pa'i.

412. S omits pa.

413. N: 'ni; S omits dbang po'o 'di ni; P: dbang po.

414. N, S: bzhag.

415. N, S, P omit ro.

416. Verse 8bcd commentary.

417. N omits pa.

418. N, P: bar.

419. S omits ni.

dad par tha snyad 'dogs te /[374] dper na tsan dan gyi dri zhes bya ba la sogs pa lta bu'o // res 'ga' ni tha mi dad pa ste / dper na gzugs la sogs pa la bum pa zhes bya ba lta bu'o //

de ltar phyogs gnyi[420] ga la yang dmigs pa nang gi yin par bstan nas mjug bsdu ba'i phyir / de ltar na nang gi[421] zhes bya ba la sogs pa smos te / de ltar na bshad pa'i rnam pas rnam par shes pa dang tha mi dad pa'i dmigs pa la chos nyid gnyis dang ldan pa yod pas yul nyid du 'thad pa yin no //

dmigs pa yongs su brtag pa yi //
rnam par 'grel ba gsal byas pas //
dge ba thob pa gang yin des //
'gro ba[422] sangs rgyas nyid thob shog/ /
dang po'i las can dga' bya'i phyir //
rgya cher bshad pa dul ba'i lhas //
khams[423] bcu dang ni bral bar byas //
de phyir mkhas rnams bzod[424] par gyis //
nyes pa 'dzin[425] pa lhur len pas //
'di ni 'dod 'dod dpyad du med //
rang gi[426] rnam rtog dbang gis na //
nyes pa med pa'am[427] blo la snang //

dmigs pa brtag pa rgya cher bshad pa slob dpon dul ba'i lha shes bya'i dmigs pa mtha' dag la gzhol[428] ba smra ba'i seng ge mu stegs can glang po che'i glad pa 'gims[429] par mdzad pas sbyar ba rdzogs so //

rgya gar gyi mkhan po shā kya siṃha[430] dang / zhu chen gyi lo tsā ba[431] ban de dpal brtsegs kyis bsgyur cing zhus nas gtan la phab pa'o //

---

420. N: gnyis.

421. Verse 8bcd commentary.

422. C: 'gro bas.

423. S: kham.

424. N, P: brjod.

425. N: zin.

426. S, N, P: rang gis.

427. N, S, P: pa'ang.

428. N: gzhal.

429. T: glad pa 'gims; N, S, T, P: klad pa 'gems.

430. S: shā kya sing ha.

431. S, N, P: lo tsa ba.

14

Ornament for Dignāga's Thought in Investigation of the Percept

TIBETAN TEXT

14.1 *Introduction*

This edition of Gungtang Denbe Drönme's *Ornament for Dignāga's Thought Regarding Investigation of the Percept* (*Dmigs pa brtag pa'i 'grel pa phyogs glang dgongs rgyan*) follows TBRC W7043. This has been compared to a version (unpaginated) in *Gungtang's Collected Works* (*Gung thang bstan pa'i sgron me'i gsung 'bum*): Beijing: Nationalities Press, 2003. The formatting follows that of the translation in order to help readers locate passages and terms.

dMigs pa brtag pa'i 'grel ba phyogs glang dgongs rgyan zhes bya ba bzhugs so

Gung thang dKon mchog bstan pa'i sgron me

Edited by Douglas Duckworth, Kalsang, and John Powers

[1] RIM PAR gzung 'dzin dmigs pa'i rgya / rnam grol sangs rgyas la btud nas / mkhas par brten te mkhas pa'i gzhung / mkhas pa'i dgongs pa bzhin bshad bya / gang bshad par bya ba'i chos ni dmigs pa brtag pa'o /

mtshan dang 'gyur phyag ni / rgya gar skad du / ā laṃ ba na ba rīkṣa / bod skad du / dmigs pa brtag pa /

sangs rgyas dang byang chub sems dpa' thams cad la phyag 'tshal lo / zhes te sla'o /

don dngos ni 'di ltar / gzhan gyi dmigs pa'i mtshan nyid skyes 'dra ba 'gog par dpe'i sgo nas khyab pa 'gog pa chen po gnyis sogs kyis sna tshogs par gsungs la / phyogs chos 'gog pa 'di lta ste / dmigs pa 'di ni nges par 'dzin pa yin na phra ba dag ji ltar 'dzin / rnam par skyed dam / bus pha'i gzugs 'dzin pa ltar phyi mar 'dod dgos kyang / de ni skabs 'dir don du mi phan te / des ni / dbang po rnam par rig pa'i rgyu / phra rab rdul de dag yin par 'grub tu chug mod / (1ab)

khyod kyi ngor bdag gis mi 'gog cing / de las nyes pa ches mngon sum sgrub sla ba 'di so na 'dug ste / brtag pa'i phyogs snga ma ma blangs pa nyid kyis khyod ltar yang de mi snang ba'i phyir (1c) dbang shes des / dmigs pa'i bdag nyid nges par 'dzin pa'i yul ni / rdul phran ma yin (1bc) te de rgyu tsam yin yang mi snang ba'i dngos su tshul gcig dang de'i [2] sgo nas rnam par skyed pa'i rgyu'ang ma yin pas don gyis rtags gnyis ka nyams te dmigs par mi rung ba dbang po bzhin / (1d) zhes gzhi bsal lo /

'dus pa'ang min par gsungs pa / re re bsal zhing mi snang bar bshad pa'i 'os med kyi rigs pas snang zhing lhag mar lus pa'i spyi sgra gang ni skabs 'dir 'dus pa ste /

de'ang shes pa tshogs pa las phyi'i rdul tshogs pa ma yin kyang / bag chags kyi dbang las de ltar snang (2a) ba'i phyir ltar zhes smos so / de la ni snga ma las bzlog nas snang ba de 'thad du chug kyang 'dus pa de las dbang po'i shes pa skye ba min pas yang tshul gcig shos nyams te dmigs pa min no / mi skyed de rdzas su med pa'i phyir zla gnyis bzhin / (2b)

'dis chos can phyogs snga'i zhe la bzhag pa'i steng nas yin pas dpe la sbyor tshul yang / kha cig tu zla gnyis snang la de'ang zla ba gnyis pas skyed du med pa'i phyir dbang po nyams pa kho nas yin pa ltar phyi rol bsags pa'i 'dus pa ltar snang ba'ang de la de bskyed pa'i nus pa'i rdzas yod pa ma yin yang nang du yid bdag lta'i bag chags kyis nyams pa las yin te dpe 'di ni 'gal ba spong pa la'ang nus pa can no / de nas de ltar phyi rol phra rags gnyis ka yang / blo yi dmigs rkyen nam dmigs yul du mi rung ngo (2cd) zhes bsdus so /

rgyas par skyon spong dgag pa sogs [3] 'phros don ni pha khol sogs kha cig rdul phran rang gi rnam pas mi snang yang / ji ltar til la snum bzhin tshogs par yod pa'i rdzas de ni / re re ba la'ang cung zad yod dgos pas na de la'ang 'dus pa'i rnam pa dag / (3a) yod cing de ni shes pa rang gi rnam ldan du / bsgrub par ram skyed par byed pa yin par 'dod do / (3b)

de la rags pa'i rnam pa snang du rung pa can yod na go / de'i chos su mtshungs pa'i phyir / phra ba'i rnam pa de'ang ci'i phyir bstan du med ces bya ba'i skyon spong bar 'dod nas / 'ga' zhig la mngon sum du yin pas thams cad du ga la dgos /

des na rdul phran nyid kyi rnam pa ni rnam rig gi don min (3cd) kyang mtshungs pa'i nyes pa med de sa la yod pa'i kha dog bstan du yod la / de'i bdag nyid sra ba nyid la sogs (3d) sa der yod pa'i chos su mtshungs kyang dbang po'i nus pa so sor nges pa nyid kyis mthong ba ma yin pa bzhin du rnam pa'ang cha gnyis su rung ngo /

zhes bya ba ni phyogs snga mas so / 'thad pa ma yin te / de dag ltar na bum pa dang / kham phor dang ka ba sogs blo (4ab) la shar ba'i tshe rnam pa mtshungs par gyur ro / ci'i phyir blo ni rang dgar ma yin pa'i yul la rang gi ngo bo'i rjes su byed cing / yul rdul phran ni ngo bo mtshungs pa kho nar dbye ba med pa'i phyir blo sna tshogs par mi rigs so / mang nyung yod pas mi 'grub ste / ngo bo la dbye ba med na bum pa che chung du 'gyur gyi kham phor gyi blor mi 'gyur ro /

gal te rnam pa'i dbye ba (4c) kha zhabs sogs mi 'dra bas khyad par dbye'o / snyam na dbyibs kyi khyad par de lta bu ni rdul phran [4] char dbye ba sogs kyi rnam pa bsgyur du med pa'i tshugs can gyi rdzas yod 'di lta bu la / bzhag du med de tshad kyi dbye ba (4c) mi 'dra ba med par chung ba'i mthar gtugs par mtshungs pa'i phyir ro / gzugs kyi cha dbyer med pa la bkod pa'i khyad par mi rung ba de phyir rnam pa'i dbye ba de skabs 'di'i rdzas su med pa'i kun rdzob kho na la yod (5b) de / cha dbyer rung pa'i phyir / rdul phran la de mi rung ste / rdul phran gyi cha so sor / yongs su bsal na ni / der snang gi shes pa nyams te gzugs snang 'gag par 'gyur (5cd) ba'i phyir /

de ltar gzhan gyi bkag nas grags pa'i gnod pa spangs pa'i phyir / rang la 'thad pa'i dmigs pa ston pa ni / dmigs pa gang zhe na / nang gi 'dzin pa'i rang mdangs de nyid shes bya'i dngos po la bzhag gi gzhan du med pa ni / zhes pa'i nges gzung ngo / rang la bya ba 'gal ba'i phyir ji ltar snang zhe na / ji ltar gnas pa'i rnam pa'i snang ba ma yin te / me long la zla gzugs shar ba na nam mkha'i khams kyang shar bas byed pa las zla ba rgyang ste chad pa'i rnam par 'byung ba ji lta bar phyi rol ltar snang ba'i tshul gyis gzung bar gyur kyang dngos po la nang du gnas pa gang yin pa de ni / don zhes bya ba ste yul du mar 'jug kyang 'dir skabs kyi dbang las dmigs rkyen yin no /

de'ang rgyu mtshan gang gi phyir na / mngon par brjod pa'i bag chags goms pa las gzung ba dang 'dzin pa'i tshul du rnam par shes pa yul de'i dngos po'i rnam par skyed pa'i [5] phyir dang / yul de med na mi skye ba'i cha nas de'i rkyen nyid do zhes kyang bshad pa yin pa'i phyir ro /

gtan tshigs gnyis las rim par bdag nyid la byed pa 'gal ba'i skyon dang dus mnyam pa ni ba lang gi rwa ltar phan tshun rkyen du mi rung ba'i ha cang thal ba bsu nas / de gnyis dus gcig cing bdag nyid gcig pa'i cha (7a) yin na'ang me ltar rang la bya ba cung zad 'jug pa srid kyang dbye ba gtan med pa'i tshul gyis ma yin pa sngar gzung 'dzin du 'gyur tshul bshad pa'i shugs kyis kyang shes pas lan 'dir mi ston la phyi ma ni yod med rjes su 'gro ldog gi nges pa mi 'khrul ba'i phyir na rkyen du gdags pa yin no /

de ltar dmigs rkyen btags pa ba ste snang ba'i dmigs rkyen rnam par bzhag nas / rang gi 'dod pa'i gtso bo nyid ston pa ni kun gzhi'i sgrar bstan pa'i yid la shes pa snga mas gang yul gyi rnam par skyed pa'i nus pa bzhag pa des ni phyi ma yul gyi rnam par 'jog pa'i phyir rim gyis (7b) phyi ma phyi ma'i dmigs rkyen yin te 'di ni dngos kyi don no /

gal te byad bzhin dang me long ji lta bar phyi'i gzugs dang dmigs las rnam par shes pa bskyed na / khyod la dmigs pa ni nang kho na las mdun du gyur pa med pa'i phyir / ji ltar shes pa skyed ce na /

yul dang lhan cig pa'i dbang po 'byung ba'i bdag nyid kyi bem por smra ba khyed dag la yul yang de dang mthun pa phyi'i bem po zhig tu 'gyur mod kyang / kho bo cag ni dmigs pa de dang lhan cig byed pas dbang po'ang khyod ltar mi smra yi / 'bras bu las rgyu'i chos rjes su dpog [6] pa'i tshe na yid kyi steng du mig shes thun mong ma yin par 'grub ba'i nus pa yi / ngo bo zhig yod par las 'gag kyang 'bras bu 'byin par sgrub pa'i rigs pa sogs kyis 'grub la / de lta bu gang yin pa de ni dbang po'ang yin par 'dod do / 'ang sgra nus pa gcig tu bzhag pa ma yin gyi gnyis ka nus par mtshungs pa ston to / dul lhas nus pa rgyu tsam la bshad kyang 'og dang sbyar na dpyad gzhir snang /

khyed cag dbang po 'byung ba'i bdag nyid las bzlog ste nus par 'dod na'ang / nus pa brten med pa ni mi gnas pas rten 'byung ba'i khyad par zhig dgos so zhes pa'i rtsod pa bsus te / rnam par shes pa'i rten gyi dbang po nus par bzhag pa de yang kho bo cag rnam par rig pa tsam du smra ba rnams la 'gar yang mi 'gal te / nus pa shes pa la gnas shing shes pa'ang nus pa las 'byung ba'i phyir khyed cag ltar phyi nas tshol ba'i ngal ba mi dgos so /

mjug bsdu ba ni / de ltar yul gyi rnam pa'i ngo bo nyid kyi shes pa dang / dbang po'i ngo bo nyid kyi nus pa (8bc) gnyis ni res mos kyi tshul du skye 'gag dus mnyam pa'i 'brel ba'i sgo nas phan tshun gyi rgyu can dang / tshul de nyid kyis thog ma med pa'i dus nas rim par 'jug pa yin (8cd) pas / sngar ltar rgol ba dag gi phugs btsal te dpyad pas kyang sun byung bar nus pa ma yin no / gzhan gyi dmigs pa ni gzung don gyi ngo bo yin la de ni 'di ba'i chos kyi bdag ste de 'gog par byed pa'i dmigs pa brtag pa slob dpon / [7] phyogs kyi glang pos mdzad pa 'di ni grub pa'i mtha'i rtsa ba ches mchog tu gyur pa zhig ste de'i don bshad pa re zhig rdzogs so / tshul 'di ni brtsun pa dkon mchog bstan pa'i sgron mes rang lo nyer drug pa la gzhung 'dir zhib dpyod cung zad bgyis skabs yid la shar tshod kyi rim rnams brjed du phangs pas spros pa rgya che ba dor te tho tsam sug bris su bagyis pa'o /

15

Beautiful String of Pearls

A COMMENTARY ON INVESTIGATION OF THE PERCEPT TIBETAN TEXT

15.1 Introduction

This edition of *dMigs pa brtag pa'i 'grel pa mu tig 'phreng ba* follows TBRC W7301, Sku 'bum edition. *Ngag dbang bstan dar gsung 'bum, ja*: 21ff. It has been compared with a typeset edition of the Sku 'bum edition, "*Mkhas pa'i dbang po a lag sha bstan dar lha rams pa'i gsung 'bum*" (*stod cha*) (Gansu: Bla brang tshug lag deb phreng, kan su'u mi rigs dpe skrun khang, 2004) (G). The formatting follows that of the translation.

dMigs pa brtag pa'i 'grel pa mu tig 'phreng mdzes zhes bya ba bzhugs so //

Ngag dbang bstan dar
Edited by Douglas Duckworth, Malcolm David Eckel, John Powers, and Sonam Thakchöe

[216] legs bshad ngḁg gis thub dbḁng bstan pa la / /
blo̥ gros mchog yangs sbyin pas 'gro ba kun / /
[217] skal bzḁng bgyid mdzad bshes gnyen mchog dran no / /
dpag med shis pa dam pas bsrung gyur cig / /
[218] tshogs gnyis sna tshogs khams can sprin las 'khrungs / /
mkhyen brtse'i gting zab yon tan tshogs kyis gang / /
gzhung bzang stong gi gru char 'jo ba'i khungs / /
thub dbang rin chen 'byung gnas la phyag tshal / /
gzhal bya'i gnas gsum lha lam yangs pa'i khyon / /
mkhyen dpyod go la'i 'gros kyis pha mtha' gzhal / /
rigs pa'i zer gyis log rtog mun 'joms pa'i / /
phyogs glang chos grags nyi zla zung de bsngags / /
mkhas pa phal gyi spyod yul las 'gongs pa'i / /
mdo rgyud zab chos blo̥ gros bzḁng po'i mthus / /
gsal bar phye ba'i grḁgs snyan srid 'di yi / /
khongs las ches brgal rgyal ba gnyis par 'dud / /
gtso bor rang gi yid la goms phyir dang / /
blo gsal 'gas kyang 'phags yul gzhung lugs la / /
tshegs chung 'jug slad 'grel pa 'grel bshad las / /
btus te dmigs pa brtag pa 'chad la spro / /
de phyir tshad ma'i gzhung la gus ldan pa'i / /
snod ldan dag la rigs pa'i srad pu ru / /
lung gi mu tig spel te sbyin yod kyi / /
mgrin pa mdzes pa'i rgyan du bdag gir byos / /

de la 'dir tshad ma'i bstan bcos dmigs pa brtag pa bshad la gnyis / klad kyi don dang / gzhung gi don no / /

dang po ni / rgya gar skad du / a laṃ ba na pa ṭī kā / bod skad du / dmigs pa brtag pa / sangs rgyas dang byang chub sems dpa' thams cad la phyag 'tshal lo / zhes byung /

gnyis pa gzhung don la gnyis / dgos sogs chos bzhi spyir bshad pa dang / gzhung don dngos bshad pa'o //

[219] **dang po la** / dgos sogs chos bzhi'i 'brel ni / bstan bcos la dgos pa yod na rtog ldan rnams 'jug gi med na mi 'jug pas dgos pa bstan la / dgos pa de yang brjod byas stongs pa'i bstan bcos la mi 'thad pas dgos pa'i sngon du brjod bya bstan dgos / dgos pa de yang bstan bcos de nyid la brten nas 'grub dgos pas bstan bcos dang 'brel lo / /

gnyis pa gzhung don bshad pa la gnyis / spyi'i don dang / yan lag gi don no /

dang po la gsum / phyi rol don du grub tshul dang / de blo la snang tshul dang / des dmigs rkyen byed tshul lo / /

dang po ni / phyi don 'dod pa dag gi lugs la / phyi rol gyi don zhes pa nang shes pa la ma ltos par grub pa'i don dang / de yang snod bcud kyi 'jig rten nang shes pa la brten nas grub tshul dang mi 'dra bar nang shes pa'i rdzas ma yin par 'dod cing / de yang mthar gtugs na phyi don rags pa rtsom byed kyi rdul phra rab la thug pas rdul phra rab ces pa ni blo ngor yang cha gsil[1] rgyu med pa'i gzugs kun gyi chung shos su 'dod cing / de la shar gyi phyogs dang nub kyi phyogs zhes blos btags pa'i cha du ma yod kyang de dag de'i bdag nyid ma yin pa dang de la cha gnyis su phye ba'i cha ma yin pa'i rgyu mtshan gyis / nyan thos sde pa dag gis cha med du 'dod pa yin te / sde bdun rgyan yid kyi mun sel las /

> 'di ltar rang gi bdag nyid yin zhing rang ma yin pa'i shar cha dang nub cha rdzas tha dad du ma med pa cha med pa'i don yin gyi / spyir [220] shar nub kyi stong pa[2] cha med pa'i don ma yin la / rdul phra rab de shar rdul phra rab dang rdzas tha dad yin gyi / de de'i cha ma yin pas de'i shar yod kyang de phyogs cha dang bcas par mi 'gyur ro //de bzhin du dus mtha'i skad cig ma la'ang rang gi bdag nyid du gyur pa'i snga phyi med pa cha med pa'i don yin gyi / spyir rang gi snga phyi yod pas dus cha dang bcas par mi 'gyur te / de lta ma yin na dus mtha'i skad cig ma don byed nus stong dang rgyu med par 'gyur ro // zhes gsungs pa'i phyir / rdul phra rab skye tshul ni / mdzod las[3] / sgra med phra

1. G: gsal.

2. G: stong ba.

3. G: mdzod la.

rab rdul rdzas brgyad // ces gsungs pa ltar / 'dod pa'i khams na gzugs gcig skye phyin chad 'byung bzhi'i rdul bzhi dang gzugs dri ro reg bya'i rdul te rdzas brgyad dang lhan cig tu skye bas khyab bo / de lta bu rdzas brgyad tshogs pa'i rdul la bsags rdul dang de'i ya gyal la rdzas rdul gyi tha snyad sbyar zhing de gnyis ka'ang rdul phra rab yin par mtshungs pa yin te / gang spel las / rdul phra rab ni rnam pa gnyis te / rdzas kyi rdul phra rab dang bsags pa'i rdul phra rab bo // zhes gsungs pa'i phyir / kho na re / de mi 'thad par thal / bsags rdul phra rab rdzas rdul las bongs tshod che dgos pa'i phyir te / rdzas rdul brgyad tshogs pa las bsags rdul gcig grub dgos pa'i phyir na / ma khyab ste / dper na / bye ma phor gang gi steng du chu phor ba gang blugs pa'i tshe sa phor gang dang chu phor gang gnyis go sa gcig tu tshogs kyang bye ma phor gang de nyid bongs tshod che ru mi 'gro ba bzhin no //

'o na sa rdul [221] thogs bcas ma yin par thal / rang gi go sar chu rdul shong ba la gegs mi byed pa'i phyir zhe na / skyon med de / rdul gyis go sa 'gegs pa'i don ni rigs mthun gyi rdul la yin gyi rigs mi mthun gyi rdul go sa gcig tu shong ba khas len dgos te / gzugs kyi go sar dri rdul dang dri'i go sar gzugs yod par khas len dgos pa'i phyir / 'di mdzod ṭi kā[4] mngon pa'i rgyan du bkag kyang gsar bu pa dag gi blo rgya bskyed pa'i phyir du bshad pa yin no / rdul phra rab dang rdul phran gnyis mi gcig ste / mdzod las / skad cig phra rab rdul dang ni / rdul phran dang ni de bzhin du / zhes gsungs pa ltar / rdul phran ni rdul phra rab bdun 'dus pa las grub pa yin pas rdul phra rab las cung rags pa yin no //

yang kha cig gis / nyan thos sde pas[5] rdzas rdul khas len mi rigs te / bzhi brgya ba'i 'grel pa las / bye brag pa ltar rang gi sde pas rdzas kyi rdul phra rab khas blang par mi rigs so / zhes gsungs pa'i phyir na ma khyab ste / bye brag pas rdzas brgyad kyi tshogs pa dang 'byung ba gzhan gsum gyi tshogs pa sogs la gtan nas ma ltos pa'i rdzas brgyad so sor phral ba'i rdzas rdul kher rkyang re'am / me rdul rkyang ba re khas blang zhing / de yang rtag pa yin te / bskal pa 'jig pa'i tshe rags pa thams cad thor ba'i shul du de lta bu rdzas rdul gcig pu lus shing slar rags pa thams cad de las mched par 'dod la / nyan thos sde pas[6] de lta bu rdzas brgyad kyi tshogs pa la ma ltos pa'i rdzas rdul mi 'dod kyang [222] rdzas brgyad dang 'dab 'byar du yod pa'i rdzas rdul yan gar ba dang zla med kyi rdul phra rab zer ba 'dod do / slob dpon legs ldan 'byed kyis kyang rdul phra rab zhal gyis bzhes par ma zad de rdul phran cha med yin par yang bzhed par gsal te / slob dpon 'di'i 'dod pa 'chad pa'i skabs kyi lam rim chen mo

4. G: ti ka.

5. G: sde bas.

6. G: sde bas.

las / rdul phra ba'i mthar thug bar yang bzhed par snang bas rdul phran cha med dmigs rkyen tu bzhed do / zhes gsungs pa'i phyir /

de la 'o na slob dpon legs ldan 'byed kyis bden grub khas len par thal / cha med kyi dngos po khas len pa'i phyir / de la khyab pa yod de / dus 'khor 'grel chen de nyid snang ba las / grub mtha' smra ba gong 'og su'i lugs la'ang cha med kyi dngos po 'dod phyin chad de bden dngos su 'dod pa yin la / zhes gsungs pa'i phyir na ma khyab / slob dpon 'dis rdul phra rab kyi skye sogs mtshan nyid bzhi rdul phra rab dang bdag nyid gcig pa'i sgo nas de'i cha yin pa'i rgyu mtshan gyis rdul phra rab cha bcas su bzhed cing / rdul phra rab rang la cha 'byed rgyu med pa'i sgo nas de la rdul phran cha med kyi tha snyad mdzad pa yin pas de'i phyir rdul phra rab chos can / cha med yin par thal / rdul phran cha med yin pa'i phyir zer na slob dpon 'dis khyab pa 'gal ba'i lan mdzad do //

da ni rdul phra rab kyis rags pa rtsom tshul ni / de ltar rdzas rdul dang bsags rdul gnyis la che chung med pa'i phyir rdzas rdul re re ba bdun gyis mi chog par bsags rdul bdun 'dus pa'i tshe rags pa'i mgo rtsom zhing / de yang [223] 'byung bzhi'i rdul phra rab ci tsam tshogs pa de tsam gyis bongs tshod che ru 'gro la / dri dang ro yi rdul phra rab bsags kyang bongs tshogs che ru mi 'gro ste / dper na sgra'i rdul ci tsam bsags kyang mig shes la snang du med pa bzhin no //sgra'i rdul de ltar mi snang ba'i rgyu mtshan la / kha cig gis / sgra'i rdul phra rab du[7] ma tshogs kyang sdeb gcig tu bsgril rgyu med pas phung por gyur pa mi srid zer ro / /

la las sgra'i tshogs pa na 'byung bzhi'i rdul shas chung zhing sgra rdul gtso bas de ltar mi snang zer / 'on kyang dung sgra lta bu gzugs rags pa yin par khas len dgos /

mdo sems gnyis kas rags pa dang rgyun rdzas su ma grub pas dngos po ma yin par khas len cing / mdo sde pas rags pa dang rgyun yin na rdzas grub dang dngos po yin pas khyab pa khas len pas / des na gzugs rags pa rtag pa yin par yang khas len pa 'dra ste / de'i sgrub byed ni gzugs chos can / khyod rags pa rtag pa yin par thal / khyod rags pa yod pa'i phyir zhes pa lta bu'i tshad ma pa'i rigs pa'i 'phrul la brten nas sgrub nus so / /

de mi nus na bum pa'i bye brag rtag pa yin par ci ltar sgrub par byed / de la yang dpyod ldan dag gis 'di ltar rgol te / 'o na bum pa chos can / khyod ma yin pa las log pa rtag pa yin par thal / khyod ma yin pa las log pa yod pa'i phyir zer / kha cig gis de mi mtshungs te / bum pa ma yin pa las log pa bum pa'i don rang mtshan gyi gzhan [224] sel yin pas de dngos po yin par khas len dgos zer ro / /

---

7. G: tu.

de la yang kha cig de mi 'thad de / bum pa yin pa rtag pa yin pas bum pa ma yin pa las log pa rtag pa yin par khas len dgos te / de lta min na yin pa srid pa'i shes bya yin na khyod yin pa rtag pa yin par sgrub mi nus zer /

mdor na rdul du ma tshogs pa'i rags pa rdzas su ma grub ces pa'i don ni / dmigs brtag rang 'grel las / rdzas su yod pa ma yin pa nyid kyis rgyu ma yin pa'i phyir / zhes gsungs pa ltar / rdzas su med pa'i rgyu mtshan gyis dbang shes kyi rgyu ma yin zhing /

dbang shes kyi rgyu ma yin pa'i don yang de'i dmigs rkyen ma yin pa'i don yin pas / des na rdul rags pa rgyu ma yin pas rtag pa las gzhan du mi 'thad cing / de bzhin du rdul 'dus pa yang rdzas su med par gsal te / lam rim chen mo las /

> sems tsam pas rdul phra rab re re ba dbang shes kyi yul ma yin te / mi snang ba'i phyir zhes pa dang / du ma 'dus pa'ang de'i yul ma yin te rdzas su med pa'i phyir /

zhes gsungs pa'i phyir / 'o na rdul bsags pa dang tshogs pa dag kyang dngos po ma yin nam zhe na / de yang dngos po ma yin zhes mkhas pa'i gsung las byung ste / tshad ma rigs rgyan las / des na dbang shes kyis spyi dang tshogs pa dang bsags pa la dmigs pa ma yin te / de gsum ga dngos po ma yin pa'i phyir / zhes gsungs pa'i phyir / rgyas par shes 'dod na / mngon sum le'u las / bsags pa dang ni tshogs pa yin / zhes sogs [225] kyi don rgyal tshab mkhas grub rnam gnyis kyis bkral ba ltar dang rigs rgyan sogs las shes par bya zhing / de dag tu gsungs pa'i gnad 'gag tsam 'dir bkod na / spyir zla med kyi rdul phran re re bas dbang shes skyed mi nus kyang bum pa lta bu'i tshogs pa na rdul phra rab mang po 'dab 'byar tu gnas pa'i tshe de'i nang gi rdul phra rab re re ba la bsags pa zhes ming gis btags nas de lta bu rdul phra rab re re la dmigs pa la bsags pa la dmigs zhes bshad pa tsam ma gtogs bsags pa dang tshogs pa rang ldog la dmigs pa ma yin zhes bshad pa ltar ro / /

de ltar bshad mod kho bo la rnam rtog 'di 'char te / sems tsam pas rdul phra rags gang yang khas mi len pas de bsags pa dngos med du 'dod pa bden du chug kyang / mdo sde pas bsags pa dngos med du 'dod na des phung po lnga'i tshogs pa gang zag tu mi 'dod dam / de mi 'dod do zhe na / dbu ma 'jug pa'i rnam bshad dgongs pa rab gsal las / rang gi sde pa[8] mang pos bum pa'i gzugs la sogs pa'i rdul brgyad de ltar 'dab 'byar[9] tu gnas pa'i tshogs pa rnams bum pa yin pas de la bum pa'i blor 'gyur ro zhes smra ba /

---

8. G: sde ba.

9. Text correction: read *'byar* for *'byor*. Both Tibetan texts read *'byor*.

zhes gsungs pa dang ci ltar mi 'gal / gal te phung po lnga'i tshogs pa gang zag tu 'dod na'ang dogs pa 'di yod de / tshogs pa btags yod yin pas gang zag gi gdags gzhir ci ltar rung btags yod kyi gdags gzhi la rdzas yod dgos pa dang 'gal pa'i phyir snyam du dogs so / /

'on kyang slob dpon [226] legs ldan 'byed kyis rdul du ma bsags pa dbang shes la snang yang rdul du ma 'dus pa dbang shes la mi snang zhes bsags pa dang 'dus pa gnyis la khyad phye zhing / de yang bum pa'i tshogs pa na yod pa'i rdul phra rab rnams rigs mthun gyi rdul yin pas de la bsags pa zhes bya zhing bsags pa dbang shes la snang ba'i tshe de'i rdul phra rab re re nas kyang dbang shes la snang bar 'dod de / dper na / khu tshur dmigs pa la sor mo dmigs dgos pa bzhin zer ro / nags tshal gyi tshogs pa na yod pa'i shing sna tshogs kyi rdul phra rab rnams rigs mi mthun gyi rdul yin pas de la 'dus pa zhes bya zhing de dbang shes la mi snang bar 'dod do / /

gzhan yang rdul mang po dngos po yin zer dgos sam snyam ste / mngon sum le'u las / khyad par skye 'gyur mang po dag / cig car blo yi rgyur gyur kyang / / zhes dang / de bzhin du rdul du ma yang dngos po yin nam snyam ste / rigs rgyan las / dbang shes skyed nus kyi rdul du ma la dmigs pa la bsags pa la dmigs pa zhes brjod pa tsam yin pa'i phyir zhes gsungs pa'i phyir / de ltar na thung mtha'i skad cig ma brgya rgyun yin zer dgos sam / yang na / sde bdun yid kyi mun sel las / dus mtha'i skad cig ma brgya mthud pa rgyun yin yang dus mtha'i skad cig ma brgya po dus thung ba'i mthar thug pa yin no / zhes pa ltar khas len nam /

phyi ma ltar khas len na thung mtha'i skad cig ma sum brgya drug cu re lnga yang thung mtha'i skad cig mar khas len dgos pas de lta na bya rdzogs kyi skad cig ma'i yun tshad dang mnyam pa'i thung mtha'i skad cig khas len dgos mi dgos shin tu zhib pa'i blo gros dang ldan pa [227] dag gis dpyod cig /

gnyis pa phyi don snang tshul bshad pa la /

bye brag smra bas rags pa rdzas su ma grub pas dbang shes la mi snang zhing phra rab snang yang rnam pa ma shar bar 'dod de / sngon 'dzin mig shes kyis sngon po rnam med thug phrad du 'dzin pa'i phyir zer[10] / de ci ltar zhe na / gzung 'dzin yin na 'dzin byed lag pa dang gzung bya skyu ru ra ltar dus mnyam pa dgos shing / de yang yul gyi rnam pa yul can shes pa'i don ji bzhin 'pho ba'i stobs kyis yul can yul de yi rnam pa can du gyur pa mi 'dod pa'i gnad kyis rnam med khas len kyang spyir shes pa'i rnam pa tsam zhig shin tu khas len te / mdzod las / rnam pa shes rab dang bcas pa'i / dmigs dang bcas pas 'dzin par byed / ces gsungs pa'i phyir / 'di legs par shes na / de nyid las / rten

10. G omits zer.

dang dmigs dang rnam bcas dang / mtshungs par ldan pa'ang rnam pa lnga / zhes dang / zhi sogs rags sogs rnam pa can / zhes pa la zhi ba cha legs par phye yod ba yin /

mdo sde pa yan chad kyis shes pa rnam bcas su khas len pa'i tshul ni / dbu ma 'jug pa las / ji ltar sems ni gang gi rnam pa can du gyur pa de yi yul // zhes yul can sngon 'dzin mig shes yul sngon po gang gi rnam pa can du skye bar 'gyur ba na de la sngon 'dzin kyis sngon po gzung ba dang 'dzin par bshad pa ltar yul can shes pa yul dang 'dra bar gyur pa las logs su [228] shes pas yul 'dzin tshul gtan nas med de / dper na ras sngon po shel dang 'phrad pa'i tshe shel gyi ngo thams cad sngon por 'gro ba bzhin du / sngon 'dzin mig shes kyis sngon po la blta ba'i tshe yul sngon po nyid sngon 'dzin mig shes kyi ngor 'pho ba na yul can mig shes yul sngon po dang 'dra bar 'gyur zhing de la sngon 'dzin mig shes sngon po'i rnam ldan du skye ba zhes bya ba yin pas sngon po dngos su 'dzin pa'i tshad kyang de yin no /

mdo sde pas rags pa rdzas su ma grub pas dbang shes la mi snang bar ma zad rags par yang mi snang ste / de ltar snang na cha bcas su snang dgos / de snang na dbang shes ma 'khrul ba la cha shas cha can de'i cha yin par snang dgos pas de ltar na cha dang cha can gnyis ngo bo tha dad du 'gyur zer / 'on kyang sngon 'dzin mig shes sngon po la sgrub 'jug yin pas sngon po'i tshogs pa na yod pa'i rdul phra rab thams cad snang bar 'dod de / sngon po'i rdul phra rab dang sngon po gnyis grub pa de dbyer med kyi rdzas gcig yin pa'i phyir / dbang shes kyis rdul phra rab de ltar snang na'ang de ni de'i nges pa 'dren nus su snang ba'i yul ma yin te / dbang yul de'i phyir rdul phran min / zhes gsungs pa'i phyir /

sems tsam pas rags pa gzhi ma grub kyang sngon 'dzin dbang shes 'khrul shes yin pas de la sngon po rags par snang bar 'dod do / /

gsum pa / dmigs rkyen byed tshul bshad pa la /

bye brag smra ba dang mdo sde pa dang sems tsam pas 'dod tshul gsum las /

dang po ni / bye brag smra bas rnam med [229] khas len pas rdul rags pa dang phra ba'i rnam pa dbang shes la gtad par khas mi len cing / rgyu 'bras dus mnyam pa khas len pas sngon po sngon 'dzin mig shes kyi dmigs rkyen yin yang de gnyis dus mnyam par 'dod de / dmigs rkyen yin na rang 'dzin shes pa 'gag pa la mngon du phyogs pa ste da ltar ba la bya ba byed par 'dod pa'i phyir ro //de gang las shes zhe na / mdzod las /

rgyu gnyis po dag 'gag pa la / /
bya ba byed do gsum po ni / /
skye la'o de las gzhan pa yi / /
rkyen dag de las bzlog pa yin / /

zhes byung ba las shes pa'i phyir / shes tshul yod de / lhan cig 'byung rgyu dang mtshungs ldan gyi rgyu gnyis rang gi 'bras bu dang dus mnyam yin pas 'bras bu 'gag pa la mngon du phyogs pa ste da ltar ba la bya ba byed ces 'chad pa la / rgyu gnyis po dag 'gag pa la / bya ba byed do zhes gsungs / skal mnyam dang kun 'gro dang rnam smin gyi rgyu gsum rang gi 'bras bu dang snga phyi yin pas 'bras bu skye ba la mngon du phyogs pa ste ma 'ongs pa la bya ba byed ces 'chad pa la / gsum po ni skye la'o zhes gsungs / rgyu tshan pa gnyis po de las gzhan pa'i de ma thag rkyen dang dmigs rkyen gnyis po bshad ma thag pa las go bzlog ste de ma thag rkyen ni rang 'bras ma 'ongs pa dang / dmigs rkyen ni rang 'bras da ltar ba la bya ba byed ces 'chad pa la / de las gzhan pa yi / rkyen dag de las bzlog pa yin / zhes gsungs pa yin pa'i phyir / /

gnyis pa mdo sde pas 'dod tshul ni /

dbang shes de'i dmigs rkyen [230] yin na dbang shes de la rang gi rnam pa gtad pa dang dbang shes de'i rgyu yin pa'i khyad chos gnyis ka tshang dgos shing / de yang dbang shes kyi dmigs rkyen ces pa'i dmigs pa dang gzung yul zhes pa'i gzung ba'i don rgyu'i don du yang khas len te / mngon sum le'u las / rgyu yi ngo bo ma gtogs pa / / gzung ba zhes bya gzhan ci'ang med // ces gsungs pa'i phyir / rgyu'i don yang 'bras bu las snga bar khas len pas rgyu 'bras dus mnyam pa mi 'dod de / de nyid las / rgyu rnams thams cad sngar yod yin / / zhes gsungs pa'i phyir /

'o na sngon 'dzin mig shes kyis sngon po ci ltar 'dzin te / sngon 'dzin mig shes skyes pa'i dus na sngon po 'gags nas med pa'i phyir ro zhe na / bshad par bya yi skal ba dang ldan pa yod na nyon cig / sngon 'dzin gyi dus na sngon po med kyang de gnyis gzung 'dzin tu mi 'gyur ba'i skyon med de / mig shes de'i bdag rkyen mig dbang dang dmigs rkyen sngon po gnyis mnyam du tshogs nas de ma thag skad cig gnyis par sngon 'dzin mig shes sngon po'i rnam ldan du skyed pa yin pas de'i tshe na sngon po med kyang sngon po'i rnam pa shes pa'i ngo na[11] lus yod pa de nyid sngon 'dzin shes pas sngon po 'dzin pa'i don yin pa'i phyir /

'on kyang bye brag smra ba'i lugs la de ring gi dus su sngon gyi bskal pa dran pa'i dran shes yod dgos shing / de nyid rang gi yul thug phrad du 'dzin na de ring gi dus su 'das pa'i bskal pa yod par 'gyur ro zhe na / 'das pa da ltar ba'i dus su yod par 'dod pa'i lugs yin pas skyon med pa'am [231] yang na sngon gyi bskal pa'i ming de'i dmigs rkyen yin zhe na rung bar sems so / /

gal te mngon sum gyi shes pa da ltar ba'i yul can ma yin nam ci'i phyir rang dus na 'das pa'i don rtogs par byed ce na / de yang mngon sum gyi shes pa

11. G: rnam par shes pa'i don.

rnams da ltar ba'i yul can du bshad ni / mngon sum gyi shes pa gang gi yul yin na mngon sum de'i dus su yod dgos pa de'i don ma yin te / gal te yin na rang gi rgyu mngon sum du rtogs pa'i mngon sum med par 'gyur ro // yul de spyir da ltar ba yin pa tsam la byed na'ang mi 'thad de / de ltar na de ring gi dus su khar sang gi nyi ma dran pa'i blo de yang da ltar ba'i yul can du 'gyur ro / /

des na 'di ltar bshad par bya ste / 'das ma thag pa la da lta yod ma thag pa zhes brjod pa ltar / so skye'i mngon sum la rang gi snga logs de ma thag tshun chad kyi rnam pa 'char ba'i nus pa yod cing de phan chad kyi rnam pa 'char ba'i nus pa med pa de'i phyir da lta yod ma thag pa'i yul rtogs pa'i nus pa can yin pa'i cha nas mngon sum da ltar ba'i yul can du bshad pa tsam yin no // 'dir mdo sde pa'i lugs la / sngon 'dzin mig shes skad cig dang po nyams su myong ba'i rang rig gi dmigs rkyen gang yin zhes dpyad dgos so / gzhan yang mngon sum le'u las / don rig 'das pa dpe dag dang // bral zhing rtags ni yod min te // zhes pa dang mi 'gal te / 'dis rang dus na 'das pa tsam ma [232] yin par rang gi dngos rgyu'i dus na 'das pa dag bshad pa yin pas 'gal ba med do //

gsum pa sems tsam pas 'dod tshul ni /

'di pas[12] rdul phra rags gang yang khas mi len kyang / dbang shes la rags par snang ba ni bag chags kyi dbang gis 'khrul pa'i snang ba yin gyi yul rang gi sdod lugs kyi dbang gis gtad pa'i rnam pa ma yin pas de'i phyir gzugs rags pa dang phra ba dmigs rkyen tu mi 'dod do / /

'o na sngon 'dzin mig shes kyi dmigs rkyen gang zhe na / de ltar sngon po sogs dbang shes kyi yul du snang ba thams cad bag chags kyi stobs las grub pa de'i phyir shes pa snga ma'i steng gi sngon po snang byed kyi bag chags de nyid sngon 'dzin mig shes kyi dmigs rkyen yin pa'i phyir / 'di yang rgyal tshab rje'i dgongs pa yin te / de nyid kyis rje'i drung du gsan pa'i mngon sum le'u'i brjed byang las /

> de'ang sgos byed[13] shes pa snga mas bzhag pa'i sngor snang dbang shes kyi de ma thag rkyen kyi steng na sngor snang shes pa de / gzung bya sngon po'i rnam ldan du skyed pa'i lag rjes 'jog pa'i nus pa yod la / nus pa de nyid dbang shes kyi dmigs rkyen yin te /

zhes gsungs pa'i phyir / de yang slob dpon ka ma la shī las mdzad pa'i de kho na nyid bsdus pa'i 'grel ba las /

12. G: 'di bas.

13. Text correction: read *sgos byed* for *sgod byed*. Both Tibetan texts read *sgod byed*.

> gzhan yang yang na / nus pa 'jog phyir rim gyis kyang // don du snang ba de ni rang dang mthun pa'i 'bras bu skyed par byed pa'i nus pa rnam par shes pa'i rten can byed pa mi 'gal lo zhes bya ba ste / 'dis ni don gzhan [233] ma yin pa'i shes pa la rang dang rjes su mthun pa'i 'bras bu skyed pa'i rgyu'i mtshan ma nus pa 'jog pa'i phyir so sor snang ba de rgyu nyid du bsgrub pa yin no / /

zhes gsungs pa la brten par snang ngo / mkhas grub rje'i dgongs pa yang yin te / sde bdun yid kyi mun sel las /

> shes pa snga ma'i steng gi rigs mthun pa'i bag chags kyi ngo bor gyur pa'i nus pa de nyid / rang 'bras dbang shes phyi ma yul gyi rnam ldan du skyed pa'i gtso bo'i rkyen yin pa'i rgyu mtshan gyis / de'i dmigs rkyen tu bzhag pa'i tshul 'di ni grub pa'i mtha' las 'ongs pa'i rnam bzhag rab tu brling ba kho na'o / /

zhes gsungs pa'i phyir / mdor na 'di pa'i[14] lugs la sngon po snang ba'i dbang shes de nyid bag la zha tshe nus pa'i ngo bor 'pho zhing nus pa de yang slar smin pa na cha gcig sngon 'dzin mig shes la snang ba'i sngon po dang cha gcig sngon po'i rnam pa can gyi mig shes su gyur pa yin pa'i rgyu mtshan gyis sngon po dang sngon 'dzin mig shes gnyis nyer len gyi shes pa'i rdzas gcig las skye ba'i phyir rdzas gcig ces bya zhing / rdzas gcig yin pas rgyu 'bras su mi rung ba de'i phyir sngon po sngon 'dzin mig shes kyi rkyen kyang ma yin zer ro / /

'o na dbang shes kyi dmigs rkyen yin na dbang shes dang lhan cig dmigs nges su 'dod pa'i lugs ma yin nam / ci'i phyir shes pa snga ma'i steng gi nus pa dmigs rkyen tu 'dod ce na /

shes pa snga ma'i steng gi sngon po snang byed kyi bag [234] chags nyid slar sngon por snang ba yin pas / de'i tshe bag chags nyid sngon por brdzus pa la sngon po dmigs so snyam du rlom yang don la bag chags la dmigs par song ba yin te / dper na zla ba gcig gnyis su snang ba'i tshe zla ba gcig po de las logs su zla ba gnyis med pas zla ba gcig la don gyis dmigs par song ba bzhin no // tshul 'di ni kun gzhi khas len pa dag gis bag chags kun gzhi'i dmigs yul du 'dod pa dang gnad gcig go /

gzhan yang 'di pa'i[15] lugs la sngon po sngon 'dzin mig shes dang rdzas gcig yin pas de gnyis dus mnyam par grub la / des na sngon 'dzin mig shes ma

14. G: 'di ba'i.

15. G: 'di ba'i.

skyes gong du sngon po med pa'i phyir mig shes de'i bdag rkyen mig dbang gis sngon po ma mthong zer dgos sam /

spyir yang 'di pas[16] mig dbang nus pa dang bag chags su yang 'dod pas de la mthong yul yod med dpyad dka' zhing / gal te bdag rkyen mig dbang gi dus su sngon po yod na de dang de 'dzin pa'i mig shes gnyis rim can du skye bar 'gyur bas de lta na sngon po rang 'dzin shes pa'i bdag nyid du 'bad pas sgrub pa ci ltar yin / yang na sngon po mthong ba'i bdag rkyen mig dbang dang de la brten pa'i mig shes gnyis dus mnyam par 'dod dam mdzangs pa'i blo gros kyis dpyad par bya'o //

gnyis pa gzhung gi don ni /

slob dpon phyogs kyi glang pos mdzad pa'i gzhung gi rtsa ba sho lo ka brgyad las med kyang don shin tu rgya che ba yin zhing / de yang don gyi gtso bo bsdu na dbang shes kyi snang yul phyi rol don [235] du grub pa bkag nas nang shes pa'i ngo bor grub pa yin pas de'i don rang 'grel dang sbrags nas bshad par bya ba la gnyis / dmigs rkyen phyi don 'gog tshul dang / de sems kyi bdag nyid du sgrub pa'i tshul lo / /

dang po la gsum / spyir dgag pa dang / bye brag tu dgag pa dang / de dag gi don bsdu ba'o // dang po la yang gsum / rdul phra rab gzung don yin pa dgag pa dang / rags pa gzung don yin pa dgag pa dang / de dag gi mjug bsdu ba'o / /

dang po ni / mdo sde pa gang dag mig la sogs pa rnam par shes pa'i dmigs pa phyi rol gyi don yin par 'dod pa de dag gi ltar na ni dbang shes de'i rgyu yin pa'i don tshang ba'i phyir rdul phra rab dag dbang shes kyi dmigs rkyen yin pa'am / yang na rdul 'dus pa la dmigs nas rang 'dra'i rnam pa der snang ba'i dbang po'i shes pa skye ba'i phyir snang yul gyi don tshang ba'i phyir rdul phra rab de dag 'dus pa dmigs rkyen yin par rtog grang na /
de la re zhig phyogs dang po mi 'thad ces snga 'grel gyis mtshams sbyar te /

> dbang po'i rnam par rig pa'i rgyu / /
> phra rab rdul dag yin mod kyi / /
> der mi snang phyir de yul ni / /
> rdul phran ma yin dbang po bzhin // (1abcd)

zhes gsungs so / don ni slob dpon phyogs glang gis re zhig rdul phra rab dbang shes kyi rgyu yin pa'i phyogs zhal gyis bzhes pa ltar mdzad nas dbang po'i rnam par rig pa ste mig sogs dbang po'i rnam par shes pa'i rgyu rdul phra rab kyi rdul dag yin mod kyi / 'on kyang dbang shes la rdul phra rab rang 'dra'i

16. G: 'di bas.

rnam pa der mi snang [236] ba'i phyir dbang shes de'i snang yul ni rdul phran ma yin te / dper na / mig gi dbang po mig shes kyi rgyu yin yang de'i dmigs yul ma yin par khyed cag gis 'dod pa bzhin no / /

'grel pa[17] ni / rdul phra rab dbang shes kyi yul ma yin zhes bya ba ni shes pa gang gis yul rang gi ngo bo nges par 'dzin pa yin te / yul de'i rnam par skye ba'i phyir ro / /

sngon po'i tshogs pa na yod pa'i rdul phra mo dag ni sngon 'dzin dbang shes de'i rgyu nyid yin du zin kyang dbang shes de'i snang yul du de ltar rung ba ma yin te dbang po bzhin no / de ltar na re zhig rdul phra mo dag dmigs rkyen ces pa'i skabs kyi dmigs pa ma yin no / /

'dir rdul phra rab dbang shes kyi rgyu yin mod kyi zhes pa dang rgyu nyid yin du zin kyang zhes pa re zhig brtag pa mtha' bzung gis bshad pa yin gyi / sems tsam pa rang lugs la rdul phra rags gang yang khas mi len te / rnam 'grel rnam bshad thar lam gsal byed las /

> dmigs brtag tu / dbang po'i rnam par rig pa'i rgyu //phra rab rdul dag yin mod kyi // zhes pa dang / kun las btus don gcig pas rdul phran tshad grub mdzad bzhed pa ma yin gyi / de yod na rgyu yin du chug kyang dmigs rkyen du mi rigs so zhes re zhig brtag pa mtha' bzung du khas blangs nas dmigs rkyen la dgag pa mdzad do / /

zhes dang / ṭik chen rigs pa'i rgya mtsho las kyang /

> gal te rang rgyud du khas len na / rang lugs la rnam rig pa'i skabs su mig dbang gi rdul phran mig shes kyi rgyur khas len dgos pas [237] rdul phran khas len pa'i sems tsam pa ches ngo mtshar che'o / /

zhes gsungs pa'i phyir / 'o na sems tsam pas gzugs khas len nam zhe na / gang yang mno bsam mi gtong ba dag gis khas len mod ces chags thogs med par smra mod / rje rin po ches dbu ma'i rnam bshad du / theg bsdus dang gtan la dbab pa'i bsdus pa dang rten 'brel mdo 'grel gyi lung shes byed du drangs nas sems tsam pas gzugs khas len ces gsungs pa'i mthar / sems tsam pa'i lugs 'di la yang phyi rol bkag na gzugs sogs kyang med par 'gro zhing / gzugs sogs bzhag na phyi rol kyang bzhag dgos par mthong 'dug pa'i phyir ro /

de dag dka' mod kyang mangs pas 'jigs nas ma bris so zhes dka' gnas su mdzad 'dug pas ci 'dod du smra nus pa zhig min par sems so / /

---

17. G: 'grel ba.

gnyis pa rags pa gzung don yin pa 'gog pa ni /

'dus pa ni re zhig brtag pa mtha' bzung gis der snang ba nyid yin du zin kyang de'i rgyu ma yin pas /

> gang ltar snang de de las min / /
> rdzas su med phyir zla gnyis bzhin // (2ab)

zhes so / don ni sngon 'dzin mig shes gang gis sngo rdul du ma 'dus pa ltar snang mod / 'on kyang sngon 'dzin mig shes de sngon po'i rdul 'dus pa de las skye ba min te / sngo rdul du ma 'dus pa rdzas su med pa'i phyir / dper na / zla gcig zla gnyis yin pa bzhin no / sngon po la sogs pa'i don gang zhig / rang snang ba ste rang gi bdag nyid dam rang dang 'dra ba'i rnam par rig pa skyed par byed pa de ni [238] dmigs rkyen ces pa'i dmigs pa yin par rigs te / de ltar de ni bstan bcos las /

> don gang zhig sems dang sems las byung ba rnams skye ba'i rgyu mtshan yang yin la de rnams skyes na don de nyams su myong ba'i tha snyad 'dogs par yang byed pa de ni dmigs pa yin no /

zhes dbang shes gang gi dmigs rkyen yin na dbang shes de la rang 'dra'i rnam pa shar ba dang dbang shes de skye ba'i rkyen nyid du bshad pas so / rdul du ma 'dus pa ni dbang shes skyed byed de ltar yang ma yin te / rdzas su med pa yin pas dper na dbang po ma tshang ba ste rab rib kyis dbang po nyams pa de'i phyir zla ba gcig gnyis su mthong ba de ni zla gcig zla gnyis su der snang ba tsam nyid yin du zin kyang / zla gcig zla ba gnyis yin pa dbang shes kyi rgyu ma yin pa'i phyir de'i dmigs rkyen ces pa'i yul ma yin no / dpe de bzhin du rdul phra rab 'dus pa rdzas su yod pa ma yin pa nyid kyis rgyu ma yin par grub pa de'i phyir rdul 'dus pa skabs 'di'i dmigs pa ma yin no / /

'dir rdul phra rab dang 'dus pa dag dbang shes kyi yul ma yin par bshad pa ni snang yul lam sgro 'dogs chod pa'i yul la dgongs shing / sngon 'dzin mig shes kyis sngon po bzung zhes pa'i don yang sngon 'dzin mig shes sngon po dang 'dra ba tsam la byed pa ma gtogs de la lag pas bum pa gzung ba lta bu 'dzin pa'i mtshan nyid kyi byed pa 'ga' yang med de / dper na / pha dang 'dra ba'i bu la pha'i gzugs 'dzin pa zhes brjod kyang de la bu 'dzin byed dang pha'i gzugs gzung byar gyur pa 'ga' [239] yang med pa bzhin no / /

zla ba gcig zla ba gnyis yin pa rdzas su ma grub kyang zla ba gcig rdzas su grub zer dgos te / zla ba gcig dngos po yin pa'i phyir te / zla ba gcig zla ba gnyis su snang ba'i dbang shes kyi dmigs rkyen yin pa'i phyir / rtags sde bdun rigs rgyan gnyis kas grub / des na zla ba gnyis su snang ba'i dbang shes la zla ba gcig gi rnam pa gtad kyang ji bzhin ma gtad do / /

gsum pa bsdus pa'i don ni /

de ltar phyi rol gnyis kar yang / /
blo yi yul du mi rung ngo // (2ab)

zhes pa ste / de ltar phyi rol gyi rdul phra rab dmigs rkyen tu 'dod pa'i phyogs dang 'dus pa dmigs rkyen tu 'dod pa'i phyogs gnyis kar yang phyi don blo yi snang yul du mi rung ngo // ci'i phyir mi rung zhe na / dmigs rkyen yin na shes pa gang la rang gi rnam pa 'jog byed yin pa dang shes pa de'i rgyu yin pa'i khyad chos gnyis ka tshang dgos shing / de yang phra ba dmigs rkyen tu 'dod pa'i phyogs la rang gi rnam pa 'jog byed yin pa'i yan lag ma tshang / 'dus pa dmigs rkyen tu 'dod pa'i phyogs la rgyu yin pa'i yan lag ma tshang ba'i phyir phyi rol gyi rdul phra mo dang tshogs pa zhes bya ba'i don de dag ni dmigs rkyen kyi skabs kyi dmigs pa ma yin no / /

gnyis pa bye brag tu dgag pa la gnyis / rdul phra rab kyi rnam pa'i dbye ba dgag pa dang / rnam pa'i dbye ba dgag pa'i bsdus don no / dang po la yang gnyis / 'dod pa brjod pa dang / de mi 'thad par dgag [240] **pa'o / dang po ni /**

kha cig 'dus pa'i rnam pa dag / /
sgrub pa yin par 'dod par byed // (3ab)

ces byung / phyi don 'dod pa'i phyogs 'di la ni ste 'di la yang kha cig gis rdul phra rab rdzas su yod pa'i phyir rgyu yin zhing rdul rdzas brgyad 'dus pa'i bdag nyid kyang yin pas dbang shes la 'dus pa'i rnam pa ste rags pa'i rnam pa dag kyang 'char ba'i phyir / des na dmigs rkyen tu 'jog byed kyi yan lag tshang bas sgrub pa ste dbang shes kyi rgyu yin par 'dod par byed ces pa'o / rdul phra rab cha med yin pas ci ltar rags pa'i rnam par 'char zhe na / phyi rol gyi don thams cad ni 'byung ba bzhi dang gzugs dri ro reg bya'i bdag nyid yin pa'i phyir rnam pa du ma can yin pas so / /

'o na bum pa'i gzugs 'dzin mig shes bum pa'i reg bya'i rdul la mngon sum du 'gyur ro zhe na / bum pa'i rdul phra rab de 'ga' zhig la rnam pa 'ga' zhig gis mngon sum nyid du 'dod kyi mig gis gzugs mthong lus kyis reg bya reg pa sogs dbang po lnga'i nus pa so sor nges pa'i rgyu mtshan gyis rnam pa thams cad du mi 'dod do / de'i phyir rdul phra rab rnams la yang 'dus par snang ba'i shes pa skyed pa'i rgyu yod do zer ro / /

gal te rdul phra rab rags pa'i rnam par dbang shes la 'char na rdul phra rab kho rang nyid ci'i phyir mi 'char zhe na /

rdul phran rnam pa rnam rig gi /
don min sra nyid la sogs bzhin // (3bcd)

zhes smos so / don ni / bum pa'i tshogs pa na yod pa'i rdul phra rab thams cad mig gi rnam rig gi gzung don min te / bum pa'i tshogs pa na yod pa'i sra ba nyid dang sogs pas 'jam rtsub kyi rdul mi snang ba bzhin no / dper na [241] ji ltar sra nyid la sogs pa ni yul gi go sa na yod bzhin du yang dbang po lnga'i nus pa so sor nges pa'i rgyu mtshan gyis mig gi blo'i yul ma yin pa ltar rdul phra mo nyid kyang de dang 'dra zhes smra'o / /

kha cig 'dus pa'i rnam pa dag / ces sogs kyi rtsa 'grel las rdul phra rab cha bcas su bshad pa tshig zin la mi snang yang / gsung gi bab la bltas na dbang shes la rdul phra rab 'dus pa'i rnam par snang bar 'dod pa'i phyogs snga zhig yin pas / dbang shes ma 'khrul ba la 'dus pa'i rnam par snang na rags par snang dgos shing rags par snang na cha bcas su snang bar don gyis grub pas de'i phyir / kun mkhyen 'jam dbyangs bzhad pa'i grub mtha'i rnam bshad du /

> dmigs brtag rtsa 'grel las / mdo sde pa dang sems tsam pas brtsad pa'i tshe mdo sde pas cha dang bcas pa'i rdul phra rab tshogs tshe re res kyang rang 'dra'i rnam par gtod[18] par khas blangs pa'i phyir /

zhes gsungs pa legs bshad du 'khums so // 'grel bshad las skabs 'di'i phyogs snga pha khol yin par gsungs so / /

gnyis pa de mi 'thad par dgag pa la gsum / pha rol po'i 'dod pa dgag pa dang / pha rol po'i dogs pa gzhan bsu ba dang / de'i lan dgag pa'o //dang po ni /

> de dag ltar na bum pa dang / /
> kham phor sogs blo mtshungs par 'gyur // (4ab)

zhes gsungs so //don ni / rdul phra rab dbang shes la rags pa'i rnam par snang zer ba 'di ci ltar yin / rags pa ni bum pa dang kham phor lta bu la zer bas rdul phra rab kyi rnam [242] pa bum pa lta bu yin nam kham phor lta bu yin de dag gang byas kyang khyed kyi 'dod pa de dag ltar na bum pa la dmigs pa'i tshe kham phor dang kham phor dmigs pa'i tshe bum pa'o snyam pa'i blo phan tshun mtshungs par 'gyur ro / /

gal te bum pa kham phor las che ba yin pas bum pa dang kham phor la sogs pa'i rdul phra mo rnams la ni mang nyung yod pa'i dbang gis yin no zhe na / khyad par de yod du zin kyang rdul phra rab la rags pa'i rnam pa de ltar yod pa'i khyad par ni 'ga' yang med do / /
gnyis pa pha rol po'i dogs pa bsu ba ni /

> gal te rnam pa'i dbye bas dbye // (4c)

---

18. See translation p. 154. Both Tibetan texts read *gtod*, but *gtad* or *btad* are more probable.

zhes gsungs te / gal te pha rol pos 'di snyam du bum pa la mgrin pa ring ba dang lto ba ldir ba la sogs pa'i rnam pa yod la kham phor la de med pas / des na rnam pa'i khyad par las mi 'dra bar dbye ba gang gis ni kham phor gyi blo las bum pa'i blo'i khyad par du gyur pa'i khyad par dbye rgyu yod do snyam du sems na zhes pa ni pha rol po'i 'dod pa'o / /

gsum pa de'i lan dgag pa ni /

mgrin pa ring ba la sogs pa'i khyad par 'di ni bum pa la sogs pa la yod mod kyi zhes mtshams sbyar nas /

> de ni rdul phran rdzas yod la / /
> med de tshad dbye med phyir ro // (4d, 5a)

zhes gsungs te / rnam pa'i dbye ba de ni rdul phran rdzas yod la med de / de ci'i phyir zhe na / rdul phra rab la che chung gi tshad dang dbyibs mi 'dra ba'i dbye ba med pa'i phyir ro / de la che chung gi tshad med de / chung shos mthar thug yin pa'i phyir / dbyibs mi 'dra ba med de / mdo sde pa khyod ltar na / zlum po kho nar nges pa'i phyir / de'i phyir bum pa dang kham phor la [243] sogs pa'i rdul phra rab rnams ni rdzas gzhan yin du zin kyang / de'i dbyibs zlum por mtshungs pa la ni dbye ba med do / /

gnyis pa rdul phra rab kyi rnam pa'i dbye ba dgag pa'i bsdus don la gnyis / dbyibs mi 'dra ba'i khyad par rags pa la 'thad tshul dang / rags pa btags yod du grub pa'i tshul lo //dang po ni /

> de phyir de rdzas med la yod // (5b)

ces gsungs te / rdul phra rab la rnam pa mi 'dra ba mi srid pa de'i phyir dbye ba de ni rdzas su med pa ste kun rdzob tu yod pa dag kho na la yod kyi rdul phra mo rnams la yod pa ma yin no / bum pa la sogs pa'i gzugs rags pa ni kun rdzob tu yod pa nyid do // zhes pa'o / /

'dir bum pa kun rdzob tu yod par bshad pa ni / mdzod rjes 'brang gi mdo sde pa la yin gyi rnam 'grel rjes 'brang gi lugs ma yin te / mngon sum le'u las / don dam don byed nus pa gang / / de 'dir don dam yod pa yin // zhes don byed nus pa thams cad don dam par yod par bshad pa'i phyir ro //

rdul phra rab kyi dbyibs zlum por bshad pa ni rnam 'grel rjes 'brang gi mdo sde pa la yin gyi mdzod lugs la mi 'thad de / mdzod las / gnyis gzung 'gyur te rdul la med // ces rdul phra rab la dbyibs med par bshad pa'i phyir / 'di ci'i phyir zhe na / nyan thos sde pas dbyibs kha dog la btags par 'dod pas / gal te rdul phra rab kyi dbyibs yod na de'i kha dog las logs su med cing de'i kha dog kyang de'i bdag nyid du 'dod dgos pas de lta na [244] rdul phra rab cha bcas su 'gyur du dogs sam snyam / dbyibs kha dog la btags pa'i tshul 'di legs par ma shes na /

rgyal dbang blos bzhed pa ltar dung ser 'dzin gyi dbang shes dung gi kha dog la 'khrul yang dbyibs la tshad mar 'dod pa de byung zhing / rgyal dbang blos de ltar bzhed pa'i rgyu mtshan ni dung dkar por snang ba'i mig shes kyis mthong ba'i dbyibs dang ser por snang ba'i mig shes kyis mthong ba'i dbyibs gnyis la khyad par med pa gang zhig // de gnyis ka dung gi dbyibs yin pa'i phyir zer /

slob dpon chos mchog gis de mi 'thad de / dung ser 'dzin kyi mig shes kyis dung gi dbyibs snang ba na dung dkar po'i dbyibs su mi snang bar dung ser po'i dbyibs su snang ba gang zhig / ser po'i dung gzhi ma grub pa'i phyir / des na mig shes de dung gi dbyibs la 'khrul ba yin te / ring po la sogs pa'i dbyibs su snang ba ni kha dog gi rdul mang po gral bsgrigs te gnas pa la ring po sogs su snang ba yin gyi ring po tshugs thub tu yod pa'i dbang gis snang ba ma yin pa'i rgyu mtshan gyis dung gi dkar po ma bzung bar dung gi dbyibs rkyang pa 'dzin tshul med pa'i phyir zhes 'gog par byed do / /

'o na gang zag des dung ci ltar thob ce na / gang zag des dpyad dus na dung ser po dpyad cing thob dus na dung dkar po thob dgos pa'i gnad kyis dung gi reg bya 'dzin pa'i tshad ma gzhan las nges sam snyam ste / rgyal tshab rje'i mngon le'i brjed byang las / dung gi sgra'ang dbyibs kyi khyad par can gyi kha dog la 'jug la [245] dung thob pa'ang tshad ma gzhan la brten nas yin gyi / zhes gsungs pa'i phyir / mdor na bum pa'i lto ba ldir ba dang mgrin pa ring ba sogs bum pa yin zhing lto ba ldir ba dang mgrin pa ring ba'i dbyibs bum pa ma yin pa'i zhib cha zhig kyang yod par mngon te / lhag mthong chen mo las / gang gi lto ba ldir ba dang mgrin pa ring ba sogs de ni bum pa yin par 'dod kyi lto ba ldir ba sogs kyi dbyibs bum par mi 'dod de / zhes gsungs pa'i phyir / gal te sems tsam pa'i lugs la rdul du grub pa med kyang rdul yod de / rags pa rtsom byed kyi rdul phra rab yod pa'i phyir te / de'i dbyibs zlum po yin pa'i phyir te / dmigs brtag rang 'grel las / rdul phra rab rnams ni rdzas gzhan yin du zin kyang zlum po la ni dbye ba med do / zhes gsungs pa'i phyir zer na /

spyir sems tsam pa'i gzhung las gzugs rags pa dang rdul zhes pa'i tha snyad mang du byung ste / dbyig gnyen gyi las grub pa'i rab byed las / bsags pa'i don gyis na lus yin te / 'byung ba dang 'byung ba las gyur pa'i rdul phra rab bsags pa'i phyir ro // zhes dang / de bzhin du gtan la dbab pa'i bsdu ba sogs sa sde'i lung mang du snang bas brtag par bya ba yod las che /

'on kyang rags pa yod na bum pa rags pa yang yod dgos la de ltar na bum pa phyi rol don du 'khrul ba'i gzhi gang zhe na bum pa rags pa de'o zhes brjod chog bzhin du rje rin po ches de skad mi gsung bar / dbu ma 'jug pa'i rnam bshad du [246]

thag pa'i rgyu mtshan gyis sbrul du 'khrul pa ni thag pa med pa'i gzhir mi skye la / bum pa la sogs pa'i rgyu mtshan can gyi 'khrul ba ni sa la sogs pa med pa'i nam mkha'i phyogs su skye bar mi 'gyur ba bzhin du / phyi rol gyi don med na sngon po la sogs pa phyi rol tu 'khrul pa'i rtog pa 'khrul gzhi ci 'dra zhig gi rgyu can du 'gyur / de'i phyir gdon mi za bar phyi rol tu 'khrul ba'i rgyu / gzung 'dzin rdzas tha dad pa gnyis su snang ba'i ma dag gzhan dbang khas blangs dgos te zhes ma dag gzhan dbang zer ba zhig btsal[19] nas bzhag pa la rgyu mtshan zhig yod do snyam nas / kho bo ni sems tsam rnam brdzun pa'i skabs su gzugs rags pa dang rdul phra rags gang yang med ces mgrin pa btegs nas smra nus shing / rnam bden pas 'dod tshul ni / 'byung 'gyur gyi mkhas pa dag gis smos shig ces skabs dbye bar bya'o / /

gnyis pa rags pa btags yod du grub pa'i tshul ni /

rdul phran yongs su bsal na ni / /
der snang shes pa nyams 'gyur phyir // (5cd)

zhes so // don ni bum pa lta bu gzugs rags pa btags yod rnams la ni de dag gi rdul phran re re nas yongs su bsal na ni bum pa la sogs pa'i rnam pa der snang ba'i shes pa nyams par 'gyur ba'i phyir / gal te bum pa rags pa rdzas su yod par 'gyur na de rnams la ni rang dang 'brel ba can gyi rdul phran bsal du zin kyang kha dog la sogs pa bzhin du rang gi blo 'dor bar mi byed pa'i skyon du 'gyur ro // de ltar rdul phra rags gang yang dmigs rkyen tu mi rung ba de lta bas na dbang po'i blo rnams kyi snang yul [247] ni phyi rol gyi don ma yin par 'thad do / /

gnyis pa dmigs rkyen nang sems kyi bdag nyid du sgrub pa la gnyis / dmigs rkyen dus mnyam pa'i phyogs dgod pa dang / slob dpon gyi rang lugs dgod pa'o // dang po la yang gnyis / phyogs snga mas 'dod tshul dang / de la rtsod pa spong ba'o // dang po ni /

nang gi shes bya'i ngo bo ni / /
phyi rol ltar snang gang yin te / /
don yin rnam shes ngo bo'i phyir / /
de rkyen nyid kyang yin phyir ro // (6abcd)

zhes gsungs te / don ni / phyi don med kyang dmigs rkyen mi rung ba'i skyon med de / nang gi shes pa'i ngo bor gyur pa'i shes bya'i ngo bo ni phyi rol gyi don du med bzhin du phyi rol lta bur snang ba nang[20] na yod pa gang yin pa de kho na don te dmigs pa'i rkyen yin no / /

sngon 'dzin mig gi rnam par shes pa sngon po'i ngo bor song ba de'i phyir mig shes la sngon por snang ba de mig shes de'i snang yul yin par ma zad de'i rkyen nyid kyang yin pa'i phyir ro /

19. Text correction: *btsal*, from *'tshol ba*.

20. G omits ni phyi rol gyi don dun med hzhin du phyi rol lta bur snang ba nang.

de ci'i phyir zhe na / nang gi rnam par shes pa ni don du snang ba dang de las skyes pa yang yin pas / des na shes pa de'i dmigs pa yang yin la rkyen kyang yin pa'i chos nyid gnyis dang ldan pa'i phyir nang na yod pa kho na dmigs pa'i rkyen yin no / /

gnyis pa rtsod pa spong ba ni /

re zhig pha rol pos de ltar nang na yod pa kho na snang ba'i yul nyid yin la ni rag la ste yin du chug na / sngon 'dzin mig shes de sngon por snang ba de'i ya gyal phyogs gcig po yin pas de gnyis lhan cig skyes pa ma yin nam go ste de nyid ci ltar na rkyen dang rkyen can yin zhe [248] na /

> gcig cha'ang mi 'khrul phyir na rkyen // (7a)

ces mig shes la sngon por snang ba dang mig shes gnyis gcig car yin na'ang gcig yod na cig shos skye zhing de las bzlog na mi skye ba la mi 'khrul pa'i phyir rkyen dang rkyen can gnyis lhan cig par gyur tu zin kyang rgyu dang 'bras bu'i dngos por 'khrul pa med pa'i phyir de ma thag rkyen dang bdag rkyen gnyis las gzhan pa'i dmigs rkyen las skye ba'i rkyen can du 'gyur te / 'di ltar gtan tshigs te de'i rgyu mtshan ni / gang zhig yod na gang yod pa dang gang zhig med na gang med pa dag ni / gdung khyim ltar phan tshun brten pa'i tshul gyis yod na yod pa dang med na med pa dag gi rgyu 'bras su 'jog byed kyi mtshan nyid de dang ldan pa nyid yin pas na mtshan nyid de ni rgyu 'bras cig car ba'i skabs su ma zad rgyu dang 'bras bur ldan pa rim gyis skyes pa dag gi yang mtshan nyid yin par smra'o / /

kha cig 'di'i rkang pa snga ma phyed dang gsum gyis rnam bden pa dang phyi ma phyed dang gsum gyis rnam brdzun pa'i lugs kyi dmigs rkyen 'chad byed yin zer la / mkhas grub rje ltar na rgyu 'bras dus mnyam khas len pa'i sems tsam pa'i 'dod pa 'chad byed yin par mngon zhing / rnam nges dar ṭīka las de 'dra ba'i sems tsam pa mi 'thad ces bkag mod / 'on kyang sems tsam pa spyi'i lugs la rgyu 'bras dus mnyam pa mi 'thad cing / de ltar 'dod pa'i sems tsam pa kha cig yod dam snyam ste / theg bsdus las /

> kun gzhi rnam par shes pa dang kun nas nyon mongs pa'i chos de dag dus mnyam du gcig gi [249] rgyu nyid du gcig 'gyur bar ci ltar zhe na / dper na mar me'i me lce byung ba dang snying po tshig pa phan tshun dus mnyam pa dang / mdung khyim[21] yang dus mnyam du gcig la gcig brten nas mi 'gyel ba de bzhin du 'dir yang gcig gi rgyu nyid du gcig 'gyur bar blta'o zhes dang / de'i don slob dpon dbyig gnyen gyis de ltar na lhan cig 'byung ba'i rgyu yang bstan pa yin no / /

---

21. Text correction: *mdung khyim* for *gdung khyim*.

zhes dang / de'i phyir sde bdun rgyan yid kyi mun sel las /

> rgyu 'bras dus mnyam srid pa dang rgyu 'bras la rdzas gzhan gyis ma khyab par 'dod pa chos mngon pa pa'i slob dpon dbyig gnyen la sogs pa snga ma dag gis 'dod pa tsam yin gyi /

zhes gsungs pa legs bshad yin no / /

gnyis pa slob dpon phyogs glang gi rang lugs 'god pa la lnga / rang lugs 'god pa dngos dang / de la rtsod pa spong ba dang / rnam shes nus pa'i rten du bshad pa dang / de dag gi mjug bsdu ba dang / zhar la byung ba gzhan bshad pa'o // dang po ni /

slob dpon snga ma dag gis bshad pa de ltar ram / yang na /

> nus pa 'jog phyir rim gyis yin // (7b)

zhes smos te / de'i don mthar chags su 'grel na / sngon 'dzin[22] shes pa snga ma'i steng gi sngor snang dbang shes phyi ma sngon po'i rnam ldan du skyed pa'i nus pa de sngor snang dbang shes phyi ma sngon po'i rnam ldan du 'jog byed kyi rkyen yin pa'i phyir rim gyis dbang shes phyi ma'i dmigs rkyen byed pa yin / zhes pa ste / sbyor ngag tu bsgril na sngor snang dbang shes de'i de ma thag rkyen rang 'gag pa [250] rnam shes kyi steng du bzhag pa'i nus pa chos can / rim gyis dbang shes phyi ma'i dmigs rkyen byed de / rang 'bras sngor snang dbang shes phyi ma la sngon po'i rnam pa 'jog pa'i rkyen yin pa'i phyir zhes 'god dgos shing / 'di la nus pa 'jog pa'i dmigs rkyen ces grags kyang kho bos bsam na rnam pa 'jog pa'i dmigs rkyen ces tha snyad btags na legs par sems so / /

sbyor ngag tu bsgril tshul 'di sde bdun yid kyi mun sel ltar yin la / rang 'grel ltar na rim gyis kyang dmigs rkyen byed tshul gzhan yod de / dbang shes la phyi rol don du snang ba de ni rang snang ba dang mthun pa'i 'bras bu phyi ma skyed par byed pa'i nus pa yid kyi rnam par shes pa'i rten can byed pas mi 'gal lo zhes pa ste go bar zad do / /

gnyis pa rtsod pa spong ba ni /

gal te 'o na khyod ni nang gi gzugs kho na dmigs pa'i rkyen yin par 'dod pa de lta na nang gi gzugs de dmigs rkyen dang mig dbang bdag rkyen byas pa la brten nas mig gi rnam par shes pa ci ltar skye ste / khyod kyi nang gi gzugs zhes pa de mig dbang las 'os med kyang de ni mig shes la mi snang bas dmigs rkyen tu ci ltar 'gyur zhe na / de la slob dpon gyis /

---

22. G: sngo 'dzin.

> lhan cig byed dbang nus pa yi / /
> ngo bo gang yin dbang po'ang yin // (7cd)

zhes smos te / mig gi dbang po gzugs su 'dod na bden yang kho bo cag gis sngon po dang sngon 'dzin mig shes gnyis lhan cig tu 'byung bar byed pa la lhag par dbang ba'i nus pa de yi ngo bo gang yin pa dbang shes phyi ma'i [251] rkyen yin par ma zad mig gi dbang po'ang yin par 'dod pas skyon med la / sngon po mthong ba'i mig gi dbang po ni nus pa yin te / rang gi 'bras bu sngon 'dzin[23] mig shes de dmigs rkyen dang de ma thag rkyen gnyis yod kyang skabs 'gar mi skye ba'i rtags las / sgra dang dri sogs mthong mi nus par sngon po kho na mthong nus zhes nus pa'i ngo bo spyi bam tsam yod pa nyid du rjes su dpag gi / 'byung ba'am 'byung ba las gyur pa'i gzugs sogs kyi khyad par zhib mo nyid du rjes su dpog pa ni ma yin no /
gsum pa rnam shes nus pa'i rten du bshad pa ni /

> de yang rnam rig la mi 'gal // (8a)

zhes so / dbang po ni nus pa yin pas de yang nus pa can rnam rig la lhan cig tu rten dang brten pa mi 'gal ba'o / sems tsam pa ltar nus pa rnam par shes pa la brten nas yod kyang rung / mdo sde pa ltar mig sngar bstan du med pa'i 'byung 'gyur gyi gzugs de'i rang gi ngo bo la brten nas yod kyang rung ste / 'bras bu skyed par byed pa la khyad par med do / /
bzhi pa de dag gi don bsdu ba ni /

> de ltar yul gyi ngo bo dang / /
> nus pa phan tshun rgyu can dang / /
> thog med dus nas 'jug pa yin // (8bcd)

zhes bya ba smos te / de ltar yul gyi rnam pa can gyi mig gi shes pa'i ngo bo dang mig dbang nus pa'i ngo bo gnyis phan tshun rgyu can du 'brel ba dang / 'brel pa de'i sngon mtha' ded na thog ma med pa'i dus nas 'jug pa yin no / / mig ces bya ba'i nus pa la brten [252] nas rnam par shes pa skyes pa dang / nang gi gzugs la brten nas rnam par shes pa skyes kyang rung / gzung don gyi mthu las don du snang ba'i rnam par shes pa skyes par mi 'dod pa'i rgyu mtshan gyis don du snang ba'i rnam par shes pa dmigs kyis ma bstan pa ste dmigs kyis ma phye bar skye'o zhes bshad do /

nus pa dang nus pa can gyi rnam shes 'di gnyis kyang phan tshun rgyu can dang brgyud pa de yang thog ma med pa'i dus can yin te / res 'ga' ni nus pa

---

23. G: sngo 'dzin.

ste rigs mthun gyi bag chags yongs su smin pa las rnam par shes pa yul gyi rnam pa nyid du 'byung la / res 'ga' ni yul de'i rnam pa can gyi shes pa las nus pa skye'o /

nus pa de ni nus pa can gyi rnam par shes pa las rdzas su yod pa'i tshul gyis gcig dang tha dad du brjod du med kyang / btags par yod pa'i tshul gyis de gnyis ldog pa gzhan nyid dang ngo bo gzhan ma yin pa nyid du ci dgar brjod par bya'o / /

de ltar phyi don med kyang dmigs rkyen dang dmigs byed gnyis cig car ba dang rim gyis pa gang gi 'dod pa ltar na yang nang gi dmigs pa ni chos nyid gnyis dang ldan pa'i phyir dmigs pa'i yul du 'thad do / /

lnga pa zhar la byung ba bshad pa la /

ni zhes pa'i sgra dgar ba dang nges bzung dang tshig gi kha skong la 'jug ces pa grags che yang / de las gzhan du 'jug tshul mang du mchis te / dmigs brtag las /

> der mi snang phyir[24] de yul ni // (1c)

zhes pa'i ni sgra ci'i phyir zhes pa'i don can yin te / slob dpon 'dul ba [253] lhas mdzad pa'i dmigs pa brtag pa'i 'grel bshad las /

> ni zhes bya ba'i sgra ni gang gi phyir zhes bya ba'i don no //

zhes gsungs pa'i phyir / de ni dper na / bum pa ni mi rtag go zhes pa la bum pa ci'i phyir mi rtag ces brjod chog pa lta bu'o // yang dmigs brtag rang 'grel las /

> 'di la ni zhes pa'i ni sgra yang sgra la 'jug ste / 'grel bshad de nyid las /
> ni zhes bya ba'i sgra ni yang zhes bya ba'i sgra'i don du blta bar bya'o / /

zhes gsungs pa'i phyir / de yang 'di la ni zhes pa la 'di la yang zhes brjod chog pa lta bu'o /

yang rang 'grel las / ci ltar sra nyid la sogs pa ni zhes pa'i ni sgra nyid ces pa'i don can yin te / 'grel bshad de nyid las / ni zhes bya ba'i sgra ni nyid ces bya ba'i don du blta bar bya'o // zhes gsungs pa'i phyir / de yang bum pa ni / mi rtag go zhes pa la bum pa nyid mi rtag ces brjod pa lta bu'o / /

yang rtsa bar / nang gi shes bya'i ngo bo ni / / zhes pa'i ni sgra nges bzung gi don dang tshig gi gcod mtshams gnyis char la 'jug pa yin te / 'grel bshad de

24. Text correction: bsTan dar mistakenly has *byed*.

nyid las / ni zhes bya ba'i sgra ni nges par bzung ba dang / bar du chod pa'i don du blta bar bya'o / / zhes gsungs pa'i phyir / de yang dper na / dang po ni / lhas sbyin ni mi zer rgyu la lhas sbyin mi nges par yin zer chog pa lta bu dang / gnyis pa 'di'i bar du chod pa ni tshig gi gcod mtshams yin te / dper na / 'dod chags zhe sdang gti mug dbang gis ni / zhes pa'i ni sgra lta bu'o / smras pa /

phyi don bkag nas 'di snang dngos po [254] kun / /
sems kyi ngo bor grub pa'i tshad ma'i gzhung / /
dus kyi mtha' 'dir ci dgar shes 'dod pa'i / /
kho bo'ang skal ba bzang po ci ste min / /
'gro ba bzhi yi dbang gyur 'byung po'i bya / /
tshul 'dir mi bzod ltas ngan gtong na yang / /
legs bshad snang bas blo ldan yid kyi khyim / /
gsal bar nus pa'i rten 'brel su yis 'gog /
rnam dag khungs btsun gzhung las btus pa dang / /
rang gi blos kyang dpyad pas dag pa'i phyir / /
gtsug lag gzhung las ha cang phyir thal ba'i / /
log bshad nyes pa shas cher med dam snyam / /
'on kyang rnam rig grub mtha' brling bas na / /
bdag gis ji bzhin gting dpog ma nus dbang / /
zhwa dpe lham la 'gebs pa yod gyur na / /
de ni nges par bdag blo'i skyon du byos / /
byis pa chung ngus 'khrul gtam smra ba'i tshe / /
de la pha mas lhag par brtse ba ltar / /
bdag kyang mi shes 'ol tshod bgyis gang la / /
ches cher brtse bas bskyang ba shin tu rigs / /
tshul 'di phyogs glang chos grags yab sras kyi / /
spyan sngar kun bzang mchod sprin tshogs gyur te / /
mchod yul dam pa rab dgyes 'dzum mdzad pas / /
'jig rten rgud tshogs 'di kun zhi gyur cig /
lung rigs sprin sngon 'khrigs pa'i bag ma[25] nas / /
legs bshad dbyar skyes rnga gsang 'di bsgrags pas / /
mang thos don gnyer mdongs mtha' gar bsgyur cing / /
phan dang bde ba'i mngal gyis sgeg gyur cig /
tshad ma'i lugs bzang 'dab brgya'i tshal yangs por / /
thos bsam bung ba'i [255] phur lding rtag rol cing / /
blo gsal zab don sbrang rtsir longs spyod pa'i / /

25. G: 'grigs pa'i ba gam.

dpal 'di nam yang nyams pa med gyur cig /
bdag kyang skye ba kun tu tshad ma pa'i / /
gzhung bzang 'di la gzhan dring mi 'jog pa'i / /
spobs pa brnyes shing gtan tshigs rig pa'i don / /
smra la 'gran zla med pa'i dbang thob shog /

ces dmigs pa brtag pa'i 'grel pa mu tig 'phreng mdzes zhes bya ba 'di ni a lag sha lha rams pa ngag dbang bstan dar zhes bgyi bas sbyar ba'o // 'dis kyang rgyal ba'i bstan pa rin po che yun ring du gnas par gyur cig / zhes pa 'di ni sku 'bum byams pa gling du dpar du bsgrubs pa'o // sa rba manggalaṃ / /

16

dMigs brtag 'grel pa snying po bsdus pa

Yeshes Thabkhas
Edited by John Powers and Sonam Thakchöe

gnyis stong zab mo'i gnad don 'byed pa la //
mchog tu mkhas pa phyogs glang chos grags sogs //
rgya bod mkhas pa'i tshogs la gus btud nas /
dmigs pa brtag pa mdo tsam bshad par bya //

zhes gus phyag dang bcas slob dpon phyogs glang gis mdzad pa'i gzhung ā lamṃ ba na pa rī kṣa bṛtti don gnyer can kha cig nas gzhung 'di la 'grel bshad byed dgos bskul ma gnang ba bzhin kho bos 'dir cung zad bshad par bya'o // gzhung gi mtshan legs sbyar skad la ā lamṃ ba na pa rī kṣa bṛtti / bod skad du / dmigs pa brtag pa'i 'grel pa zhes bya la / de'ang ā lamṃ ba na zhes pa ni bod skad du dmigs pa dang / pa rī kṣa ni brtag pa dang / bṛtti ni 'grel pa zhes pa'i don no //

gzhung mtshan la dpyad pa /

'dir kha cig gis dmigs pa dang / yul dang / don gsum la khyad par ji yod dam zhe na / spyir btang byas na / dmigs pa dang / yul dang / don / gsum don gcig la 'jug / dper na gzugs sgra dri ro reg bya bcas la yul lnga dang don lnga dmigs pa lnga bzhag srol yod pa bzhin no // 'on kyang de dag gsum la gzhi gzung bya'i sgo nas khyad par dbye rgyu yod de / blo de dang de'i dmigs pa yin na blo de'i yul dang don du 'jog mi dgos /

dper na / stong nyid mngon sum du rtogs pa'i ye shes lta bur mtshon na / dmigs pa chos thams cad la dmigs nas de dag gzung 'dzin gnyis stong rtogs pa'i shes rab zhig la 'jog dgos pa'i skabs / chos thams cad shes rab de'i dmigs pa yin kyang yul ma yin /

dper na / dmigs pa gzugs la dmigs nas gzugs 'dzin rdzas gzhan gyis ma grub par mngon sum du rtogs pa'i tshe / gzugs ye shes de'i dmigs pa yin yang de'i yul ma yin pa bzhin no // yang sngon 'dzin mig shes lta bu mtshon na / sngon po de sngon 'dzin mig shes de'i yul yang yin / don yang yin dmigs pa'ang yin dgos /

spyir dmigs pa brtag pa'i gzhung 'dir / dmigs pa gang yin dang de'i rang bzhin gang yin brtag pa'i skabs yin pas / blo la rnam pa gtad pa'i sgo nas shar ba'i dmigs rkyen de phyi rol yul gis rnam pa gtad nas yong gi yod dam / yang na nang shes pa'i steng gi bag chags sad pa las yong gi yod brtag pa na /

dngos smra ba mdo sde pa rnams kyis phyi rol yul gyis rnam pa gtad nas 'byung zhes lan 'debs pas / 'o na de 'dra'i dmigs pa de'i rang bzhin gang yin zhes brtag par mdzad do //

yang na gal te dmigs pa dang don dang yul gsum don gcig yin pa'i dbang du byas te / gzhung 'di'i mtshan la / dmigs pa brtag pa zhes ma btags par / yul brtag pa'am don brtag pa zhes btags na gzhung don 'grel brjod byed stangs la khyad par 'gro 'am mi 'gro ce na /

skabs 'dir rtog pa'i blo'i yul la dpyad pa ma yin par / mngon sum gyi blo rnams kyis yul gzugs sgra dri ro reg bya sogs dmigs rkyen byas nas 'dzin pa'i tshe rang rang gi yul gyi rnam pa blo la gtad pa'i sgo nas myong dgos tshul la dpyad pa'i gzhung yin zhing / rtog blo yul la 'jug pa'i rnam gzhag ma yin pas / dmigs pa brtag pa zhes mtshan bzhag na legs / yul brtag pa zhes gzhung mtshan du bzhag na khyab che drags pa'i skyon yod de / yul ni rtog pa lta bu blo thams cad la yod pa'i phyir ro //

sangs rgyas dang byang chub sems dpa' thams cad la phyag 'tshal lo // zhes bya ba ni lo tsā ba'i 'gyur phyag mdzad pa'i tshig go /

spyi bshad /

sangs rgyas bcom ldan 'das kyis chos kyi 'khor lo rim pa gsum bskor ba las / dang po bden bzhi'i chos 'khor ni phyi don yod pa lta bur mdzad nas gsungs la / de yang ston pa sangs rgyas kyis gtso bor nyan thos sde gnyis la dgongs nas chos 'khor dang po'i skabs 'jig rten tshang mas gzugs sgra sogs phyi rol du mngon sum du mthong rgyu yod pa ltar snang bar dgongs nas phyi rol don du grub pa gsungs pa las / de dag gis mthong tshul ltar gnas lugs la yod med sogs kyi dpyad pa ma mdzad par snang / de ltar yang tshad ma rnam 'grel le'u gsum pa las /

des de nyid don btang snyoms can //
glang chen gzigs stangs nyid mdzad nas //
'jig rten thugs ni 'ba' zhig gis //
phyi rol dpyod la 'jug par mdzad //

ces gsungs pa ltar / sangs rgyas kyis bden bzhi'i chos 'khor bstan skabs gzugs sogs phyi rol don du ma grub pa la sogs don la gnas shing / de ltar gzigs kyang re zhig btang snyoms su bzhag nas ma gsungs la / dper na glang po che sa cha gcig nas gzhan la bskyod skabs lam g.yas g.yon la yod pa'i dngos rdzas mang po mngon sum gyi spyod yul du 'gyur kyang / ma mthong ba ltar byas nas rang gi 'dod pa'i phyogs su bskyod pa bzhin du / sangs rgyas kyis kyang phyi rol don du ma grub pa gzigs kyang de ltar ma gzigs pa ltar byas nas 'jig rten pa'i bsam blo'i nang phyi rol don du grub par mthong ba ltar de gzhir bzhag byas nas de ltar gdul bya la chos bstan par mdzad shing /

ston pa sangs rgyas kyis 'khor lo dang po'i skabs su chos rnams phyi rol don du snang ba ltar du med pa sogs 'grel bshad ma gsungs pas rgyu mtshan gyis / 'khor lo dang po'i gdul bya kha cig nas chos rnams phyi rol don du yod do dang / rang gi mtshan nyid kyis yod pa don la gnas pa de ltar 'khor lo dang po'i dgongs pa yin no snyam pa'i bsam tshul byung /

gzhan yang / 'khor lo dang po'i skabs gzugs sgra dri ro reg bya bcas yul lnga rang gi dbang po'i blo la shar ba'i tshe rang gis rnam pa gtad pa'i sgo nas rnam par shes pa skyed tshul yang gsungs la / de yang / gzugs kyi dmigs rkyen dang / mig dbang gi bdag rkyen / yid shes skad cig snga ma de ma thag rkyen byas nas mig gi rnam par shes pa skyes zhes gsungs pas / mdor na / phyi rol gyi yul de rgyu dang / mig gi rnam shes de 'bras bur gsungs pas / phyi don yod pa bstan no // des na 'khor lo dang po'i ched du bya ba'i gdul bya phyi don yod par smra ba'i don smra gnyis sam nyan thos sde gnyis ste bye brag smra ba dang mdo sde ba rnams rjes su gzung ba'i ched du phyi don yod par gsungs so //

'o na phyi don bzhed pa'i lugs la dmigs rkyen ces pa'i dmigs pa'i mtshan nyid gang yin nam zhe na /

dmigs pa ni dmigs rkyen byas nas myong ba dang / gzung don du byas nas myong ba'i don no / dmigs pa'am gzung don ni phyi rol don du grub la / de mig sogs dbang po rnams kyis mngon sum gyi spyod yul yin no //

'o na mig sogs dbang po'i mngon sum rnams kyis phyi don mngon sum du myong ba'i rgyu mtshan gang yod dam zhe na / mdo sde pa ltar na / phyi rol don du grub tshul 'di ltar te / sngon po phyi rol na yod la / de'i rnam pa mig shes la tshur gtad pa'i sgo nas dmigs rkyen byed pas sngon 'dzin mig shes kyis sngon po gzung don du byed pa'i sgo nas myong zhes 'dod do //

de la sems tsam pas mdo sde par phyi don yod pa'i rgyu mtshan gang yod dam / yang na phyi rol gzung don du byed tshul ji ltar yin zhes dris pas lan du / mdo sde bas tshad ma rnam 'grel las / de 'dra ba dang de las byung // gal te myong ba'i mtshan nyid yin //

zhes byung ba bzhin /

dmigs rkyen gzugs sgra dri ro reg bya rnams rang rang gi rnam pa gtad nas dbang mngon gyi blo de yul de'i rnam pa can du skyes pas de las byung zhes dang / de dang 'dra zhes pa ni shes pa de yul de dag gi rnam pa can du skyes pas na / shes pa de yul de dang 'dra ba yin no zhes so //

gung thang gis dmigs brtag 'grel par gzhan gyi dmigs pa'i mtshan nyid skyes 'dra ba zhes bkod pa bzhin mdo sde ba'i lugs la / mdor na yul can de yul de las skyes shing / yul can la yul gyi rnam pa shar bas de dang 'dra ba'i khyad chos gnyis ldan gyi sgo nas phyi don gyis nang shes pa'i dmigs rkyen byed do zhes smra bar byed do // de ni dmigs pa dmigs rkyen du byas nas myong ba'i don dang / dmigs pa mngon sum gyis gzung don du byas nas myong ba'i don yang yin no // bstan dar lha rams pas kyang dmigs rkyen gi mtshan nyid 'di ltar 'jog ste /

> sngon po la sogs pa'i don gang zhig rang snang ba ste rang gi bdag nyid dam rang dang 'dra ba'i rnam par rig pa skyed par byed pa de ni dmigs rkyen ces pa'i dmigs pa yin par rigs te / de ltar de ni bstan bcos las / don gang zhig sems dang sems las byung ba rnams skye ba'i rgyu mtshan yang yin la de rnams skyes na don de nyams su myong ba'i tha snyad 'dogs par yang byed pa de ni dmigs pa yin no / zhes dbang shes gang gi dmigs rkyen yin na dbang shes de la rang 'dra'i rnam pa shar ba dang dbang shes de skye ba'i rkyen nyid du bshad pas so //

zhes gsungs so // bye brag smra ba'i lugs la ni / phyi don yod / phyi don blo'i dmigs rkyen yang yin / 'on kyang phyi don de dbang shes kyis mngon sum gyis spyod yul yin pas / blo des yul la thad kar 'jug pa ma gtogs / yul de yul can la rnam pa tshur shar pa'i sgo nas dmigs rkyen byed par mi 'dod pas / sngon 'dzin mig shes yul de dag gi rnam pa can du mi skye bas na / shes pa de yul de dang 'dra ba'i khyad chos tshang mi dgos so //

sems tsam pa'i lugs ltar na / sngon po la sogs pa'i phyi don yod pa lta bur snang yang / don la de dag thams cad nang sngon 'dzin mig shes sogs kyis bzhag pa'i kun gzhi'i steng gi bag chags sad pa las byung ba 'ba' zhig yin /

bag chags sad tshul la'ang rnam pa mi 'dra ba gnyis yod pa las / rmi lam gyi shes pa bzhin du / bag chags gi cha kha gcig shes pa'i ngo bor skyed pa'i tshul du sad pa dang / cha shas gcig yul gyi rnam pa'i ngo bor skyed pa'i sgo nas sad pa'i rgyu mtshan de gnyis kyi phyir na / sngon 'dzin mig shes dang sngon po'i rnam pa gnyis nang shes pa'i steng gi bag chags sad pa kho na las myong ba rigs pas grub bo //

mthong tshul la yul can gyis bzhag pa min par / yul gyis sgo nas tshur rnam pa gtad pa lta bur mthong yang / don dngos la rmi lam lta bur ste / phyi rol yul steng nas med bzhin du kun gzhi'i steng gi bag chags sad stobs kyis dbang gis rmi lam gyi shes pa'i ngor yul sna tshogs snang ba bzhin no / rmi lam gyi shes pa la yul yid du 'ong ba dang / yid du mi 'ong dang / bde ba dang sdug bsngal / skye rga na 'chi la sogs pa'i rnam pa sna tshogs myong skabs / thams cad nang shes pa'i steng na 'dug kyang phyi rol na yod pa lta bur mthong ba bzhin no //

gzhung don dngos 'chad pa la sa bcad gnyis las /

dang po / dmigs pa phyi don yin par bzhed pa'i dngos smra ba don smra gnyis kyi 'dod pa dgag pa dang /

gnyis pa dmigs pa nang na yod par bsgrub pa'i sems tsam pa'i rang lugs gzhag pa gnyis las /

dmigs pa phyi don yin par bzhed pa'i dngos smra ba'i 'dod pa dgag pa ni /

dang po dmigs pa phyi don yin par bzhed pa'i dngos smra ba'i 'dod pa dgag pa la gsum /

dang po / rdul phra rab gzung don yin pa dgag pa dang /

gnyis pa / rags pa gzung don yin pa dgag pa dang /

gsum pa / rdul 'dus pa'i rnam pa gzung don yin pa dgag pa'o //

dang po / rdul phra rab gzung don yin pa dgag pa ni /

gang dag zhes pas tshig gis nang pa'i grub mtha' smra ba'i khongs nas 'ga' shas te / phyi rol don du grub par bzhed pa'i bye brag smra ba dang mdo sde pa ste nyan thos sde gnyis rnams zur bton mdzad la / de gnyis ni 'khor lo dang por phyi don gang gi ched du gsungs pa'i gdul bya yin pa'i phyir ro // grub mtha' smra ba de dag ni mig dang rna ba dang sna la sogs pa'i rnam par shes pa rnams kyi dmigs pa ni phyi rol gyi don yin par 'dod la / sems tsam pas phyi rol don du grub ba 'gog cing / 'gog byed kyi rigs pa'ang gtso bo bzhi bkod srol 'dug pas / de dag ni /

(1) slob dpon thogs med kyi theg bsdus su rmi lam dang gzugs brnyan la sogs pa'i rigs pa /
(2) slob dpon dbyig gnyen gyi nyi shu par rdul phran cha med 'gog byed kyi rigs pa /
(3) slob dpon chos grags kyi tshad ma rnam 'grel las (gong du bshad pa ltar) gzugs 'dzin gyi mtshan nyid skye la 'dra ba 'gog byed kyi rigs pa /
(4) slob dpon phyogs glang gi dmigs pa brtag pa'i 'grel par rdul 'dus pa dang phra rab gzung don yin par 'gog byed kyi rigs pa bcas so //

dmigs brtag gzhung 'dir bye mdo sde gnyis ka'i dmigs rkyen bkag mod kyang / mdo sde pas gzugs 'dzin mig shes lta bu gzugs dmigs rkyen du byas nas myong ba'i mtshan nyid la tshad ma rnam 'grel las / de 'dra ba dang de las skye // gal te myong ba'i mtshan nyid yin // zhes pa'i 'dod pa la dgag pa gtso bor byas yod / dgag pa de yang gung thang gis 'grel par gsungs pa bzhin dpe'i sgo nas khyab pa 'gog pa'o //

mdo sde pas dmigs rkyen phyi don yod par sgrub pa'i rigs pa ni 'di ltar / gzugs 'dzin mig shes chos can / khyod kyis gzugs dmigs rkyen du byas nas myong ba dang gzung don du byas nas myong ba yin te / gzugs 'dzin mig shes gzugs de las skyes shing / gzugs 'dzin mig shes kyis gzugs 'dzin pa'i tshe shes pa de la gzugs kyi rnam pa shar ba'i sgo nas 'dzin pas de dang 'dra ba yin pa'i phyir / dper na sngon 'dzin mig shes sngon po las skyes zhing sngon po'i rnam pa can du skyes pas de dang 'dra ba bzhin no // zhes bkod do //

mdo sde pa'i dmigs pa phyi don bsgrub pa'i rigs pa sems tsam pas 'gog skabs gung thang gi gsungs ltar na phyogs chos ma grub pa'i skyon brjod pas sgo nas bkag go / 'gog tshul yang / gzugs 'dzin mig shes kyis gzugs dmigs rkyen dang gzung don du byas nas myong ba re zhig kho bo cag 'dod mod / 'ong kyang mdo sde pa khyod kyis gzugs 'dzin mig shes la dmigs rkyen phyi rol gyi gzugs yod par sgrub byed kyi rigs pa de rigs pa yang dag dang rtags yang dag ma yin te / rtags yang dag gi mtshan nyid tshul gsum yin pa ma tshang ba'i phyir / tshul gsum tshang na phyogs chos dang rjes khyab ldog khyab gsum tshang dgos pa las khyod kyi rtags de la phyogs chos ma grub ste / phyogs chos zhes pa'i phyogs rtsod gzhi gzugs 'dzin mig shes la chos rtags gzugs las skyes ba med cing / gzugs des gzugs 'dzin mig shes de la tshur rnam pa ltas te de dang 'dra ba'i rnam pa shar ba'ang med pa'i phyir / zhes dgag go /

phyogs chos 'gog pa de'ang rgyas par bshad phyir slob dpon phyogs glang gis 'dri ba 'di ltar / phyi don dmigs pa bzhed pa bye brag smra dang mdo sde ba de dag ni rdul phra rab dag dbang shes de'i rgyu yin pa'i phyir dmigs pa yin par 'dod dam / yang na rdul phra rab 'dus pa de dbang shes der snang ba'i shes pa skye ba'i phyir dmigs pa yin par rtog grang na ste 'dod dam /

de gnyis gang yang 'dod mi rigs te / slob dpon phyogs glang gis / de la re zhig rdul phra rab dag dbang shes skye ba'i rgyu yin pa'i dbang du btang na yang de'i dmigs rkyen du mi rung / de bzhin phra rab 'dus pa'i rnam pa dag dbang shes la snang ba'i dbang du btang na yang de'i dmigs rkyen du mi rung ngo zhes gsungs so //

dbang po rnam par rig pa'i rgyu //
phra rab rdul dag yin mod kyi //
der mi snang phyir de yul ni //
rdul phran ma yin dbang po bzhin // (1abcd)

mig rna sna'i dbang po sogs kyi rnam par rig pa'am rnam par shes pa rnams bskyed par byed pa'i rgyu rdul phra rab ches shin tu chung ba mthar thug pa dag yin pa'i dbang du byas mod kyang / rdul phra rab dag dbang shes der tshur rnam pa gtad pa'i sgo nas snang dgos pa gang zhig la mi snang ba'i phyir dang /

dbang shes des yul de dag rang gi rnam pa dang 'dra ba'i sgo nas 'dzin dgos pa gang zhig la mi 'dzin pa'i phyir na / dbang po'i rnam par shes pa dag gi dmigs pa'i yul ni rdul phran ma yin te / yin na rdul phran gyi rnam pa dbang shes la gtad pa'i sgo nas 'dzin cing / yul de dang 'dra ba'i nges shes 'dren dgos pa gang zhig rdul phran dmigs nas de 'dra ba'i nges shes mi 'dren pa'i phyir / dper na mig gi dbang po de mig shes skye ba'i rgyu tsam yin kyang mig shes de la rnam par gtad pa'i sgo nas mi snang ba bzhin no //

skabs 'dir rdul phra rab dbang shes kyi rgyu yin mod kyi zhes pa dang rgyu nyid yin du zin kyang zhes pa bstan dar lha rams pa'i dmigs brtag 'grel pa ltar na zhes gsungs pas re zhig brtag pa mtha' bzung gis bshad pa yin gyi / sems tsam pa rang lugs la rdul phra rags gang yang khas mi len te / ces rgyal tshab rje'i rnam 'grel rnam bshad thar lam gsal byed dang / mkhas grub rje'i ṭika chen rigs pa'i rgya mtsho'i lung 'dren byas te / gsal bshad mdzad /

'o na sems tsam pas gzugs khas len nam zhe na / bstan dar lha ram pa ltar na gang yang mno bsam mi gtong ba dag gis khas len mod ces chags thogs med par smra mod / rje rin po ches dka' gnas su mdzad 'dug pas ci 'dod du smra nus pa zhig min par sems so //

bstan dar lha ram pas rje rin po ches dbu ma'i rnam bshad du / theg bsdus dang gtan la dbab pa'i bsdu pa dang rten 'brel mdo 'grel gyi lung shes byed du drangs nas sems tsam pas gzugs khas len ces gsungs pa'i mthar / sems tsam pa'i lugs 'di la yang phyi rol bkag na gzugs sogs kyang med par 'gro zhing / gzugs sogs bzhag na phyi rol kyang bzhag dgos par mthong 'dug pa'i phyir ro //

mdor na / sems tsam pa'i lugs la mkhas pa kha cig gis gzugs med ces 'dod la / kha cig gis gzugs med na sems tsam la rten 'brel yan lag bcu gnyis kyi bzhi ba ming gzugs kyang med par thal lo / de med na / dbang po lnga dang / gzugs sogs don lnga med par thal ba dang / sangs rgyas kyi gzugs sku yang med par thal ba sogs kyis skyon du ma 'jug pas nges par du sems tsam pa'i lugs la'ang gzugs yod ces 'dod dgos so zhes so // gzugs 'dod pa tsam gyis phyi rol gyi gzugs yod ces 'dod pa'i khyab pa mi dgos so // zhes khyad par phye nas grub mtha' smras so //

mkhas pa kha cig ni / sems tsam lugs la gzugs yod ces 'dod phyin chad phyi rol gyi gzugs yod ces dngos su ma brjod kyang shugs la khas blangs song pa'i phyir ro // zhes 'dod /

spyir sems tsam pa'i gzhung lugs nas phyi don gyi gzugs med ces gsungs srol yod pa ma gtogs gzugs med ces gsungs srol med / sems tsam par gzugs yod phyi rol don du grub ba'i gzugs med ces yongs su grags / gang ltar yang / sems tsam lugs la gzugs yod dang med dka' gnas su mdzad nas gnad don de la zhib 'jug gis dpyad pa 'jug mkhan ma byung ba lta bur snang bas zhib mor dpyod dgos so //

gang ltar yang / slob dpon phyogs glang gi lugs la / rdul phran ni dbang shes rnams kyi yul ma yin te / yul zhes bya ba ni shes pa la tshur rnam par gtad nas shes pa de yul rang gi rnam par can du skye dgos pa gang zhig yul sngon po dang ser po sogs ci 'dra yod pa gang gis rang gi ngo bo nges par 'dzin pa'i sgo nas rtogs dgos pa yin te shes pa de dmigs rkyen yul de'i rnam par skye ba'i phyir ro //

rdul phra mo dag gi ni nyan thos sde gnyis kyis 'dod pa bzhin dbang po'i shes pa de'i re zhig rgyu nyid yin du zin pa'i dbang du btang na yang / rdul phran gyis rnam pa gtad nas dbang shes kyis 'dzin pa'am nyams su myong ba'i yul gyi mtshan nyid de lta bu tshang ba zhig ma yin te / rnam pa gtad mi nus pa'i phyir / mig gi dbang po sogs mig shes skye ba'i rgyu yin pa'i dbang du btang yang mig shes la rnam ba gtad pa'i sgo nas dmigs rkyen mi nus pa bzhin no // de ltar na zhig rdul phra mo dag dbang shes rnams kyi dmigs pa ma yin no //

gung thang ltar na rdul phran ni dmigs pa'i nges par 'dzin pa'i yul ma yin te / de rgyu tsam yin yang mi snang ba'i phyir dang de'i sgo nas rnam par skyed pa'i rgyu yang ma yin pas don gyis rtags gnyis ka nyams te dmigs par mi rung zhes gsungs so //

gnyis pa / rags pa gzung don yin pa dgag pa /

gung thang ltar byas na rdul re re bsal na 'dus pa mi snang bar bshad pa'i 'os med kyi rigs pas 'dus pa dmigs pa yin par dgag go / slob dpon gis 'dus pa ni der snang ba nyid yin du zin kyang zhes gsungs don ni bstan dar lha rams pa ltar byas na 'dus pa ni re zhig brtag pa mtha' bzung gis shes par snang ba nyid yin du zin kyang de'i rgyu ma yin pas / zhes gsungs pas rdul phran kho rang blo la mi snang ba ma zad rdul phran 'dus pa'ang sems tsam rang lugs la shes par mi snang ba bzhed pas rgyu mtshan gyis 'dir brtag pa mtha' bzung gi dbang du byas nas 'dus pa shes par snang ba'i tshul byas par zad do //

> **gang ltar snang de de las min //**
> **rdzas su med phyir zla gnyis bzhin //** (2ab)

rdul phra rab dang mi 'dra bar 'dus pa gang dag phyi rol don du grub pa ltar mig shes sogs la 'dus pa'i rnam pa mi 'dra ba du ma snang ba yod kyang / nang gi bag chags sad ba las snang ba yin pas /

dbang shes de rnams phyi'i yul tshogs pa 'dus pa de las rnam pa gtad pa'i sgo nas skyes pa min te / 'dus pa de dbang shes bskyed pa'i nus can gyi rgyu ma yin pa'i phyir te / 'dus pa ni dngos med rdzas su grub pa med pa'i phyir zla gcig la zla gnyis 'dzin pa'i mig shes bzhin no // zla gnyis 'dzin pa'i mig shes yod kyang de bskyed byed kyi rgyu zla gnyis ma yin te / zla gnyis rdzas su med pa'i phyir te gzhi ma grub pa'i phyir ro //

gung thang gis bzhed pa la / 'dus pa blo la snang zhes pa de 'dis chos can phyogs snga'i zhe la bzhag pa'i steng nas yin la / dpe la sbyor tshul yang /

> kha cig tu zla gnyis snang la de'ang zla ba gnyis bas skyed du med pa'i phyir dbang po nyams pa kho nas yin pa ltar phyi rol bsags pa'i 'dus pa ltar snang ba'ang de la de bskyed pa'i nus pa'i rjas yod pa ma yin yang nang du yid bdag lta'i bag chags kyis nyams pa las yin te dpe 'di ni 'gal ba spong ba la'ang nus pa can no //

skabs 'dir 'dus pa dang bsags pa gnyis la khyad par ji yod dam / sems tsam pas de gnyis phyi don yin par bkag pa'i tshe 'gog byed kyi rigs pa gcig mtshungs yin nam yang na de gnyis rigs pa mi 'dra bas sgo nas bkag ce na /

sems tsam pas 'dus rdul dang bsags rdul gnyis la dbye ba gzhag pa ma mthong la / phyi don bzhed pa'i rang rgyud pa'i slob dpon legs ldan 'byed kyis sems tsam slob dpon phyogs glang gis / de mi snang phyir de yul ni // zhes dang / rdzas su med phyir zla gnyis bzhin // zhes pa'i lan du rtog ge 'bar ba las /

> rdul phra rab bsags pa ni dmigs pa yin par dam bcas pas khyod kyis 'dus pa dmigs pa ma yin par 'gog pa ni kho bo cag la gnod pa med do // bsags pa dang 'dus pa gnyis la khyad par ci yod ce na / rdul phra rab rigs mthun pa dag ni gzhi gcig la brten pa ni tshogs pa zhes bya'o // glang po che dang rta la sogs pa dang / skyer pa dang seng ldeng la sogs pa'i rigs mi mthun pa gzhi tha dad pa 'dus pa la dmag dang nags tshal la sogs par gdags pa ni 'dus pa zhes bya'o //

zhes gsungs so // gong gsal gyi don cung zad spros na slob dpon legs ldan 'byed kyis dbu ma snying po las /

> de la gal te pha rol po //
> bsags pa min pa'i gzugs sems kyis //
> spyod yul min par sgrub byed na //
> der ni grub pa nyid sgrub 'gyur //

zhes pa'i don 'grel pa na / rtog ge 'bar ba las /

> gal te pha rol po dag bsags pa ma yin pa'i gzugs rdul phra rab gcig pu sems kyi spyod yul nyid ma yin par sgrub par byed na / phyogs snga ma de grub pa nyid sgrub par 'gyur te / kho bo cag kyang de ltar 'dod pa'i phyir ro //

zhes rdul 'dus pa rdzas su med pas dbang po'i shes pa'i dmigs rkyen du mi 'dod la / yang de nyid las /

> ci ste bsags pa'i gzugs la ni /
> gtan tshigs ma grub nyid 'gyur te //
> gzugs gzhan dag gi bsags pa ni //
> der snang blo ni skye phyir ro //

zhes pa'i don 'grel pa na /

> ci ste rdul phra rab rigs mthun pa bsags pa'i phyogs su byas nas de la rdzas su yod pa ma yin pa nyid gtan tshigs su brjod na ni / de lta na gtan tshigs gang yang rung ba la ma grub par 'gyur te / ci'i phyir zhe na / 'di ltar rdul phra rab mthun pa'i gzugs gzhan dag gis de la bsags shing kun sbyar ba na de yul gyi dngos por khas blangs shing / der snang ba'i blo rdul phran 'dus pa'i rnam par skye ba'i phyir ro // kho bo cag ni rdul phra rab rigs mthun pa'i bsags pa bum pa la sogs pa nyid dang phra rab kyang kun rdzob pa'i rdzas su 'dod do //

zhes gsungs so // de dag gi don gsal bar bsdus te rje tsong kha pas drang nges legs bshad snying po las /

> gzugs sgra la sogs pa bsags pa'i skabs su ni rdul phra rab re res kyang dbang po'i shes pa'i dmigs rkyen byed pas de dag de la mi snang ba ma yin no // dmag dang nags tshal la sogs pa rigs tha dad la brten pa rnams ni 'dus pa yin la / de rdzas su med kyang brten gcig la brten pa'i rigs mthun pa'i phra rab rnams ni bsags pa yin zhing de bzhin du bum pa la yang yin pas de ni rdzas su yod do //

zhes gsungs / mngon pa mdzod las bye brag smra ba sogs kyis 'dod pa bshad pa'i skabs / rdul ches phra mo rnams kyang nyung mthar chos brgyad kyi bdag nyid can du 'dod cing rdul de dag la bsags rdul zhes dang / bsags rdul re re'i nang na yod pa'i sa chu me rlung byung ba bzhi dang / gzugs sgra dri ro reg bya ste 'byung 'gyur lnga bcas brgyad po re re la rdzas rdul zhes khyad par byed /

rdul phran mi 'dra ba gnyis las / rdzas rdul chung ba dang bsags rdul chi ba yod dgos tshod lta bu yin kyang / byed smras rang lugs la / rdzas rdul dang bsags rdul gnyis che chung gi khyad par med par 'dod / dper na bye ma phor ba gang la chu phor gang blug pa'i tshe phor pa'i nang bongs tshod che ru mi 'gro ba bzhin / bsags rdul re re'i nang rdzas rdul brgyad brgyad yod kyang rdzas rdul las bsags rdul kyi bongs tshad che ba med ces 'dod do //

gang ltar sems tsam pas phyi don dgag pa'i tshe 'dus pa dang bsags pa gnyis kar phyi rol na yod pa dgag dgos la / de gnyis 'gog byed kyi rigs pa'ang gcigs mtshungs ma gtogs rigs pa mi 'dra ba gnyis yod pa mi snang / sems tsam pa'i lugs la 'dus rdul dang bsags rdul gang yang rung gnyis kar rtog brtag tsam las rdzas su grub pa min pas 'dus byas ma yin / dngos po'ang ma yin / zhes 'dod do //

gzugs sgra dri ro la sogs pa don gang zhig rang dang rang rnam par gtad pa'i sgo nas snang ba'i rnam par rig pa ste mig shes sna shes la sogs pa'i dbang shes bskyed pa de ni dmigs pa yin par rigs te 'di ltar don de ni mig gi dbang shes la sogs pa rnam par gtad pa'i sgo nas skye ba'i rkyen nyid du bshad pas so //

zla gcig zla gnyis su 'dzin pa'i mig shes la dbang po 'khrul bas rkyen gyis yul gyi gnas tshul ji lta ba 'dzin pa'i shes pa bskyed pa'i cha rkyen ma tshang ba'i phyir zla ba gnyis mthong ba ni mig shes der snang ba nyid yin du zin kyang zla gcig zla gnyis su 'dzin pa'i mig shes de'i dmigs rkyen gyi yul ma yin te zla gnyis yod pa ma yin te gzhi ma grub pa'i phyir ro // dpe de bzhin du 'dus pa de yang rdzas su yod pa ma yin pa nyid kyis dbang shes bskyed pa'i rgyu ma yin pa'i phyir dmigs pa ma yin no //

'dir rdul phra rab dang 'dus pa dag dbang shes kyi yul ma yin par bshad pa ni snang yul lam sgro 'dogs chod pa'i yul la dgongs shing zhes bstan dar lha rams pas gsungs pa bzhin / yul la sna tshogs yod pas shugs rtogs la sgro 'dogs ma chod pa sogs min par / skabs 'dir yul la nges par snang yul la sgro 'dogs chod pa'i yul yin dgos te / yul gis rnam pa gtad nus shig dang dngos su rtogs bya'i yul zhig dgos pas so /

skabs 'dir sngon 'dzin mig shes kyis sngon po bzung zhes pa'i don yang sngon 'dzin mig shes sngon po dang 'dra ba'am sngon 'dzin mig shes la sngon po'i rnam pa gtad nas de sngon po'i rnam pa can yin pas rgyu mtshan gyis sngon po dang 'dra ba tsam la byed pa ma gtogs /

> de la lag pas bum pa gzung ba lta bu 'dzin pa'i mtshan nyid kyi byed pa 'ga' yang med de / dper na / pha dang 'dra ba'i bu la pha'i gzugs 'dzin pa zhes brjod kyang de la bu 'dzin byed dang pha'i gzugs gzung byar gyur pa 'ga' yang med pa bzhin no //

kha cig gis zla gcig zla gnyis 'dzin pa'i blo la mtshon na / yul dang / don / dmigs pa bcas kyi rnam gzhag ji ltar 'jog gam zhe na /
zla gnyis 'dzin pa'i blo'i dmigs pa ni zla ba gcig yin kyang blo de'i ngor zla ba gcig ji bzhin dmigs pa med / blo de'i 'dzin pa'i yul lam don ni zla gnyis la 'jug pas zla gcig ma yin /

yang na mdo sde pa'i lugs la yul dang dmigs pa gnyis tha dad yin pa'i rgyu mtshan gis shes pa la yang log gi khyad par gzhag sla / shes pa'i yul la phyi rol gyi gzugs sgra dri ro sogs dang / dmigs pa la shes pa de nyid kyi snang ba'i yul gyi rnam pa de 'jog go / zla ba gnyis 'dzin gyi shes pa log shes yin te / shes pa de'i dmigs pa zla ba gcig las med kyang de'i yul la zla ba gnyis yod par snang ba'i phyir / zla ba gcig 'dzin gyi blo yang dag pa yin te / dmigs pa la zla ba gcig snang ba bzhin yul la'ang zla ba gcig yin pa'i phyir ro zhe na / 'on kyang slob dpon phyogs glang gi lugs la dmigs pa dang yul gnyis tha dad mi 'jog par gnyis kar shes pa'i steng gi bag chags yin par bzhag pa'i rgyu mtshan gyis shes pa la yang log gi khyad par gzhag dka' ba lta bur snang bas lugs 'di la zla ba gnyis 'dzin gyi shes pa log shes yin pa dang / zla ba gcig 'dzin gyi blo yang dag pa yin pa'i khyad par gang la brten nas 'jog dgos sam zhe na /

phyi don yod med gang yang rung / zla ba gcig gis mthong ba bzhin bya ba byed nus shing zla gnyis kyis mthong ba bzhin bya ba byed mi nus su med pa'i phyir na / zla gcig 'dzin pa'i shes pa yang dag pa dang zla gnyis 'dzin pa'i shes pa log pa yin par shes nus so // dper na / dbu ma pa'i lugs la yang yul rang ngos nas ma grub na yul de gang zhig yin zhes 'dri ba'i tshe / dbu ma pas rang bzhin gyis ma grub pa la'ang don byed nus pa yod ces pa'i lan gtab pa dang 'dra ba'o //

yin na yang gong gi rgyu mtshan de phyi don bzhed pa'i dbu ma pa la 'thad kyang phyi don mi bzhed pa'i phyogs glang gi lugs la mi 'thad / phyogs glang gi lugs la zla gnyis 'dzin byed kyi shes pa yod phyin chad / shes pa de'i rgyu zla gnyis yin / shes pa de la shar ba'i rnam pa'ang zla gnyis de yin pa'i phyir / zla gnyis la dmigs pa'i mtshan nyid gnyis kar ldan pas phyir na / phyogs glang gis mdo sde par zla gnyis 'dzin pa'i shes pa de skyon can nam log shes yin pa'i lan ji ltar mdzad dam zhe na /

phyogs glang gi lugs la blo la yang log gi khyad par de'ang bag chags kyi sgo nas 'jog dgos la / bag chags la'ang rigs mi 'dra ba gnyis su dbye nas / kha cig brtan pa'i bag chags dang kha cig mi brtan pa'i bag chags / blo don mthun dang bya ba byed nus pa'i bag chags la brtan pa'i bag chags ces dang blo don mi mthun dang bya ba byed mi nus pa'i bag chags la mi brtan pa'i bag chags ces dbye bar mdzad / brtan pa'i bag chags la brten nas yang dag pa'i blo skyes / mi brtan pa'i bag chags la brten nas blo log pa rnams skyes zhis 'grel brjod byed do //

sems tsam pa'i lugs la phyi don med kyang bag chags kho na'i dbang gis bya ba byed nus pa dang bya ba byed mi nus pa'i rnam gzhag nges par du 'jog dgos pas zla gcig don byed nus pa dang zla gnyis don byed mi nus par 'jog nus /

de bzhin blo la'ang phyin ci log pa dang phyin ci ma log pa'i khyad par zhig nges can du 'jog dgos pas zla gcig 'dzin pa'i blo yang dag dang zla gcig zla gnyis su 'dzin pa'i blo phyin ci log par yin par 'jog nus /

de bas bstan dar lha rams pas kyang / zla ba gcig zla ba gnyis yin pa rdzas su ma grub kyang zla ba gcig rdzas su grub zer dgos te / zla ba gcig dngos po yin pa'i phyir te / zla ba gcig zla ba gnyis su snang ba'i dbang shes kyi dmigs rkyen yin pa'i phyir / rtags sde bdun rigs rgyan gnyis kas grub / des na zla ba gnyis su snang ba'i dbang shes la zla ba gcig gi rnam pa gtad kyang ji bzhin ma gtad do //

zhes gsungs / de bzhin sems tsam pa'i lugs la de dang de dngos gnas yin pa dang gzhan dang gzhan dngos gnas ma yin pa'i rnam gzhag mi 'khrul ba zhig 'jog thub dgos te / de 'dra'i rnam gzhag 'jog mi thub na dngos po'i gnas lugs gtan la 'bebs mi nus par thal ba dang / gnas lugs gtan la 'bebs byed kyi rigs pa'ang med par thal ba sogs kyis skyon du ma 'jug go /

yang na phyogs glang gi lugs la dmigs pa dang yul gnyis ngo bo gcig yin pa'i rgyu mtshan gyis / zla gnyis 'dzin byed kyi blo'i ngor yul dang dmigs rkyen gnyis kar zla gnyis de nyid yin la / zla gnyis blo de skyed byed kyi rgyu yin cing / blo de yang zla gnyis kyi rnam pa skyed byed kyi rgyu yin pa'i phyir na / des na zla gnyis med pa'i chos yin bzhin du lugs de la don byed nus pa lta bu 'dug pas zla gnyis 'dzin pa'i blo phyin ci log pa ji ltar yin / ci'i phyir yang dag pa'i blo ma yin / lugs de la blo la don byed nus dang mi nus pa'i khyad par blo'i de'i dmigs pa dang yul gnyis mthun mi mthun gyis sgo nas 'jog mi nus / de med pas blo la yang log khyad par 'byed byed kyi rnam gzhag gang yin gsal po med pa lta bu 'dug ce na /

zla ba gcig mthong ba ltar zla gcig gis don byed nus / zla ba gcig zla gnyis dang zla ba brgya sogs su mthong ba ltar don byed mi nus / gnad don de 'gro ba rigs drug so sos dngos po la lta tshul dang myong tshul la gzhigs na gsal po red / spyir gzugs sgra sogs sems can rnams kyi 'tsho rten nam longs spyod yin / longs spyod de dag la brten nas tshor ba bde sdug 'dra min myong / tshor ba bde sdug las chags sdang sogs kyi blo sna tshogs byung /

'dod pa'i dngos po yin rung mi 'dod pa'i dngos po yin rung chu mo gangga lta bur chos gcig la mtshon na / 'gro ba rigs drug gis lta ba'i tshe / mthong tshul mi 'dra ba sna mang yod / mis chu mthong / lhas bdud rtsi / sems can chu phag dang nya lta bus sdod gnas kyi tshul du longs su spyad / chu longs su spyod rgyu'i las med mkhan gyi rigs yi dwags lta bus snag khrag mthong ba'am yang na gang yang mi mthong /

de bzhin sems can kha cig la rang rang gis las kyis mthus zla ba'i 'od kyang mes 'tshig pa lta bus tsha ngar che ba dang / nyi ma'i 'od kyang 'khyag roms ltar grang ngar can bzod mi thub pa'i myong ba yong / gzhan yang nga tsho mi'i lus la nad na tsha dmigs bsal zhig yod na / gnam gshis dro po dang gos ga tshod gyon yang grang ngar gyis 'dar ba dang / skabs 'gar gnam gshis grang mo dang lus la gyon chas gcig kyang ma gyon yang tsha bas 'tshig pa lta bu yong ngo //

nam mkha' mtha' yas kyi lhas nam mkha' kho nar mthong ba las thogs reg yod pa'i chos gtan nas mi gzigs / phag pa lta bu yin na mi gtsang ba'i bsti gnas kho na la skyid snang 'byung zhing sa gtsang ma rgyal khang lta bur la bzhag na btson bcug byas pa ltar sdug bsngal gyi rgyur 'gro ba gsal po red / de bzhin du mi gsum gyis gang zag gzhan zhig la bltas pa'i tshe / mthong snang mi 'dra ba gsum 'byung ste / gnyen gyi phyogs la 'dod pa dang / dgra'i ngor la mi 'dod pa dang / bar ma'i ngor la bar ma mthong /

chos gcig la myong tshor 'dra min de dag yong dgos pa'i rgyu mtshan yang / sems can rang rang gi blo'i steng gi bag chags sad stobs las 'byung ba ma gtogs / phyi rol yul nyi ma dang zla ba lta bu kho rang nas 'byung ba min / gal te phyi rol yul ngos nas yin na ni / skye bo kun la myong tshor dang mthong snang gcig pa yong dgos ste / phyi rol yul ngos nas blo la rnam pa gtad stangs la khyad par cung zad tsam yang med pa'i phyir ro //

phyi rol yul ngos nas sems can la nye ring dang dbye 'byed kyis bsam pa mi srid pas sems can kha shas la yul yid du 'ong ba'i rnam pa gtad pa dang kha shas la yul de nyid yid du mi 'ong ba'i rnam pa gtad mi srid pa'i phyir dang / sems can kha shas la bde ba'i rgyu dang kha shas la sdug bsngal gyi rgyur 'gyur ba mi srid pas yul yid du 'ong dang mi 'ong / bde sdug gang gis rgyu 'gro dang mi 'gro / longs su spyad du rung dang mi rung sogs sems can rang rang gi las dbang 'ba' zhig yin pas so so'i nang shes pa'i steng gi bag chags sad stobs kho na las 'byung ba bsgrub bo //

rmi lam ji srid du gnyid ma sad kyis bar du rmi lam gyi shes pa la yul thams cad phyi rol na yod pa lta bur snang ba las rang gis sems steng gi bag chags sad stobs las 'byung ba zhig nam yang mthong mi nus ba bzhin no // gnyid ma sad bar rmi lam gyi dga' yul la dga' ba dang / sdang yul la sdang ba 'byung la / rmi lam nang mi gzhan zhig gis yul de dag khyed rang gi sems kyis bcos pa 'ba' zhig yin zhes 'grel brjod byas kyang nam yang yid ches byed mi nus / nam gnyid sad pa dang rmi lam med par 'gyur ma thag sems kyi dga' snang dang zhed snang gang yod kyang rang bzhin gis zhi 'gro bar 'gyur ba bzhin / so so skye bos gzung 'dzin rdzas gzhan du 'dzin pa'i zhen pa yod phyin chad phyi rol don du grub pa 'dug snyam pa'i bsam pa ldog mi thub la / 'on kyang gzung 'dzin rdzas gzhan gyi stong pa de nam rtogs tshe phyi don yod pa la zhen pa'i blo de rang bzhin gyis ldog des na sems tsam bshad pa'i dgos pa mthar thug ni / phyi don la zhen chags zlog pa'i phyir yin no // da ni gzhung 'grel dngos la 'jug par bya'o //

> **de ltar phyi rol gnyis kar yang //**
> **blo yi yul du mi rung ngo //** (2cd)

de ltar phyi rol gyi rdul phra mo dang tshogs pa gnyis kar yang dbang po'i blo yi gzung don du byas nas myong ba'i yul du mi rung ngo //

gzung don du byas nas myong ba'i yul du mi rung ba'i rgyu mtshan ci yin zhe na /

gzung don gyi cha rkyen la rgyu yin pa dang de dang 'dra ba'i rnam par gtad pa gnyis dgos pa las de re re la yan lag gcig gcig ma tshang ba'i phyir / rdul tshogs pa la ni dbang shes skyes ba'i rgyu yin pa'i yan lag ma tshang / rdul phra mo la ni rnam pa can du skye ba med pas de dang 'dra ba'i yan lag ma tshang pa'i phyir / rgyu mtshan de bas na phyi rol gyi rdul phra mo dang tshogs pa zhes bya ba'i gzung don ni dmigs pa ma yin no // bstan dar lha rams pas /

> de ltar phyi rol gyi rdul phra rab dmigs rkyen tu 'dod pa'i phyogs dang 'dus pa dmigs rkyen tu 'dod pa'i phyogs gnyis kar yang phyi don blo yi snang yul du mi rung ngo // ci'i phyir mi rung zhe na / dmigs rkyen yin na shes pa gang la rang gi rnam pa 'jog byed yin pa dang shes pa de'i rgyu yin pa'i khyad chos gnyis ka tshang dgos shing / de yang phra ba dmigs rkyen du 'dod pa'i phyogs la rang gi rnam pa 'jog byed yin pa'i yan lag ma tshang / 'dus pa dmigs rkyen du 'dod pa'i phyogs la rgyu yin pa'i yan lag ma tshang ba'i phyir phyi rol gyi rdul phra mo dang tshogs pa zhes bya ba'i don de dag ni dmigs rkyen gyi skabs kyi dmigs pa ma yin no //

zhes don bsdus nas gsungs so // gung thang gi 'grel par gong gi tshig bcad dang po dang gnyis pas phyi don phra rags gnyis ka yang blo yi dmigs rkyen nam dmigs yul du mi rung ngo // zhes don bsdus nas bstan na / tshig bcad gsum pa bzung nas rgyas par skyon spong dgag pa sogs 'phros don gi gzhung yin no zhes gsungs so //

gsum pa / rdul 'dus pa'i rnam pa gzung don yin pa dgag pa ni / 'di la ni /

> **kha cig 'dus pa'i rnam pa dag //**
> **sgrub pa yin par 'dod par byed //** (3ab)

skabs 'di'i kha cig 'di su yin / kha cig 'di'i bzhed pa de rgya nag gi dmigs brtag gi 'grel pa khag la bshad pa ltar na / gong gi kha cig dang pos rdul phra mo dmigs rkyen du bzhed / kha cig gnyis pas rdul 'dus pa dmigs rkyen du 'dod / kha cig gsum pa 'di'i 'dod lugs ni / dang po gnyis dang mi 'dra bar rdul phran 'dus pa'i rnam pa de dmigs rkyen du 'dod pa ltar 'grel brjod byas yod pas de'i thog dge bshes lags nas dgongs tshul gang yod dam zhe na /

rang 'grel la skabs 'di'i kha cig de su yin dang min dngos su ma gsungs kyang slob dpon 'dul ba lha'i dmigs brtag 'grel bar pha khol la ngos 'dzin gnang yod / de'i rjes su 'brangs nas gung thang dang / bstan dar lha rams pa'i bod 'grel rnams la'ang pha khol yin par bshad /

rgya nag 'grel byed rnams kyis bshad pa bzhin spyir rang 'grel la dngos su mi mngon yang khas blangs 'gal ba med pa lta bu 'dug // kha cig gsum pa'i 'dod pa dang phyi don zhal gyis bzhed pa kha cig gis 'dod pa gcig pa lta bu snang te / rdul phran cha med re re ba snang mi nus kyang / de dag tshogs pa'i tshe tshogs pa blo la snang ba ma zad / tshogs pa'i nang la yod pa'i rdul phran rnams kyang blo la snang nus pas de dag gis dmigs rkyen byed / dper na til du ma tshogs pa na / til tshogs snang ba'i tshe re re ba yang snang / de bzhin du skra'i nyag ma re re mi mthong yang / skra rkang du ma tshogs pa'i tshe skra'i tshogs pa dang skra rkang re re mthong zhes zer ro // bstan dar lha rams pas kyang /

> kha cig 'dus pa'i rnam pa dag // ces sogs kyi rtsa 'grel las rdul phra rab cha bcas su bshad pa tshig zin la mi snang yang / gsung gi bab la bltas na dbang shes la rdul phra rab 'dus pa'i rnam par snang bar 'dod pa'i phyogs snga zhig yin /

'on kyang sems tsam ltar na skyon yod de / dbang shes ma 'khrul ba la 'dus pa'i rnam par snang na rags par snang dgos shing rags par snang na cha bcas su snang bar don gyis grub pas de'i phyir / pha khol la sogs pa kha cig gis rdul phra rab re re ba kho rang gi ngo nas dbang shes la rnam pa gtad nas de dang 'dra bar bskyed pa'i nus pa med mod / rdul du ma 'dus pa'i rnam pa can du sgrub pa te bskyed pa'i nus pa yod pas rdul 'dus pa rnam dbang shes kyi dmigs yul yin par 'dod par byed do // bstan dar lha rams pa'i kha cig 'dis 'dod pa 'di ltar 'kod /

> phyi don 'dod pa'i phyogs 'di la ni ste 'di la yang kha cig gis rdul phra rab rdzas su yod pa'i phyir rgyu yin zhing rdul rdzas brgyad 'dus pa'i bdag nyid kyang yin pas dbang shes la 'dus pa'i rnam pa ste rags pa'i rnam pa dag kyang 'char ba'i phyir / des na dmigs rkyen tu 'jog byed kyi yan lag tshang bas sgrub pa ste dbang shes kyi rgyu yin par 'dod par byed ces pa'o //

sems tsam pas / 'o na / rdul phra rab cha med yin pas ci ltar rags pa'i rnam par 'char zhe na /

kha cig gis / phyi rol gyi don thams cad ni 'byung ba bzhi dang gzugs dri ro reg bya'i bdag nyid yin pa'i phyir rnam pa du ma can yin pas so // zhes zer ro //

'o na rdul phran rnams dbang po'i shes pa la 'dus pa'i rnam pa can du bskyed nus na / rdul phran re re ba ci'i phyir shes pa la rnam par gtad nas snang mi nus so zhe na /

rdul phran re re ba ni shes pa la snang mi nus te / chos thams cad la snang ba'i cha dang mi snang ba'i cha gnyis gnyis yod pa'i phyir / bum pa lta bu'i don 'dus pa thams cad la ni dbyibs kyi cha / kha dog gi cha / reg bya'i cha la sogs pa'i rnam pa du ma can yin pa'i nang dbyibs dang kha dog mig shes kyis mngon sum du mthong yang / reg bya mi mthong ba bzhin /

rdul phran la'ang gzugs kyi cha / sgra'i cha / dri'i cha la sogs pa'i rnam pa du ma yod pas 'dus pa'i rnam pa kha shas mngon sum gyi spyod yul yin yang kha shas ni mngon sum la mi snang / rdul re re ba'i rnam pa mngon sum ma yin kyang rdul 'dus pa **de la rnam pa 'ga' zhig gis mngon sum nyid du** rnam par gtad par '**dod do** // de bas na **rdul phra rab rnams la yang 'dus par snang ba'i shes pa skyed pa'i rgyu yod do** // ces kha cig gsum pa 'dis 'dod do //

gal te rdul phra rab rags pa'i rnam par dbang shes la 'char na rdul phra rab kho rang nyid ci'i phyir mi 'char zhe na / slob dpon phyogs glang gis /

> **rdul phran rnam pa rnam rig gi //**
> **don min sra nyid la sogs bzhin //** (3cd)

zhes tshig rkang gnyis po 'dis kha cig gsum pa de'i 'dod pa gsal bshad mdzad la / rdul phran rnams kyi 'dus pa'i rnam pa gtad rung rdul kho rang gi rnam pa gtad mi rung ste / rdul phran de shes pa'am rnam rig gi dmigs rkyen nam gzung don min pa'i phyir ro // dper na bum pa lta bur mtshon na / bum pa'i dbyibs dang kha dog sogs mig shes kyis mngon sum gyis mthong yang / bum pa'i sra ba nyid dang reg bya la sogs pa mig gis mngon sum gyis mi mthong ba bzhin /

rgyu mtshan de bas na / bum pa lta bur ji ltar sra ba reg bya nyid dang kha dog la sogs pa rnam pa ni du ma yod bzhin du yang bum pa'i kha mdog dang dbyibs mig gi blo'i yul yin kyang sra ba'i reg bya la sog pa mig gi blo yul ma yin pa ltar / rdul phra mo nyid kyang 'dus pa'i rnam par blo'i yul du gtad nus kyang kho rang re re ba'i rnam par blo yul du gtad mi nus pa de dang 'dra'o //

> **de dag ltar na bum pa dang //**
> **kham phor sogs blo mtshungs par 'gyur //** (4ab)

slob dpon phyogs glang gis lan 'di ltar mdzad / rdul phran tshogs pa'i rnam pa blo la 'char na skyon 'di ltar yod te / rdul phran tshogs pa'i tshe gzugs dbyibs sogs che chung gi khyad par gang yang med par gnas dgos la /

de dag ltar na 'dus pa'i rnam pa mthong tshe rags pa'i rnam pa zhig nges can du mthong dgos la / 'dus pa'i rnam pa de rags pa bum pa'i rnam pa lta bu zhig mthong dgos sam / yang na rags pa kham phor gyi dbyibs lta bu'i rnam pa zhig mthong dgos smra dgos so //

gnyis kar ltar yang rigs pa ma yin te / rdul phran re re ngos nas dbyibs dang kha dog sogs kyi khyad par cung zad tsam yang med par mtshungs pas na / gal te rdul phran rang ngos nas bum pa lta bu'i rnam par gtad par 'dod na / rdul phran thams cad kyang bum pa'i rnam pa can du snang dgos / gal te rdul phran rang ngor nas kham phor gyi rnam pa lta bur snang bar 'dod na / rdul phran thams cad kham phor gyi rnam can du snang bar 'dod dgos so //

rgyu mtshan de bas na rdul phran rnams bum pa snang ba'i blo dang kham phor snang ba'i blo sogs la khyad par cung zad tsam yang dbye rgyu med par bum blo dang kham blo sogs thams cad mtshungs par 'gyur ba'i skyon yod do //

rdul phran rnams la phan tshun che chung gi dbye ba sogs gtan nas med pas / bum pa dang kham phor la sogs la rnam 'gyur mi 'dra bar lto ba ldir ba dang zhabs zhum pa la sogs pa'i khyad par ni rdul phra mo rnams la bzhag du med pas rdul phra mo ni mang po yod du zin kyang bum pa dang kham phor gnyis ltar blo la snang tshul la khyad par 'ga' yang med do //

gal te rnam pa'i dbye bas dbye // (4c)

gal te kha cig gis mgrin pa dang lto ldir ba dang zhabs zhum pa la sogs pa'i rnam pa'i khyad par blo la shar la / rnam pa'i khyad par mi 'dra de dag las gang gis blo'i khyad par du 'gyur ba'i khyad par yod do snyam du sems na / slob dpon gyi khyad par 'di ni bum pa la sogs pa rags pa'i chos rnams la yod kyi /

de ni rdul phran rdzas yod la //
med de tshad dbye med phyir ro // (5ab)

de 'dra'i rnam pa'i khyad par mi 'dra ba de ni rdul phran rdzas yod la med de de dag la che chung la sogs tshad kyi dbye ba med pa'i phyir ro // rdul phra rab rnams ni rdzas gzhan te tha dad so sor yin du zin kyang de dag thams cad dbyibs zlum po yin par blo la snang ba tsam las de dag la dbyibs dang kha dog sogs kyi ni dbye ba med do //

de phyir de rdzas med la yod // (5b)

rgyu mtshan de bas phyir na dbyibs dang kha dog la sogs pa'i rnam pa mi 'dra ba'i dbye ba de dag ni rdzas su med pa'i chos rnams la yod kyi rdzas yod kyi rdul phran rnams la med de / **rnam pa'i dbye ba ni** rags pa'i chos **kun rdzob tu yod pa dag kho na la yod kyi rdul phra mo rnams la ma yin no // bum pa la sogs pa ni kun rdzob tu yod pa nyid** yin pas de dag la kha dog dang dbyibs sogs kyi bkod pa mi 'dra ba yod do //

'dir lung gi rjes 'brang gi mdo sde pa'i 'dod pa 'god pa'i skabs yin la / lung gi rjes 'brang gi mdo sde pa'i bzhed pa ni bye brag smra ba'i bzhed pa ltar dang ches mthun pas / bum pa la sogs pa bcom pa'am blos cha shas so sor bsal ba na rang 'dzin gyi blo zhig pa kun rdzob kyi bden pa dang / rdul phran cha med dang shes pa skad cig cha med sogs rdzas grub rnams bcom pa'am blos cha shas so sor bsal ba na rang 'dzin gyi blo ma zhig pas don dam bden par 'dod do //

rigs pa'i rjes 'brang gi mdo sde pa ltar na rnam 'grel las bshad pa bzhin / don dam par don byed nus pa don dam bden pa'i mtshan nyid dang / don dam par don byed mi nus pa kun rdzob bden pa'i mtshan nyid du 'dod pas gang mngon sum la snang du rung ba don dam bden pa dang / gang mngon sum la snang du mi rung ba ni kun rdzob bden par bzhed do //

> **rdul phran yongs su bsal na ni //**
> **der snang shes pa nyams 'gyur phyir //** (5cd)

bum pa la sogs pa'i chos rnams kun rdzob kho nar yod pas rgyu mtshan gis de dag gi rdul phran rnams yongs su bsal na ni / bum pa la sogs pa chos der snang ba'i shes pa nyams par 'gyur ba'i phyir / rdzas su yod pa rnams la ni 'brel pa can cha shas sogs blos so sor bsal du zin kyang kha dog la sogs pa 'gyur med don dam bden pa bzhin du rang gi blo 'dor bar mi bye da do // **de lta bas na dbang po'i blo rnams kyi yul ni phyi rol na yod pa ma yin par 'thad do** //

gnyis pa / sems tsam pa'i rang lug gzhag pa ni /

dmigs rkyen phyi rol don du grub par 'dod pa'i lugs bkag nas / 'o na sems tsam rang lugs la dmigs rkyen gang la 'jog gam / yul dmigs rkyen du byas nas myong ba dang / gzung don du byas nas myong ba'i rnam gzhag med na 'jig rten grags pa'i gnod pa mi yong ngam zhe na / sems tsam rang lugs la 'jig rten grags pa'i gnod pa spangs pa'i phyir dmigs pa nang na yod pa bsgrub pa'i sems tsam pa'i rang lug gzhag pa ni /

> **nang gi shes bya'i ngo bo ni //**
> **phyi rol ltar snang gang yin de //** (6ab)

sems tsam pa'i lugs la dmigs rkyen gzhag du yod de / nang gi shes pa'am kun gzhi'i steng gi bag chags de de yin pa'i phyir / skabs 'dir gung thang gi 'grel par dmigs pa gang zhe na / nang gi 'dzin pa'i rang mdangs ste shes pa rang gi snang ba de nyid shes bya'i dngos po blo la shar ba bzhag gi shes pa las rdzas gzhan du phyi rol du med pa ni rang lugs la nges par gzung ngo //

'o na shes pa rang la bya ba 'gal ba'i phyir dang dus mnyam yin pa'i phyir dang ngo bo gcig pa yin pa'i phyir / shes pa rang gis bdag nyid gsal ba'i yul de shes pa kho rang gi dmigs rkyen la ji ltar snang zhe na /

nang gi yul de shes pa'i rdzas dang shes pa'i ngo bo yin kyang shes pa dang 'brel med phyi rol yin pa lta bur snang la / phyi rol du snang ba de ji ltar gnas pa'i rnam pa'i snang ba ma yin te / me long la zla gzugs shar ba na nam mkha'i khams stong sangs kyang shar bas byed pa las zla ba dang gzugs brnyan 'brel med rgyang ste chad pa'i rnam par 'byung ba ji lta bar phyi rol ltar snang ba'i tshul gyis gzung bar gyur ba'i dngos po nang du gnas pa gang yin pa'am shes pa'i bdag nyid gang yin pa de nyid don zhes bya ba ste / don ni yul du mar 'jug kyang 'dir skabs kyi dbang las dmigs rkyen yin no // de'ang rgyu mtshan gang phyir na dmigs rkyen yin zhe na / gung thang ltar na /

> mngon par brjod pa'i bag chags goms pa las gzung ba dang 'dzin pa'i tshul du rnam par shes pa yul de'i dngos po'i rnam par skyed pa'i phyir dang / yul de med na mi skye ba'i cha nas de'i rkyen nyid do //

zhes kyang bshad pa yin pa'i phyir ro // kun gzhi'i steng gi mig shes kyis sngon po lta bu mthong ba'i bag chags smin pa las / phyogs gcig shes bya sngon po'i rnam pa'i ngo bor skyes la / phyogs gcig sngon po'i rnam pa can gyi blo'i ngo bor skyes so // des na sngon po lta bu shes pa la 'char ba'i skabs 'char tshul mi 'dra ba gnyis yod pa'i rgyu mtshan gyis nang gi shes bya'i ngo bo phyi rol du yod pa ltar snang ba gang yin pa de ni dbang shes de dag gi dmigs rkyen yin no //

des na nang gi bag chags sad stobs kyis shes pa la snang ba'i don nam yul de nyid dmigs rkyen yin no // shes pa'i yul de la phyi rol gyi don med bzhin du rmi lam gyi shes pa ltar phyi rol na yod pa'i rnam pa lta bur snang ba kho no zad do // nang shes pa'i mdun na yod pa'i bag chags sad stobs kyis byung ba'i yul sngon po dang dkar po sogs kho na dmigs pa'i rkyen yin no //

> **don yin rnam shes ngo bo'i phyir //**
> **de'i rkyen nyid kyang yin phyir ro //** (6cd)

nang gi shes pa la snang ba'i yul de nyid dmigs rkyen yin pas rnam shes kyi don yin la / don de dang rnam shes gnyis ngo bo tha dad med cing / don de rnam shes de'i ngo bo yin pa'i phyir / nang shes pa'i yul de ni rnam shes de'i dmigs rkyen nyid kyang yin pa'i phyir ro //

nang gi rnam par shes pa ni don te yul gyi rnam pa can **du snang ba yin pas** / de dang 'dra zhes pa'i khyad chos dang po tshang ba dang / nang gi yul de las dmigs rkyen byas nas shes pa de skyes pa yin pas / de las skyes zhes pa'i khyad chos gnyis pa tshang bas / mdo sde pa khyed cag gi 'dod pa'i dmigs rkyen gyi chos nyid gnyis dang ldan pa'i phyir na nang na yod pa'i don kho na dmigs pa'i rkyen yin no //

yang phyogs sngas dwogs 'dri 'di ltar zhus pa / re zhig sems rtsam pa khyod rang gi smras ba de ltar shes pa la snang ba'i yul nyid dmigs rkyen yin la ni rag la ste dmigs rkyen yin pa'i dbang du btang yang / shes pa de dang de'i phyogs gcig po shes pa la snang ba'am gsal ba'i yul de gnyis dus mnyam pa'am lhan cig skyes pa go ste yin pas / yul de'i ji ltar shes pa de'i dmigs rkyen byed / rgyu 'bras dus mnyam pa ni ba lang gi rwa gnyis ltar phan tshun rkyen du mi rung bas ha cang thal ba'i skyon 'jug go zhe na /

kha cig gis brjod pa'i skyon 'di rgyu 'bras dus mnyam du bzhed pa'i lugs la mi 'jug kyang / rgyu 'bras rim can du 'dod pa'i lugs la 'jug go /

gcig cha'ang mi 'khrul phyir na rkyen // (7a)

rgyu 'bras dus mnyam du bzhed pa'i lugs la shes pa dang de'i dmigs rkyen yul gnyis dus mnyam pa yin na rgyu 'bras rnam gzhag ji ltar 'thad ce na /

'thad de / de gnyis dus mnyam yin na'ang shes pa de yis yul mi 'khrul ba'i rgyu byed / de bzhin yul de yis shes pa mi 'khrul ba'i rgyu byed pas / phan tshun gcig gis gcig la rgyu byed / lhan cig 'byung ba'i rgyu dang mtshungs ldan gyi rgyu sogs la rgyu 'bras dus mnyam du 'jog rung ba'i phyir / dper na shing gdung ma gsum gcig gis gcig la brten nas ma 'gyel bar gnas tshe / phan tshun dus mnyam kyang gcig gis gcig la mi 'khrul bar brten pa'i rgyu 'bras byed pa bzhin no //

dus gcig pa'am lhan cig par gyur du zin kyang gcig gis gcig la phan tshun rgyu byas nas gcig gis gcig la 'bras bu 'byin pa la nges pa can yin pas 'khrul pa med pa'i phyir / gcig shos de gcig shos gzhan las skye ba'i rkyen du 'gyur rung te / 'di ltar gtan tshigs pa'am rtog ge ba dag ni gcig de yod pa la gzhan de'i grogs byed pa dang gcig de med pa na gzhan de'ang med par 'gyur na / de dag gi phan tshun rgyu 'bras kyi 'brel ba de dang ldan pa nyid kyis phyir na rgyu dang rgyu dang ldan pa'am 'bras bu rim gyis skye zhes smra'o //

sems tsam pas rgyu 'bras dus mnyam yod pa'i dper gdung ras 'tshig pa dang me gnyis la bzhag / gdung ras 'tshig pa de me la brten / me skyes ba gdung ras 'tshig pa la brten kyang / me dang gdung ras 'tshig pa gnyis dus mnyam yin / mdung ras 'tshig pas me skye ba dag gi yang rgyu 'bras kyi mtshan nyid yin par smra'o // yang na /

nus pa 'jog phyir rim gyis yin // (7b)

yang na / skabs 'dir rgyu 'bras rim gyi ba bzhag na'ang rung ste / shes pa ni gung thang 'grel par ltar na dmigs rkyen dngos sam nus pa 'jog pa'i dmigs rkyen dang / shes pa de la rnam par gtad pa'i yul ni dmigs rkyen btags pa ba snang ba'i dmigs rkyen nam rnam par bzhag pa'i dmigs rkyen yin pas phyir na de gnyis rgyu 'bras rim gyis pa yin no //

rim gyis kyang yin te / zhes pa'i tshig gis yul yul can rgyu 'bras rim can pa'ang bzhag chog te / bag chags de dmigs rkyen yin pa'i phyir na / bag chags smin pa'i tshe cha gcig las yul sngon po'i rnam pa skye ba dang cha gzhan las yul can sngon po 'dzin ba'i shes pa'i rnam pa skyes bas / shes rnam dang don rnam gnyis kar bag chags smin pa las 'byung bas /

bag chags de yul lam don gyi rnam par skyed byed kyang yin / shes pa'i rgyu yang yin pas / bag chags smin pa'i tshe yul sngon po'i rnam pa'i don gyi rnam par snang ba dang bag chags de nyid ni shes pa snga ma sngon 'dzin mig shes rang snang ba dang / shes pa snga ma sngon 'dzin mig shes des bag la bzhag pa de dang mthun pa sngon po 'dzin pa'i shes pa phyi ma 'bras bur skyed par byed nus pas / bag chags kyis rnam par shes pa'i rten byed pa mi 'gal lo //

dper na khong khro lta bur mtshon na / kun gzhi'i steng gi bag chags sad stobs las khong khro yid du mi 'ong ba'i shes pa bskyed / khong khro des nus pa kun gzhi'i steng du bag la bzhag ba'i tshul du gnas / de nas slar yang yid du mi 'ong ba 'thong ba'i khong khro'i rnam pa can gyi shes pa bskyed /

de bzhin du bag chags de dmigs pa yin pas / bag chags sad ba'i stobs las yul sngon po'i rnam pa snang zhing yul can sngon po 'dzin pa'i shes pa yang skyes bas so // kun gzhi'i dmigs pa la'ang bag chags 'jog yul sngon po mthong ba'i tshe bag chags de nyid yul sngon po'i rnam par rdzus nas snang zhes 'dod do //

gal te 'o na sems tsam pa khyed rang gis bshad pa ltar yin na ni nang gi shes pa'i bag chags sad stobs kyis gzugs kho na dmigs pa'i rkyen yin na / ji ltar nang gi gzugs de dang mig dbang la brten nas mig gi rnam par shes pa skye'o zhes bshad pa de ji ltar yin zhe na /

nang gi shes pa'i gzugs de nyid dmigs rkyen yin na mig shes skye ba mig dbang la brten pa'i dgos pa med pa'i phyir / sems tsam pa'i 'dod pa ltar na dmigs rkyen gzugs de dbang shes la 'char mi dgos par / nang gi shes pa'i bags chags 'ba' zhig la brten nas mig gi rnam shes skye ba'i phyir ro / zhes pa ni kha cig gi dwogs pa bkod pa'o // kha cig gis dwogs pa 'di gung thang gi 'grel par 'di ltar bkod /

> gal te byad bzhin dang me long ji lta bar phyi'i gzugs dang dmigs pa las rnam par shes pa bskyed na khyod la dmigs pa ni nang kho na las

mdun du gyur pa med pa'i phyir / ji ltar shes pa skyed ce na / yul dang lhan cig pa'i dbang po 'byung ba'i bdag nyid kyi bem por smra ba mdo sde ba'i lugs la yul yang dbang po mthun phyi'i bem po zhing tu gyur mod kyang / kho ba cag ni dmigs pa de dang lhan cig byed pas dbang po'ang khyod ltar mi smra yi / 'bras bu las rgyu'i chos rjes su dpog pa'i tshe na yid kyi steng du mig shes thun mong ma yin par 'grub ba'i nus pa yi ngo bo zhig yod par las 'gag kyang 'bras bu 'byin par sgrub pa'i rigs pa sogs kyis 'grub la de lta bu gang yin pa de ni dbang po'ang yin par 'dod do //

lhan cig byed dbang nus pa yi //
ngo bo gang yin dbang po'ang yin // (7cd)

bag chags 'di nyid dmigs pa yin pas sngon po'i rnam par 'char ba tsam du ma zad / mig gi dbang po'ang mdo sde pa bzhin du phyi'i rdul du grub ba'i gzugs zhig min par lhan cig byed pa'i rgyu nang shes pa'i steng gi nus pa yi ngo bo gang yin pa zhig la 'dod do //

dbang po ni rang gi 'bras bu de la brten nas **nus pa'i ngo bo nyid du** sngon la yod pa rjes su dpag thub pas / mdo sde pas 'dod pa ltar 'byung ba las gyur pa'i dbang po gzugs can pa **nyid du ni ma yin no** // sems tsam pa'i lugs la dbang po nus pa'i ngo bor 'jog tshul 'di slo dpon zla grags kyi dbu ma 'jug pa las gsal bar gsungs ste /

rang gi rnam shes rten gyi nus de la //
dbang po gzugs can mig ces bya bar rtogs //

rnam shes kyi rten gyi nus pa zhig la dbang po gzugs can mig zhes bya bar rtogs so // thal 'gyur bas lugs de dgag pa'i skabs /

mig dbang med par rang gi sa bon ni //
smin las long ba la 'dir cis mi skye //

mig dbang med par rang gi sa bon nam nus pa smin pa la brten nas gzugs mthong nus na long ba la ci'i phyir gzugs mthong ba'i rnam she mi skye / long bas gzugs mthong rigs ste mig shes skye ba'i nus yod pa'i phyir / ces thal 'gyur ba'i sems tsam pa'i 'dod pa 'gog par byed do //

sems tsam pa khyed cag dbang po 'byung ba'i bdag nyid las bzlog ste nus par 'dod na'ang / nus pa brten med pa ni mi gnas pas rten 'byung ba'i khyad par zhig dgos la de dgos na khye rang gis tshig dang 'gal lo // zhe na /

de yang rnam rig la mi 'gal // (8a)

dbang po nus pa'i ngo bor bzhag pa de yang rnam par rig pa tsam smra ba'i lugs la 'gal ba med de / nus pa shes pa la gnas shing shes pa'ang nus pa las 'byung ba'i phyir khyed cag ltar phyi nas tshol ba'i ngal ba mi dgos so //

nus pa de dang ldan pa'i rnam par shes pa la nus pa de yod kyang rung / phyi'i gzugs su grub pa la sogs pa bstan du med pa'i shes pa rang gi ngo bo la yod kyang rung ste / 'bras bu rnam shes bskyed pa la khyad par med do //

de ltar yul gyi ngo bo dang //
nus pa phan tshun rgyu can dang //
thog ma med du 'jug pa yin // (8bcd)

de ltar yul ser po dang sngon po sogs kyi rnam pa can gyi shes pa'i ngo bo dang / shes pa de skyed byed kyi nus pa'am shes pa bag la gnas pa'i tshul gnyis phan tshun rgyu can yin ste / gcig gis gcig la rgyu byed pa'i phyir / shes pa bag la gnas pa'i tshe ni nus pa yin la / nus pa de smin pa'i tshe shes pa yin pas / shes pa skyes pa nus pa snga ma zhig yod pa la rag las shing / nus pa skyes pa'ang shes pa snga ma yod pa la rag las so //

shes pa dang de skyed byed kyi nus pa gnyis phan tshun rgyu can byed tshul de ni dus thog ma med du 'jug pa yin ste / dge mi dge'i bsam pa gang 'dra zhig yin yang sems steng du bag chags 'jog // bag chags de las slar yang dge sdig gi sems byung / de dag las dge sdig gis las bsags /

las kyis mthus 'khor ba'i bde sdug myong tshor sna tshogs byung / bde sdug gi tshor ba las chags zhen dang sdang sems sogs nyon mongs pa'i sems skyes / nyon mongs dbang gis sems kyis steng du dge mi dge'i bag chags bzhag // slar yang bag chags de dag las dge mi dge ba'i sems skyes pas 'khor ba'i sdug bsngal rnams 'jug pa yin no //

mig dbang de nus pa la bzhag pas rgyu mtshan gis / mig ces bya ba'i nus pa dang nang gi shes pa'i mdun la yod pa'i gzugs dmigs rkyen yin pa de la brten nas rnam par shes pa don du snang ba dmigs kyis de gnyis la ma brten par phyi rol gyi yul la brten nas rnam shes mi skye'o //

nus pa dang nang gi shes pa 'di gnyis kyang gcig gis gcig bskyed pas **phan tshun gyi rgyu can dang / thog ma med pa'i dus can yin te** / rigs 'dra snga ma'i bag chags las phyi ma skye dgos pa'i phyir na / kun gzhi'i steng du shes pa bag la nyal ba'i nus pa de nyid smin pa las rnam shes skyes / rnam shes 'gag tshe de'i bag la gnas pa'i nus pa kun gzhi'i steng du bzhag yang de smin pa las shes pa skyes pa'i phyir ro //

res 'ga' ni nus pa yongs su smin pa las rnam par shes pas yul gyi rnam pa nyid 'byung la res 'ga' ni rnam par shes pa'i yul gyi rnam pa mi gsal ba'i tshul du gnas na **de'i rnam pa la nus pa'o** // rnam par shes pa dang rnam par shes pa la snang ba'i yul sngon po lta bu las de gnyis ldog pa gzhan nyid dang rdzas gzhan ma **yin pa nyid du ci dgar brjod par bya'o** // de ltar nang gi dmigs pa ni shes pa de'i rgyu yang yin / shes pa de de'i rnam pa can du skyed byed kyang yin pas chos nyid gnyis dang ldan pa'i phyir dmigs rkyen nam yul du mthong ngo //

'dir mdo sdo pa kha cig gis sems tsam pa la skyon brjod 'di ltar byed de / sems tsam pa khyod shes pa'i steng gi nus pa dmigs rkyen dngos dang yul ni dmigs rkyen btags pa ba tsam yin zhes pa'i khas len 'di la kho cag mdo sde pa la 'jug pa'i skyon de ci'i phyir mi yong ngam / sems tsam khyod ltar na / rdul phran gyis blo skye ba'i rgyu byed kyang dmigs rkyen ma yin te / de blo la mi snang ba'i phyir dang / dmigs rkyen gyi khyad chos gnyis pa ma tshang ba'i phyir zhes 'dod pas / nus pa'ang dmigs rkyen ma yin par thal / des blo skyed par byed kyang nus pa kho rang blo la mi snang ba'i phyir dang dmigs rkyen gyi mtshan nyid gnyis pa ma tshang ba'i phyir ro // zhe na //

sems tsam pas rdul phran rgyu byed pa'i dbang du btang yang zhes brtag pa mtha' bzung gi sgo nas mdo sde pa'i 'dod pa bzhin smras na yang / sems tsam rang lugs la rdul phran shes pa skye ba'i rgyur khas mi len pa'i phyir ste / shes pa bskyed byed kyi rgyu dngos ni nang shes pa'i steng gi bag chags sam nus pa de yin pa'i phyir /

sngon po'i rnam pa can gi blo la mtshon na nus pa'am bag chags ni / sngon po'i rnam pa can gi shes pa mngon par mi gsal ba'i tshul du bag la gnas pa de yin la / nus pa des sngon 'dzin mig shes kyi dmigs rkyen byed pa'i tshe nus pa de smin pa'am mngon par gsal nas yul gyi rnam pa'i ngo bo dang yul can shes pa'i ngo bo red 'gro ba de yin /

nus pa'am bag chags ni me tog gi the'u lta bu yin la the'u las me tog shar ba bzhin / nus pa mngon par gsal skabs nus pa de nying yul dang yul can gyi ngo bor 'gro ba'i phyir na nus pa de yul gyi rnam pa'i ngo bor rdzus pa lta bu yin zhes gzhung las gsal /

'o na / bag chags dang nus pa gnyis la khyad par gang yod dam zhe na /

spyir btang shes pa lta bur mtshon na / bag chags dang nus pa dang sa bon gsum don gcig la 'jug // shes pas bzhag pa'i bag chags dang sa bon dang nus pa gsum gcig go / 'on kyang sa bon la myu gu skye ba'i nus pa yod zhes brjod kyang sa bon la myu gu skye ba'i bag chags yod zhes mi smra'o / sa bon chos thams cad la yod pa'i nus pa la 'jug kyang / bag chags ni shes pa kho na dang 'brel ba'i nus pa zhig ste / bag chags sad pa las shes pa skye shing / shes pa 'gag tshe bag chags kyi ngo bor gnas pa'i phyir ro //

mdo sde pa ltar bye brag smra bas kyang sngon po dang sngo 'dzin mig shes rig bya rig byed yin pa dang / sngo 'dzin gyi blos sngon po ngo bo nyid kyis gzung don du byas nas myong bar 'dod pas de la sems tsam pa dang rtsod pa gang yang med la / de ltar na yang bye brag smra bas sngo 'dzin de sngon po'i rnam pa can du mi 'dod pas / sems tsam pas sngo 'dzin de yul sngon po'i rnam pa can du sgrub dgos shing / sngo 'dzin de sngon po'i rnam pa can du grub ste / ngas sngon po mthong snyam du dran pa na yul can mthong ba po dang sngo 'dzin de sngon po'i rnam pa can du dran pa de las yul gyi rnam pa can gyi blo tshul gnyis pa can du 'gru pa yin no // de ltar yang rnam 'gral las /

de dag nyid kyis myong ba la //
brtsad pa 'ga' yang yod ma yi //
de don rang bzhin nyid ma grub //
de yang yang dag dran las grub //

ces gsungs pas so // gal te bye brag smra ba'i 'dod pa ltar / yul can rnam rang rang gi yul gyi rnam pa tha dad du shar ba las yul de dang de rtogs pa'i yul can so sor phye ba med na / de ltar na gzugs 'di ni 'di ltar yin la 'di ltar ni ma yin no // zhes yul rnams tha dad dam so sor dran pa'i blo 'di skye ba med par 'gyur ro // de ltar yang rnam 'grel las /

rang spyod yul gyi phye mod cing //
tha dad par myong med de la //
'di ni 'di lta'am 'di ltar ni //
min zhes tha dad 'di med 'gyur //

ces gsungs shing / gal te sngo 'dzin lta bu rgyud la ldan pa'i gang zag gis rang gis sngo 'dzin la sngon po'i rnam pa ji ltar yod pa ma shar zhing rang gi sngon po mthong ba'i mig gi shes pa yang shes pa med na rang gis yul ci dang ci 'dra zhig mthong thos rig pa med pa dang / rang gis yul gang dang gang mthong ba dang thos pa dang de dag la reg pa sogs mi shes par 'gyur bas skye bo rnams long ba dang lkug pa lta bur 'gyur bar gsungs so // de ltar yang slob dpon lha dbang blos tshad ma rnam 'grel gyi dka' 'grel las /

> shes pa'i 'dra ba nyid kyang mi 'dod pa'i rgol ba gang yin pa de'i gnyis mthong mod / don grub pa ma yin zhing shes pa yang ma yin no // de ltar 'dra ba las don 'di'i mthong ba 'di yin par 'gyur ba de yang yod pa ma yin pa de ltar na gang las don rig par 'gyur / shes pas kyang bdag nyid myong ba ma yin zhing / gzhan 'ga' zhig gis kyang ma yin te mi rung ba'i phyir ro // de bas na shes pa'am shes bya grub pa ma yin no // gang gi tshe de ltar yin pa de'i tshe don 'di 'am shes pa 'di zhes don dang shes pa gnyis po dag shes pa ji ltar yod / brjod pa ldog pa de ltar na 'gro ba ma lus pa long ba dang lkugs par 'gyur ro //

zhes gsungs so // de yang blo snga ma 'ga' zhig la yul gyi rnam pa so sor gsal bar shar ba med pa la phyis su dran pas tha dad du so sor 'byed mi nus shing de ltar 'byed pa'i dran pa med do // dper na tshe ma spun gnyis kyi rnam pa mi 'dra ba yod pa so sor ma shes na de gnyis so sor 'byed mi nus pa bzhin no // de ltar yang rnam 'grel las /

> nyams su myong ba tsam gyis ni //
> tha dad 'ga' zhig rnam 'byed min //
> tha dad gsal ba med pa la //
> rnam 'byed blo med tshe sogs bzhin //

zhes gsungs pa ltar ro // gzhan yang blo la yul gyi rnam pa shar ba med na blos thag nye ring dang gzugs gzhan gyis bar du chod pa'i yul rnams la dbang blos gsal mi gsal dang / mthong ba dang mi mthong ba'i khyad par med par 'gyur te de ltar khyad par 'jog byed med pas so // de ltar yang rnam 'grel las /

> nye ring la sogs khyad par gyis //
> gsal dang mi gsal mi rung ngo //

zhes gsungs so // gong du bshad pa ltar sems tsam pa'i lugs la phyi rol gyi gzugs med pa bzhin du gzugs kyang med par 'dod ces pa dang / yang lugs 'dir phyi rol gyi gzugs med kyang gzugs yod ces pa'i go ba len phyogs mi 'dra ba'i 'dod tshul gnyis byung zhing rje tsong kha pa'i bzhed pa ni sems tsam pa'i lugs 'dir phyi rol gyi gzugs med kyang gzugs yod ces pa 'di yin te /

'jug pa rang 'grel gyi skabs su sems tsam pa'i 'dod pa brjod pa na phyi rol gyi gzugs med pa mang du gsungs shing de bzhin du rnam par shes pa las tha dad pa'i gzung ba dang / rnam par shes pa la tha dad pa'i mig dbang med ces dgag bya la khyad par phyi rol gyi zhes dang rnam par shes pa las tha dad pa'i zhes sbyar nas gzugs med ces sogs gsungs so // de ltar yang / rje tsong kha pas dbu ma dgongs pa rab gsal las /

> 'grel par dbu ma 'jug pa rang 'grel / sems tsam pa'i 'dod pa brjod pa na / phyi rol med ces pa mang du gsungs shing / rnam par shes pa las tha dad par gyur ba'i gzung ba ni cung zad kyang yod pa min zhes / gzugs sogs kyi gzung ba med pa la rnam shes las tha dad pa'i zhes khyad par smos pa dang / dbang po gzugs can mig ces bya bar rtogs zhes pa'i 'grel pa las / rnam par shes pa las tha dad pa'i mig gi dbang po ni yod pa ma yin no //

zhes gsungs shing / 'o na gzugs dang dbang po gzugs can pa sogs med ces khas blangs rgyu yin nam snyam na / sher phyin gyi mdo sogs su don dam par yod pa ma yin zhes pa'i khyad par sbyar ba dang ma sbyar ba gnyis yod pa ltar 'jug pa rang 'grel gyi skabs su yang khyad par sbyar ma sbyar gnyis ka yod kyang skye ba 'gog pa na don dam par skye ba med ces khyad par sbyar nas gsungs pa rnams khyad pa ma sbyar ba'i skye ba med par gsungs pa'i skabs su yang de ltar sbyar ba de 'khyer dgos pa bzhin du sems tsam pa'i skabs 'dir yang gzugs med ces gsungs pa rnams la phyi rol gyi gzugs med ces khyad par sbyar dgos par gsungs te / dbu ma dgongs pa rab gsal las /

> rnam par shes pa las tha dad pa'i mig gi dbang po ni yod pa ma yin no // zhes dgag bya la khyad par sngar ltar sbyar ba bzhin sems tsam gyi skabs su 'dod rgyu yin nam / 'on te gzugs sogs lnga dang dbang po gzugs can lnga med ces khyad par ma sbyar bar khas blang rgyu yin snyam na / 'grel pa 'dir khyad par sbyar ma sbyar gnyis ka 'dug kyang / skye ba 'gog pa la dgag bya la khyad par sbyar ba mang du byung na / ma byung ba'i skabs thams cad du yang de 'khyer ba bzhin du / 'dir yang de ltar bya ste /

zhes gsungs pa ltar ro // sems tsam pa'i lugs 'dir / phyi rol gyi gzugs med kyang spyir gzugs yod dgos pa yin te / 'phags pa thogs med kyis theg bsdus kyi skabs su kun gzhi rnam shes kyis dbang po gzugs can thams cad kyi rgyu byed pa dang / mi la sogs pa'i lus thams cad nye bar len pa'i gnas su gyur ba dang / tshe ji srid 'tsho ba'i bar du dbang po gzugs can lnga po ma zhig par gzung ba dang / kun gzhi'i steng gi snod kyi 'jig rten grub byed kyi sa bon nam bag chags la tshor ba med pa'i sa bon du gsungs shing /

de bzhin rten 'brel mdo 'grel gyi skabs su yang kun gzhi rnam shes kyi rkyen gyis bzhi pa ming gzugs 'grub par bshad la / de 'dra'i gzugs de 'byung ba dang 'byung 'gyur gyi gzugs la bshad cing / gzugs de gzugs med khams na med la 'dod khams dang gzugs khams gnyis na yod par bshad pas / de ltar sems tsam pa'i lugs la gzugs khas len pa mtha' yas pa zhig yod par gsungs so // de ltar yang rje tsong kha pas dbu ma dgongs pa rab gsal las /

> 'dir phyogs snga ma brjod pa'i gzhung theg bsdus su / ci'i phyir len pa'i rnam par shes pa zhes bya zhe na / dbang po gzugs can thams cad kyi rgyu yin pa dang / lus thams cad nye bar len pa'i gnas su gyur pa'i phyir te / 'di ltar tshe ji srid par rjes su 'jug gi bar du des dbang po gzugs can lnga po dag ma zhig par nye bar gzung ba dang / zhes dang / thun mong ni snod kyi 'jig rten gyi sa bon gang yin pa'o // thun mong ma yin pa de ni so so rang gi skye mched kyi sa bon gang yin pa'o // thun mong gang yin pa de ni tshor ba med pa 'byung ba'i sa bon no // zhes kun gzhi'i steng gi snod kyi 'jig rten gyis sa bon tshor ba med pa'i dngos

> po'i sa bon du gsungs pa dang / bsdu ba las kyang de bzhin du gsungs shing / rten 'brel mdo 'grel du / kun gzhi rnams kyi rkyen gyis ming gzugs 'grub par bshad pa'i ming phung po lhag ma bzhi dang / gzugs 'byung ba 'byung 'gyur gyi gzugs la 'chad cing / de 'dra de gzugs med na med kyang khams gzhan gnyis na yod par bshad pa sogs sems tsam gyi lugs la gzugs khas len pa mtha' yas pa cig snang ngo //

gal te sems tsam pa'i lugs 'dir gzugs la sogs pa yod par gsungs pa yod kyang / de dag ni gzugs sogs blo la snang ba tsam yod pa la dgongs nas gsungs pa yin gyi don la gzugs sogs yod pa ma yin na de ltar na lugs 'dir tshor ba med pa'i snod kyi 'jig rten sa gzhi ril po 'di yang yod pa ma yin zhing de dag la longs spyad bya'i gzugs sgra dri ro reg bya sogs med la /
longs spyod pa po'i skyes bus gzugs kyi phung po blangs te de la / gzugs sgra sogs la longs spyod byed kyi mig dang rna ba'i skye mched sogs kyang med par thal zhing / de ltar na mig sogs gang la ldan pa'i longs spyod pa po dang bde sdug myong ba po'i skye bu yang med par 'gyur bas lugs 'di la de 'dra'i tha snyad gang yang bya mi rung bar 'gyur zhing / de 'dra'i tha snyad gang yang bya mi rung yang da dung grub mtha' 'di legs so zhes sus kyang mi smra bar gsungs so // de ltar yang dbu ma dgongs pa rab gsal las /

> sems tsam gyi lugs la gzugs khas len pa mtha' yas pa cig snang ngo // de lta ma yin na sems tsam gyi skabs su gzugs phung gi steng nas / de ltar gzugs sgra sogs tha snyad mdzad pa thams cad la / gsar du ma bcos pa tha snyad btags pa de nyid kyis tha snyad byed du mi rung ba kho nar 'gyur bar snang la / de 'dra ba'i tha snyad byar mi rung bar mthong yang da dung grub mtha' 'di legs so zhes pa ni 'phags yul gyi sangs rgyas pa su la yang mi snang ngo //

zhes gsungs so // des na dbang mngon rnams kyi shes bya gzugs sgra la sogs pa gzugs 'dzin dbang pa'i shes pa las rgyang chod de phyi rol du yod par mi 'dod par nang shes pa'i dngos por smra ba la shes bya nang gir smra ba zhes zer ba yin gyi shes bya gzugs med la shes pa yod ces zer ba'i don ma yin no // de ltar yang dbu ma dgongs pa rab gsal las /

> shes bya nang gir smra ba zhes pa'i ming don kyang shes bya ni gzugs sgra sogs yin la / de phyi rol tu mi 'dod kyi nang shes pa'i dngos por smra ba la zer ba yin no //

zhes gsungs shing / des na sems tsam pa'i lugs 'dir yul gzugs yid du 'ong mi 'ong las dga' sdug myong ba'i shes pa tshor ba gsal bar nyams su myong ba las de dag yod par 'dod pa de bzhin du sngon po la sogs pa'i gzugs sogs kyang de ltar gsal bar nyams su myong ba yod pas de dag med pa ma yin par yod pa yin la / 'on kyang sngon po la sogs pa'i gzugs sogs phyi rol du yod pa ma yin pa'i khyad par phye dgos so // de ltar yang slob dpon lha dbang blos mdzad pa'i tshad ma rnam 'grel gyi 'grel bshad las /

> rnal 'byor spyod pa ba gzhan dag ni sngon po la sogs pa thams cad med pa ma yin te / dga' ba la sogs pa bzhin du gsal bar nyams su myong ba nyid kyi phyir ro // 'on kyang sngon po la sogs pa phyi rol gyi ngo bo nyid du yod pa ma yin zhing / shes pa 'dzin par 'dod pa gcig gi yang cha gnyis par gyur pa yod pa ma yin no //

zhes gsungs pa ltar bzang ngo //

> bdag gis 'dir 'bad rnam dkar dge ba'i chogs //
> ston ka'i zla ltar gang zhig bsags pa 'dis //
> 'gro ba'i yid kyi mun pa yongs bsal te //
> shes rab snang ba rgyas pa'i rgyar gyur cig //

dmigs brtag 'grel pa snying po bsdus pa zhes bya ba re zhig rdzog /

English-Tibetan-Sanskrit Glossary

English	Tibetan	Sanskrit
actual percept condition	dmigs rkyen dngos	
aggregation	bsags pa	upacita
appearance	snang ba	ābhāsa
appearing percept condition	snang ba'i dmigs rkyen	
apprehended aspect	gzung ba'i cha	grāhyāṃśa
apprehended object	gzung bar bya	grāhya
appropriating cognition	nyer len gyi shes pa	upādāna-vijñāna
aspect	snang ba	ākāra
capacity	nus pa	śakti
cause	rgyu	hetu
cause	rgyu mtshan	nimitta
Cittamātra	sems tsam	Cittamātra
cognition	rnam par rig pa/rnam par shes pa	vijñāna
cognition that appears as itself	rang snang ba'i rnam par rig pa	svābhāsa-vijñapti
cognitive object	shes par bya	jñeya
collection	'dus pa	samūha
combined features	'dus pa'i rnam pa	saṃcitākāra
composite	tshogs pa	samūha/saṃghāta
compound	phung po	skandha
configured together	'dab byar	
condition	rkyen	pratyaya
contrapositive entailment	ldog khyab	vyatireka-vyāpti
conventionally real	kun rdzob du yod pa	saṃvṛti-sat
convey an aspect	rnam pa gtod pa	ākārārpaṇa
corresponds to	rjes su byed	anukaroti
defective sense faculties	dbang po ma tshang ba	vikalpendriya

English	Tibetan	Sanskrit
definition	mtshan nyid	lakṣaṇa
direct cause	dngos rgyu	sākṣāt-kāraṇa
dominant condition	bdag rkyen	adhipati-pratyaya
dormant	bag la zha	nyagbhāva
effect	'bras bu	phala
effect	rgyu dang ldan pa	hetumān
emptiness	stong pa nyid	śūnyatā
entity	dngos po	bhava
external object	phyi rol gyi don	bāhyārtha
eye sense faculty	mig gi dbang po	cakṣur-indriya
false representationalist	rnam brdzun pa	alīkākara
feature	snang ba	ākāra
fundamental consciousness	kun gzhi rnam par shes pa	ālaya-vijñāna
fundamental particle	rdul phra rab	paramāṇu
immediately preceding condition	de ma thag rkyen	samanantara-pratyaya
inference	rjes dpag	anumāna
inherent existence	rang bzhin	svabhāva
internal cognitive object	nang gi shes bya	antar-jñeya
invariably concomitant	mi 'khrul	avyabhicāra
macro-object	rags pa	sthūla/audārika
material form	gzugs	rūpa
maturation	yongs su smin pa	pariṇāma
mental phenomenon	sems las byung	caitta
mind	sems	citta
Mind Only	sems tsam	Cittamātra
minute particle	rdul phran	aṇu/paramāṇu
nominal percept condition	dmigs rkyen btags pa	
nominally real	btags yod	prajñapti-sat
object	yul/don	viṣaya/artha
object of engagement	spyod yul	gocara
omnipresent	kun 'gro	sarvatraga
particular	rang gi mtshan nyid	svalakṣaṇa
percept	dmigs pa	ālambana
percept condition	dmigs pa'i rkyen	ālambana-pratyaya
percept condition that is transferred	rnam par 'jog pa'i dmigs rkyen	
percept condition that transfers capacity	nus pa 'jog pa'i dmigs rkyen	

English	Tibetan	Sanskrit
perception	mngon sum	pratyakṣa
positive entailment	rjes khyab	anvaya-vyāpti
predisposition	bag chags	vāsanā
reflexive awareness	rang rig	svasamvedana
representation	snang ba	ākāra
Sautrāntika	mDo sde pa	Sautrāntika
seed	sa bon	bīja
self-presenting	rang mdangs	
sense faculty	dbang po	indriya
sensory cognition	dbang shes	indriya-jñāna
simultaneous cause	lhan cig 'byung ba'i rgyu	sahabhū-hetu
Śrāvaka	nyan thos	Śrāvaka
stable predispositions	bag chags brtan pa	
substance	rdzas	dravya
substantial particle	rdzas rdul	dravya-paramāṇu
substantially real	rdzas su yod pa	dravya-sat
thing	dngos po	bhava
true representationalist	rnam bden pa	satyākara
Vaibhāṣika	Bye brag smra ba	Vaibhāṣika
Vaiśeṣika	Bye brag pa	Vaiśeṣika
visible form	gzugs	rūpa
Yogācāra	rNal 'byor spyod pa	Yogācāra

Bibliography

ACIP: Asian Classics Input Project: http://www.asianclassics.org.

Aodeng Qimuge 敖登其木格. 2007. "A-lag-sha Ngag-dbang Bstan-dar's Thought about Writing: Translation, Assembled Notes, and Study of the Tibetan Text "Light of Fine Words" (Awang danda laranbade chuangzuo sixiang Zangwen jiayan riguangde fanyi pingzhuhe yanjiu 阿旺丹达拉然巴的创作思想—藏文《嘉言日光》的翻译、评注和研究). M.A. thesis, Inner Mongolia University.

Arai Ikkō. 2003. "Critiques of the Vijñānavāda by Udayana: A Study of the Chapter on bāhyārthabhaṅga of the Ātmatattvaviveka (1)." [ウダヤナの唯識説批判: Ātmatattvaviveka「外境滅」章研究 (1) Udayana no yūishikisetsu-hihan—Ātmatattvaviveka 外境滅 sho kenkyū (1)]. *Komazawa Daigaku Bukkyōgaku-bu Ronshū* 34: 37–56.

Aramaki Noritoshi. 2000. "Toward an Understanding of the Vijñapti-mātratā." Jonathan Silk (ed.). *Wisdom, Compassion and the Search for Understanding: The Buddhist Studies Legacy of Gadjin Nagao*. Honolulu: University of Hawai'i Press: 39–60.

Arnold, Dan. 2005. *Buddhists, Brahmins, and Belief: Epistemology in South Asian Philosophy of Religion*. New York: Columbia University Press.

Arnold, Dan. 2010. "Self-Awareness (*svasaṃvitti*) and Related Doctrines of Buddhists Following Dignāga: Philosophical Characterization of Some of the Main Issues." *Journal of Indian Philosophy* 38: 323–378.

Asaṅga. n.d. *Bodhisattva Levels* (*Bodhisattva-bhūmi*). GRETL e-text: http://gretil.sub.uni-goettingen.de/gretil/1_sanskr/6_sastra/3_phil/buddh/bsa034_c.txt; accessed 28/08/2014.

Asaṅga. n.d. *Compendium of Ascertainments of the Levels of Yogic Practice* (*Yogācārabhūmi-iniścaya-saṃgrahaṇī*; Tib. *rNal 'byor spyod pa'i sa rnam par gtan la dbab pa bsdu ba*). sDe dge 4038, Sems tsam, vol. *zhi*; 1b1-289a7; zi 1b1-127a4.

Asaṅga. n.d. *Compendium of Mahāyāna* (*Mahāyāna-saṃgraha*; Tib. *Theg pa chen po'i bsdus pa*. sDe dge #4048, *sems tsam*, vol. *ri*; Ch. *She dasheng lun* 攝大乘論. T 31, no. 1594.

Asaṅga. n.d. *Ornament for Mahāyāna Discourses* (*Mahāyāna-sūtrālaṃkāra*). Tib. *Theg pa chen po mdo sde'i rgyan*. sDe dge #4020, Sems tsam vol. *phi*; 1b1-39a4 GRETL e-text: http://gretil.sub.uni-goettingen.de/gretil/1_sanskr/4_rellit/buddh/asmahsbc.txt; accessed 28/8/2014.

Bhāviveka. n.d. *Blaze of Reasoning: A Commentary on the Verses on the Heart of the Middle Way* (*Madhyamaka-hṛdaya-vṛtti-tarkajvālā*; Tib. *dBu ma snying po'i 'grel pa rtog ge 'bar ba*). sDe dge edition, dBu ma vol. *dza*.

Bhāviveka. n.d. *Verses on the Heart of the Middle Way* (*Madhyamaka-hṛdaya-kārikā*; Tib. *dBu ma'i snying po'i tshig le'ur byas pa*), sDe dge edition, dBu ma *dza*.

Bianchi, Ester. 2009. "The 'Chinese Lama' Nenghai (1886–1967): Doctrinal Traditions and Teaching Strategies of a Gelukpa Master in Republican China." Matthew T. Kapstein (ed.). *Buddhism between Tibet and China*. Somerville, Mass.: Wisdom Publications: 295–346.

Bianchi, Ester. 2004. "The Tantric Rebirth Movement in Modern China." *Acta Orientalia* 57(1): 31–54.

Bingenheimer, Marcus. 2003. "Chinese Buddhism Unbound—Rebuilding and Redefining Chinese Buddhism on Taiwan." K. Sankarnarayan (ed.). *Buddhism in Global Perspective*. Mumbai: Somaiya Publications: 122–146.

Blofeld, John. 1938. "Lamaism and Its Influence on Chinese Buddhism." *T'ien Hsia Monthly*, September: 151–160.

Broughton, Jeffrey. 1983. "Early Chan Schools in Tibet." Robert Gimello and Peter Gregory (eds.). *Studies in Ch'an and Hua-yen*. Honolulu: University of Hawaii Press: 1–68.

Buescher, Hartmut (ed.). 2007. *Sthiramati's Triṃśikāvijñaptibhāṣya: Critical Editions of the Sanskrit Text and Its Tibetan Translation*. Vienna: Österreichische Akademie der Wissenschaften, Phil.-hist. Kl., Sitzungsberichte, 786; Beitrḥge zur Kultur- und Geistesgeschichte Asiens, 57.

Burke, David. 1983. "On the Measure 'Parimaṇḍala'." *Philosophy East and West* 33(3): 273–284.

C: Co ne edition of the Tibetan canon.

Cabezón, José (ed.). 1998. *Scholasticism: Cross-Cultural and Comparative Perspectives*. Albany: State University of New York Press.

Candrakīrti. n.d. *Commentary on the Four Hundred* (*Catuḥśataka-ṭīkā*; Tib. *dBu ma bzhi brgya pa'i ṭīka*). sDe dge edition, dBu ma vol. *ya*.

Candrakīrti. n.d. *Introduction to the Middle Way* (*Madhyamakāvatāra; dBu ma la 'jug* pa). sDe dge edition, dBu ma vol. *'a*.

CBETA: Chinese Electronic Buddhist Electronic Text Association: http://www.cbeta.org.

Chatterjee, Amita. 2012. "Naturalism in Classical Indian Philosophy." Edward N. Zalta (ed.). *The Stanford Encyclopedia of Philosophy* (Spring 2012 Edition), URL: http://plato.stanford.edu/archives/spr2012/entries/naturalism-india/.

Chatterjee, D. C. 1933. "*Hetucakranirṇaya*." *Indian Historical Quarterly* 10: 266–272, 511–514.

Chatterjee, D. C. 1930. "Two Quotations in the *Tattvasaṃgraha-pañjikā*." *Annals of the Bhandarkar Oriental Research Institute* 11: 196–199.

Chen, Bing 陈兵, and Deng Zimei 邓子美. 2000. *Twentieth Century Chinese Buddhism* (*Ershishiji Zhongguo Fojiao* 二十世纪中国佛教). Beijing: Minzu Chubanshe.

Chi, Richard S. Y. 1984. *Buddhist Formal Logic*. Delhi: Motilal Banarsidass.

Chia Ning. 1992. *The Li-fan Yuan in the Early Qing Dynasty*. Ph.D. dissertation, Johns Hopkins University.

Chim Jambeyang (mChims 'Jam pa'i dbyangs). n.d. *Ornament for the Treasury of Abhidharma* (*mDzod 'grel mngon pa'i rgyan*; Skt. *Abhidharmakośālaṃkāra*). (1) n.d. TBRC W2CZ8096. Khun grub zil gnon rje 'bum lha khang, [lha sa] (1 volume: 430 ff.); (2) 2009. *Chos mngon pa mdzod kyi tshing le'ur byas pa'i 'grel pa mngon pa'i rgyan*. New Delhi: Institute of Tibetan Classics.

Chu, William. 2010–2011. "The Timing of Yogācāra Resurgence in the Ming Dynasty (1368–1643)." *Journal of the International Association of Buddhist Studies* 33(1–2): 5–25.

Cook, Francis (trans.). 1999. *Three Texts on Consciousness Only*. Berkeley, Calif.: Numata Center.

Cox, Collett. 1995. *Disputed Dharmas: Early Buddhist Theories on Existence. An Annotated Translation of the Section on Factors Dissociated from Thought from Saṅghabhadra's Nyāyānusāra*. Tokyo: International Institute for Buddhist Studies.

Cox, Collett. 1988. "On the Possibility of a Nonexistent Object of Consciousness: Sarvāstivādin and Dārṣṭāntika Theories." *Journal of the International Association of Buddhist Studies* 11: 31–87.

D: sDe dge edition of the Tibetan canon.

Dalai Lama and Alexander Berzin. 1997. *The Geluk/Kagyü Tradition of Mahamudra*. Ithaca: Snow Lion Publications.

Dargyay, Geshe Lobsang. 1981. *A Concise Biography of Guṅ Thaṅ Dkon Mchog Bstan Pa'i Sgron Me*. Vienna: Arbeitskreis für Tibetische und Buddhistische Studien Universtität Wien.

Das, Sarat Chandra. 2000. *A Tibetan-English Dictionary*. Delhi: Motilal Banarsidass.

Davenport, John (trans.). 2000. *Ordinary Wisdom: Sakya Pandita's Treasury of Good Advice*. Boston: Wisdom Publications.

Demiéville, Paul. 1952. *Concile De Lhasa: Une controverse sur le quiétisme entre bouddhistes de l'Inde et de la Chine au VIIIe siècle de l'ère chrétienne*. Paris: Collège de France, Institut des hautes études chinoises.

Dessein, Bart (trans.) 1999. *Saṃyuktābhidharmahṛdaya: Heart of Schlasticism with Miscellaneous* Additions. Delhi: Motilal Banarsidass (3 vols.).

Devendrabuddhi. n.d. *Subcommentary to the Commentary on the Compendium of Epistemology* (*Pramāṇavārttika-pañjikā*; Tib. *Tshad ma rnam 'grel gyi dka' 'grel*). sDe dge *bsTan 'gyur, Tshad ma* vol. *che*, (Toh. **4217**): 3.242b6.

Dhammajoti, Bhikkhu K. L. 2012. "Abhidharma Debate on the Nature of the Objects of Sensory Perception." *Journal of Buddhist Studies* (Centre for Buddhist Studies, Sri Lanka) 10: 203–234.

Dhammajoti, Bhikkhu K. L. 2007b. "Ākāra and Direct Perception (Pratyakṣa)." L. Kawamura and S. Haynes (eds.). *Pacific World Journal*, third series, no. 9: 245–272. Berkeley: Institute for Buddhist Studies.

Dhammajoti, Bhikkhu K. L. 2004. "Logic in the Abhidharma-mahāvibhāṣā." *Journal of Buddhist Studies* (Centre for Buddhist Studies, Sri Lanka) 2: 180–197.

Dhammajoti, Bhikkhu K. L. 2007a. *Sarvāstivāda Abhidharma*. Hong Kong: University of Hong Kong.

Dharmakīrti. 2007. *Ascertainment of the Instruments of Knowledge* (*Pramāṇa-viniścaya*). Ernst Steinkellner (ed.). *Dharmakīrti's Pramāṇaviniścaya, Chapters 1 and 2*. Beijing & Vienna: China Tibetology Publishing House / Austrian Academy of Sciences Press. For corrigenda, see: *Wiener Zeitschrift für die Kunde Südasiens* 51 (2007–2008): 207–208, as well as http://ikga.oeaw.ac.at/Mat/steinkellner07_corrigenda.pdf.

Dharmakīrti. n.d. *Commentary on the Compendium of Epistemology* (*Pramāṇa-vārttika*; Tib. *Tshad ma rnam 'grel*). (1) Miyasaka Yūsho (ed.). 1971–1972. *Pramāṇavarttika-Kārikā* (Sanskrit and Tibetan). *Acta Indologica* #2. Narita: Naritasan Shinshoji. (2) Dvārikādāsa Śāstri (ed.). 1968. *Pramāṇavārttika of Ācārya Dharmakīrti*. Varanasi: Bauddha Bharati. (3) Ramcandra Pandey (ed.). 1989. *Ācāryadharmakīrteḥ pramāṇavārttikam*. Delhi: Motilal Banarsidass. (4) Tibetan: sDe dge edition, Tshad ma, vol. *ce*.

Dharmapāla (Hufa 護法). n.d. *Clarification of Entry into the One Hundred Dharmas* (*Śatadharma-prakāśa-mukha-śāstra*; Tib. *Chos brgya gsal pa'i sgo'i bstan bcos*). sDe dge edition #4063, Sems tsam vol. *shi*: 145a7–146b2.

Dharmapāla (Hufa 護法). n.d. *Explanation of Investigation of the Percept* (*Guan suoyuan lun shi* 觀所緣論釋), T 1625, CBETA version: http://21dzk.l.u-tokyo.ac.jp/SAT/ddb-sat2.php?mode=detail&useid=1625_,00,0891&nonum=&kaeri=, vol. 00.0889b28; accessed 8/5/2014.

Dharmottara. 1971. *Commentary on the Drop of Logic* (*Nyāyabindu-ṭīkā*. Dalsukhbhai Malvania (ed.). *Paṇḍita Durvekamiśra's Dharmottarapradīpa*. Tibetan Sanskrit Works Series 2. Second edition. Patna: Kashi Prasad Jayaswal Research Institute.

Dharmottara. n.d. *Investigation of the Instruments of Knowledge* (*Pramāṇa-parīkṣā*; Tib. *Tshad ma brtag pa*). sDe dge edition, Tshad ma vol. *zhe*.

Dignāga. n.d. *Autocommentary to Investigation of the Percept* (*Ālambana-parīkṣā-vṛtti*). Tib. *dMigs pa brtag pa'i 'grel pa*. (1) sDe dge (D) edition, TBRC *bsTan 'gyur*,

W23703-1490: 171.5–174; (2) Co ne (C): TBRC W1GS66030, vol. 174: 175–177; (3) dPe bsdur ma (B): TBRC W1PD95844, vol. 97: 432–436; (4) gSer bris (S): #3705; TBRC W23702, vol. 183: 474–476; (5) Peking (Pe cing) (P): #5703, *tshad ma* vol. *ce*: 86a.5–87b.2 (vol. 130, p. 73); (6) sNar thang (N): #3702, *tshad ma* vol. *ce*: 180b1–182a2.

Dignāga. n.d. *Commentary on the Treasury of Abhidharma Called "Lamp of the Essence" (Abhidharmakośa-vṛtti-marmapradīpa-nāma*. Tib. *Chos mngon pa'i mdzod kyi 'grel pa gnad kyi sgron me zhes bya ba*). sDe dge #4095, *mngon pa*, vol. *nyu*: 95b1–214a7; TBRC W23703.

Dignāga. 2005. *Compendium of Epistemology* (*Pramāṇa-samuccaya*; Tib. *Tshad ma kun las btus pa*). (1) Ernst Steinkellner (ed.). "*Dignāga's Pramāṇasamuccaya*, Chapter 1: A hypothetical reconstruction of the Sanskrit text with the help of the two Tibetan translations on the basis of the hitherto known Sanskrit fragments and the linguistic materials gained from Jinendrabuddhi's Ṭīkā.": http://www.ikga.oeaw.ac.at/Mat/dignaga_PS_1.pdf; corrections: http://www.ikga.oeaw.ac.at/mediawiki/images/f/f3/Dignaga_PS_1_revision.pdf; (2) sDe dge #4203, Tshad ma vol. *ce*: 1b1–13a7.

Dignāga. n.d. *Hair in the Hand Treatise* (*Hastavāla-prakaraṇa*). Ch. *Jiejuan lun* 解捲論. T 1620.31. Trans. Paramārtha.

Dignāga. n.d. *Interpretation of the Verses Condensing the Perfection of Wisdom* (*Prajñāpāramitā-saṃgraha-kārikā-vivaraṇa*; Ch. *Fomu ban ruo boluomiduo yuanji yaoyi shi lun* 佛母般若波羅蜜多圓集要義釋論. T 1517.25. Trans. Dānapāla.

Dignāga. n.d. *Introduction to Logic* (*Nyāya-mukha*). Ch. *Yinming zhengli men lun* 因明正理門論. T 1628.32.3b26-7. Trans. Xuanzang.

Dignāga. n.d. *Investigation of Universals* (*Sāmānya-lakṣaṇa-parīkṣā*). Ch. 觀總相論頌. T 1623.31. Trans. Yijing.

Dignāga. n.d. *Investigation of the Percept* (*Ālambana-parīkṣā*). Tib. *dMigs pa brtag pa*. (1) sDe dge edition (D), #4205, *Tshad ma* vol. *ce*: 86a1–86a5. TBRC W23703-1490: 171.1–5; (2) Co ne (C): TBRC W1GS66030, vol. 174: 174–175; (3) dPe bsdur ma (B): TBRC W1PD95844, vol. 97: 430–431; (4) gSer bris (S): #3705; TBRC W23702, vol. 183: 474–476; (5) Peking (Pe cing) (P): #5703, *tshad ma* vol. *ce*: 177a7-177b5 (vol. 130: 73–74); (6) sNar thang (N): #3702, *tshad ma* vol. *ce*: 119.3-6.

Dignāga. n.d. *Treatise on Apprehending the Designations of Causes* (*Quyin jiashe lun*取因假設論, T31.88. SAT Daizōkyō edition: http://21dzk.l.u-tokyo.ac.jp/SAT/ddb-sat2.php?mode=detail&useid=1622_,31,0887c21.

Dignāga. n.d. *Verses Condensing the Perfection of Wisdom* (*Prajñāpāramitā-saṃgraha-kārikā*). Ch. 佛母般若波羅蜜多圓集要義論. T 1518.25. Trans. Dānapāla.

Dreyfus, Georges B. 1997. *Recognizing Reality: Dharmakīrti's Philosophy and Its Tibetan Interpreters*. Albany: State University of New York Press.

Dreyfus, Georges B. 2003. "Would the True Prāsaṅgika Please Stand? The Case and View of 'Ju Mi Pham." Georges Dreyfus and Sara McClintock (eds.). *The*

Svātantrika-Prāsaṅgika Distinction: What Difference Does a Difference Make? Boston: Wisdom Publications: 317–347.

Dreyfus, Georges, and Christian Lindtner. 1989. "The Yogācāra Philosophy of Dignāga and Dharmakīrti." *Studies in Central and East Asian Religions* 2: 27–52.

Dunne, John D. 2004. *Foundations of Dharmakīrti's Philosophy*. Boston: Wisdom Publications.

Durveka Miśra. 1955. *Light on Dharmottara* (*Dharmottara-pradīpa*). Dalsukh Malvania (ed.). *Paṇḍita Purveka Miśra's Dharmottara-pradīpa*. Patna: Kashiprasad Jayaswal Research Institute.

Eckel, M. David. 2008. *Bhāviveka and His Buddhist Opponents*. Harvard Oriental Series 70. Cambridge, Mass.: Harvard Department of Sanskrit and Indian Studies.

Eckel, M. David. 1987. *Jñānagarbha's Commentary on the Distinction Between the Two Truths*. Albany: State University of New York Press.

Edgerton, Franklin. 1985. *Buddhist Hybrid Sanskrit Grammar and Dictionary (Vol. 1: Grammar; Vol. 2: Dictionary)*. Delhi: Motilal Banarsidass.

Eichman, Jennifer. 2013. "Humanizing the Study of Late Ming Buddhism." *Chung-hwa Buddhist Journal* 26: 153–185.

Eltschinger, Vincent. 1999. "Śubhagupta's *Śrutiparīkṣākārikā* (vv. 10cd-19) and its Dharmakīrtian Background." Katsura Shoryu (ed.). *Dharmakīrti's Thought and its impact on Indian and Tibetan Philosophy*. Vienna: Verlag der Österreischischen Akademie der Wissenschaften: 47–61.

Eshō Mikogami. 1986. "Bāhyārthasiddhikārikā." *Ryukoku Daigaku Ronshū* 429: 2–44.

Eshō Mikogami.1983. "Śubhagupta no gokumi-ron no yōgo." *Ryukoku Daigaku Bunko Kenkyūjo Kiyō* 22: 1–17.

Fazun 法尊. 1990a. "Author's Experiences in Tibet" ("Zhuzhe ru Zang de jing-guo" 著者入藏的經過). *Collected Buddhist Studies Essays of Venerable Fazun* (*Fashi foxue lunwen ji* 法尊法师佛学论文集). Beijing: Zhongguo fojiao wenhua yanjiusuo: 358–371.

Fazun 法尊. 1990b. "Fazun Fashi's Autobiography." ("Fazun Fashi zi shu" 法尊法師自述). *Collected Buddhist Studies Essays of Venerable Fazun*: 372–376.

Fazun 法尊 (trans.). 1939. *Great Exposition of Mantra* [*sNgags rim chen mo*; Ch. *Mizongdao cidi guanglun* 密宗道次第廣論]. Reprint, Shanghai: Shanghai Foxue shuju, 1996.

Fazun 法尊 (trans.). 1935. *Great Exposition of the Stages of the Path* [*Lam rim chen mo*; Ch. *Puti dao cidi guanglun* 菩提道次第廣論]. Reprint, Shanghai: Shanghai Foxue shuju, n.d.

Fazun 法尊. 1940. *Political and Religious History of the Tibetan People* (*Xizang Minzu zhengjiao shi shi* 西藏民族政教史). Peking: Quanguo tushuguan wenxian suowei fuzhi zhongxin.

Fazun 法尊. 1980. *Tibet and Tibetan Buddhism* (*Xizang yu Xizang fojiao* 西藏与西藏佛教). Taipei: Tian hua chuban shiye gufen youxian gongsi.

Franco, Eli. 2006. "A New Era in the Study of Buddhist Philosophy." *Journal of Indian Philosophy* 34: 221–227.

Franco, Eli. 1986. "Once Again on Dharmakīrti's Deviation from Dignāga on Pratyakṣābhāsa." *Journal of Indian Philosophy* 14: 79–97.

Franco, Eli. (ed.). 2013. *Periodization and Historiography of Indian Philosophy*. Publications of the de Nobili Research Library 37. Vienna.

Franke, Herbert. 1987. "Tibetans in Yuan China." John D. Langlois (ed.). *China under Mongol Rule*. Princeton, N.J.: Princeton University Press: 296–328.

Frauwallner, Erich. 1930. "Dignāgas *Ālambanaparīkṣā*: Text, Übersetzung und Erläuterungen." *Wiener Zeitschrift für die Kunde des Morgenlandes* 37, heft 1 und 2: 174–194.

Frauwallner, Erich. 1959. "Dignāga: sein Werk und seine Entwicklung." *Wiener Zeitschrift für die Kunde Süd- und Ostasiens* 3: 93–164.

Frauwallner, Erich. 1953. *Geschichte der indischen Philosophie*. II. Band. Salzburg: Otto Müller Verlag.

Frauwallner, Erich. 1961. "Landmarks in the History of Indian Logic." *Wiener Zeitschrift für die Kunde Süd und Ostasiens* 5: 125–148.

Frauwallner, Erich. 1957. "Vasubandhu's *Vādavidhi*." *Wiener Zeitschrift für die Kunde Südasiens* 1: 104–146.

Funayama, Toru. 1995. "Arcaṭa, Śāntarakṣita, Jinendrabuddhi, and Kamalaśīla on the Aim of a Treatise (prayojana)." *Wiener Zeitschrift für die Kunde Südasiens* 39: 181–203.

Funayama, Toru. 2007. "Kamalaśīla's Distinction between the Two Sub-schools of Yogācāra: A Preliminary Survey." Birgit Kellner et al. (eds.). *Pramāṇakīrtiḥ: Papers dedicated to Ernst Steinkellner on the occasion of his 70th birthday, Part 1*. Vienna: Wiener Studien zur Tibetologie und Buddhismuskunde 70.1: 187–202.

Funayama, Toru. 2001. "On the Date of Vinītadeva." Raffaele Torella (ed.). *Le Parole e i Marmi: Studi in Onoore di Raniero Gnoli*. Rome: Serie Orientale Roma 92. Rome: Istituto Italiano per Africa e l'Oriente: 309–325.

Funayama, Toru. 1992. "A Study of *Kalpanāpoḍha*. A Translation of the *Tattvasaṇgraha* vv. 1212–1263 by Śāntarakşita and the *Tattvasaṇgrahapañjikā* by Kamalaśīla on the Definition of Direct Perception." *Zinbun: Annals of the Institute for Research in Humanities, Kyoto University* 27: 33–128.

Gangopadhyaya, Mrinalkanti. 1980. *Indian Atomism: History and Sources*. Calcutta: Bagchi. WID-LC B132.A83 G36.

Gangopadhyaya, Mrinalkanti. 1971. *Vinītadeva's Nyāyabindu-ṭīkā*. Indian Studies Past and Present. Calcutta: R. D. Press.

Gardner, Alexander P. 2006. "The Twenty-Five Great Sites of Khams: Religious Geography, Revelation and Nonsectarianism in Nineteenth Century Eastern Tibet." Ph.D. dissertation, University of Michigan.

Gendün Drup (dGe 'dun grub). n.d. *Ornament of Reasoning: Great Exposition of Epistemological Treatises* (*Tshad ma'i bstan bcos chen mo rigs pa'i rgyan; Gsung 'bum*, vol. 5 (*ca*).

Gómez, Luis O. 1983a. "The Direct and Gradual Approaches of Zen Master Mahāyāna: Fragments of the Teachings of Moheyan." Robert Gimello and Peter Gregory (eds.). *Studies in Ch'an and Hua-yen*. Honolulu: University of Hawai'i Press: 69–168.

Gómez, Luis O. 1983b. "Indian Materials on the Doctrine of Sudden Awakening." Whalen Lai and Lewis Lancaster (ed.). *Early Ch'an in China and Tibet*. Berkeley: University of California Press: 393–434.

Gungtang Könchok Denbe Drönme (Gung thang dKon mchog bstan pa'i sgron me). 1990. *A Biography of Lord Jikme Wangpo, The Omniscient Second Jamyang Sheba* (*Kun mkhyen 'jam dbyangs bzhad pa sku 'phreng gnyis pa rje 'jigs med dbang po'i rnam thar*). Lanzhou: Gansu's Nationalities Press.

Gungtang Könchok Denbe Drönme (Gung thang dKon mchog bstan pa'i sgron me). n.d. *Entrance to the Scholars' Explanations of the Difficult Points of Mind and the Fundamental Consciousness* (*Yid dang kun zhi'i dka' gnad rnam par bshad pa mkhas pa'i 'jug ngogs*). *Gungtang's Collected Works* (bLa brang ed.), vol. 2, 243–362.

Gungtang Könchok Denbe Drönme (Gung thang dKon mchog bstan pa'i sgron me). 2003. *Gungtang's Collected Works* (*gung thang bstan pa'i sgron me'i gsung 'bum*). Beijing: Nationalities Press.

Gungtang Könchok Denbe Drönme (Gung thang dKon mchog bstan pa'i sgron me). 1991. *A Hundred Waves of Elegant Sayings*. Yeshi Tashi (trans.). The Dalai Lama Tibeto-Indological Series-X. Sarnath: Central Institute of Higher Tibetan Studies.

Gyeltsap (rGyal tshab Dar ma rin chen). 2006. *Clarifying the Thought: Great Commentary Definitively Elucidating Epistemological Treatises* (*bsTan bcos tshad ma rnam nges kyi ṭīk chen dgongs pa rab gsal*). *dPal dge ldan pa'i tshad ma rig pa'i gzhung gces btus. Bod kyi gtsug lag gces btus.* (1) New Delhi: Institute of Tibetan Classics, vol. 21. (2) TBRC W669.

Gyeltsap (rGyal tshab Dar ma rin chen). n.d. *Good Explanation of the Four Hundred Commentary* (*bZhi brgya pa'i rnam bshad legs bshad snying po*). Asian Classics Input Project (ACIP) http://www.asianclassics.org/release6/flat/S5428I_T.TXT.

Gyeltsap (rGyal tshab Dar ma rin chen). n.d. *Illumination of the Path to Liberation: Explanation of the Commentary on the Compendium of Epistemology, an Unerring Illumination of the Path to Liberation* (*Tshad ma rnam 'grel gyi tshig le'ur byas pa'i rnam bshad thar lam phyin ci ma log par gsal bar byed pa*). Lhasa: Zhol Par khang edition, vol. *cha*.

Hallisey, Charles. 2007. "Sautrāntika." Damien Keown and Charles S. Prebish (eds.). *Encyclopedia of Buddhism*. London: Routledge: 675–677.

Hanneder, J. 2007. "Vasubandhu's Viṃśatikā 1 2 anhand der Sanskrit- und tibetischen Fassungen." K. Klaus and J.-U. Hartmann (eds.). *Indica et Tibetica: Festschrift für Michael Hahn, zum 65 Geburtstag von Freunden und Schülern überreicht.*

Vienna: Arbeitskreis für Tibetische und Buddhistische Studien Universtität Wien: 207–214.

Hattori, Maasaki. 1960. "Bāhyārthasiddhikārikā of Śubhagupta." *Indogaku Bukkyōgaku Kenkyū* 8-1: 400–395.

Hattori, Maasaki. 1968. *Dignāga, On Perception*. Cambridge, Mass.: Harvard University Press.

Hattori, Maasaki. 1961. "Dignāga's Criticism of the Mīmāmsaka Theory." *Journal of Indian and Buddhist Studies* 9(2): 711–724.

Hattori, Maasaki. 1988. "Realism and the Philosophy of Consciousness-Only" Trans. William Powell. *The Eastern Buddhist* 21: 23–60.

Hayes, Richard. 1987. *Dignāga on the Interpretation of Signs*. Dordrecht: Kluwer Academic Publishers.

Hayes, Richard. 1993. "Jinendrabuddhi." *Journal of the American Oriental Society* 103 (4): 709–717.

Hirakawa Akira. 1973. *Index to the Abhidharmakośabhāṣya (P. Pradhan Edition)*. Tokyo: Daizo Shuppan Kabushikikaisha.

Holmes-Tagchungdarpa, Amy. 2014. *The Social Life of Tibetan Biography: Textuality, Community, and Authority in the Lineage of Tokden Shakya Shri*. Lanham, Md.: Lexington Books.

Hopkins, Jeffrey. 2003. *Maps of the Profound: Jam-Yang-Shay-Ba's Great Exposition of Buddhist and Non-Buddhist Views on the Nature of Reality*. Ithaca, N.Y.: Snow Lion Publications.

Ichigō Masamichi. 2000. "Śāntarakṣita and Bhāviveka as Opponents of the Mādhyamika in the Madhyamakāloka." Jonathan Silk (ed.). *Wisdom, Compassion and the Search for Understanding*. Honolulu: University of Hawai'i Press: 147–170.

Jaini, Padmanabh S. 1985. "The Sanskrit Fragments of Vinītadeva's *Triṃśikā-ṭīkā*." *Bulletin of the School of Oriental and African Studies* 48: 470–492.

Jamyang Gyatso ('Jam dbyangs rgya mtsho). 2012. *Religious Biography of Geshe Yeshes Thabkhas (dGe bshes Ye shes thabs mkhas rnam thar)*. Unpublished pdf.

Jamyang Shebe Dorje ('Jam dbyangs bzhad pa'i rdo rje). 1999. *Sun of the Field of Samantabhadra: Explication of Tenet Systems (Grub mtha'i rnam bshad kun bzang zhing gi nyi ma). Grub pa'i mtha' rnam par bzhag pa 'khrul spong gdong lnga'i sgra dbyangs kun mkhyen lam bzang gsal pa'i rin chen sgron me*. Mundgod: Drepung Gomang Library. Taiwan reprint: Corporate Body of the Buddha Educational Foundation.

Jangchup Dzüntrül (Byang chub rdzu 'phrul). 1985. *Explanation of the Noble Discourse Explaining the Thought (Ārya-saṃdhinirmocana-sūtrasya-vyākhyāna*; Tib. *'Phags pa dgongs 'grel nges par 'grel pa'i mdo'i rnam par bshad pa*. sDe dge edition. Delhi: Delhi Karmapae Choedhey, vol. *cho* [205]: 1–293.

Jhā, Gaṅgānāṭha (trans.). 1986. *Tattvasaṃgraha of Śāntarakṣita with the Commentary of Kamalaśīla* (2 vols.). Delhi: Motilal Banarsidass.

Jinendrabuddhi. 2005. Ernst Steinkellner, Helmut Krasser, and Horst Lasic (eds.). *Viśālāmalavatī. Jinendrabuddhi's Viśālāmalavatī Pramāṇasamuccayaṭīkā*. Beijing and Vienna: China Tibetology Research Center and Austrian Academy of Sciences.

Kajiyama, Yūichi 梶山雄一. 1966. *An Introduction to Buddhist Philosophy: An Annotated Translation of the Tarkabhāṣā of Mokṣākaragupta*. Memoirs of the Faculty of Letters: Kyoto University 10: 1–173.

Kajiyama, Yūichi 梶山雄一. 1965. "Controversy Between the *Sākāra-* and *Nirākāra-vadins* of the Yogācāra School—Some Materials." *Journal of Indian and Buddhist Studies* 14: 26–37.

Kajiyama, Yūichi 梶山雄一. 1999. "Do Other People's Minds Exist?" [創價大學國際佛教學高等研究所年報] *Annual Report of the International Research Institute for Advanced Buddhology at Soka University* 3: 3–35.

Kajiyama, Yūichi 梶山雄一. 1977. "Realism of the Sarvāstivāda School." Leslie S. Kawamura and Keith Scott (eds.). *Buddhist Thought and Asian Civilization*. Emeryville, Calif.: Dharma Publishing: 114–131.

Kamalaśīla. n.d. *Commentary on the Rice Seedling Discourse* (*Śālistambaka-ṭīkā*; Tib. *'Phags pa sā lu ljang pa rgya cher 'grel pa*). sDe dge #4001, *mDo 'grel*, vol. *ji*: 145b–163b.

Kamalaśīla. 1968. *Extended Commentary on the Compendium of Metaphysics* (*Tattvasaṃgraha-pañjikā*). Ed. Dvārikādāsa Śāstri. Varanasi: Bauddha Bharati Series.

Kapstein, Matthew T. (ed.). 2009. *Buddhism between Tibet and China*. Somerville, Mass.: Wisdom Publications.

Kapstein, Matthew T. (ed.). 2001. *Reason's Traces: Identity and Interpretation in Indian and Tibetan Buddhist Thought*. Boston: Wisdom Publications.

Kapstein, Matthew T. (ed.). 2000. *The Tibetan Assimilation of Buddhism: Conversion, Contestation, and Memory*. Oxford: Oxford University Press.

Kapstein, Matthew T., and Sam van Schaik (eds.). 2010. *Esoteric Buddhism at Dunhuang: Rites and Teachings for This Life and Beyond*. Leiden: E. J. Brill.

Karma Phuntsho. 2005. "Shifting Boundaries: Pramāṇa and Ontology in Dharmakīrti's Epistemology." *Journal of Indian Philosophy* 33: 401–419.

Karunadasa, Y. 1967. *Buddhist Analysis of Matter*. Colombo: Department of Cultural Affairs.

Katsura Shoryu (ed.). 1999. *Dharmakīrti's Thought and Its Impact on Indian and Tibetan Philosophy. Proceedings of the Third International Dharmakīrti Conference (Hiroshima, November 4–6, 1997)*. Vienna: Verlag der Österreischischen Akademie der Wissenschaften.

Kawamura, Leslie S. 1975. "Vinītadeva's Contribution to the Buddhist Mentalist Trend." Ph.D. dissertation, University of Saskatchewan.

Kedrup (mKhas grub dGe legs dpal bzang). 2006a. *Clarification of the True Nature of the Great Commentary on the Wheel of Time* (*Dus 'khor 'grel chen de nyid snang ba;*

full title: *dPal dus kyi 'khor lo'i 'grel chen dri ma med pa'i 'od kyi rgya cher bshad pa de kho na nyid snang bar byed pa*. ACIP: http://asianclassics.org/release6/webdata/tibhtml/sungbum_author.html; accessed 5/5/2012

Kedrup (mKhas grub dGe legs dpal bzang). 1990. *Ocean of Reasoning: Extensive Exposition of the Commentary on the Compendium of Epistemology, Chapter on Direct Perception (Tshad ma rnam 'grel gyi rgya cher bshad pa rigs pa'i rgya mtsho las mngon sum le'u rnam bshad bzhugs so*. Beijing: Mi rigs dpe skrun khang. (2) Tokyo: Zhol edition, Tohoku #5505.

Kedrup (mKhas grub dGe legs dpal bzang). 2006b. *Ornament for Seven Epistemological Texts That Dispels Darkness in the Mind (Tshad ma sde bdun gyi rgyan yid kyi mun sel). dPal dge ldan pa'i tshad ma rig pa'i gzhung gcas btus. Bod kyi tsug la gces btus. Gsung 'bum*, vol. 5 (*ca*). New Delhi: Institute of Tibetan Classics, vol. 21.

Keenan, John. 1980. "A Study of the *Buddhabhūmy-upadeśa*: The Doctrinal Development of the Notion of Wisdom in Yogācāra Thought." Ph.D. Dissertation, University of Wisconsin.

Keenan, John. 2006. *The Summary of the Great Vehicle*. Berkeley: Numata Center.

Kellner, Birgit. 2014. "Changing Frames in Buddhist Thought: The Concept of Ākāra in Abhidharma and in Buddhist Epistemological Analysis." *Journal of Indian Philosophy* 42 (2–3): 275–295.

Kellner, Birgit. 2011. "Dharmakīrti's Criticism of External Realism and the Sliding Scale of Analysis." Helmut Krasser et al. (eds.). *Religion and Logic in Buddhist Philosophical Analysis: Proceedings of the Fourth International Dharmakīrti Conference, Vienna, August 23–27, 2005*. Vienna: Verlag der Österreichischen Akademie der Wissenschaften: 291–298.

Kellner, Birgit. 2010. "Self-Awareness (*svasaṃvedana*) in Dignāga's *Pramāṇasamuccaya* and *–vṛtti*: A Close Reading." *Journal of Indian Philosophy* 38: 203–231.

Khenpo Shenga (mKhan chen gZhan phan Chos kyi snang ba). 1978. *Commentaries by Khenpo Shenga Expanding the Texts of the Chief Indic Buddhist Śāstras in Their Tibetan Translations (Gzhan-dga' Gzhan-phan-cho-kyi-snan-ba, G'zun chen bcu gsum gyi mchan 'grel)* (6 vols.). Dehra Dun: D. G. Khochlen Tulku.

Khotse Tsültrim (Kho tshe Tshul khrims) (ed.). 2006. *Summary of the Essential Points of the Uncommon Liberation Story of Alasha Dendar Lharampa (A lag sha bstan dar lha rams pa'i thun mong ba'i rnam thar gnad bsdus bkod pa). Gangs ljongs rig bcu'i snying bcud chen mo bzhugs so*, vol. 1. Lhasa: Mi rigs dpe skrung khang.

Kolås, Ashild and Monika P. Thowsen. 2005. *On the Margins of Tibet: Cultural Survival on the Sino-Tibetan Frontier*. Seattle: University of Washington Press.

Könchok Denbe Drönme, Gungtang (Gung thang dKon mchog bstan pa'i sgron me). n.d. *Ornament for Dignāga's Thought in Investigation of the Percept (dMigs pa brtag pa'i 'grel pa phyogs glang dgongs rgyan)*. TBRC W7043.

Krasser, Helmut. 1992. "On the Relationship of Dharmottara, Śāntarakṣita, and Kamalaśīla." *Tibetan Studies, Proceedings of the 5th Seminar of the*

International Association of Tibetan Studies (Narita 1989). Narita-shi: Naritasan Shinshoji: 151–158.

Kuiji 窺基. n.d. *Account of the Treatise on Mere Cognition* (*Cheng weishilun shuji* 成唯識論述記). T 43, no. 1830.

Kuiji 窺基. n.d. *Account of the Twenty Verses on Mere Cognition* (*Weishi ershi lun shuji* 唯識二十論述記, 2 *juan*. T 43, no. 1834.

Kumārila. 1971. *Commentary on Verse Composition* (*Ślokavārttika*). Uṃveka Bhaṭṭa. *Ślokavārttikavyākhyā Tātparyaṭīkā*. S. K. Ramanatha Sastri (ed.); revised by K. Kunjunni Raja and R. Thangaswamy. Second edition. Madras: University of Madras.

La Vallée Poussin, Louis de. 1971. *L'Abhidharmakośa de Vasubandhu*. Brussels: Institut Belge des Hautes Études Chinoises.

La Vallée Poussin, Louis de. 1930. "Note sur l'*Ālambanaparīkṣā*." *Journal Asiatique* 217: 296–297.

La Vallée Poussin, Louis de. 1929. *Vijñaptimātratāsiddhi: la siddhi de Hiuan-Tsang*. Paris: Paul Geuthner.

Lai, Whalen, and Lewis R. Lancaster (eds.). 1983. *Early Ch'an in China and Tibet*. Berkeley: Asian Humanities Press.

Lamotte, Étienne. 1973. *La Somme du Grand Véhicule d' Asaṅga (Mahāyānasaṃgraha)*. Louvain: Université de Louvain, Institut Orientaliste.

Lamrim Chenmo Publication Committee. 2000. *The Great Treatise on the Stages of the Path to Enlightenment: Lam rim chen mo*. Ithaca, N.Y.: Snow Lion Publications.

Lévi, Sylvain. 1932. *Un système de philosophie buiddhique. Matériaux pour l'étude du système Vijñaptimātra*. Paris: Honoré Champion.

Liang Shuming 梁漱溟. 1994. *Outline of Mere Cognition* (*Weishi shuyi* 唯識述義). *Liang Shuming quanji* 梁漱溟全集. Shandong: Shandong renmin chuabshe, vol. 1: 301–302, n. 1.

Lin, Chen-kuo. 2008. "Object of Cognition in Dignāga's *Ālambanaparīkṣāvṛtti*: On the Controversial Passages in Paramārtha's and Xuanzang's Translations." *Journal of the International Association of Buddhist Studies* 29(2): 55–76.

Lin, Hsiao-Ting 2006. *Tibet and Nationalist China's Frontier: Intrigues and Ethnopolitics*. Vancouver: UBC Press.

Lobsang Rabgye. 1990. "What Is Non-Existent and What Is Remanent in Śūnyatā?" *Journal of Indian Philosophy* 18(1): 81–91.

Lü Cheng 呂澂. 1928b. "Evidential Study of *Introduction to Logic*" (Yinming zhengli men lun ben zhengwen 因明正理門論本證文). *Neixue* 內學 4: 237–264.

Lü Cheng 呂澂1928a. (L). *Translation and Comparative Exposition of Investigation of the Percept* (*Guan suoyuan shi lun huiyi* 觀所緣釋論會譯). *Neixue* 內學 4: 123–164.

Lusthaus, Dan. 2002. *Buddhist Phenomenology: A Philosophical Investigation of Yogācāra Buddhism and the Ch'eng Wei-shih Lun*. London: Routledge.

Lusthaus, Dan. 2013. "Lü Cheng's Chinese Translation of the Tibetan Version of Dignāga's *Ālambana-parīkṣā-vṛtti*: An English Translation." Sarah F. Haynes and

Michelle J. Sorensen (ed.). *Wading into the Stream of Wisdom: Essays in Honor of Leslie S. Kawamura*. Berkeley: Institute of Buddhist Studies: 97–127.

Lusthaus, Dan. 2014. "Lü Cheng, Epistemology, and Genuine Buddhism." John Makeham (ed.). *Transforming Consciousness: Yogācāra Thought in Modern China*. New York: Oxford University Press: 317–342.

Lusthaus, Dan. 2008. "A Pre-Dharmakīrti Indian Discussion of Dignāga Preserved in Chinese Translation: The *Buddhabhūmy-upadeśa*." *Journal of the Centre for Buddhist Studies, Sri Lanka*, 6: 1–65.

Lutgendorf, Philip. 1991. *The Life of a Text: Performing the Rāmcaritmānas of Tulsidas*. Berkeley: University of California Press.

Macdonnell, Arthur. *A Practical Sanskrit Dictionary*. 2014. http://dsalsrv02.uchicago.edu/cgi-bin/romadict.pl?query=etAvAt&display=simple&table=macdonell; accessed 12/05/2014.

Makeham, John. 2013. "The Significance of Xiong Shili's Interpretation of Dignāga's *Ālambana-parīkṣā (Investigation of the Object)*." *Journal of Chinese Philosophy* 40: 205–225.

Makeham, John (ed.). 2014. *Transforming Consciousness: Yogācāra Thought in Modern China*. New York: Oxford University Press.

Makley, Charlene. 2007. *The Violence of Liberation: Gender and Tibetan Buddhist Revival in Post-Mao China*. Berkeley: University of California Press.

Manabe, T. 2010. "Are Distinction of Direction and Unity Compatible in an Atom? Discussion between Kamalaśīla and Śubhagupta." *Journal of Indian and Buddhist Studies* 8 (1): 400–395 (= 9-14).

Matilal, Bimal Krishna. 1986. *Perception: An Essay on Classical Indian Theories of Knowledge*. Oxford: Clarendon Press.

Matsuoka Hiroko. 2012. "On the *Ālambanaparīkṣā* as Cited in the Bahirarthaparīkṣā of the *Tattvasaṃgraha*." *Journal of Indian and Buddhist Studies* 60: 1242–1247.

Matsuoka Hiroko. 2014. "On the Buddha's Cognition of Other Minds in the Bahirarthaparīkṣā of the Tattvasaṅgraha." *Journal of Indian Philosophy* 42: 297–307.

Matsuoka Hiroko. 2013. "Śāntaraksita in Defence of the Ālambanaparīkṣā v. 2ab." *Journal of Indian and Buddhist Studies* 61: 1241–1247.

McCrea, Lawrence J., and Patil, Parimal G. 2010. *Buddhist Philosophy of Language in India: Jñānaśrīmitra on Exclusion*. New York: Columbia University Press.

McClintock, Sara. 2014. "Kamalaśīla on the Nature of Phenomenal Content (ākāra) in Cognition: A Close Reading of TSP and TS 3626 and Related Passages." *Journal of Indian Philosophy* 42: 327–337.

Mingyu 明昱. n.d. *Explanation of Investigation of the Percept (Guan suoyuan yuan lunshi ji* 觀所緣緣論釋記). XZJ 83.363a-399b.

Mingyu 明昱. n.d. *Reconciled Explanation of Investigation of the Percept* (*Guan suoyuanyuan lun huishi* 觀所緣緣論會釋). CBETA vol. 51, No. 830: 0810b05-813c24.

Monier-Williams, Monier. 1979. *A Sanskrit-English Dictionary*. Delhi: Motilal Banarsidass.

Moriyama Shinya. 2010. "On Self-Awareness in the Sautrāntika Epistemology." *Journal of Indian Philosophy* 38: 261–277.

Moriyama Shinya. 2014. "Ratnākraśānti's Theory of Cognition with False Mental Images (*alīkākāravāda) and the Neither-One-Nor-Many Argument." *Journal of Indian Philosophy* 42: 339–351.

N: sNar thang edition of the Tibetan canon.

Nāgārjuna. n.d. *Fundamental Verses on the Middle Way* (*Mūlamadhyamaka-kārikā*). http://gretil.sub.uni-goettingen.de/gretil/1_sanskr/6_sastra/3_phil/buddh/nagmmk_r.txt.

Negi, J. S. 2000. *A Tibetan-Sanskrit Dictionary*. Sarnath: Central University of Tibetan Studies.

Ngawang Belden (Ngag dbang dpal ldan). 1964. *Annotations for* the *"Great Exposition of Tenets," Freeing the Knots of the Difficult Points, Precious Jewel of Clear Thought* (*Grub mtha' chen mo'i mchan 'grel dka' gnad mdud grol blo gsal gces nor*). Sarnath: Pleasure of Elegant Sayings Printing Press.

Ngawang Dendar (Ngag dbang bstan dar). n.d. *Advice on Seven Topics on Mind Training: Short Path of Mahāyāna* (*bLo sbyong don bdun ma'i gtam theg mchog nye lam*). TBRC W25275.

Ngawang Dendar (Ngag dbang bstan dar). n.d. *Beautiful String of Pearls: A Commentary on Investigation of the Percept* (*dMigs pa brtag pa'i 'grel pa mu tig 'phreng mdzes*). Tibetan Buddhist Resource Center (TBRC) W7301, sKu 'bum edition. *Ngag dbang bstan dar gSung 'bum, ja*: 21ff.

Ngawang Dendar (Ngag dbang bstan dar). n.d. *Ornamental Gem for the Crown Jewel of the Wise: Explanation of the "Crown Jewel of the Wise, Praise of Tārā"* (*Grol bstod mkhas pa'i gtsug rgyan gyi rnam bshad mkhas pa'i gtsug nor gyi phra rgyan, Ngag dbang bstan dar gsung 'bum*. Zi ling [Xining]: sKu 'bum byams pa gling, n.d., vol. 1: 1443–1472; TBRC W29009.

Nietupski, Paul. 2011. *Labrang Monastery: A Tibetan Buddhist Community on the Inner Asian Borderlands, 1709–1958*. Plymouth, UK: Lexington Books.

Nietupski, Paul. 2009. "The 'Reverend Chinese' (Gyanakpa tsang) at Labrang Monastery." Matthew T. Kapstein (ed.). *Buddhism between Tibet and China*. Somerville, Mass.: Wisdom Publications: 181–213.

Norbu, T. J. 1995. "Gungthangpa's Text in Colloquial Amdowa." Ernst Steinkellner and Helmut Tauscher (eds.). *Contributions on Tibetan Language, History and Culture*, vol. 1. Delhi: Motilal Banarsidass: 222–242.

Nordrang Orgyen (Nor brang o rgyan). 2006. "A lag Sha Ngag dbang bstan dar." *Collected Literary Works of Nor bu o rgyan* (*Nor brang o rgyan gyi gsung rtsom phyogs btus*). Beijing: Krung go'i bod rig pa dpe skrun khang.

Obermiller, E. 1970. *Indices Verborum Sanscrit-Tibetan and Tibetan-Sanscrit to the Nyāyabindu of Dharmakīrti and the Nyāyabinduṭīkā of Dharmottara*. Osnabrück: Bblio Verlag.

Ouyang Jingwu 歐陽竟無. 1914. *Interpretive Exposition of Investigation of the Percept (Guan suoyuan yuan lun shijie* 觀所緣緣論釋解). *Foxue congbao* 佛學叢報 11: 1–29.

P: Peking edition of the Tibetan canon.

Pandey, Ramcandra (ed.). 1989. *Ācāryadharmakīrteḥ pramāṇavārttikam*. Delhi: Motilal Banarsidass.

Paramārtha (Zhendi 眞諦). n.d. *Treatise on the Object of Cognition Devoid of Attributes* (*Wuxiang sichen lun* 無相思塵論). T 1619.31.882-883. CBETA: http://21dzk.l.u-tokyo.ac.jp/SAT/ddb-sat2.php?mode=detail&useid=1619_,00,0882&nonum=&kaeri=.

Pārthasārathimiśra. 1978. *Jewel Mine of Logic* (*Nyāya-ratnākara*). *Ślokavārttika of Śrī Kumārila Bhaṭṭa with the Commentary Nyāyaratnākara of Śrī Pārthasārathi Miśra*. Dvārikādāsa Śāstri (ed.). Varanasi: Prāchyabhāratī Series, #10.

Potter, Karl H. (ed.). 1977. *Indian Metaphysics and Epistemology: The Tradition of Nyāya-Vaiśeṣika up to Gaṅgeśa*. Princeton, N.J.: Princeton University Press.

Powers, John. 2007. *Introduction to Tibetan Buddhism* (2nd ed.). Ithaca, N.Y.: Snow Lion Publications.

Powers, John, and David Templeman. 2012. *Historical Dictionary of Tibet*. Metuchen, NJ: Scarecrow Publications.

Pradhan, Prahlad (ed.). 1975. *The Abhidharmakośa of Vasubandhu: With the Commentary*. Patna: K. P. Jayaswal Research Institute.

Prajñākaragupta. 1953. *Subcommentary on the Commentary on the Compendium of Epistemology*. Rahul Samkrtyayana (ed.). *Pramāṇavārttikabhāṣya of Prajñākaragupta*. Patna: K.P. Jayaswal Research Institute.

Pruden, Leo (trans.). 1988–1990. *Abhidharmakośabhāṣyam of Vasubandhu*. 6 vols. Berkeley: Asian Humanities Press.

Pudon (Bu ston Rin chen grub). 1986. *History of Buddhism* (*Chos 'byung*). *The History of Buddhism in India and Tibet*. Eugene Obermiller (trans.). Delhi: Sri Satguru.

Pūrṇavardhana n.d. *Supplement on the Features of the Commentary on the Treasury of Abhidharma* (*Abhidharmakośa-ṭīkā-lakṣaṇa-sariṇī; Chos mngon pa mdzod kyi 'grel bshad mtshan nyid kyi rjes su 'brang* ba). sDe dge edition, mNgon pa, vol. *cu*.

Rahula, Walpola. 1971. *Le Compendium de la Super-Doctrine (Abhidharmasamuccaya) d' Asaṅga*. Paris: École d'Extrème-Orient.

Randle, H. N. 1981. *Fragments from Diṅnāga*. Delhi: Motilal Banarsidass.

Roerich, George N. (trans.). 1995. *The Blue Annals*. Delhi: Motilal Banarsidass.

Saccone, Margherita Serena. (2014). "Śubhagupta on the Cognitive Process." *Journal of Indian Philosophy* 42: 377–399.

Sadhukhan, Sanjit Kumar. 1994. "A Short History of Buddhist Logic in Tibet." *Bulletin of Tibetology*, no. 3: 7–56.

Śāntarakṣita. 1968. *The Compendium of Metaphysics* (*Tattvasaṃgraha*). Swami Dwarikadas Shastri (ed.). *Tattvasaṃgraha with the Commentary Pañjikā of Śrī Kamalaśīla*. 2 vols. Bauddha Bharati Series 2. Varanasi.

Sastri, Aiyaswami. 1938. "*Ālambanaparīkṣā* and *Vṛtti* by Diṅnāga: With the Commentary of Dharmapāla." *The Brahmavidyā: Adyar Library Bulletin* 3. Reprint Madras: Adyar Library, 1942.

Scharfe, Harmut. 2002. *Education in Ancient India*. Leiden: E. J. Brill. Widener OL 330.7 Bd. 16.

Schmithausen, Lambert. 1999. "A Further Note on *Hetucakraḍamaru* 8–9." *Journal of Indian Philosophy* 27: 79–82.

Schmithausen, Lambert. 2005. *On the Problem of the External World in the Ch'eng Wei Shih Lun*. Occasional Papers Series 13. Tokyo: International Institute for Buddhist Studies.

Schmithausen, Lambert. 1976. "On the Problem of the Relation of Spiritual Practice and Philosophical Theory in Buddhism." *German Scholars on India: Contributions to Indian Studies*. Vol. II. Edited by the Cultural Department, Embassy of the Federal Republic of Germany, New Delhi. Bombay: Nachiketa Publications Limited.

Schmithausen, Lambert. 1973. "Spirituelle Praxis und Philosophischen Theorie im Buddhismus." *Zeitschrift für Missionswissenshaft und Religionswissenschaft* 3.

Schott, Magdalene. 1935. *Sein als Bewußtsein: Ein Beitrag zur Mahāyāna-Philosophie*. Heidelberg: Carl Winters Universitätsbuchhandlung, Materialien zur Kunde des Buddhismus 28: 25–50.

Sellars, W. 1977. "Berkeley and Descartes: Reflections on the 'New Way of Ideas'." Peter K. Machamer and Robert G. Turnbull (eds.). *Studies in Perception: Interpretations in the History of Philosophy and Science*. Columbus: Ohio State University Press: 259–311.

Siderits, Mark, Tom Tillemans, and Arindam Chakrabarti (eds.). 2011. *Apoha: Buddhist Nominalism and Human Cognition*. New York: Columbia University Press.

Siṃhasūri. 1966. *Commentary on the Wheel of Logic According to the Nyāya Text-Tradition* (*Nyāyāgamānusāriṇī Nyāyacakravṛtti*). Muni Jambūvijayajī (ed.). *Dvādaśāraṃ Nayacakram of Ācārya Śrī Mallavādi Kṣamāśramaṇa with the Commentary Nyāyāgamānusāriṇī of Śrī Siṇhasūri Gaṇi Vādi Kṣamāśramaṇa. Part I*. Bhavanagar: Śrī Jain Ātmānand Granthamālā Series (#92).

Smith, E. Gene. 2001. *Among Tibetan Texts: History and Literature of the Himalayan Plateau*. Somerville, Mass.: Wisdom Publications.

Sparham, Gareth. 1993. *Ocean of Eloquence: Tsong kha pa's Commentary on the Yogācāra Doctrine of Mind*. Albany: State University of New York Press.

Speijer, Jakob S. 1886. *Sanskrit Syntax*. Leiden: E. J. Brill.

Sperling, Elliot. 1983. "Early Ming Policy toward Tibet: An Examination of the Proposition that the Early Ming Emperors Adopted a 'Divide and Rule' Policy toward Tibet." Ph.D. Dissertation, Indiana University.

Sperling, Elliot. 2009. “Tibetan Buddhism, Perceived and Imagined, along the Ming-Era Sino-Tibetan Frontier.” Matthew T. Kapstein (ed.). *Buddhism between Tibet and China*. Somerville, Mass.: Wisdom Publications: 155–180.

Stcherbatsky, Th. 1916. *The Tibetan Translation of the Treatises Samtānāntarasiddhi by Dharmakīrti and Samtānāntarasiddhiṭīkā by Vinītadeva along with the Tibetan Commentary Written by Ngag dbang bstan dar lha rams pa* [*Тибетский перевод сочинений Samtānāntarasiddhi Dharmakīrti и Samtānāntarasiddhiṭīkā Vinītadeva вместе с тибетским толкованием, составленным Агваном Дандар-Лхарамбой*]. Petrograd: Bibliotheca Buddhica, 38.

Steinkellner, Ernst. 2005. “Dignāga's *Pramāṇasamuccaya*, Chapter 1: A hypothetical reconstruction of the Sanskrit text with the help of the two Tibetan translations on the basis of the hitherto known Sanskrit fragments and the linguistic materials gained from Jinendrabuddhi's *Ṭīkā*.” www.oeaw.ac.at/ias/Mat/dignaga_PS_1.pdf; accessed 22/08/2014.

Steinkellner, Ernst. 1981. *Rnam Thar Sgo Gsum Gyi Rnam Par Bźag Pa, Legs Bśad Rgya Mtsho'i Rba Rlabs*. Vienna: Arbeitskreis für Tibetische und Buddhistische Studien Universtität Wien.

Sthiramati (Anhui 安慧). 2014. *Commentary on the Real Meaning of the Treasury of Abhidharma* (*Apitdamo Shelun shi* 阿毗達磨俱舍論實義疏; Skt. *Abhidharmakośa-tattvārtha-ṭīkā*), three *juan*. (CBETA, ZW01, no. 7; accessed 22/08/2014.

Sthiramati (Anhui 安慧). n.d. *Subcommentary on the Commentary to the Treasury of Abhidharma, Called “Meaning of Truth”* (*Abhidharmakośa-bhāṣya-ṭīkā-tattvārtha-nāma*; Tib. *Chos mngon pa mdzod kyi bshad pa'i rgya cher 'grel pa, don gyi de kho na nyid ces bya ba*). sDe dge edition, *sna tshogs*, vol. *tho*.

Śubhagupta. 1967. *Subcommentary on the Establishment of External Objects* (*Bāhyārthasiddhikārikā*). N. A. Sastri (ed.). *Bulletin of Tibetology* 4. http://himalaya.socanth.cam.ac.uk/collections/journals/bot/pdf/bot_04_02_01.pdf: 1–97.

Sullivan, Brenton. 2007. “Fazun and His Influence on the Life and Education of the Sino-Tibetan Buddhist Institute.” M.A. Thesis, Kansas University.

Sullivan, Brenton. 2008. “Venerable Fazun at the Sino-Tibetan Buddhist Institute (1932–1950) and Tibetan Geluk Buddhism in China.” *Indian International Journal of Buddhist Studies* 9: 199–239

T: *Taishō shinshū daizōkyō*. Takakusu Junjirō, Watanabe Kaikyoku, et al. (eds.). 100 vols. Tokyo: Taishō Issaikyō Kankōkai, 1924–1932.

Taber, John. 2005. *A Hindu Critique of Buddhist Epistemology. Kumārila on Perception. The “Determination of Perception” Chapter of Kumārila Bhaṭṭa`s Ślokavārttika*. London: RoutledgeCurzon.

Taber, John. 2010. “Kumārila's Buddhist.” *Journal of Indian Philosophy* 38: 279–296.

Tachikawa, Musashi. 1971. “A Sixth-century Manual of Indian Logic.” *Journal of Indian Philosophy* 1: 111–145.

Tāranātha. 1990. *History of Buddhism in India* (*rGya gar chos 'byung*). Lama Chimpa and Alaka Chattopadyaya (trans.). *Tāranātha's History of Buddhism in India*. Delhi: Motilal Banarsidass.

Tashi Ngödrup (bKra shis dngos grub) (ed.). 2008. *Collected Works of Dendar Hlarampa* (*Bstan dar lha rams pa'i gsung 'bum*. Compiled by gSer gtsugs nang bstan dpe rnying 'tshol bsdu phyogs sgrig kha; *Collected Outstanding Texts from the Land of Snows* (*Gangs can khyad nor dpe tshogs*), vol. 99. Lhasa: Bod ljongs mi dmangs dpe skrun khang.

TBRC: Tibetan Buddhist Resource Center: http://www.tbrc.org/#home.

Tenzin Gyatso. 1995. *The World of Tibetan Buddhism*. Somerville, Mass.: Wisdom Publications.

Thurman, Robert A. F. 2008. *Why the Dalai Lama Matters: His Act of Truth and the Solution for China, Tibet, and the World*. New York: Atria Book.

Tillemans, Tom F. 1990. *Materials for the Study of Āryadeva, Dharmapāla, and Candrakīrti*. Wiener Studien zur Tibetologie und Buddhismuskunde 24. Vienna: Arbeitskreis für Tibetische und Buddhistische Studien Universität Wien.

Tillemans, Tom F. 1993. *Persons of Authority: The sTon pa tshad ma'i skyes bur sgrub pa'i gtam of A lag sha Ngag dbang bstan dar, A Tibetan Work on the Central Religious Questions in Buddhist Epistemology*. Stuttgart: Franz Steiner Verlag.

Tillemans, Tom F. 1999. *Scripture, Logic, and Language: Essays on Dharmakīrti and His Tibetan Successors*. Boston: Wisdom Publications.

Tillemans, Tom F. 2007. "Transitivity, Intransitivity, and the *tha dad pa* Verbs in Traditional Tibetan Grammar." *Pacific World* 9: 49–62.

Tillemans, Tom, and Donald S. Lopez. 1998. "What Can We Reasonably Say about Nonexistence? A Tibetan Work on the Problem of *Āśrayasiddha*." *Journal of Indian Philosophy* 25: 99–129.

Tola, Fernando, and Carmen Dragonetti. 2004. *Being as Consciousness: Yogācāra Philosophy of Buddhism*. Delhi: Motilal Banarsidass.

Tola, Fernando, and Carmen Dragonetti. 1982. "Dignāga's *Ālambanaparīkṣāvṛtti*." *Journal of Indian Philosophy* 10: 105–134.

Töndor and Tenzin Chödrak (Don rdor and bsTan 'dzin chos grags). 1993. "A Concise Biography of Dendar Hlarampa" (*bsTan dar lha rams pa'i lo rgyus nyung bsdus*). *Histories of Eminent Himalayan Masters* (*Gangs ljongs lo rgyus thog gi grangs can mi sna*). Lha sa: Bod ljongs mi dmangs dpe skrun khang, vol. 2: 344–346; TBRC W19803, vol. 4201.

Tsongkhapa (Tsong khą pa bLo bzang grags pa). 2006a. *Clarifying the Thought: Explanation of the Introduction to the Middle Way* (*dBu ma 'jug pa'i rnam bshad dgongs pa rab gsal*): *dPal dge ldan pa'i tshad ma rig pa'i gzhung gces btus. Bod kyi gtsug lag gces btus*. New Delhi: Institute of Tibetan Classics, vol. 19.

Tsongkhapa (Tsong kha pa bLo bzang grags pa). n.d. *Essence of Eloquence Differentiating the Interpretable and the Definitive* (*Drang nges legs bshad snying po*). (1) 1988. Zhol edition: Sera Monastery printing, *gSung 'bum* vol. *pha*, 114ff.; (2) 1975. bKra shis lhun po edition, *Collected Works of Rje Tsoṅ-kha-pa Blo-bzaṅ-grags-pa*, vol. 21 (*pha*). Delhi: Ngawang Gelek: 478–714.

Tsongkhapa (Tsong kha pa bLo bzang grags pa). n.d. *Great Exposition of Calming Meditation* (*Lhag mthong chen mo*). ACIP: (http://www.asianclassics.org/release6/flat/S5392L_T.TXT; accessed 8/3/2013).

Tsongkhapa (Tsong kha pa bLo bzang grags pa). 2006b. *Great Exposition of the Stages of the Path to Awakening* (*Lam rim chen mo*). New Delhi: Institute of Tibetan Classics, *Gsung 'bum*, vol. 13 (*pa*).

Tsongkhapa (Tsong kha pa bLo bzang grags pa). n.d. *Instructions on the View of the Profound Path of the Middle Way Consequence School* (*dBu ma thal 'gyur pa'i lugs kyi zab lam dbu ma'i lta khrid*). Collected Works, vol. *sha*. Dharamsala: Paljor Press.

Tsongkhapa (Tsong kha pa bLo bzang grags pa). 1982. *Memorandum to the Perception Chapter* (*mNgon sum le'u'i brjed byang*). *gSung 'bum* (*sku 'bum par ma*); rGyal tshab Dar ma rin chen, *Mngon sum le'u'i brjed byang. rGyal tshab rje gSung 'bum.* Zhol par ma, vol. 5: 581–678. TBRC W676. New Delhi: Mongolian Lama Guru Deva). http://tbrc.org/link?RID=O2CZ7509|O2CZ75092CZ7561$W676; accessed 10/10/2013.

Tsültrim Rinchen (Tshul khrims rin chen). 1982–1985. *Tshad ma rnam 'grel gyi tshig le'ur byas pa.* sDe dge *bsTan 'gyur*. TBRC W23703. Delhi: Delhi Karmapae Choedhey, Gyalwae sungrab partun khang: 189–304. http://tbrc.org/link?RID=O1GS6011|O1GS60111GS36425$W23703.

Tubb, Gary Alan, and Emery Robert Boose. 2007. *Scholastic Sanskrit: A Handbook for Students.* New York: American Institute for Buddhist Studies.

Tucci, Giuseppe. 1929. "Buddhist Logic before Diṅnāga (Asaṅga, Vasubandhu, *Tarka-śāstras*)." *Journal of the Royal Asiatic Society*: 451–488.

Tuttle, Gray W. 2006. "Tibetan Buddhism at Ri bo rtse lnga/Wutai shan in Modern Times." *Journal of the International Association of Tibetan Studies*, no. 2: 1–35.

Tuttle, Gray W. 2005. *Tibetan Buddhists in the Making of Modern China.* New York: Columbia University Press.

Ui Hakuju 宇井伯壽. 1953. *Shiyaku-taisyō Yuisiki nijū-ron Kenkyū (Daijō-bukkyō Kenkyū* 4) [Comparative Study of the *Viṃśatikā vijñaptimātratāsiddhi* with Four Translations (Studies of the Mahāyāna Buddhism, 4)]. Tokyo: Iwanami Shōten: 20–21.

Ui Hakuju 宇井伯壽. 1958. *A Study of Dignāga's Works* (*Jinna chosaku no kenkyū* 陳那著作の研究). Tōkyō: Iwanami Shōten: 167–231.

Vāgbhaṭa (Pha khol). n.d. *Eight-Limbed Compendium* (*Aṣṭāṅga-saṃgraha*). SARIT version, R.P. Das and R. E. Emmerick (ed.), revised by Dominik Wujastyk: http://sarit.indology.info/exist/apps/sarit/works/sarit_aṣṭāṅgasaṅgraha; accessed 4/4/2016.

Vāgbhaṭa (Pha khol). n.d. *Eight-Limbed Essential Collection*](*Aṣṭāṅga-hṛdaya-saṁhitā*). SARIT version, R.P. Das and R. E. Emmerick (ed.), revised by Dominik Wujastyk: http://sarit.indology.info/exist/apps/sarit/works/sarit_aṣṭāṅgahṛdayasaṃhitā; accessed 4/4/2016.

Vasubandhu. n.d. *Commentary on the Compendium of Mahāyāna* (*Mahāyāna-saṃgraha-bhāṣya*; Tib. *Theg pa chen po bsdus pa'i 'grel pa*). sDe dge edition, Sems tsam vol. *ri*.

Vasubandhu. n.d. *Commentary on the Distinction of the First Factor of Dependent Arising* (*Pratītyasamutpādādivibhaṅga-bhāṣya*; Tib. *rTen cing 'brel bar 'byung ba dang po dang rnam par dbye bshad pa*): (1) Peking 5496, vol. 104: 277–306; (2) Tohoku 3995: *bsTan 'gyur* (*dpe bsdur ma*); W1PD95844: 717–876.

Vasubandhu. n.d. *Commentary on the Treasury of Abhidharma* (*Abhidharma-kośa-bhāṣya*). (1) Prahlad Pradhan (ed.). 1975. P. Pradhan. *Abhidharmakośabhāṣyam of Vasubandhu*. Patna: K. P. Jayaswal Research Institute; (2) GRETL e-text (http://gretil.sub.uni-goettingen.de/gretil/1_sanskr/6_sastra/3_phil/buddh/vakobhau.htm; accessed 6/6/2014).

Vasubandhu. n.d. *Differentiation of the Middle and Extremes* (*Madhyānta-vibhāga*). GRETL e-text: http://gretil.sub.uni-goettingen.de/gretil/1_sanskr/6_sastra/3_phil/buddh/bsa010_c.txt; accessed 28/08/2014.

Vasubandhu. n.d. *Exposition Establishing How Action Works* (*Karma-siddhi-prakaraṇa*; Tib. *Las grub pa'i rab byed*). sDe dge edition, Sems tsam vol. *shi*.

Vasubandhu. n.d. *Thirty Verses* (*Triṃśikā*). (1) Buescher, Hartmut (ed.). 2007. *Sthiramati's Triṃśikāvijñaptibhāṣya: Critical Editions of the Sanskrit Text and its Tibetan Translation*. Vienna: Österreichische Akademie der Wissenschaften, Phil.-hist. Kl., Sitzungsberichte, 786; Beitrḫge zur Kultur- und Geistesgeschichte Asiens, 57; (2) GRETL E-text: http://gretil.sub.uni-goettingen.de/gretil/1_sanskr/6_sastra/3_phil/buddh/sthtvbhc.txt; accessed 8/9/2014.

Vasubandhu. n.d. *Treasury of Abhidharma Commentary* (*Abhidharma-kośa-bhāṣya*). (1) Prahlad Pradhan (ed.). 1975. P. Pradhan. *Abhidharmakośabhāṣyam of Vasubandhu*. Patna: K. P. Jayaswal Research Institute; (2) GRETL e-text (http://gretil.sub.uni-goettingen.de/gretil/1_sanskr/6_sastra/3_phil/buddh/vakobhau.htm; accessed 6/6/2014).

Vasubandhu. 1975. *Treasury of Abhidharma* (*Abhidharma-kośa*; Tib. *Chos mngon pa'i mdzod*). (1) Prahlad Pradhan (ed.). *The Abhidharmakośa of Vasubandhu: With the Commentary*. Patna: K.P. Jayaswal Research Institute; (2) GRETL e-text: http://gretil.sub.uni-goettingen.de/gretil/1_sanskr/6_sastra/3_phil/buddh/vakobhac.txt; accessed 12/3/2014.

Vasubandhu. n.d. *Twenty Verses* (*Viṃśatikā* (or *Viṃśaka*). (1) Sylvain Lévi (ed.). 1925. *Vijñaptimātratāsiddhiḥ Deux traités de Vasubandhu: Viṃśatikā (La Vingtaine) accompagnée d'une explication en prose et Triṃśikā (La trentaine) avec le commentaire de Sthiramati*. Paris: Librairie Ancienne Honoré Champion; (2) GRETL e-text: http://gretil.sub.uni-goettingen.de/gretil/1_sanskr/6_sastra/3_phil/buddh/vasvvmsc.txt; accessed 28/08/2014; (3) Corrections to Lévi edition: Ui (1953).

Vinītadeva. n.d. *Subcommentary on Investigation of the Percept* (*Ālambana-parīkṣā-ṭīkā*). Tib. *dMigs pa brtag pa'i 'grel bshad*). sDe dge bsTan 'gyur, Tshad ma vol. *zhe* (190), ff. 175a3-187b.5: TBRC, vol. 3452, Work #22704: 349–374.

Wang-Toutain, Françoise. 2000. "Quand les maîtres chinois s'éveillent au bouddhisme tibétain: Fazun: le Xuanzang des temps modernes." *Bulletin de l'École Française d'Extréme Orient* 87: 707–727.

Warder, A. K. 1975. "Objects and Distinctions among Ālambana, Viṣaya, Vastu, Artha, Grāhya, Karman, Gocara, Dharma, Svalakṣaṇa, and Prameya, Sanskrit Words with Assumed Synonymous Meanings." *Journal of Indian Philosophy* 3: 355–361.

Wayman, Alex. 1979. "Yogācāra and the Buddhist Logicians." *Journal of the International Association of Buddhist Studies* 2(1): 65–78.

Welch, Holmes. 1968. *The Buddhist Revival in China*. Cambridge, Mass.: Harvard University Press.

Welch, Holmes. 1967. *The Practice of Chinese Buddhism, 1900–1950*. Cambridge, Mass.: Harvard University Press.

Welmang Könchok Gyaltsen (dPal mang dkon mchog rgyal mtshan). 1974. *Religious Biography of Gungtang Könchok Denbe Drönme: Sun of the Lotus Blossom of Faith (Gung thang dkon mchog bstan pa'i sgron me'i rnam thar dad pa'i padmo bzhad pa'i nyin byed). Könchok Gyaltsen's Collected Works*, vol. 7. New Delhi: Gyalten Gelek Namgyal.

Whitney, Dwight. 1945. *The Roots, Verb-Forms and Primary Derivatives of the Sanskrit Language*. New Haven, Conn.: American Oriental Society.

Wilson, Joe B. 1984. "The Meaning of Mind in the Mahāyāna Buddhist Philosophy of Mind-Only (Cittamātra): A Study of a Presentation by the Tibetan Scholar Gung-tang Jam-pay-yang (gung-thang-'jam-pa'i-dbyangs) of Asaṅga's Theory of Mind-Basis-of-All (*ālayavijñāna*) and Related Topics in Buddhist Theories of Personal Continuity, Epistemology, and Hermeneutics." Ph.D. dissertation, University of Virginia.

Wogihara Unrai. 1932–1936. *Sphuṭârtha Abhidharmakośavyākhyā by Yaśomitra*. Tokyo: The Publishing Association of Abhidharmakośavyākhyā.

Xuanzang 玄奘. 1997. *Great Tang Dynasty Record of Western Regions* (*Da Tang xiyu ji* 大唐西域記). T 2087.51.867–947. (1) Li Rongxi (trans.). *The Great Tang Dynasty Record of the Western Regions*. Berkeley: Numata Center for Buddhist Studies. (2) SAT Daizōkyō Text Database: http://21dzk.l.u-tokyo.ac.jp/SAT/T2087.html; accessed 2/9/2014.

Xuanzang 玄奘. (X). n.d. *Treatise Investigating the Percept Condition* (*Guan suoyuanyuan lun* 觀所緣緣論). T 1624.31.888–889). CBETA: http://21dzk.l.u-tokyo.ac.jp/SAT/T1624.html; accessed 8/23/2012.

Xuanzang 玄奘. n.d. *Treatise on Mere Cognition* (*Cheng weishi lun* 成唯識論). T 1585.31.1a-59a.

Xing Suzhi 邢肃芝. 2003. *Record of a Search for the Dharma in the Land of Snows: A Chinese Lama's Oral History* (*Xueyu qiufa ji: yi ge hanren lama de koushu shi* 雪域求法記: 一個漢人喇嘛的口述史). Zhang Jianfei 张健飞 and Yang Nianqun 杨念群 (ed.). Beijing. Shenghuo dushu xinzhi san lian shudian.

XZJ. *Xuzangjing.* 續藏經. (1905–1912). Taiwanese Reprint of *Dai nihon zokuzōkyō.* Kyoto: Zokyō sho.

Yamabe Nobuyoshi 山部能宜. 1998. "Self and Other in the Yogācāra Tradition." *Kitabatake Tensei hakushi koki-kinen rombunshū* 北畠典生博士古稀記念論文集. Kyoto: 15–41.

Yamaguchi, Susumu 山口益. 1929. "Dignāga, *Examen de l'Objet de la Connaissance* (*Ālambanaparīkṣā*): Textes tibétain et chinois et traduction des stances et du commentaire, éclairissement et notes d'après le commentaire tibétain de Vinītadeva." *Journal Asiatique* 214: 1–65.

Yamaguchi, Susumu 山口益. 1974. *Index to the Prasannapadā Madhyamaka-vṛtti.* Kyoto: Heirakuji Shoten.

Yamaguchi, Susumu, and Nozawa Jōshō 野澤靜證. 1953. *Philological Explanations of Vasubandhu's Vijñaptimātratā* (*Seshin yuishiki no genten kaimei* (世親唯識の原典解明). Kyoto: Hōzōkan: 409–484.

Yamaguchi, Susumu, and Harriette Meyer. 1929. *Examen de l'objet connaissance.* Paris: Imprimerie Nationale.

Yao, Zhihua. 2009a. "Empty Subject Terms in Buddhist Logic: Dignāga and His Chinese Commentators." *Journal of Indian Philosophy* 37: 383–398.

Yao, Zhihua. 2009b. "Tibetan Learning in the Contemporary Chinese Yogācāra School." Matthew T. Kapstein (ed.). 2009. *Buddhism between Tibet and China.* Somerville, Mass.: Wisdom Publications: 281–294.

Yaśomitra. n.d. *Subcommentary on the Treasury of Abhidharma* (*Abhidharmakośa-ṭīkā / Abhidharmakośa-sphuṭārthā*). GRETL etext: http://gretil.sub.uni-goettingen.de/gretil/1_sanskr/6_sastra/3_phil/buddh/yabhkvyu.htm; accessed 19/6/2014.

Yeshes Thabkhas (Ye shes thabs mkhas). 2010. *A Comprehensive Commentary on Āryaśālistambasūtra by Ācārya Kamalaśīla*, translated and edited by Prof. Geshe Yeshe Thabkhey. Sarnath: Central University of Tibetan Studies (Bibliotheca Indo-Tibetica Series #72).

Yeshes Thabkhas (Ye shes thabs mkhas). 1997. *Straightforward Analysis of Interpretable and Definitive Meanings in the Treatise "Essence of Eloquence" Composed by Tsongkhapa Losang Drakpa* (*Shar tsong kha pa blo bzang grags pas mdzad pa'i drang ba dang nges pa'i don rnam par 'byed pa'i bstan bcos legs bshad snying po*). Varanasi: Vāṇa dbus bod kyi ches mtho'i gtsug lag slob gnyer khang.

Yijing 義淨. 2000. *A Record of Buddhist Practices Sent Home from the Southern Seas* (南海寄歸內法傳). (1) Li Rongxi (trans.). *Buddhist Monastic Traditions of Southern Asia: A Record of the Inner Law Sent Home from the South Seas.* Berkeley: Numata Center for Buddhist Studies. (2) T 2125, vol. 54. SAT Daizōkyō Text Database: http://21dzk.l.u-tokyo.ac.jp/SAT/T2125.html; accessed 3/9/2014.

Yijing 義淨. n.d. *Explanation of Investigation of the Percept* (*Guan suoyuan lunshi* 觀所緣論釋). T31 no. 1625.

Yongming Yanshou 永明延壽. n.d. *Records of the Mirror of Orthodoxy* (*Zongjing lu* 宗鏡錄). T 48.2016.415a–957b.

Yü, Chün-fang. 1981. *The Renewal of Buddhism in China: Chu-hung and the Late Ming Synthesis*. New York: Columbia University Press.

Yu, Dan Smyer. 2012. *The Spread of Tibetan Buddhism in China: Charisma, Money, Enlightenment*. London and New York: Routledge.

Zhang Kecheng 張克誠. n.d. *Superficial Interpretation of Investigation of the Percept* (*Guan suoyuan yuan lun qianshuo* 觀所緣緣論淺說).

Zhang Yisun et al. (eds.). 1993. *The Great Tibetan Dictionary* (*Bod rgya tshig mdzod chen mo*; Ch. *Zang Han dacidian* 藏汉大辞典). Beijing: Mi rigs dpe skrun khang.

Zhang Zhiqiang. 2009. "From the 'Alternative School of Principles' to the Lay Buddhism: On the Conceptual Features of Modern Consciousness-Only School from the Perspective of the Evolution of Thought during the Ming and Qing Dynasties." *Frontiers of Philosophy in China*: 64–87.

Zhenjie 真界. n.d. *Anthology of Commentaries on Investigation of the Percept (Guan suoyuanyuan jijie* 觀所緣緣論集解). Woodblock print, n.d.

Zhixu 智旭. n.d. *Straightforward Explication of Investigation of the Percept* (*Guan suoyuanyuan lun zhijie* 觀所緣緣論直解). XZJ 83 CBETA X51. No. 831.

Index

Abhidharma 12, 15–16, 55, 59, 62, 106, 128, 157, 163
Abhidharma-kośa. See *Treasury of Abhidharma*
Account of the Treatise on Mere Cognition (*Cheng weishilun shuji*) xviii, 26 n. 42
ālambana. *See* percept
Ālambana-parīkṣā. See *Investigation of the Percept*
Ālambana-parīkṣā-ṭīkā. See *Subcommentary to Investigation of the Percept*
Ālambana-parīkṣā-vṛtti See *Autocommentary on Investigation of the Percept*
ālambana-pratyaya. *See* percept condition
ālaya-vijñāna. *See* fundamental consciousness
Anthology of Commentaries on Investigation of the Percept xix
Arcaṭa 51
Aristotle xviii
Asaṅga 10, 26 n. 42, 107, 125, 150, 181, 210–211
atadābhatayā 56–57
Autocommentary on Investigation of the Percept xv–xvi, xxviii, 6–8, 14, 20–22, 27–28, 33, 37, 49, 58–59, 67, 70, 75, 138, 148, 158, 164, 166, 175, 195, 209, 216
  English translation 40–47
  Tibetan text 219–223
autopoiesis 44 n. 38, 111, 117, 129

Bahir-artha-parīkṣā. *See* Investigation of External Objects
Beautiful String of Pearls: A Commentary on Investigation of the Percept xvii, 118–130
  English translation 131–168
  Tibetan text 262–286
Bhadanta 89 n. 42–43
Bhāviveka xvi, 20 n. 37, 41 n. 13, 57–61, 65, 72–74, 76, 136–137, 139, 186–188
Blaze of Reasoning xvi, 186–188
Brentano, Franz 11
Buddhism x, xvi–xvii, xix–xxii, xxiv, xxvi, xxviii–xxx, 10, 13, 16, 29, 32, 36, 48–50, 59, 71, 121–122, 124, 129, 173–174, 181
  Chinese xviii, xxii–xxvii, xxix
  Indian 3, 5, 7, 36, 65, 170–172, 212
  Tibetan xxii–xxiv, xxvii, xxix, 3, 36

Cabezón, José 37 n. 47
Candrakīrti 111, 204, 209–210
capacity 8, 26–27, 39, 45–46, 71–74, 76, 98–102, 115–117, 128–130, 141–142, 146, 163–165, 202–206
Cheng weishi lun. See *Account of the Treatise on Mere Cognition*
China, history of *Investigation of the Percept* in xvii–xx, xxiii–xxvi
China Institute for Inner Learning xx, xxiii
Cittamātra 33, 111, 122, 124–129, 137–139, 142, 145, 150–151, 155, 158–160, 162, 165, 172–174, 178–186, 189, 191–192, 194, 196, 199–213
  False-Representation 36, 159
  True-Representation 36, 160, 162
Clarifying the Thought: Explanation of the Introduction to the Middle Way 139, 150, 159 n. 81, 162–163, 184, 209–212
Clarifying the Thought: Great Commentary Definitively Elucidating Epistemological Treatises 163–164
cognition xv, xix, xxvii, 6, 8–35, 38–46, 49, 52–71, 73–88, 90–103, 110–111, 113–117, 123–124, 127–130, 133, 137–158, 160–161, 163–167, 172–173, 176–183, 185–209, 211–213
collections 7–11, 13–19, 22, 25, 29, 34, 39–42, 52, 58–63, 66–68, 79–82, 85–91, 112–114, 126–127, 138–139, 148, 151–158, 173, 181–183, 185–187, 189, 194–197, 213
Commentary on Epistemology 157
Commentary on the Compendium of Epistemology xvii, 6, 66, 142 n. 36, 143 n. 38, 144 n. 39, 145 n. 41, 146, 149–150, 177–178, 181, 184, 199, 207–208, 213
Commentary on the Compendium of Metaphysics 44 n. 34, 146
Commentary on the Distinction of the First Factor of Dependent Arising 150, 184, 210, 211
Commentary on the Four Hundred 135–136
Commentary on the Treasury of Abhidharma 46, 55, 119, 125
Commentary on the Treasury of Abhidharma Called "Lamp of the Essence" 6
Compendium of Ascertainments 150, 159, 184
Compendium of Epistemology xvi–xvii, 4, 6, 66, 69, 74, 76–77, 126, 139 n. 25, 140 n. 29, 149–150, 151 n. 61, 177–178, 181, 183, 184, 199, 207–208, 213
Compendium of Mahāyāna 27 n. 42, 162, 181, 184, 210, 211
Compendium of Metaphysics xvi, 64, 146
conditions 12–13

Democritus 16
Dendar Lharampa 118–119, 179, 183–185, 189–191, 194–196. *See also* Ngawang Dendar
Devendrabuddhi 208, 213
Dharmakīrti xvii–xviii, xxvii, 6, 27, 49–50, 66, 126, 132, 139 n. 25, 140 n. 29, 142 n. 36, 143 n. 38, 144 n. 39, 145 n. 41, 167, 172, 175, 181, 199, 207–208
Dharmapāla xv–xviii, xx, xxvii–xxviii, xxx, 7, 17, 20, 24, 48, 56–59, 70, 80, 83 n. 16, 85, 87, 173
  third position 7–8, 15, 17–20, 59–68, 88, 90, 173
Dharmottara 50, 51, 157
Differentiation of the Precious Lineage 107
Difficult Points of Mind and the Fundamental Consciousness 107

Dignāga x, xv–xxx, 3–28, 30, 32–37, 46–50, 52–77, 80–87, 89–103, 105, 108–113, 117, 124–130, 132, 146–157, 160–161, 163–165, 167, 171–177, 181–183, 185–186, 190–192, 195, 197–198, 204, 217, 219, 257
  biography 3–6
  and idealism 7–9
  opponents 14–20, 52–59, 109, 112–115, 148–160, 181–199
  own position 20–24, 115–117, 160–167, 199–213
  vocabulary 9–12, 175–177
Discourse Explaining the Thought 24
Dorjieff, Agvan xxiv
double moon 25, 29–31, 34–35, 39, 42, 52, 58–59, 86–87, 95, 113, 115–116, 132, 147, 151–153, 173, 186, 189–193, 200
  Autocommentary 42
  Dendar on 151–153
  Gungtang's use of 29–30, 115–116
  Vinītadeva on 86–87
  Yeshes Thabkhas on 173, 189–193
doxography 27–32, 36, 64, 118–130, 146, 172
Drepung Monastic University xxiv, 106, 118–119, 169, 172
Dreyfus, Georges 64 n. 28, 77
Drop of Logic 50
Dunne, John 66 n. 30

epistemology xv–xvii, xix–xx, xxx, 6, 8–10, 13, 16, 30, 36, 51, 56, 67, 119, 129, 132, 173–174
Epistemology xvi, xix, 50, 138, 167–168, 171
Essence of Eloquence 107, 171, 188
Explanation of Investigation of the Percept xviii–xix, xxvii, 18
Exposition Establishing How Action Works 159
external object xvi, 3, 8–14, 17, 20–32, 34–36, 39–40, 42–44, 53–54, 56, 59, 61, 64, 67, 70–73, 75, 77–81, 87–88, 94–95, 101, 109–111, 113–115, 117, 123–124, 127–130, 133, 141, 148, 150, 152–154, 159–160, 164–165, 167, 173–174, 176–186, 189–191, 193–196, 199–200, 203–205, 209–210, 212–213. *See also* idealism

Fazun xxiv–xx, xxv–xxvi
Franco, Eli xviii n. 2
Funayama, Toru x, 49–52
fundamental consciousness 98, 107, 110–111, 116, 124, 126, 147, 162, 180, 199–200, 202–203, 205, 210–211
fundamental particles xv, 6–9, 14–19, 24–25, 28, 32–34, 36, 38, 40–43, 52, 54–57, 59–70, 79, 81–94, 109, 112–114, 123–124, 127, 133–142, 148–149, 152–166, 173, 180–183, 185–188, 194–198

Geluk xvi–xvii, xxii, xxv–xxvi, 27, 29–32, 36, 106–108, 111, 118–119, 122–127, 137, 171–172
  doxography 122–127
  epistemology 29–32, 118–119
Gendün Drup (dGe 'dun grub) 138 n. 24
Gómez, Luis xxii
Great Commentary on the Wheel of Time 137
Great Exposition of Calming Meditation 158
Great Exposition of the Stages of the Path xxv, 136, 138, 171
Guan suoyuan lunshi. See *Explanation of Investigation of the Percept*
Guan suoyuan shi lun huishi. See *Translation and Comparative Exposition of Investigation of the Percept*

Guan suoyuanyuan lun huishi. See *Reconciled Explanation of Investigation of the Percept*
Guan suoyuanyuan lun qianshuo. See *Superficial Interpretation of Investigation of the Percept*
Guan suoyuanyuan lun shijie. See *Interpretive Exposition of Investigation of the Percept*
Guan suoyuanyuan lun zhijie. See *Straightforward Explication of Investigation of the Percept*
Gungtang. *See* Könchok Denbe Drönme
Gyeltsap (rGyal tshab Dar ma rin chen) 107, 136 n. 16, 139, 145, 146, 158, 162, 163 n. 93, 183

Hallisey, Charles 125
Heart of the Middle Way, 187

idealism xxvii, 7–9, 12, 22–27, 30–31, 33, 35, 79, 110–111, 127–130, 173, 182 n. 6. *See also* external object
Illumination of the Path to Liberation: Explanation of the Commentary on the Compendium of Epistemology, an Unerring Illumination of the Path to Liberation 149, 183
intentional object 11–12, 14, 22–23, 28, 30, 81, 111, 172–176, 178, 180–181, 189–190, 200–205, 208
intentionality 11, 14, 23–24, 27–32
Interpretive Exposition of Investigation of the Percept xx
Introduction to Logic 6
Introduction to the Middle Way 141–142, 159, 204, 209–210
invariable concomitance, 44–45, 44 n. 38, 97–98, 128–130, 161–163
Investigation of External Objects xvi, 64, 67
Investigation of the Percept x, xi, xv–xxiii, xxvi–xxx, 3, 6–7, 10–11, 15, 18, 20, 22, 24, 27, 29, 32, 36–37, 48–49, 54, 64, 66–67, 72–73, 75–78, 107–109, 112, 117, 122, 132, 149, 155, 171–177, 181, 195, 216
  English translation 38–39
  Tibetan text 217–218

Jamyang Sheba I ('Jam dbyangs bzhad pa Ngag dbang brtson 'grus) 105–106
Jamyang Sheba II ('Jam dbyangs bzhad pa dKon mchog 'Jigs med dbang po) 102, 106, 126, 154–155
Jinendrabuddhi 4, 75–76, 157
Jñānagarbha 76

Kamalaśīla xxii, 20 n. 37, 41 n. 9, 45 n. 41, 51, 65, 69, 82 n. 12, 146, 171
Kapstein, Matthew xxiii n. 19
Kawaguchi, Ekai xxiv
Kedrup (mKhas grub dGe legs dpal bzang) 134 n. 8, 137 n. 22, 139, 140 n. 30, 146, 150, 162, 183–184
Kellner, Birgit 71, 75, 77
Könchok Denbe Drönme, Gungtang (Gung thang dKon mchog bstan pa'i sgron me) x, xv, xvii, xxii, xxx, 7, 24, 27–32, 34–36, 105–117, 129, 172–174, 179, 181–182, 185, 195, 199–200, 202–204, 257
  biography 105–108
  on intentionality 27–32
Kumārila 59, 65, 67, 71

Legs bshad snying po. See *Essence of Eloquence*
logic xix–xx, 4–5, 9, 49, 72, 99, 106, 168, 180
Logician 45, 97–98, 201

Losang Drakpa, Tsongkhapa xxv, 30–31, 107–108, 122, 136 n. 21, 138 n. 23, 139, 145, 150–151, 159, 171, 174, 184, 188, 208–212
Lü Cheng xx, xxii–xxiii, xxvi–xxvii, 43 n. 31
Lusthaus, Dan xi, xx n. 14, 7 n. 12, 23 n. 41

macro-object 17, 19, 68, 88, 93, 109, 124, 133, 136–138, 142, 145, 148, 151, 153–160, 185, 196–198
Madhyamaka xxi, xxv, 57, 67, 70, 106–109, 111, 118, 123–125, 191
Madhyamaka-hṛdaya. See *Heart of the Middle Way*
Madhyamaka-hṛdaya-kārikā-tarkajvālā. See *Blaze of Reasoning*
Mahāyāna-saṃgraha. See *Compendium of Mahāyāna*
Mahāyāna-sūtrālaṃkāra. See *Ornament for Mahāyāna Discourses*
Makeham, John x, xxi
Memorandum to the Perception Chapter 145, 158
methodology xxviii–xxx, 9–12
mind-only 48, 50, 53, 64, 67, 72, 107, 108, 110, 111
Mingyu xviii, xix, xxvii, 18–19, 83 n. 16
minute particles, 84

Nālandā xxii, xxvii, 5, 24
Ngawang Dendar (Ngag dbang bstan dar) xv–xviii, xxii, xxx, 7, 24, 32–36, 92 n. 44, 97 n. 70, 118–168, 172–174. *See also* Dendar Lharampa
  biography 118–122
  on doxography 122–130
  on representations 32–36
Ngawang Losang (Ngag dbang blo bzang) 131 n. 1
Non-sectarian (Ris med) xxi–xxii
Nyāya-bindu. See *Drop of Logic*
Nyāya-bindu-ṭīkā. See *Subcommentary on the Drop of Logic*
Nyāya-mukha. See *Introduction to Logic*

Ocean of Reasoning: Extensive Exposition of the Commentary on the Compendium of Epistemology 150, 183
ontology 8–10, 12–13, 27, 186
opposing positions 14–20
Ornament for Dignāga's Thought in Investigation of the Percept x, xvii, 105–117
  English translation 112–117
  Tibetan text 257–261
Ornament for Epistemological Treatises 138, 152, 192
Ornament for Mahāyāna Discourses 10
Ornament for Seven Epistemological Texts That Dispels Darkness in the Mind 134, 140, 146, 152, 192
Ornament for the Commentary on the Treasury of Abhidharma 135
Ornament of Reasoning: Great Exposition of Epistemological Treatises 138 n. 24
Ouyang Jingwu xx

paramāṇu. *See* fundamental particles
Paramārtha xviii, xxviii, 45 n. 40, 46 n. 46
percept xv–xvi, xix, 6–15, 17, 21–30, 34–36, 40–42, 46, 52, 54–63, 67, 69–71, 73, 77–90, 94–97, 99, 101–103, 110–117, 127–129, 138–139, 141, 143, 148–153, 161, 165, 172–176, 178–182, 185–186, 189–192, 194, 199, 202–203, 205
percept condition xix, 12–14, 18, 21, 23, 25, 31, 33–35, 44–45, 55, 70, 85–86, 95–97, 99, 114–116, 128, 130, 133, 136, 138, 142–148, 151–153, 160–165, 176–179, 181–183, 185, 187–189, 192, 194–196, 199–206

perception xv–xvi, 5–6, 8–18, 21–24, 26–29, 31–36, 53, 60, 62–63, 67–68, 71, 108–111, 123, 127–129, 141, 144–145, 147, 159, 172–174, 178–179, 181, 183, 196, 199, 211–212
Perception Chapter 139–140, 143–145, 157
Plato xviii
Prajñākaragupta 41 n. 14, 82 n. 12
Pramāṇa-vārttika. See *Commentary on the Compendium of Epistemology*
Prāsaṅgika-Madhyamaka 107–108, 111, 124, 204
Precious Garland of Tenet Systems 122, 154–155
Pudön (Bu ston) 4–5
Pūrṇavardhana 134

Radich, Michael x, 70
Ratnagotra-vibhāga. See *Differentiation of the Precious Lineage*
Reconciled Explanation of Investigation of the Percept xix
Records of the Mirror of Orthodoxy xix
Rendawa (Red mda' ba) 108
representation 7–8, 12–13, 19, 22–26, 28, 31–36, 41, 46, 55, 60–61, 64, 70–76, 83–84, 86–88, 95–98, 101–102, 109–111, 113–117, 122–124, 127–130, 141–156, 159–160, 163, 165, 176, 178–180, 182–183, 185–186, 188–198, 200–203, 205–208
representationalism 12–14, 19, 24, 32, 36, 122–123, 142, 162
Rules for Debate 4

Sakya (Sa skya) xvi, xii, 108
Sakya Paṇḍita (Sa skya Paṇḍita Kun dga' rgyal mtshan) 108
Śākyamuni xii
Śākyasiṃha 103
Saṃdhinirmocana-sūtra. See *Discourse Explaining the Thought*
Samye Debate xxii–xxiii
Saṅghabhadra 62–63
Śāntarakṣita xvi, 64–65, 67, 69
Sarvāstivāda 125
Sautrāntika 13–14, 32–33, 35, 62, 122–123, 125–130, 137, 139, 141–143, 145, 148, 155–157, 165, 172–173, 176, 178–179, 181–182, 190–191, 198–199, 201, 203, 206
Sautrāntika-Cittamātra 137
scholasticism 37
Sellars, Wilfrid 30
Siṃhasūri 41 n. 11
Sino-Tibetan Institute of World Buddhist Studies xxv
Smith, E. Gene xxi
Śrīlāta 62
Sthiramati 24, 49, 60–63, 65
Straightforward Analysis of Interpretable and Definitive Meanings in the Treatise "Essence of Eloquence" Composed by Tsongkhapa Losang Drakpa 171
Straightforward Explication of Investigation of the Percept xix
Subcommentary on the Drop of Logic 51
Subcommentary to Investigation of the Percept 24, 27, 48–77, 166
  English translation 78–104
  Tibetan text 224–256
Subcommentary to the Commentary on the Compendium of Epistemology 208, 213
Śubhagupta 64–65, 67–68
Sumati 65
Summary of the Essence: A Commentary on Investigation of the Percept 169–174
  English translation 175–213
  Tibetan Text 287–316
Superficial Interpretation of Investigation of the Percept xx

supervenience 109–110
Svātantrika 124, 186

Taber, John 71
Taixu xxv
Tāranātha 4–5
Tattva-saṃgraha. See *Compendium of Metaphysics*
Thirty Verses 24, 49–50, 60
Translation and Comparative Exposition of Investigation of the Percept xx
Treasury of Abhidharma 6, 10, 63, 93 n. 59, 134–135, 141, 143, 156, 172, 188
Treatise on the Levels of Yogic Practice 5, 159
Triṃśikā-kārikā. See *Thirty Verses*
Tsongkhapa. *See* Losang Drakpa
Tuttle, Gray xxiii n 20
Twenty Verses 24–25, 49–50, 53, 109, 181

Uddyotakara 59, 67

Vāgbhaṭa 59, 88, 114, 155, 195–196
Vaibhāṣika 13–14, 32, 62, 100, 122–123, 126, 141–145, 173, 178–179, 182, 188, 198, 206–207
Vaiśeṣika 54, 68–69, 93, 136
Vasubandhu xxi, 4, 6, 10, 24–25, 49, 53–55, 63, 93 n. 59, 109, 125, 128, 141, 143, 150, 159, 162–163, 181
Verses on the Heart of the Middle Way xvi, 60, 63, 74, 187
Viṃśatikā. See *Twenty Verses*
Vinītadeva xv–xxix, 7, 11–12, 19–20, 24–27, 29–31, 33, 36, 42 n. 19, 42 n. 21–23, 48–104, 117, 166, 174, 195
  biography 49–50
  and idealism 24–27, 69–77, 79

Wheel of Reasons 6

Xuanzang xviii–xix, xxviii, 4–5, 47

Yao, Zhihua xxvi
Yaśomitra 62–64
Yeshes Thabkhas xv, xvii, 12, 24, 36, 169–213, 287–316
  biography 169–171
  on Cittamātra 174
  on the double moon 173
  on ethics 173–174
Yijing xviii–xix, xxviii, 4
Yogācāra xviii–xxi, xxiii, xxv–xxvi, 24, 27, 29, 31, 33, 35–36, 48, 72, 100, 107–108, 110, 115–117, 123, 125, 150–151, 174, 178–185, 199–213
Yogācāra-bhūmi. See *Treatise on the Levels of Yogic Practice*
Yongming Yanshou xix

Zhang Kecheng xx
Zhenjie xix
Zhixu xix
Zongming lu. See *Records of the Mirror of Orthodoxy*

CPSIA information can be obtained
at www.ICGtesting.com
Printed in the USA
BVHW031007140422
634236BV00010B/17

9 780190 623708